The Life
and Reign of
EDWARD
the Fourth

The Life and Reign of EDWARD the Fourth

KING OF ENGLAND AND OF FRANCE AND LORD OF IRELAND

CORA L. SCOFIELD

IN TWO VOLUMES

Volume Two

 FONTHILL

Fonthill Media Limited
Fonthill Media LLC
www.fonthillmedia.com
office@fonthillmedia.com

First published in the United Kingdom 1923
This revised edition published in the United Kingdom
and the United States of America 2016

British Library Cataloguing in Publication Data:
A catalogue record for this book is available from the British Library

ISBN 978-1-78155-476-0

Typeset in Minion Pro 10pt on 15pt
Printed and bound by CPI Group (UK) Ltd, Croydon, CR0 4YY

CONTENTS

BOOK IV—ENGLAND AND FRANCE

BOOK V—LOUIS XI's PENSIONER

BOOK VI—MISCELLANEA

BOOK IV

ENGLAND AND FRANCE

1

READJUSTMENTS

Henry VI had been dead only a few hours when the Duke of Gloucester started for Kent with a part of the army that had returned to London with Edward, and the next day, while the funeral barge was on its way to Chertsey, the king followed his brother with the rest of the troops and with Clarence, Arundel, Rivers, Hastings, and other lords in attendance.[1] Edward travelled slowly, for he stopped here and there to punish some of those who had assisted in the Bastard of Fauconberg's insurrection. He did not reach Canterbury until 26 May, and when he did arrive, he found a very repentant city and magistrates bedecked with white roses.[2] No sudden display of devotion to the house of York, however, could save Canterbury from paying the penalty of her sins. Her liberties and franchises were taken from her; some of her citizens were hanged; many others were arrested, and Mayor Faunt, who before this time had been seized and placed in the Tower, was brought home to be kept in ward until a full inquiry could be made into the crimes attending the recent disturbances.[3] But the tedious task of dealing with the mass of offenders in Kent was left to a commission to be appointed later and, after a short stay in Canterbury, the king went on to Sandwich, where the guiltiest of the guilty was abiding his

---

1. Kingsford, *Eng. Hist. Lit. in Fif. Cent.*, 374-375; *Chron. of John Stone*, 116; *Three Fif. Cent. Chron.*, 185.
2. Canterbury spent 9*d.* for white kersey "ad faciendum inde rosas." Hist. MSS. Com., *Report 9*, p. 176.
3. *Ibid.*, p. 142; Issue Roll, Easter 11 Edw. IV, 19 May; *Cal. Patent Rolls*, 296. For proof that Vaunt was in ward as late as 25 July, when the king's commissioners held their inquest at Canterbury, see Hist. MSS. Com., *Report 9*, p. 176. A list of Warwick's adherents was found in Faunt's pocket when he was arrested, but Sir George Browne managed to get hold of it and sent it down to Canterbury. *Ibid.*, p. 142. The Cinque Ports also lost their liberties and franchises. *Cal. Patent Rolls*, II, 260.

coming. As the Bastard of Fauconberg had made an offer to surrender his ships as soon as he heard that the king and his army were starting for Kent, Gloucester had already gone ahead to receive the ships, and all that Edward had to do when he reached Sandwich was to accept the Bastard's submission.[1] This he did at once and then, leaving Sir John Scott in charge at Sandwich, the Earl of Arundel at Dover, Thomas St Leger at Rochester, and a captain named John Brumston at Canterbury, he went back to London and took the Bastard with him.[2] A few days later (4 June) the Archbishop of York was released from the Tower, and shortly after the Bastard of Fauconberg received his pardon and undertook to serve under the Duke of Gloucester in the marches towards Scotland. Letters of protection were granted to the Bastard on 16 June, and he probably went north with Gloucester soon after.[3]

When Edward returned to London from Kent in May 1471, he must have felt that he was master of England as he had never been master of her before, since not only was his long struggle with Warwick over, but the great earl whose power had been only less than his own had dragged down to the grave with him both Henry VI and Henry VI's son. The only surviving representative of the house of Lancaster was young Henry Tudor, and the likelihood that those who had been ready to fight against all odds for Henry VI and his son would extend their devotion to the son of Margaret Beaufort and Edmund Tudor seemed slight. Probably the bitter experiences of the last ten years kept Edward from supposing that, even under these circumstances, the last stubborn adherent of the house of Lancaster would accept defeat, forget a lost cause, and become his loyal subject; and though to outward appearances he had forgiven Clarence, he knew that so long as Clarence lived there was one potential, if not actual, traitor in his own family circle. All things considered, however, the future looked much less difficult than the past had been, and the victory begun at Mortimer's Cross and Towton now appeared to be complete.

But if out of the troubles of the last ten years Edward the king had come forth triumphant, Edward the man, sad to say, had gone down in defeat. Very different from the brave, frank, generous, well-intentioned youth who

---

1. *Arrivall*, 39.
2. Issue Roll, Easter 11 Edw. IV, 19 May; *Cal. Patent Rolls*, II, 296; Hist. MSS. Com., *ut sup.*
3. Stow, 425; *Cal. Patent Rolls*, II, 262; French Roll 11 Edw. IV, m. 31. I have found nothing to support Stow's statement that Edward not only pardoned the Bastard, but "made him knight and vice-admiral."

had taken the crown from Henry VI with Warwick's aid in 1461 was the man who came back to England in 1471 to slay Warwick on the battlefield and Henry in a dungeon in the Tower. Edward of York was still a young man in 1471, for the battle of Towton was fought a few days before, the battle of Tewkesbury a few days after, his twenty-ninth birthday. He was also a brave man still. But ten years of kingship had taught him many bitter truths, and adversity, instead of making him wiser and better, had coarsened and brutalized him.

The men to whom Edward turned chiefly for advice during the second half of his reign were not more self-seeking nor more unscrupulous than the Woodvilles had shown themselves to be, and certainly not more cruel than Tiptoft, Earl of Worcester. But neither were they, unhappily, the kind of men to teach him wisdom and self-restraint or to lead him into paths of righteousness and peace. They were his chamberlain, Lord Hastings, who was neither a wise man nor a good, and his brother Gloucester, whose virtues now shone very bright by contrast with the ingratitude and faithlessness of Clarence but whose actions in years to come were to show that he was just as ambitious and untrustworthy as Clarence himself and, because he had more ability, really more dangerous.

Plenty of Woodvilles cumbered the earth even after Warwick's massacre of the summer of 1469, as four of the queen's brothers, Anthony, Earl Rivers, Lionel, who was to become near the end of Edward's reign chancellor of the University of Oxford and Bishop of Salisbury, Edward and Richard, were still living; but no one of these men seems ever to have exercised much influence over Edward. Indeed, for Anthony, second Earl Rivers, who was a knight of the tourney and a poet and lover of letters rather than a man of affairs, Edward appears to have felt a genuine contempt despite the fact that the earl had shared his days of exile in Burgundy and helped him more or less to regain his throne. When, soon after the battles of Barnet and Tewkesbury, Rivers asked permission to go to Portugal to fulfil a vow he had taken to fight the Saracens, Edward lost his temper, accused him of cowardice, because he wanted to leave the country at a time when there was so much to be done, and refused the request. Later the king relented, told the earl he might go and gave him a letter to all the potentates of Europe requesting a safeconduct for him, but though after Christmas there was a report that the earl had embarked for

Portugal on Christmas Eve, he did not leave England, and the Saracens never felt his steel.[1]

Perhaps Rivers gave up his crusade in the hope of pleasing the king, but if that was the case he made his sacrifice too late for his own good, as in the meantime he had lost the most important office he had ever held, the lieutenancy of Calais. The lieutenancy had been granted to him before Edward's flight from England, and there was no obvious reason why he should not have it again when Edward returned. Yet in July it was given to Lord Hastings.[2] No doubt Hastings was a fitter man for the post, but Rivers's chagrin was very deep, and it led to an enmity between Hastings and the Woodvilles which was scarcely less bitter, or less disastrous to the house of York in the long run, than the enmity which had existed between Warwick and the Woodvilles. Queen Elizabeth's dislike for the lord chamberlain was particularly intense, because it was based not only on the slight that had been put upon her brother for his sake, but on a suspicion that he was "secretly familiar with the king in wanton company."[3] Like any wife, she hated the encourager of her husband's infidelity.

The day on which he first reached London after his return from Burgundy Edward had ordered the appointment of new sheriffs throughout the kingdom and had required Henry's appointees to surrender their offices upon penalty of a fine of ten thousand pounds;[4] but on the whole he displayed the same desire to avoid all changes not actually imperative that Warwick had shown during Henry's readeption. He picked up the reins of government again as if he had dropped them voluntarily to go away on a few months' pleasure trip, rather than as if he had been driven out of his kingdom by open rebellion. The treasurership, which the dead Earl of Worcester had held, was given to the Earl of Essex; the great chamberlainship, left vacant by Warwick's death, to the Duke of Gloucester, and the chief butlership, which had been in Lord Wenlock's hands from 1460 till the day he fell at Tewkesbury, to the Earl of Wiltshire; and Chief Justice

---

1. *Paston Letters*, V, 106, 110, 131; Rymer, XI, 727; *Cal. Patent Rolls*, II, 292.
2. Writs of Privy Seal, file 834, no. 3232; French Roll 11 Edw. IV, m. 18.
3. More, *Hist. of Richard III*, 9. More says in another place that at one time, owing to some accusation which Rivers made against him, Hastings was "for the while (but it lasted not long) far fallen into the king's indignation and stood in great fear of himself."
4. Fine Roll 11 Edw. IV, m. 10.

Danby and Sir Richard Illingworth, chief baron of the Exchequer, were superseded, probably because they had shown more complacency towards Warwick than could well be overlooked.[1] But Stillington slipped back into his old place as chancellor, and Rotherham into his as keeper of the privy seal, as if the months of Henry's readeption had never been, and not only was Gloucester again constable of England and admiral, but Clarence, in spite of all that had occurred, was allowed to resume his old office, the lieutenancy of Ireland.[2] The care of the northern border was also divided again, as it had been in the last weeks before the flight to Burgundy, between Gloucester and Northumberland, though the power of Northumberland, who was warden of the east and middle marches, was subordinate to that of Gloucester, who was warden of the west march.[3]

The pleasantest task Edward had to perform after his home-coming and his two great victories was to make suitable provision for the son and heir born to him during his absence. On 26 June the child that had first seen the light in the Westminster sanctuary seven months before was created Prince of Wales, and on 3 July, in the parliament chamber, many lords spiritual and temporal, including the Archbishop of York, took the oath of allegiance to him as the undoubted heir to "the crowns and realms of England and of France and lordship of Ireland."[4] Straightaway, too, a bevy of officers were appointed to look after the Prince's needs. For the present the only really vital person in his entourage was his nurse; and Avice Welles, as she was named, must have performed her duties to the king's satisfaction and pleasure, for she was granted, soon after her charge celebrated his second birthday, a tun or two pipes of Gascon wine yearly and at another time was given silk for a gown that cost nearly ten pounds.[5] But the king's son was also provided with a chancellor, the Abbot of Westminster, who was already his godfather;

---

1. *Cal. Patent Rolls*, II, 258, 262; Writs of Privy Seal, file 832, no. 3150. Essex retained the treasurership until his death, which occurred only a few days before Edward's. Wiltshire died early in 1473, and Rivers was then made chief butler. Writs of Privy Seal, file 834, no. 3639; *Cal. Patent Rolls*, II, 415.
2. *Cal. Patent Rolls*, II, 272. For proof that Gloucester was exercising the offices of constable and admiral in July 1471, see *Ancient Correspondence*, Vol XLIV no. 61.
3. *Cal. Patent Rolls*, II, 313, 439, etc.; Hist. MSS. Com., *Report 6*, app., 223.
4. *Rolls of Parl.*, VI, 9, 234; Rymer, XI, 714. The heralds and minstrels received a largess of twenty pounds for their services on 26 June. Issue Roll, Easter 11 Edw. IV, 15 May.
5. *Cal. Patent Rolls*, II, 358; Tellers' Roll, Easter 17 Edw. IV.

a steward, Lord Dacre, and a chamberlain, Thomas Vaughan; and as he was burdened with the possession of the principality of Wales, the duchy of Cornwall, and the county of Chester, these three men, together with his mother, three of his uncles, Clarence, Gloucester and Rivers, Lord Hastings, John Alcock, and others, were appointed to administer his affairs for him until he attained his majority.[1]

Yet great as was the satisfaction the king took in thus starting his son and heir on life's journey with all the proper accoutrements, that pleasure was offset to some degree by the furious quarrel which broke out between his two brothers almost as soon as he was seated on his throne again and which, added to the animosity between Hastings and the Woodvilles, must have made the atmosphere of his court anything but pleasant and peaceful.

That the king should look with more favour and affection upon a brother who had been faithful to him than upon one who had tried to steal his crown was only natural, and in the distribution of offices Gloucester had been given three to Clarence's one. That much Clarence, with all his stupid selfishness, might have endured in silence, but as soon as he learned that Gloucester wanted to marry the young widow or fiancée of Henry VI's son, Anne Neville, who had been captured with Margaret of Anjou after the battle of Tewkesbury, his jealous wrath began to rise; and when, during the summer, all the vast estates which the Earl of Warwick had owned in Yorkshire and Cumberland were granted to Gloucester instead of to him,[2] the husband of Warwick's elder daughter, his anger and disappointment passed all bounds. Evidently he found out that the Lady Anne herself shrank from the thought of marrying his brother, for to escape Gloucester's attentions she seems to have suffered Clarence to carry her off and disguise her as a housemaid. But a very brief experience of kitchen life sufficed to alter the lady's feelings, and when Gloucester discovered her whereabouts, she allowed him to take her to the sanctuary of St Martin's. Naturally Clarence was made still angrier by this foiling of his plans, and at length Edward felt so disturbed about the dissension between his brothers that he called them both before his council. Nothing was gained by that, however, as each of the dukes brought forward so many arguments in favour of his own wishes and pretensions and pleaded

---

1. *Cal. Patent Rolls*, II, 283; Signed Bills, file 1502, no. 4385.
2. *Cal. Patent Rolls*, II, 260, 266.

his cause with so much skill and eloquence that even men learned in the law, it is said, listened to them with wonder and admiration.[1] The quarrel not only went on, but waxed hotter and hotter, until Clarence, if he had ever had any chance of redeeming himself in Edward's eyes, lost it for all time. More and more the king grew to feel that his brother Clarence was a viper, and perhaps his estimate of the duke's character was not far wrong. On the other hand, he seemed to pass on to Gloucester the affection Clarence had forfeited, and this enraged Clarence the more.

Abroad as well as at home Edward saw some clouds on the horizon as he scanned the skies in the months immediately following his recovery of his throne. But take it all in all, his position had never been stronger or his prospects brighter than now, and it was not long before the only really storm-like clouds showed signs of breaking up or drifting away.

The result of the battle of Barnet was known to the Duke of Burgundy within four days after the event.[2] The news was sent to him by his wife, who had it from Edward himself. As Margaret seasoned her message with a statement that her brother was far from satisfied with the niggardly amount of help he had received from Burgundy, Charles's first feeling was not one of pleasure. But fortune had not been smiling on him of late in his struggle with the king of France, and a moment's reflection sufficed to make him realize how much cause he had to rejoice that Warwick was not the victor instead of Edward. It was Charles who had solicited the truce with Louis which had so angered and alarmed Warwick as the earl was marching towards Barnet and death, and had the battle of Barnet terminated in a different way, he might have been forced to go down on his knees before Louis and beg for a treaty of peace. Consequently, though he never forgave Edward for finding fault with what he had done for him, Charles hastened to announce his brother-in-law's victory to his subjects and to Louis himself. He also bestowed pensions of a thousand pounds a year on Earl Rivers and Lord Hastings in recognition of the aid they had given to the king.[3]

---

1. *Hist. Croy. Cont.*, 557.
2. La Marche, III, 73, says that the news of Warwick's death reached Charles at Corbie. The duke was at Corbie from 11 to 18 April. Commynes-Lenglet, II, 198.
3. Commynes, I, 218-219; *Chronique Scandaleuse*, I, 256-257; Basin, II, 275; Commynes-Lenglet, II, 198, III, 617-620. Hastings continued to receive his pension from Charles until 1475, if not longer.

As for Louis, he did not know at first whether to believe what Charles told him about events in England or to think that the duke was lying to him. On 5 May Bettini informed the Duke of Milan that there had been a meeting at Peronne of representatives of the king of France and the Duke of Burgundy, but that nothing had been decided and that "things seem very different since the last news from England. The duke is very haughty and they now fear that there will be great difficulty in obtaining Picardy from him." The Burgundians, Bettini said further, had spread a report that the Earl of Warwick was dead, but an English herald who had just arrived at the French court declared that the earl was well and strong, and also that there was no truth in the story that the Duke of Clarence had been killed. Though the duke had been slightly wounded, he had recovered and was with his brother Edward. "I wish the country and the people were plunged deep in the sea," Bettini growled, "because of their lack of stability, for I feel like one going to the torture when I write about them, and no one ever hears twice alike about English affairs."[1]

Three weeks after Bettini wrote this letter, France was still in doubt about the situation in England. On 18 May another Milanese declared that Louis had received a letter from Queen Margaret the evening before in which the queen asserted that Warwick was not dead, but had merely withdrawn to a secret place to recover from the wounds he had received in the battle with Edward, and that her son was in London with many men. And on the 26th Bettini reported again:

> There is no news of English affairs except by way of Burgundy. They are masters of the sea together with the Bretons and Easterlings; not a bird can pass without being taken by them. However, two friars arrived here some days ago. They say that the affairs of the Prince of Wales are very prosperous and he has a countless number of men. The Burgundians here do not deny it and fear that the Prince may give King Edward a great deal of trouble. The friars also say that the death of the Earl of Warwick is not true, but in this people do not believe them.[2]

Edward was too busy immediately after the battle of Tewkesbury to give much thought to friend or foe beyond the sea, but at the end of May, while he was at Canterbury, he dispatched letters to the Duke of Burgundy, to his

---

1. *Cal. Milanese Papers*, I, 153-154.
2. *Ibid.*, I, 155.

kind host, the Seigneur de la Gruthuyse, and to the magistrates of Bruges; and with each letter he enclosed a "mémoire en papier" which contained an account of his fortunes since he sailed from Flushing and which was an abridgment of the now well-known *Historie of the Arrivall of Edward IV in England*.[1] The letter to Charles, which is dated 28 May, and that to the magistrates of Bruges, written just a day later, have been preserved,[2] and they show that if Edward had spoken somewhat impolitely and ungratefully of Charles when writing to his sister, he did not fail to be courteous and appreciative when writing directly to the duke himself. For he now expressed his gratitude for the hospitality extended to him during the months of his exile and, promising Charles that he would proclaim anew the league and intercourse of merchandise between England and Burgundy which had been in force at the time of his flight, he asked the duke to do the same.

Of Edward's letter to the Seigneur de la Gruthuyse no copy has ever come to light. Probably it never reached its destination, as Stephen Dryver, who set out with it from Sandwich while Edward was there, was captured by the French and held a prisoner at Dieppe for a month and three days—in other words, until he succeeded in furnishing ransoms for himself and his men to the amount of twenty-one pounds.[3] But the letter to the magistrates of Bruges was received at Bruges on 7 June,[4] and the one to Charles, which Edward intrusted to Pierre Courtois, one of the ducal secretaries who had apparently accompanied him to England, may have made even a speedier journey. At all events, on 2 June Bettini, after informing the Duke of Milan that the day before the king of France had learned that the Prince of Wales had fallen in battle and that Queen Margaret was a prisoner, closed his letter by saying that the Duke of Burgundy was showing his joy and satisfaction "by public demonstrations, constant processions, ringing of bells and bonfires, so that

---

1. See Bruce's introduction to the *Arrivall*, vi-vii.
2. The letter to Charles may be found in Plancher, IV, 306, that to the magistrates of Bruges in Gilliodts-van-Severen, VI, 62, Waurin, III, 146, Commynes-Dupont, III, 292, and *La Revolte du Conte de Warwick* (Caxton Society, 1849). A translation of the latter is printed in *Archæologia*, XXI, 23.
3. Writs of Privy Seal, file 836, no. 3323—the king's notification to the chancellor that he had granted Dryver a year's safeconduct for a ship or Ships of 600 tons burden. Cf. *Ibid.*, file 838, no. 3410.
4. Van Praet, *Recherches sur Louis de Bruges*, II.

one would imagine the whole country to be on fire. It is expected to make him so haughty that he will no more consent to a year's truce."[1]

It goes without saying that the king of France lighted no bonfires to celebrate the battles of Barnet and Tewkesbury. Edward's triumph meant to Louis not only the loss of the English alliance he had hoped to secure through Warwick; it probably meant also that Edward, with his desire for revenge whetted by recent events, would soon be renewing his plans for that invasion of France which his subjects had already shown their willingness, even eagerness, to support. More anxiously than ever, therefore, Louis pressed his negotiations with Charles for a longer truce, although there was fear, according to Bettini again, that if the duke consented to the truce, it would be merely to give himself a better chance to perfect his plans for an attack on France with the help of the English. And before many days had passed it was reported that Edward was already making preparations for war. On 17 June Bettini wrote: "We hear that King Edward is devoting all his attention to gathering a large force to send it to war against this kingdom." But he went on to say that, although the French were not without uneasiness, no one thought the English would make a descent this season, and in the meantime a complete agreement might be made with the Duke of Burgundy. "If this takes place, there will be little to fear from the English afterwards," he declared; "but if it does not, they will have more to fear than they may want." There would be one advantage in a war with the English, he added, for in such a war there would be no danger of a secret understanding with the French lords, as there was when it was a case of war with the Duke of Burgundy alone. At the same time he confessed that Edward and Charles would probably make many conquests from the king of France, and that the war was likely to be long and bloody. Two days later he was writing again. "Rumours and advices," he said this time, "continue to increase that the English are getting ready to come at present and land in Normandy and Guienne. They are very anxious about it here, and their suspicions are strengthened by this new attitude of the Duke of Burgundy in refusing to accept the truce as arranged by his ambassadors by his order. The king on his side does not relax any of his preparations for war." Even a month later the scare was not over.

---

1. *Cal. Milanese Papers*, I, 156. The Duchess of Burgundy celebrated her brother's victory with a huge bonfire at Ghent on 12 June. Commynes-Lenglet, II, 198.

"His Majesty has a large fleet at sea," Bettini wrote at that time, "and he increases it every day with the intention of fighting the English before they land, should they attempt to come here as talked of."[1]

But, in reality, whatever developments the future might bring forth, Louis had little to fear from the English at present. Edward had accomplished wonders in a few weeks, but even with that he did not yet have his kingdom well enough in hand to undertake a war with France. Calais had not been brought to submission; Kent was still in such a state that it was necessary to keep garrisons in the chief towns, and Jasper Tudor, Earl of Pembroke, as Louis well knew, was at large in Wales.

The subduing of Calais proved less difficult than Edward probably anticipated. It was not until the middle of July that Hastings was appointed lieutenant of Calais,[2] and when he crossed the sea in August, he took with him Lord Howard, who was to be his deputy,[3] and fifteen hundred armed men, besides two hundred members of the "old retinue." The new lieutenant was also provided, however, with letters of pardon for Gate, Wrottesley, and all other persons in Calais and Guines, as well as with a commission to pay the wages of the garrison and to dismiss the more than five hundred extra men that had been added to the garrison by Warwick.[4] Very likely these documents were of more service to him than his troops. For Gate and Wrottesley decided to submit at once rather than attempt to resist or to seek asylum in France, and their submission enabled Hastings to enter Calais "peaceably." Gate and Wrottesley were then sent to London, and with them probably went the late Marquis of Montagu's eleven year old son, George Neville, who had certainly been in Calais in June and whose name was included in Edward's letters of pardon.[5]

---

1. *Cal. Milanese Papers*, I, 156-158, 160.

2. Writs of Privy Seal, file 834, no. 3232; French Roll 11 Edw. IV, m. 18. The terms of Hastings's indenture with the king may be found in a warrant to the treasurer of Calais, Exchequer Accounts, France, bundle 197, no. 17.

3. Writs of Privy Seal, file 834, no. 3240; French Roll 11 Edw. IV, m. 18.

4. Signed Bills, file 1502, no. 4394; French Roll 11 Edw. IV, m. 26 and 30; Writs of Privy Seal, file 835, nos. 3261, 3263; Warrants for Issues, 11 Edw. IV, 16 July; Tellers' Rolls, Mich. 11 and 12 Edw. IV; Issue Roll, Easter 11 Edw. IV, 19 May; Foreign Roll 12 Edw. IV, m. E; *Cal. Patent Rolls*, II, 270, 290.

5. *Paston Letters*, V, III; *Hist. Croy. Cont.*, 557; *Lettres de Louis XI*, IV, 244; Writs of Privy Seal, file 835, no. 3261. For proof that George Neville was at this time eleven years of age, see Inquisitions *post mortem*, 16 Edw. IV, no. 29. The Marchioness of Montagu was ultimately granted the custody of her son. *Cal. Patent Rolls*, II, 335.

When Calais saw fit to yield, Guines could hardly attempt to resist even if she wished to do so. And perhaps it was not her wish, as Richard Whetehill had already been reappointed lieutenant of Guines on 28 June,[1] a fact from which it would appear that, in spite of his close relations with Warwick in earlier years, he had either remained faithful to Edward during the recent troubles or had bought the king's favour by submitting at the earliest possible moment. Hammes Castle too seems to have submitted without a struggle this time, and John Blount continued to be, or became again, the king's lieutenant there.[2]

Although Calais had been deeply implicated in the Bastard of Fauconberg's insurrection, Edward had been glad to deal gently with her. But towards Kent and Essex, the counties from which the Bastard had drawn most of his men, he pursued quite a different policy. In their case there was no king of France just over the wall watching and waiting for a chance to slip in, and Edward chose to make an example of the Kentishmen and their neighbours which neither they nor the rest of his subjects would soon forget. Although the names of the Earls of Essex and Arundel headed the list of commissioners who were appointed on 15 July to inquire into the late insurrections, the actual work of the commission devolved on Lord Dynham, Sir Thomas Bourchier, Sir John Fogg, and two other men;[3] and they adopted thoroughness rather than justice as their watchword. However, though two petty captains, Spising of Essex, the man who had led the Bastard's attack on Aldgate, and Quint of Rochester, were executed and their heads sent to London to be set up on Aldgate,[4] in general money was preferred to heads. The king's commissioners "sat upon all Kent, Sussex, and Essex that were at the Blackheath," declares Warkworth, "and upon many other that were not there; for some men paid two hundred mark, some a hundred pound, and some more and some less, so that it cost the poorest man seven shillings which was not worth so much, but was fain to sell such clothing as they had

1. Writs of Privy Seal, file 834, no. 3245; French Roll 11 Edw. IV, m. 28. For the terms of Whetehill's indenture, see Exchequer Accounts, bundle 71, no. 5. Hastings was afterwards made joint lieutenant with him. French Roll 11 Edw. IV, m. 11.
2. Writs of Privy Seal, file 843, no. 3699; French Roll 13 Edw. IV, m. 28.
3. *Cal. Patent Rolls*, II, 287, 299-300; Hist. MSS. Com., *Report 9*, app., 177.
4. Kingsford's *London Chron.*, 185; Fabyan, 662; Stow, 425; Hist. MSS. Com., *Report 9*, app., 141.

and borrowed the remnant and laboured for it afterward. And so the king had out of Kent much good and little love."[1]

Calais' submission had been obtained with little effort, and the frightened followers of the Bastard of Fauconberg had been powerless to oppose the officers of the law. But the Earl of Pembroke was a trouble not so quickly disposed of, as not only the Welsh mountains and castles, but the Welsh people, whose devotion to all who represented the house of Lancaster nothing seemed to destroy, gave shelter to Jasper Tudor.

If Margaret of Anjou had succeeded in effecting a junction with Tudor, as she hoped to do, before Edward overtook her at Tewkesbury, the subsequent battle might have had a very different ending. But Edward's quickness spoiled all, and Tudor, who probably was not far away at the time of the battle, retired to Chepstow when he heard of the day's disaster. Soon after the battle Edward sent one Roger Vaughan in pursuit of the earl, but not only did Vaughan fail to capture the prey he sought, but he was himself captured and beheaded. From Chepstow Tudor withdrew to Pembroke, taking his nephew Henry with him, and there he was immediately besieged by one Ap Thomas; yet though the odds were so much against him that it seemed as if he must inevitably surrender, at the end of a week Ap Thomas's own brother came to the rescue and raised the siege.[2]

Ready as his Welsh friends were to help him, it was not from them alone that the Earl of Pembroke was getting support. Early in July Paston wrote to his mother that "the Scots and the Welsh men be busy," but that "what they mean" he could not say.[3] Something of what the Welsh and the Scots meant, however, is revealed by two of Bettini's letters. On 16 July Bettini told the Duke of Milan that the king of France entirely agreed with his suggestion

---

1. Warkworth, 21-22. Anyone questioning the thoroughness of Kent's punishment need only consult some reports of the king's commissioners which are preserved in *Ancient Correspondence*, Vol. LVII, nos. 107-110, and the one printed in Hist. MSS. Com., *ut sup.* "Gifts" from various persons in Kent and Essex are entered on Tellers' Roll, Mich. 11 Edw. IV. Cf. Ramsay, II, 391.
2. According to Vergil, from whose history the above facts are derived, Tudor was attacked by Morgan Thomas and rescued by David Thomas; but. as Edward gave a reward of £20 to one John Seynolo, knight, for capturing Morgan ap Thomas (Tellers' Roll, Mich. 11 Edw. IV), it looks rather as if it were David ap Thomas who besieged Pembroke and Morgan who came to Tudor's relief.
3. *Paston Letters*, V, 107.

that it would be well to "try and keep up some disturbances in England" and that he was doing all he could to that end. "He still has there the Earl of Pembroke, brother of the late King Henry on his mother's side, who has a good number of places in Wales, a strong country and near to Scotland, which is in constant opposition to King Edward with the help of the Scots. He has arranged to give assistance to this earl and to the Scots also, and to do what he can for them, so that they may keep up the war and disturbance." And on 6 August Bettini wrote again: "It seems that the Earl of Pembroke, with some other lords and the help of the Scots, is still keeping matters unsettled in England. His Majesty has sent an ambassador to the said earl and to the king of Scotland."[1]

As long as Louis could keep the Welsh and the Scots "busy," he was not likely to see an English army landing in Normandy or Guienne. Nevertheless, he had need of all his courage and all his cleverness; for it was as he feared—another league hostile to him was taking shape, mainly through the efforts of the Duke of Brittany, and despite the assertion of Bettini, who evidently had not studied the history of past wars between England and France, that the loyalty of the lords of France could be counted on in case of a war with the English, the king of England was again being urged to join the league. On 17 June Bettini had written, in cipher, that it was thought that if Louis and the Duke of Burgundy reached an agreement, a marriage between Charles's daughter and the Duke of Guienne would follow. But Bettini or anyone else who thought that Louis would favour, or even tolerate, a marriage between his brother and the Burgundian heiress was very much mistaken. Since the birth of the Dauphin the Duke of Guienne had become refractory and seditious again, and Louis' feeling towards his brother was very like Edward's feeling towards Clarence. That there was talk of such a marriage was true, but the plan was not of Louis' making. It emanated from Francis II and his confederate, the Count of St Pol, who were proposing to make Louis' brother the nominal head of their new league against Louis, just as he had been the nominal head of the League of the Public Weal six years before, and who thought that, by leading the Duke of Burgundy to think that through the league he would be able to recover the lost Somme towns, they could win his consent to the marriage.

---

1. *Cal. Milanese Papers*, I, 160.

Francis had drawn other important persons into his league besides the Duke of Guienne and the Count of St Pol. The most powerful nobleman of the south of France, Gaston de Foix, whose daughter Francis had recently married, was also a party to it. So was the man Louis hated most of all, the husband of another daughter of the Count of Foix, the Count of Armagnac, who, in September 1460, had been condemned to forfeit all his goods, chiefly on the ground that he had been guilty of intriguing with the English, and who was now bent on recovering what had been taken from him.[1] Yet Francis wanted, in addition, the help of Edward, whose goodwill he had some right to count on, as he had responded to the urgent appeal for help which Edward had sent to him from Flanders and, since Edward's recovery of the throne, had ordered his subjects to observe the treaties made with England before the king's flight.[2] According to report, the Abbot of Bégard was the envoy whom Francis sent to England in July, or about that time, with a request for help against Louis; and probably the report was true, as a messenger of the Abbot of Bégard carried letters from Edward to Francis not long after.[3]

Of far greater weight in Edward's estimation than the desire the Duke of Brittany showed to make him a partner in the new league against the king of France were the signs the Duke of Burgundy also gave of a wish to enter into an alliance with him against Louis. On 5 July Charles renewed his truce with Louis until 1 May 1472, but that did not prevent him from receiving in the same month some envoys from Francis and the Duke of Guienne who brought him further messages regarding the league and the proposed marriage between his daughter and the Duke of Guienne;[4] and even at the moment that he signed the renewal of his truce with Louis, Charles had an embassy in England on an errand which boded anything but good for France. For shortly after he heard of Edward's final victory, Charles had sent Baudoin de Lannoy, Seigneur de Molembais, and one of his secretaries to England, and these ambassadors, one of whom, the ducal

---

1. Commynes-Lenglet, III, 141-145; Dupuy, *Réunion de la Bretagne a la France*, I, 276, *et seq.*; Samaran, *La maison d'Armagnac*, 176-178. At the beginning of November John of Aragon concluded an alliance with the Dukes of Burgundy and Brittany. He was looking for the opportunity to recover Roussillon and Cerdagne which came a year later.
2. 19 June. Diplomatic Documents (Exchequer, T. of R.), box 19, no 541; 45th Report of Deputy Keeper, app., 333.
3. Issue Roll, Easter 11 Edw. IV, 13 July; Tellers' Roll, Mich. 11 Edw. IV.
4. Dupuy, I, 281; Plancher, IV, cccvii.

secretary, died in England, probably of the plague, as did also the clerk of the Seigneur de Molembais, were directed by Charles not simply to extend his congratulations to Edward on his success, but to urge the king to unite with him in an attempt to crush Louis. The king of France was as much the enemy of England as of Burgundy, Charles argued, and this mutual attack on him, the duke maintained, would give the king of England an opportunity both to revenge his wrongs and to recover his rights.[1]

Edward replied to Charles's invitation by sending Doctor John Russell to ask for fuller information about the duke's proposal, and to Francis he seems to have sent word that, if he supported the league, he would expect to be repaid with assistance to recover Guienne or Normandy.[2] But the prospect of a marriage between Mary of Burgundy and Louis' brother filled Edward with such intense alarm that even the possibility of recovering Guienne or Normandy seemed by comparison a small matter. Louis' only son was a sickly child, and if the Duke of Guienne married Mary of Burgundy and afterwards, by the death of the Dauphin, became king of France, England would be confronted with a union of France and Burgundy which would spell her ruin. When Russell hastened to point out this danger to Charles, the duke tried to make it clear, without saying so in plain words, that he had no intention of permitting his daughter to marry the Duke of Guienne; but notwithstanding this, Edward's fears grew daily until he seems to have contemplated a complete *volte-face*, a joining of forces with Louis against Francis's league and the reopening of the negotiations Louis had attempted

---

1. Haynin, II, 193; *Hist. Croy. Cont.*, 556-557. Edward presented "Master Simon," ambassador of the Duke of Burgundy, with three pieces of cloth and £33 6*s* 8*d* in money. Issue Roll, Easter 11 Edw. IV, 13 July; Tellers' Roll, Mich. 11 Edw. IV. William Bysse of Burgundy, knight (Guillaume de Bische, Seigneur de Clery-sur-Somme?), also received a small sum of money. Issue Roll, *ut sup.*

   From the "Confidences d'Henri Millet," *Lettres de Louis XI*, IV, 358, one would conclude that the first suggestion of a joint war against France came, not from Charles, but from Edward. But that does not seem to have been the case, though probably Charles wanted the Dukes of Brittany and Guienne to think it was.

2. *Hist. Croy. Cont.*, 557; *Lettres de Louis XI, ut sup.*; Issue Roll, *ut sup.* According to a marginal note to the third continuation of the Croyland chronicle, the author of that continuation served as Edward's ambassador to Burgundy on this occasion. He may have accompanied Russell, who, the entry on the Issue Roll shows, was absent from England twenty-eight days.

to begin with Rotherham in 1468 for a marriage alliance between the houses of York and Valois.[1]

As it proved, Edward was not the only person who was nervous and ready to take fright. His intimation that, if he joined the league, he would expect help to reconquer Guienne or Normandy so alarmed the Duke of Guienne that the duke began to make preparations to protect his duchy against the English.[2] In the end both the Duke of Guienne and Francis decided that it would be safer to drop Edward out of their plans altogether, and they entreated the Duke of Burgundy not to seek the assistance of the ancient enemies of France.[3] Charles, in consequence, gave Russell an evasive answer, merely telling him that he would send an embassy to England with a definite reply sometime before All Saints' Day, while, to cheer Francis and the Duke of Guienne, he declared that he was "mauvais Anglois," that he loved the crown of France, and that when all had been arranged with the lords of France, he would listen no more to the king of England's demands.[4]

It was when the prospects of the league were in this rather gloomy state that Louis managed to pick up pretty full information about it. He sent Oliver le Roux to the Count of Foix on some mission, and Le Roux, happening to be lodged in the same house with one Henri Millet, who had come from the Duke of Brittany, succeeded in extracting from his fellow lodger almost all there was to know concerning the league and its plans and difficulties.[5] The immediate result of Le Roux's discoveries seems to have been a decision on Louis' part to respond quickly and graciously to Edward's advances, as scarcely had Le Roux's letter telling of what he had learned from Millet been received and read, when Louis sent over to England Pierre de Cerisay, son of the Guillaume de Cerisay who had gone to England with the Bishop of Bayeux during Henry VI's readeption, and not long after Bettini was writing from the French court:

> His Majesty still continues the negotiations for an understanding and marriage alliance with the king of England which I reported in my previous letter had been begun . . . . and I feel sure there will be no failure on his side to carry it into

1. Commynes, I, 226-228; *Cal. Milanese Papers*, I, 160-161.
2. See a letter which the duke wrote to the Sire d'Albret on 4 August. Mèrtene and Durand, *Veterum Scriptorum Amplissima Collectio*, I, 1602-1603.
3. Commynes, *ut sup.*
4. *Lettres de Louis XI, ut sup.*
5. *Ibid.*

effect, though there is considerable doubt as to whether the king of England may not break off. It is thought that he may have started the proposals in order to lull his Majesty to sleep to prevent him from sending help to the Earl of Pembroke or to any other of his opponents, so as to secure himself thoroughly in that kingdom of England and then snap his fingers at his Majesty.[1]

Edward knew too much about the feeling of his people towards the French not to be a little apprehensive in regard to what they might say and do when they discovered that an embassy from Louis had arrived in England. So he inserted in the safeconduct he gave to Cerisay an order to his subjects to show the stranger and his companions "all such cheer and humanity as ye can make, the more tenderly for our pleasure, as we may have cause to thank you."[2] Probably even this did not save the French ambassador from a pelting with taunts and gibes by the populace, but at least he escaped serious violence, and on 1 September Goldwell and Vaughan were appointed to treat with him. Edward was ready not only to consider a truce with France, but even to arrange with Cerisay for the holding of a diet to negotiate a final peace. But a truce was the only thing agreed on, and even that was to endure only until 1 May 1472, the date at which the truce between Louis and Charles would expire. Edward ratified this truce on 5 September, and Cerisay seems to have hurried home immediately after to lay it before Louis for his approval and ratification.[3]

At this moment, as far as the Duke of Brittany's league was concerned, the gods seemed to be siding with Louis. Yet not everything was going Louis' way; for even before Cerisay went to England, the king of Scotland had grown tired of playing Louis' game, and about the time Cerisay came home the Earl of Pembroke, though not by his own volition, slipped out of reach.

As early as 7 August Edward had received word from James III that he was willing to send the Bishop of Glasgow and other commissioners to Alnwick on 23 September to treat for redress of infractions of the truce between England and Scotland. The message had so friendly a sound that Edward gave to three of the representatives he chose to go to Alnwick, Alcock, Hatclyf, and Sir William Parre, authority to negotiate with the Scots

---

1. *Cal. Milanese Papers, ut sup.*
2. Warrants under the Signet, file 1381, 25 August 1471; French Roll 11 Edw. IV, m. 15.
3. Rymer, XI, 721-722.

for a marriage alliance.[1] As for Jasper Tudor, when the Scots retired from the field, his position became dangerous in the extreme, as at once Edward gave a commission to William Herbert, Earl of Pembroke, and Lord Ferrers to call out the men of South Wales and the marches against him.[2] The Yorkist Earl of Pembroke was not to have the satisfaction, however, of capturing his Lancastrian rival, for before he could reach the neighbourhood of Pembroke Castle, Tudor and his nephew fled to Tenby, where they hired a boat to take them to France. But the master of the boat was a Breton, and owing either to his treachery or to a storm, the voyage of Tudor and his nephew ended in the port of Brest, where they found themselves guests, not of the king of France, but of the Duke of Brittany.[3]

Had Jasper Tudor and his nephew succeeded in their intention of taking shelter at Louis' court, Edward's anxieties would scarcely have been lessened by their flight from Wales; and even as it was, there was no certainty that they would not ultimately make their way into Louis' open arms. For though Francis had just set his seal to a renewal of the thirty years' treaty which he had signed with Edward in 1468,[4] he did not hesitate to give his unexpected guests, enemies of Edward though they were, a cordial welcome and a promise of his protection, and what he would decide to do with them even he did not yet know. As soon as he learned that Tudor and his nephew were in Brittany, Edward began to make large offers to Francis to induce the duke to hand them over to him, but at the same time Louis was insisting that Francis must surrender them to him, or at least promise not to let them pass into the control of anyone else.[5] On 28 September Paston wrote that it was said "the Earl of Pembroke is taken on to Brittany; and men say that the king shall have delivery of him hastily, and some say that the king of France will see him safe and shall set him at liberty again."[1] But as it turned

---

1. *Ibid.*, XI, 716-719; *Cal. Documents relating to Scotland*, IV, 282-283. Alcock was paid £20 in advance for his expenses, and Hatclyf £40. Warrants for Issues, 11 Edw. IV, 17 and 18 August; Issue Roll, Easter 11 Edw. IV, 13 July.

2. *Cal. Patent Rolls*, II, 289.

3. Vergil, 674; Commynes-Lenglet, III, 138; Morice, III, 266-270; Bernardi Andreæ *Vita Henrici VII* (*Memorials of King Henry VII*), 15-18; Alain Bouchart, *Grandes Croniques de Bretaigne*, III, 220.

4. 23 August. Rymer, XII, 22.

5. Vergil, 674, 676; Commynes-Lenglet and Morice, *ut sup.* The records contain no trace of the bribes Vergil says Edward offered Francis.

out, neither the king of England nor the king of France had anything to say about Tudor's fate. On 30 September Edward in his turn sealed the renewal of the thirty years' treaties between England and Brittany, but if he did so in the belief that Francis would yield in the matter of Tudor and his nephew, he was doomed to disappointment, as the most the duke would promise him was that the fugitives should be kept under a surveillance so strict that they would have no chance to do him harm.[2] Francis realized that the sea had cast up on his shore a valuable and useful prize, and that prize he meant to keep at least for the present.

The Earl of Pembroke and his nephew were not the only foes from whom Edward was delivered at the close of the summer. The end of another was reported by Paston in the same letter in which he spoke of Pembroke's flight. Sometime before 11 September it was learned that the Bastard of Fauconberg had deserted Gloucester's service and fled.[3] Perhaps the Bastard, like Pembroke, was trying to get away to France, or perhaps he was hoping to join Sir Thomas Fulford, who about this time succeeded, with the help of some of his friends, in escaping from the Westminster sanctuary and in making his way to Devon, where he began to stir up commotions. But whatever the Bastard's plan may have been, he quickly came to grief, as he was captured by Gloucester and beheaded at Middleham. On 15 September Paston wrote that he understood "the Bastard Fauconberg is either headed or like to be, and his brother both; some men say he would have deserved it, and some say nay." And afterwards, in his letter of the 28th, he said: "Thomas Fauconberg his head was yesterday set upon London bridge looking into Kent ward; and men say his brother was sore hurt and escaped to sanctuary at Beverley."[4]

This last letter from Paston was full of interesting news, for in addition to what he wrote about the Earl of Pembroke and the Bastard of Fauconberg, he told his brother that the king and queen had gone on a pilgrimage to

---

1. *Paston Letters*, V, 112-113.
2. Rymer, XI, 722; Vergil, *ut sup.*
3. *Cal. Patent Rolls*, II, 288.
4. Warkworth, 20; *Paston Letters*, V, 109, 111, 113;   Waurin, III, 145; Fabyan, 662-663; Kingsford's *London Chron.*, 185; Stow, 425. The statement by Fabyan that the Bastard was captured near Southampton must be incorrect, as he was executed at Middleham. The brother escaped to sanctuary must have been William Neville, another Bastard of Fauconberg. He was given a pardon in October 1477. *Cal. Patent Rolls*, III, 57.

Canterbury with so large a company that it was said that never before had so many people been seen in one pilgrimage. Europe had been in the grip of the plague all summer, and in an earlier letter Paston had described the epidemic as "the most universal death that ever I wist in England."[1] The king had taken such fright that, before the danger was past, he swallowed ten pounds' worth of medicine "contra pestem."[2] Yet happily he and all the members of the royal family escaped unharmed, and the great pilgrimage to Canterbury was probably one of thanksgiving. But if the king's journey was first of all a pilgrimage, it seems to have had another object as well; for while the noble company was at Canterbury, Mayor Faunt was hanged, drawn, and quartered.[3] The Bastard of Fauconberg's attempt to escape may have sealed Faunt's fate.

It is pleasant to know that Faunt's execution terminated the tragedy of the Bastard of Fauconberg's insurrection. Edward had now had all the vengeance he wanted, and shortly after he returned to London he offered a general pardon—an offer which was so welcome to his subjects that the entries on the Pardon Roll of this first year of his recovered sovereignty fill thirty-five membranes of parchment.[4]

Among the many persons who sought the king's pardon at this time were two notable prisoners of the battle of Tewkesbury, Sir John Fortescue and the already once pardoned Doctor Ralph Mackerell.[5] Fortescue had been the

---

1. *Paston Letters,* V, 110. Cf. *Ibid.,* 119, *Chronique Scandaleuse* I, 262, and *Caspar Weinreich's Chron.,* 737.
2. Issue Roll, Easter 11 Edw. IV, 15 May.
3. Warkworth mentions Faunt's execution twice. The first time he speaks as if it occurred after the Bastard of Fauconberg's execution, but the second time as if it took place during the king's visit to Canterbury in May. And this latter date has usually been accepted by historians. It cannot have taken place in May, however, since there is proof, as has been stated above, that the mayor was alive and in ward at Canterbury as late as 25 July.
4. *Paston Letters,* V, 116; Signed Bills, file 1503, no. 4422; Pardon Roll 11 Edw. IV; *Cal. Patent Rolls,* II, 299-303. One person who obtained a pardon was the antiquarian and chronicler, William of Worcester. Pardon Roll 11 Edw. IV, m. 26. In his pardon he is described as William Worcestre of Pokethorp, co. Norfolk, gentleman, *alias* William Worcetyr, *alias* William Wyrcestre, *alias* William Botener, *alias* William Wursetur, *alias* William Worsetyr, *alias* William Worceter! May not the modern historian be pardoned if he is sometimes inconsistent in his spelling of fifteenth century names?
5. Fortescue's pardon was granted on 13 October, Mackerell's on 4 November, and Fulford's, which is mentioned below, on 4 December. *Cal. Patent Rolls,* II, 296, 303; Pardon Roll 11 Edw. IV, m. 13.

wisest and most devoted friend Margaret of Anjou and her son had found during all their years of exile and poverty, but he was too valuable a man to be allowed to spend his remaining years in obscurity, even though he had adhered to the wrong cause. After a little while he was induced to refute "by large and clear writings" all the arguments against the right of the house of York to the throne which he had advanced in the earlier productions of his pen; then his attainder was reversed, and he became a member of Edward's council.[1] Even to Sir Thomas Fulford, in spite of his recent escapade, a pardon was not denied; and Sir Thomas Cook also ultimately obtained grace. Though Edward had ordered the seizure of Cook's goods when he first came back from Burgundy and found that the mercer had fled, Cook's wife received a pardon on 20 December and when, some months later, her husband and her son were released from their captivity in Flanders and delivered into Edward's hands, they too were pardoned. Poor Cook seems to have spent the rest of his days in peace, which probably means in comparative poverty, and he finally passed out of this world of trouble on 28 April 1478.[2]

Yet while it is evident that Edward, even now when he had learned to punish with such a heavy hand, really preferred to pardon, there were a few persons towards whom he relented slowly. Of the ecclesiastics he had sent to the Tower immediately after he came home, the Archbishop of York had received a pardon a few days after the battle of Tewkesbury, and the Bishops of Winchester, Lincoln, and Chichester obtained theirs during the summer; but the two Welsh bishops, who may have been suspected of taking too much interest in Jasper Tudor, were kept waiting longer. The Bishop of Llandaff did not get his pardon until 12 February 1472, while that of the Bishop of St David's seems to have been withheld until the following September.[3] Even then the Welsh bishops went free long before two other persons whose fate the fortunes of war had placed in Edward's hands. Edward had no wish to

---

1. Warkworth, 19; *Rolls of Parl.*, VI, 69; Plummer, Fortescue's *Governance of Eng.*, 72. "The Declaration made by John Fortescu, knyght, upon certayn Wrytinges sent oute of Scotteland ayenst the Kinges Title to the Roialme of England" may be found in Lord Clermont's edition of Fortescue's works. Fortescue became a member of Edward's council before the end of 1474, for he was present at a council meeting held in the Star Chamber on 26 November of that year. Signed Bills, file 1508, no. 4671.
2. Fabyan, 660, 662; Pardon Roll 11 Edw. IV, m. 28; *Cal. Patent Rolls*, II, 347; Inquisitions *post mortem*, 18 Edw. IV, no. 51.
3. *Cal. Patent Rolls*, II, 259, 261, 294, 299; Pardon Roll 12-17 Edw. IV, m. 18.

treat the Duke of Exeter as he had treated the duke's associate, Somerset, for Exeter had been his sister's husband; but before 26 May, seemingly in defiance of all sanctuary rights, the duke was removed from the Westminster sanctuary to the Tower, and though a chaplain, a cook, and a number of other servants were hired to look after his wants, in the Tower he was destined to languish for many a day to come.[1]

Harder still was the lot of one who was sometimes Exeter's neighbour in the Tower. Happily there is reason to believe that Margaret of Anjou was not in the Tower the night her husband was murdered there; for though she had been brought to London in Edward's train immediately after the battle of Tewkesbury, she spent her first few months of captivity at Windsor. After those first months she was sometimes in the custody of Edward's sister, the Duchess of Suffolk, at Ewelme in Oxfordshire, and sometimes at the Tower under the eye of Lord Dudley, the constable. When she was in the Duchess of Suffolk's charge, the allowance made to the duchess for her "diets" was eight marks a week, but when she was at the Tower, Dudley drew as much as a hundred shillings a week for her expenses. Her wardrobe was also replenished, to some extent at least, at the public expense, for on one occasion seven yards of woollen cloth called puke, which was provided for her by a London tailor, and on another six yards of black velvet for "frontlets, tippets, and other necessaries," which she received from Caniziani, were paid for at the Exchequer.[2] She was also permitted to keep Lady Katharine Vaux with her, and two other women, Petronilla and Mary, were appointed to wait on her. Still, it is easy to imagine the mental sufferings of the proud and high-spirited queen. Probably her father made some effort to obtain her release, as Edward's council at one time sent one Guillaume de la Barre to the king of Sicily, "father of Margaret, late called queen of England."[3] But the only person who could give her much help was the king of France, and even if Louis' hard heart felt some pity for her, his relations with Edward were in so delicate a state that it was too much to hope that he would take the risk of making a plea on her behalf.

---

1. Issue Roll, Easter 11 Edw. IV; Tellers' Roll, Mich. 11 Edw. IV; Devon, *Issues of the Exchequer*, 496; Rymer, XI, 713-714.
2. *Paston Letters*, V, 131; Warrants for Issues, 11 Edw. IV, 26 Sept.; Tellers' Rolls, Easter and Mich. 13 and 14 Edw. IV.
3. Tellers' Roll, Mich. 13 Edw. IV.

There was no apparent reason why the Duke of Burgundy should raise objections to the truce Edward was proposing to sign with Louis, as it was to end on the same day on which his own truce with Louis would expire. But as nothing could serve Louis' ends better than to increase the ill-feeling between Edward and Charles which he knew existed beneath the surface, it is not unlikely that an embassy which he sent to Charles in August let fall a few hints about the desire Edward had been showing for a marriage alliance with the house of Valois. As it happened, too, Edward gave Charles further cause to feel irritated with him by sending Hastings, Hatclyf, and others, towards the end of October, to say that the merchants of the staple found themselves unable to pay the thirteen thousand pounds of the Duchess Margaret's dowry which they had undertaken to have ready at some date already past, and to ask from the duke not only an extension of time in which to make the payment, but a reduction of the amount to be paid.[1]

What reply Charles made to this unpalatable request concerning his wife's dowry there is nothing to show, though he was probably forced to agree at least to the extension of time. But the duke's temper was evidently so upset either by Edward's failure to send the money due to him or by something Louis' ambassadors let drop that he seems to have sought comfort in the thought that a day might come when he could throw off the Yorkist alliance he had never liked and himself lay claim to the throne of England. For on 3 November Charles of Burgundy, descendant of John of Gaunt, signed at the Abbey of St Bertin in Arras, in the presence of his chancellor and two other witnesses, a statement that his mother, Isabella of Portugal, had declared herself to be the rightful heir to all of the possessions of Henry VI, late king of England, that she had ceded her claims to him, that he accepted this gift, and that it was his intention to make good his title to the kingdom of England as soon as a suitable opportunity offered. He declared further that if, for reasons concerning the welfare of the Faith and of the house of Burgundy, he delayed to establish his claim, and even if in the meantime he called another by the title of king of England, his rights would not suffer prejudice thereby.[2]

---

1. Warrants under the Signet, file 1382, 23 Oct.; French Roll 11 Edw. IV, m. 15. Hatclyf spent forty-four days on this embassy and was paid as many pounds for his services, besides five marks for his passage and re-passage, Warrants for Issues, 11 Edw. IV, 9 Dec., 22 Jan.
2. Gachard *Trésor national* (Brussels, 1842), II, 122-127.

Had one of Louis' numerous eavesdroppers been hidden in the Abbey of St Bertin the day Charles signed this declaration, the king might have decided that he need worry no more about a joint attack on France by the Duke of Burgundy and Edward of England. But Charles's secret was well kept, and about a fortnight later Louis offered to give back to him St Quentin and Amiens, the most important of the Somme towns, if he would renounce his alliance with the Dukes of Guienne and Brittany and promise to give his daughter's hand to the Dauphin instead of to the Duke of Guienne.[1] Such a bribe as this Louis thought Charles could not possibly resist and, probably because he was convinced that he had drawn the fangs of the most dangerous of his enemies, he pretended to feel quite indifferent about the truce Cerisay had negotiated with Edward. He found fault with it because it did not provide for free mercantile intercourse between England and France and proposed to limit it to forty days; and when, early in December, an English herald who was on his way to Burgundy came to him to ask for a safeconduct for an embassy from Edward, he wrote to the ambassadors through whom he had made his marriage offer to Charles that, until he received the duke's answer, he would make no treaty with anyone in the world.[2]

There is nothing to show that Cerisay's truce ever received Louis' ratification. But perhaps by this time Edward cared little whether it was accepted or not, as he probably knew nothing of Louis' offer to affiance the Dauphin to Mary of Burgundy, while he did know that the Duke of Guienne had become ill unto death. It was his fear of a marriage between Louis' brother and Mary of Burgundy that had led him to open negotiations with Louis, and when all danger of such a marriage seemed to be removed, or about to be removed, he may have been glad to recover his self-respect by showing that he was quite as indifferent about Cerisay's truce as Louis appeared to be.

---

1. Plancher, IV, cccviii.
2. *Lettres de Louis XI*, IV, 289.

A TREATY WITH THE DUKE OF BRITTANY AND A VISIT FROM THE SEIGNEUR DE LA GRUTHUYSE

Edward spent the whole winter of 1471–1472 at Westminster Palace, and he made use of the midwinter festivals to remind his subjects in a pleasant way that he was king again. On Christmas Day both he and Queen Elizabeth wore their crowns, and afterwards, when he "kept his estate" in the White Hall, there were music and a mass at which the Bishop of Rochester officiated, a dinner during which the Bishop of Rochester sat on the king's right and the Duke of Buckingham on his left, and after dinner a "disguising," which must have been a fairly elaborate affair, as it cost fifty marks.[1] On New Year's Day, and likewise on Twelfth Day, the king and queen "went in procession," and on the latter day the king again wore his crown, though the queen forbore to wear hers "because she was great with child." On Twelfth Day the king also kept his estate in the White Hall again, and on this occasion he honoured the mayor and aldermen of London and many of the wealthy citizens—probably the creditors who had been so glad to see him come home—with an invitation to the dinner that followed.[2]

All this pomp and pageantry probably gave quite as much enjoyment to the king as to his guests, as it helped to blot out the memory of unfortunate events. Moreover, Edward had the satisfaction, as the winter was drawing to a close, of getting rid of one of the most unpleasant survivals from the recent rebellion by composing the quarrel between his brothers. On 17 February Paston wrote that the day before the king and queen and the Dukes of Clarence and Gloucester had gone "to Sheen to pardon, men say not all in charity," that the king "entreateth my Lord of Clarence for my Lord of Gloucester, and, as it is said, he answereth that he will have my lady his sister-

---

1. Tellers' Roll, Mich. 11 Edw. IV.
2. Kingsford, *Eng. Hist. Lit. in Fif. Cent.* (printing from Cotton MS. Julius C VI, and Additional MS. 6113), 379. Cf. Stow, 425.

in-law but they shall part no livelihood, as he saith."[1] Nevertheless, soon after Paston's letter was written an agreement which involved some sacrifice on the part of everyone was reached. Gloucester secured his bride and married her without even waiting for the papal dispensation which was just as necessary to the legality of this marriage as it had been to that of Clarence and Isabel Neville. Clarence, on the other hand, was granted all the lands and other property which the Earl of Warwick had held by his own or by his wife's right, and though at the king's special request he surrendered a part of these lands to Gloucester, on receiving a promise that no other lands which had been granted to him would be taken away from him, he was rewarded a week later with the earldoms of Warwick and Salisbury. Even that was not all Clarence gained, as in the meantime the lieutenancy of Ireland had been granted to him again for twenty years and in May Gloucester surrendered to him the great chamberlainship, taking in exchange the office of warden of the forests beyond the Trent.[2] From the sanctuary of Beaulieu Abbey, where she was still living under strict guard, the Countess of Warwick, to whom most of the lands so carefully divided between the king's brothers belonged by right, penned many a protesting letter not only to the king and to Clarence and Gloucester themselves, but also to the queen, to the queen's mother, to the king's mother and sisters, and even to the little Princess Elizabeth. But all was labour thrown away. Not even parliament, to which the countess finally appealed sometime during the autumn or winter of 1472, paid any attention to her entreaties.[3]

Although the restoration of peace between his brothers must have brought much relief to Edward's mind, it gave him no new faith in Clarence, and he seems to have decided to seize upon this moment when Clarence had just been appeased by large concessions to disencumber himself of another person whom he distrusted and in whom Clarence might someday find a confederate, if he had not already done so.

In April the king was staying at Windsor, and there, on the 10th, Queen Elizabeth gave birth to another daughter. The Princess Margaret was to be granted only a few months of life, for shortly before Christmas she was laid

---

1. *Paston Letters*, V, 135-136.
2. *Cal. Patent Rolls*, II, 330, 335, 338, 344; Charter Roll 11-14 Edw. IV, m. 4; Signed Bills, file 1504, no. 4454 Nicolas, *Hist. Peerage*.
3. Wood, *Letters of Royal and Illustrious Ladies*, I, 100-104.

to rest in Westminster Abbey, "at the altar end before Saint Edward's shrine," where her little sarcophagus of grey marble may still be seen nestling close to the tomb of her mighty ancestor, Edward III.[1] But the coming grief cast no shadow before to mar the gaieties at Windsor Castle. The feast of the Order of the Garter was kept on St George's Day, and the Duke of Norfolk, the Earl of Wiltshire, and Lords Ferrers, Mountjoy, and Howard were welcomed into the Order, while the Prince of Wales had a stall reserved for him, if he was not actually made a knight of the Garter at this time.[2] The king devoted most of his leisure, however, to the chase, and in the hunting parties riding out from the castle with him one of his most frequent companions was the Archbishop of York. In truth, no one seemed to enjoy more of the royal favour at this time than George Neville, and one day the king told him that he would "come for to hunt and disport with him in his manor of Moor." So the archbishop hurried away to The Moor, sent for the plate and other valuables he had kept hidden since the battles of Barnet and Tewkesbury, "borrowed more stuff of other men," laid in supplies of meat and drink, and altogether "arrayed as richly and as pleasantly as he could." Yet the guest for whom all these preparations were made never came. The day before the king was expected at The Moor the archbishop received orders to return to Windsor, and as soon as he reached the castle, he was put under arrest. When the citizens of London woke up on Sunday morning, 26 April, they were startled to hear that the Archbishop of York had been brought to the Tower during the night, and before they had recovered from their surprise, he was carried off to a more remote and inaccessible prison. On Monday, at midnight, he was removed to a ship which took him to Calais, and from Calais he was sent to Hammes Castle, there to remain at the will of the king, who, in the meantime, seized the temporalities of his bishopric, made a crown out of his mitre set with precious gems, and gave all his other "jewels, plate, and stuff" to the Prince of Wales.[3]

Of what was the Archbishop of York accused? Of holding communication with his sister's husband, the Earl of Oxford, who, though he had taken

---

1. *Paston Letters*, V, 137; Green, *Princesses of Eng.*, III, 437; Madden, *Gent. Mag.*, Jan., 1831.
2. Kingsford, *Eng. Hist. Lit. in Fif. Cent.*, 380-381; Anstis, *Register of the Order of the Garter*, I, 50-51.
3. Warkworth, 24-25; *Paston Letters*, V, 137. Edward seems to have made an unsuccessful effort to have the archbishop deprived of his see. *Cal. Milanese Papers*, I, 165.

refuge in Scotland immediately after the battle of Barnet, had since gone to France and of late had been turning his energies to making raids on Calais and the marches.[1] The ultimate object which Oxford and the archbishop had in mind, if they really had been plotting together, is an untold secret on which at this distance of time it is difficult to throw any light. But it is a fact which must have some significance that whenever Oxford's name is mentioned, either at this time or later, Clarence is uneasy or in trouble; and though the evidence is merely presumptive, there is little room to doubt that conspiring of some sort was going on and that Clarence was concerned in it.

If it is impossible to determine just what the Archbishop of York and the Earl of Oxford were aiming at, there is no mystery about the sources from which Oxford was getting help. In his raids on Calais the earl was assisted by the French and the Easterlings[2]—by the French because Louis XI saw in Oxford just what he had seen in Margaret of Anjou, in Warwick, and in Jasper Tudor, namely, a means of keeping Edward IV busy at home, and by the Easterlings because the old war between Edward and the Hanseatic League had broken out again. Edward had been very ready to make promises to the Hansards when he was a fugitive and hungering for friends, but he had been equally ready to forget his promises as soon as he was on his throne once more. Within four months from the time Hanseatic ships had helped to convey him and his little army to Ravenspur, he had again granted to the merchants of Cologne the exclusive enjoyment of the privileges which had formerly belonged to all Hanseatic merchants in England;[3] and the other Hanseatic towns, in consequence, had resumed their war on English merchantmen. Evidently, too, the Hansards were waging this war with as much success as of yore, since in January Edward had found it necessary to send out a fleet to keep the sea against his enemies[4] and by the beginning of March had decided to make another effort to reach a settlement with the

---

1. Account of John Thrisk, mayor of the staple and victualler of Calais, from 6 April, 12 Edw. IV, to 6 April, 13 Edw. IV. Foreign Roll 13 Edw. IV, m. J.
2. *Ibid.*
3. *Cal. Patent Rolls*, II, 272, 307; *Hanserecesse*, II, 6, pp. 435, 475.
4. The fleet was under the command of John Cheyne and four other captains and carried 420 men-at-arms and archers. *Cal. Patent Rolls*, II, 305, 318; Tellers' Roll, Mich. 11 Edw. IV. More than £200 was expended on the *Grace Dieu* at this time. *Cal. Patent Rolls*, II, 313; Tellers' Rolls, Mich. 11 and 12 Edw. IV.

Hanseatic League through the Duke of Burgundy, to whom he was about to send an embassy for other negotiations.

Irresistible as Louis considered the offer he had made to detach Charles from the Duke of Brittany's league, Charles did not snatch at it. The duke replied by demanding the surrender of Amiens and St Quentin, not at some future time, but at once, and as Louis had no thought of making such a sacrifice, all that he got from Charles in the end was an extension of his truce with him until 15 June.[1] In the meantime, too, Louis laid up further trouble for himself by taking the offensive against his brother and the Duke of Brittany. He stopped the payment of his brother's pension, sent an army to the frontiers of Guienne, and began to attack Breton ships. Worse than all, he sent Monypenny to Scotland to offer James III a part of Brittany in exchange for the services of a Scottish army,[2] and Francis, getting a hint of this, began to crave again that help from England which he had renounced when the Duke of Guienne took fright at Edward's demands.

Apparently the Duke of Burgundy never sent to England the embassy he had promised Russell to dispatch thither before All Saints' Day. But in spite of that, and also in spite of the secret longing for the crown of England which he had begun to cherish, the duke must have intimated to Edward in some way that he was ready to continue the negotiations begun in the preceding summer, since, on 29 February, Rotherham (who was about to exchange the bishopric of Rochester for that of Lincoln),[3] Hastings, Hatclyf, and Russell were empowered to go to Burgundy to treat with Charles for a perpetual peace or league. A few days later Hatclyf, Russell, John Pickering, consul of the English merchants in the Netherlands, and others were also commissioned to treat with the Hansards and to try to come to some understanding with Charles and his subjects in regard to the commercial grievances which for so long had been a source of disagreement between England and Burgundy and which the last diet, held at Bruges in 1469, had failed, like the diets that went before, to settle.[4]

Hatclyf, if not his fellow ambassadors, too, set out for the court of

---

1. *Chronique Scandaleuse*, I, 265.
2. Dupuy, I, 302.
3. Alcock succeeded Rotherham as Bishop of Rochester.
4. Rymer, XI, 737-740; *Hanserecesse*, II, 6, pp. 456, 544.

Burgundy immediately after he received his commissions from the king.[1] Nevertheless, it was nearly a month before the Englishmen appeared at Bruges, and probably the cause of their delay was the arrival in England of two ambassadors from the Duke of Brittany, Michel de Partenay, the duke's chamberlain, and Guillaume Guillemet. For it was but natural that Edward should wish to hear what Francis had to say to him before he listened to any further proposals from Charles or made any further proposals of his own.

What Francis wanted, as soon appeared, was just what he had wanted in 1468, to wit, some English archers to help him defend his duchy against the king of France. He begged Edward to send him six thousand archers in case Louis should attack him, and to prove his need he told of Louis' plan to obtain an army from Scotland.[2] Edward was on fairly good terms with James III by this time, and there was to be another meeting of English and Scottish commissioners at Newcastle on 25 April which was to arrange for the redress of infractions of the truce and which, it was hoped, would lead to a treaty of peace with Scotland.[3] But the thought of a Scottish army going over to France to strengthen Louis' hand was a very alarming one, and no sooner had Francis's ambassadors delivered their message than Edward gathered together a few ships and sent Earl Rivers, Sir Edward Woodville, ten or a dozen other gentlemen, and about thirty archers to Brittany to give Francis such assistance as they could and to tell him that an English fleet would follow to help prevent the king of France from bringing troops from Scotland. The six thousand archers, however, were another matter. Rivers landed in Brittany on 6 April, but though one of Louis' spies who was on the watch at St Malo reported that Francis received the English earl with "la plus grande chère de tout le monde" and that it was rumoured Edward had given the duke to understand that he would come to Brittany himself if necessary, evidently Rivers brought no promise about the archers, as some

---

1. He was paid 20s a day from 4 March to 5 July. Warrants for Issues, 12 Edw. IV, 3 October.
2. Morice, III, 242-243; Blancher, IV, cccxvii-cccxviii; Commynes-Lenglet, III, 181.
3. All that resulted from the meeting at Newcastle, however, was a renewal of the truce and agreements that the wardens of the marches should meet every twenty days to redress breaches of the truce and that another diet should be held in July 1473. Rymer, XI, 733, 740, 748-750, 758, 790.

Breton ambassadors who went to the Duke of Burgundy soon after the earl's arrival were told to ask Charles to urge Edward to send them.[1]

It was on 2 April that Edward's ambassadors at last reached Bruges. Charles was not in Bruges at the moment, but he arrived on the following day, and on the 4th Gruthuyse, who had done the honours meanwhile, conducted the Englishmen to the duke to present their credentials. On the 5th they dined with the Bastard of Burgundy "in his chamber;" on the 6th they went to Male to dine with the Duchess of Burgundy, and on the 7th they dined with Gruthuyse himself.[2] But in spite of all this hospitality, the negotiations for which they had come resulted in little or nothing, though Hatclyf, and perhaps some of the others, tarried at the Burgundian court until about the first of July.[3] No league for waging war on the king of France or for any other purpose was signed, and no progress was made towards settling the commercial differences between England and Burgundy, unless an enactment by the English parliament a few months later that for five years, beginning with Michaelmas, 1474, Newcastle wool was to be stapled at Middleburg or Calais[4] grew out of some agreement reached at this time.

The attempt to negotiate with the Hanseatic League also proved futile. The English ambassadors and the Hansards of Bruges held numerous conferences, but they exchanged more hard words than courteous ones, and when the conferences were over, matters were in much the same state as before. The Hansards' instructions were to insist that the sentence pronounced against their fellows by Edward's council must be annulled as "unjust and wrongful," that all goods seized at the time of the sentence must be restored to their owners, and that the Hanseatic merchants must be reinstated in all their old privileges in England; and they had been charged to refuse to consider any overtures of peace until these concessions had been promised. But the only effect their demands had on the Englishmen was to

---

1. Plancher, *ut sup.*; Morice, III, 239-243; Warrants for Issues, 12 Edw. IV, 9 April. Edward presented Francis's ambassadors with £26 13s 4d for their expenses and with jewels of the value of £78 3s. Tellers' Roll, Mich. 12 Edw. IV.
2. Commynes-Lenglet, II, 201; Kingsford, *Eng. Hist. Lit. in Fif. Cent.*, 380.
3. According to Stow, 426, the English ambassadors went from Burgundy to Brittany "to have gotten there the two Earls of Pembroke and Richmond." But there is nothing in the records to support this statement.
4. Statute 12 Edw. IV, c. 5.

make them turn stubborn. Not for an instant would Edward's ambassadors admit that the sentence of the king's council against the Hanseatic merchants was unjust. Even when their opponents "offered to stand at law upon might of that sentence and it were aforne the Emperor," they haughtily refused to consider the subject. Consequently the only decision reached was that the Hanse towns should be asked to agree to the holding of another peace diet at Utrecht. In the meantime the Hansards went on seizing English ships and the English went on seizing Hanseatic ships.[1]

Probably one reason why Edward's negotiations with Charles produced no definite results at this time was that, in the midst of them, on 25 May, the Duke of Guienne died. Yet the Duke of Guienne's death did not cause the Duke of Brittany's league to fall to pieces, as Louis probably hoped it would. Rather it seemed to bring Francis and Charles closer together, as they united, almost before the duke had drawn his last breath, in accusing Louis of having poisoned the brother whose death he was so obviously awaiting with impatience, and early in June Charles, ignoring the fact that his truce with Louis had not yet expired and confidently expecting that Francis would come to his aid, set off from Arras, sacked one or two small towns, crossed the Somme, and on the 28th laid siege to Beauvais.

As soon as Charles thus boldly threw down the gauntlet, Louis repeated his tactics of 1468. Instead of sending every man he could muster to put a stop to Charles's operations, he marched suddenly against Brittany to prevent Francis from going to Charles's support and to scare him, if possible, into another treaty of Ancenis. This time, however, Louis was not as successful as he had been in 1468, as Francis had an unusually fine army ready to take the field and, in spite of the delay that had been disastrous to him in 1468, was again counting on speedy succour from England.[2] For when Edward learned that the Duke of Guienne was actually dead and that Louis was advancing against Brittany, his hesitancy about sending Francis further aid disappeared at once. This does not mean that Francis got the whole six thousand archers he had so urgently requested. But when Earl Rivers asked to be allowed to transport a thousand men-at-arms and archers to Brittany at his own expense,

---

1. *Hansisches Urkundenbuch*, X, 64, 83, note, 144; *Hanserecesse*, II, 6, pp. 482 *et seq.*, 511, 514, 544-549, 560-561; *Caspar Weinreich's Chron.*, 734-735.

2. Dupuy, I, 312.

Edward gladly gave his consent and permitted proclamation to be made that anyone wishing to join the earl in Brittany might do so. The king also began preparations to send an additional thousand men to Francis under the command of Lord Duras, as well as to send a fleet to sea, as he had promised. According to his indenture, which was drawn up on 15 July, Duras was to "do service of war unto the Duke of Brittany under the rule and guiding of the right noble and worthy lord, the Earl Rivers, now being with the same duke," for thirteen weeks; his men were to be mustered at Southampton on the last day of July, and when their term of service was completed, if Francis wished to retain them for another thirteen weeks at his own expense to fight the king of France or any other enemy of the king of England, they were to be at liberty to enter the duke's service for such wages as the duke and Duras might agree on.[1]

A few days after the signing of his indenture with the king, Duras received a grant of the castle and town of La Sparre in "our duchy of Aquitaine," which probably points to the region in which it was expected his services would be employed; and as his commission as commander of the force going to Brittany was sealed on 4 August, he probably left England soon after that date.[2] But in the meantime Edward had seen in Francis's need an opportunity to secure a treaty which would enable him to invade France by way of Brittany, should he desire to do so, and on 23 July he had commissioned William Slefeld, one of his secretaries, and John Sapcote to go over to Brittany and, with Rivers's help, negotiate a treaty of alliance with Francis.[3] The terms he offered, however, so appalled Francis's councillors, particularly the Seigneur de Lescun, that, though Louis had taken Ancenis on 7 July and had announced his intention of marching into the very heart of Brittany, it was not until 11 September that the treaty of alliance between England and Brittany was signed at Châteaugiron.

The treaty of Châteaugiron provided that Edward should land in Guienne or Normandy before 1 April 1473, to begin a war of conquest in France, or, if for any valid reason he could not come himself, should send an army

---

1. *Cal. Patent Rolls*, II, 339, 340; K. R. Exchequer Accounts 71/5. Duras's men were to be archers, with the exception of twenty spears, and he was to have £100 "in great" for himself, for each spear 18*d* a day, and for each archer 6*d* a day. Francis was to provide for the shipping and reshipping, and Edward was to have a third of the winnings of war.
2. Rymer, XI, 761; *Cal. Patent Rolls*, II, 342.
3. Rymer, XI, 760.

under the command of a lieutenant general. He was to pay the expenses of his army, but Francis was required to support him in every way, and if the king came in person, the duke too must take the field in person. Francis had to permit the English troops to land in Brittany at the ports nearest to the section of France which was to be attacked, and he had to allow them to come and go through his domains as freely as did his own subjects. If Edward chose to cede to Francis some of the conquered territory rather than pay in money for the services of the duke's troops, he was to be free to do so, and he was also to have the option of redeeming later on by money payment any lands so ceded. If Francis needed assistance to defend his domains while the invasion of France was going on, Edward was to supply it at the duke's expense; and for the protection of Brittany meanwhile, until the English army arrived, Edward was to furnish Francis with a thousand archers, either those already in Brittany (meaning, apparently, those serving under Rivers) or others to be sent over from England (meaning, probably, Duras's men). On the other hand, if Francis wished to make a truce with the king of France until 1 April, he might do so, but after the arrival of the English army he was to make no truce without the consent of Edward or his lieutenant; and if he made any conquests in France before 1 April, he must hand over to Edward any lands or places among those conquests which had formerly belonged to the kings of England and be ready to hold the rest of them of the king of England in the same manner in which their present possessors held them of the king of France. Finally, Edward was to ratify the treaty by 1 November, and after it had been ratified he, as well as Francis, was to sign no treaty of truce or peace with Louis without the consent of his ally, unless it might be a truce until 1 April.[1]

That Edward was beginning to cherish a serious intention of invading France the treaty of Châteaugiron proves. But he was too well acquainted with the Duke of Brittany's weaknesses not to realize that Francis alone would be exceedingly poor backing for an undertaking so important and so hazardous, and for that reason he was making, at the same time that he was negotiating with Francis, another effort to come to a definite understanding with the Duke of Burgundy. At the end of July Charles had been obliged to abandon the siege of Beauvais, and though after that he ravaged the country

---

1. Morice, III, 246-249.

near Eu and Dieppe and made a vain attempt against Rouen, by the first of September it was so evident that he would get no help from Francis, who had all he could do to protect his own possessions, that, in discouragement, he turned his face towards home. At the village of Blangy, southeast of Eu, on the very day the treaty of Châteaugiron was being signed, he was overtaken by William Hatclyf, who had sailed from Winchelsea some little time before but had had to wait at Abbeville until 8 September before he could learn where the duke was to be found.[1]

Bluemantle Pursuivant accompanied Hatclyf to Burgundy, and he has left a painstaking account of their journey. But unluckily either he knew nothing about the instructions Hatclyf carried or else he thought it unwise to commit his knowledge to paper; for while his pen lingers over petty details that could well be spared, he leaves his readers wholly in the dark regarding what would interest them most. It is a safe guess, however, that Hatclyf was intrusted with a definite proposal from Edward that Charles as well as Francis should help him to invade France, for immediately after the interview at Blangy, Gruthuyse, with his son Jean, and with Guillaume Rochefort[2] and other ambassadors, set out for London not simply to accept an urgent invitation which he had received from Edward to pay him a visit, but to carry important messages from the Duke of Burgundy to the king of England. In fact, Gruthuyse carried to Edward nothing less important than a list, "signed of the duke's name above and beneath with his hand," of the lands Charles would expect Edward, in case the proposed war with France was successful, to grant to him and his heirs to hold for ever in the same way in which the duke now held, or pretended to hold, such of his hereditary lands as lay within the kingdom of France. The list was an ample one, too, for it included the counties of Champagne, Nevers, and Rethel, with the barony

---

1. Kingsford, *Eng. Hist. Lit. in Fif. Cent.*, 381. Bluemantle says they sailed in a ship "well furnished with men of war." And yet one of Hatclyf's servants and some of his goods were captured by the French and taken to Dieppe. See Warrants for Issues, 12 Edw. IV, 3 Oct. and 20 Feb. Bluemantle received 40s for his expenses during the journey. Tellers' Roll, Mich. 12 Edw. IV.

2. For proof that Rochefort accompanied Gruthuyse to England, see the instructions given to Hastings, Scott, Hatclyf, and Russell on 19 January 1473. Signed Bills, file 1505, no. 4521A (printed in *State Papers, Henry VIII*, 1849, Vol. VI, Part V, 1-8). Cf. *Cal. Milanese Papers*, I, 170. Rochefort went over to Louis XI in 1477 and was made chancellor of France in 1483.

of Douzy, the county of Eu, the county of Guise and the city of Tournai, the duchy of Bar and all lands in France held by the Count of St Pol (a man Charles greatly disliked), Langres and its appurtenances, the town and lordship of Picquigny, which Charles had taken by assault in February 1471, and the other Somme towns to which the duke laid claim—in a word, all that part of the kingdom of France which adjoined Charles's present domains.[1]

Gruthuyse, as we learn from Bluemantle, who probably returned to England with him, was treated with most unusual honours from the day he entered English territory. At Calais he was feasted "daily and nightly" for three or four days by Lord Howard, Sir John Scott, Sir William Pecche, and Geoffrey Gate, and at the end of that time Gate escorted him to Dover with several ships "well furnished with men of war." At Dover he was welcomed by the magistrates of the town, as well as by two esquires sent by Edward to conduct him to London, and as he passed through Canterbury and Rochester, presents of fruit, wine, and game were bestowed upon him.[2] From Gravesend he went up the river to "Lyon Key," close by London bridge, and after he had been regaled with "an honourable and a plenteous dinner" at the house of one of the sheriffs, he returned to his boat and proceeded to Westminster, where lodgings had been made ready for him in Cannon Row, in the house of the Dean of St Stephen's Chapel. More splendid lodgings, however, were waiting for him at Windsor Castle, and thither he went a day or two later.

Bluemantle describes very minutely Gruthuyse's reception and entertainment at Windsor, and the intimate picture of life in the royal castle which his account furnishes is pleasing and unusual. Upon Gruthuyse's arrival at Windsor, Bluemantle says, Lord Hastings and other noblemen took him at once to speak with the king and queen, and later they supped with him in the three chambers "richly hanged with cloths of Arras and with beds of estate" which had been set aside for his use. In the evening the king accompanied his guest to the queen's chamber to watch the queen's ladies and gentlewomen dance and play games, and though Gruthuyse seems to have contented himself with looking on, Edward danced with his little daughter, my Lady Elizabeth. The following morning, before breakfast, the

---

1. Instructions to Hastings, Scott, etc., *ut sup.*
2. Cf. *Hist. MSS. Com, Report 9*, pp. 142-143.

mass of Our Lady was celebrated, and immediately after the king presented
Gruthuyse with a covered cup of gold which was enriched not only with
precious stones, but with something more precious than precious stones,
"a great piece of an unicorn's horn." After breakfast Gruthuyse had the
honour of being presented to the Prince of Wales, who was brought out by
his chamberlain, Master Vaughan, and then the king took him into the "little
park," where he made him ride on his own horse, "a right fair hobby," and
afterwards gave the horse to him, together with "a royal crossbow, the string
of silk, the case covered with velvet of the king's colours, and his arms and
badges thereupon." The only game killed before dinner was a doe, which
was given to Gruthuyse's servants, but after dinner, which was served in the
lodge, the sport seems to have been better, as near the castle were "found
certain deer lying, some with greyhounds and some run to death with
buckhounds," and half a dozen exhausted bucks were slain and presented
to Gruthuyse. Finally, although by this time it was growing dark, the king
exhibited his garden and "vineyard of pleasure," and then all returned to the
castle to hear evensong in their chambers before going to bed.

Most of Gruthuyse's first day at Windsor had been spent in the open air,
but the chief event of the second one was a banquet given by the queen in
her chamber. Gruthuyse and his son sat at the main table with the king and
queen, the Princess Elizabeth, the Duchess of Exeter, the Duke and Duchess
of Buckingham, and other lords and ladies, while at a side table were seated
"a great view of ladies all on one side," and at a third table, spread in the
outer chamber, the queen's gentlewomen and Gruthuyse's servants. After
the banquet there was dancing again, during which the Princess Elizabeth
danced with the Duke of Buckingham, and then, about nine o'clock, the
king, accompanied by the queen and her ladies, conducted his guest to three
"chambers of pleasance all hanged with white silk and linen cloth and all the
floors covered with carpets." In the first chamber was a bed "of as good down
as could be gotten," with sheets of fine linen, a counterpoint of cloth of gold
furred with ermine, a tester and a celer also of cloth of gold, and curtains
of white sarsenet, while "as for his head suit and pillows, they were of the
queen's own ordinance." In the second chamber there was another bed of
estate, all in white, and in addition" a couch with featherbeds hanged with
a tent knit like a net," and a cupboard; and in the third had been prepared
baths "covered with tents of white cloth." When all these luxuries had been

displayed, the king and the queen departed to their own chambers, leaving Gruthuyse to the tender mercies of the lord chamberlain, who undressed him, shared the bath with him, and finally, as an invitation to sweet dreams, partook with him of "green ginger, divers sirups, comfits, and hippocras."

The next morning Gruthuyse returned to Westminster. But he was followed thither a few days later by the king, who came both to open parliament[1] and to create his guest, on 13 October, Earl of Winchester, granting him at the same time two hundred pounds a year out of the revenues and customs of the county and port of Southampton to sustain his new dignity.[2] The investiture took place in the House of Lords, and William Alyngton, Speaker of the House of Commons, made a lengthy address in which he did not content himself with praising Gruthuyse for his "great humanity and kindness" to the king, but took occasion to heap encomiums upon many other persons, including even the Duke of Clarence, for their good behaviour during the recent troubles. Afterwards there was a procession to the tomb of Edward the Confessor in which the king and queen, wearing their crowns, and the Prince of Wales, in his "robes of estate," took part, while the new Earl of Winchester carried the sword of state. There was a dinner, too, in honour of the new earl, who did not forget to give a generous largess to the officers of arms,[3] and it was not until six o'clock or later that the guest of the day took leave of the king and was escorted to his lodgings by many noblemen and heralds, including Bluemantle himself, the chronicler of the ceremonies.[4]

When Edward opened parliament on 6 October, neither he nor the Duke of Brittany had yet ratified the treaty of Châteaugiron, and the outcome of his negotiations with the Duke of Burgundy was also still in doubt. He felt so sure, however, that he would soon arrive at a complete agreement with

---

1. The writs of summons had been sent out on 19 August. *Reports touching Dignity of a Peer*, IV, 980-984; Writs of Privy Seal, file 840, no. 3550.
2. *Archæologia*, XXVI, 285; Charter Roll 11-14 Edw. IV, m. 3; Signed Bills, file 1528, no. 5651. Gruthuyse's annuity was soon in arrears, and on 16 February 1477, Edward ordered £620 to be paid to him. Warrants for Issues, 16 Edw. IV, 16 Feb. The grant of the earldom of Winchester was cancelled in 1500, eight years after Gruthuyse's death, by Henry VII at Calais.
3. Cf. Lansdowne MS. 285, f. 211b.
4. *Archæologia*, XXVI, 280-284; Kingsford, *Eng. Hist. Lit. in Fif. Cent.*, 382-388.

both dukes that he did not hesitate to cause announcement to be made of his intention to "set outward a mighty army" and to invite the Commons to make a grant to him for that purpose.[1] Nor did he lack all reason for his feeling of confidence, since Charles, though his asking price was large, was so eager for an English invasion of France that he had offered, apparently through Gruthuyse, to hand over the county of Eu as a pledge of his support.[2] Moreover, soon after parliament opened Michel de Partenay and Jacques de la Villéon arrived in London to exchange ratifications of the treaty of Châteaugiron.[3] Believing that all was going well, on 24 October Edward sealed his ratification of the treaty with Francis, and about the same time commissioned Sir Robert Grene to take four hundred archers to Burgundy to assist Charles.[4] Yet, as it turned out, Grene and his archers were destined to stay at home because before the time came for them to cross the sea Edward learned that first Francis and then Charles had signed a truce with Louis and that there was to be at least a pretence of peace negotiations.

Francis's truce with the king of France, which in the beginning was for six weeks only, was signed on 15 October,[5] and the duke seems to have dispatched an embassy to Edward immediately after it was concluded. For Paston, writing on 4 November, said he heard that some ambassadors from Brittany would reach London the next day, that the report was that Earl Rivers would "hastily come home" from Brittany with such of his men as had not died "of the flux and other epidemics," and that some declared

---

1. *Rolls of Parl.*, VI, 3-4.
2. See the address to the Commons cited below.
3. Diplomatic Documents (Exch. T. of R.), box 19, no. 544; *45th Report of the Deputy Keeper*, app., 334. Cf. Palgrave, *Kal. of the Exchequer*, III, 13.
4. A copy of Edward's ratification of the treaty of Châteaugiron, dated Westminster Palace, 24 October, 12 Edw. IV, is preserved in Legrand's collections, MS. français 6979, ff. 118-121. Cf. an injured document in Exchequer T. R., Council and Privy Seal, file 90, no. 51. Grene's commission as "leader and governor" of the archers to be sent to Charles was not sealed until 1 December, but he drew pay for them from 14 November. *Cal. Patent Rolls*, II, 363; Tellers' Roll, Mich. 12 Edw. IV; Signed Bills, file 1505, no. 4506. It is from the entry on the Tellers' Roll that we learn that he and his men were going to Burgundy. On 25 November the Duke of Milan was told: "For this winter at any rate it is enough that the English have cheated the duke [of Burgundy], promising to send him men every day, while he had sent them money. But they did not choose to cross." *Cal. Milanese Papers*, I, 165.
5. Commynes-Lenglet, III, 228-230; Dupuy, I, 316.

the Breton ambassadors were coming to ask for more men.[1] But accurate as was the information which Paston often picked up from his friends and fellow gossips, in regard to the errand of the Breton ambassadors he was mistaken; for whether or not Rivers was on his way home, certainly Francis was not asking for more men at present. The Seigneur de Lescun, if not Francis himself, had been growing more convinced every day that the treaty of Châteaugiron was a disastrous bargain and that it would be a great deal better to make peace with Louis than to suffer an English army to set foot in Brittany for the purpose of making war on France. In other words, Francis, who in 1468 had been frightened into submission to Louis by dread of a hostile invasion of his duchy by a French army, had now been frightened once more into submission by dread of a peaceful invasion of his duchy by an English army; and apparently what the Breton ambassadors really came to England for was to persuade Edward to abandon his intention of invading France and sign a truce with the French king.[2] There is even reason to believe that Francis's ambassadors requested Edward to receive an embassy from Louis, as at the end of October Louis was seeking advice about the choice of an envoy to be sent to England and, if a letter written to the Duke of Milan by one Pietro Aliprando on 25 November is to be trusted, two ambassadors from France, as well as four from Burgundy and others from Brittany, were in England at that time waiting to see what Edward and the English parliament would decide to do.[3]

The Duke of Burgundy's truce with Louis was signed on 3 November. It was to last until 1 April 1473, and it contained an agreement that negotiations for a permanent peace should begin at Amiens on 1 December.[4] But as

---

1. *Paston Letters*, V, 157. The writer also says that there was a story that the Duke of Brittany was dead.
2. On 6 October the Duke of Milan was told that the Duke of Brittany, by the mediation of the king of England's brother, was negotiating a league between the king of France and the king of England. *Cal. Milanese Papers*, I,163.
3. *Cal. Milanese Papers*, I, 166, 169. At the close of his letter the writer makes the interesting, but hardly credible statement that the king of France had offered "pro forma" to surrender the duchy of Aquitaine and the county of Poitou to the king of England. This, he said, would "cause discord in the parliament, as Burgundy desires to cut down the duchy of Normandy. He also desires that Flanders and all his dominions may be exempt from the parliament of Paris and from the crown of France, to which the king cannot consent."
4. Commynes-Lenglet, III, 231; Commynes, I, 249.

Charles went on with his preparations for war,[1] it was pretty evident that he put no faith in any peace negotiations, and Edward, notwithstanding Francis's change of feeling, continued to urge parliament to make a war grant. "In England," wrote one from Bruges on 17 November, "they are at present holding the general parliament and the conclusion is expected from day to day. There is nothing certain as yet, but it seems that the English are disposed to do great things against the king of France, and it also seems that they mean to put a large force in Normandy at the cost of the island." Yet in another letter of the same date the same writer declared that, if the Duke of Burgundy made peace with the king of France, all the others would do likewise. "God in his mercy grant what is best for Christians."[2]

The prospect of a renewal of the wars of conquest in France called forth many eloquent speeches in parliament,[3] but the Commons had not forgotten how, four years before, they had voted money for a war with France which never came to pass, and this time it cost the king more of an effort to get what he wanted. A "declaration in writing," setting forth the danger in which the realm stood through the "great conspired malice" of the king's ancient enemies, was distributed among the members,[4] and afterwards someone, perhaps the Archbishop of Canterbury, was sent to address them. Through God's grace and by the king's "most victorious prowess," the Commons were told, the civil war was now over, but the "multitude of riotous people which have at all times kindled the fire" were still spread over the entire kingdom and were committing so many crimes that, if a speedy remedy were not found, the wealth and prosperity which the king's subjects so much desired could never be realized. On the other hand, the population of the kingdom had already been so much reduced by civil war and "strait execution of the law" that if all were put to death who deserved to be, the result might be, in a few years, "such destruction of people" who were needed to defend the kingdom that England's enemies would take courage to attack her. A defensive war, the king's spokesman pointed out, is always more terrible than a foreign one, and requires a far greater number of men; and for that

---

1. *Cal. Milanese Papers*, I, 163.
2. *Ibid.*, I, 164.
3. *Hist. Croy. Cont.*, 557.
4. *Rolls of Parl.*, VI, 4.

reason, he argued, it would be better to keep the idle and riotous people in the kingdom busy with an "outward war."

The speaker also dwelt on the "subtle and crafty enterprises" of the king of France and declared that Louis had continually held out hope of peace and of "recompense for the king's inheritance of that side," yet would never make a reasonable agreement, though the king had sent to him, first the Archbishop of York, the Earl of Essex, and other great men, afterwards the Earl of Warwick, and finally the Bishop of Rochester. Louis had even endeavoured, he said, through the many French embassies sent to England, to destroy the king and his land by stirring up sedition and civil war. In fact, it was Louis who had been the chief instigator of the "most unnatural inward trouble" which had prevented the king from carrying out his intention of invading France after the announcement made by him during his last parliament. At all times Louis was on the lookout for some way to put England "out of quiet and surety," and at this very moment he was inciting the kings of Denmark and Scotland to make war on her.

Surely then, the speaker contended, the king was right in thinking that the best thing for him to do was to follow the example of Scipio, who, when the Romans despaired of being able to defend their country against Hannibal, went to Carthage and won the victory there. And acting on this belief, the king, at an expense of over a hundred thousand pounds, had purchased alliances with two of the mightiest princes of France, the Dukes of Burgundy and Brittany—alliances which had already done so much to reduce the power of the French king that the Duke of Burgundy had been able to seize many lordships and places in France, including the county of Eu in Normandy, which, through his ambassadors, he was now offering to the king, if he would send an army to receive it. All this went to show that if the king invaded France now, he would be able to accomplish his purpose with little bloodshed or difficulty; and every day the Dukes of Burgundy and Brittany were urging him to assert his rights in France and were offering their assistance "so largely as afore these days was never like offer made by any stranger." Nor were these two dukes the only allies on whom the king could count, as no doubt the king of Aragon and other great lords whom Louis had wronged would also be ready to take a hand in the war. And how great would be the honour and profit of the war! For with Brittany "standing as it doth," if Normandy and Gascony belonged to England, the French would have no place to keep a navy, Englishmen would no longer have to buy safe-conducts, and much less money would be needed for the keeping of the sea. "Many gentlemen, as well younger brothers as other," could go to Normandy and Gascony to live there and guard them, and the "men of war" who were now making mischief in England could be got rid of by sending them to do garrison duty.

Not since the Norman Conquest, the speaker pointed out in conclusion, had justice, peace, and prosperity continued in England for any length of time except when the king "made outward war." Even Henry VI, he said, in spite of his "simpleness of wit," had "stood ever in glory and honour while the war was continued beyond." And as a last argument before calling on the Commons to make a generous grant to the king, he warned his hearers that, if the Dukes of Burgundy and Brittany were denied the help they sought, they might cease to be friends of England and become her enemies; or they might be overthrown, in which case the king of France would be mightier than ever and not only would England's commerce, especially her vital commerce with Burgundy, be utterly destroyed, but she would be surrounded with powerful adversaries and forsaken by her old friends.[1]

Whether it was hope of great benefits or fear of dark possibilities that moved them, the Commons ultimately yielded to the king's wishes, and on the last day of November, when parliament was prorogued until 4 February, the desired war grant was announced. Put on their guard by past experience, however, the Commons had tried to make their grant in such a way that the king would be unable to use the money for any purpose except the one for which it was meant. Instead of granting him a fifteenth and tenth, they had availed themselves of a precedent set by the Reading parliament of 1453 and had granted him the services of thirteen thousand archers for a year. And while for the wages of these men—sixpence a day for each archer—a

---

1. *Literæ Cantuarienses* (Rolls Series), III, 274-285. The editor has given 1474 as the probable date of this address, but that cannot be correct, as the speaker stated that the king was "in good trust and hope" of a treaty with the Hanseatic League, and the treaty with the League was signed on 28 February 1474. In fact, a reference to "certain chapters of instructions given to the Lord Gruthuyse" by the Duke of Burgundy, and a statement that "this last summer" the Duke of Burgundy had "lain long time upon the ground that is under the obeissance of the said adversary," make it certain that the address was delivered during the first session of the parliament of 1472-1475.

tenth was to be levied before 2 February, the money was not to be put at the king's disposal after it was collected, but was to be kept in some castle, town, or house of religion until parliament gave further orders concerning it; and if the king's army "held not" before Michaelmas Day, 1474, the money was to be paid back to its former owners. The king had also been required to renounce any claim that might possibly arise out of the grant of archers made to Henry VI in 1453 and to release his subjects from the payment of the still unpaid portion of the fifteenth and tenth granted to him in 1468.

Even the Lords were so affected by the excitement of the hour that they taxed themselves with a tenth. Yet they too were careful to stipulate that the money they gave was not to be placed at once in the king's hands, but was to be kept in St Paul's Cathedral until parliament gave directions regarding its use, and that it was to be returned to its former owners in case the king passed "not forth of this realm" before Michaelmas Day, 1474.[1]

Edward's subjects had again signified their willingness to begin anew the old war with France which had ended so disastrously in Henry VI's reign. But though the king had intimated that the Dukes of Burgundy and Brittany were clamouring for war, a month after the prorogation of parliament he had to announce that, owing to the representations of the Duke of Brittany's ambassadors, Michel de Partenay and Jacques de la Villéon, he had postponed his intended attack on France for a few weeks.[2] On the same day, as was afterwards learned, Francis sealed a new truce with Louis which was to last until 23 November 1473, in other words until eight months after the date by which Edward was bound by the treaty of Châteaugiron to begin his invasion of France.

It was the Seigneur de Lescun who had persuaded Francis to desert Edward in this way, and Louis, in addition to giving Francis a pension of forty thousand francs, bestowed on Lescun one of six thousand francs, besides a gift of twenty-four thousand gold crowns in hand and several offices well worth having.[3]

Edward must have suspected, even before he heard of the new truce, that

---

1. *Rolls of Parl.*, VI, 4-9. During the session the attainders of several Lancastrians, including that of Doctor John Morton, who for some months past had been Master of the Rolls (*Cal. Patent Rolls*, II, 334), had been reversed.
2. 8 Dec. Exchequer T. R., Council and Privy Seal, file 90, m. 44, 47.
3. Commynes-Lenglet, III, 234; Dupuy, I, 319.

Francis was going to yield to Louis. But the suspicion made no apparent change in his intention to invade France. If Francis withdrew, Charles, his stronger ally, still remained, and when, about 10 December, the Seigneur de la Gruthuyse started for home, after receiving as a final mark of favour the privilege of bearing the ancient arms of the Earls of Winchester with a canton of the arms of England and a grant to two towns on his estates in Flanders, Aemstede (Hamste) and Westenschouen, of special trading privileges in England similar to those granted to Veere a year before,[1] William Hatclyf and three merchants of the staple, William Rosse, John Barton, and John Chaney, accompanied him.

Some time before this the Hansards had entrusted to William Rosse at Bruges a letter accepting the proposal which had been made to them in the spring that another diet should be held to adjust their quarrel with the king of England and suggesting that the diet should meet on 1 May 1473, but at Hamburg instead of at Utrecht. But as Rosse had the bad luck to fall ill at Calais, Edward did not receive the letter of the Hansards until after Michaelmas, the date by which they had asked him to let them know his decision, and Gruthuyse and Hatclyf, as well as Rosse and the two other merchants, were now empowered to explain the king's delay to the Hansards and to try to obtain a treaty with them.[2] Hatclyf, however, had also another mission to perform, for he was to announce to the Duke of Burgundy that the king of England was ready to bring an army across the sea to conquer France and to conclude an offensive and defensive alliance with the duke. He carried with him a "minute" or outline, drawn up by the king's council,[3] of the terms Edward was prepared to offer Charles and he was directed to come to a full understanding with the duke both in regard to the way in which the war against France was to be conducted and in regard to the concessions which Edward was to make to the duke out of the territories conquered.[4]

---

1. Rymer, XI, 765; *Cal. Patent Rolls*, II, 338; Van Praet, 14; Writs of Privy Seal, file 841, no. 3599; French Roll 12 Edw. IV, m. 5; Signed Bills, file 1505, no. 4505. This grant to Aemstede and Westenschouen, like the grant to Gruthuyse of the earldom of Winchester, was cancelled by Henry VII at Calais. See the entry on the French Roll just cited.
2. *Hanserecesse*, II, 6, pp. 577-579; Rymer, XI, 765.
3. Instructions to Hastings, Scott, Hatclyf, and Russell, Signed Bills, file 1505, no. 4521A; *State Papers, Henry VIII, ut sup.*
4. Signed Bills, file 5505, no. 4514; French Roll 12 Edw. IV, m. 10, 11 Dec.

Just what suggestions Hatclyf was authorized to make for Edward, except that he was to propose to Charles a joint declaration against Louis and an agreement that, after Edward landed in France, neither he nor the duke should reply to any letters or embassies from Louis without the knowledge and consent of the other,[1] it is impossible to say. But he was followed to Burgundy a month later by Hastings, Scott, and Russell, and fortunately the instructions given to these ambassadors for their guidance and Hatclyf's are still in existence.[2]

What Edward bade his ambassadors say to Charles was that his "affection" was now "greatly set to the expedition" to France, and that he was willing to land with an army in Normandy or the neighbourhood in the coming April, May, or, at the latest, June to begin the war. He was ready to agree, too, that the duke should have the lands in France mentioned in the list brought to him by Gruthuyse, but he charged his ambassadors that, if the duke or his council "devised a minute of a letter of transport and grant" of those lands, or any part of them, which he was expected to sign, they must "take a deliberation thereupon" and send or bring the minute to England "to be ripely seen and understanden." The ambassadors were also to persuade the duke to allow the king of England and his successors to hold the city, church, and archbishopric of Rheims, "where the kings of France have right to be sacred and by the hands of the said archbishop," or, if that was more than could be obtained, they were to procure a written promise that, notwithstanding the transference to Charles of the county of Champagne, the king and his successors could go to Rheims at their pleasure and "enter, abide, and challenge there to be sacred."

Edward also expected Charles to assist him to recover the crown of France. He wanted the duke to promise to serve him with ten thousand men for a year, if not longer, after he landed in France, and for repayment proposed to assign to him each year a portion of the conquered territories, other than those the duke was to own in perpetuity, to hold until through the profits and revenues therefrom he should recover the sum he had paid out in wages to his men. The king clearly intended to keep the conduct of the

---

1. *Ibid.*
2. For the commission for Hastings, Scott, and Russell, which is of the same purport as the one given earlier to Hatclyf alone, see Signed Bills, file 1505, no. 4521, and French Roll 12 Edw. IV, m. 1, 19 Jan.

war in his own hands, as he expected Charles to serve him at such times and in such places as he might deem wise; but in general he wanted his army and the duke's to attack the enemy at different points, at the same time that each held himself in readiness to go to the support of the other in case of need.

Finally, as it had been suggested that a special agreement concerning the aid "which that one prince should be bound to find to the other in case he were thereunto lawfully required" ought to be added to the treaty of alliance, Edward empowered his ambassadors to sign, after the alliance had been secured, "letters of assistance" providing that, in the event that either prince became engaged in war, he might call upon the other for aid to the extent of five thousand men. This was to be on the understanding that if the war was a defensive one, the prince supplying the men would pay the wages of two thousand of the men, while if it was not a defensive one, the prince receiving aid would pay the wages of the whole five thousand. Edward was not willing, however, that these letters of assistance should go into effect until after Normandy or some other considerable part of France had submitted to him.[1]

Hastings, Scott, and Russell received these instructions on 19 January 1473, and they must have started for Flanders immediately after, as they had their first meeting with Charles at Ghent just six days later.[2]

On 8 February 1473, parliament reassembled at Westminster, and Paston's brother no doubt voiced the feelings of most Englishmen when he wrote to him: "I pray God send you the Holy Ghost among you in the parliament house, and rather the devil, we say, than ye should grant any more taxes."[3] Nevertheless, on the plea that the grant previously made to him was insufficient to enable him to invade France and that he was "verily disposed" to take an army across the sea "in brief time," Edward again asked for money. He made his request without referring to the fact that his treaty with the Duke of Brittany had miscarried, and without admitting that there was any doubt whatever about a satisfactory agreement with the Duke of Burgundy. Yet, as a matter of fact, Francis was urging Charles to sign another truce with Louis[4] and Charles was on the point of yielding—not to Francis's urgings, but to the fear that, if he

---

1. Signed Bills, file 1505, no. 4521A; *State Papers, Henry VIII, ut sup.*
2. Commynes-Lenglet, II, 204.
3. *Paston Letters*, V, 178.
4. Dupuy, I, 324-326.

plunged into a war with Louis, he would lose the opportunity circumstances were just now holding out to him to get possession of Gueldres. About the beginning of March Edward's ambassadors in Burgundy sent him word that, in spite of his readiness to meet Charles's terms, the invasion of France would have to be postponed for another year and, bowing to the inevitable, on 7 March the king sent a commission to Hatclyf to treat with Louis for a truce on land and sea. A fortnight later a truce which included both England and Burgundy and which was to last until 1 April 1474, was signed with the French king.[1]

Edward did not feel called upon to hurry to the parliament chamber to make known that he had signed a truce with the king of France which would necessitate the postponement of his invasion of France for at least another year, and on 8 April, when parliament was prorogued until 8 October,[2] the Commons, admitting that their previous grant was inadequate and also that it had proved difficult to collect, announced that they had added to it a fifteenth and tenth. Only by giving notice, when he accepted the grant, that payment of the money would be deferred from St John's Day, the date the Commons had named, until Michaelmas, unless for urgent reasons affecting the defence of the realm it was necessary to call for it sooner, did the king confess that there would be no expedition to France in the immediate future. But the Commons had again shown their distrust of him by providing that the proceeds from the fifteenth and tenth were not to pass into his hands until he had actually "indented" with the captains of the archers and the day of muster had been proclaimed in every shire. The Lords, on the other hand, had displayed a more trusting spirit than before. The wages of his troops were not the only expense the king would have to meet if he set out to conquer France; he would also have to lay in "great provision" of bows and arrows, guns and gunpowder, and other war supplies long before he left

---

1. Signed Bills, file 1505, no. 4531A, 7 March; Commynes-Lenglet, III, 247; Palgrave, *Kal. of the Exchequer*, III, 17. It should be noticed that Rymer, XI, 750, has overlooked the fact that the dates are "avant Pasques" and has assigned this treaty to the year 1472.
2. The prorogation was pronounced by Stillington, but he resigned the great seal two months later, and after a brief time, during which it was in the hands, first of Doctor John Morton, Master of the Rolls, and then of the Earl of Essex, the seal was given to Lawrence Booth, Bishop of Durham. Rymer, XI, 782; Signed Bills, file 1505, nos. 4539, 4543. Stillington was summoned to Rome in 1475 to answer grave charges of some sort. Martène and Durand, *Veterum Scriptorum Amplissima Collectio*, II, 1506.

England, and the Lords, with the consent of the Commons, permitted him to take the money that had been raised in pursuance of their grant and use it for the purchase of such necessaries.[2]

The Lords and Commons had scarcely dispersed after the prorogation when news of the truce that had been signed with the king of France spread through England. "As for tidings," wrote Paston on 16 April, as he was on his way to Calais, "there was a truce taken at Brussels about the 26th day of March last past between the Duke of Bourgogne and the French king's ambassadors and Master William Hatclyf for the king here, which is a peace by land and water till the first day of April now next coming between France and England and also the duke's lands."[2] As the writer added, "God hold it for ever and grace be," it would appear that to him at least the news was not displeasing; but even to those who were not sorry to have the war with France delayed, it must have looked as if the king had deliberately deceived his people by keeping back the truth about his negotiations with the Dukes of Burgundy and Brittany.

To offset the revelation in regard to the postponement of the invasion of France, Edward had some really good news to impart which might prove to have important bearing on his war plans. This news was that the prospect of a treaty of peace with the Hanseatic League was improving and that a truce was about to be concluded with the king of Denmark, whose seizure of the English ships in 1468 had led to the imprisonment of the Hanseatic merchants in London and who was still lending his aid to the Hansards, with results which had been particularly disastrous of late to English merchants.[3]

On 21 January Hatclyf, Rosse, and Challey, who were then at Bruges, had written a letter to the city of Lübeck. In this, after telling of Rosse's illness at Calais and the consequent delay in the delivery of the message he was carrying from the Hanseatic League to the king of England, they expressed their disappointment because they had found no one at Bruges who had authority to treat with them and said that, as they did not want to go home without doing anything, they had told the aldermen of the Hanseatic merchants at Bruges that, if the League would send ambassadors to Utrecht

1. *Rolls of Parl.*, VI, 39–42. The convocation of Canterbury granted the king a tenth. Wilkins, III, 607; Wake, 379; Fine Roll 12 Edw. IV, m. 4.

2. *Paston Letters*, V, 184.

3. *Cal. Milanese Papers*, I, 166.

on 1 July, they would ask their king to do the same.[1] This letter was well received by the Hanse towns, and as they now made up their minds to allow the diet to be held at Utrecht, no further difficulties arose. On the same day on which Edward authorized Hatclyf to sign the truce with the king of France, he also empowered Gruthuyse, Hatclyf, and Russell to treat with the Hanse towns regarding a truce, mercantile intercourse, and the time and place of the diet;[2] and almost at the same moment the League empowered Heinrich Kastorp, Doctor Johann Osthusen, and Johann Luneborg to treat with England for a perpetual peace and the redress of injuries or, in case a treaty of peace could not be agreed on, to arrange for a ten years' truce and for further peace negotiations or arbitration. Shortly after it was agreed that before 25 June both Edward and the League should send to Bruges a written declaration stating that a diet was to be held at Utrecht on 1 July and that there was to be a suspension of hostilities until 1 October, and also safeconducts for the ambassadors who were to attend the diet.[3] Bluemantle carried to Bruges in May the documents Edward was to furnish, and as the League was almost equally prompt in doing its part, there seemed to be every reason to hope that the quarrel between England and the Hanseatic League, which had cost both parties dear, would soon be settled and forgotten.[4]

The truce with the king of Denmark was signed in the midst of these negotiations with the Hanseatic League. Denmark Herald came over to England with friendly messages from King Christian; Norroy King-of-Arms went over to Denmark with a gift of ten yards of green cloth, ten yards of murrey cloth, and ten yards of violet cloth for King Christian's consort, and finally, on 1 May, announcement was made that a two years' truce between England and Denmark had been concluded. During the two years all differences were to be referred for arbitration to the king of Scotland, the Duke of Burgundy, or other princes chosen by both parties, and Englishmen and Danes were to enjoy mutual freedom of trade, except

---

1. *Hanserecesse*, II, 6, pp. 577-579. Cf. *ibid.*, pp. 579-582.
2. Signed Bills, file 1505, no. 4531; French Roll 13 Edw. IV, m. 31, 7 March.
3. *Hanserecesse*, II, 6, pp. 587-589, 591-593.
4. *Ibid.* II, 7, pp. 12-13; Rymer, XI, 780; Writs of Privy Seal, file 844, no. 3736; French Roll 13 Edw. IV, m. 19, 24; instructions given to the ambassadors sent to Utrecht, cited below.

that, as of old, Englishmen were not to go to Iceland without the permission of the king of Denmark.[1]

With still another foreign power Edward was carrying on negotiations during the spring of 1473, and in this instance too the interests of English traders were concerned. Edward had been in no way responsible for the attack made by the Bastard of Fauconberg in March 1471, on the Portuguese ships returning home from Flanders, and although Alphonso V had authorized reprisals and revoked all safeconducts previously granted by him to English merchants,[2] any further revenge he may have contemplated was renounced when he heard of the overthrow of Henry VI and Warwick. But though Edward ratified the old treaty between England and Portugal on 11 March 1472, and Alphonso did likewise on 30 August following, the outrage committed by the Bastard of Fauconberg still rankled in the minds of the Portuguese, and John d'Elvas, who brought to England, during the winter of 1472–1473, Alphonso's ratification of the treaty, was commissioned to demand compensation for the ships and goods which had been seized. As the Bastard had already been executed for another cause, it was impossible to punish him further, but on 23 February a commission was appointed to make the desired reparation and to arrest and bring before the king and his council those who had shared in the Bastard's guilt. Three days later John d'Elvas gave an acquittance in Alphonso's name which contained a promise that neither the king of England nor his subjects should be made to suffer for the Bastard's offence.[3]

---

1. Tellers' Roll, Easter 13 Edw. IV; Rymer, XI, 775; *45th Report of the Deputy Keeper*, app. II, 5.
2. Stillington and Chapmen, *The Commercial Relations of England and Portugal* (London, 1907), 21, 100.
3. Rymer, XI, 741, 762-764, 767, 769; *Cal. Patent Rolls*, II, 379.

A SETTLEMENT WITH THE HANSEATIC LEAGUE

However his subjects may have felt about the truce with France, the king of England himself must have heaved a sigh of relief when it was signed, though the common belief in France that Edward was indolent and less eager for war than his subjects[1] was probably unwarranted. It is not likely that the man who had fought and won the battles of Barnet and Tewkesbury had lost all his martial spirit in two years, and Edward had excellent reasons for feeling that the present moment was no time to commit his kingdom to the care of a regent while he crossed the sea for any enterprise however glorious. For one thing, he was still not quite sure of the Scots, and so obvious was it that he ought not to leave home before his northern border had been made entirely secure from attack that the Duke of Burgundy sent a couple of ambassadors, Fulpard de Amerongen and Georges Baert, to Scotland by way of England to see what could be done to bring James III to terms. But though Charles prevailed on James to renew his truce with England until 10 April 1475, and also to agree that there should be another conference of English and Scottish commissioners at Alnwick on 16 June, this was hardly enough, and Edward's efforts to obtain a treaty of peace and a marriage alliance with James continued to be unavailing.[2] At this very time, moreover, as Edward and Charles probably suspected, if they did not actually know, some Scottish ambassadors who had gone to France were not merely assuring Louis that James had rejected all Edward's proposals, but were offering to find means to prevent the English from landing in France. James shared the belief that Edward was less anxious than his subjects to attempt to recover England's lost

1. *Cal. Milanese Papers*, I, 177, 183.
2. Rymer, XI, 772-775, 776-778; Warrants under the Signet, file 1383, 26 May.

possessions beyond sea, and for the sum of ten thousand crowns he offered to keep Edward at home, by attacking him, if that proved to be necessary, or by promising to protect him against his subjects should they rise in revolt when he gave up his expedition to France and disbanded his army.[1]

Another thing which gave Edward pause, and which also helps to explain why James was so confident that he could keep the English away from France, was the fact that England was filled with a mysterious unrest and teeming with crime. At the close of the autumn session of parliament the Commons had made bold to call the king's attention to the crimes of all sorts which were being perpetrated by "such persons as either been of great might or else favoured under persons of great power," and to request him to proclaim anew the statutes against maintenance and the giving of liveries.[2] But though Edward did not fail to act upon this recommendation,[3] the disorders seemed to increase. In Herefordshire, Shropshire, and the Welsh marches generally conditions became so serious that in the winter the Prince of Wales was sent to the marches in the hope that the presence of the heir to the throne would evoke the loyalty of the people and serve as a restraining influence in case there was anything of a treasonable nature behind the disturbances. On 20 February the Prince's council was strengthened by the addition of ten new members, including William Alyngton, Speaker of the House of Commons, and given fuller powers,[4] and shortly after the Prince was taken to Hereford by his mother. A body of royal commissioners, including some of the judges, accompanied the queen and the Prince for the purpose of punishing the offenders against the king's peace, and before all was over many persons were indicted. But the king's commissioners found their task no easy one, as the people were afraid

---

1. See a copy of some instructions given by Louis to Alexander Monypenny (not to William Monypenny, Seigneur de Concressault, as both Dupuy, I, 343, and Legeay, II, 129, intimate) going to Scotland. Legrand's collections, MS. français 6981, ff. 214-217. Legrand assigned this document to the year 1474, which may be correct; but there is little doubt that the offer to which Monypenny was to reply was identical with the one the Milanese ambassador in France speaks of in a letter written on 12 May 1473 (*Cal. Milanese Papers*, I, 174-175), although he reported that James wanted a pension of some sixty thousand crowns as his reward.

2. *Rolls of Parl.*, VI, 8.

3. See letters he sent to Salisbury and Coventry on 11 February. Hatcher, *Old and New Sarum*, 179; *Coventry Leet Book*, 373 (reprinted in Thornley, *Eng. under the Yorkists*, 166).

4. *Cal. Patent Rolls*, II, 366; Signed Bills, file 1505, no. 4525.

to give evidence against their neighbours "for dread of murdering and to be mischiefed in their own houses, considering the great number of the said misdoers and the great bearers-up of the same";[1] and so evident was it that only by constant vigilance and pressure could law and order be maintained in that far-away and difficult part of the kingdom that it was decided that the Prince should remain in the Welsh marches as the representative of the royal authority. Alcock, Bishop of Rochester, was appointed the Prince's teacher and president of his council and Earl Rivers his governor, and about the time he celebrated his third birthday, Edward IV's son took up his permanent residence in Ludlow Castle, where his father had spent so much of his own childhood.[2]

Rivers and Alcock were by no means left to bring up the Prince of Wales according to their own fancy. Before the Prince was intrusted to their care, minute instructions were drawn up for their guidance, and it was far from an idle life that was mapped out for the king's little son. For the Prince was to arise every morning "at a convenient hour, according to his age," hear matins in his chamber, go, as soon as he was dressed, to his chapel or closet to attend mass, after mass eat his breakfast, between breakfast and dinner give his time to "such virtuous learning as his age shall suffer to receive," during dinner listen to the reading of "such noble stories as behooveth to a prince to understand and know," and after dinner return again to his learning. Later in the day he was to be given instruction in "such convenient disports and exercises as behooveth his estate to have experience in," then he was to go to evensong, and after evensong he was to eat his supper. Only when supper was over was the poor little fellow to be allowed to relax and enjoy "all such honest disports as may be conveniently devised for his recreation." But happily eight o'clock was to find him in bed with the curtains drawn, and those who attended at the last ceremonies of the ceremonious day were bidden to "enforce themselves to

---

1. *Rolls of Parl.*, VI, 160.
2. The ordinances of the Prince's household were drawn up on 27 September, but the appointments of Alcock and Rivers were not sealed until 10 November. Signed Bills, file 1506, no. 4578; *Cal. Patent Rolls*, II, 401, 417. The Milanese ambassador in France wrote on 6 July that he heard that the king of England had taken his son to Wales, "and styled him prince, as is customary with their firstborn, and has left him in the country." *Cal. Milanese Papers*, I, 176. On the question of whether Edward IV is to be credited with the origination of the Council in the Marches of Wales, which became an important body in the Tudor period and continued to exist until 1689, see Miss C. A. J. Skeel's, *The Council of the Marches of Wales* (London, 1904).

make him merry and joyous towards his bed." Around that bed careful watch was to be kept every night and all night, and that disease might not steal in and rob the king of God's "precious sonde and gift and our most desired treasure,"[1] a physician and a surgeon were to be ever at hand. Nor was the moral welfare of the child forgotten; for no swearing or ribald words were to be tolerated in his household, least of all in his presence, and no "customable swearer, brawler, backbiter, common hazarder, [or] adulterer" was to be retained in his service.[2]

Yet it is greatly to be feared that if no adulterer was to be permitted to approach the Prince of Wales, his own father ought to have been excluded from his presence. In an account of one George Lovekyn, tailor and yeoman of the wardrobe (and an undoubted authority on fashions, as he was a Frenchman born),[3] which the king sent to the Exchequer for payment in 1477, appears under the heading, "For my Lord the Prince," charges for the making of a doublet of purple velvet, a doublet of purple satin, a doublet of black satin, a doublet of green satin, two doublets of black velvet, a long gown of purple velvet, a long gown of purple satin, a long gown of black satin, a long gown of green satin, a long gown of black velvet, a bonnet of purple velvet lined with green satin, two bonnets of black velvet lined with black satin, and a long gown of cloth of gold upon damask. But alas! the next items in the account are "For my Lord the Bastard". However, the royal bastard (Arthur was his name and Lady Elizabeth Lucy was understood to be his mother)[4] seems to have had to put up with much fewer and plainer clothes than the Prince, as he had received from Lovekyn only a coat of black velvet, a gown of black, and a gown of russet.[5]

---

1. Signed Bills, *ut sup.*

2. Halliwell, *Letters of the Kings of Eng.*, I, 136-144; *Ordinances and Regulations for the Government of the Royal Household*, 27-33. A few weeks before his death Edward sent to the Prince's council another set of ordinances "concerning our said son's person" which contained several additional articles and changed the Prince's bed hour from eight to nine o'clock. Nichols, *Grants of King Edward the Fifth* (Camden Society), vii-viii.

3. *Cal. Patent Rolls*, II, 472, 594. He was granted letters of denization in 1476, and in 1480 he was "sergeant tailor of the Great Wardrobe." See Nicolas, *Wardrobe Accounts of Edward IV*, 155, where his name is spelled "Lufkyn."

4. Stow, 433; Hall, 367; More, *Hist. of Rich. III*, 61-62. Arthur Plantagenet married Elizabeth, daughter of Edward, third Viscount Lysle, was created Viscount Lysle in 1523, and died in 1541. Nicolas, *Hist. Peerage.*

5. Accounts, etc. (Exchequer K. R.), bundle 412, no. 8.

The establishment of the Prince of Wales and his council at Ludlow may have put a check on crime in that neighbourhood, but unfortunately it was not in the Welsh marches only that the peace and good order of England, if not the sovereignty of Edward IV, were threatened. The whole kingdom appeared to be in a state of apprehension and nervous irritability. At Norwich one Hogan was predicting that serious rebellions would take place in the month of May, and so sensitive had Edward become to every hint of danger that he had the prophet brought up to London. But London itself felt premonitions of trouble. "As for the world, I wot not what it meaneth," wrote Paston from the capital on 2 April. "Men say here, as well as Hogan, that we shall have ado in haste. I know no likelihood but that such a rumour there is." And ten days later he wrote again: "Every man saith that we shall have ado or May pass. Hogan the prophet is in the Tower; he would fain speak with the king, but the king saith he shall not avaunt that ever he spake with him."[1]

Although Edward pretended to scorn the Norwich prophet, he determined not to let the grass grow under his feet until Hogan's predictions came true. In April, about a week after parliament was prorogued, he left London, with Speaker Alyngton as a companion, to make an extended progress through his kingdom, and even if the truth was much exaggerated in the stories which reached France about the condition of things in England, it was high time for him to bestir himself. For on 20 April the Milanese ambassador in France reported:

> His Majesty told me that yesterday evening he heard from Bordeaux, from some of his subjects who had come from England, how Edward of York, to use his Majesty's own words, had his hands full in England because about sixty thousand persons had risen against him and were waging active war on him. I offered his Majesty my congratulations on this.[2]

Why was England so restless and uneasy? Some months later it was being told in France that the northern counties of Edward's kingdom had refused to give him any money for the expedition to France, though they were willing to provide their share of troops; and there is a confession in the records of parliament that the king's assessors were unsuccessful in performing their task

---

1. *Paston Letters*, V, 177-179, 181.
2. *Cal. Milanese Papers*, I, 174.

in Cheshire, Northumberland, Cumberland, Westmoreland, the bishopric
of Durham, the town of Newcastle, the city of Lincoln, a certain wapentake
in Yorkshire, and a certain hundred in Herefordshire.[1] But on the whole,
apparently, England had shown herself to be in favour of renewing the wars in
France, and if one section of the country insisted on being permitted to give men
only, instead of men and money, that would hardly account for the widespread
conviction that the whole kingdom was on the verge of a serious rebellion. At
first glance one might even suspect that Englishmen had become too prone
to look for civil war and that there was no real occasion for so much anxiety.
But between the lines of Paston's letters, which are almost the only source of
information we have about the troubles in England at this moment, this much
at least can easily be read: the ill-feeling between Clarence and Gloucester,
which, notwithstanding the supposedly satisfactory settlement recently made
concerning the Warwick estates, was still very strong, was regarded by Edward's
subjects as a menace to the peace of the entire kingdom. Paston's meaning is not
always as clear as could be wished, but if Clarence was believed to be still in a
vindictive mood, not only towards Gloucester but towards Edward, and to be
endeavouring to stir up another rebellion in the hope of accomplishing what
he had failed to accomplish before, Paston might well shrink from mentioning
names and from being very explicit in his statements.

If Clarence had succeeded in laying the train for another explosion,
one thing is certain, and that is that he had not done it alone. Aid and
encouragement had been given to him by someone, and not only probability
but positive evidence points to the king of France as his helpmate. Louis had
apparently told the duke that, if he would engage in another conspiracy against
his brother's throne, he would send the Earl of Oxford to make a descent on
the coast of England and would also, if he could, get the king of Scotland to
give assistance. "The Earl of Oxford was on Saturday at Dieppe," said Paston
in his letter of 16 April telling of the truce with France, "and is purposed into
Scotland with a twelve ships. I mistrust that work. Item, there be in London
many flying tales, saying that there should be a work, and yet they wot not
how."[2] And a "work" there might have been in very truth had Oxford's plans
turned out as he hoped they would. But luckily James's ambassadors were
slow in striking a bargain with Louis, and in the meantime Edward, who had

---

1. *Ibid.*, 177-178; *Rolls of Parl.*, VI, 113.
2. *Paston Letters*, V, 184.

been growing more and more suspicious that negotiations hostile to him were going on between James and Louis, succeeded in frightening the Scots both by withholding his safeconduct for the Scottish commissioners who were to come to Alnwick for the diet of 16 June and by directing the Earl of Northumberland to send a pursuivant to Scotland to complain of certain violations of the truce and especially of James's reception of the Earl of Oxford after his flight from England.[1] Oxford, in consequence, grew discouraged about getting help from James and, instead of going to Scotland, changed his plans and headed straight for England. On 18 May Paston reported more rumours about the earl.

> I heard say that a man was this day examined, and he confessed that he knew a great treasure was sent to the Earl of Oxford, whereof a thousand pounds should be conveyed by a monk of Westminster, and some say a monk of Charterhouse. Item, that the same man should accuse a hundred gentlemen in Norfolk and Suffolk that have agreed to assist the said earl at his coming thither, which, as it is said, should be within eight days after St Dunstan, if wind and weather serve him.

Paston again spoke of his news as "flying tales," but events were to prove that the story-mongers were very near the truth this time, as on 28 May, just nine days after St Dunstan's Day, Oxford landed at St Osith's.[2]

At the moment of Oxford's landing Edward was far away, at Ludlow,[3] but the Earl of Essex and Lords Dynham and Duras at once set out for Essex, and the news that they were coming sufficed to send Oxford back to his ships. "Men look after they wot not what," remarked Paston after telling of Oxford's landing and its sequel,

> but men buy harness fast; the king's menial men and the Duke of Clarence's are many in this town; the Lord Rivers come today, men say to purvey in like wise. Item, how that the Countess of Warwick is now out of Beaulieu sanctuary, and Sir James Tyrell conveyeth her northward, men say by the king's assent, whereto some men say that the Duke of Clarence is not agreed. Item, men

---

1. See a letter from James to the Earl of Northumberland dated 13 July. *Cal. Documents relating to Scotland*, IV, 408-409. That this letter and the reply of the Scottish ambassadors concerning Oxford belong to 1473 is readily determined by a comparison of the names appended to the reply with those appearing in James's commission of 10 September 1473. Rymer, XI, 787.
2. *Paston Letters*, V, 186, 188. Cf. *Cal. Milanese Papers*, I, 175.
3. Privy Seals.

say that the Earl of Oxford is about the Isle of Thanet hovering, some say with great company, and some say with few.[1]

The very order in which Paston mentions his items of news is enough to show that it was generally believed that some kind of an agreement existed between Oxford and Clarence. Edward did not venture to accuse Clarence openly of treason, but he was evidently on his guard, and it was well understood that, if he was not actually assisting Gloucester, he was at least conniving at the attempts of one of his brothers to get the better of the other. The removal of the Countess of Warwick from Beaulieu appears to have been the work of Gloucester, and another letter writer speaks of a rumour that the king had restored to the countess the whole of her inheritance in order that she might grant it to Gloucester. "And of this folks marvel greatly."[2]

Edward spent the whole summer moving from place to place, and all the time he kept Speaker Alyngton with him.[3] During June he was at Ludlow, Coventry, Kenilworth Castle, and Leicester, during July at Nottingham, Leicester, Stamford, and Fotheringay. In August he spent some time at Shrewsbury, where, on the 17th, his heart was made glad by the birth of his second son, Richard of Shrewsbury;[4] and from Shrewsbury he went to Lichfield. During September he visited Burton-upon-Trent, spent a week or more at Nottingham, and about the 21st reached Leicester again.[5] And all this journeying to and fro seems to have had just one purpose, which was to make the people feel that they were under the royal eye. For all the summer the Earl of Oxford, in spite of his repulse from St Osith's, hovered about the coast of England, capturing passing ships and accumulating "great good and riches,"[6] and all the summer the curious uneasiness within the kingdom continued. While the king was hurrying from place to place, his councillors in London,

---

1. *Paston Letters*, V, 188-189.
2. See a letter to William Calthorp which is dated 1 June and which clearly belongs to the same month of June as Paston's letter cited above. *Hist. MSS. Com., Report 11*, app. 7, p. 95.
3. In December Edward ordered the payment of £26 13s 4d to Alyngton in consideration of the expenses the Speaker had incurred while attending upon him during the summer in the counties of Leicester, Nottingham, Derby, Stafford, Salop, and Hereford, and in the marches of Wales. Warrants for Issues, 13 Edw. IV, 5 Dec. Cf. *Rolls of Parl.*, VI, 160.
4. According to the notes in Add. MS. 6113 which have already been cited on several occasions, Richard was born on 17 August 1472. But this is impossible, as Princess Margaret was born in April 1472.
5. Privy Seals.
6. Early Chancery Proceedings, bundle 48, no. 270; Warkworth, 26.

cudgelling their brains to determine who was spreading the mischief, grew suspicious of every idler and beggar—even of the indigent student eking out a living by begging from door to door. On 12 July the sheriffs of London were ordered to make proclamation that, in as much as many persons,

> being strong and mighty of body to do service in husbandry and other labours, feign them to be sick and feeble, and some feigning them in going of pilgrimages and not of power to perform it without alms of the people, and some also feign them to be clerks in universities, using study and not of power to continue it without help and relief of the people, by means of the which feignings divers and many fall into the said beggings, as well in cities and boroughs as other places, and so, living idly, will not do service, but wander about from town to town as vagabonds, sowing seditious languages,

the king commanded that every person who was able to work should "serve in husbandry and other businesses" according to the laws and statutes; that no person should set out on a pilgrimage who could not make the journey without begging or who did not have "letters testimonial" under the king's great seal stating the reason of his pilgrimage, where he came from and whither he was going, and that no clerk of any university should "go a-begging for his sustenance or finding" unless he had letters from the chancellor of his university saying he was "a clerk of poverty entending his learning, not able to continue without relief of begging."[1]

But what saved England from another outbreak of civil war in the summer of 1473 was probably not so much the activity of the king and the vigilance of his councillors as the failure of the Earl of Oxford's plans. At the beginning of July, according to the Milanese ambassador in France, Oxford sent Louis XI twenty-four "original seals of cavaliers and lords and one duke" who had pledged themselves to make war on Edward. But Louis, though he was not afraid to acknowledge that it was he who had sent Oxford to stir up Edward's enemies, had so far lost faith in the earl by this time that he questioned the genuineness of the twenty-four seals and, instead of sending the "good sum of money to begin this war" which the earl asked for, he decided to look after the defences of the coast of Normandy and to send out a fleet to scour the

---

1. Close Roll 13 Edw. IV, m. 23 dorso. Cf. London Journal 8, f. 52b. There is a slight reference to this proclamation in Richard Parker's *History and Antiquities of the University of Cambridge* (London, 1721), 220.

near-by seas.[1] For should the uprising in England fail to come to pass, what was more likely than that Edward, knowing full well who had sent Oxford to attack him, would take revenge, as he had done once in years gone by, by dispatching some of his trusty friends to swoop down on the coast of France?

Scotland failed Oxford no less completely than did France, for James, whatever his intentions may have been at the start, was by this time so convinced of the inadvisability of having anything to do with Oxford that he was trying to prove to Edward that he had been blameless in regard to him from the first. To the message the Earl of Northumberland's pursuivant had brought him, James replied that he had never been asked to surrender Oxford, and that the earl had long had in his possession a safeconduct from him which even now had not expired. He also intimated that if he had offended Edward in the matter of Oxford, the score might be considered even, since he had written several times in vain to request the surrender of his rebel and traitor, Lord Boyd, who some time before this had fled to England and recently had been granted a pension by Edward.[2] In July, when the Scottish parliament met, the Scottish lords, not knowing, they said, whether it was through "ignorance, recklessness, or malice" that the English had failed to do their part in regard to the Alnwick diet, advised that the king of England should be asked why he had stopped the safeconduct and should be informed that no truce could be kept "without reformation of attemptates"; and when Edward received this message, he at once sent a new safeconduct for the Scottish commissioners and agreed that the diet should meet on 21 September.[3]

When the English and Scottish commissioners assembled, Edward's representatives took James's sharply to task for the friendly reception which had been given to Oxford in Scotland, declaring that James had violated his truce with England not only by allowing Oxford to take refuge in his

---

1. *Cal. Milanese Papers*, I, 176.
2. *Cal. Documents relating to Scotland, ut sup.* In the first place Boyd's pension of 200 marks was granted for three years, Michaelmas, 1472, to Michaelmas, 1475, but in June 1475, it was renewed for seven years more. *Cal. Patent Rolls*, II, 466, 536; Warrants for Issues, 14 Edw. IV, 5 August; Signed Bills, file 1508, no. 4655. He was receiving money from Edward at least as late as 1480. Tellers' account, Exchequer T. R., Council and Privy Seal, file 92, m. 24.
3. *Acts of Parl. of Scot.*, II, 104-105; *Rotuli Scotiæ:*, II, 437; Signed Bills, file 1505, 110. 4547, 27 July. Edward's commissioners were named on 24 August, James's on 10 September. Rymer, XI, 786-787.

kingdom, but by permitting the earl to sell the English ships and goods he had stolen. But the Scots replied, as James himself had already done, that Oxford had a safeconduct which had been granted to him when he was "in good grace of his sovereign lord," and that this safeconduct would not expire until Michaelmas Day. They also declared that at the time he came to Scotland the earl had been refused a year's extension of his safeconduct, which caused him to depart "right evil content," and that the only ships he had with him were the French one which brought him to Scotland and a small carvel of Zealand which King James had been careful to hold for more than twenty days to see if any man would "say aught till her." Finally, they said that if the earl was engaged in any conspiracies at the time he came to Scotland, the fact was unknown to James, who, they promised, would so keep his truce with England in the future that, God willing, no failure on his part would be found. With these explanations and assurances the Englishmen pretended to be content, and in the end it was agreed that the compacts made at the meeting at Newcastle the year before should be kept and that the "days of redress upon the borders" should be observed more carefully hereafter.[1]

In spite of Oxford's ultimate disappointment, his movements and Clarence's behaviour had kept Edward in a state of anxiety all summer, and it is not surprising that the plans for the invasion of France had been advancing very slowly, especially as the Duke of Burgundy's mind was still taken up with Gueldres. But the plans had not been dropped, and any progress of any nature that was made in the direction of a better understanding between England and Scotland was a help towards their realization. A settlement Edward effected with the Hanse towns, after months of negotiation, was also a highly important gain, as the seas must be made safe for English ships before an English army could be transported to France.

In the middle of May, Scott, Hatclyf, Russell, Doctor Henry Sharp, Sir John Crosby, William Rosse, William Bracebridge, and Hugh Bryce had been appointed to go to Utrecht for the diet with the Hanse towns, and they had also been empowered to treat with the king of Denmark, should any

---

1. *Cal. Documents relating to Scotland*, IV, 409-410; Rymer, XI, 788. Edward also had to pay £911 8s to nine Scottish merchants who had grievances against some of his subjects. £200 of this sum was paid before Easter. Tellers' Roll, Mich. 13 Edw. IV.

Danish ambassadors come to Utrecht while they were there.[1] But it was not simply to negotiate with the Easterlings, and perhaps the king of Denmark, that all these envoys were sent across the sea; for, in conjunction with Lords Hastings and Howard, they were to attend another diet at Bruges in June, at which once more an effort was to be made to settle the commercial differences between England and Burgundy. Moreover, to Hastings, Howard, Scott, Hatclyf, and Russell was given a commission to treat with the Duke of Burgundy for a perpetual peace and an offensive and defensive alliance, or, in other words, to complete the negotiations between Edward and Charles for "the great enterprise which by them both is intended against their common adversary, Louis of France," and upon which they were now "well-nigh agreed."[2]

The chief objection which Charles had raised to the treaty proposed to him by Hastings, Hatclyf, Scott, and Russell in the preceding winter seems to have been that, while he was required to bind himself to send a specified number of men into the field, Edward, who, theoretically at least, was to receive the lion's share of the benefits of the invasion of France, made no definite promise in regard to the number of men he would bring, but merely stated that he would prepare himself and his army "magnifice prout decet." Uncomfortably aware that Louis would be able to retaliate upon him much more easily than upon Edward, the duke wanted a more exact statement about the size of Edward's army and a postponement of the joint declaration of war which he and Edward were to make against Louis until the war had been begun by one or both of them. He also wanted a definite agreement, first, that the two armies, while acting separately, should keep so close together that they could assist each other if necessary, and, second, that neither ally should withdraw from the war as long as the other continued to fight. Finally, the duke seems to have demanded that the special treaty of mutual aid should be signed when the other treaty was signed, instead of being delayed, as Edward wished, until Edward had mastered a part of

---

1. Writs of Privy Seal, file 844, no. 3742, 14 May; French Roll 13 Edw. IV, m. 24, 20 May; *Hanserecesse*, II, 7, pp. 13-14. On 27 July Edward granted a safeconduct for a Danish embassy, and one for King Christian himself. Rymer, XI, 784-786. But no negotiations with Denmark took place at Utrecht.
2 Rymer, XI, 778; Cotton MS. Galba B I, f. 213; Writs of Privy Seal, file 844, no. 3744; French Roll 13 Edw. IV, m. 30. Cf. *Hansisches Urkundenbuch*, XI, 140.

France; and he proposed to make it obligatory upon either ally to send to the other upon demand, not five thousand men as Edward had suggested, but six thousand, the prince supplying the men to pay the wages of thirty-six hundred of them if the war was a defensive one, but not otherwise.

Before his instructions to his ambassadors were drawn up, Edward had made up his mind to let Charles have his own way as far as possible, and the men who were going to Bruges were told that the treaty with Burgundy might state that the king of England was to take to France in April 1474, an army of more than ten thousand men, while the Duke of Burgundy was to bring between ten and twenty thousand men. But on one point Edward was "desirous to have more liberty." As the treaty now stood, he was required to "descend in Normandy or in the parties of France near thereunto"; but as it remained to be seen if Normandy would be the best part of France to attack, he charged his ambassadors to "endeavour them to get that article accorded in such wise" that he could land in whatever place he thought "most convenient for the weal of his conquest." He told them, too, that "the letter of perpetual amity and alliance" must antedate the treaty of mutual assistance, and that in case the duke objected to the mutual fulmination against Louis being made before the English army had "descended beyond the sea," they might yield to him in that matter, but only on condition that he would give his "bond under seal for taking of his full part in our quarrel." Finally, he directed his ambassadors to ask for a change in the wording of the "bill of transport" conveying to Charles the territories he had demanded as the price of his co-operation, so that the clause concerning the Count of St Pol's lands would state that reference was made only to such lands as "the Earl of St Pol, now being constable of France, holdeth as his inheritance, and not to such as he now holdeth by virtue of his office or otherwise of the French king's grant and assignment."[1]

While such was the gist of the instructions given to the ambassadors who were to treat with Charles in regard to the invasion of France, the men who were to attend the diet at Bruges were told to make demands concerning seven matters, the more important of which had already been discussed, but never settled, at previous diets. To begin with, they were to dig up the old

---

1. Chancery Miscellanea, bundle 30, no. 10/15 (formerly Chancery Diplomatic Documents, 366 P).

bone of contention. "First, for the party of the king's subjects upon the article touching coming and distribution of English cloth in the duke's countries other than Flanders, they shall insist to have it enlarged in such form as in other diets hath been desired." But Edward wanted not only a free market for England's cloth in the Netherlands; he also wanted to secure for England a monopoly of the wool trade with the cloth manufacturers there, who, owing to the exactions of the English staplers and the high price of English wool, had been turning more or less to Spain and Scotland for their supplies, in spite of the fact that the wool of those countries was admittedly inferior in quality to English wool. Consequently the king's second order to his ambassadors was to "insist with all diligence" upon the "proscribing of Spanish and Scottish wool and for provision for Newcastle wool." His third was that they should demand that all moneys circulating in Charles's domains should be given true and fixed values, and that the correct weight of both gold and silver coins should be maintained. Fourth, they were to insist that "searches made upon Englishmen hereafter be not made in fields and highways without the towns, but in good towns and more honestly than hath been used aforne and in late days"; fifth, that all kinds of tolls and customs should be "set in certain," and that no new ones should be added; sixth, that Charles should permit (although traffic in arms was prohibited by the treaty of 1467) the exportation from his dominions of "horses, harnesses, all manner artillery, and habiliments of war, wrought and unwrought"; and seventh, that "good provision" should be made to keep "rovers, men of war, or enemies unto England" out of the duke's ports and territories. Other matters which were to be treated of were redress of violations of the truce, the staple regulations to which Charles's subjects had raised objections in 1468, and tolls, customs, etc. It had been claimed that the king's officers, especially those of the city of London, were making unjust exactions of Burgundian merchants, and Edward told his ambassadors that, when this subject was brought up, they were to "take good inspection unto the answers that they of London" had made to him in regard to it, though he authorized them to promise that no tolls or customs would be demanded except the old and customary ones, provided English merchants were equally well treated in Charles's lands.[1]

---

1. Chancery Miscellanea, bundle 30, no. 10/14 (formerly Chancery Diplomatic Documents 366 P).

"Touching them of the Hanse" Edward's instructions were just as explicit and, in view of past events, surprisingly polite. At their first meeting with the representatives of the Hanse towns at Utrecht, Scott and Hatclyf and their companions were to say that their king had been told on several occasions that certain well-disposed Englishmen and Hansards—"merchants such as loven peace and tranquillity"—had many times, "in their meeting at marts and other places" in the Duke of Burgundy's countries, "broken their hearts together and sorrowed the breach of the old amities and friendships which were betwixt the king's subjects and them," and that, as a prince "that would rest in peace with all Christian people," he had been glad to approve when a diet had been arranged. But though, as this friendly greeting half betrayed, Edward had made up his mind to offer a compromise in regard to the sentence pronounced against the Hanseatic merchants in 1468 which practically amounted to an abandonment of his whole position, his ambassadors were by no means to confess this at once. On the contrary, if the Hansards insisted, as they had done before, on discussing the injuries they claimed to have sustained, they were to be asked what they had in mind, and if it was found that they referred to the sentence of the king's council, they were to be told, though "in courteous wise," that no "indifferent man" would believe that the council of any prince, "proceeding by great and many deliberations like as the king's council did, would give of any likeliness a wrong judgment," and that "the manner of all princes and sovereigns, from whom is none appeal, is such that one deferreth alway to the sentence and judgment given by the other in all such cases as the one hath jurisdiction upon the subjects of that other." Nevertheless, if they persisted in their demand, the king's ambassadors, "rather than break finally," were to yield, after defending the sentence as far as they thought best, and tell the Hansards that the king, in consideration of the old friendship between England and the Hanse towns and because, as he would never forget, "divers persons of their nation and company have acquitted themself thankfully toward his Highness at the time of his great business," would find a way to "appease the hearts" of those who felt themselves injured by the sentence. If the Hansards seemed inclined to be content with this and wished to know what indemnity or recompense would be given them, the king's ambassadors were to tell them that for a time, "be it one year more or less," he would permit all members of the Hanse to import into and export from England all lawful merchandise duty free "in the name and to the behoof of" those who had suffered by the sentence. Hope was also held out to the Hansards that their ancient privileges would be restored to them in toto if they renewed the arrangement ratified by the Hanse at Lübeck in 1437. But on one point Edward refused to yield an inch. His ambassadors were to "forbear to enter the matter" of old injuries committed by either party in the time of Henry VI or since.[1]

Hatclyf and Russell, who were to have a hand in all these negotiations, whether with Charles or with the Hansards, left Westminster on 28 May and crossed to Calais on the 31st. One of their colleagues, Lord Howard, had preceded them by a few days, and as three Hanseatic ships had attacked him while he was crossing from England, driving his ship upon the sands, and killing sixteen of his men,[2] Howard at least must have felt the desirability of success at Utrecht. Rosse too was already at Calais and, having arranged with Howard and Rosse to follow them, Hatclyf and Russell went on to Bruges, arriving there on 3 June.

To their surprise, the Englishmen found no one at Bruges with whom they could treat. They were told that the Duke of Burgundy had empowered the president of Flanders, Georges Baert, and others to discuss the "matter of merchandise" with them and that these men were at Ghent awaiting word of their coming; but, so far as they could learn, no one had yet been appointed to negotiate with them regarding the "secret matter of pactions." Two days after their arrival, therefore, Hatclyf and Russell dispatched Bluemantle to Charles, who was then at Maastricht and on the point of entering Guelderland, to ask him to send someone to treat with them about the invasion of France. While they were waiting for a reply, the president of Flanders and his colleagues came over from Ghent, but even after that it was impossible to do anything until Howard and Rosse arrived from Calais, since Edward's commission called for at least four persons. Charles's representatives waited five or six days, but then, as Howard and Rosse did

---

1. Chancery Miscellanea, bundle 30, no. 10/16 (printed in *Hanserecesse*, II, 7, pp. 13-16).
2. *Hist. MSS. Com.*, *Report 11*, app. 7, p. 95. The accounts of the victualler of Calais, both for this year and for the following one, speak of Easterlings and other "spoliatores marls" pursuing English ships "usque terram juxta le Ruysbank le Rode versus portus Calesii." Foreign Roll 14 Edw. IV, m. B.

not appear, they departed, "and nothing was done in that matter." Nor was this the only disappointment. Rosse, though not Howard, finally came from Calais, and Bluemantle returned from Maastricht bringing word that Charles was sending the Seigneur de la Gruthuyse, Jean Gros, and other persons to Bruges; but though Hatclyf and Russell now waited in their turn for six days, the duke's commissioners neither came nor were heard from, and as by this time the date appointed for the diet with the Hansards was drawing "fast on," the Englishmen at length set out for Utrecht. It was well that they did so, for, when they reached Ghent, they learned that the reason why Gruthuyse and Gros had not come to Bruges was that Charles had sent them to Utrecht to treat with the Hansards.

On arriving at Utrecht on the last day of June, Hatclyf and Russell found that the Hanseatic ambassadors had been detained by contrary winds and so, "to avoid idleness," they went off on a pilgrimage to Amersfoort. But they were back in Utrecht in time to pay their respects to the Bishop of Utrecht when he arrived there on 6 July, and on the 7th both the aldermen of the Hansards of Bruges and the burgomasters of Utrecht came to tell them that those who were to treat with them were at Hamburg "abiding the wind" and had sent excuses for their "long tarrying." Two days later the wind was considerate enough to shift to the east, and on the 13th the belated Hansards, twenty of them, at last arrived. Thereupon negotiations commenced at once. On the 14th there was a meeting to exchange first courtesies, and on the 15th another for the exhibition of commissions. But the Englishmen began to make trouble immediately, first, because the Hansards were so many, second, because they had brought no "writing under seal" to show that they represented any city except Lübeck, and third, because their commission held good only until Assumption Day (15th August). The Hansards met these objections by consenting to let three or four of their number act for all and by promising that, if an agreement were reached, they should be "sufficiently purveyed of power and authority"; but they complained on their part because no mention was made in Edward's commission of "authority to repair and make restitutions." They were satisfied, however, when the Englishmen replied—not quite truly, it would seem—that this authority was conveyed by the general clause giving them power to settle differences by such means as they thought best, and, after a little discussion about the order to be observed in speaking, the Hansards said that, out of deference to the king of England, they would give his commissioners the "first room."

On Friday, 16 July, the really serious conversations began. But alas! they began badly, as the Hansards immediately demanded not only the revocation of the sentence of 1468, but also compensation for what they had suffered at the hands of the English even before Edward's accession to the throne. The Englishmen retorted that the war the Hanseatic League had waged against England "unrightwisely and without cause" was the main source of trouble, and that to seek the best means of putting an end to it would be "the best way to come to peace." Instantly the Hansards were up in arms. The entire responsibility for the war, they maintained, lay with England, and the sentence which had been pronounced against the Hanseatic merchants was entirely unjust, first, because so many had been condemned who had never been "cited nor called," second, because the condemned had been denied "advocates and learned counsel," third, because some who were "actors and parties against them were also judges in the sentence," and fourth, because the deed which had occasioned the sentence was not done by the Hanse men, but by the king of Denmark, who was not "of their confederacy." They declared, too, that King Edward had refused to make reparation, although the Duke of Burgundy had requested him to do so, and that the Englishmen who came to the diet at Bruges the year before "would not hear speak the orators of the Hanse, but departed them."

To all this the Englishmen answered haughtily that they had not been sent to defend the sentence of the king's council, which was "of the self rightwise," though they did go to the trouble of declaring that all the Hansards in England had been duly "cited to their answer, called, and heard," that without doubt they had had "sufficiency of advocates and counsel," and that there was not a member of the king's council at the time who was a party to the matter except the Marquis of Montagu, the Earl of Warwick's brother. To the assertion that the king of Denmark, not the Hanseatic League, was the guilty party, the Englishmen's only reply was to cite the facts brought out at the trial, while for what had occurred at Bruges they threw the blame on the instructions given to the League's representatives, which "went directly and notorily to the infamy of our prince." The Hansards were also told that the sentence, even if it could be proved to contain "inquity," was not sufficient cause for war, that it was a reprisal for injuries done to Englishmen by the men of the Hanse, and that if the men of the Hanse felt themselves wronged by it, they should have made use of "a counter-marque or a counter-reprisal" instead of resorting to war.

By this time both Englishmen and Hansards had worked themselves up into such a temper that there was great danger that the negotiations would break down completely. But fortunately in their inmost hearts all were longing for a settlement, and after a while the Hansards suggested that it would be better to steer away from subjects which threatened to wreck the whole diet to the consideration of such matters as "best might conduct towards the peace." To this the Englishmen gladly gave their consent, and when they were pressed to say something to "quiet the spirits" of those who felt themselves "greatly hurted and grieved," they dwelt on their king's benevolent feeling towards the people of the Hanse and his gratitude for their kindness to him in the days of his "adverse fortune." Then they announced that they were authorized to say that, if the Hansards would agree to a peace, Edward would open the ports of his kingdom to them again and would restore all their old privileges, harmful though those privileges were to his own subjects. But the Hansards were not satisfied with this. They still insisted upon having reparation both for what they had suffered at the hands of the Earl of Warwick and others before Edward's accession and for the sentence of the king's council, and they also brought up another sore point. "They marvelled," they said, "that Englishmen, which thought the sentence good," would make an exception of the merchants of Cologne, since those merchants belonged to the Hanse and were nearer to the king of Denmark, "that did the deed," than were those who were condemned by the council. Whereupon the Englishmen took umbrage again. If old scores were going to be raked up, they thought they could rake up some on their side, such as the seizure by the Hansards on one occasion of fourteen English ships, which were "better than forty or sixty of theirs." And as for the sentence, a subject it had just been agreed to drop, if that was going to be mentioned again, they would demand reparation for what Englishmen had suffered through the unjust war the Hansards had been carrying on against them. Yet in the end the Englishmen calmed down so far as to suggest that, as their proposal seemed to be unacceptable, their opponents should make one. And thereupon the Hansards went off to deliberate till the morrow.

The narrow escape from a rupture during the first discussions ought to have taught both parties the need of being more conciliatory, but the same obstinacy and ill temper showed themselves on the following days. On Saturday the Hansards sent word that the offer to restore their former privileges was not enough, since those privileges were granted, as the words of the grant showed, more for England's profit than for theirs; and they went on to say that, while it was true that they were required to pay less customs than Englishmen paid, at the time the grant was made to them Englishmen paid nothing, and what Englishmen paid now they paid by their own consent. They pointed out, too, that the renewal of their privileges was no great favour to them, as those privileges were "nothing but their own, no new thing." On these statements the Englishmen pondered till Monday, but when they spoke, it was with emphasis. They had seen copies of the grants made to the Hansards by Henry III, Edwards I, II, and III, Richard II, and Edward IV himself, they said, and not one of them stated that the grants were made for the profit of England or in recognition of the merits of the Hansards. They also maintained that, even if English merchants were paying no customs at all at the time the Hanseatic merchants bargained to pay threepence, "at this day to pay less than an Englishman" was "a great privilege" for which many would willingly pay "a million of gold"; and they added that, as other nations which had enjoyed the privilege of paying but threepence had forfeited it as soon as they became hostile to England, it was only reasonable that the Hansards too should forfeit it when they became hostile.

But, in spite of their seeming firmness, the Englishmen were ready for a compromise. So they ended by requesting the Hansards to tell them what more they wanted, though at the same time they entreated them to ask only for what was "honest" and "possible" and reminded them of the king's "great occupations since the last trouble" and that whatever was awarded to them would have to be "at his charge only," in as much as many of those for whose satisfaction the sentence had been rendered were dead, some were impoverished, and some were "come to naught." Then the Hansards, though they stuck to their demand for restitution, even refusing to change the word to "recompense" to spare the king's feelings, promised to be content with such restitution as was just and as the king could pay; and when the

Englishmen asked for time for deliberation before saying how much the king would be willing to pay, as they did not want their opponents to "suck out all our milk and then drink not," they were given to understand that a reasonable offer would be accepted.

But again alas! When on the following day the Englishmen announced that Edward would allow the Hansards, "or them that pretended them hurted," to content themselves out of the customs due on such merchandise as they should import into England, the Hansards, though willing to agree to this method of obtaining satisfaction, mentioned terrible figures. They asserted that their injuries entitled them to two hundred thousand pounds, though they would accept, they said, twenty-five thousand; and they demanded in addition, "for the harms and rebukes that Londoners and other Englishmen had done them," a free gift of the Steelyard in London and of a house in Boston and one in Lynn. To this the Englishmen replied that the king was willing to do something to comfort the men of the Hanse, but he was not prepared to bind himself to pay any fixed sum, and also that they had no authority to make any promises about the Steelyard or about houses in Boston and Lynn. If their offer was rejected, they said, the only thing left to do was to hold another diet. When the Hansards, protesting that if they had known that the Englishmen had such limited powers they would have "biden at home, nor they would not have spent so much money in vain," continued to insist that a definite sum must be named and declared that they had no authority to agree to another diet, the Englishmen told them that they had made demands which the king and his council, not being "gods nor knowers of men's thoughts," could not foresee, and that evidently one party or the other would have to send home for larger powers.

The Hansards were willing to give the Englishmen a month to obtain fuller instructions, but at this juncture they stirred up another hornets' nest by demanding that the merchants of Cologne should be excluded from the benefits of any treaty which was signed and should be deprived of the privileges they were now enjoying in England until they had been readmitted to the Hanseatic League. When the Englishmen objected to this on the ground that the men of Cologne had always been the king's good friends, the reply made to them was that "either the king should lack the Cologniers or all them of the Hanse." Longing to find a little comfort somewhere, the Englishmen then asked what reduction they might hope for in the amount of restitution that had been mentioned and how English merchants visiting Hanseatic towns would be treated. The Hansards replied that, if the king gave them the London Steelyard and the houses in Boston and Lynn, they would deduct five thousand pounds from the sum they had named, and that English merchants trading with the Hanse towns would be received "as they have been wont to be in times past." This sounded so little promising that the Englishmen, in order that Edward might have more time to prepare for war, if war instead of peace it was to be, strove hard to induce the Hansards to let them have more than a month to get their new instructions; but they were refused even this, and finally it was agreed that the Hansards should draw up their demands in writing and that their "book" should be sent to Edward.

The Hansards took three days to prepare their book, and while their pens were busy, Hatclyf hurried off to consult with the Duke of Burgundy, who was now laying siege to Nijmegen, and to make three requests of him: first, that he would instruct his own commissioners to be "difficile to accord" with the Hansards unless the English did so, second, that he would consent to act as arbitrator between the English and the Hansards if Edward wished him to do so, and third, that he would ask the Hansards to agree to another diet and to a truce. As soon as Charles had given him the desired promises, Hatclyf returned to Utrecht, and on the 26th the Hansards presented their book.[1] The Englishmen claimed that their offers had been misstated, but the Hansards permitted them to rewrite a part of the articles, and then, on the 30th, both parties agreed to a prorogation of the diet until 1 September.[1] After that the Englishmen withdrew to Dordrecht and from there sent Bluemantle to England to make a report to the king.[3]

Hatclyf and Russell made use of the month of grace the Hansards had given them to go back to Bruges and take up the negotiations with Charles which were so important a part of their mission. They were at Bruges

---

1. For the full text of the book, see *Hanserecesse*, II, 7, pp. 92-100.
2. *Ibid.*, p. 121.
3. Russell's chaplain, John Canyng, was also sent to the king about this time. After seeing Edward at Lichfield he returned to Utrecht. Warrants for Issues, 14 Edw. IV, 3 April.

from 4 to 24 August, and during that time they came to some sort of an agreement with the duke "upon the forms and number of all the minutes of pactions" relating to the invasion of France. But this time too "for default of number" they could do nothing in the "matters of merchants." On the 24th Bluemantle returned from England with letters from Edward, and, after sending him on to Charles, Hatclyf and Russell went back to Utrecht, though with the understanding that Charles's commissioners would meet them at Bruges again on 20 September to inform them of the duke's decision about the war treaty. They reached Utrecht on the morning of 1 September, but in their desire to hide from the Hansards the fact that Bluemantle had gone to see Charles, they pretended that he had not yet come back from England with their instructions. Two days later, however, Bluemantle arrived at Utrecht with letters from Charles asking the Hansards to grant the king of England's requests,[1] and the next day the Englishmen made known Edward's message, which was, in substance, that he could not give the Hanseatic League a final answer until he had consulted parliament, which would meet in October. In the meantime the Hansards ought to agree, the king thought, either to another diet or to the continuation of the present one "with abstinence of war," but, if they wished, he was ready to make an agreement with them on such points as could be settled at once and leave the rest for further negotiation.

Edward's proposal sounded fair, but not to the ears of the Hansards, who had begun to suspect that all the English really wanted was to make them "lose the profit of this summer in the war." Consequently, far from accepting it, they declared once more that they had no authority to agree to another diet and, complaining that their expenses were so heavy that they could not afford to continue the present one much longer, they threatened to go home within a couple of days. Not until they were given a written copy of Edward's answer[2] and were told that, if they would not agree to either of his suggestions, it would be best to call on the Duke of Burgundy or some other prince to arbitrate, did they consent to give the king the additional time he wanted. And then, just when their opponents seemed to have become "more quiet, softer, and more inclined," the Englishmen learned that, without any

---

1. See *Hanserecesse*, II, 7, pp. 133-134.
2. Cf. *ibid.*, pp. 100-101.

warning to them, the Duke of Burgundy's commissioners had come to a separate agreement with the Hansards. Alarmed at the prospect of having to carry on their struggle without Charles's help, the Englishmen were led to show a milder disposition, and finally, when the debate had narrowed down to the question of "which articles should be put in the letter apart, which should condition all that should be concluded," it was decided that the essential points were the amount of money Edward was to pay, the grant of the London Steelyard and the houses in Boston and Lynn, and the expulsion of the Cologne merchants from England. But the Englishmen intimated that a further reduction of the sum demanded from the king would be expected, warned the Hansards that a gift of the three houses would entail "great perpetual charges" for which the Hanseatic League would have to assume responsibility, and urged them to listen to the excuses of the Cologne men, who by this time had sent representatives to Utrecht to try to ward off the blow they feared was coming. Ultimately the Hansards went so far as to say that they would be satisfied with fifteen thousand pounds from the king. But as for mercy for the Cologne men, never would they promise that!

On 17 September the Hansards brought in a "book of articles from which they would in no wise depart," and then began more bickering about the length of time Edward was to be given to make his reply and the date at which another diet should meet to finish the negotiations. At first the Hansards declined to wait longer than until 1 December for the king to make up his mind or to continue the truce beyond 1 January, but after the Englishmen had shown them how impossible it would be for the king to be ready so soon, they reluctantly agreed that the diet should meet on 15 January and that the truce should last until 1 March. Even then they wanted the assurance that Edward would supply the necessary "writings and seals" without cost to the Hanseatic League, that the Englishmen would procure an extension of their safeconduct for them from the Duke of Burgundy, and that the men who had represented Edward at this diet would represent him at the next as well. These promises they finally received, but when the Englishmen ventured to ask that, should a treaty be signed, the League would obtain a confirmation of it from the king of Poland and other princes having "power and seignory upon any person or places of the Hanse," the Hansards answered that never before had they been asked for a confirmation of any agreement they made by any prince except the Master of Prussia, "in whose place and right is now succeeded the king of Poland." They also refused a last entreaty that they would make a further reduction in the amount of money they claimed from the king.

On 19 September the Englishmen and the Hansards met for the last time and exchanged a "book in Latin of articles." Stated briefly, the agreements contained in the articles were as follows:

I. There was to be a truce between England and the Hanseatic League on land and sea until 1 March.

II. If a final peace should be signed, the king of England was to give a promise, confirmed by parliament, that the Hansards would not suffer injury in any way in consequence of any sentence pronounced by the king's council or of any letters of marque granted against them.

III. Trade was to be resumed between England and the Hanse towns, merchants being required to pay the same customs and other duties as of old.

IV. The liberties and privileges formerly enjoyed by Hanseatic merchants in England were to be granted to them again by letters patent confirmed by parliament.

V. Hanseatic merchants were not to be subject to the jurisdiction of the admiral of England, but, when controversies arose in which they were concerned, the king was to name two or more judges to hear and determine them.

VI. The Hansards were to recover the Steelyards in London and Boston[1] and be given a house in Lynn near the water's edge.

VII. In full satisfaction of all injuries done to Hanse men by Englishmen, the king of England was to grant to the Hanse towns, "of his grace and royal munificence," fifteen thousand pounds out of the customs due to him on merchandise imported into and exported from England by Hanseatic merchants.

VIII. The king of England was to repay to the Hanseatic merchants a loan of four hundred and eighty-four pounds which they had made to him while they were imprisoned in England.

IX. The merchants of Cologne were not to share the privileges re-granted to the members of the Hanseatic League.

X. The city of London was to accept the agreements made between the king and the Hanseatic League, and the Hansards were to recover their old privileges in the city, including the custody of Bishopsgate.

XI. The king of England was to make due provision for the reform of English cloth, both as to its length and breadth and as to the quality of the wool used in the making of it.

---

1. "Item in villa de Boston curiam de Staelhoff alias dicta Steelyard."

XII. The Hansards were to be permitted to sell Rhenish wine in England as they had done in days gone by.

XIII. The king of England and the Hanse towns were to send representatives to another diet to be held at Utrecht on 15 January.

XIV. The Hansards were to see to it that the king of Poland either sent ambassadors to the coming diet or confirmed any treaty which might be signed.[1]

Edward's envoys had little cause to feel proud of the results of their long battle with the Hansards, as they had made a good many more concessions than their opponents. But at least the chief obstacles to peace now appeared to be overcome, and with the "book in Latin of articles" they set out for England,[2] whither they were soon followed by Herman Wanmate, formerly secretary of the Hanseatic merchants in London, who was sent not merely to talk matters over with Edward and his councillors but to distribute a little money in the right quarters.[3] Wanmate's money was hardly necessary, however, so anxious was Edward for peace, and, parliament having readily done what was desired of it, on 22 December Scott, Hatclyf, Russell, and Rosse were commissioned to return to Utrecht for the final diet with the Hansards.[4]

Edward had approved, on the whole, of what his representatives had agreed to, though in return for the restoration of the old privileges of the Hanseatic merchants in England he thought he ought to have a promise that the privileges which Englishmen had formerly enjoyed "in the east parties" would be confirmed anew by the king of Poland and the whole Hanseatic League. He also instructed his ambassadors to try again to persuade the Hansards to accept less money from him, but he was resigned to paying

1. For the account of these long negotiations with the Hansards, see *Hansisches Urkundenbuch*, X, 140-163. Cf. *Hanserecesse*, II, 7, pp. 21-57, 852-852. For the text of the "book in Latin of articles," see *Hanserecesse*, II, 7, pp. 121-131.
2. Hatclyf was engaged on this embassy 134 days and was allowed as many pounds for his expenses, besides five marks for his passage and re-passage and £5 for going "into Guelderland" to the Duke of Burgundy and for sending messages to him divers times. Warrants for Issues, 13 Edw. IV, 15 Oct.
3. *Hansisches Urkundenbuch*, X, 163; *Hanserecesse*, II, 7, p. 56. Edward granted a safeconduct for Wanmate on 13 October, and it was carried over to Calais by a pursuivant and delivered to Wanmate on his arrival there. French Roll 23 Edw. IV, m. 10; *Hanserecesse*, II, 7, pp. 204-206.
4. *Rolls of Parl.*, VI, 65-68; Signed Bills, file 1506, no. 4589; French Roll 13 Edw. IV, m. 5; *Hanserecesse*, II, 7, pp. 202-203.

the fifteen thousand pounds, and also to repaying the loan of four hundred and eighty-four pounds, if there was no escape from it. To punish the merchants of Cologne he was still exceedingly loth, especially as they were now offering to submit their quarrel with the League to arbitration,[1] and he told his ambassadors to inquire at Bruges and other places which they were to visit on their way back to Utrecht if there were not some hope of a reconciliation between Cologne and the League and to dwell, when talking with the Hansards, upon "the inconvenience and unreasonableness of their intent" towards the Cologne men. At least, he thought, the League ought to be considerate of his honour to the extent of permitting the article relating to the Cologne men to be couched in general terms, making it obligatory upon him, when he was notified that a certain town had ceased to be a member of the Hanseatic League, to treat the citizens of that town as "strangers and nothing privileged within his realm" until he was informed that it had been received into the League again. Yet not even for the sake of the Cologne men did the king wish his ambassadors to "break" with the Hansards. Rather than that, they were to "put the orators of the Hanse in comfort and hope" that, when they came to England, they would have "the residue of their intents accomplished in such wise as of reason they shall be content."[2]

As Edward had reached the point where he was ready to let the Hansards have practically everything they had demanded, the second diet of Utrecht was successful. Neither the representatives of England nor those of the League were in Utrecht on 15 January, but by 1 February all had arrived, and on 28 February a treaty of peace, ratifications of which were to be exchanged at Bruges on 1 August, was signed by Hatclyf, Russell, and Rosse for Edward, and by Doctor Johann Osthusen and Johann Bersenbrugge of Lübeck, Heinrich Murmester of Hamburg, and Bernard Pawest of Danzig for the League. The treaty was based on the articles drafted in September, but, after long haggling, the Hansards had agreed to be content with ten thousand pounds from the king in place of fifteen thousand, and also to let the king have his way about the form of the article relating to the Cologne men. A separate supplementary treaty provided that the king of England should hand over the Steelyards in London and Boston and the house in Lynn, as well as his bond for the ten thousand pounds to be retained by

1. *Hanserecesse*, II, 7, p. 221.
2. *Hanserecesse*, II, 7, pp. 213-220; Schanz, *Englische Handelspolitik*, II, 388-397.

the Hansards out of the customs, to whomsoever the League might send to England to receive them, and that if he did not do this before 1 August, the League's ratification of the treaty was to be deposited with some disinterested person, such as the Prior of the Carmelites at Bruges, until it was done. The Hansards also certified that the city of Cologne was at present excluded from the Hanseatic League, and Edward promised that, from the day the ratifications of the treaty were exchanged, the men of Cologne should lose their privileges in England. Lastly, it was provided that, although the renewal of commercial intercourse between England and the Hanse towns was not to begin until after the exchange of the ratifications, peace was to be proclaimed in the meantime.[1]

The treaty of Utrecht—to complete a long story—did not at once still the troubled waters. The Hanseatic League ratified the treaty on 1 May, and on the following day Herman Wanmate and Arnd Brekerfeld were appointed to go to England to receive the Steelyards in London and Boston and the house in Lynn.[2] But Edward, whose heart still rebelled against the humiliating price he was paying for peace, did not do his part so promptly. The Cologne men, who had been given friendly warning immediately after the signing of the treaty of Utrecht of what they must prepare for, struggled hard to save themselves, and Edward, glad to do as much for them as he could, on 4 April confirmed their privileges until the last possible day, 31 July, though on the understanding that they would withdraw from their guildhall and the Steelyard before 1 July.[3] Writing from Antwerp on 22 June to his friend Avery Cornburgh in London, Gerhard von Wesel complained bitterly of the harsh treatment Cologne was receiving from ungrateful England. "We poor merchants of Cologne," he wrote, "may well greatly marvel us what that moved the king's good grace so suddenly to give us that have so long time continued within England such hasty and short warning to avoid our houses and our hall that his ancestors have given only to us many years before that any other of the *stedes* were within England there, as we never trespassed, neither offended, howbeit that we had as good and rightfully a

---

1. Rymer, XI, 793-803; *Hanserecesse*, II, 7, pp. 341-353. For a minute account of the negotiations at this second diet of Utrecht by the Hanseatic ambassadors, see *Hanserecesse*, II, 7, p. 239 *et seq.*
2. *Hanserecesse*, II, 7, pp. 353, 394.
3. *Ibid.*, p. 383; Writs of Privy Seal, file 847, no. 3881; French Roll 14 Edw. IV, m, 29.

cause of grudge against the commons of England as other that indeed have showed it alway." "Shall this be our reward," he exclaimed, "for sparing of recoverance of our great hurts and losses to us done by the king's subjects, and suffering divers other injuries? Is this our reward for because we would not assist the king's enemies at their desire, and now to stand with them in like case? Is this for loaning of our money to the king, as yet without restitution? Is this the reward that we shall have for our loving dealing and abiding when that other warred?" The men of Cologne were not driven, he said, to ask pardon of those they had never offended except "in pleasing to the king's good grace." They had "trusted too much in fair language not fructuous, leaving the hen and taking the egg, whereof we must beware hereafter, and when fortune and stablesse cometh to have ready our net to receive it; but, forsooth, we knew none rather that England was so weak and so lightly to overcome by a small fellowship. I am sorry that strangers shall know it, God wot full well." But of what avail was it to protest? The king himself, as Gerhard confessed, was "not culpable in this our expulsion"; he had only done what he was compelled to. The day set for the surrender of the Steelyards was very near at hand, and Gerhard was deeply concerned because he had heard that the rent-gatherer was "loth that John my child should take away such reparations as I have made in my chamber, as glass windows and other things." The poor man had spent twenty pounds on those reparations, and yet it was not so much the loss of the value of his money that troubled him, thrifty merchant though he was, as the dread that "other should mock me to scorn with my father's arms and marks in glass windows and other places."[1]

As it turned out, Gerhard did not have to give up his glass windows quite as soon as he feared, for a few days after he wrote his wailing letter to Cornburgh, Edward gave the Cologne men permission to stay in the Steelyard until 31 July and to continue to enjoy their privileges during his pleasure.[2] The Hanseatic League had been so importuned to make peace with Cologne that it had begun to listen, and the Archbishop of Trèves, whom

---

1. *Hansisches Urkundenbuch*, X, 200-201. For another anxious letter Which Gerhard wrote to Wanmate and Brekerfeld about his windows, see *ibid.*, 271. He was regarded with suspicion by the other Cologne merchants. *Ibid.*, 228-229, 275-276.

2. Signed Bills, file 1507, no. 4638; *Cal. Patent Rolls*, II, 445, 452; *Hansisches Urkundenbuch*, X, 202, 205.

the Emperor selected as arbitrator, wrote to Edward asking him to permit both parties to enjoy their old privileges in England until their differences had been adjusted. But what really procured for the Cologne men another month's occupancy of the Steelyard was not the letter of the Archbishop of Trèves—for, as Edward afterwards wrote to the Emperor, joint occupancy of the Steelyard by the Cologne men and the merchants of the other Hanseatic towns was out of the question so long as they hated each other as they now did—but the fact that the journey of Wanmate and Brekerfeld to England was delayed by the refusal of Danzig to ratify the treaty of Utrecht and by the slowness with which the other Hanseatic towns sent in their ratifications.[1]

On 20 July Edward ratified the treaty of Utrecht; on the 22nd he empowered his chaplain and almoner, Alexander Legh, to carry his ratification to Bruges and ordered the drawing up of the letters patent granting to the merchants of the Hanseatic League ten thousand pounds out of the customs or subsidies on merchandise imported and exported by them; and on the 28th he restored to the Hansards the privileges they had enjoyed in England before the sentence of 1468.[2] But Wanmate and Brekerfeld lingered at Bruges, waiting for better news from Danzig, and when Legh arrived there and met John Duerkoep, the League's representative, Duerkoep discovered defects in the writing and sealing of the three documents he had brought and he found fault with the two the League had sent. So in the end it was agreed that all the documents should be left in the care of the Prior of the Carmelites and that more satisfactory ones should be deposited with him by 1 November.[3]

On 4 October Wanmate and Brekerfeld at last arrived in London. Edward was not in the city at the time, and neither were Hatclyf and Russell, who had conducted the negotiations at Utrecht; but the chancellor was directed to receive the League's envoys and to do what was necessary to fulfil the terms of the treaty, and Wanmate and Brekerfeld were summoned before the council in the Star Chamber. Several conferences followed, and on 30 October the king's councillors ordered the proclamation of the treaty

---

1. *Hanserecesse*, II, 7, pp. 354-355, 408, 427, 453-455.
2. *Ibid.*, pp. 353, 427; Rymer, *ut sup.*; French Roll 14 Edw. IV, m. 25, 26; Writs of Privy Seal, file 849, no. 3964.
3. *Hanserecesse*, II, 7, pp. 427-430.

between England and the Hanseatic League with a statement that the merchants of the League were to enjoy their former privileges.[1] But it was not until 14 December that the grant to the Hansards of the ten thousand pounds out of the customs was sealed,[2] and although the Cologne men were now at last turned out of the London Steelyard, it was not handed over to Wanmate and Brekerfeld, as they, on finding that there would be heavy rents of uncertain amount to pay, decided to wait for further instructions. Nor was it until the beginning of January 1475, that Hatclyf and Scott, who were at that time going on an embassy to the Duke of Burgundy, stopped at Bruges to offer again to exchange ratifications of the treaty of Utrecht; and even then it was found that, as Legh had failed to say that new copies must be made of all the documents he had taken to Bruges, they had brought but one document instead of three. So again the ratifications, although now satisfactory to both parties, had to be deposited with the Prior of the Carmelites, and Hatclyf and Scott promised to procure the lacking documents before Easter and send them to the prior.[3]

All these delays notwithstanding, matters were finally straightened out. Early in 1475 parliament confirmed Edward's agreement to allow the Hanseatic merchants to occupy the Steelyard, with certain lands and tenements adjoining it, in perpetuity, on condition that they would pay "like charges for deeds of alms and pity" as other proprietors had paid and rents amounting to £85 19s 6d. On 28 April following five messuages situated in Windgoose Lane and a tenement and quay adjoining them were also granted to the Hansards, and the next day certain tenements and a quay in Lynn were given to them for their Steelyard there. About the same time they got possession of their Steelyard in Boston, and on 12 May the city of London granted the special confirmation of their privileges which the treaty of Utrecht called for. Yet it was not until 4 September 1475, that William Caxton and William Dollyng, notary, placed in the hands of Duerkoep and two other representatives of the League at Bruges the three corrected documents Edward had sent and received from them the two the League was to

1. *Ibid.*, pp. 439-442.
2. *Cal. Patent Rolls*, II, 473; *Hansisches Urkundenbuch*, X, 225.
3. *Hanserecesse*, II, 7, pp. 442-443, 445; Diplomatic Documents (Exchequer, T. of R.), no. 1424; *48th Report of Deputy Keeper*, app., 604.

give in exchange.[1] When this was done, all the provisions of the treaty of Utrecht had been carried out except two: Edward had still to repay the loan of four hundred and eighty-four pounds, and the Cologne merchants had still to be punished with the loss of their privileges. But perhaps the matter of the four hundred and eighty-four pounds was not pressed, and Edward's evasion of his promise regarding the Cologne men was excusable, because Cologne was about to be given a chance to make her peace with the League. The first attempt to reconcile Cologne and the League failed, and in August 1476, Edward was forced to tell the Cologne men that he would have to take their privileges from them. But fortunately it proved unnecessary to follow up this threat with the deed, as in November the city of Lübeck announced that Cologne had been reinstated as a member of the Hanseatic League.[2]

1. *Rolls of Parl.*, VI, 123-124; *Cal. Patent Rolls*, II, 509-510, 519, 540; *Hanserecesse*, II, 7, pp. 462-465, 478; *Hansisches Urkundenbuch*, X, 257-258; Sharpe, *Cal. Letter Book L*, 129; Diplomatic Documents (Exchequer, T. of R.), box 19, no. 554; *45th Report of Deputy Keeper*, app., 335. One John Bolles was paid £160 for tenements bought from him by the king "pro mansione de lez Esterlinges in Boston." Tellers' Roll, Easter 15 Edw. IV.
2. *Hanserecesse*, II, 7, pp. 479-480, 581, 647-650, 654-656; Rymer, XII, 36.

BARGAINS WITH BURGUNDY AND SCOTLAND

When Edward came to London at the beginning of October 1473, to open parliament, he was greeted with the news that the Earl of Oxford had descended on the coast of Cornwall on the last day of September and seized St Michael's Mount. Oxford had only about eighty men with him, including his three brothers, George, Thomas, and Richard de Vere, and his companion in flight from the battlefield of Barnet, Viscount Beaumont; but the Cornishmen, far from trying to drive him off, had welcomed him with "right good cheer," and what with his neighbours' good will and the natural strength of the Mount—a steep rocky promontory at low tide and an island at high tide—he seemed to have found an excellent lair.[1] Yet perhaps to Edward Oxford looked less dangerous after he settled down in Cornwall than he had looked while he was in France or sailing about in search of unwary merchantmen. Or perhaps, as parliament began at once to busy itself about the treaty with the Hanseatic League and about a new act of resumption and a plan for a general clearing up of such of the royal debts as went back to the days before the flight to Burgundy,[2] the king's mind was too much occupied with what was going on at Westminster to leave him time to worry about what had happened at St Michael's Mount. For almost a month passed before any notice was taken of Oxford's presence, and even when an effort was at last made to oust him from his stronghold, it was not because any fear was felt of him but because his proximity began to react on London and on Clarence. Dark rumours about Clarence's intentions commenced to float about again, and London grew more and more "queasy," until finally it became necessary to prohibit the bearing of arms and to require all tavern keepers to close their doors at nine o'clock at night.[3]

---

1. Worcester, Itinerarium, 122; Warkworth, 26; *Cal. Patent Rolls*, II, 418.
2. *Rolls of Parl.*, VI, 71-72.
3. Close Roll 13 Edw. IV, m. 13 dorso; London Journal 8, f. 64.

The proclamation forbidding the carrying of arms was issued on 23 October, and four days later the king commissioned Sir John Arundell, John Fortescue, a Cornishman named Henry Bodrugan, and others to array his subjects in Cornwall, and in the adjoining counties too, if necessary, for the purpose of reducing St Michael's Mount to obedience.[1] But as the days passed, the plot seemed to thicken. Paston wrote to his brother from London that most of the men about the king had:

> ... sent for their harness, and it is said for certain that the Duke of Clarence maketh
> him big in that he can, showing as he would but deal with the Duke of Gloucester;
> but the king intendeth, in eschewing all inconvenients, to be as big as they both and
> to be a stifler atween them. And some think, that under this there should be some
> other thing intended and some treason conspired; so what shall fall can I not say.

That the king sent at this moment for the great seal, which since the end of July had been in the keeping of Lawrence Booth, Bishop of Durham, was also interpreted as a bad sign.

> Some say we shall have a new chancellor, but some think that the king doth
> as he did at the last fields, he will have the seal with him; but this day Doctor
> Morton, Master of the Rolls, rideth to the king and beareth the seals with him.

However, no change was made at the Chancery, and in a fortnight the atmosphere had apparently cleared somewhat, as Paston then expressed the hope that Clarence and Gloucester would be "set at one by the award of the king."[2]

Perhaps because Sir John Arundell died two weeks after the commission for the reduction of St Michael's Mount was issued,[3] the conduct of the siege of the Mount devolved on Bodrugan, who, if the statements of his enemies are to be believed, instead of doing his duty, used the authority the king had given him to extract "great notable sums" from his fellow Cornishmen and then pocketed the money. There must have been a few skirmishes, as on one occasion Oxford "issued out" and took a prisoner and on another,

---

1. *Cal. Patent Rolls*, II, 399. Fortescue was probably the great-nephew of Sir John Fortescue. He married a daughter of Edward's godmother, Lady Saye. *Letters of Margaret of Anjou*, 106. Bodrugan had married the widow of the late Viscount Lysle. *Rolls of Parl.*, II, 399.
2. *Paston Letters*, V, 195, 196, 199.
3. Inquisitions *post mortem*, 33 Edw. IV, no. 26.

when he attempted a similar sally, he was wounded in the face by an arrow; but in general Bodrugan seems to have preferred parleying to fighting, and, still worse, he allowed Oxford to gather in an abundance of supplies.[1] Consequently a whole month passed and Oxford was still master of his rock. Then Edward decided that it was time to make a change. On 7 December the king issued a new commission for the reduction of the Mount which gave his commissioners power to offer pardon to every man in the Mount who was willing to take the oath of allegiance, with the exception of Oxford and his brothers and Viscount Beaumont; and though he did not venture to leave Bodrugan's name out of the commission altogether, he transferred the command of the siege to Fortescue. At the same time he sent to Fortescue's assistance some cannon and other artillery from the storehouses at the Tower and several ships.[2] William Fetherston (or Fedyrston) and Edward Brampton were ordered to proceed to Cornwall with the *Garce*, the *Carican*, the *Cristofre* of Calais, and the *Mary* of Calais, carrying altogether six hundred men, and to keep as near the Mount as they could without danger to their ships in order that they might do "all the hurt and noisance" possible to Oxford and his friends and prevent aid from the outside world from reaching them.[3]

Fetherston and Brampton were retained by the king for two months, and Fortescue's commission was for the same length of time.[4] Nor was this more

---

1. *Rolls of Parl.*, VI, 139; *Paston Letters*, V, 201; Warkworth, *ut sup.*
2. *Cal. Patent Rolls*, II, 412, 418; Tellers' Roll, Mich. 13 Edw. IV. A proclamation was also issued forbidding the bearing of arms in Devon, and probably in the adjoining counties as well. Close Roll 13 Edw. IV, m. 8, dorso.
3. Exchequer Accounts, K. R., bundle 71, no. 5. Cf. Scofield, *Eng. Hist. Review*, April 1914, p. 240. Brampton was Portuguese by birth but had obtained letters of denization in October 1472, and also a grant of certain messuages, tenements, etc., in London in recognition of good services rendered in many battles. *Cal. Patent Rolls*, II, 357; Exchequer T. R., Council and Privy Seal, file 90, m. 45. It also appears, from a petition sent to the king in February 1482, by one Druot Curtoys, that, by taking the name of Edward, Brampton had become the king's godson. Curtoys says that one day as he was passing through the High street in London, he "stooped down to the earth and would have taken up a pin from the same," and that when some bakers, "thinking that he had taken up money, asked of him the half part and, with menacing words, there, to the great fear of your said orator, came out upon him the number of eight bakers," he slew one of them in self-defence. He asks for a pardon and tells the king that he has been in his service "eversithens he was of lawful age upon the sea, as Edward Brampton, your godson, and Fetherston can well report." Signed Bills, file 1520, no. 5300.
4. Tellers' Roll, *ut sup.*

time than was needed to dispose of Oxford. Bodrugan's wrath, when he found that he must give place to Fortescue, betrayed him into acts which ultimately caused him to be outlawed,[1] and probably his opposition held Fortescue back for some days, as it was not until 23 December that the siege of the Mount began in earnest. Even then Oxford's men seem to have scored quite as many successes as the king's men, and though the earl was ready enough to "speak and commune" with Fortescue whenever there was a brief truce, he was secretly looking day by day for help from the king of France, to whom he had managed to send his brother Richard while the easy-going Bodrugan was conducting the siege. Louis, however, though he was, as anxious as ever to make life uncomfortable for the king of England, was still suspicious of Oxford and proved poor support. Richard de Vere seems to have been arrested as soon as he reached Normandy, and though, after hearing his story, Louis decided to do something for Oxford and in the course of time sent the earl two shiploads of supplies, the first ship ran into so fierce a gale that her master jettisoned his cargo and returned home, while the second was either frightened away by Fetherston and Brampton or reached the Mount too late to be of service.[2]

Even without the hoped-for aid from France, Oxford might have been able to hold out a considerable time longer had it not been for the power of pardon with which Fortescue was armed. One by one the earl's men were seduced, and all but eight or nine of them had been secretly won over before he woke up to what was happening. Under such conditions it was impossible to go on fighting, and in desperation Oxford asked for a pardon. He did not sue wholly in vain, as on 1 February 1474, Edward granted a pardon to him, to two of his brothers, George and Thomas, to Thomas Clifford, and to all other persons in the Mount except Viscount Beaumont and one Richard Laumarth. But the pardon was one of life only, and so uncertain was the king that Oxford would accept it that he retained Fetherston to serve with the *Carican* for another six weeks. However, Oxford's day was done, and on the 15th he surrendered to Fortescue, who, when he entered the Mount, found that its defenders, far from being reduced to extremity, still had "victual enough till midsummer after."[3]

---

1. *Cal. Patent Rolls*, II, 491; *Rolls of Parl.*, VI, 132-143.
2. Warkworth, 27, 71; *Cal. Milanese Papers*, I, 177-178. It must have been Richard de Vere who went to France, since George and Thomas surrendered with Oxford.
3. Warkworth, *ut sup.*; Signed Bills, file 1507, no. 4602, 1 Feb., 13 Edw. IV; *Rolls of Parl.*, VI, 149; Tellers' Roll, Easter 14 Edw. IV.

Oxford, his two brothers, Beaumont, and Clifford were all carried in triumph to the king, and in a short time the earl was sent to Hammes Castle, where his fellow conspirator of two years past, the Archbishop of York, was already a prisoner. As the lieutenant of Hammes was allowed fifty pounds a year for Oxford's "costs and sustentation," the earl was evidently amply provided with all the necessaries of life, but a year after his capture he and his two brothers were attainted and all their lands and goods declared forfeit to the king;[1] and though the Countess of Oxford, who had been in the sanctuary of St Martin's perhaps ever since the battle of Barnet, succeeded in obtaining a general pardon for herself on 17 March 1475, she was never allowed to visit her husband, and it is said that all she had to live on was what was given to her in charity or "what she might get with her needle or other such conning as she exercised."[2] It is an ill wind, however, that blows no man good, and Oxford's downfall brought relief to the Archbishop of York. For as soon as Oxford was behind prison bars, Edward's fear of the archbishop seems to have died away, and as Gloucester had already been pleading for Neville, it happened that a few months after the brother-in-law of the late Earl of Warwick disappeared behind the gates of Hammes Castle, the brother of that earl emerged from them. George Neville received a pardon on 11 November and was permitted to return to England. But two years and a half of prison life had broken the archbishop's health as well as his spirit, and he died, of sorrow, it was said, on 8 June 1476.[3]

The capture of the Earl of Oxford removed one more difficulty from Edward's path, and if Louis XI had been a wiser man, he would have put more faith in the earl and given him enough help to enable him to get back to France, if nothing more. For now that Oxford had passed out of reach, who was there that Louis could use to stir up the enemies Edward still had at home and thereby keep the English from attacking France? Welcome rumours of dissensions in England growing out of Edward's inability to collect the money granted for the invasion of France and of wrangling still going on between Clarence and Gloucester continued to reach Louis' ears

1. Foreign Rolls, 17 Edw. IV, m. B, and 21 Edw. IV, m. B; *Rolls of Parl.*, VI, 144 *et seq.*
2. *Paston Letters*, V, 137; *Cal. Patent Rolls*, II, 507; Fabyan, 663.
3. *Paston Letters*, V, 199; *Cal. Patent Rolls*, II, 47; Vergil, 675; Le Neve, *Fasti Ecclesiæ Anglicanæ.*

during the winter; but a Florentine who came over from England early in February, before the fall of St Michael's Mount, told a tale not so comforting. He declared that Edward was "obeyed by his brothers and every one," that peace reigned in England, and that, though no preparations to invade France seemed to be going on, an embassy from the Duke of Burgundy was always at the English court urging the matter forward.[1]

In spite of what the Florentine reported, it was the king of England rather than the Duke of Burgundy who was taking the most interest at this moment in the invasion of France. For though Hatclyf and Russell had succeeded in getting some kind of satisfaction from Charles in August, the duke was carrying on his negotiations with Edward in a half-hearted way, with his eyes fixed on the east. Ever since Sigismund of Austria's visit to him in 1469, Charles had been dazzled by the hope that, if he consented to the marriage of his daughter Mary to the Archduke Maximilian—the marriage Sigismund had suggested—the Emperor would promise to bring about his election as King of the Romans; and to such a height had this hope risen in his breast by the summer of 1473 that the invasion of France had begun to look to him like a minor thing and a hindrance to greater schemes. Consequently, even while he was making agreements with Hatclyf and Russell, he had been engaged in peace negotiations with Louis.[2] But in the autumn of 1473 the duke met with a great disappointment; for when, after Hatclyf and Russell had returned home, he went to Trèves to meet the Emperor, all that he obtained was the investiture of the duchy of Gueldres.[3] So little was Frederick III pleased by the greater requests Charles made of him that he ran away in the night rather than promise to procure the duke's election as King of the Romans or to grant another desire of Charles's heart, the erection of his ducal domains into a kingdom. The lesson was a bitter one, and Charles ought to have taken it to heart, renounced his imperial ambitions, and turned back to the policy of his earlier years. But he had dreamed a dream he could not forget, and till the day he met his death in the snow before Nancy the imperial diadem glittered tantalizingly before his eyes and determined his every move.

When Hatclyf and Russell went back to Utrecht early in January 1474, to

---

1. *Cal. Milanese Papers*, I, 178.
2. Commynes-Lenglet, II, 208; *Chronique Scandaleuse*, I, 299.
3. John Paston possessed a "book of the Meeting of the Duke and the Emperor." *Paston Letters*, V, 207.

meet the Hansards again, Doctor John Morton and Lord Duras accompanied them to continue the war negotiations with Charles, and when parliament reassembled on 20 January, after a brief prorogation, it was prorogued again almost at once because the ambassadors who had been sent to Burgundy could not reach home before Easter.[1] But as it turned out, Morton and Duras did not come home until nearly midsummer. Perhaps the first thing which delayed their return was the fact that representatives of the king of France and of the Dukes of Burgundy and Brittany met at Compiègne in February and once more there was talk of a treaty of peace. But, more than that, Charles, being less eager than he had been to participate in an invasion of France, was hindering his negotiations with Edward by increasing his demands. He now wanted a promise from Edward that he would be allowed to hold the fiefs he already possessed in France, and also the lands he was to receive when the war was won, as "true, sole, direct, and supreme lord," without rendering any homage or service to the crown of France, and that this grant would be ratified by the States General of France.[2] Edward was not unwilling to concede even this, however, and when the negotiations at Compiègne terminated in nothing more alarming than an extension of the truce between Charles and Louis until 15th May,[3] the king felt so sure that not only Charles but the Duke of Brittany also would ultimately agree to do what he wanted them to do, that to please the two dukes and to help them to hold their own against Louis until his arrival with his army, he began preparations to send a thousand archers and a few men-at-arms to Charles, and two thousand archers, under the command of Lords Duras and Audley, to Francis.[4]

That Edward was getting troops ready for some purpose was soon known in France. Report said that six thousand Englishmen were coming across

---

1. Warrants under the Signet, file 1384, 7 Dec., 1473; French Roll 13 Edw. IV, m. 5, 7 Jan.; *Rolls of Parl.*, VI, 98-99.
2. See the text of the treaty as signed. Rymer, XI, 811-812.
3. Commynes-Lengiet, II, 293-295, 302-311.
4. Rymer, XI, 791; *Cal. Patent Rolls*, II, 440. In Signed Bills, file 1526, no. 5564, will be found a proclamation which was to be sent to the sheriffs of London and the chancellor of the duchy of Lancaster and which probably belongs to this date. It states that, as the king was planning to send a certain number of archers to his brother, the Duke of Burgundy, good and able archers who wished to join the expedition and receive the offered wages should present themselves before the last day of February before the ambassadors of the duke at the hostelry of the sign of the Great Horn in Christchurch Street, London, there to enter their names, learn the day of muster, etc.

the sea to swell Charles's forces, and Louis hurriedly sent out a small fleet. News of the fall of St Michael's Mount had not yet reached France, and Louis pretended that his ships were going to Oxford's relief; but as he also began to inspect his frontier fortresses, to lay in supplies of food, and to move his heavy artillery about, it was evident that he feared he was going to be attacked.[1] France, however, was to escape invasion for another year, and for the reason that again the Duke of Burgundy's attention was diverted to other matters.

The lands which Sigismund of Austria had pledged to him in 1469 had brought Charles into delicate relations with the Swiss cantons. Although friendship with the Swiss was a policy handed down to him by his father and he had had no thought, when he took over the Hapsburg domains in Alsace, of assuming with them the quarrel of the Hapsburgs with their stalwart neighbours, Sigismund had looked at the matter in another light— and so, unluckily, had the Swiss, in spite of all Charles could say to reassure them. After the meeting with the Emperor at Trèves the situation became still worse, as that meeting resulted not only in the disappointment of Charles's vaulting ambitions, but in a rupture between him and Sigismund and in still greater tension between him and the Swiss, who had no desire to be swallowed up in a new kingdom of Burgundy. Shortly after Sigismund entered into an alliance with the towns of the Upper Rhine, which had also been alarmed by Charles's schemes, and finally Louis XI, always on the lookout for an opportunity to create new enemies for Charles, saw his chance. By working upon the fears of the Swiss, Louis brought about a reconciliation between Sigismund and the Swiss confederacy, a feat which Charles himself had many times attempted but without success; and a few months, later he even enticed the Swiss into an alliance with himself. The League of Constance took shape in March and the early part of April 1474, and immediately after its formation Sigismund, without waiting to hear what answer Charles would make to a letter in which he had announced his intention to redeem the lands he had pledged to the duke in 1469, proceeded to repossess himself of Alsace, where, on account of the brutality of Charles's governor, Peter von Hagenbach, he received a hearty welcome. Hagenbach was seized and executed at Brisach on 9 May, and Charles at once sought revenge by dispatching an army to lay waste the province.

---

1. *Cal. Milanese Papers*, I, 178-179.

The day Hagenbach was put to death at Brisach the English parliament assembled once more at Westminster. Edward had devoted the months of March and April, while waiting for further word from Charles, to another progress through the midland counties,[1] but when he got back to Westminster there was still no treaty with Burgundy to announce. Morton and Duras had taken leave of Charles at Luxembourg on 22 April and had received as parting gifts some silver vessels and a horse for each,[2] but perhaps the disturbing news which was just beginning to come in from Alsace had induced them to linger a little longer to learn the outcome of what was happening there; for they had not yet come home, and parliament sat only long enough to take action on a few domestic matters, including the old quarrel between the king's brothers.

If there had been any truth in the story going about after the Countess of Warwick was carried off from Beaulieu that Edward meant to give her inheritance back to her in order that she might hand the whole of it over to Gloucester, the king must have changed his mind, as nothing of the sort was done. But though Clarence had escaped that blow, his feelings had been hurt again by the recent resumption act, because it contained an exemption clause in Gloucester's favour but none in his;[3] and evidently Edward felt the need of doing something more to placate him. Ever since her removal from Beaulieu, the Countess of Warwick had been in Gloucester's custody, as, indeed, she was destined to remain until after the battle of Bosworth;[4] and to purchase peace between the king's brothers parliament now sanctioned unblushingly the partition of the countess's estates between Clarence and Gloucester and their wives and gave the recipients the right to hold them "in like manner and form as if the said countess were now actually dead." If it should happen that Clarence outlived his wife, he was to enjoy her share of the estates as well as his own to the end of his days, and Gloucester was granted the same privilege in regard to his wife's share; and as there was some doubt about the validity of the marriage of Gloucester and Anne Neville, because of the lack of a papal dispensation, it was stated that this disposition of the estates was to hold good if Gloucester and his wife should be "divorced and after the

1. Privy Seals.
2. Commynes-Lenglet, II, 212-213.
3. *Hist. Croy. Cont.*, 561; *Rolls of Parl.*, VI, 75.
4. Gairdner, *Richard III*, 24.

same be lawfully married," or if they should be divorced and not afterwards lawfully married, provided the duke had done his utmost to procure a lawful marriage and did not wed any other woman.[1]

On 28 May Rotherham, who a few days before had succeeded the Bishop of Durham as chancellor, pronounced an adjournment of parliament until 6 June in order, as he said, that the members might the "more quietly and devoutly" observe the feast of Pentecost.[2] But as, on the same day, the king created his son Richard Duke of York, and splendid jousts, in which Earl Rivers took a leading part,[3] were held in honour of the event, the legislators of the land probably went to the tournament field before they went to church.

Before 6 June Morton and Duras at last came back from Burgundy.[4] They must have brought an account of Charles's troubles in Alsace, and also the news that the duke had extended his truce with Louis until 15 June;[5] yet they had not been altogether unsuccessful in their mission, and when parliament reassembled, the chancellor confidently announced that the king intended to "hold the voyage royal" to France "in as goodly haste as shall please God." Confession had to be made, however, that, owing to "briefness of time," it would be impossible for the king to leave England before Michaelmas, as he was required to do by the terms of the grant of thirteen thousand archers made to him in November 1472, and the Commons were asked to give him an extension of time. Indeed, as word soon came that Charles—to please, he asserted, the king of England and the Duke of Brittany—had now consented to prolong his truce with the French king until 1 May 1475,[6] it was obvious that the invasion of France would have to be postponed for a whole year. Nevertheless, with the excuse that the grant of 1472, because of the refusal of certain sections of the country to pay their share of it, had brought in only £31,410 14s 1d ob. and that the fifteenth and tenth granted in the spring of 1473 was still unlevied and unpaid, Edward ventured to ask for another war

---

1. *Rolls of Parl.*, VI, 100-101; *Cal. Patent Rolls*, II, 455. Cf. Ramsay, II, 399-400.
2. *Rolls of Parl.*, VI, 104; Foss, *Judges of Eng.*, IV, 382-383.
3. *Excerpta Historica*, 242-243.
4. Morton was engaged on this embassy to Burgundy 126 days and was paid £126 for his services. Warrants for Issues, 14 Edw. IV, 18 June; Exchequer T. R., Council and Privy Seal, file 91, no. 20; Tellers' Roll, Mich. 13 Edw. IV.
5. Commynes-Lenglet, III, 315; Plancher, IV, 335.
6. *Cal. Milanese Papers*, I, 181; Commynes-Lenglet and Plancher, *ut sup.*

grant. And the Commons, obedient to his wish, gave him until St John's Day, 1476, to start for France, granted him another fifteenth and tenth in place of the one that had not been collected, authorized him to collect a year's wages for five hundred and ninety archers (£5,383 15s) from the districts which had refused to pay their share of the grant of 1472, and, lastly, granted him the additional sum of £51,147 4s 7d ob. q^a. to bring the total amount he would receive up to £118,625, the cost of the wages of the thirteen thousand archers. However, this time too the Commons tried to be cautious. Although one half of the £51,147 4s 7d ob. q^a. was to be levied on St John's Day, 1475, the other half on St Martin's Day following, the money was not to be given to the king until he and his ships were ready to go to France.[1]

When Speaker Alyngton had announced the new grant to the king, on 18 July, parliament was prorogued until 23 January 1475.[2] Just a week later the treaty with the Duke of Burgundy, which was drawn up in six separate documents,[3] was promulgated, and then it came out that the king was not to make his descent on France until the following year, by the first day of July. In other respects the final treaty differed little from the one Edward had been ready to accept in May 1473, except that he was given "more liberty," as he had wished, in regard to where he should land, the agreement now being that he was to land in Normandy "or in other parts of France." Charles had not been willing to allow the city of Rheims to be reserved out of the grant to be made to him of the county of Champagne, but he did promise that Edward and his successors should have the privilege of going to Rheims to be crowned, and also that, should some other place be chosen for the coronation ceremony, the sacred *ampulla* which had been used at the coronations of the kings of France since the days of Clovis might be taken to that place, on condition that it would be sent back to Rheims when the coronation was over. Edward's demand that the treaty of "perpetual amity and alliance" should antedate the treaty of mutual aid Charles had

---

1. *Rolls of Parl.*, VI, 111-119.
2. *Ibid.*, 120. Alyngton received £200 from the king for his services during this parliament. Warrants for Issues, 14 Edw. IV, 16 July. Cf. Tellers' Roll, Easter 14 Edw. IV, and also Tellers' Roll, no. 51A, a roll which evidently belongs to Mich. 14 Edw. IV.
3. All are printed in Rymer, XI, 804-814. Edward's counterpart of the treaty of 27 July, regarding the payment of the duke's troops, may be found in Writs of Privy Seal, file 849, no. 3972.

evidently conceded, as the former treaty was sealed on 25 July, the latter on the 26th. But on the other hand, the declaration of war against Louis was to be postponed, as Charles had desired, until he or Edward or both had begun the attack.

Charles had won still another important promise from his ally, though it did not appear in the treaty. The final negotiations relating to the treaty had apparently taken place in England, and to conduct them Charles had sent over to England, probably with Morton and Duras when they went home, an embassy which was headed by Guillaume de Clugny, prothonotary of the Apostolic See.[1] Clugny, it will be remembered, was the man who had brought to Edward, in 1466, the first request from Charles for the hand of Margaret of York, and on the present occasion he seems to have been instructed to insist that Edward must make an earnest effort to complete the payment of his sister's dowry, less than half of which—one hundred and fifteen thousand crowns—had been paid thus far, although the marriage treaty had stated that the whole amount must be paid within three years after the marriage. Charles was willing, however, probably because he knew that Edward was having difficulty in finding the money he needed to prepare for the invasion of France, to grant his brother-in-law easy terms; and the agreement he finally accepted was that Edward should send him five thousand crowns every Annunciation Day and every Michaelmas Day, beginning with the year 1475, until the entire eighty-five thousand crowns still owing to him had been paid. Edward gave his bond to this effect on 29 July.[2] The last five thousand crowns would be due, according to this arrangement, on 25 March 1483, or, as it proved, six years after the death of Charles and two weeks before the death of Edward himself.

Now that he had obtained a satisfactory treaty with Charles, Edward began at once to make contracts with many lords, knights, and esquires to accompany him on his expedition to France with retinues, large or small, of men-at-arms and archers.[3] He also sent Falcon Herald to France to make a formal demand for the surrender of Guienne and Normandy and to say

---

1. £89 were paid to Clugny and other ambassadors of the Duke of Burgundy for their expenses. Tellers' Roll, Easter 24 Edw. IV.
2. Signed Bills, file 1507, no. 4649. (See Appendix VIII).
3. Rymer, XI, 817; Exchequer Accounts, bundle 72, nos. 5 and 6, bundle 72, nos. 1 and 2.

that a refusal would mean war.[1] Or at least this was Falcon's alleged errand, though, if reliance is to be placed on what Christoforo di Bollati, now Milanese ambassador at the French court, was told, the messages the herald carried to Louis were in reality far less belligerent in character. Bollati wrote on 18 August:

> A herald has been here from King Edward of England, who desired to present himself before his Majesty. He brought the king a letter containing the declaration that that sovereign was satisfied with the mention made of him by the Duke of Burgundy in the last truces, which he approved and ratified. The letters then contain a clause about giving credence to the person of this herald, upon which he has already been twice to very intimate discussions with his Majesty, at which no one else was present but my Lord of Concressault. The subject of these discussions is a marriage alliance which King Edward asks for between his daughter and my lord the Dauphin, showing that he is inclined to return again to those designs which were suggested upon other occasions against the Duke of Burgundy and for the ruin of his state. An English lord who had this matter in hand on a previous occasion, in the time of the Earl of Warwick, with King Edward's consent and by his instigation, has sent one of his servants with this herald to present a pair of greyhounds to his Majesty and to ask for a safeconduct to come as ambassador with all instructions upon this matter in the name of King Edward. This safeconduct has been made out, so that he is expected to come from that sovereign.

The purport of the transactions between Edward and Louis, Bollati gave the Duke of Milan to understand, was that Louis should cede to Edward a part of Guienne or Normandy in return for assistance to destroy the Duke of Burgundy, and that, after Charles had been crushed, Edward should accept a part of the duke's territories as an equivalent for all that he claimed in the kingdom of France. But in the midst of his extraordinary story Bollati interrupted himself to say that reports were coming in all the time that the English were getting a large army ready and that they were already putting their artillery on board their ships. This, he said, caused many conjectures,

> which resolve themselves into two suspicions: either that this King Edward suggests this marriage alliance as a sham and pretence so that he may afterwards be able to claim that he tried the way of peace and concord before

---

1. Tellers' Roll, Easter 14 Edw. IV; *Chronique Scandaleuse*, I, 319.

war, and by this negotiation see to cooling and delaying the provisions and preparations of his Majesty against the English; or else that King Edward is proceeding sincerely in this alliance, owing to some hidden indignation and wrath he may have against the Duke of Burgundy because of the constant incitement with which he stirs up the English people to make war on this kingdom to recover their ancient rights. And as King Edward is by his nature more inclined to quiet and peace than to war, many adhere to the latter opinion.

In another letter which he wrote on 6 September Bollati stated that the English herald was still at the French court, and that when the herald asked Louis to agree to freedom of trade between England and France during the truce, the king refused unless the truce was to be for more than a single year. But six days later there were more stories about the preparations for war going on in England. A letter from Bordeaux said that a man who had recently returned from England declared that King Edward had been holding a long council, and that he intended to come to France in March to reconquer the duchy of Guienne; while from Scotland came word that three thousand Englishmen were ready even now to start for France. It was said that these troops, by pretending to be merchants on their way to Bordeaux to buy wine, would make their way up the Garonne and go to the assistance of Perpignan, which Louis was trying to wrest from the king of Aragon. Fanciful as this tale sounded, when Louis was suddenly inspired to send a present of a couple of coursers to King Edward, the Milanese ambassador decided that the French king's real purpose was "to investigate thoroughly the truth and certitude of all these things."[1]

Remembering what happened afterwards, it would be rash to say that there was no truth whatever in Bollati's story about Edward's offer of a marriage alliance to Louis at this time. Rather do later events seem to justify the belief that the offer was not only made, but made in sincerity. And if, even now when his bargain with Charles was concluded, Edward felt misgivings about attempting to invade France and feared that, after all, he might have to change his plans and make peace with Louis, that is nothing to wonder at, in as much as Charles was apparently still pursuing an *ignis-fatuus* in the east. During the summer Charles marched to the support of one

---

1. *Cal. Milanese Papers*, I, 182-185.

of two rival claimants to the archbishopric of Cologne and, on 30 July, laid siege to the strongly fortified city of Neuss. Yet it was impossible that Edward should want to see Burgundy crushed by France for any consideration, and if help to overthrow Charles and willingness to accept a slice of Burgundy instead of a slice of France as his reward was what Louis required of him in return for a marriage alliance, it is not surprising that Edward pressed the subject no farther. Nor is it surprising, on the other hand, that Louis doubted the sincerity of Edward's offer, since it was true not only that a great English army was gradually being formed, but that Edward was making every effort to secure alliances with other enemies of Louis besides Burgundy.

In August, while Falcon Herald was in France, William Slefeld went over to Brittany to see if Francis II would sign another treaty binding himself to take part in an attack on Louis;[1] and about the same time the Abbot of Abingdon and Bartelot de Rivière departed for Italy to invite Ferdinand of Naples, to whom Rivière had carried the insignia of the Garter eleven years before, to become a member of the alliance against France, and also to offer the Garter to Frederico Ubaldi, Duke of Urbino.[2] But the journey of the Abbot of Abingdon and Rivière seems to have effected little or nothing, and the negotiations with the Duke of Brittany, though at first they seemed to be proceeding well, also ended disappointingly. Francis had just assured Louis (much as he had done in 1464) that he was not in league with the English, that he had never treated with them except for commercial intercourse, and then with Louis' consent, and that, unless he were driven to it, he never would treat with them for any other purpose;[3] but some of his councillors, chief among them being the Seigneur d'Urfé, were much in

---

1. See two commissions given to Slefeld, French Roll 14 Edw. IV, m. 11, 22 August. It was intended at first that Louis de Bretaylle should accompany Slefeld, but for some reason the king decided otherwise. See Signed Bills, file 1508, no. 4666. Slefeld received £26 13s 4d for his expenses. Tellers' Roll, Easter 14 Edw. IV.

2. Rymer, XI, 816-817; Anstis, II, 190-191. The Duke of Urbino was elected to the stall formerly occupied by Lord Mountjoy, who had died on 1 August of this year. Inquisitions *post mortem*, 14 Edw. IV, no. 24. The Garter sent to the duke cost £4 4s 6d, the robe £33 13s 3d. Tellers' Roll, Mich. 14 Edw. IV. Rivière was allowed £66 13s 4d for his expenses on the journey, while the Abbot of Abingdon received, in place of money, the privilege of shipping forty sacks of wool, duty free, "beyond the mountains," in other words, to Italy. Tellers' Roll, Easter 14 Edw. IV; Writs of Privy Seal, file 850, no. 4007.

3. Morice, III, 273-275.

favour of his accepting Edward's proposal, and some time after Michaelmas he went so far as to send an envoy to England.[1] Afterwards Slefeld paid another visit to Brittany, accompanied by Louis de Bretaylle, and towards the close of the year Jacques de la Villéon arrived in London and, on 12 December, made an agreement with Edward about the indemnity to be paid to certain Breton merchants who had suffered loss at the hands of some of the king's subjects.[2]

Yet it was soon evident that, while Francis's timid heart was undoubtedly with the enemies of Louis XI, he was much more ready to participate in their plans than in their battles. The Seigneur d'Urfé wrote to Edward and Lord Hastings that his master, the Duke of Brittany, could accomplish more for the cause in one month by his intelligent diplomacy than the king of England and the Duke of Burgundy could accomplish by force of arms in six months; but this boast would not have given much satisfaction to Edward even if he and Hastings had received the letters which contained it. As it happened, they never did receive them. Louis had already found out a good deal about what his enemies were saying to one another; for when, in the preceding winter or spring, John of Aragon and his son Ferdinand had sent on a mission to Edward, Charles, and Francis that same Doctor de Lucena who had visited England during Henry VI's readeption, Louis had succeeded, by means he knew so well how to use, in obtaining from that gentleman all the information he had to convey.[3] And now by a present of sixty marks to an English secretary Louis also secured the Seigneur d'Urfé's letters.[4] Later on the Seigneur d'Urfé, having learned the dangers of plotting by letter, went over to England in person, but apparently all that he took to Edward was the assurance that Francis was in sympathy with his plans and was acting as he did simply to deceive Louis. Edward then sent Lord Duras to Brittany with messages which Francis interpreted as meaning that

---

1. Dupuy, I, 345; Tellers' Roll, Easter 14 Edw. IV—an entry of a reward of 66s 8d given to some Breton whose name is left blank and nine persons in his company.
2. Tellers' Roll, Mich. 14 Edw. IV; Writs of Privy Seal, file 852, no. 4103, 15 March 1475; *Cal. Patent Rolls*, II, 521.
3. Dupuy, I, 343-344; *Lettres de Louis XI*, V, 321, note 2. Edward gave the Doctor de Lucena £66 13s 4d for his expenses while in England. Tellers' Roll, Mich. 13 Edw. IV.
4. Commynes, I, 268-269.

the king approved of his "dissimulations," and there, for the present, the negotiations with Francis ended.[1]

If Edward failed to get what he wanted from Francis, he had ample reason to congratulate himself on the success which at last crowned his efforts to secure a treaty with the Scots, as peace with the Scots was much more essential to the success of his expedition to France than a promise of aid from the Duke of Brittany. To the offer James III had made to keep Edward at home by offering to support him against his subjects if they rebelled when he gave up his intention to attack France, or by making war on him if necessary, Louis had ultimately replied by sending Alexander Monypenny to Scotland to say that, while, "grace à Dieu," he was quite able to give the English a suitable reception if they dared to come to France, he would be glad to be free to attend to other matters, and therefore would willingly pay James the ten thousand crowns he had named as the price of his help, though only when it was certain that the descent of the English had been prevented by James's agency. Louis was even willing to unite with James in promising to help Edward in case of a rebellion in England; and should Edward express a wish to establish "plus grande intelligence" with his neighbours of France and Scotland by means of a treaty of peace or a long truce, Louis was ready for that also.[2] But to James, who probably recalled the unfulfilled promise about the surrender of Saintonge, pledged to his grandfather by Louis' father on another occasion when France needed help against the English, Louis' answer did not sound altogether satisfactory, and when a definite offer of a marriage between his son and heir and Edward's daughter Cecily was brought to him by Ireland King-of-Arms, he inclined his ear to it. Ireland carried back word to Edward that "in the matter that he was sent unto him for" King James was "of full loving and toward demeaning," and that he would send an embassy to England in all haste "for the more firm communication and conclusion of the same." Edward at once dispatched a safeconduct for James's embassy, and though there was some delay and a second safeconduct had to be granted in May, in July the Bishop of Aberdeen, Lyon King-of-Arms, and other Scottish

1. Tellers' Roll, no. 51A; Morice, III, 282; Plancher, IV, 353—an undated letter from Francis to Edward.
2. Instructions to Alexander Monypenny, Legrand collections, MS. français 6981, ff. 214-217.

envoys arrived at Westminster. On 30 July a preliminary agreement was reached and Edward promised to send an embassy to Scotland by 8 October to sign the marriage treaty.[1]

Of course Louis was not long in finding out what was going on between Edward and James, and of course he strove to the utmost to thwart Edward's plans. In September Louis was endeavouring anxiously, with the aid of the Seigneur de Concressault, to arrange a marriage between James's heir and the daughter of the Duke of Milan.[2] But though some of the lords of Scotland favoured, in fact, had suggested, the Milanese match, James preferred the English one, and promptly on 8 October the Bishop of Durham, Lord Scrope, Doctor John Russell, and Robert Bothe arrived at Edinburgh with power not only to complete the negotiations for the marriage of Prince James and Princess Cecily, but also to offer redress for a particularly heinous breach of the truce which had been committed in March 1473, when the famous Scottish ship, the *Salvator*, or the *Bishop's Barge*, as it was sometimes called, had been wrecked near Bamburgh and some Englishmen had plundered it and held one of its passengers, the Abbot of Colme, for ransom.[3] Two weeks sufficed for the making of the full agreement. On 25 October James granted an acquittance for all claims connected with the *Salvator*, after a promise of redress to the amount of five hundred marks had been given, and at noon the next day the betrothal of Prince James of Scotland, aged two, and Princess Cecily of England, aged four, was solemnized in the presence of a goodly company of Scottish nobles, public notaries, and other persons, Lord Scrope, as Cecily's proxy, and the Earl of Crawford, as Prince James's, clasping hands and, in the name of their respective kings, swearing that the marriage contract should be fulfilled.[4]

---

1. Warrants under the Signet, file 1384, 24 March, 14 Edw. IV; *Rotuli Scotiæ*, II, 441; Signed Bills, file 1507, no. 4625; Rymer, XI, 834, 825. The Scottish ambassadors received £100 13s 2d from Edward for their expenses. Tellers' Roll, Easter 14 Edw. IV.
2. *Cal. Milanese Papers*, I, 186-187.
3. Rymer, *ut sup.*; *Rotuli Scotiæ*, II, 445; Signed Bills, file 1508, nos. 4663, 4664; Lesley, 39-40. James had requested the Duke of Burgundy to write to Edward and ask him to make redress for "the barge broken at Bamburgh." Facsimiles of National MSS. of Scotland, Part II, no. 76. The *Salvator* was known as the *Bishop's Barge* because it had been built by the order of Kennedy, late Bishop of St Andrews.
4. Several writers, reading Rymer's documents carelessly, have stated that the betrothal took place on 18 October. James's commission to Crawford was given on that day, but the betrothal occurred on the 26th.

The marriage treaty which was expected to bind England and Scotland together in everlasting friendship provided that James and Cecily should be married "after the form and by the authority of Holy Kirk" within six months after they reached the marriageable age; that Cecily should be endowed during the lifetime of James III with all the lands, rents, and revenues of the "old heritage" of the Prince of Scotland ("the duchy of Rothesay, the earldom of Carrick, and the lordships of the Stuart lands of Scotland") and should be entitled, upon the accession of her husband to the throne, to the third part of all his property, and that her father should give her a dot of twenty thousand marks "English money," which was to be paid in yearly instalments—two thousand marks a year for the first three years and after that one thousand marks a year—each time on 3 February and in the church of St Giles at Edinburgh. It was also stipulated that if, through the death of James or Cecily or for any other cause, their marriage never took place, "whensoever the king of Scotland should hap to have a son, his heir, the same that is now or other, and the king of England a daughter of like age or within three or four years above or beneath the age of the same son and heir," every effort should be made to marry the said "son of Scotland" to the said "daughter of England." But even if that effort failed, James was to retain all the dower money that had been paid to him, provided the amount he had received did not exceed twenty-five hundred marks. If he had received more than twenty-five hundred marks, he was to refund the excess amount within four years, making the payments on 3 February of each year in the church of St Nicholas at Newcastle. Lastly, ratifications of the marriage treaty and bonds for the payment and for the possible refunding of the dowry were to be exchanged in the parish church at Norham on 4 January, unless the two kings arranged for an earlier exchange.

The treaty was ratified by King James, under whose eye it had been negotiated, on 3 November; and after he had given his bond for the refunding of the dowry should occasion to refund it arise, he sent Lyon King-of-Arms to London with the English ambassadors to exchange confirmations of the truce which had been agreed on the day the betrothal took place and to receive Edward's bond.[1]

---

1. Rymer, XI, 820-834, 850; *Cal. Documents relating to Scotland*, IV, 289; Palgrave, *Cely Papers*, III, 20, 21; Accounts of Lord High Treasurer of Scot., I, 54. James gave the herald who came to Scotland with Edward's ambassadors a gown of cloth of gold lined with satin. *Ibid.*, I, lix.

On 26 November, at a meeting held in the Star Chamber, Edward's council decreed that the chancellor of England should draw up and seal the bond to be given to James; but as it was a risk to send large sums of money across the Scottish border, where thieves abounded, Lyon was required, before he left for home, to sign an agreement with the clerk of the council that, whenever an instalment of Cecily's dowry was to be paid, James would send to Norham not only a safeconduct for those who were bringing the money, but also a guard to escort them to Edinburgh.[1]

The new truce and marriage treaty with Scotland was the most important advantage, next to his treaty with Charles, which Edward had yet gained over Louis, and the most necessary to the success of an English invasion of France. But there was still another serious difficulty which must be overcome, and during the time his ambassadors were in Edinburgh negotiating with James, Edward had been wandering through his kingdom in search of money to help pay for the equipment of his army. He might have raised the extra money he needed by loans, but as forced loans were unpopular and had the added disadvantage of requiring repayment sooner or later, he had decided to be bold and ask for gifts. He began his experiment in London. First of all, he called the lords spiritual and temporal before him one by one and inquired of them what they "of their free wills" would give him for the war with France. And the lords were so taken by surprise, or so beguiled by his pleasant way of appealing to their generosity, that they promised him considerable sums. Then he summoned the mayor and aldermen of London to his presence, and when the mayor had promised him thirty pounds and each of the aldermen from ten to twenty marks, he sent for "all the trusty commoners" of the city, women as well as men. Many a commoner promised "the wages of half a man for a year," which is to say, £4 11s 3d; and there is a story that a kiss from the handsome royal lips induced one widowed dame, "much abounding in substance and no less grown in years," to increase her gift from twenty pounds to forty.[2] As his experiment had succeeded so well in London, the king was encouraged to try it in other parts of his kingdom, and the journey which he made through Warwickshire, Nottinghamshire, Worcestershire, and Gloucestershire

---

1. Signed Bills, file 1508, no. 4671; Rymer, XI, 836.
2. Fabyan, 664; Kingsford's *London Chron.*, 186; Hall, 308.

during the autumn[1] had no other purpose than to enable him to reach the pockets of the men and women of property who could not be summoned to Westminster Palace.

Edward had a very retentive memory, especially, it is said, in regard to the names of his subjects and the estates they owned,[2] and that gift now proved a highly serviceable one. An Italian gentleman who was visiting England at this time was greatly impressed by Edward's success in "plucking out the feathers of his magpies without making them cry out," and he tells how the king went from place to place, sending for his subjects one by one, telling them that he wanted to cross the sea to conquer France, and contriving to obtain money from everyone who had the value of forty pounds and upwards. What surprised the Italian most was that everyone seemed to give willingly. He wrote:

> I have frequently seen our neighbours here who were summoned before the king, and when they went they looked as if they were going to the gallows; when they returned they were joyful, saying that they had spoken to the king and he had spoken to them so benignly that they did not regret the money they had paid. From what I have heard, the king adopted this method: when anyone went before him, he gave him a welcome as if he had known him always; after some time he asked him what he could pay of his free will towards this expedition; if the man offered something proper, he had his notary ready, who took down the name and the amount; if the king thought otherwise, he told him, 'such a one, who is poorer than you, has paid so much; you, who are richer, can easily pay more'; and thus by fair words he brought him up to the mark. And in this way it is argued that he has extracted a very large amount of money.[3]

Such well-to-do men and women as the king could not appeal to with his own persuasive lips were reached through the sheriffs and mayors or through other persons specially commissioned for the purpose, and the order given to these agents was that they should ask those whom they thought would be most likely to prove accommodating to "show by way of their good will and benevolence with what sums of money or otherwise it shall please them"

---

1. Privy Seals.
2. *Hist. Croy. Cont.*, 564.
3. *Cal. Milanese Papers*, I, 193-194. Cf. *Hist. Croy. Cont.*, 558, and Fabyan, *ut sup.*

to assist the king, and to secure from them a sealed statement of what sum they would give and when. The word "benevolence" was quickly singled out by those to whom the king's request came, and *benevolence* was the name which became attached not only popularly but officially to Edward's new method of taxing his people without authority of parliament. The excuse the king gave for himself was that the grants he had received from parliament for the war were "appointed only to serve for men's wages, archers, and to none other use," although it was quite apparent to any "well-advised" person that he would have to have large sums for "other huge and manifold charges belonging to such an army," and that he was unable to get the money he must have "without the assistance, love, and kindness of such persons, his faithful subjects, as God had endued with His gifts of honour and goods specially before other."[1]

But unhappily it was not only those to whom much of this world's goods had been given who had to help pay for the expedition to France. "The king goeth so near us in this country, both to poor and rich," groaned Margaret Paston in the spring of 1475, "that I wot not how we shall live but if the world amend."[2] And to make matters worse, the farmers got lower prices than usual for their produce—in Norfolk only tenpence a comb for malt and oats and eighteen pence for wheat[3]—because the king, taking thought for the provisioning of his army, issued a proclamation forbidding the exportation of wheat, malt, barley, rye, beans, peas, oxen, sheep, kine, and mares.[4]

Edward returned to London from his money-collecting tour on 16 November to find the marshal of the household of the king of France, "Christopher de Phailly, *alias* Christopher Lailler," for whom he had granted a safeconduct on 27 September, waiting to see him.[5] Probably Lailler had brought the two coursers which, according to the Milanese ambassador's

---

1. Cotton MS. Cleopatra F VI, f. 310 (a letter to the sheriff and other persons in Berkshire); *Coventry Leet Book*, II, 409.
2. *Paston Letters*, V, 233.
3. *Ibid.*
4. Signed Bills, file 1508, no. 4680, 4 Dec., 2474, and file 1527, no. 5454. (undated). Cf. *Paston Letters*, V, 222.
5. French Roll 14 Edw. IV, m. 9; *Paston Letters*, V, 216. According to the *Chronique Scandaleuse*, Lailler's given name was Jean. But he is called Christopher in the safeconduct.

letter of 12 September, Louis had seen fit to send as a present to the king of England. But the story runs that the gift Edward received from Louis consisted, not of horses, but of a donkey, a wolf, and a boar, and that Louis intended the donkey to represent Edward himself, the wolf the Duke of Burgundy, and the boar the Duke of Brittany.[1] And certain it is that for some reason Louis' marshal met with a very chilly reception from Edward. "As for the French embassy that is here," wrote Paston on 20 November, "they come not in the king's presence by likelihood, for men say that the chief of them is he that poisoned both the Duke of Berry and the Duke of Calabria." Bollati himself, writing soon after Lailler had returned to France, declared that Louis' envoy "did not have audience of King Edward or access to him. When he asked to see him, they took him to a room, but he did not come within forty feet of him. When the king of France heard this, he said it was due to the ambassador of the Duke of Burgundy, who gave King Edward to understand that the man was sent to poison him."[2] But if Edward kept the Frenchman at a safe distance, he not only appointed two yeomen of his chamber to wait upon him, which evidently means to keep watch of him, but gave him a reward of twenty pounds—perhaps for not poisoning him!—and on Christmas Day, when his safeconduct was about to expire, granted him another of a month's duration.[3]

One piece of information which Lailler must have carried back to Louis was that, at the beginning of December, Edward had sent another embassy to the Duke of Burgundy. This embassy consisted of Doctor John Morton, Sir Thomas Montgomery, and William Hatclyf, and with the help of William Caxton and several other merchants, these men were to seek from Charles a new agreement in regard to the rate of exchange between England and Burgundy, and also one about a staple in the duke's dominions for Newcastle wool.[4] But, as Lailler probably learned, Morton, Montgomery, and Hatclyf were charged with a third errand as well. Although Charles had expected to win an easy victory at Neuss, even now, after a four months' siege, the city was

---

1. *Chronique Scandaleuse*, I, 319; Dupuy, I, 343. Louis' gift recalls the tennis balls sent to England by the Dauphin in 1414.
2. *Paston Letters, ut sup.*; *Cal. Milanese Papers*, I, 190.
3. Tellers' Roll, Mich. 24 Edw. IV; French Roll 14 Edw. IV, m. 10.
4. Writs of Privy Seal, file 850, no. 4044, 28 Nov.; French Roll 14 Edw. IV, m. 6, 1 December.

neither conquered nor likely to be, as the princes of the Empire, frightened into united action for once by the duke's aggressions on the Rhine, had come to its aid. Added to this, Louis had incited the Swiss to make war on Charles in Alsace. But while Charles was really getting into deeper water every day, Edward had so little understanding of the situation that he gave Morton, Montgomery, and Hatclyf commissions to sign treaties of alliance against the king of France both with Matthias Corvinus, king of Hungary, who was one of Charles's friends, and with the Emperor, who was now one of the duke's foes.[1]

If some of Edward's hopes were foolish, however, some were not; and in addition to the victory he had won over Louis in Scotland, he won another over him in Spain. Soon after the battle of Barnet, Peter Sans de Venesse, the man who had obtained from Edward, shortly before his flight to Burgundy, a general protection for the merchants of Guipuscoa, Biscay, Old Castile, Asturias, and Galicia and an annuity of twenty pounds for himself which was to be paid as long as the peace between England and the five provinces lasted,[2] had returned to England, with John de Andia of Guipuscoa, to do his work over again. Edward proved as well-inclined towards the provinces as before, and in August 1471, both the letters of protection and Peter Sans' annuity were renewed and John de Andia too was granted twenty pounds a year.[3] But there had been many breaches of the letters of protection since August 1471, and early in 1474 the five provinces sent ambassadors to England for the second time to seek redress.[4] Edward then granted the provinces fresh letters of protection and sent Bernard de la Forsse and William Pykenham, archdeacon of Suffolk, to Castile to make a bargain with Henry the Impotent.[5] Shortly after a special embassy from Guipuscoa came to England and secured six hundred

---

1. Rymer, XI, 834-836.
2. See above, Vol. I, p. 508, note 3.
3. Rymer, XI, 720; *Cal. Patent Rolls*, II, 273; Issue Roll, Easter II Edw. IV, 13 July.
4. In the spring of 1472 an embassy had come from the five provinces, and at that time Edward issued a proclamation commanding any of his subjects who had grievances against the provinces to appear before his commissioners and the ambassadors of the provinces at Westminster Palace with proofs of their claims. Warrants of the Council, file 1547, 20 April 1472.
5. French Roll 13 Edw. IV, m. 2, 26 Feb.; Exchequer T. R., Council and Privy Seal, file 91, no. 10. Cf. Writs of Privy Seal, file 487, nos. 3869-3870, Signed Bills, file 1507, no. 4628, and Tellers' Roll, Mich. 13 Edw. IV. This was by no means the last journey of Bernard de la Forsse to Spain. He went thither again, apparently in the spring or summer of 1475, with

crowns in reparation for certain deeds which had been committed by those incorrigible pirates, the men of Fowey, and finally, in the autumn of 1474, John de Andia and other ambassadors arrived in London bringing letters of protection for English merchants trading with Biscay which Henry the Impotent had granted on 26 September.[1] Then followed a settlement which was pleasing to all parties; for Edward granted the merchants of the five provinces, in satisfaction of all their claims, eleven thousand crowns out of the customs due on merchandise imported or exported by them and was rewarded with a promise of the aid of the five provinces against the king of France.[2]

As it happened, Henry the Impotent died a week before the great seal of England was affixed to this bargain with the five provinces, and at once a struggle to secure his vacant throne began between his sister Isabella, the wife of Ferdinand of Aragon, and Alphonso of Portugal, who announced his intention of marrying Henry's daughter, Joanna, and assumed the title of king of Castile. Louis XI forthwith espoused the cause of Alphonso and demanded from him as a reward—and probably obtained—a renunciation of the ancient alliance between Portugal and England, which had been confirmed once more in 1472.[3] But Edward took sides with Ferdinand and Isabella, and eventually, in May 1475, obtained a renewal of the alliance which had been signed by England and Castile in 1467 but which had been nearly, if not entirely, sundered by the treaty Louis had persuaded Henry the Impotent to sign with him in 1470.[4]

In these months when he was preparing for his expedition to France, Edward even made some effort to improve conditions in Ireland. But he did not act without being prodded, and if the Anglo-Irish were justified in their fears, the

---

Windsor Herald to deliver to King Ferdinand Edward's confirmation of the league between England and Castile, if it proved that Ferdinand was ready to give a similar confirmation. Signed Bills, file 1527, no. 5537 (undated); Tellers' Roll, Easter 15 Edw. IV—an entry of a payment of £20 to Windsor Herald sent to the king of Castile and Leon.

1. French Roll 14 Edw. IV, m. 20; Tellers' Rolls, Easter and Mich. 14 Edw. IV; Cotton MS. Vespasian C XII, ff. 164-165. A letter written to Edward on 10 September 1474, by the junta and procurators of Guipuscoa may be found in *Ancient Correspondence*, Vol. XLI, no. 99.
2. Rymer, XI, 841-842; *Cal. Patent Rolls*, II, 480; Gorosabel, *Memoria sobre las Guerras y Tratados de Guipuzcoa con Inglaterra* (Tolosa, 1865), 53. 96-99.
3. Rymer, XI, 741, 762.
4. *Lettres de Louis XI*, V, 388-394; Daumet, *L'alliance de la France et de la Castile*, 115-122; Rymer, XII, 2-3.

treaty he signed with the king of Scotland was probably of greater help to his subjects in Ireland than any steps he took to assist them directly. For when, in the autumn of 1473 or the following winter, the Anglo-Irish appealed to him for aid, they declared that they were in danger not only from his "Irish enemies and English rebels," but from the Scots, who had been settling in Ulster in such numbers in recent years that there was chance of a repetition of the events of 1315–1318, when Edward Bruce, brother of the famous Robert Bruce, invaded Ireland at the invitation of the native Irish and, with the assistance of Donal O'Neill and other Irish chiefs, all but succeeded in putting an end to English rule in the island. On receiving this appeal, Edward sent Sir Gilbert Debenham, James Norris, and David Keting, an old supporter of his father in Ireland,[1] to Dublin with "comfortable answers"; and this encouraged the Irish parliament to send Sir Robert Bold[2] with Debenham, Norris, and Keting, when they went home, to thank the king for having spared a few thoughts for Ireland and to tell him about "the piteous decay of the said land and subjects and how it might be best relieved and rescued."

The woeful state of things in Ireland was due in part, the king was told by the Irish parliament, to his Irish enemies and his English rebels, but also in part to the Scots, of whom ten thousand or more were now living in Ulster and, remembering the success of Bruce, were daily conspiring to reduce Ireland to the obedience of the king of Scots, a "malicious intent" which the faithful Anglo-Irish, being "but of petty number" in comparison with the Irish, the English rebels, and the Scots, were not strong enough to resist. In view of the seriousness of the situation, the king was urged to see that his friends in Ireland had help before August, lest their enemies should destroy the crops and leave no food for the troops, and either to come in person or to send the Duke of Clarence, his lieutenant, or some other lord of the blood royal, with at least a thousand archers and money for their wages. The king's friends would do their part if the king did his. The Irish parliament had already granted tunnage and poundage to carry on the wars, and if the king confirmed this grant, the Anglo-Irish would also supply forty Irish spears and one hundred English archers yearly at their own expense.

---

1. *Cal. Patent Rolls*, III, 390.
2. Sir Robert Bold, Baron of Ratoath, was not trusted by all persons in the Pale. See Gilbert, *Viceroys of Ireland*, 397.

Suggestion was also made to the king that, before the army of relief was sent, all persons of Irish birth living in England, save students at Oxford and Cambridge or in the courts of London, should be ordered by proclamation to return to their native land, and that he could raise the money he would need for the work in Ireland by levying "his royal service called escuage" in England. The full subjugation of Ireland ought to be accomplished easily, the king was assured in closing, since all the cities, castles, and walled towns were already in his possession. And, "considering the great treasure of mines of all manner metals and alums within the same, with the great commodities of lands and lordships, and the great richesse and revenues of rivers and havens of the same," the profits derived from the island would soon amount, as they had "of old time," to a hundred thousand marks a year, a sum so large that, "with little help of the realm of England," it would enable the king—"which is reputed here in prophecies the white lion and *sextus Hiberniæ*, which by the said prophecies shall win this land and many other realms"—to devote his whole attention to "the subduing of his great enemies of France and Scotland and all other adherent friends."[1]

What the Irish parliament told him could hardly fail to produce some effect on Edward's mind; and the first precaution he seems to have taken was to win by some means the good will of Henry O'Neill, the Ulster chief most to be feared. For in the summer of 1474 O'Neill sent a messenger to England, and in the record of the payment of a reward of forty shillings to this messenger the chief is described as "magnus Dominus vocatus Henricus Oneyll amicus Regis."[2] But while this was good as far as it went, more needed to be done. The Archbishop of Dublin also came over to England during the summer of 1474, and he probably gave a further account of Ireland's distressful and dangerous state and urged afresh the need of doing something to relieve and protect the island. For on 5 August the king excused the city of Waterford from sending its semi-annual account of the fee farm to the Exchequer at

---

1. "Enstruccyons youen and opened by the iij astates of our souerayn liege lord the kynges high Court of Parlement in Irland and his counsell of the same to the kynges dyscrete seruantes, Gilbert Debenham, knyght, James Norres, Esquyer, Dauid Ketyn, and Sir Robert Bold, knyght. To be presented & shewed for the hasty socour and Relief of the said land to the kinges highnes in England." Chancery Miscellaneous Rolls, bundle 19, no. 9. This document is not dated, but its date is fixed approximately by the fact that a payment made to Debenham and Norris for their journey to Ireland is entered on Tellers' Roll, Mich. 13 Edw. IV.

2. Tellers' Roll, Easter 14 Edw. IV.

Dublin because there was so much rebellion, robbery, and war abroad in the country roundabout that the journey to Dublin was too dangerous. About the same time, too, he made Sir Gilbert Debenham chancellor of Ireland and sent him over to the island.[1] But Debenham took with him only four hundred archers instead of the thousand or more the Irish parliament had mentioned as necessary, and such a force could not possibly subdue Ireland. Even when two hundred and thirty more men were sent to him in the following spring,[2] Debenham was able to do little or nothing to bring peace and order out of the chaos. Although the fear that the Scots would attempt to repeat the exploits of Bruce was not realized, bloody wars with the ill-treated Irish and jealous wranglings among the English settlers themselves went on as of old and kept Ireland in its usual state of turmoil.

---

1. *Cal. Patent Rolls*, II, 461, 474, 491; Tellers' Roll, *ut sup.*
2. *Cal. Patent Rolls*, II, 524.

THE EXPEDITION TO FRANCE

Edward usually spent the Christmas season either at Westminster Palace or at Windsor or one of the other royal manors near London, but during the winter of 1474–1475 he was still pursuing his quest for money and had little time to spare for festivities. On Christmas Day he was at Coventry, and before he finished the "plucking of his magpies" he went as far north as Lincoln. But about the middle of January he came back to London,[1] and soon after Morton and Montgomery returned from Neuss.

It was not a cheering report that Morton and Montgomery brought. They had not succeeded in obtaining a treaty with the Emperor, who had signed one with the king of France instead, and although they had met an embassy from the king of Hungary in the Duke of Burgundy's camp, any efforts they may have made to draw Matthias Corvinus into the league against Louis had failed.[2] Still more discouraging was the story they had to tell about Charles; for instead of bending all his strength to preparation for the invasion of France, the duke was apparently thinking only of the conquest of Neuss. Nothing seemed to shake Charles's infatuation—not even the fact that Louis, who was being advised by the Duke of Milan not to wait until the English arrived but to deal with Charles while he could deal with him alone,[3] appeared to be making ready to strike. When, at Christmas time, it was rumoured that an English fleet was sailing towards Mont St Michel and Louis, fearing that the English were about to invade Normandy with the aid of the Duke of Brittany, dispatched an army to the Somme, Paston

---

1. Privy Seals.
2. Commynes-Lenglet, II, 215, III, 459; Haynin, II, 258.
3. Gingins la Sarra, *Dépêches des ambassadeurs milanais our les campagnes de Charles-le-Hardi, Due de Bourgogne*, I, 26-30; *Cal. Milanese Papers*, I, 191.

wrote from Calais that it was thought that "at the day of breaking of truce, or else before," the French king would "set upon the duke's country here."[1]

But in spite of the bold front he assumed, Louis was really very nervous. His subjects were protesting loudly against the taxes he was imposing on them to defray the expense of defending his kingdom, and he feared a defeat in the field would mean a rebellion at home. His most heartfelt desire, therefore, was to persuade Charles to prolong his truce with him again or, better still, to sign a treaty of peace that would put a stop altogether to the coming of the English; and his knowledge of Charles's eagerness to push his enterprise on the Rhine gave him great hope of success.[2] "His Majesty is more discomposed than words can describe," declared Bollati, "and has almost lost his wits. In his desperation and bitterness he uttered the following precise words among others: 'Ah, Holy Mary, even now when I have given thee fourteen hundred crowns thou dost not help me one whit.'" And the Milanese added: "His Majesty is trying his hardest to obtain the truces with the Duke of Burgundy." At the beginning of January there was a report that the English had actually landed in Normandy and, though this story proved to be untrue, when Christopher Lailler reached Paris, he stated that thirty thousand English troops would be mustered on the 20th and would soon be embarking for France. An English herald who came with Lailler brought nothing worse, according to Bollati, who was present when the herald was received by Louis in full council, than letters demanding the restitution of goods taken from Englishmen during the truce and offering like restitution if any Frenchmen had been robbed by the English. But though this did not sound very war-like, it was suspected that the herald's real mission was "to see the condition in which things are here."[3] To Louis' great disappointment, too, Charles, though his persistence in the siege of Neuss was causing Edward great anxiety, refused every inducement to betray his ally by consenting to a longer truce or a treaty of peace. And in the meantime Edward's preparations for war were evidently advancing towards completion.

When parliament met at Westminster on 23 January, the furtherance of the king's intended "voyage" was again the first thought of all. The royal

---

1. *Paston Letters*, V, 219; *Chronique Scandaleuse*, I, 320.
2. Commynes, I, 265, 267, 271; Gingins la Sarra, *ut sup.*; *Cal. Milanese Papers*, I, 190, 191.
3. *Cal. Milanese Papers*, I, 189-190.

finances, it was revealed, had become badly tangled, partly through the postponing of the war from year to year and partly through the peculiar way in which the grants for the war had been made. There were also some losses to be made good, as not a little of the money intended for the expenses of the war had vanished since its collection, in some cases by theft, in others because the collectors had converted it to their own use or died while it was still in their hands. But a proclamation commanding all persons who had in their possession any of the money collected for the king's use to bring it to the Receipt of the Exchequer before Ascension Day, on pain of forfeiture of three times the amount they had received, probably checked any further leakages of this sort, and the Commons were moved to be kind once more. The collection of the £51,147 4s 7d ob. q^a. granted to the king in the past summer was proving so troublesome, and the results so unsatisfactory, that the likelihood was that the half of the grant which was payable on St John's Day would not be ready for delivery on that date; and as the king was hoping to start for France before St John's Day, it was obvious that some change would have to be made. So the Commons, remembering that "the most easy, ready, and prone payment of any charge to be borne within this realm by the commons of the same is by the grant of fifteenths and tenths," substituted for the £51,147 4s 7d ob. q^a. a whole fifteenth and tenth, payable in the quizaine of Easter, and three-quarters of another fifteenth and tenth, payable at Martinmas. Even now, however, the king was told that he could have the money only when he was ready to set sail, and that if he did not start for France before St John's Day, 1476, the whole grant would be void and the money would have to be given back to those from whom it had been collected.[1] The clergy too made a new grant to the king, those of the province of Canterbury giving him a tenth and a half and those of the province of York two tenths.[2]

The fourth parliament of Edward IV, which had been sitting at intervals for two years and a half, was dissolved on 14 March 1475, and immediately after Edward made hasty trips to Gravesend and Sandwich, probably to

1. *Rolls of Parl.*, VI, 120-121, 149-153.
2. Wilkins, III, 608, and Wake, 379, mention the grant made by the convocation of York, but they seem to have known nothing about the tenth and a half obtained from the convocation of Canterbury. See, however, Fine Roll 15 Edw. IV, m. 3-5.

look for ships for the transportation of the army which was now nearly ready to leave England.[1] If the story reaching France that thirty thousand Englishmen were going to Calais to join the Duke of Burgundy, while ten thousand more went to Normandy and six thousand to Gascony,[2] was an exaggeration of the facts, nevertheless the army with which Edward was preparing to recover England's lost possessions in France and to restore the glory and renown of English arms was a very large one. It was also as perfect and magnificent in all its appointments as the victor of Towton and Barnet and Tewkesbury could make it. So anxious was Edward to appear in France "en état grand" that, at the time he sent his embassy to Charles at Neuss, he had told William Rosse to seek out Oliver de la Marche and obtain from him a written description of the estate kept by Charles both in his household and on the battlefield.[3] In order to satisfy the king's requirements, a number of goldsmiths were impressed for his service and more than four hundred pounds were expended on cloth of gold. A part of this cloth of gold was made into a robe which must have been a very gorgeous garment inside as well as outside, as it was lined with red satin which cost fifty shillings a yard. But it could hardly be too beautiful for the occasion for which it was probably intended, the coronation of Edward of York as king of France.[4]

Philip de Commynes, who had every opportunity to inform himself about the matter, declares that the English army which came to France in 1475 was the largest and best armed force ever brought to that country by an English king; and he thinks that Edward had with him fifteen hundred men-at-arms and fifteen thousand mounted archers, besides a host of foot soldiers, artillery men, men in charge of the tents and pavilions, trench diggers, etc.[5] These figures may be a little too large, but they are not far wrong, for the records of the English Exchequer—and the records may not tell the whole story, as they were somewhat carelessly kept in those days— indicate that the men-at-arms who followed Edward to France numbered between eleven and twelve hundred, the archers between ten and eleven

1. *Rolls of Parl.*, VI, 153; Privy Seals.
2. *Cal. Milanese Papers*, I, 191.
3. La Marche, IV, 1 *et seq.*, 153-157.
4. Tellers' Roll, no. 51A.; Rymer, XI, 852; *Cal. Patent Rolls*, II, 496.
5. Commynes, I, 286-287. Charles understood at first that Edward had brought 24,000 men and sent 6,000 to the Duke of Brittany. Gingins la Sarra, I, 192-195.

thousand.[1] The Duke of Clarence's retinue consisted of one hundred and twenty men-at-arms, including himself, and one thousand archers. The Duke of Gloucester, who had promised the same number of men as Clarence, in the end brought even more.[2] The Dukes of Norfolk and Suffolk each brought forty men-at-arms and three hundred archers, the Earl of Northumberland sixty men-at-arms and three hundred and fifty archers, the Earls of Pembroke and Rivers each forty men-at-arms and two hundred archers, the Earl of Douglas four men-at-arms and forty archers, the other Scottish refugee, Lord Boyd, half of that number, and Lords Hastings and Stanley each forty men-at-arms and three hundred archers, while many other noblemen, including Lords Howard, Scrope, Ferrers, Lysle, and Fitzwarine, and the queen's son, Sir Thomas Grey, who in April was created Marquis of Dorset,[3] and also many knights and esquires from all parts of the kingdom, came with as many men as they could afford to furnish for the king's service.[4]

It is said that in Edward's army there were also many natives of Guienne and Normandy who had formerly sworn allegiance to the kings of England and now carried in their pockets deeds and other documents with which they expected to establish their claims, when the war had been won, to the estates they had once owned in the land of their birth.[5] Whether this be true or not, there was at least one Norman nobleman who hoped that the English expedition to France would bring some benefit to him, though it might not be more than his personal freedom. Jean Malet, Seigneur de Graville, who had been a prisoner in England ever since his capture on Holy

---

1. Tellers' Rolls, Mich. 14 and Easter 15 Edw. IV, and no. 51A; Rymer, XI, 844-848 (printing from Tellers' Roll, no. 51A). The city of Salisbury seems to have sent the king 24 men, under Sir Edward Darell, of whom the Exchequer records contain no mention. See Hatcher, *Old and New Sarum*, 195. And at the end of Tellers' Roll, no. 51A the Duke of Buckingham's name appears followed by a blank space in which it was evidently intended to state the number of men he brought.

2. He afterwards received an extra payment of £666 13s 4d because he had taken to France a larger retinue than he had indented for. Tellers' Roll, Easter 15 Edw. IV; Exchequer T. R., Council and Privy Seal, file 91, m. 28.

3. Charter Roll 15-22 Edw. IV, m. 13. He had been created Earl of Huntingdon in August 1472 (not 1471, as Nicolas states). Charter Roll 11-14 Edw. IV, m. 5. But this title he seems to have resigned when he was made Marquis of Dorset.

4. Rymer, XI, 817-819, 844-848; Exchequer Accounts, bundles 71/5, 71/6, 72/1, 72/2; Tellers' Rolls, Mich. 14 Edw. IV and no. 51A.

5. *Chroniques de Jean Molinet*, Vol. I, c. xxiii.

Island in 1462, had lost all hope by this time that his son, Louis Malet, one of Louis XI's councillors, would ever do anything to secure his release. So he now swore allegiance to Edward as "roi d'Angleterre et de France" and, for the sum of thirty thousand gold crowns, transferred all his hereditary estates in France to John Forster, esquire, "provost of the king's army beyond the seas" and probably the same John Forster whom Margaret of Anjou had once been so anxious that Charles VII should deliver into her hands. This large sum of money probably represented the unfortunate man's ransom and something besides, but as it turned out that France was not conquered, his sacrifice availed him nothing, and he continued to be a prisoner in England for three years longer. Then at last his cold hearted son advanced to him, though not without demanding excellent security, ten thousand crowns; and with this amount he seems to have purchased his freedom and the privilege of returning to France, where Louis XI gave him a pension of two thousand livres in consideration of his good services in former days, especially in the conquest of Normandy and Guienne from the English.[1]

One part of Edward's preparations for war was to lay in huge supplies of wheat, flour, oats, wine, ale, beef, mutton, fish, and other food stuffs.[2] Although his soldiers would forage for themselves when they could, it was not safe to trust to foraging alone, as Louis never hesitated to lay waste the fertile fields of France to check the advance of an enemy. The king also signed an agreement with two London grocers, William Banke and Henry Denys, and a London draper, Walter Fletcher, who undertook to supply "at their own adventure" everything he wanted for his army, and who received from him a licence to take throughout England, except from the lands of the Church, all things needed, staple merchandise not included, at reasonable prices and to ship the goods, without paying export duties, from any port or ports of the realm.[3] As the archers were still the best part of an English army and it was essential that there should be bows and arrows in plenty and of the best quality, the king issued, too, a proclamation forbidding any fletcher to make any kind of "tackle for shooting but only sheaf arrows" and ordering all bowyers to turn their bowstaves into

---

1. Scofield, *Eng. Hist. Review*, July 1910, p. 548. The Dame Agnes Foster, or Forster, who had had the Seigneur de Graville in her "ward and rule" while he was a prisoner in England was probably the wife or mother of John Forster.
2. *Cal. Patent Rolls*, II, 515, 516, 526, 527, 529, 532, 537.
3. French Roll 15 Edw. IV, m. 17.

bows and all fletchers, bowyers, and makers of arrow-heads and bowstrings to see that their wares were "good and sufficient, so that no fault be found in them."[1] Yet he was not less mindful of his artillery than of his archers. William Rosse, who had been made comptroller of the royal ordnance, was assigned £1,160 12s 8d ob. with which to make purchases, besides being empowered to impress workmen and ships to convey the ordnance across the sea; and he apparently did his work admirably, as the Duke of Milan was told that, incredible as it seemed, the king of England's artillery was greater than the Duke of Burgundy's. One writer mentions that the English brought to France as a novelty "un instrument à manière de charue" which it took fifty horses to drag into the field.[2] There is other proof that Edward went to France with an ample number of engines of war. For in the following September, when the invasion of France was over and John Sturgeon, master of the ordnance, handed over to Rosse at Calais "divers parcels of the king's ordnance and artillery such as weren brought by the said John out of England for the king's great voyage," in those parcels were included—in addition to hundreds of "shot of stone," thousands of bows and arrows, many barrels of gunpowder, sulphur, brimstone and saltpetre, a crane and two gins with which to "ship and unship" or "cart and uncart" the heavy guns, "great hooks of iron with chains" for pulling down drawbridges, etc., assaulting ladders, "a boat of leather of three pieces" and "leather of two boats shapen and sewed ready to ye frame," pieces of a floating bridge, and numerous smaller necessaries, such as shovels, spades, pickaxes, crowbars, hammers, pincers, horse-shoes, and horse-shoe nails—the following pieces of artillery:

> First, a chariot with a great iron gun.
> Item, a chariot with the chamber of the said great iron gun and the chamber of the long fowler called the *Edward*.
> Item, a chariot with the great brazen gun.
> Item, a chariot with the chamber of the same brazen gun and one pot-gun of iron.
> Item, a chariot with a great bombard of iron.
> Item, a chariot with a great bastard gun and Her chamber called the *Messenger*.

---

1. Rymer, XI, 837. Cf. *Cal. Patent Rolls*, II, 492.
2. Exchequer Accounts, bundle 67/24; *Cal. Patent Rolls*, II, 494; *Cal. Milanese Papers*, I, 201; Molinet, I, c. xxiii. There is a list of the purchases made by Rosse in a much injured document, Exchequer Accounts, bundle 55/11. It includes some articles for "le gross Brasyn gon."

Item, a chariot with a bombardell called the *Edward*.

Item, a chariot with a fowler and her chamber called the *Fowler of Chester*.

Item, two chariots with two great pot-guns of brass.

Item, a chariot with a fowler and her chamber called *Megge*.

Item, a chariot with a fowler and her two chambers called the Fowler of the Tower.

Item, a chariot with a fowler and her chamber called the Less Fowler of the Tower."[1]

The daily wage which Edward's soldiers were to receive was 13*s* 4*d* for a duke, 6*s* 8*d* for an earl, 4*s* for a baron, 2*s* for a knight, 12*d* for a man-at-arms, with 6*d* in addition as a reward, and 6*d* for an archer; and a quarter's wages were paid in advance on 31 January, one day before proclamation was made that all lords and captains who had indented to accompany the king to France and had received wages on that account were to be ready to meet him with their retinues at Portsdown (near Portsmouth), on 26 May.[2] Yet, strange to say, even now when the day of departure was so near, Edward was not quite sure on what part of the coast of France he was going to disembark. Some of his councillors were of the opinion that he ought to begin with an attack on Guienne; others urged him to land in Normandy, while still others were in favour of his crossing to Calais and advancing into France from that point. Distracted by so much contradictory advice, he finally decided to do what one would think he ought to have done in the first place, namely, consult his ally, Through Guillaume de Clugny, who had been in England again on some errand and was now returning home,[3] Edward sent word to Charles that he would be glad to know where the duke thought he ought to land; and Charles at once replied that in his judgment Normandy would be the most favourable landing place. If the landing were made in Guienne, Charles said, the English, while not beyond reach of help

---

1. Indenture respecting the Kings artillerie brought owte of England for the Kings grete viage," Exchequer Accounts, bundle 55/7. Compare a list of articles headed, "The Remnant of habiliments of war left with William Rosse at Calais of that that was purveyed against the kings Royal voyage in France," which is entered in a paper book entitled "The Castell of Guynes." Exchequer Accounts, France, bundle 198, no. 13. Although this book seems to have been written in the reign of Henry VII, it contains some entries belonging to the reigns of Edward IV and Richard III.
2. Rymer, XI, 848. See also the indentures printed by Rymer and those to be found among the Exchequer Accounts.
3. Edward gave jewels worth £80 10*d* to Clugny and the other ambassadors who came with him. Tellers' Roll, Easter 15 Edw. IV.

from the Duke of Brittany, would be "far from my aid" and too long a march from Paris; and if they landed at Calais, not only would they be too far from the Duke of Brittany but, owing to the difficulty of finding enough provisions for two armies in so, small a territory, there would probably be quarrelling between the English and the Burgundians. On the other hand, the duke said, if the landing were made at the mouth of the Seine or at La Hogue, Edward would be within easy reach of both his allies; and he closed his letter with a promise that, if the king would let him know how many ships he needed for the transportation of his army, he would send them to him.[1]

After weighing Charles's advice, Edward decided to follow it, and by a second proclamation he ordered his troops to meet him on Barham Downs—about six miles from Canterbury—instead of at Portsdown.[2] He was also glad to accept Charles's offer of help in transporting his army to France, although many a ship was already being fitted up for that purpose in the ports of England and on 8 March the Cinque Ports were ordered to have "at the Downs between our ports of Sandwich and Dover" the fifty-seven ships they were bound to furnish for fifteen days' service at their own expense and for a still longer time at the king's expense if he asked them so to do.[3] About a week later the Italian gentleman whose account of Edward's method of collecting benevolences has already been quoted wrote that the king now had everything in order for his expedition and was constantly engaged in inspecting his artillery, which had been assembled at St Katharine's. Although the king had a great many bombards, the Italian said, he was having new ones made every day, and recently he had paid money to a large number of his captains, all of whom had been told to be ready with their men on 26 May. "Indeed," the Italian declared, "everyone is putting his harness in order and everything necessary for a campaign, to such an extent

---

1. Commynes-Dupont, I, 336, note. Charles's letter is undated.
2. A proclamation concerning the day of the king's muster at "Barham-down" near the city of Canterbury was sent to the different counties and to divers captains going with him to the parts of Normandy and France, and the treasurer of England was allowed £20 for his labours in connection with "the muster of this our army royal prepared towards our duchy of Normandy and realm of France to be taken at Berham Down within our shire of Kent." Tellers' Roll, no. 51A; Warrants for Issues, 15 Edw. IV, 23 June. Apparently the place of muster was not changed until after 21 April, as in a letter of that date Edward refers to the muster about to take place at Portsdown. *Records of the Borough of Nottingham*, II, 387-388.
3. Tellers' Roll, no. 51A; Close Roll 15 Edw. IV, m. 32 dorso.

as to show their great desire to cross." But he added: "I do not know what they will do. Many are kinsmen to St Thomas, but the expenditure of the money goes to show that the business will be carried out. The ships which are to take them over are all to gather at Amthona (Southampton), and it is said they will go to sea. They are expecting daily a Venetian ship laden with malvasie. According to what the Venetians say, she will take pay from the king to take him across."[1]

Evidently there were some who still believed that Edward would never go to France and had never really intended to do so. Yet if there was any doubt about the departure of the English army, it was the fault of Charles, not of Edward. Charles seemed to be as ready as ever to make promises, but, apparently forgetting that the date designated for the beginning of the invasion of France was now only a few weeks away, he still went on with the hopeless siege of Neuss. At last Edward sent Lord Dacre and William Hatclyf to Burgundy to consult the Duchess Margaret.[2] Margaret, however, was powerless to recall her husband from Neuss, though she must have shown a desire to be helpful, as she was rewarded with a licence to export annually from England, without paying customs, fifty pieces of cloth to her husband's domains (in defiance, seemingly, of the unrepealed edict against the importation of English cloth into Burgundy) and one thousand pieces through the Straits of Marrok in the "Great Ship of Burgundy" or other ships.[3] By the middle of April Lord Dynham, who some weeks before had been commissioned to keep "the narrow sea" with an army of three thousand men, had his fleet ready at Erith, and he seems to have been sent out about that time to begin his task.[4] But naturally Edward

---

1. *Cal. Milanese Papers*, I, 194. Edward probably hired ships from the Genoese as well as from the Venetians, as on 22 May orders were given to Dynham and to all other captains, masters of ships, etc., not only to suffer any Genoese carrack, ship, or boat sailing to any place except France to pass in peace, but to protect it, if it should be attacked. Close Roll 15 Edw. IV, 26 dorso.
2. Dacre and Hatclyf were away forty days. Tellers' Roll, *ut sup*.
3. French Roll 15 Edw. IV, m. 20; *Lettres de rois, reines, etc., des tours de France et d'Angleterre*, II, 491-492. Cf. French Roll 15 Edw. IV, m. 1-2.
4. K. R. Exchequer Accounts, bundle 72/2—an indenture made by the king on 12 March with Sir William Pirton, who undertook to serve under Dynham with 360 "fightingmen" for four months; Tellers' Roll, Easter 15 Edw. IV—an entry of a payment to Thomas Bulkeley sent to Erith with money for Dynham, who was at that place in the *Grace Dieu*. Dynham's men were to be mustered on 10 April in the port of London, according to Pirton's indenture, and his appointment as captain of the fleet was sealed on 25 April. *Cal. Patent Rolls*, II, 527; Rymer, XII, 1.

was unwilling to leave England until he had received positive assurance that Charles would be on hand, and, finding that Margaret could not help him, he sent Earl Rivers and Richard Martyn all the way to Neuss to beg and entreat the duke once more not to forget his promises to his ally.[1]

Rivers and Martyn reached Charles's camp before Neuss on 29 April,[2] and they found there both an embassy from the Duke of Brittany and an envoy sent by the Count of St Pol, who was supposed to be urging Charles to conclude a new truce with Louis but was in reality making some secret offers to the duke on his own account. Little dreaming that Charles had received from Edward a promise that he should have his possessions when France had been conquered, St Pol had already offered to let Edward into Amiens, Peronne, and Abbeville, if Edward would pledge his word to give him Champagne, and the Duke of Brittany the county of Poitou, when Louis had been overthrown; and now he was secretly offering to hand over St Quentin to Charles and provide him with four hundred lances, if Charles would make him captain general of his army.[3] Yet it was easy to see that the invasion of France was doomed to failure unless Charles could be persuaded to give up the siege of Neuss, and the Breton ambassadors and St Pol's envoy united with Rivers and Martyn in trying to get a definite promise from the duke that he would abandon his foolish enterprise and march with his entire army to meet the king of England upon his arrival. Rivers and Martyn seem to have told Charles flatly that, if he did not do his part, Edward would not cross the sea at all.[4] But though the duke could have made an honourable peace quite easily, as an apostolic legate came and went daily between his camp and that of his enemies, seeking to negotiate a peace, and the king of Denmark, returning home from Rome, spent some time in the neighbourhood of Neuss and did his best to terminate a conflict which he feared would hinder the crusade he had just proposed to the Pope, Charles kept replying that it was impossible for him to give up the siege of Neuss, as both his honour and his

---

1. Warrants for Issues, 15 Edw. IV, 15 April—a warrant to pay £100 to Rivers and Martyn; Tellers' Roll, Easter 15 Edw. IV. According to Commynes, I, 271-272, Rivers was sent twice to Charles to try to induce him to abandon the siege of Neuss.
2. Commynes-Lenglet, II, 216.
3. St Pol's confession, Commynes-Lenglet, III, 457; Gingins la Sarra, I, 132-134. Cf. Commynes, I, 281 note.
4. *Cal. Milanese Papers*, I, 195-196.

reputation were at stake. "Luy avoit Dieu troublé le sens et l'entendement" is the only explanation Commynes could think of for the duke's obstinate persistence in an undertaking so obviously doomed to end in defeat and to bring to naught, if continued longer, the invasion of France which he had desired so long and for which all was now ready.[1] And while Charles refused to listen to reason, Louis, grasping the situation, determined to make the most of it. Two days after Rivers and Martyn reached Neuss, and the very day his truce with Charles expired, Louis sent his army across the Somme to overrun Charles's domains.[2]

All that Edward had to cheer him during the weeks which Charles's stubborn foolishness filled with doubt and anxiety was the growing desire the Duke of Brittany was manifesting to take a leading part in the invasion of France. For though at first Francis had preferred to avoid making a definite treaty to attack Louis, in the end something—very likely his hope of getting Poitou—overcame his caution, and at the beginning of May the Seigneur d'Urfé and Jacques de la Villéon arrived in England with authority to conclude a treaty of alliance. Edward appointed the Earl of Essex, Duras, and Russell to negotiate with Francis's ambassadors, and on 16 May a treaty was drawn up which bound Francis to join Edward with eight thousand men and assist him to recover the kingdom of France and the duchies of Normandy and Aquitaine. Nothing seems to have been said in the treaty about Poitou, but Edward promised that, in case Francis needed help against Louis, Lord Dynham, captain of the fleet, should go to his assistance, landing his men at whatever place the duke might designate, and also that a force of English archers should be sent to Brittany.[3] On 19 May Lords Audley and Duras signed an indenture with Edward by which they bound themselves to do him "service of war" with two thousand archers for a year under the Duke of Brittany in Brittany and such other parts of France as the duke thought "most behooveful and expedient" for the conquest of that kingdom; and the muster of their men was to take place at Weymouth on 23 June.[4]

---

1. Commynes, I, 271-272, 283-284; Gingins la Sarra, I. 132-134.
2. *Chron. Scandaleuse*, I, 329.
3. Signed Bills, file 1509, no. 4735, file 1511, no. 4829; French Roll 15 Edw. IV, m. 12.
4. Warrants for Issues, 15 Edw. IV, 20 May. Cf. *Cal. Patent Rolls*, II, 542; Rymer, XII, 12. Two payments to Audley and Duras of £4,586 10s each, representing the first and second quarters' wages for their men, are recorded in Tellers' Roll, no. 51A.

While carrying on his negotiations with Francis II and waiting for the return of Rivers and Martyn with what he hoped would be better news from Charles, Edward was making his final arrangements for leaving England. The Prince of Wales was to bear the title of "keeper of the realm" during his father's absence, and he was brought up from Ludlow on 12 May. He made a state entry into London and, to give additional dignity to his small person, was knighted on Whit Sunday at Westminster.[1] The new keeper of the realm was to be left, however, in his mother's charge, and the queen was allowed twenty-two hundred pounds a year for the expenses of her household while her husband was in France and as much again "because that my Lord Prince is assigned by the king to be in household."[2] The actual control of the affairs of his kingdom while he was away Edward delegated to "our great council in England," which was so called to distinguish it from "our great council in France and Normandy," the body of councillors which followed the king beyond sea;[3] and among the members of the council in England were the Archbishop of Canterbury, Alcock, Bishop of Rochester, already president of the Prince's council, the Bishops of Ely, Durham, Bath, Carlisle, and Norwich, the Earls of Essex and Arundel, Lords Dacre, Dynham, and Dudley, Doctor John Russell, Sir John Say, Sir John Wingfield, Richard Fowler, chancellor of the duchy of Lancaster, William Huse, attorney general, Thomas Vaughan, and William Alyngton.[4] As Rotherham was to accompany the king to France, Alcock was to be acting chancellor of England during the expedition, and there are royal writs addressed to Alcock as "our chancellor" of a date as early as 27 April and as late as 28 September, the day on which Edward returned to London. Rotherham

---

1. London Journal 8, f. 98; Sharpe, *London and the Kingdom*, I, 317; *Cal. Patent Rolls*, II, 534-535; Rymer, XII, 13.
2. Cotton MS. Vespasian C XIV, f. 244.
3. On two occasions Thomas Bulkeley was sent by the advice of "our great council in England" over the sea to "our council at Calais" with divers and great sums of money and instructions and "secret writings." Warrants for Issues, 18 Edw. IV, 6 Feb. The term "nostre grant Consel en France et Normendie" occurs in the grant of the office of marshal of France to the Duke of Norfolk. Signed Bills, file 1510, no. 4798.
4. Signed Bills, file 1510, no. 4794A, file 1511, no. 4801A. Dacre was appointed one of the king's councillors by letters patent and was granted 100 marks a year for his services. Writs of Privy Seal, file 854, nos. 4202-4204; *Cal. Patent Rolls*, II, 534, 550, 559.

received the title of "chancellor of France" as soon as the king landed on the other side of the sea, but at the same time he continued to bear the title of chancellor of England, with the curious result that for five months England had two chancellors.[1]

Not many days after the Prince of Wales came up to London, Rivers and Martyn reached home with nothing better to report than that Charles was still at Neuss and evidently determined to stay there no matter what happened. So dismaying was this news that had Edward, on receipt of it, renounced the expedition to France entirely, Charles could not justly have blamed him. And in all probability Edward would have decided to stay at home had Charles been the only person to whom he was answerable. But how were the people of England to be pacified? The king of Scotland had not spoken without knowledge of the situation when he gave Louis to understand that, in order to persuade Edward to give up his intention of making war on France, it would be necessary to promise him aid against his subjects; and if there had been danger, even when the plans for the expedition were only half formed, that an abandonment of it would cause a rebellion, that danger was much greater now when the splendid army was assembled and all that remained to be done was to transport it to France. No, it was too late for Edward to turn back. He must cross the sea and at least make a feint of attacking Louis. So on Tuesday, 30 May, he left London to join his army. The wardens of the guilds had been charged to be ready to assist at the king's departure at nine o'clock in the morning "with as many of your fellowship, as well householders as other sad and well advised persons, as goodly may be purveyed," but it was six o'clock in the evening before Edward, attended by many armed men, left the Bishop of London's palace and rode through streets lined with mercers, fishmongers, butchers, bakers, and other worthy citizens to the bridge, where boats were waiting to take him to Greenwich. A day or two later he seems to have returned to Westminster on some errand, but on 7th June he arrived

---

1. Writs of Privy Seal, files 852-854; Foss, *Judges of Eng.*, IV, 474-475. The form "Dominus Cancellarius Francie" will be found in a number of the Writs of Privy Seal and Signed Bills. Edward afterwards granted the Bishop of Rochester, late chancellor of England, a reward of £100 for his good services to him and to the Prince of Wales and for his expenses "in attending to our councils in our absence out of this our realm." Warrants for Issues, 15 Edw. IV, 6 Oct.

at Canterbury, where his soldiers were mustered and waiting for him on Barham Downs.[1]

What took the king back to Westminster after making his state departure was probably a desire to confer with the officers of the Exchequer about the proceeds of the fifteenth and tenth which he was not to receive until he was ready to start for France. For when he finally proceeded to Canterbury, he was followed by Thomas Bulkeley and other officials of the Receipt bringing "divers and great sums of money" from the "great treasury within Westminster" for the wages of his soldiers.[2] Unfortunately, however, the withdrawal of these divers and great sums left an almost empty Exchequer, and now, on the very eve of his sailing, Edward was sorely troubled by "lack of gold." From Canterbury he was able to send back word to the treasurer and chamberlains of the Exchequer that he had succeeded in obtaining a loan of five thousand pounds from the Medicis and the Portinaris, and another of a thousand marks from Caniziani, now a London citizen and mercer;[3] but even these additions to his funds were not sufficient to relieve his difficulties. Audley and Duras, with their two thousand archers, were ready to sail for Brittany, and Oliver King, one of the royal secretaries, was to go with them to exchange with Francis the ratifications of the treaty recently signed at London and to assist in the negotiation of a further treaty of peace and alliance.[4] But Audley and Duras could not go without money, and on 17 June the king wrote to the mayor and aldermen of London explaining the situation and commanding them, with the aid of the two chief justices, the chief baron of the Exchequer, and Richard Martyn, to obtain a "good and loving grant" from everyone in the city who was known to be worth a hundred marks or more and who had not already "showed to us their benevolence."[5] Less than three hundred pounds seems to have

---

1. London Journal 8, ff. 100b-101; Sharpe, I, 318; Privy Seals.
2. Warrants for Issues, 17 Edw. IV, 6 Feb.
3. Warrants for Issues, 15 Edw. IV, 12 and 22 June. Cf. Rymer, XII, 7-9; *Cal. Patent Rolls*, II, 547; Close Roll 15 Edw. IV, m. 17; Receipt Roll, Easter 15 Edw. IV.
4. French Roll 15 Edw. IV, m. 17; Signed Bills, file 1510, nos. 4770, 4771; Rymer, XII, 12; *Cal. Patent Rolls*, II, 536. King was made Edward's chief secretary in the French tongue in March 1476. Rymer, XII, 26; *Cal. Patent Rolls*, II, 582. After Hatclyf's death, which occurred sometime between 23 June and 22 October 1480, he succeeded to the office of "first and chief secretary" to the king, an office which gave him charge of the royal signet. Signed Bills, file 1518, no. 5197. Cf. *Cal. Patent Rolls*, III, 196.
5. Halliwell, *Letters of Kings of Eng.*, I, 144 (from Harleian MS. 543, f. 148). The correct date of this letter is 17 June, not 22 June, as Halliwell gives it.

been gleaned by this proceeding, as the records of the city of London contain a memorandum that on 18 August, 15 Edward IV, the clerk of the city delivered to Thomas Bulkeley of the Receipt two hundred and eighty-two pounds "granted now late unto the king our sovereign lord by way of benevolence by certain of his subjects inhabited within this city."[1] But with this the king had to make shift.

On 20 June Edward left Canterbury for Sandwich,[2] and one of the first things he did after reaching Sandwich was to have Rotherham attach the great seal to a will which he had drawn up in anticipation of the moment of his departure for France. "Remembering inwardly that we, as other creatures in this world, be transitory and have none abidunt therein certain, considering also that we be now upon our journey and in taking our passage, by God's sufferance and assistance, toward our realm of France, for the recovering of our undoubted right and title unto the same," were the words in which Edward confessed that even kings are mortal; and while he bequeathed his soul to "Almighty God and to His glorious Mother, Our Lady Saint Mary, Saint Edward, and all the Holy Company of Heaven," he gave orders that his body should be buried "low in the ground" in St George's Chapel, the beautiful church of the Order of the Garter at Windsor which he had recently begun to rebuild. The particular place in the chapel in which he wished to lie he had already pointed out to the Bishop of Salisbury, and he directed that over his grave should be placed a stone "wrought with the figure of death, with scutcheon of our armour and writings convenient about the borders of the same remembering the day and year of our decease," over the stone a vault, and over the vault a chapel or closet containing an altar and a tomb. Upon the tomb was to rest "an image for our figure" made of silver and gilt, or at the least of copper and gilt, and near by was to be erected a chantry in which two priests were to pray daily for the souls of their royal benefactor, his wife, and his ancestors.

It was not only for the proper burial of his body that Edward took thought when he drew up his will. His lengthy testament made careful provision for the payment of his debts, for the completion of St George's Chapel, for the distribution of two hundred pounds a year "for ever more" in alms, for the maintenance of his wife and his younger son, and for the marriage of his

---

1. London Journal 8, f. 105.
2. Privy Seals.

daughters. In February Alexander Legh had carried to Edinburgh the first instalment of Princess Cecily's dowry, together with the five hundred marks promised as indemnity for the Salvator and a message from Edward to the effect that he had made such arrangements for the "rule of the marches" during his absence in France that he hoped there would be no breaches of the truce by his subjects.[1] But eighteen thousand marks of Cecily's dowry still remained to be paid, and Edward's will contained an order that the money should be paid to the king of Scotland according to agreement, or, in case the Scottish marriage failed to take place, to any other bridegroom the queen and the Prince of Wales might select for Cecily. As for the Princesses Elizabeth and Mary, for whom no marriages had yet been arranged, they were to have ten thousand marks each if they accepted husbands chosen for them by the queen and the Prince, but if either of them should be so wilful as to marry to suit herself, instead of her mother and brother, "so that they be thereby disparaged," her ten thousand marks were to be used to help pay her father's debts. And if the unborn child the queen was now carrying proved to be a daughter, that daughter was to have ten thousand marks towards her marriage on the same conditions.[2]

Good reason did Edward have to meditate on the dangers he was about to face, as he was setting out for France with the almost certain knowledge that his chief ally was going to fail him. But since Charles was so far away and the Duke of Brittany had not yet ratified the treaty negotiated by the Seigneur d'Urfé and Jacques de la Villéon, he was not going to land in Normandy, as Charles had advised him to do. Under the circumstances that would have been utter folly, and he had resolved to take his army to Calais and there await developments. First of all, however, he sent Garter King-of-Arms to Louis with a letter in which he demanded the surrender of the kingdom of

---

1. Rymer, XI, 850; Cotton MS. Vespasian C XVI, ff. 118-120—Edward's instructions to Legh. Before entire harmony between England and Scotland was possible, Edward had to make redress for two other "attemptates," viz., the capture of the king of Scotland's "own proper carvel," the afterwards famous *Yellow Carvel*, by the Duke of Gloucester's ship, the *Mayflower*, and the capture of a ship belonging to the Lord of Luss by one belonging to Lord Grey. See Legh's instructions. There was also a dispute over a fishgarth, or weir, on the river Esk which was not settled without an amount of negotiating out of all proportion, one would think, to its importance. See Rymer, XI, 837, 851; *Rotuli Scotiæ*, II, 550; and Legh's instructions.

2. *Excerpta Historica*, 366-379.

France and announced that he was coming for the purpose of restoring the ancient liberties of the Church and the people of France and of lifting from them the heavy burdens now oppressing them. But the herald was also told, if not to make proposals of peace to Louis, at least to be attentive to anything Louis might say about a treaty.[1]

In one respect Charles was as good as his word. If what Commynes says is to be believed, the duke sent Edward no less than five hundred ships, of a type particularly well suited for the transportation of horses, to help carry the English army to France. But however many ships Edward may have had, it took him more than three weeks to get his army across to Calais,[2] and Commynes remarks that, if Louis had understood how to manage his affairs on the sea as well as he understood how to manage them on land, the king of England would not have found himself in France in the year 1475.[3] As it was, although Louis apparently had a fleet in readiness and was on the alert,[4] the only accident which seems to have occurred was the capture of two or three of Edward's little transports by a ship of Eu. At the beginning of June the Count of St Pol, anxious to get Louis out of the Somme neighbourhood, reported that the English were on the point of landing in Normandy, and Louis hurried to Rouen, but only to learn that the English fleet—Dynham's, no doubt—had withdrawn.[5] And when an English herald, Scales, who was carrying some letters for Edward, fell into Louis' hands and told him that by 22 June Edward would bring twelve or thirteen thousand soldiers to Calais, where it was understood four or five thousand men had already gathered, all that Louis could do was to send troops into Picardy to lay waste the country so that the English would find a bare cupboard.[6]

But if Louis' fleet could neither destroy Edward's transports nor drive them back, perhaps by diplomacy he could attain his ends. When Garter arrived and presented Edward's letter, which was composed in so fine a style that Commynes, who stood at Louis' elbow in these days, was of the opinion

---

1. Commynes, I, 288-289, 325. Cf. Molinet, I, c.xxiii.
2. The transportation of the army seems to have commenced at the very beginning of June. Haynin, II, 274.
3. Commynes, I, 288.
4. *Lettres de Louis XI*, V, 337.
5. *Chron. Scandaleuse*, I, 332-333; *itineraire de Louis XI*.
6. *Chron. Scandaleuse*, I, 334; *Lettres de Louis XI*, V, 361, 363, 366.

that no Englishman could possibly have written it, Louis forthwith invited the herald to a private audience and, after telling him quite gently that he knew the king of England was coming to France only to please the Duke of Burgundy and the English people, remarked that the fighting season was already nearly past and that the Duke of Burgundy was really a defeated man. He gave Garter to understand, too, that he was aware of St Pol's intrigues and predicted that Edward would find that the count was deceiving him, just as he deceived everyone else. In short, Louis offered plenty of reasons why Edward, if he were a wise man, ought to be glad to listen to overtures of peace; and finally he squeezed three hundred gold crowns into Garter's hand and promised him a thousand more should a treaty be concluded. Garter accepted Louis' money without hesitancy and, after assuring the king that he would do what he could for him, admitted that he thought his royal master would not be sorry to receive proposals of peace, though it would be useless to try to do anything about the matter until after the English army had crossed the sea. Then it would be well, he suggested, to send a herald to King Edward to ask for a safeconduct for an embassy, and at the same time letters to Lords Howard and Stanley, as well as one to himself, so that he might assist and introduce the herald.

As Louis had already made an attempt to win the heart of Lord Hastings with gracious letters and a "très grand et beau présent" sent to Calais but had gained nothing thereby except a letter of thanks,[1] he was particularly pleased to receive a hint in regard to which of the English lords he would find most approachable, and after his conversation with Garter he called Commynes to him and told him to present the English herald with thirty ells of crimson velvet and not to let anyone speak with him. He also rehearsed the contents of Edward's letter to those who were present when he received it, and to a small group of his intimates even read it aloud. And all the time his face wore a very cheerful expression, because he felt confident, from what the Garter had let fall, that he would have little difficulty in securing a treaty with the English king.[2]

On 4 July Edward crossed from Dover to Calais,[3] and on the 6th the

---

1. See a letter from Hastings to Louis written on 27 June, year not stated. MS. français 2902, f. 33. Legrand, who made a copy of this letter (MS. français 6980, f. 196) assigned it to 1475, and M. Mandrot, (Commynes, II, 4, note„ has done the same.
2. Commynes, I, 288-290.
3. Privy Seals; Gingins la Sarra, I, 192-195.

Duchess Margaret arrived at Calais bringing not only handsome presents but also, probably, the tidings that Charles had at last signed a truce with the Emperor and was now coming to meet his ally. For scarcely had Margaret departed for St Omer, escorted by Clarence and Gloucester, when, on 14 July, Charles himself appeared.[1] But the only armed force the duke brought with him was a small bodyguard, and all that he had come for was to talk over plans. He at once proposed that Edward should overrun Normandy, with the help of the Duke of Brittany and the Count of St Pol, and then push his way into Champagne, while he himself, he said, after returning to get his troops, which on leaving Neuss he had sent into Lorraine to pillage, would enter Champagne from the east and come to meet the English army in the heart of Louis' kingdom, at Rheims, where Edward could be crowned king of France.[2]

If Edward kept his temper when it was found that Charles had come without an army, his soldiers did not. There was much murmuring against the duke, and the advice of some of the English lords was that the invasion of France should be given up at once. But there were others who still wanted to fight, since that was what they had come for, and who declared that the English army was better off without Charles's troops. If the duke's army came, these men said, there would surely be quarrels about quarters, provisions, or something of the sort, and what could give the French king greater pleasure than to see his enemies drawing swords against each other? Charles was also clever enough to say flattering things. He assured the English, who already felt sufficiently confident that France would shiver with fright at the sight of them, that they really had no need of his help, as with an army so splendid their king could march in triumph through France, aye, to the gates of Rome, if he wished. In this way the duke avoided a quarrel with the allies he had treated so strangely, and in the end it was decided that, as the Count of St Pol was still offering to hand over St Quentin, Edward should advance towards that place by way of Doullens and Peronne.[3]

---

1. *Stonor Letters and Papers*, I, 158; Commynes-Lenglet, II, 217; Basin. II, 356; Molinet, *ut sup.*

2. Gingins la Sarra, I, 154-160, 192-195; *Cal. Milanese Papers*, I, 196-197; *Lettres de Louis XI*, VI, 3-7; Commynes, I, 292; *Hist. Croy. Cont.*, 558.

3. *Hist. Croy. Cont.*, Molinet, and Comnaynes-Lenglet, *ut sup.*; Commynes, I, 293-294.

After Charles had spent four days at Calais, the English army was put in readiness to march. Then, leaving Sir John Scott, Sir John Donne, Thomas Thwaytes, chancellor of the Exchequer, and others at Calais to constitute his council there and to keep in touch with the council in England,[1] Edward and all his troops accompanied the duke to Guines. There Charles took his leave for the moment and went to St Omer to join the Duchess Margaret, while Edward advanced slowly through the county of Boulogne. For several days the whole English army was encamped on the "field of Fawconbergh" (Fauquembergues), where Edward set up a tent described as "la plus riche de jamais" and where Charles, on whom Clarence and Gloucester and other English lords seem to have remained in attendance, was with him again from 22 to 24 July. Afterwards two nights were spent on the field of Agincourt, where thoughts of Henry V's glorious victory must have filled the minds of all, and then one or two at Blangy. On the 29th, by which time the neighbourhood of Doullens had been reached, Charles came once more and reviewed the army, and on 6 August Edward and Charles arrived together at Peronne, where Edward discovered, to his disgust, that, though Charles himself entered the town, he and his army must be content to encamp at St-Christ-sur-Somme.[2]

Thus far, apparently, Edward had remained outwardly courteous to Charles. But he was thinking anything but kind thoughts about his brother-in-law, and he knew that the French were now advancing in large numbers. It is proof of how well Dynham had kept the "narrow sea" while the English army was crossing to Calais that as late as 17 July Louis was still uncertain whether his enemies had landed on the continent or were still in England but soon after all his doubts were removed, and by the 27th he was at Beauvais with a powerful army.[3] He still hoped for the intervention of providence, however, and the hope was much encouraged when to Beauvais came another English herald, Ireland, and a couple of pursuivants, who, like Garter, were received in secret audience and presented with

---

1. On 13 July, and again on 17 August, Thomas Bulkeley delivered £2,000 to Scott, Donne, and Thwaytes at Calais. Tellers' Roll, Easter 15 Edw. IV. Thwaytes had been chancellor of the Exchequer since 11 August 1471. *Cal. Patent Rolls*, II, 272.
2. Privy Seals; Commynes-Lenglet, *ut sup.*; Commynes I, 292-293; *Journal de Dom Gerard Robert, religieux de l'Abbaye de Saint Vaast d'Arras* (Arras, 1852), 3-4.
3. *Lettres de Louis XI*, V, 373; *itinéraire de Louis XI*.

generous gifts.[1] From Beauvais Louis proceeded to Compiègne, and he was at Compiègne when Edward and Charles arrived at Peronne. Some of the English troops, angered by their exclusion from Peronne, took to foraging in the neighbourhood, and one party of soldiers seems to have wandered as far as Noyon, where some of Louis' men discovered them and killed about fifty of them. Then Charles, seeing that the English were getting out of hand, grew very anxious that they should move on, and he suggested to Edward that they should both proceed at once to St Quentin, as the Count of St Pol had just repeated his promises once more. Edward was glad enough to do this, and with the duke and his whole army he started on; but when St Quentin came in sight, the big guns of the town opened fire on the first Englishmen who appeared, and after two or three soldiers had been killed and several others taken prisoners, the rest turned and fled, bitterly denouncing the Count of St Pol as a traitor.[2]

The much heralded invasion of France was certainly beginning very badly, and if Charles did not see that Edward was already sick of the whole venture, he was indeed a blind man. Yet on 12 August, the day after the unfortunate occurrence at St Quentin, the duke went off to rejoin his army, while Edward seems to have moved his troops to Lihons-en-Santerre.[3] Charles declared, as he went away, that he was going to do great things for his allies, but Edward had lost all faith in him, and the campaign which had been mapped out at Calais and was to have terminated in Edward's coronation at Rheims was destined to end here and now. For Charles was scarcely out of sight when Edward entered openly into negotiations with Louis. One Jacques de Grassay, who by some chance had fallen into Edward's hands, was set at liberty, and as the Frenchman took his leave, Howard and Stanley slipped a noble into his hand and requested him to recommend them to the king of France. Guessing what this meant, Grassay hurried to Louis at Compiègne, and though at first he was listened to with suspicion, as he had a brother in the Duke of Burgundy's service, the fact that his message came from Howard and Stanley, the very men Garter had mentioned, gave it an appearance of

---

1. *Cal. Milanese Papers*, I, 200.
2. *Ibid.*, 200-201; Basin, II, 358; Commynes, I, 293-295.
3. On 13 August the English army appears to have been "beside a village called Santerre within Vermandois, a little from Peronne." Rymer, XII, 14-15.

truth, and Louis, after a moment's hesitation, decided to send a messenger to Edward. Louis had not prepared for war in Edward's showy and elaborate way, and he had no herald with him, but a frightened and reluctant youth was arrayed in as correct a herald's costume as could be devised on a moment's notice and dispatched to the English king.

When Louis' messenger arrived, Edward was at dinner, but as soon as he rose from the table, Howard and Stanley brought in the youth. It had long been the desire of the king of France, the young man told Edward, to have peace with England, and never since his accession to the throne had he wilfully committed any act hostile to the king or kingdom of England; for though it was true that he had received the Earl of Warwick, this he had done in order to punish the Duke of Burgundy, not the king of England. And if the Duke of Burgundy had invited the king of England to cross the sea, the duke's only object was to secure better terms for himself from the king of France. If others had offered assistance, they too were merely looking after their own interests and would desert the king of England the moment they saw that it would be to their advantage so to do. Louis also reminded Edward that the winter season would soon be at hand to force a cessation of war and, finally, he let him know that he was prepared to be generous. The king of France realized, said his messenger, that the king of England had been put to heavy expense. He knew, too, that there were many persons in England, both noblemen and merchants, who really desired a war with France. Yet should the king of England be willing to consider a treaty, Louis thought he could offer terms which would please both him and his people, and, on receiving a safeconduct for a hundred men, he would gladly send some ambassadors to proceed with the matter, or, if the king of England preferred, there might be a meeting of ambassadors at some village half-way between the two armies.[1]

Edward felt no scruple about listening to Louis' offer. Why should he? So he immediately agreed to send some ambassadors to a halfway meeting place, and an English herald returned to Compiègne with Louis' messenger to obtain a safeconduct for them. Edward did not, however, take this step without advice. Clarence and Gloucester, the Duke of Norfolk, who had been made marshal of "our realm of France" while the army was at Calais,[2]

---

1. Commynes, I, 295-300.
2. Signed Bills, file 1510, no. 4798.

the Duke of Suffolk, Rotherham, the Marquis of Dorset, the Earls of Northumberland, Rivers, Pembroke, and Douglas, Lords Hastings, Stanley, Howard, and Ferrers, and a dozen or so more men had been called in for consultation, and although Gloucester and a few others opposed making peace with the French,[1] it was with the approval of the majority that response was made to Louis' overtures. On 13 August, Howard, Morton, Dudley, dean of the chapel, and Thomas St Leger were chosen to treat with Louis and to offer the following terms: if Louis would bind himself, his country, and his subjects to pay the king of England seventy-five thousand crowns within fifteen days and twenty-five thousand crowns every Easter and every Michaelmas as long as both of them lived, and if he would marry his son, the Dauphin, at his own expense, to the first or second daughter of the king of England and endow her with rents of the value of sixty thousand pounds yearly "after the estimation of France," then the king of England, as soon as he received the seventy-five thousand crowns, would take his army back to England, leaving behind him hostages who must be set free when the greater part of his army had landed in England. Edward also asked for a "private amity" binding Louis and himself to aid each other "in case any of them both were by their subjects wronged or disobeyed," and for a truce with intercourse of merchandise for seven years.[2]

As the one king was as eager as the other for a treaty, there were no delays. Louis delegated the Bastard of Bourbon, admiral of France, the Bishop of Evreux, Jean Blosset, Seigneur de St Pierre, and Jean de Daillon, Seigneur du Lude, to conduct the negotiations for him,[3] and on the morning of the 15th Howard, Morton, Dudley, and St Leger met these Frenchmen at a village not far from Amiens. As a matter of form, the Englishmen began by declaring that Louis must surrender to Edward his crown and his kingdom, or at least the duchies of Normandy and Guienne; and when they introduced the subject of the marriage of the Dauphin with one of Edward's daughters, they asked Louis either to give the duchy of Guienne outright to the bride for her maintenance or to pay her fifty thousand crowns a year for nine years and at the end of that time surrender the revenues of the duchy to her and

---

1. Molinet, *ut sup.*; Commynes, I, 319.
2. Rymer, XII, 14-15; *Cal. Patent Rolls*, II, 583.
3. Commynes, I, 300; *Cal. Milanese Papers*, I, 210.

her husband. But in the outcome their demands narrowed down to those mentioned in their commission, and to show their king's goodwill, they offered to name the traitors in Louis' kingdom and furnish written proof of their treachery—"qui estoit chose bien estrange," remarks the righteous Commynes.

When Louis learned what Edward's ambassadors had said, some of his councillors were inclined to think the king of England's readiness to treat was merely a trick. Louis himself, however, was inclined to believe, partly because the summer was so nearly over, partly because the Duke of Burgundy had virtually failed his ally and, more than all, because he was so convinced that Edward loved ease and pleasure above all things, that his foe was in earnest. So he decided not to delay, but to buy Edward off before he had time to change his mind. And his decision to act quickly was a wise one—not because Edward was trying to trick him, but because by this time a rumour of what was going on had reached Charles's ears. On the 18th Charles rushed back to Peronne, and there were stormy interviews between him and Edward on the two following days. Charles demanded to know if it were true that Edward had made peace with the king of France, and when he was told that a truce, in which he and the Duke of Brittany were to be included if they wished, had been agreed upon, he flew into a towering rage. In English, so that everyone within hearing could understand what he said, the duke referred insinuatingly to the great victories which other kings of England had won in France, and then, after informing Edward that he had invited him to cross the sea not because he needed his help, but only to give him a chance to recover his rights in France, he declared he would prove that he was capable of taking care of himself by refusing to make any truce with the king of France for three months after the English army went home. Having thus freed his mind, he mounted his horse and rode away to Namur.[1]

The Count of St Pol also tried to interfere when he heard that Edward and Louis were on the point of making peace. The count did not come to make his protest in person, as Charles had done, but, terrified by the thought that the two kings might compare notes about him, he wrote to Edward begging him for the love of God not to trust Louis' promises but to go into winter quarters at Eu and St Valery. If it was a question of money, he wrote, he

---

1. Commynes, I, 302-303, 307-308; Commynes-Lenglet, *ut sup.*

would furnish a loan of fifty thousand crowns. But aside from the fact that Louis had already burned Eu and St Valery, Edward knew St Pol pretty well by this time, and he sent back word to his wife's uncle that the truce with the French king was already an accomplished fact but that if he, the count, had kept his promises, it would never have been signed.[1]

Edward did not allow himself to be disturbed either by Charles's upbraidings or by St Pol's supplications. Both the duke and the count had forfeited all right to consideration. Although Charles told the Duke of Milan's ambassador, Panicharolla, who joined him at Namur, that before he left Peronne, Edward had promised him to do nothing without his consent, three days after Charles reached Namur, Thomas Danet came to him to say that Edward had received certain offers from the king of France which he felt he must accept, partly because of his heavy expenses, partly because of the approach of winter, and partly because his allies, the Duke of Brittany and the Count of St Pol, as well as Charles himself, had not given him the support they had promised. Charles was informed, however, that, not wanting to appear ungrateful, Edward had secured from Louis, by great effort, a promise that he should be included in the truce if he expressed a wish to be within three months, and also that he, Edward, should be allowed to arbitrate the differences between Charles and Louis. After the defiant words he had thrown at Edward as he left Peronne, Charles could not be expected to receive this message in a calm spirit, and he hastened to send the Bishop of Tournai, the Count of Chimay, and two other knights of the Golden Fleece to Edward to persuade him to renounce his purpose or at least "to try," as Panicharolla wrote, "for better terms than those arranged, if he must enter into a truce and agreement."[2] But Charles was too late, even if Edward had been disposed to listen to him. About 19 August, Howard, Morton, Dudley, and St Leger went to see Louis, who had withdrawn to the neighbourhood of Senlis, and by the 23rd Louis had received a letter from the Seigneur de St Pierre which caused him to praise God, Our Lady, and St Martin and to tell his chancellor that, as he valued the honour and welfare of his king and of the whole realm, he must have the money for King Edward, with something besides for gifts for Lord Howard and others who had been helpful, at Amiens before Friday evening, and that he must also

1. Commynes, I, 309-310.
2. *Cal. Milanese Papers*, I, 202-204, 206, 208, 218.

either bring or send the great seal of France, as the English would be content with nothing less.[1]

Louis might well praise God and the Saints, for his danger was past. To satisfy the English soldiers, it was agreed that Edward and his army should march towards Amiens in battle array and that Louis and his army, also in battle array, should advance to meet them there. But after this mock display of preparation for battle the two kings were to meet on a bridge and put the final touches to the peace negotiations.[2] On 25 August, therefore, Louis proceeded to Amiens, and when Edward and his troops arrived, he welcomed them as guests.[3] The Duke of Burgundy had succeeded in flattering the English soldiers out of a bad humour, but Louis knew a still surer road to their hearts. He sent them from eighty to a hundred—Commynes declares as many as three hundred—cartloads of the finest French wines, and the gates of Amiens stood open to every Englishman who cared to enter them. Not only that, but huge tables loaded with food and wine stood ready, and attendants "fort gros et gras" urged every man who passed to eat and drink his fill. Three or four days the gormandizing lasted, and so completely was military discipline forgotten that, had he wished, Louis might have cut down with the sword great companies of the would-be conquerors of his kingdom. Instead the king took fright when he found that the streets and taverns were full to overflowing with Englishmen. He sent Commynes to beg the English captains to take their men away, and though Commynes reported that Edward's soldiers were too drunk to be dangerous, the king was not satisfied until he went to the gate of the town and saw with his own eyes just what was going on. After a time Edward heard of the disorderly conduct of his men and requested Louis to shut them out of the town. Louis replied politely that he could not think of doing such a thing, but he told Edward that if he wanted to send some of his own archers to guard the gate, he might do so, and as Edward was glad to avail himself of this permission, many an Englishman was ejected from Amiens by order of his own king.[4]

---

1. *Lettres de Louis XI*, VI, 12-13; *itineraire de Louis XI*; Gingins la Sarra, I. 203-209; *Cal. Milanese Papers*, I, 200.

2. Gingins la Sarra, *ut sup.*; *Cal. Milanese Papers*, I, 200, 210.

3. *Itineraire de Louis XI*. Gerard Robert says that Edward "fit son camp a trois lieues d'Amiens, et contenoit bien trois lieues de pays."

4. Commynes, I, 308-312; Basin, II, 359; Molinet, *ut sup.*

It was a relief to everyone when the meeting of the two kings at last took place. Commynes and the Seigneur du Bouchage had been appointed by Louis, and a herald by Edward, to pick out the best place for the meeting, and the choice fell on the village of Picquigny, apparently because at that point the Somme was narrow and yet not fordable. A bridge was hastily constructed across the river, and as Louis had not forgotten how in his grandfather's reign the then Duke of Burgundy had been murdered on just such a bridge at Montereau, strong bars were built across the middle of the bridge with no opening except a little wooden grating through which two or more persons could talk but could not draw swords on each other. There were wooden awnings, too, to protect those who stood on the bridge from the weather, but unhappily they proved to be too small, as there was a deluge of rain on 29 August, the day of the meeting, and many a fine cloak was ruined.[1]

About eight hundred men followed the king of France to Picquigny, while the king of England brought his entire army. But it had been agreed that only a dozen men should attend each king on the bridge, and though Edward did not notice the fact—thereby confirming Commynes' oft-expressed opinion that the English were never as clever as the French when it came to making treaties—Louis was given another opportunity for treachery, as on his side of the river there was fine open country, while on Edward's side the bridge could be approached only by a causeway built across the marshes. However, four Englishmen were posted on Louis' end of the bridge and four Frenchmen on Edward's to keep close watch of all that was done, and there was no attempt at foul play, though Louis took the added precaution, not unusual with him, of inviting one of his attendants to divide the chances of murder with him by appearing in garments exactly like those he himself had chosen to wear. On this occasion it was Commynes whom Louis honoured in this way, and among the other eleven men who attended the French king on the bridge were the Duke of Bourbon and his brother, Cardinal Bourbon, the Bastard of Bourbon, the Bishop of Evreux, and the Seigneur de St Pierre. Among Edward's attendants too there were men of very high rank, for though Gloucester, who to the last objected to making peace with Louis, was conspicuous by his absence, Clarence was with his brother, and so were

---

1. Commynes, I, 313-315; *Chron. Scandaleuse*, I, 343.

the Earl of Northumberland, Lord Hastings, and Rotherham, the chancellor.

As Edward stepped upon the bridge, he wore on his head a black velvet cap adorned with a large fleur-de-lis of precious stones, and from his tall shoulders fell the magnificent robe of cloth of gold lined with red satin which he had had made for himself at such great expense before he left home. The king of England had lost something of his remarkable personal beauty with the passing of the years, for he was growing too fat, and to French eyes his costly robe of cloth of gold looked a little out of style, as it was made in the fashion of the days of Charles VII;[1] yet he made a very striking figure as he advanced to the barrier to meet Louis, who was never remarkable either for good looks or for fine clothes. When he reached the barrier beyond which Louis stood, he doffed his velvet cap and half knelt in salutation, while Louis responded with an equally deferential greeting. Then through the grating kisses were exchanged, and as Edward made a low bow, Louis said: "My cousin, you are most welcome. There is no man in all the world I so much desired to see as yourself, and I thank God that we have met for this happy purpose." To this speech Edward replied with the same friendly politeness and in quite good French, and after Rotherham had delivered a brief harangue in which he predicted that the treaty about to be signed would establish a memorable peace between England and France, the documents were produced, and each king, with one hand resting on a missal and the other on one of those pieces of the "true Cross" which were already strewn over Europe, swore to keep the treaty.

The documents to be signed were four in number, and their contents prove that Louis had consented to make practically all the concessions Edward had named as the price of peace. The first document contained two agreements: first, that all differences between the kings of England and France—meaning primarily Edward's claim to the crown of France—should be referred for settlement to four arbitrators, the Archbishops of Canterbury and Lyons, the Duke of Clarence, and the Count of Dunois,

---

1. Commynes, I, 316; *Chron. Scandaleuse*, II, 343. Cf. with Commynes' polite tribute to Edward's handsome appearance on this occasion Fabyan's statement that Louis was "apparelled more like a minstrel than a prince royal."

2. There is in existence a French treatise entitled "Pretensions des Anglois à la Couronne de France," which was written at or about this time for the purpose of proving the illegality of Edward's claim to the crown of France. It is printed in *La Vraie Cronicque d'Escoce*, Roxburghe Club 1847.

who were to hold their first meeting in England before Easter, their second in France before the following Michaelmas, and whose decision must be rendered within three years and must be accepted by both kings on penalty of paying a fine of three million crowns; second, that the king of England, on receiving seventy-five thousand gold crowns from the king of France, should take his army home without committing any act of hostility and should leave Lord Howard and Sir John Cheyne in France as hostages until the larger part of his army had landed in England. The second document provided for a seven years' truce between England and France in which the allies of both kings were to be included, if they so desired, which did away with the necessity of safeconducts for Englishmen going to France or Frenchmen going to England, and which abolished all charges paid by English merchants in France and by French merchants in England that had been established within the last twelve years. The third document was a treaty of amity which was intended to create a lifelong friendship, "true, sincere, and perfect," between Edward and Louis. It forbade either king to enter into any league or agreement with any ally of the other without his knowledge and consent, provided that within a year a diet should he held to determine the rate of exchange between England and France and, most important of all, arranged for a marriage between the Dauphin of France and Elizabeth, "daughter of the most victorious king of England," when they should reach the marriageable age. Louis was to defray the expenses of the bride's journey to France for her marriage and give her, "as soon as she shall come to years of marriage," a dowry in the form of rents amounting to sixty thousand pounds a year;[1] and if Elizabeth should die before the marriage took place, the Dauphin was to marry her sister Mary instead. Lastly, the treaty of amity contained an agreement that if either king found himself confronted by an armed rebellion of his subjects, the other must support him not only by giving him an asylum in case he had to flee from his kingdom, but even by making war on his behalf "with all diligence and affection."[2] But naturally Edward did not care to have his subjects know

---

1. It has been erroneously stated by several writers that this amount was to be paid by Louis to Elizabeth until she reached the marriageable age.
2. *Archæologia*, XXXII, 326; Rymer, XII, 15-20; Commynes-Lenglet, III, 397-400, 402-405. There is also a transcript of "The Promise of Matrimonie" by Stow in Harleian MS. 543, f. 174b.

that Louis had promised to help him if they rebelled when he went home without drawing his sword, and the treaty of amity was "made secretly, the better to content the people."[1]

The arbitration treaty, the truce, and the treaty of amity were signed by both kings and sealed with the great seals of England and France, but the fourth document brought forth on the bridge, which was Louis' promise to pay Edward the large pension he had demanded, required only Louis' signature and seal. Every year, as long as both of them lived, Louis was to pay to Edward in the city of London at Easter, and again at Michaelmas, the sum of twenty-five thousand gold crowns; and as security he promised to procure and send to Edward before the feast of the Purification either a bond for the payment of the pension given by the Medici or a "bull apostolic sealed with lead" confirming all the promises he had made and threatening him with the punishment "of interdicting our realm, countries, and lordships and of cursing our own person" if he failed to keep them.[2] It is said that Louis made still another promise on the bridge at Picquigny, a promise that, in Edward's honour, a sun should be stamped on every crown coined in France. And it is a fact that in the following November orders were given for the minting of a new French crown, the "ecu au soleil."[3] Mere appearances never troubled Louis, and the presence of the king of England's badge on all the coins of his realm would not have chilled his pleasure in getting rid of Edward's "dampnable entreprise."

After the signing of the treaties, the two kings talked together on the bridge for some time. During their conversation Louis jokingly invited Edward to visit Paris and make merry with the ladies, adding that Cardinal Bourbon, who was present to hear the jest, would grant him absolution for

---

1. See a report of what was said by some English ambassadors sent to France in, February 1477. *Portefeuilles de Fontanieu*, 138-139, ff. 58-59; Legrand coll., MS. français 6984, ff. 192-195. Compare the statement of one writing at the time about the treaty between Edward and Louis that "the only things announced and really published, without further particulars, are a truce for seven years with the English, during which period both nations can have intercourse and trade without demanding or having any safe-conducts; and the allies, that is Burgundy and Brittany, can enter if they wish." He adds that he understands, however, that "there are many other things in secret, to wit, a marriage alliance and an even closer understanding, which are not made public for good reasons." *Cal. Milanese Papers*, I, 213.

2. *Archæologia, ut sup.*; Rymer, XII, 20-21; Commynes-Lenglet, III, 401-402.

3. Molinet, *ut sup.*; Commynes-Lenglet, IV, 431.

any peccadillos he might be guilty of. And Edward, who knew the Cardinal by reputation and could enjoy a joke even when it was partly at his own expense, laughingly accepted the invitation. But there were some matters of importance which the two kings wished to discuss in private and, sending their attendants away, they remained for a few moments longer conversing quite alone. The behaviour of the man nobody trusted, the Count of St Pol, seems to have been one of the subjects they talked over, and perhaps another was what was to be done with Margaret of Anjou. But Margaret's fate was left to be decided by negotiation, and if Edward offered proof of St Pol's treachery towards Louis, Louis was able to match it by showing a letter in which the count had promised to attack the English army as soon as it appeared.[1] Finally, Louis called Commynes to his side and asked Edward if he knew him. Edward at once recognized the former servitor of the Duke of Burgundy, and as he began to recall the occasions on which he had met Commynes before, Louis was given a chance to introduce the subject of Charles. What would Edward do, Louis inquired, if Charles refused to be included in the truce? Edward answered that he would make the offer a second time, and if Charles still refused, he would wash his hands of the matter and leave Louis and the duke to make a settlement to suit themselves. Then Louis ventured to mention the Duke of Brittany and to ask Edward what he would do in case Francis too refused the truce. Instantly, however, Edward was on his guard. Saying that in his hour of need he had found no better friend than the Duke of Brittany, he begged Louis not to molest Francis, and Louis saw that he must drop the subject. Both kings then recalled their attendants and, after exchanging a few more pleasant words with Edward and also with Edward's attendants, as he was bent on making as many friends among the English as possible, Louis bade them all farewell. The two kings left the bridge at the same moment, and while Edward rejoined his army, Louis returned to Amiens, where on the following day he acknowledged, in the presence of an apostolic notary, his obligation to pay to the king of England fifty thousand crowns a year on pain of excommunication and cursing.[2]

Louis' courtesies to Edward and his soldiers continued as long as they remained within reach. He supplied Edward with everything he wanted,

---

1. Molinet.

2. Commynes, I, 318-319; *Archæologia, ut sup.*

even to candles, and Amiens was as full of hungry and thirsty Englishmen the day after the interview at Picquigny as it had been before. Lord Howard and two or three other English noblemen had apparently accompanied Louis to Amiens after the meeting on the bridge, for they supped with him that evening; and perhaps Louis' wine went to Howard's head, as he proposed in a whisper to bring Edward to Amiens, and even to Paris, for a frolic. But Louis had already confided to Commynes that he had been frightened, after he gave his jocular invitation to Edward, lest it should be accepted, and he by no means relished Howard's proposal. Though the subject was brought up a second time, he finally disposed of it by saying that he must now give his time and attention to the Duke of Burgundy. In fact, Louis had both the Duke of Burgundy and the Duke of Brittany still on his mind, and though the rupture between Edward and Charles seemed to be as complete as even he could desire, he had been disappointed by Edward's reply in regard to Francis. On the following day the Seigneur de St Pierre and the Seigneur du Bouchage again approached Edward on the subject of Francis, but this time the king showed temper and declared that if anyone invaded Brittany, he would come back and defend its duke.[1]

That Edward had not made peace with Louis without fear and misgivings is evident from the contents of the treaty of amity. Yet his army, which had been so bounteously feasted by Louis, seems to have displayed no disappointment or resentment, as Louis de Bretaylle told his old acquaintance, Commynes, that because a white pigeon happened to alight on Edward's tent on the day of his meeting with Louis, his soldiers were convinced the peace was the work of the Holy Ghost.[2] Nevertheless, the Duke of Gloucester was not the only person who disapproved of what had been done. Louis de Bretaylle himself thought Edward had made a mistake, and in talking with Commynes he predicted that the French would make fun of the English after they went home. Of course Commynes declared the French would do nothing of the kind and, after adroitly praising Edward for his valour, he inquired how many battles the king had won and how many he had lost. Bretaylle replied that Edward had won nine battles and lost only one, the present one, but he added that in his opinion the disgrace of this one defeat outweighed the honour of the

---

1. Commynes, I, 319-320.
2. Cf. Molinet.

whole nine victories. When Commynes repeated this remark to Louis, the king forthwith invited Bretaylle to dinner and offered him large inducements to leave Edward's service and enter his; and though Bretaylle declined to change his allegiance, Louis pressed a gift of a thousand crowns on him and promised to do great things for his brothers, who, unlike him, had never deserted Gascony for England, while Commynes begged him in a whisper, as he was leaving, to use his influence towards the continuance of the good understanding now established between the kings of England and France.[1]

Bretaylle's prediction that the French would laugh at the foes they had vanquished so easily very quickly came true. Louis himself was already laughing in his sleeve and boasting about how much more successful he was in driving the English out of France than his father had been, since his father had had to fight them, whereas the only weapons he had employed were venison pasties and fine wines.[2] Yet in reality it had cost Louis a good deal more than venison pasties and fine wines to get rid of Edward and his army. His jest, like many another, was more witty than true. For he had had to bestow generous pensions not only on Edward himself but on Edward's chief friends and councillors. With Edward's full knowledge and consent, apparently, Rotherham, chancellor of England, accepted from the king of France a pension of a thousand crowns a year, Doctor John Morton, Master of the Rolls, one of six hundred crowns, and Lord Howard and Sir Thomas Montgomery each one of twelve hundred crowns. But the largest pension of all, next to Edward's own, went to Lord Hastings. The influence which Hastings exercised over his royal master was fully understood by the king of France as well as by the Duke of Burgundy, and as Charles was already paying the lord chamberlain a thousand crowns a year, Louis promised him two thousand a year. Proof of all this is furnished not simply by the statement of Commynes, who makes some errors concerning the amounts of the different pensions, but by the accounts of Jean Restout, merchant of Rouen, whom Louis sent to London in 1476, 1477 and 1478 to pay the pensions, King Edward's as well as the others.[3]

---

1. Commynes, I, 321-322.
2. *Chron. Scandaleuse*, II, 344.
3. Compte de Guillaume Restout commis par le roi Louis XI pour payer certaines sommes au Roi d'Angleterre et ses officiers pour les années 1476, 1477, 1478. MS. français 10,375,

According to Commynes, the Marquis of Dorset, Sir John Cheyne, and Thomas St Leger were also promised pensions, but if that is true, the money was delivered to them in some other way than through the hands of Restout, as their names do not appear in his accounts.

Even these pensions were not the only gifts Louis had had to make in order to send the English home without fighting and in a good humour with him. He had also distributed presents of plate and other valuables with the same generosity he had displayed at the time of Warwick's visit to him at Rouen. Even the Duke of Gloucester, who to the end had stood out against making peace, consented to visit Louis at Amiens and to accept from him gifts of plate and richly caparisoned horses. Clarence too was remembered, and Commynes states that in less than two years' time Lord Howard received from Louis, in addition to his pension, as much as twenty-four thousand crowns in money and plate, and that Lord Hastings gathered in at one sweep a thousand marks' worth of plate. The English chronicler, Fabyan, was also impressed by Hastings's good luck. He says the lord chamberlain came home from France with no less than twenty-four dozen bowls, "whereof half were gilt and half white" and which weighed "upon seventeen nobles every cup or more." And of course Louis had not forgotten to reward the heralds and trumpeters, who received their donation with cries of "Largesse an très noble et puissant roy de France! Largesse! Largesse!"[2]

But anxious as he was to please the English in every way, Louis appears to have found it impossible to lay his hands on the entire seventy-five thousand crowns he had agreed to pay Edward before the English army took its departure. In the end he seems to have offered fifty-five thousand crowns in cash and a promise, given under the great seal of France and his sign-manual, that the remaining twenty thousand crowns should be paid within a certain brief time.[2] With this pledge Edward had to be content and, escorted by the Bishop of Evreux as Louis' representative, he departed for Calais with his army. Only the hostages, Lord Howard and Sir John Cheyne,

---

ff. 1-27. This is the original account, written on parchment. It has been briefly referred to by M. Mandrot, Commynes, I, 307, notes 1-3.

1. Commynes, I, 307, 319, II, 3-4; Fabyan, 665; *Chron. Scandaleuse*, I, 344-345.

2. This seems to be the most likely explanation of the sending of twenty thousand crowns by Louis to Edward in October. See later.

remained behind, and as they were sent to Paris for a week's festivities and afterwards entertained in Louis' household, they probably did not regret that it had fallen to their lot to stay a little longer in France.[1]

On the way back to Calais, some of Edward's soldiers indulged in a little plundering, and the inhabitants of the county of Boulogne, who, being near neighbours of Calais, already had an accumulation of grievances against the English, took what revenge they could. But the king marched as rapidly as possible, as he had no desire to linger in the territory of the Duke of Burgundy, who was not to be appeased by his apologies—scarcely due under the circumstances—and expressions of desire for continued friendship.[2] Yet Charles was glad to take into his service some two thousand or more English soldiers who disliked to go home without seeing some real fighting. It was better for these men to be fighting the French than to be cutting one another's throats in England, was the excuse the duke gave at the time for this inconsistency, but not long after he told Panicharolla, who asked him "how he stood with the king of England," that Edward was afraid of him, in fact, hated him, on account of his claim to the English crown. "For he has a most just title to the succession, and much better than the king's," explained Panicharolla, who seemed to think that the duke would attempt to enforce his claim "once things have settled down a little," and that it was in order to win popularity in England, "in which, he says, he has a strong party and is much beloved," that he was taking English soldiers into his service. "Once he has that kingdom, he need only lift his other shoulder and forthwith he would be king of France."[3]

Edward and his army reached Calais on 4 September, the very day on which the truce between France and England was being published in Paris, and the king at once set about transporting his troops back to England.[4] But he himself

---

1. *Chron. Scandaleuse*, I, 345-346.
2. It was told that Charles tore up the Garter with his teeth when he heard of the treaty between Edward and Louis. *Cal. Milanese Papers*, I, 216.
3. *Ibid.*, I, 217-218, 221. According to Commynes, I, 266, Charles had three thousand English soldiers in his service about this time. Sir John Middleton, Thomas Stanley, and "Talbot" are mentioned as the captains of these men. Molinet, I, 35, 40; Commynes-Lenglet, II, 214. On 21 March 1476, Paston wrote that Sir John Middleton had taken leave of the Duke of Burgundy "to sport him, but he is set in prison at Brisach." *Paston Letters*, I, 259.
4. *Paston Letters*, V, 237; *Chron. Scandaleuse*, I, 344, and note; Molinet, I, c. xviii.

remained at Calais until sometime after 18 September,[1] and while he was still there, he received a letter from the Count of St Pol. Frightened by his failure to prevent the treaty between Edward and Louis, St Pol had tried to curry favour with Louis by offering to persuade the Duke of Burgundy to help destroy Edward and his whole army. The only reply Louis had made to him, however, was that his proposal came too late, and now, boiling with wrath, the count found such consolation as he could in writing to Edward that, by making peace with Louis, he had shown himself a poor, dishonourable, cowardly king and that he would soon find out that Louis had hoodwinked him. Edward had no need to make answer to this taunt. He sent the count's letter to Louis, who soon settled everyone's account with the deceiver. For though St Pol fled to the Duke of Burgundy for protection, Charles handed him over to Louis, and on 19 December he was beheaded as a traitor after being tried before the Parliament of Paris.[2]

Although St Pol's vituperative letter caused Edward no concern, the days the king spent at Calais were not happy ones. Charles had proudly asserted that he would sign no truce with the king of France for three months after the English army went home, but not long afterwards he told Panicharolla that, if he did not have help, he would have to make peace with Louis as the English had done.[3] And, as it turned out, he was very soon offering Louis a truce. Louis took pains to have the English hostages, Howard and Cheyne, present when he received the ambassadors who brought Charles's offer,[4] and when Edward learned, as he did at Calais, that Charles was seeking to make a treaty on his own account with Louis, he was no less angry than Charles had been when he heard of the negotiations which ended in the treaty of Amiens. At the time the news reached him, Edward was on the point of sending Sir Thomas Montgomery back to Louis to make a bargain concerning Margaret of Anjou, and he immediately instructed Montgomery to beg Louis not to

---

1. Privy Seals.
2 *Chron. Scandaleuse*, I, 346 *et seq.*; Commynes, I, 330-337; Molinet, I, 178-179; Haynin, II, 292-293; Commynes-Lenglet, III, 424-426.
3. *Cal. Milanese Papers*, I, 208-209.
4. Commynes, I, 327-328. Charles drew up the treaty he was willing to sign with Louis as early as 13 September, and the truce was published on 16 October, although Commynes says the Burgundian ambassadors asked that its publication might be delayed to spare Charles's honour. Commynes-Lenglet, III, 409, *et seq.*; La Marche, III, 214 *et seq.*; *Chron. Scandaleuse*, I, 347-348.

accept a separate treaty with Charles. Commynes declares Edward's anger and excitement were so great that he even told Louis that, if he would continue to fight Charles, he would come back to France in the following summer and assist him. All that he asked in return, according to Commynes, was that Louis should pay the wages of half of his men and compensate him for what he would lose in customs receipts by the suspension of the English wool trade with Charles' territories. However, by the time Montgomery reached Vervins, where Louis was staying at the time and where the negotiations with Charles's ambassadors were taking place, the truce between Louis and Charles was already concluded, and Louis, whose chief wish was that Edward should go home and stay there, sent back only his thanks.[1]

It was on 28 September that Edward finally arrived in London. The mayor and aldermen and more than six hundred members of the guilds met him at Blackheath, and he was escorted through the city to Westminster with as much blowing of trumpets as if he had won another battle of Crecy or Agincourt.[2] Yet never before had an English army returned from France with no battles to recount and so few gaps in its ranks. Of the common soldiers who had crossed the sea with the king, only those who had entered the Duke of Burgundy's service and the few who had fallen in the foraging raid near Peronne or before the inhospitable gates of St Quentin were missing, and of those of higher rank, only Lord Howard and Sir John Cheyne, who had been left behind as hostages, and the Earl of Douglas, who, after the army returned to Calais, had obtained permission "to do certain pilgrimages at ye high court of Rome and other places" for the weal of his soul.[3] No, one other man had failed to return. The Duke of Exeter, whose wife, King Edward's sister, had long since obtained a divorce from him and married Thomas St Leger, had been a prisoner in the Tower as late as 16 May 1475,[4] but he had probably won his liberty soon after that date by offering to join the expedition to France. At any rate, he had accompanied Edward across the sea, and while the king's troops were voyaging homeward, he was "found dead, as it was said, between Dover and Calais." Fabyan says that how the

1. Commynes, I, 329-330.
2. London Journal 8, f. 110b; Sharpe, I, 318; Fabyan, 665; Kingsford's *London Chron.*, 387.
3. Signed Bills, file 1511, no. 4802, 8 Sept.
4. An allowance of 6s 8d was made for his "diets" in the Tower on Whit Sunday, 16 May. Tellers' Roll, Easter 15 Edw. IV.

duke was drowned "the certainty is not known," but the Duke of Burgundy told Panicharolla that the king of England had his one-time brother-in-law thrown into the sea. As Charles was in a venomous mood towards Edward, he may have invented this tale, but the fact remains that Polydore Vergil too intimates that Exeter was helped to his death.[1]

Nor did the two thousand archers who had gone with Audley and Duras to Brittany come home with any heroes to mourn or any laurels to display. Anxious to throw the blame for the fiasco in which the invasion of France had ended on to other shoulders than his own, Charles gave Panicharolla to understand that Francis had refused to accept the English archers after he had asked for them, and that this was why the English grew suspicious and abandoned their entire enterprise.[2] Charles may also have been responsible for an apparently false story, reported to Louis by Bourré the day before the treaty of Amiens was signed, that Audley and Duras had made a descent on St Malo.[3] For although Edward felt that Francis as well as Charles had deserted him, the replies he had made to Louis about Francis showed that he had no quarrel with the duke. Francis, like Charles, hastened to make his peace with Louis as soon as Edward had gone home, and in the treaty he signed on 9 October he renounced, without mentioning names, all alliances he had formed against France.[4] But such renunciations did not mean much, especially when made by Francis. Only a few days before, on 28 September, the duke had written to Edward expressing his intention to keep "loyally" his thirty years' truce and intercourse of merchandise with him, no matter what happened, and his belief that Edward would wish to do the same. Francis sent his letter to England by Morice Gourmel, whom he described as "mon secrétaire et bien sear serviteur que ray autrefois envoié devers vous," and with Gourmel travelled home Lord Duras and Oliver King.[5] Lord Audley and the two thousand archers had probably already gone back to England.

---

1. Fabyan, 663; Kingsford's *London Chron.*, 186; *Cal. Milanese Papers*, I, 220; Vergil, 678. Both Fabyan and Kingsford's *London Chronicle* put Exeter's death in the wrong year. The Duchess of Exeter died a few months after her former husband, on 14 January 1476. Inquisitions *post mortem*, 35 Edw. IV, no. 36; *Paston Letters*, V, 250.
2. *Cal. Milanese Papers*, I, 208.
3. MS. français 20,489, f. 29.
4. Commynes-Lenglet, III, 430 *et seq.*; *Chron. Scandaleuse*, I, 347.
4. Cotton MS. Vespasian F III, f. 26b. Edward gave Gourmel £6 13s 4d. Tellers Roll, Mich. 15 Edw. IV.

BOOK V

LOUIS XI's PENSIONER

1

A QUIET YEAR

The great expedition to France was over and not an inch of territory had
been conquered. According to Hall, Edward had picked up the tertian ague
during his absence to be a plague to him as long as he lived,[1] and for all the
money he had squeezed out of his subjects for the war he had come home
with nothing to show, which he dared announce, except a seven years' truce
with France with intercourse of merchandise. No wonder he had dreaded the
reception awaiting him in England! Of course those who had suspected that
the only reason why he talked about invading France was that he wanted an
excuse for extorting money could now boast of their wisdom; and if some of
Louis' subjects thought their king had agreed to concessions derogatory to the
honour and dignity of France,[2] more of Edward's subjects felt that the treaty
of Amiens was a disgrace to England and to England's king. Those who had
accepted Louis' money insisted on calling their pensions "tribute money,"[3] and
Edward lamely explained that, "after many great and importable charges and
expenses in our last voyage by us borne and sustained, which were indeed more
greater than any man could of likelihood have esteemed before," God had been
pleased to put into the mind of Louis of France to offer him "a good and an
honourable appointment" which he hoped would prove to be "for the universal
weal and profit of us and of all our subjects, as well by free communication and
intercourse of merchandise to be had betwixt both parties as in many other
wises."[4] But no words could hide the truth. Edward had sold himself to the king
of France, and if the treaty of amity had been made known at the moment of

---

1. Hall, 338.
2. Molinet.
3. Commynes, I, 328, II, 3.
4. *Records of the Borough of Nottingham*, II, 388-389.

his home-coming, possibly the prediction of one who had heard from afar of the proposed marriage between the Dauphin of France and Elizabeth of York that Edward would be "torn to pieces the moment he returned to England"[1] would have been fulfilled. Even the truce with intercourse of merchandise, which Edward tried to think was for the profit of his people, bore much less resemblance to what his subjects had hoped for than to what Louis had long desired and had so nearly obtained at one time through the Earl of Warwick. For the people of England had not given their money to buy a chance to trade freely with France for the next seven years, but to recover the rich provinces beyond the sea which Henry VI had lost.

Panicharolla stated in a letter he wrote the day before Edward reached London that the Duke of Burgundy asserted he was "advised from England that the people there are extremely irritated at this accord, cowardly as it is, because they paid large sums of money without any results," and that King Edward "did not want his brothers to proceed to England before him, as he feared some disturbance, especially as the Duke of Clarence, on a previous occasion, aspired to make himself king."[2] Yet though Charles was evidently trying to comfort himself with the belief that Edward would have trouble when he reached home—in fact, Panicharolla added, "I gather that some revolution would give secret satisfaction to the duke here"—no rebellion occurred in England. No doubt Clarence would have been found to be just as ready as before to snatch at his brother's throne, but the people of England were heartily tired of civil war, and when Edward, eight days after his inglorious return to London, remitted a part of the last war grant made to him, the three quarters of a fifteenth and tenth which was to be paid at Martinmas,[3] they seem to have preferred to let bygones be bygones rather than repeat the events of 1470–1471.

Edward probably gave up the three quarters of a fifteenth and tenth with regret, but considering the possible results of an attempt to collect it, and also considering Louis' readiness to pour money into his pocket, the sacrifice was not a great one. Already Louis' treasurer of war, Noel le Barge, was starting for England with twenty thousand crowns, probably a part of

---

1. *Cal. Milanese Papers*, I, 211
2. *Ibid.* 217.
3. *Records of the Borough of Nottingham, ut sup.*; Ramsay, II, 414.

the seventy-five thousand crowns which Louis ought to have paid before the English army turned homewards; and for this money Edward gave a receipt on 22 October sealed with England's great seal.[1] Howard, Cheyne, and Montgomery, moreover, were now on their way home, and they were bringing with them not only the presents of gold and silver plate which Louis had bestowed on themselves,[2] but a promise from the French king that he would ransom Margaret of Anjou for fifty thousand crowns. According to the agreement Howard and Montgomery had made, Edward was to receive ten thousand crowns, as well as Louis' "obligation and seal" for the payment of the remaining forty thousand crowns, at the time Margaret was handed over, and ten thousand crowns every Michaelmas Day thereafter until the full amount of the ransom had been paid; and Louis was also to give another "seal" promising that he would not let Margaret pass from his hands until she had delivered to the king of England "letters of renunciation" drawn up according to the directions of Edward's council and containing her renunciation of all title to the crown of England and to all rights of dower or other claims which she might be able to advance against Edward. All that Edward was required to do on his part was to renounce his rights over the queen and her belongings and to promise not to hinder Louis' designs by aiding or countenancing any person who might try to lay claim to her possessions.[3]

Almost at once after his return from France, Edward issued a proclamation giving his people notice that, in spite of the new truce "with the whole intercourse of merchandise" which had been signed with France, all persons born under his "obeissance" were still forbidden to buy or even to house any wines of Gascony, Guienne, Bordeaux, or Bayonne which had been brought to England in ships not owned by Englishmen.[4] Perhaps because of this proclamation, English merchants who hurried to Bordeaux to trade found that they were not going to enjoy all the privileges they thought they were entitled to under the new truce. At any rate, it was found necessary to send Montgomery back to Louis to make a protest regarding the treatment English

---

1. Close Roll 15 Edw. IV, m. 16 dorso. (See Appendix IX).
2. Commynes, I, 330; *Chron. Scandaleuse*, I, 347.
3. *Lettres de rois, reines, etc. des cours de France et d'Angleterre*, II, 493494 (from Cotton MS. Vespasian F III, f. 30).
4. Writs of Privy Seal, file 854, no. 4238, 12 Oct., 1475; Exchequer T. R., Council and Privy Seal, file 91, m. 36. Cf. Hist. MSS. Com., *Report 5*, app., 494.

merchants were receiving at Bordeaux, and Edward decided that Margaret of Anjou should accompany Montgomery to France. On 13 November the king renounced all his rights over Margaret and authorized Thomas Thwaytes, in whose custody she seems to have been at the moment, to deliver her to Montgomery, and Montgomery to deliver her to the French king.[1] Not long after Richard Haute conducted the queen to Sandwich,[2] and from there she was taken to France. On 8 January 1476, Montgomery obtained from Louis, in addition to a proclamation forbidding acts of hostility at sea, a decree relieving English merchants going to Bordeaux from the need of showing safeconducts, exempting them from the larger part of the port and other dues, and reducing the customs they were required to pay;[3] and three weeks later, at Rouen, he surrendered Margaret to the Seigneur de Genlis, captain of Rouen, and Jean Raguier, receiver general of Normandy, after he had received from them the first ten thousand crowns of the queen's ransom and Louis' bond for the remaining forty thousand crowns.[4]

On the day on which she passed into Louis' hands, "Margaret, daughter of the king of Sicily," made the promised renunciation of all her rights and claims in England, and the receipt of this document Montgomery acknowledged on the following day.[5] But René of Anjou's daughter found that this was not the only renunciation she would be obliged to sign. Louis as well as Edward had to be paid, and on 7 March Margaret renounced in Louis' favour—to compensate him, as he claimed, for what he had spent in trying to assist her to recover the kingdom of England for her husband and her son, as well as for what he had undertaken to pay to ransom her—all rights which she inherited from her mother in the duchy of Lorraine and from her father in Anjou, Bar,

---

1. Signed Bills, file 1511, no. 4816 (see Appendix X); *Cal. Patent Rolls*, II, 571; Rymer, XII, 22.
2. Tellers' Roll, Easter 15 Edw. IV. Haute, whose mother was a sister of the first Earl Rivers, was beheaded at Pontefract by Richard III at the same time that Anthony, Earl Rivers was beheaded. Nichols, *Grants of King Edward the Fifth*, xvi, note. Anne Haute, whom Sir John Paston at one time thought of marrying, was his sister.
3. *Ordonnances des rois de France*, XVIII, 160-166; Royal MS. 13 B XI, f. 37b; Palgrave, *Kalendars of Exchequer*, III, 23.
4. *Record Transcripts*, series II, no. 136 (from Archives du Royaume, Trésor des chartres, J. 648-8); Legrand collections, MS. français 6982, f. 235 dorso *et seq.* (an extract from the account of Pierre Parent, 1476).
5. Record Transcripts, *ut sup*. (from Archives du Royaume, Trésor des chartres, suppl. J 922 and J 648-10).

and Provence.[1] Even with this Louis felt that he had been poorly paid, in as much as the duchy of Lorraine was at present in the hands of the Duke of Burgundy, and René of Anjou still lived to enjoy his rights in Anjou, Bar, and Provence; and though he granted Margaret a pension of six thousand livres,[2] he seems to have treated her with scant courtesy. "The Duke of Bourgogne hath conquered Lorraine," wrote Paston, "and Queen Margaret shall not now by likelihood have it; wherefore the French king cherisheth her but easily."[3] Ultimately Margaret retired to her father's estates, and there she spent the remaining six years of her life. Her father did what he could for her while he lived, but after he died in the summer of 1480, Louis' pension was her entire fortune; and when at last, in August 1482, death came to her relief, in her will, of which the faithful Katharine Vaux was one of the witnesses, she requested Louis, as her sole heir and chief executor, to permit her body to be interred in the cathedral of Angers near the tombs of her ancestors and, in case "le petit de biens" which God and he had given her did not suffice to pay all her debts, to provide for the payment of the rest of them for his soul's sake and hers.[4] "Madame," wrote Louis to Madame de Montsereau as soon as he heard that the widow of Henry VI had gone to her last accounting, "I am sending to you my equerry, Jean de Chasteaudreux, to bring me all the dogs you have had from the late queen of England. You know she has made me her heir, and that this is all I shall get; also it is what I love best. I pray you not to keep any back, for you would cause me a terribly great displeasure; but if you know of anyone who has any of them, tell Chasteaudreux."[5] With these heartless words the curtain drops on the tragic life-story of Margaret of Anjou.

The large sums of money which Edward received from Louis—the sums he was paid at the time of the signing of the treaty of Amiens, his pension, and Margaret's ransom—did not enrich England, but they must have contributed

---

1. Commynes-Lenglet, III, 473. Margaret had to repeat this renunciation after her father's death. *Ibid.*, 479.
2. For a copy of a receipt which Margaret gave for her pension on 2 February 1482, see *Record Transcripts*, series II, no. 138 (from Cabinet de Titres de la Bibliothèque du Roi). Cf. *Chron. Scandaleuse*, II, 15, and Legrand coll., MS. français 6983, f. 204.
3. *Paston Letters*, V, 258.
4. *Lettres de Louis XI*, IX, 276, note 2; Lecoy de la Marche, *Le Roi René*, II, 395-397. Margaret's will is dated 2 August 1482.
5. *Lettres de Louis XI*, IX, 276.

very materially to the building up of the splendid fortune which the king possessed in his later years and which enabled him, the chronicler of Croyland Abbey tells us, to outdo all his predecessors on the throne in the collection of gold and silver vessels, tapestries, and other *objets d'arts*, in the erection of costly buildings, and in the acquisition of lands and other property.[1] It was not alone to the flow of gold from Louis' treasury, however, that Edward owed his rapidly increasing wealth. He had wanted his subjects to believe that lack of sufficient money was the real cause of his failure to conquer France, and as if he were determined that such lack should never spoil his plans again, he renounced the spendthrift ways of his earlier years and "began to slide by little and little into avarice."[2] At the same time he seems to have extended greatly the commercial "adventures" in which he had been engaged more or less from the early years of his reign, if not from the day of his accession, and, according to the Croyland chronicler again, he collected the customs more carefully than they had ever been collected before and secured large amounts of money by imposing, through the courts, heavy fines on persons who had entered into estates without strict conformity to forgotten or generally unheeded laws. The same chronicler also declares that the king kept the revenues of vacant benefices in his own hands until their surrender was purchased from him by the payment of a fixed sum, but the justice of this accusation may perhaps be challenged.[3]

Edward's growing wealth did not only enable him to purchase land and to indulge his fondness for things of beauty. It also enabled him to avoid making those frequent appeals to his subjects for money which had probably been no less distasteful to him than irritating to them. And with this source of ill-will removed, he soon recovered the affection of his people in spite of the disgust they had felt when they heard how the French expedition had ended. Unfortunately, however, prosperity always brings its temptations,

---

1. *Hist. Croy. Cont.*, 559.
2. Vergil (Camden Society), 172.
3. *Hist. Croy. Cont., ut sup.* So far as the bishoprics were concerned, the only temporalities which Edward retained for more than a few months were those of St Asaph, whose bishop was deprived of his see for treason in 1463, those of Durham, which he kept in his hands from December 1462, till April 1464, became Lawrence Booth was suspected of being in league with Margaret of Anjou, those of Bath and Wells, which he held from January 1465, to January 1466, because the first man elected to succeed Thomas Beckynton died before he was consecrated, and those of the archbishopric of York, which were seized when George Neville was arrested and imprisoned.

and now that his financial worries were over, peace signed with the king of France, his only dangerous foe, and his throne practically safe from attack, Edward gave himself up to the life of ease and pleasure which Louis XI had already decided he coveted more than anything else in the world. Commynes goes so far as to declare of Edward that "nul autre chose il n'avoit eu en pensée que aux dames, et trop plus que de raison, et aux chasses, et à bien tracter sa personne"; and even the Croyland chronicler, who praises the king as a good Catholic, an enemy to heretics, and a promoter of learning, admits that he was given to debauchery and sensuality.[1] On the other hand, Sir Thomas More claims that Edward's "fleshly wantonness" did not grieve his people very much, and that in his later days it was "lessed and well left."

How much truth, if any, there was in the story of Edward's seduction, by means of a promise of marriage, of Lady Eleanor Butler, daughter of the late Earl of Shrewsbury, which was told after his death by Robert Stillington and used with such dire effect against his children by the Duke of Gloucester,[2] it is impossible to say. And concerning the king's relations with Lady Elizabeth Lucy nothing is known beyond the fact that she was probably the mother of his natural son, Arthur, and also of his natural daughter, Elizabeth, who seems to have been born about the time of his marriage to Elizabeth Woodville and who in after years became the wife of Sir Thomas Lumley.[3] But of Edward's love for another woman who was not his wife we know somewhat more. "King Edward would say that he had three concubines which in diverse properties diversely excelled, one the merriest, the other the wiliest, the third the holiest harlot in the realm";[4] and though Hall, who wrote these words, mentions no names, there is little doubt that the merry concubine was Jane Shore, a woman who will always be remembered because of her unhappy history after Edward's death, because of the tribute paid to her goodness of heart by Sir Thomas More, who knew her personally after age and misfortune had robbed her of her beauty, and because of the old ballad, "The Woefull Lamentation of Jane Shore, a Goldsmith's Wife of London, sometime King Edward IV his Concubine."

Jane Shore was the wife, not of a London goldsmith, as the ballad says, but of a London mercer, who was sufficiently well-to-do to make a considerable loan to

---

1. Commynes, I, 207; *Hist. Croy. Cont.*, 564.
2. *Rolls of Parl.*, VI, 241; *Hist. Croy. Cont.*, 566.
3. More, *Hist. of Richard III*, 61-62; Sandford, 425.
4. Hall, 363.

her paramour at the time of the expedition to France;[1] and her liaison with Edward seems to have been formed in the latter part of his reign and, when once begun, to have lasted to the end of his days. It may even have been one of the causes of that lessening of the king's "fleshly wantonness" of which Sir Thomas More speaks. At all events, Jane Shore's love was certainly not the least good influence that came into Edward's life. "This woman was born in London," More writes:

> worshipfully friended, honestly brought up, and very well married, saving somewhat too soon, her husband an honest citizen, young and goodly and of good substance. Proper she was and fair; nothing in her body that you would have changed but if you would have wished her somewhat higher. Thus say they that knew her in her youth, albeit some that now see her (for yet she liveth) deem her never to have been well visaged.

Yet men delighted not so much in her beauty

> as in her pleasant behaviour. For a proper wit had she, and could both read well and write, merry in company, ready and quick of answer, neither mute nor full of babble, sometime taunting without displeasure and not without disport.

And what was better even than her wit was the warmth of her heart and her sympathy for those in trouble.

> Where the king took displeasure, she would mitigate and appease his mind; where men were out of favour, she would bring them in his grace. For many that had highly offended she obtained pardon; of great forfeitures she got men remission; and, finally, in many weighty suits she stood many men in great stead, either for none or very small rewards, and those rather gay than rich; either for that she was content with the deed self well done, or for that she delighted to be sued unto and to show what she was able to do with the king, or for that wanton women and wealthy be not alway covetous.[2]

> Long time I lived in the courte,
> With lords and ladies of great sorte;
> And when I smil'd all men were glad,
> But when I frown'd my prince grewe sad.

---

1. Tellers' Roll, Easter 14 Edw. IV. In a general pardon granted to Shore on 24 December 1471, he is described as a citizen and mercer of London, alias late of Derby, yeoman. Pardon Roll ix Edw. IV, m. 28.
2. More, *Hist. of Richard III*, 54-55.

But yet a gentle mind I bore
To helplesse people that were poore;
I still redrest the orphan's crye,
And saved their lives condemned to dye.

I still had ruth on widowes tears,
I succour'd babes of tender yeares;
And never looked for other gaine,
But love and thankes for all my pain.[1]

Few events of interest occurred in England during the months immediately following the return of the king and his army from France, or during the subsequent year. The child the queen was carrying at the time the king went to France was born at Westminster, on 2 November, and as the gods had again seen fit to send a daughter, the infant was given the name of Anne and was soon put up in the matrimonial market like her older sisters.[2] But the king's children were so numerous now that the advent of another was not an exciting event, and soon after the queen's confinement Edward left Westminster to spend several weeks "ministering justice of our law" in Hampshire and Wiltshire.[3] The king did his work thoroughly, not even sparing his own servants from instant hanging if they were found guilty of murder or theft,[4] but it was impossible to undo at once the results of the letting loose upon the country of thousands of soldiers whose appetite for adventure and for plunder had been whetted without being satisfied by the expedition to France. The whole kingdom was so infested with thieves that neither the merchant taking his goods to market nor the pilgrim carrying pious offerings to the shrine of saint or martyr was safe on the highways.[5] It was a noticeable fact, too,

---

1. *The Woefull Lamentation of Jane Shore, a Goldsmith's Wife in London, sometime King Edward IV his Concubine*. Printed from a black-letter copy in the Pepys Collection for William Cole. (London).

2. Madden. *Gent. Mag.*, Jan., 1831; Stow, 429; Green, *Princesses of Eng.*, IV, *et seq*. In the end Anne of York married Lord Thomas Howard, son of the Earl of Surrey, and of the children she bore to this husband only one lived long enough to be carried to the baptismal font. She herself, though she lived to see Henry VIII ascend the throne, died at the age of thirty-seven or thirty-eight.

3. Cotton MS. Vespasian. C XIV, f. 572—a writ of supersedeas dated 28 November 1476; Privy Seals.

4. *Hist. Croy. Cont.*, 559.

5. *Ibid.*

that conditions were worst in the old centres of Lancastrian activity, in the northern counties and in Wales and the Welsh marches. At the beginning of January a commission of oyer and terminer, with authority to array men-at-arms and archers if necessary, was sent to the Prince of Wales, and the king planned to go to Wales after Easter to consult with the Prince's council and to assist the lords of the marches to punish crime. The journey to Wales evidently proved to be unnecessary, as in the end it was abandoned and the king spent the spring at Windsor, Westminster, and Greenwich; but in March the Duke of Gloucester and the Earl of Northumberland had to be sent to Yorkshire with a strong force—as many as five thousand men, according to the records of the city of York—to restore order in that neighbourhood.[1]

Just what happened in Yorkshire to call for the sending of so large a body of troops there is nothing to show, but it is worthy of note not only that the Croyland chronicler, when speaking of the events of this year, remarks that Edward knew well how easily his subjects might be led to thirst for change and to rise in rebellion if a suitable leader presented himself, but that Panicharolla kept writing that the men about the Duke of Burgundy were looking for a disturbance in England "because the king exacted a great treasure and did nothing" and in one letter stated plainly that Charles "foments this all he can."[2] Perhaps Charles was actually planning to lay claim to Edward's throne as soon as the disastrous war in which he was now engaged with the Swiss was over, and perhaps Edward was aware of the fact and believed the duke to be implicated in the present troubles in his kingdom. For though Edward continued to write pleasant letters to Charles and even paid him, on 4 May 1476, sixteen thousand crowns of what he still owed him for the Duchess Margaret's dowry,[3] it is clear that he was glad to do the duke an ill turn when he could. When, in March, a Milanese envoy came to him to take his leave,

---

1. *Cal. Patent Rolls*, II, 574; Privy Seals; Stow, 429-430; Davies, *York Records*, 50-52.
2. *Hist. Croy. Cont., ut sup.*; *Cal. Milanese Papers*, I, 218. About this time it was reported that another large body of English archers was going "to the pay" of Charles. *Ibid.*, 222. Probably Thomas Everingham was the captain of these men, as he was with Charles at the fatal siege of Nancy. Early Chancery Proceedings, bundle 60, no. 167.
3. Chancery Diplomatic Documents, Foreign, no. 530—two receipts, each for eight thousand crowns, given on 4 May by Nicolas de Goudeval. Panicharolla wrote on 3 May that Charles had received a very gracious letter from Edward, saying that he was sending Lancaster King-of-Arms "to impart certain matters," and that it was thought the English and the French would not long remain friends. *Cal. Milanese Papers*, I, 226.

Edward drew the man aside and told him to tell the Duke of Milan that the Duke of Burgundy had proposed to the king of France to conquer Milan for the Duke of Orleans and had said that his real purpose in attacking the Swiss was to find an excuse for getting as near to the Milanese border as possible.[1] Nor was this probably the beginning of Edward's effort to sever the alliance which Charles and Sforza had signed in January 1475.[2] A few months earlier Earl Rivers had set out on a journey to Italy, and though he went mainly for pleasure, he had carried a letter of introduction to the Duke of Milan with which Edward had provided him[3] and which was probably intended to pave the way for something more than sightseeing.

Rivers visited not only Milan during his tour but the other famous cities of Italy. His impression of that lovely land was marred, however, by an encounter, not far from Rome, with some highwaymen, who robbed him of his jewels and plate "worth a thousand mark or better." Queen Elizabeth hastened to send her brother a letter of exchange for four thousand ducats, but he still grieved over the loss of his jewels, and when he heard that some of them had been sold in Venice, he hurried thither and explained the situation to the Venetian senate, which decreed that, out of consideration for the king of England, the earl's property should be gratuitously restored to him.[5] After his stay in Venice, Rivers left Italy, and on 6 June this hero of tournaments arrived at the camp of the Duke of Burgundy and immediately offered his services to Charles, who was then advancing on Morat. Two days later, however, when he found that "the froward carls," as Paston called the Swiss, were close at hand and that there was likely to be bloodshed, he suddenly took his departure with many expressions of regret.[6] Charles laughed when the earl left and declared that the queen of England's brother was scared, but probably Rivers never felt sorry that he had not lingered to take part in the battle of Morat, as Charles was soundly beaten.

The Duke of Burgundy was not the only pretender to his throne whom

---

1. Gingins la Sarra, I, 345-346; *Cal. Milanese Papers*, I, 222-223.
2. Perret, *Relations de la France avec Venise*, II 39-40.
3. *Cal. Milanese Papers*, I, 217; *Hist. MSS. Com., Report 9*, app. II, 411.
4. *Paston Letters*, V, 258.
5. *Cal. Milanese Papers*, I, 222; *Cal. Venetian Papers*, I, 136.
6. Gingins la Sarra II 233. 235-236; *Cal. Milanese Papers* I, 227-228; Commynes-Lenglet, II, 219.

Edward had on his mind. The Duke of Brittany had promised him that the Earl of Richmond should be too well guarded to be able to do him any harm, but in spite of that he would have much preferred to have the son of Margaret Beaufort in his own hands, and he hoped that he could yet persuade Francis to surrender the earl to him. Very soon after Oliver King came home with the letter in which Francis expressed his determination to stick to his thirty years' mercantile treaty with England, he was sent back to Brittany not only to obtain an actual renewal of the treaty from Francis, but to call the duke's attention to another matter. To a degree King's second journey to Brittany was successful, for on 22 January 1476, Francis renewed the thirty years' treaty;[1] but when the duke was reminded that the troops Edward had sent to Brittany both in the past summer and in 1468 had cost him much money and was told that the king thought he ought to be recompensed, he showed no inclination to acknowledge his debt. On the contrary, he sent Morice Gourmel to England again to present claims for damages, for breaches of the truce amounting to fifty thousand crowns! It may be that Francis had justice on his side, as Edward finally consented to call the account even and, after mutual releases had been exchanged, on 16 March, in his turn confirmed the thirty years' treaty.[2] In any case, there was no complaint in the polite letter Edward dispatched to Francis by the messenger who carried to Brittany his renewal of the treaty.[3] Francis, on the other hand, was troubled by the remarks which it was said some English ambassadors had made in France, and in a short time Jacques de la Villéon arrived in England to inquire about them. Edward then seized the opportunity to talk with Villéon about Richmond, and in another letter which he wrote to Francis on 18 June, he not only denied emphatically that the remarks in question had ever been made and assured the duke that he would always find the king of England his "good cousin and friend," but asked him to give credence to the messages Villéon would bring concerning "certain other matters of which I have talked to him touching the Earl of Richmond."[4]

---

1. Rymer, XII, 22.
2. Cotton MS. Julius B VI, f. 383—a letter written by Francis to Edward on 25 Jan.; Rymer, XII, 23-24.
3. Legrand coll., MS. français 6983, f. 65.
4. *Ibid.*, f. 347.

Immediately after Villéon went home, Edward left London. There was an epidemic of the "pox" in the city, but while the king no doubt shrank from contact with a disease of whose discomforts he had already had experience, it was not on account of the epidemic alone that he was forsaking London. He was going to Fotheringhay to be present at the re-interment of the bodies of his father and his brother Edmund. For more than fifteen years the Duke of York and the Earl of Rutland had been sleeping in a humble tomb at Pontefract, and Edward was anxious to give them a more suitable resting place in the church at Fotheringhay, the college of which he had re-founded and enriched with liberal gifts early in his reign.[1]

The two bodies were exhumed on 24 July, and for the remainder of that day an image of the Duke of York, garbed in an ermine trimmed mantle and a cap of maintenance of purple and ermine, and covered with a cloth of gold, lay in state in the choir of the church of Pontefract under a hearse which was blazing with candles, decked with banners and standards, and guarded by an angel of silver bearing a crown of gold as a reminder that by right the duke had been a king. When, on the following day, the long journey to Fotheringhay began, a number of ecclesiastics, including Lawrence Booth, recently elected Archbishop of York, went on in advance to see that proper preparations had been made in the several churches in which the bodies were to find temporary shelter along the way, while the Duke of Gloucester, with other lords and many officers of arms, all dressed in mourning garb, followed with the funeral chariot, which was drawn by six horses, with trappings of black charged with the arms of England and France, and preceded by a knight bearing a banner of the ducal arms. The first night was spent at Doncaster, the succeeding ones at Blyth, Tuxford, Grantham, and Stamford, and at each place the people of the neighbourhood, dressed in black, were assembled, a hearse with many candles was ready in the church, priests celebrated mass, and every person who came to do honour to the dead received a penny, every woman with child twopence. When at length, on 29 July, Fotheringhay was reached, the members of the college and many ecclesiastics went forth to meet the cortège, while the king himself, in a habit of blue and a cap of mourning furred with miniver, waited at the entrance of the churchyard with the Duke

---

1. *Cal. Patent Rolls*, I, 392, 396, 433; Charter Roll 3 Edw. IV, pt. II, m. 18-19.

of Clarence, the Marquis of Dorset, Earl Rivers, Lord Hastings, and other noblemen. Upon the arrival of the chariot at the churchyard, Edward, with tears streaming from his eyes, kissed the image of his father and followed the coffins into the church, where two hearses were waiting, one in the choir for the body of the Duke of York and one in the Lady Chapel for the body of the Earl of Rutland; and after the king had retired to his "closet" and the princes and officers of arms had stationed themselves around the hearses, masses were sung and the king's chamberlain offered for him seven pieces of cloth of gold, each piece five yards in length, and the queen's chamberlain for her one piece of the same costly material. The next day three masses, the Mass of Our Lady, the Mass of the Trinity, and the Requiem, were sung, the Bishop of Lincoln preached a "very noble sermon," and offerings were made of many more pieces of cloth of gold, of the Duke of York's coat of arms, of his shield, his sword, his helmet, and his courser, on which rode Lord Ferrers in full armour and holding in his hand an axe reversed, and lastly, by the king and queen and two of the royal princesses in person, of the mass penny. When the funeral was over, the people were admitted to the church, and it is said that before the coffins were placed in the vault which had been built under the chancel for their reception, five thousand persons came to receive the alms, while four times that number partook of the dinner which was served partly in the castle and partly in the king's tents and pavilions.[1] Clearly it was a dinner worth eating, as the menu included capons, cygnets, herons, rabbits, butter, cream, and so many other good things that the bills for it afterwards presented by John Elryngton, cofferer of the household, amounted to more than three hundred pounds.[2]

Among the many persons of distinction who witnessed the re-interment of the father and brother of the king of England and made suitable offerings were five ambassadors from foreign princes, two from the king of France,

---

1. Harleian MS. 48, ff. 78-91—an account of the re-interment written by Chester Herald. Cf. Sandford, 391-392, who, however, has made a mistake of ten years in the date of the re-interment. When the Duchess of York died, she too was buried in the vault under the chancel of Fotheringhay church, but in Reformation days the chancel was torn down and the bodies removed to the churchyard, where they remained until Queen Elizabeth ordered them to be placed in the church again.
2. Account Book of John Elymgton, Cofferer of the Household, 11-14 Edw. IV, Exchequer Accounts, bundle 412, no. 3. Cf. Warrants for Issues, 16 Edw. IV, 24 Feb.

two from the king of Denmark, and one from the king of Portugal. The nature of the errand which had brought the king of Portugal's envoy to England can only be surmised; but the probability is that he had come to say something about Alphonso's pretensions to the crown of Castile, as a year later Edward was manifesting an interest in that subject as a would-be mediator. There is no question, on the other hand, about the purpose for which the Danish ambassador had come. In the preceding summer, while Edward's attention was taken up with his expedition to France, some merchants of Hull had gone to Iceland—that possession of the Danish crown which no Englishman was suffered to approach without a special licence—and had carried off both a ship belonging to King Christian and the money which had been collected from the customs and the royal tribute. It was primarily to seek redress for this outrage that Christian had sent Lord John Peters and Matthias Hirsberg to England, but the two men were also empowered to negotiate a new treaty between England and Denmark to take the place of the one which had been signed at Hamburg in 1465 and which Edward had confirmed again as recently as 16 March. Peters and Hirsberg had arrived in England in the spring—in fact they were already on English soil when they were granted a safeconduct on 24 May—but they had some mission to perform in Scotland as well, and they probably postponed their negotiations with Edward until after their return from the court of James III, as it was not until 9 July that Edward authorized Hatclyf and Robert Bothe to treat with them. But though the Danish ambassadors followed the king of England to Fotheringhay and did honour to his dead, they seem to have received little satisfaction. They did not succeed in negotiating a new treaty between England and Denmark, and not until the following January did Edward send Clarenceux King-of-Arms to Denmark to make arrangements for a diet for the settlement of violations of the treaty of 1465 which had been agreed upon before his renewal of that treaty in March.[1]

The two ambassadors of the king of France who were present at the re-interment of the Duke of York and the Earl of Rutland were the Rouen merchant, Guillaume Restout, and Louis de Marafin, Seigneur de Notz-en-

---

1. Rymer, XII, 25, 27, 29, 39; Diplomatic Documents (Exchequer T. of R.), no. 1096; *45th Report of Deputy Keeper*, app., 335. Clarenceux was paid £26 13s 4d for his trip to Denmark. Tellers' Roll, Mich. 16 Edw. IV.

Brenne, and what they had come for was to pay the first instalment of the pensions of King Edward and his friends.[1] On 31 July, at Fotheringhay, Restout received from Edward a receipt for twenty-five thousand crowns, from the chancellor of England one for five hundred crowns, and from Doctor John Morton one for three hundred crowns. Lord Howard, whom Restout had probably seen in London on his way north, had already received his six hundred crowns on 10 July, and Sir Thomas Montgomery gave his receipt for a like amount on 6 August. When it came to Lord Hastings, however, Restout found that he would have to forego a receipt, as Hastings declared loftily that he had not asked for the money and that he did not intend that anyone should have a chance to say that the lord chamberlain of England had been a pensioner of the king of France, or that any receipts from him should ever be found in that king's *chambre des comptes*. The lord chamberlain was not too virtuous to accept the thousand crowns Restout had brought for him, but a certification by Jean Le Gouz, a notary who had accompanied Restout and Marafin to England, that the money had been delivered in his presence and by Marafin's order to Hastings's clerk, William Lauriot, was the only proof Restout had to show that Hastings's pension had been paid. Louis was greatly disappointed when he found that no receipt from the lord chamberlain was forthcoming, for, just as Hastings suspected, he was gloating over the proofs he was laying by, for the edification of future generations, of the number of great English lords who were in his pay. Nevertheless, he admired Hastings for refusing to give a receipt, and never again did he ask him for one.[2]

Edward stayed at Fotheringhay until past the middle of August, and then, after spending a few days at Nottingham, he set out for Worcestershire,[3] very likely to "minister justice of our law" again. The pox had apparently died out

---

1. Canterbury furnished six mounted men to escort Restout from that city to Rochester. *Hist. MSS. Com., Report 9*, app., 143.

2. Restout's account, MS. français 10,373. Cf. Rymer, XII, 30, and Commynes, II, 4-6. According to Commynes, it was Pierre Cléret who asked Hastings for a receipt and was refused. But Cléret accompanied Restout on his second journey to England, not his first, and on that occasion Louis gave orders that Hastings was not to be asked for a receipt, as he had refused to give one before. In March it had been reported on the continent that the lord chamberlain was dead, and Louis was suspected of having compassed his death because he had been unable to bind him to his interests! Gingins la Sarra II, 13-16.

3. Privy Seals.

in London by this time, since on 12 September Elizabeth Stonor wrote from the city to William Stonor urging him to come to London and to send her children thither, as "the pox been past out of this country and city as far as I understand, blessed be God;" and from Worcestershire the king returned slowly through Oxfordshire to Windsor. He reached Windsor on 8 October, but he seems to have hastened at once to Westminster, as Elizabeth Stonor wrote on 9 October: "Sir, the king is come to Westminster, and I understand there shall be a great council, wherefore I wot never."[1]

If Elizabeth Stonor's news was true and a great council had been summoned, Edward must have had some weighty subject to lay before the lords of his realm, as a great council was not lightly called. And what he probably wanted to consult the lords about was the desirability of accepting a Spanish wife for his eldest son. For a Spanish ambassador was in England about this time; Thomas Langton was sent to Spain late in November to seek a confirmation of the existing treaty between England and Castile, and a marriage between the Prince of Wales and the Infanta Isabella, daughter of Ferdinand of Aragon and Isabella of Castile, was under consideration during the winter.[2] But there was another matter as well about which the king ought to have been seeking advice. Great misfortunes were befalling the Duke of Burgundy in his war with the Swiss, and, little love as Edward felt for Charles, he must have realized that if the duke met with any overwhelming disaster, a new situation would be created in Europe the outcome of which no man could foresee. At the same time the merchants of England were once more urging a settlement of the differences with Burgundy which had been discussed again and again in the diets at Bruges, and on 12 September Scott, Hatclyf, Doctor John Coke, Thomas Thwaytes, and William Rosse had been commissioned to cross the sea to treat with Charles's chancellor, Guillaume Hugonet.[3]

Not all the lords of England combined, however, were wise enough to foretell what Charles's stubbornness would wreck next or to suggest any means whereby Hugonet and the Flemish burghers could be persuaded to

---

1. *Stonor Letters and Papers*, II, 10-12.
2. Rymer, XII, 36; French Roll 16 Edw. IV, m. 9—a licence granted on 22 November, at the request of Galfrid de Sasula, ambassador of the king of Spain, to Bertram Dartigra to export 200 quarters of grain in the *Saint James*, probably the ship which had brought the Spanish ambassador to England.
3. French Roll 16 Edw. IV, m. 3-6; Rymer, XII, 32.

yield what they did not want to yield. It was the middle of December, by which time Charles had been engaged for nearly two months in his second siege of Nancy, before the English ambassadors came home from Bruges, and even then they had to confess that they had accomplished very little. Apparently the revocation of the edict against English cloth was as far away as ever, and although some kind of an agreement had been made about a staple for Newcastle wool, two demands of the Newcastle wool merchants— that the Duke of Burgundy should excuse them from the payment of tolls and that reparation for certain injuries of which the duke's subjects complained should not be exacted from them—had been left "in suspense."[1]

Even less satisfactory than the results of this effort to remove some of the causes of friction between England and Burgundy was the outcome of Edward's attempt to persuade the Duke of Brittany to surrender the Earl of Richmond. Since Jacques de la Villéon had reported to Francis what Edward had said to him about Richmond, Morice Gourmel had been going back and forth between Brittany and England carrying letters, and on 3 October Francis once more confirmed the thirty years' treaty.[2] But Henry Tudor was still in Brittany. Polydore Vergil says—and as his history was written at the request of Henry VII he should be a good authority on all facts connected with Henry's life—that Edward ultimately sent some ambassadors to Francis with a direct request for the surrender of Richmond, and that these ambassadors assured Francis that it was not for any evil intent that the king of England wanted to get possession of the young earl, but in order to settle England's dynastic problem once for all by a marriage which he proposed to arrange for the earl, presumably with one of his own daughters. Francis was either persuaded to believe this story or was tempted by the gold the English ambassadors had brought with them, for he decided to grant Edward's request, and Richmond was soon handed over to the king's envoys. At St Malo,

---

1. See the instructions given to some ambassadors sent to England by the Archduke Maximilian in January 1481. Commynes-Lenglet, IV, 18. Hatclyf was engaged on this embassy from 10 September until 14 December and was paid 20s a day, besides 40s for his passage and re-passage, £5 for the expenses of a pursuivant sent to Charles, and 20s for those of a messenger sent into Holland with letters for the Duchess Margaret. Warrants for Issues, 16 Edw. IV, 11 Feb. A payment to Coke for his journey to Flanders is entered on Tellers' Roll, Mich. 16 Edw. IV. For proof that the negotiations took place at Bruges, see Gilliodts-van-Severen, VI, 105.
2. Diplomatic Documents (Exchequer T. R.), no. 558; *45th Report of Deputy Keeper*, app., 335.

however, as he was being taken to England, Richmond either fell ill of a fever or pretended to do so, and before he was able to travel farther, Francis's treasurer, Pierre Landois, suddenly arrived and spirited him away to a sanctuary.[1] Much disappointed, the English ambassadors went home alone, and Edward had to be content with a renewal of the promise Francis had already given that the Lancastrian pretender to his throne should find no chance to injure him. Francis agreed to keep Richmond either in sanctuary or in prison, and he seems to have lived up to his promise, as the accounts of one of his officers show that in the early part of 1475 Richmond was a "prisoner" at Elven and his uncle, the Earl of Pembroke, at Josselin, that in October 1476, Richmond was at Vannes in the custody of one Vincent de la Landalle, and that in November 1476, Pembroke was also a prisoner at Vannes in charge of one Bertrand du Parc.[2]

As usual, Edward had abstained from quarrelling with Francis even when he had excuse for so doing. He pretended to be content that Richmond should stay in Brittany, and in December he renewed the promise of protection he had given Francis in 1468.[3] He seems even to have offered, in a letter Gourmel carried home at one time, to do what he had warned Louis he would do if Brittany were invaded, namely, to cross the sea again and attack France to save Francis from destruction.[4] But the offer must have had a hollow sound to Francis's ears if he knew, as he probably did, that Guillaume Restout was again in England distributing Louis' money. Edward's receipt for the second instalment of his pension from Louis was given on 7 December 1476, Montgomery's on 30 November, and Rotherham's, Morton's, and Howard's on 10, 12, and 15 December; and although this time nothing was said to Hastings about a receipt, Restout's companions, who on this occasion were Pierre Cléret, Louis' *maître-d'hôtel*, and Master Jacques Teste, clerk of the chamber of accounts, certified that the lord chamberlain was paid his thousand crowns.[5] Louis, who knew that

---

1. Vergil, 679-680.
2. Compte de François Avignon (1 Dec. 1474—1 Oct. 1477), Legrand coll., MS. français 6982, f. 326.
3. Rymer, XII, 37.
4. Bouchart, *Grandes Croniques de Bretaigne*, III, 223.
5. Restout's account, *ut sup.*; Rymer, XII, 38. Perhaps Louis feared that Hastings's example would prove contagious, as this time he had excused Restout from the necessity of returning any receipts to him except Edward's. Yet everyone except Hastings seems to have given a receipt.

the most irreconcilable enemy he had in England was not King Edward but the English people, had even sent something besides the pensions. "There is nothing fresh from England," the Milanese ambassador in France had written on 4 November, "except that his Majesty decided some time ago to send seven hundred thousand butts of wine to the king of England, and he is having them laded now. This is certainly a great and marvellous thing, but it is thought to be in order to ingratiate himself with the people of England."[1] Had Louis been familiar with the secrets of cold storage, doubtless some thousands of venison pasties would have accompanied the wine!

1. *Cal. Milanese Papers*, I, 229.

2

CLARENCE AND MARY OF BURGUNDY

The year 1477 had just opened and the king of England was taking his ease at Westminster Palace or Greenwich when he received the shocking news that, on 5 January, the Duke of Burgundy had been killed in the midst of his troops besieging Nancy. That Edward shed no tears over the death of his sister's husband may be taken for granted, as no love had ever been lost between him and Charles. If he had feared that Charles was casting covetous eyes on his throne, his first feeling may even have been one of relief that the duke had been removed to another world. But with the news of Charles's death came also the word that the king of France was helping himself to as much of Mary of Burgundy's heritage as he could lay his hands on, and if the conquest of Burgundy by France was going to be the result of Charles's death, scarcely anyone would have more reason to weep over his bier than the king of England. For aside from the fact that England and Burgundy were bound together by commercial ties so close that disaster to either of them must inevitably cause a very serious loss to the other, Artois, one of the regions in which Louis' armies were reported to be most active, adjoined Calais, and if the king of France should succeed in conquering Artois, nothing was more likely than that Calais would be the next object of his attention. To be sure, Louis' attitude towards England had been, to outward appearances, friendliness itself since the signing of the treaty of Amiens, and directly after Charles's death he seems to have dispatched some ambassadors to London to announce that he was planning to send very soon another embassy of more imposing size and dignity "for the appeasing of such debates "as still existed between Edward and himself," for the entertaining of their amities and benevolences, and for a mutual dealing "regarding commercial intercourse between their subjects.[1] He made no

---

1. See the instructions to Morton and Donne to be cited presently.

attempt, however, to explain or defend his conduct towards Mary of Burgundy, and in alarm Edward again called the lords of his kingdom to come and give him their advice. Eighty-five letters of privy seal were sent out summoning divers lords to a council meeting at Westminster,[1] and on 14 February Paston wrote:

> Yesterday began the great council, to which all the estates of the land shall come to, but if it be for great and reasonable excuses; and I suppose the chief cause of this assembly is to commune what is best to do now upon the great change by the death of the Duke of Bourgogne, and for the keeping of Calais and the marches, and for the preservation of the amities taken late, as well with France as now with the members of Flanders; whereto I doubt not there shall be in all haste both the Dukes of Clarence and Gloucester.[2]

The first decision reached by the king and the lords of the realm was that the garrison at Calais must be strengthened. Paston continued:

> It is so, that this day I hear great liklihood that my Lord Hastings shall hastily go to Calais with great company.... It seemeth that the world is all quavering; it will reboil somewhere, so that I deem young men shall be cherished.

And when Guillaume Olivier, the man who had carried Louis' wonderful gift of wine to England, reached home in the first days of March, he stated that Lord Hastings had already arrived at Calais with a thousand or twelve hundred men.[3] Yet though it was true that Hastings had been sent to Calais—because the king and his council understood that the town and marches there "stood in great jeopardy and peril for sundry encounters and comings of our enemies thither and there about"—he had not been given a thousand or twelve hundred men, but only sixteen spears and five hundred and fourteen archers; and, instead of being instructed to find out what could be done to shield Mary of Burgundy, he had been told to keep peace with the French king.[4] If Edward had done what his subjects wanted him to do, says Commynes, he would have offered Mary an English army for her protection.[5] But not even for so great a cause as the safety of Burgundy could Edward find heart to quarrel with Louis, when such

---

1. Tellers' Roll, Mich. 16 Edw. IV.
2. *Paston Letters*, V, 270.
3. *Lettres de Louis XI*, VI, 138.
4. Warrants for Issues, 18 Edw. IV, 8 Feb.; *Paston Letters*, V, 277.
5. Commynes, II, 6.

a quarrel would mean the loss both of fifty thousand crowns a year and of the hope, which had been growing dearer to him and to Queen Elizabeth with every passing day, that his eldest daughter would in a few years become Dauphiness of France.[1] Nor is it likely that his chief councillors, seeing that they too were recipients of Louis' bounty, urged him very earnestly to show his teeth. However, if Edward kept silent when Louis' attack on Mary of Burgundy began, he did not overlook the fact that by refraining from taking up the cudgels for Mary he was placing Louis under great obligations to him, and on 16 February he sent Doctor John Morton and Sir John Donne to France to solicit a few favours.[2]

A copy of the instructions given to Morton and Donne is still in existence, and though time has treated the document roughly, from such portions of it as can be deciphered it appears that the sole reason Edward gave for sending an embassy to France was a belief that if he made his wishes known beforehand, it would be possible to reach a "profitable conclusion" more quickly when Louis' ambassadors came to England. He seems also to have told Morton and Donne to make three suggestions to Louis: first, that it was only fitting, "considering the promised marriage by both princes," that the treaty of Amiens should be extended "for term of years or lives"; second, that, as it was advisable, "for the entertaining of the benevolences and creance" between them, that the "pactions and promises made and to be made be duly and surefully by everich of them observed and kept," Louis ought to send him the "collateral sureties" which he had promised for the payment of the fifty thousand crowns a year he had agreed to give him; and third, that it was high time to hold the monetary diet which had been provided for in the treaty of amity. But that Edward was very anxious at the same time to show his friendship for Louis is sufficiently proved by the fact that he also instructed Morton and Donne to inform the French king that "orators" of Spain and Brittany were in England and to tell him that he would let him know about the answers the king of Spain made to him concerning "the marriage of his daughter."[3]

Morton and Donne were not long in reaching France, and at their first meeting with those whom Louis appointed to treat with them they began by saying, as they had been instructed to do, that they had come because

---

1. *Ibid.*, I, 326, II, 7-8.
2. Signed Bills, file 1512, no. 4870 (an injured document).
3. Chancery Miscellanea, bundle 30, file 10, no. 20. Edward gave one of the Spanish ambassadors £20. Tellers' Roll, Easter 17 Edw. IV.

King Edward thought time could be saved by talking matters over before the ambassadors of the king of France came to England. Then they expressed a desire to see the treaties signed at Picquigny, remarking that they had been hastily drawn up and that it might be possible to make some additions to them which would help to preserve the good understanding between the kings of England and France and be a source of perpetual benefit to the two kingdoms. It seemed to them, they said, that while neither king was willing to renounce his rights and pretensions in favour of the other, some means of preserving peace and love might be found which would make unnecessary an exchange of embassies composed of such important persons as those the king of France was proposing to send to England. After that they delivered Edward's message about the "orators" of Spain and Brittany. Several times, they said, the king of Spain had sent to England to ask for new alliances, but the king of England had always refused to hear of anything except the old ones, for the reason that he was fully determined not to enter into any new alliance with Ferdinand of Aragon or anyone else unless the king of France approved. The Spanish ambassadors had said, however, that the king of Spain was sorry to be at war with the king of France, and this seemed to mean that Ferdinand would be glad to have the king of England mediate between him and the king of France—a task which ought not to be difficult, if the king of Spain was ready for mediation, since the king of France had now got possession of Roussillon and the other things for which he had gone to war. As for the king of Portugal's pretensions to the Castilian crown, Ferdinand was willing that that matter too should be submitted to the king of England's mediation. Morton and Donne had even brought letters to Alphonso, who had been in France for several months past trying to induce Louis to help him invade Spain by way of Biscay and Navarre;[1] but they declared that they had no intention of holding any communication with him unless the king of France wished them to do so.

The most astonishing announcement the English ambassadors had to make, however, concerned the Duke of Brittany. It was the belief of the Duke of Brittany, they said, that the king of France hated him and longed for his undoing because of his friendship for the king of England—in fact, the duke had told King Edward this. Yet they hastened to add that if Francis had

---

1. Commynes, I, 381 *et seq.*

done anything since the treaty of Amiens was signed to injure the king of France, the king of England was quite free to abandon him and would even be glad to find an excuse for doing so. They proposed that there should be a meeting of ambassadors of both kings and of the Duke of Brittany, and said that if Francis then refused to listen to reason, the king of England would throw him over.[1]

It was not until their second meeting with Louis' commissioners that Morton and Donne revealed the true object for which they had come. The main treaties signed by the kings of France and England, they said, were the truce with intercourse of merchandise, which was "toute publique," and the treaty of amity, which was kept secret "pour mieux contenter le people"; and it was strange and inconsistent, they pointed out, that while the treaty of amity was to last as long as the two kings lived, the truce was for seven years only, a period already nearly half expired. They then urged the advisability of finding some means of making the treaty of amity known "A tout le peuple," and they suggested that probably no better way to do this could be found than to sign a new truce similar in terms to the old one except that it should be made to endure, like the treaty of amity, for the lives of the two kings. They made two other suggestions as well. First, they said that the article in the treaty of amity relating to a monetary diet ought to be transferred to the truce and that, as the present state of things opened the way for the Duke of Burgundy and others to draw great quantities of gold both from France and from England, the diet ought to be held and the necessary settlement made. Second, they asked—apparently with special thought for the merchants of Italy—for the introduction into the truce of an article protecting from hindrance or injury any person who was going to or from France or England for the purposes of trade and who was provided with a certificate from the king of either country. The all-important point in the eyes of the king of England, however, was the extension of the truce to make it correspond with the treaty of amity, and, coming back to that subject, Morton and Donne stated that, if the king of France would consent

---

1. "La creance des ambassadeurs du Roy Dangleterre ensemble les ouvertures quilz ont faictes," MS. français 4054, ff. 104-105. This document has been dated 1475 by a later hand, but a comparison of it with the instructions given to Morton and Donne, and also with the document in *Portefeuilles de Fontanieu* about to be cited, proves beyond a doubt that it belongs properly to the negotiations of February–March 1477.

to treat for such an extension, they were prepared to act for the king of England and that they were very sure both that King Edward would ratify any agreement they made and that, if the king of France wanted to send a messenger to England with them, King Edward would send back by him the necessary letters patent.

The affairs of Spain, too, were mentioned again at the second conference, and this time Morton and Donne stated definitely that Edward would be glad if peace could be established between the king of Spain and the king of France and also, by the mediation of the king of France and himself, between the king of Spain and the king of Portugal. And Louis' commissioners understood them to mean that, if the king of France consented to this, he would be allowed to retain Roussillon. Finally, in regard to Brittany the two Englishmen proposed, as they had done before, that there should be a meeting of English, French, and Breton ambassadors to discuss matters, and they repeated that if the Duke of Brittany declined even then to submit to the king of France, as he ought to do, the king of England would feel himself justified in abandoning him.[1]

Thus far, seemingly, Edward's ambassadors had said nothing about the "collateral sureties" for which he had waited in vain and which they had been charged to demand. Before the conferences were over, however, that and several other weighty matters besides those already mentioned must have been discussed, for when, on 4 March, it was agreed that certain articles should be laid before the kings of France and England for their approval, those articles contained the following provisions: first, that the king of France should, if possible, send to the king of England before Pentecost the bond of the bank of Medici which he had promised as security for the payment of the pension of fifty thousand crowns a year, or, if he could not do this, that he should send before All Saints' Day the papal letter which had been mentioned in the treaty of Amiens as an alternative for the bond; second, that ten thousand crowns of Margaret of Anjou's ransom (which had been due since Michaelmas) should be paid before the English ambassadors went home; third, that the truce between England

---

1. "Cest leffect de ce que les ambaxadeurs d'Angleterre out dit à la dernière communication qu'on a eu auecques eulx," *Portefeuilles de Fontanieu*, portefeuilles 138-539, ff. 58-59; Legrand coll., MS. français 6984, ff. 192-195

and France should be extended so that it would endure not only as long as both Edward and Louis lived, like the treaty of amity, but for a year after the death of either king; and fourth, that, when the monetary diet met, values should be fixed and rules laid down which would be advantageous to both kings and to their subjects.

Morton and Donne had also asked Louis to aid in checking shipments of wool into France from other places than the lawful staple at Calais not only by confiscating such wool but by permitting the king of England to appoint his own examiners in France; but the answer they received to this request was that the king of France would seek the advice of the merchants of his kingdom on the point and instruct the ambassadors he sent to England accordingly. And to another request, too, Louis' reply was not just what was desired. He was willing to forbid his subjects to interfere with any Genoese or Florentine merchants going to England, but as for the Venetians, they were his enemies and he would not promise them security until they had made their peace with him, as the king of England might help them to do.[1] In regard to four other matters which were spoken of Louis was not asked to give any answer until his ambassadors came to England. First, Morton and Donne said, Edward wanted to know what Louis meant to do about the Duchess Margaret's jointure rights, which were endangered by the attack he was making on Mary of Burgundy. Second, Edward desired further pledges that the Dauphin of France would marry his daughter. Third, Edward would like to receive a written acknowledgment of the innocence of Sir Thomas Montgomery, who, for some reason, was suspected of having a share in the Duke of Brittany's conspiracies against the king of France and who was probably afraid that he would lose his pension from Louis. And fourth, Edward wished Louis' ambassadors to bring with them, when they came, full instructions and power to treat concerning the Spaniards, the Bretons, "and others."[2]

When Morton and Donne had completed their negotiations, the ten thousand crowns of Margaret of Anjou's ransom were handed over to them

---

1. The Venetians had entered into an alliance with the Duke of Burgundy in 1472, and since that time a maritime war had been going on between them and the French.
2. *Responsiones datæ per ambassiatores Franciæ Anglicis ambassiatoribus cum nonnullis novis articulis ex parte Anglie traditis*, Record Transcripts, series II, no. 136 (from Archives du Royaume, K 159).

at Paris, as well as two hundred marks in silver as a gift for themselves,[1] and they departed for home feeling fairly well satisfied with what they had accomplished, especially as, in addition to the agreement of 4 March, Louis had told Morton that, for Edward's sake, he would treat the Duchess Margaret with the greatest "faveur et douceur" that was possible.[2] But there is reason to believe that Louis had derived even greater satisfaction from his negotiations with the two Englishmen than they had, since it was plain from what they had told him that all he would need to do to prevent Edward from espousing the cause of Mary of Burgundy was to go on sending plenty of money to England with the addition from time to time of a few hollow promises. There was one fly in Louis' ointment, however, and that fly was the Duchess Margaret, who, he knew, hated him and would use every particle of influence she had over her stepdaughter to thwart his designs. He made up his mind, therefore, that, while continuing to pose as Edward's good friend, he would get rid of Edward's sister by hook or by crook. Only a few days, consequently, before he promised Morton to show Margaret all possible consideration, he had written to certain ones who had gone to meet a deputation from Ghent that he was sending Guillaume Olivier, "who has just come back from England and has taken the wines to the king," to tell them the news and had suggested to them that they might say to the Flemings that the king of England's object in sending Lord Hastings to Calais with so many men was "to carry off Mademoiselle de Bourgogne and that Madame de Bourgogne is directing the enterprise."[3]

It must be acknowledged that Louis was not the only person who was practising deceit in these days. Edward was just as capable of double-dealing as Louis and not half so clever about covering up his naughty deeds. Louis had so many spies here, there, and everywhere that it was next to impossible to conceal from him anything he had a wish to know, and at the moment Morton and Donne were confiding to him that Edward would be glad to find an excuse for forsaking the Duke of Brittany, he had in his pocket all the letters Morice Gourmel had recently been carrying back and forth between Edward and Francis. For Gourmel, being skilful with his pen, had

---

1. Account of Pierre Parent for 1477, Legrand coll., MS. français 6982, 235 dorso, *et seq.*; Legeay, II, 264.
2. Plancher, IV, cccxc.
3. *Lettres de Louis XI*, VI, 138.

made copies of every letter intrusted to him either by Edward or by Francis, had delivered the copies to the unsuspecting king and duke, and had sold the originals to the king of France for a hundred crowns apiece! Louis kept his secret for a time, but when, not many days after Morton and Donne had left him, an embassy from Francis, headed by Francis's chancellor, Guillaume Chauvin, came to him to say that Francis desired peace and a good understanding with him, the opportunity for revenge was too good to lose. So he arrested the Breton ambassadors, astounded Chauvin, who had been kept in ignorance of Francis's dealings with Edward, by flaunting before his eyes the letters purchased from Gourmel, and, when he finally suffered the Breton ambassadors to go home, sent Francis's own letters back to him with the message that he did not want to hear any more protestations of friendship from him until he had cast off the king of England for good and all. Gourmel was soon captured and made to confess everything, and after a short imprisonment in the château of Auray he was quietly drowned one night in the moat. But vengeance on Gourmel could not put the cat back in the bag, and Francis ordered the mobilization of his troops and made ready for the worst.[1] More than likely the duke implored Edward, as he had done so many times before, to send him some archers; but if he did, it was only to find out how unreliable is the friendship of kings, as Edward, who could not bring himself to fight Louis for Burgundy's sake, certainly was not going to fight him for the sake of Brittany.

However Louis may have expressed himself to Morton and Donne about the Spanish marriage alliance which Edward had acknowledged he was contemplating, shortly after those two gentlemen came home from France, Richard Martyn and Thomas Langton were sent to continue the negotiations for the marriage of the Prince of Wales and the Infanta Isabella and to ask Ferdinand and Isabella to send another embassy to England.[2] But just when Edward had begun to rejoice in the belief that to the very desirable marriages which he had arranged for two of his daughters he was about to add another very desirable one for his eldest son, he received a rude shock, as scarcely had Martyn and Langton set sail for Spain when

---

1. Bouchart, III, 223-224; Dupuy, I, 362-367.
2. Rymer, XII, 42. Martyn was paid £10 for this journey to Spain. Receipt Roll (really a Tellers' Roll), Mich. 17 Edw. IV, no. 632.

there arrived in London a messenger from the Duchess Margaret.[1] Although this messenger came primarily to urge Edward to send an embassy to Flanders to meet some ambassadors coming from the Emperor to press the suit of the Archduke Maximilian for Mary of Burgundy's hand, he must have brought also the information that Mary was virtually a prisoner of the burghers of Ghent and that the king of France was trying to force her to marry his son, the Dauphin.

It was no feeling of affection for the Archduke Maximilian which led Margaret to ask that an English embassy should be sent to meet his emissaries in Flanders, for had it fallen to her to decide whom Mary of Burgundy should take for a husband, she would not have chosen Maximilian but quite a different person. Ever since her husband's death it had been Margaret's great hope that she could arrange a marriage between her stepdaughter and her brother Clarence, who, despite his past misdemeanours, was still her favourite brother and whose wife, Warwick's daughter, had died at Warwick Castle just before Christmas after giving birth to a son a few weeks earlier at Tewkesbury Abbey.[2] But though Clarence's heart had leapt with joy at the thought of marrying Mary of Burgundy, the greatest heiress in Europe, Margaret had soon been forced to acknowledge to herself that such a marriage was out of the question. In the first place, Mary showed no inclination to accept Clarence. In the second place, Edward, who had so little reason to trust his brother, made it perfectly plain that he would never permit Clarence to make so great a marriage. In the third place, it was absolutely indispensable that Mary should marry a man who would be not only her husband but her defender against the king of France, and Clarence could bring no army as a bridal

1. This messenger was probably Mary of Burgundy's councillor and chamberlain, "James Douche," to whom Edward granted letters of protection on 5 May. French Roll 17 Edw. IV, m. 6.
2. *Hist. Croy. Cont.*, 561. See also a Tewkesbury Chronicle printed in Dugdale's *Monasticon Anglicanum*, II, 64-65, according to which Clarence's son Richard was born "in the new chamber of the infirmary" on 6 October 1476, and baptized seven days later. The Duchess Isabel, whom the chronicler calls "patrona nostra," was ill unto death during her confinement and was still ill when her husband took her, on 12 November, to Warwick, where she died—not on 12 December, as the chronicle says, but on 22 December (*Rolls of Parl.*, VI, 174)—and afterwards her child also, on the feast of the Circumcision (1 January). On 4 January her body was brought back to Tewkesbury, to lie in state in the Abbey for thirty-five days before it was placed in a vault behind the high altar.

present without the help and consent which Edward would refuse to give. With much regret, therefore, and with no little resentment towards Edward, who might have made the realization of her wishes possible, Margaret had given up her cherished plan and had decided to throw her influence into the scale on behalf of Maximilian, the suitor Mary herself favoured.

Needless to say, the information which the Duchess Margaret's messenger gave him roused Edward to instant action. As Mary of Burgundy was twenty years of age and the Dauphin only six, the marriage Louis had proposed to Charles's daughter was so preposterous that her acceptance of it was almost unthinkable; but what caused Edward's consternation was not doubt about Mary's decision, but the discovery that Louis felt himself free to offer the Dauphin's hand to anyone. Had Louis forgotten about the marriage treaty he had signed on the bridge at Picquigny? And if he could forget about that so easily, what were any of his promises worth? It was such thoughts as these that made Edward decide to send an embassy to Flanders forthwith, as Margaret had requested him to do, and also to instruct Doctor John Coke and Louis de Bretaylle, whom he chose as his emissaries, to treat with the Emperor's ambassadors for a renewal of the peace and league which had existed in earlier days between England and the Holy Roman Empire.[1] He did not heed quite all of his sister's advice, however; for although upon their arrival at Ghent, Coke and Bretaylle thanked the young Duchess of Burgundy for the generous provision she had made for her stepmother, King Edward's sister, and begged her on no account to think of marrying the son of the king of France, they ended by offering her the hand of Earl Rivers! Little liking as he had for his wife's brother, and ill fitted as Rivers was to be the protector of Burgundy, Edward had again allowed his judgment to be overruled by his wife's ambition for the advancement of her family, and his ambassadors not only urged Mary to marry a man whom her father had laughed at as a coward, but promised her an English army if she would accept Rivers for a husband.[2] But, much as she needed help, Mary of Burgundy had no intention of wedding a petty English earl. If the king of England had parted with his senses, the Duchess of Burgundy had not. Mary had already made up her mind to marry Maximilian and no one else and, in fact, even before Coke and Bretaylle had a chance

---

1. French Roll 17 Edw. IV, m. 7; Signed Bills, file 1512, no. 4886.
2. Haynin, II, 312-313; Commynes, II, 8; La Marche, III, 243.

to make their extraordinary proposal to her, the imperial ambassadors had arrived and the fate of her hand was practically settled.

Perhaps Edward was neither greatly surprised nor greatly disappointed when he found that Earl Rivers was not destined to become the consort of the Duchess of Burgundy. If he did feel any regret, he was sufficiently consoled by the certainty that at least Mary was not going to rob his eldest daughter of her fiancé. About 20 May he sent Sir John Donne to Flanders to assist Coke and Bretaylle in their negotiations with the imperial ambassadors,[1] and then he waited to see what would happen next. Louis could not fail to make note of the fact that English and imperial ambassadors had met in Flanders, or to realize that Edward must have learned of his effort to force Mary into a marriage with the Dauphin, but for the present neither he nor Edward seems to have cared to break silence about Mary of Burgundy's matrimonial affairs. Why should Louis apologize for a project that had failed, and what would Edward gain by reproaches? Since the duchess was not going to marry the Dauphin, least said soonest mended, both seem to have thought.

Other persons than Louis and Edward, however, were interested in what was going on in Burgundy. Edward's subjects, knowing no legitimate reason why Louis' sins should be overlooked, were both mystified and disgusted by the inactivity of Lord Hastings at Calais; and Clarence's disappointment, when he saw his briefly entertained hope of marrying Mary of Burgundy fade away, was so intense that he made no effort to conceal it. Though Clarence may have attended the council meeting in February at which the situation in Burgundy was considered, after that he rarely appeared at court, and when he did come, he showed reluctance not only to open his lips in the council chamber but, as if he feared poison, to eat or drink in the king's house.[2] Finally he lost all control of himself and gave vent to his spite in a manner which was as silly and ineffective as it was vicious. On 12 April, at Cayford in Somerset, two hirelings of the duke, with some four score other persons, broke into the house of one Ankarette Twynyho, a former servant of Clarence and his dead wife, and carried her off to Warwick, where she was first thrown into prison and then brought before the justices of the peace and indicted, at Clarence's suit, on a charge of having given to the

---

1. Rymer, XII, 42.
2. *Hist. Croy. Cont., ut sup.*

Duchess of Clarence "a venomous drink of ale mixed with poison" which had caused the duchess to sicken and die.[1] Ankarette insisted that she was innocent, but the jurors, "for fear and great menaces and doubt of loss of their lives and goods," returned a verdict of guilty. The poor woman was sentenced to be drawn from the jail through the town "unto the gallows of Myton and there upon the said gallows to be hanged until she were dead," and the sentence was carried out without delay. Ankarette did not suffer alone, as one John Thuresby of Warwick, accused of having poisoned the infant son of the Duke and Duchess of Clarence, who lived but a few weeks and whose birth without doubt had been the real cause of the duchess's death, was executed at the same time; but Sir Roger Tocotes, who was declared to be an abettor of Ankarette and Thuresby, and who was also condemned to death, happily escaped capture.[2]

In his persecution of Ankarette and Thuresby, Clarence had acted throughout "as though he had used a king's power," and that he should dare thus to interfere with the course of the law was an alarming sign of what was passing through his mind. His astounding behaviour cost him dear in more ways than one, for it reawakened all of Edward's old distrust of him and it also destroyed his chance of securing another bride who, though she did not possess the incomparable charms of Mary of Burgundy, might at another time have been quite acceptable to him. In the winter Alexander Legh had gone to Scotland to pay the third instalment of the Princess Cecily's dowry,[3] and though, owing to "distemperance" of the weather and perhaps illness, he had been a little late in reaching Edinburgh, King James had been none the less glad to see him. James, in fact, was finding his alliance with the king of England so much to his liking that when Legh started for home, apparently in the first days of May, he was intrusted with a proposal for two other Anglo-Scottish marriages, to wit, a marriage between James's brother, the Duke of Albany, and Edward's sister Margaret, the lately widowed Duchess of Burgundy, and one between James's sister

1. It is curious that, although, according to the Tewkesbury Chronicle cited above, the duchess was at Tewkesbury until 12 November, Ankarette was accused of giving her the deadly drink at Warwick on 10 October.
2. *Rolls of Parl.*, VI, 173-174; *Cal. Patent Rolls*, III, 72-73; *Third Report of the Deputy Keeper*, app. II, 224; L. Vernon-Harcourt, The Baga de Secretis, *Eng. Hist. Review*, July 1908.
3. Rymer, XII, 41.

Margaret and Edward's brother Clarence.[1] But perhaps at no time would such a wholesale union with the royal house of Scotland have appealed to Edward, and certainly at the present moment it did not attract him. He sent Legh back to Scotland to thank James for this fresh proof of "his entire love and affection anempst us" but to explain to him that, "after the old usages" of his kingdom, no honourable person ever talked about marriage within a year after their mourning; and though he promised that, when a convenient time came, he would "feel the dispositions" of his brother and sister and send word to King James, the two marriages seem never to have been spoken of again.[2] The Duchess Margaret, if James's offer was ever mentioned to her, probably declined to consider it, and as for Clarence, Edward had no desire to procure any wife for him.

Even at the moment that he was sending his courteous but evasive reply to the king of Scotland, Edward was taking his revenge on Clarence, and taking it in a manner scarcely less extraordinary than that in which Clarence had found relief for his anger. The story of what Edward did has come down to us in a much confused state, but the main facts seem to be these. One John Stacy, an Oxford clerk who called himself an astronomer but who was suspected of studying the stars for dark and evil purposes, was arrested and accused of a number of crimes, the most serious of which was an attempt, at the entreaty of the faithless wife of Lord Beauchamp, to bring about that nobleman's death by the use of leaden images. When he was examined, Stacy made a confession, and after he had named Thomas Burdett of Arowe, a member of Clarence's household,[3] as his accomplice, Burdett was arrested, and also another Oxford clerk, Thomas Blake. According to Stow's Annals,[4] the chief accusation against Burdett was that when King Edward once honoured him by hunting in his park at Arowe, he was so enraged by the killing of a white buck in which he had taken much pride that he blurted out that he "wished the buck's head in his belly that

---

1. *Cal. Documents relating to Scotland*, IV, 474.
2. Ellis, *Original Letters*, Series I, I, 56; Halliwell, *Letters of Kings of Eng.*, I, 547.
3. Hist. Croy Cont., *ut sup*. In a pardon granted to him in 1470, Burdett is described as Thomas Burdet of Saint Augustine near Bristol, esquire, alias of Arowe, co. Warwick, alias of Bell, co. Worcester, alias of Belbroughton, alias of Bristol. Pardon Roll 9-10 Edw. IV, m. 2.
4. p. 430.

moved the king to kill it," a remark which was construed to mean that he desired the death of the king himself. According to the legal records of the case, however, the crimes for which Burdett, Stacy, and Blake were tried were as follows. First, it was claimed that Burdett, "endeavouring to exalt himself in riches," on 20 April 1474, at Westminster, treasonably imagined and compassed the death of the king; that he set out, with the help of Stacy and Blake, to "calculate the nativities" of the king and the Prince of Wales and "also to know when the king and Prince should die," and that Stacy and Blake, on 6 February 1475, "worked and calculated by art magic, necromancy, and astronomy" the death of the king and his son. Second, it was asserted that on 20 May 1475, Stacy and Blake again resorted to the magic arts, in spite of the fact that "the determinations of Holy Church and the opinions of divers doctors" forbade "any liegeman thus to meddle concerning kings and princes" without their permission, and that six days later, in the hope of destroying "the cordial love of the people" for the king and of shortening his life by sadness, they and Burdett declared to certain ones that the king and the Prince would die in a short time. Third, Burdett was accused of having disseminated on 6 March 1477, and again on 4 and 5 May of that year, treasonable "bills and writings, rhymes and ballads" at Holborn to incite the king's subjects to rebellion.

The trial caused great excitement, and most of the lords of England were present when, on 19 May, all three men were condemned, in spite of their declaration of innocence, to be taken back to the Tower for the night, "to the end that they may better take care for their souls," and then to be drawn to Tyburn and hanged. Burdett and Stacy were executed accordingly the next day, although they both repeated their assertion of innocence on the gallows and Burdett made a long and spirited speech. For Blake, however, a pardon was secured at the last moment by the Bishop of Norwich, and he was finally discharged. On the day of the hanging a writ of *certiorari* was sent to Warwick, and although Ankarette Twynyho and John Thuresby could not be brought back to life, Sir Roger Tocotes, hearing that his danger was past, soon surrendered himself at the Marshalsea, and in the following Hilary term he was acquitted.[1]

---

1. *Third Report of Deputy Keeper*, app. II, 213-254; Vernon-Harcourt's article and *Hist.*

Clarence did not need to be told that Burdett's and Stacy's execution was intended as a warning to him, and, had he been wise enough to hold his peace, probably nothing worse would have happened, as Edward had shown repeatedly that he shrank from treating him as he deserved. But Clarence was always possessed to do the thing he ought not to do. A day or two after the hanging of Burdett and Stacy, Edward left London for Windsor,[1] and as soon as he had gone, Clarence hurried to Westminster with Doctor John Goddard, pushed his way into the council chamber, and there ordered Goddard to read to the king's councillors the declaration of innocence which Burdett and Stacy had made.[2] In other words, the duke appealed from the king to the king's council. And his very bold act had the uglier look because he had chosen for his spokesman the same Minorite preacher who had expounded Henry VI's right to the throne at Paul's Cross on 30 September 1470.

Clarence's strange conduct excited the greater suspicion because about this time an uprising occurred in one of the counties not far from London. Perhaps Edward himself had never felt sure that Clarence had had anything to do with the Earl of Oxford's seizure of St Michael's Mount, but it is an interesting, if not a significant fact that now when the king and his brother were at loggerheads again Oxford's name crops up once more. For in May or June 1477, there appeared in Cambridgeshire or Huntingdonshire one who announced himself to be the Earl of Oxford. Luckily the imposter—for imposter he was, as the real Earl of Oxford was safe in Hammes Castle— was soon captured and all was over, apparently, by 23 June, as on that date Paston, writing to his brother, said: "My Lady of Oxenford looketh after you and Arblaster both. My Lord of Oxenford is not comen into England that I can perceive, and so the good lady hath need of help and counsel how that she shall do."[3] Yet short as the imposter's career had been, he had evidently

---

Croy. Cont., *ut sup.*; Croke's *Reports, Reign of Charles I* (translated by Sir Harbottle Grimston, Dublin, 1793), 121-122; Inquisitions Miscellaneous, Chancery, file 328 (formerly Inquisitions *post mortem*, 17 Edw. IV, no. 66). Blake's pardon passed the great seal on 3 June, and ten days later Stacy's widow obtained a grant of her husband's goods. *Cal. Patent Rolls*, III, 40, 43. One John Bell was paid 76*s* 11*d* ob. for the expenses of the jurors impanelled for the trial of Burdett, Stacy, and Blake. Tellers' Roll, Easter 17 Edw. IV.

1. Privy Seals.
2. *Hist. Croy. Cont., ut sup.*
3. *Paston Letters*, V, 289.

gathered up enough of a following to cause anxiety, as in November, when the new sheriffs were taking office, Edward ordered that six pounds should be paid to William Alyngton the Younger, who had been sheriff of the counties of Cambridge and Huntingdon during the past year, because "to our great pleasure" he had "endeavoured himself and taken in the said counties as well one person calling himself Earl of Oxon as other great felons in the said country, to his great labour, costs, and charges, and to the appeasing and laying apart great inconveniences that might likely have followed thereof."[1]

That Clarence was implicated in the rising in Cambridgeshire and Huntingdonshire there was every reason to believe, and Edward scarcely needed further evidence than he already had to convince him that his brother had been plotting against his throne once more. He was offered further evidence, however, and by no less a person than the king of France, who, not being quite sure what Edward's ambassadors had been saying and doing in Flanders, was delighted to hear that Clarence was making trouble again and thought he saw a chance not only to add to Edward's disturbance of mind, but to sow discord and distrust between him and his sister Margaret.

Morton and Donne's journey to France had not altered Louis' plan to send to England the imposing embassy which Edward, who may have feared the effect the sight of it would have on his subjects, had sought to avoid, and on 1 June he commissioned the Archbishop of Vienne, Olivier Guérin, his *maître-d'hôtel*, Olivier le Roux, Seigneur de Beauvoir, his *maître des comptes*, and others to cross the sea to treat with Edward concerning the prolongation of the seven years' truce and the other matters of which Morton and Donne had spoken.[2] Le Roux, who was perhaps more in Louis' confidence than the other members of the embassy, preceded his colleagues to England, and his instructions are an interesting illustration of Louis' methods in diplomacy.

When he had presented his credentials, Le Roux was to tell the king of England that the king of France had been pleased to hear of his good estate and personal prosperity from the last ambassadors he had sent to England. Then, after expressing thanks for the kindness with which those ambassadors

1. Warrants for Issues, 17 Edw. IV, 23 Nov. Cf. Scofield, *Eng. Hist. Review*, April 1914, 242-243. William Alyngton the Younger was probably a son of William Alyngton, Speaker of the House of Commons, 1471-1475.
2. Rymer, XII, 47-48.

had been received, he was to add that the king of France had learned from them what matters still remained to be disposed of by negotiation and also that it had been proposed to set a day for a meeting of representatives of both kings. For this purpose, Le Roux was to say further, the king of France would send ambassadors to England with ample powers before the end of the month; and the only reason why he had not given such powers to his last ambassadors was that he had heard on all sides that, through Madame de Bourgogne and the lord chamberlain of England, an agreement had been made with the other party, and, as he himself was acting in good faith, he would have been ashamed to be refused. When he had thus reached the subject of Mary of Burgundy, Le Roux was to complain "en bonne façon" of the attitude Edward had taken in regard to her, saying that the king of France's quarrel with Mary was an affair of his kingdom and ought to be settled within his kingdom, just like many controversies which had arisen in Edward's own kingdom. He was also to remind Edward that the treaty of amity signed in 1475 bound him not to sustain or favour any rebellious or disobedient subject of the king of France and, after informing him that both the late Duke Charles and, since his death, his daughter, Mademoiselle de Bourgogne, had proved themselves rebellious subjects of the king of France, thereby forfeiting all their holdings in France, to tell him that the king of France had been astonished, in view of these things, that in the beginning he had seemed to want to assist Monsieur de Clarence to marry Mademoiselle de Bourgogne. Finally, Le Roux was to warn Edward out of the goodness of Louis' heart that a marriage between Mary and Clarence would have done more harm to him than to the king of France, as he would know if he could hear the remarks commonly made about the matter beyond sea and what Madame de Bourgogne had said secretly to her confidants and to certain great lords, who had not concealed the matter from the king of France, both about the marriage and about the things Monsieur de Clarence would do in England if he came into possession of the Burgundian dominions.[1]

The first step Edward seems to have taken after he heard what Le Roux had to say was to summon Lord Hastings home, as Paston stated, in the same letter in which he remarked that the Earl of Oxford had not come to

---

1. Régistre de Pierre Doriolle, MS. français 10,187, ff. 123-124; Legrand coll., MS. français 6984, ff. 302-303 (See Appendix XI.) According to the *Chronique Scandaleuse*, II, 63, Edward understood that Clarence was planning to go to Flanders to aid Margaret.

England so far as he knew, that the lord chamberlain had arrived from Calais and gone to the king at Windsor. But if Edward had allowed himself to doubt Hastings's faithfulness, it was only for a moment, and he was probably very soon convinced by Hastings of the innocence of the Duchess Margaret as well. There was no one, however, who felt any desire to defend Clarence, and as soon as Edward returned from Windsor, he summoned his brother to Westminster Palace. The mayor and aldermen of London happened to be at the palace when Clarence arrived, and in their presence and with his own lips Edward accused the duke, not of conspiring against his throne, but of committing acts which violated the laws of the realm and threatened the security of judges and jurors. Then he ordered the culprit to be put under arrest and taken to the Tower.[1]

It was about the first of July when Le Roux's colleagues reached England. The last bit of instruction Le Roux had received from Louis was that he was to pick up all the news he could in England and to find out especially if any embassies from the Emperor's son, from any other princes of Germany, or from Mademoiselle de Bourgogne or Flanders had been there and, if so, what they had come for. But though an imperial herald was in England sometime during the summer,[2] Edward had not as yet entered into any league with Archduke Maximilian, and the Archbishop of Vienne and his companions found a clear field. Clarence's arrest was also encouraging news, as it seemed to prove that Louis' poison was taking effect, and when Guillaume Restout, whom Louis had sent along with his ambassadors, produced the expected money for Edward and his friends—not omitting Sir Thomas Montgomery—he felt himself to be so much in favour with the king of England that he ventured to make a request on his own behalf. "Please it, your Highness," runs a petition which Edward received on 29 July and immediately granted, "of your most noble and abundant grace to grant unto William Restout, argentier to your cousin of France, that all such goods and merchandises which he shall bring or do to be brought in his name within this your noble royaulme, and also such as [he] shall do to be led out of it, may be so without paying any manner of customs and subsidies till it amounteth to the sum of 100 mark by time or times."[3]

---

1. *Hist. Croy. Cont.*, 561-562.
2. Tellers' Roll, Easter, 17 Edw. IV.
3. Signed Bills, file 1513, no. 4912. Restout made payments to Edward on 5 July, to

Among the men whom Edward chose to treat with the ambassadors of the king of France there were no less than three of that king's pensioners, Lord Howard, Sir Thomas Montgomery, and Doctor Morton;[1] and if the Frenchmen expected to find their task made easy and pleasant for them, it is hardly surprising. One of the first matters taken up when the negotiations began was the request Morton and Donne had made regarding English wool smuggled into France from other places than Calais, and as an answer to that request the Frenchmen seem to have produced a copy of some order issued by Louis on 19 June 1476, forbidding or regulating the importation of wool into Normandy.[2] Soon after the truce was mentioned, and as Louis' ambassadors at once announced that they were prepared to prolong it, on 21 July a new treaty was signed which provided that the truce of Amiens should continue so long as the present kings of France and England lived and for a year after the death of whichever one of them died first.[3] But in one or two respects the new truce fell short of Edward's wishes. For one thing, it contained no article such as he had suggested to insure the safety of merchants travelling to or from England or France, although both his representatives and Louis' seem to have signed a declaration that it would be well if an agreement could be made that not only the subjects of the kings of France and England but those of such of their allies as they might name within a year should be allowed to journey to and fro without fear of being molested.[4] In the second place, the article providing for a monetary diet was not transferred from the treaty of amity to the truce, as Edward had wished it to be, although what objection Louis could raise to such a transfer it is hard to see.

Montgomery on 6 July, to Morton on 10 July, and to Rotherham and Howard on 12 July. Restout's account; Rymer, XII, 45. It appears from Restout's account that Louis had given orders that hereafter Rotherham's and Hastings's pensions were to be paid in four quarterly instalments instead of semi-annually. Yet Rotherham gave only two receipts during the year, each one being for 500 crowns. The certification that Hastings had received his money came from the Bishop of Elne this time, and it was not made until 7 January, after the whole amount for the year had been paid to the lord chamberlain.

1. Rymer, XII, 45.
2. The copy was deposited in the treasury of England on 12 July. Palgrave, *Kalendars of Exchequer*, III, 24.
3. Rymer, XII, 46; Palgrave, *Cely Papers*, III, 25. Note that the ratification of the truce which Rymer prints really belongs to the year 1481.
4. Régistre de Pierre Doriolle, f. 117 dorso. See also Legrand coll., MS. français 6984 f. 298.

These disappointments in regard to the new truce were as nothing, however, compared to the discovery that Louis had sent by his ambassadors neither the "collateral sureties" for the payment of the pension of fifty thousand crowns nor the additional guarantees for the fulfilment of the marriage treaty which he had just shown such an alarming inclination to forget. He had also failed, apparently, to make a reply to the question concerning the jointure rights of the Duchess Margaret. His reasons for that are not far to seek. For not only was he probably hoping that the revelation Le Roux had made about Margaret's supposed intrigues with Clarence would cure Edward of all interest in the welfare of Madame de Bourgogne, but he also had a proposal to offer which, if it should prove to have any attraction for Edward, as he believed it would, must change the situation entirely. In brief, Louis had instructed his ambassadors to invite Edward to take a hand in his war on Burgundy and by so doing secure for himself a part of the spoils!

Morton and Donne had spoken of one other matter while they were in France. They had requested Louis to authorize the ambassadors he sent to England to treat regarding Brittany and Spain. But the disclosure of Gourmel's rascality had placed the Duke of Brittany in such an embarrassing position that he was now suing to Louis for peace,[1] and if Louis was led by the consciousness of his own perfidious conduct in the matter of the marriage treaty to confine his sarcasm to Francis, Edward might well congratulate himself. The situation in regard to Spain, too, was somewhat changed, as Louis had now practically abandoned his championship of Alphonso of Portugal's claims.[2] In any case, there was no need for Edward to fulfil his promise to keep Louis informed about his negotiations with Ferdinand and Isabella for a marriage alliance, as Louis had found another Gourmel in the person of a gentleman who once before had supplied him with valuable information, the Doctor de Lucena. Among some papers which Louis handed over at some time to his chancellor, Pierre d'Oriole, was a set of instructions given by Ferdinand on 11 August 1477, to the Doctor de Lucena and Lope de Valdeniesso as they were starting for England. In these

---

1. *Lettres de Louis XI*, VI, 212-214; Dupuy, I, 368-370.
2. Alphonso, fearing that Louis was going to hand him over to Ferdinand, tried to get out of France in disguise. This made Louis feel a little ashamed, and at the end of August he ordered some ships to be made ready to take the king of Portugal home. Commynes, I, 383, and note 3.

instructions, the original copy of which, with Ferdinand's seal attached, is still to be seen in the Bibliothèque Nationale, Ferdinand directed his two envoys first of all to exact from the king of England a sworn promise that he would confide nothing of what they told him to anyone except his wife and his chancellor—and not even to them except under oath—and then, when this promise had been given, to say to him that if he would help Ferdinand and Isabella to meet the expenses of war with the king of France and the king of Portugal, and if he would also help them to repay the money they had received from the king of Naples in anticipation of a marriage between the Prince of Capua and their daughter, then they, the king of Naples consenting, would be ready to conclude the marriage between the Infanta Isabella and the Prince of Wales.[1] With this document in his possession, what need had Louis of any further information about the negotiations for the marriage of the Infanta Isabella and the Prince of Wales?

Louis' ambassadors did not remain long in England, and when they set out for home, Edward sent some ambassadors with them.[2] Fain would one hear that Louis' invitation to him to do a little robbing of Mary of Burgundy on his own account had given Edward a moral shock, and that his reply was the instantaneous and indignant refusal which his subjects would undoubtedly have given had they been the ones to make the answer. But, sad to say, everything goes to show that Edward had received the invitation without surprise and, instead of declining it, had proceeded to weigh it leisurely and with cool selfishness, since he seems to have done nothing more in the beginning than to instruct his ambassadors to protest mildly against the attack that was being made on Mary and to ask Louis what excuse he had to offer for what he was doing.[3] Yet while Edward was speaking thus gently, Louis' armies were going on with their work and had begun to lay siege to St Omer. "The French king hath burned all the towns and fair abbeys that were that way about St Omer and also the corns which are there," wrote an

---

1. MS. Dupuy 760, f. 89. Cf. Legrand coll., MS. français 6985, f. 234. In MS. français 4054, f. 196, may also be found a letter written to Edward on 31 July 1477, by Pedro Velasco, Conte de Haro. It relates to the mission of Lope de Valdeniesso, and it too was probably given to Louis by the Doctor de Lucena.
2. *Cal. Milanese Papers*, 1, 229.
3. This appears from the reply which Howard, Tunstall, and Langton afterwards carried to Louis.

indignant Englishman from Calais on 17 August. It was reported at the same time that Cassel, "that is mine old Lady of Burgundy's jointure, and all the country there about" had been burned and that the French king intended, if he failed to capture St Omer, to bring his army "through these marches into Flanders." Another story was that Louis had "railed greatly" about Lord Hastings to Tiger Pursuivant "openly before two hundred of his folks," and as this looked as if he were trying to make an excuse for attacking Calais itself, Hastings grew suspicious and ordered the destruction of "all the passages except Newnham bridge, which is watched," and kept the turnpike shut at night. What made the situation doubly alarming was the fact that when Maximilian, whose marriage with Mary of Burgundy took place on 19 August, arrived for the wedding, it was found that he had brought with him, not the large army everyone had hoped for, but, according to Paston's worried friend, only four hundred men and "an hundred thousand ducats, which is but a small thing in regard for that he hath to do."[1]

When the news got abroad that Maximilian had failed to bring Mary the help that had been expected of him, Louis thought at once of the probable effect this would have on Edward. Now, he seems to have said to himself, my cousin of England will see that Burgundy is doomed and will regret that he did not accept my invitation to enter the war. For the Archbishop of Vienne and Olivier le Roux had not much more than reached home when they were sent back to England, accompanied by Monsieur de la Rocheguyon, to suggest again that Edward should enter into an alliance with the king of France against Burgundy. In reply to the question Edward had asked, Louis now explained at length why his attack on "Madame d'Autriche," as he now chose to call Mary, was "très juste et raisonnable cause" and why the king of England ought to be glad to help rather than to oppose him. He repeated his assertion that he was justified in seizing the lands the Duke of Burgundy had held in the kingdom of France, because they had been forfeited by the rebellions, disobedience, and crimes of leze-majesty committed first by Charles and afterwards by his daughter, while as for the lands Charles had held outside of France, those, he declared, he was justly entitled to by right of conquest. To strengthen his argument, he referred to the treaty of Peronne, which, he claimed, gave him the right to seize Charles's territories in case

1. *Paston Letters*, V, 297-298.

Charles violated the treaty, as he had done in many ways. He also explained that the sole right and title which the house of Burgundy had to the duchy and county of Burgundy was derived from the present King John of France once made of them to his son Philip in appanage, and as in France, he said, it was customary for all appanages to return to the crown on the failure of male heirs,[1] the duchy and county of Burgundy had returned, at the death of the late Duke Charles, to the crown of France as appanage land. For that reason Madame d'Autriche had no right whatever to the said duchy and county, and yet she had had the temerity to attempt to hold them by force and even to form an alliance with the Swiss against the king of France![2]

By such reasoning as this Louis tried to show that it was not he who had offended against Mary of Burgundy, but Mary of Burgundy who had offended against him. He realized, however, that there was another awkward fact to be explained away, the fact that he had violated the truce which he had signed with Charles and which had not yet expired at the time of the duke's death. But he felt no twinges of conscience on that score, as his truce with Charles, he maintained, could not extend to anything involving the recovery of the rights of the crown of France, and, what was more, Charles himself had broken the truce in divers ways, while he, the king of France, had kept it faithfully up to the time when Madame d'Autriche tried to retain possession of his domains and deny his rights. He threw in the statement, too, that Charles's daughter had offended in another way against the law of France and the welfare of the state; for although by the law and ancient usage of France, the daughters of princes of the blood could not marry without the consent of the king, she had taken unto herself a husband without consulting him.

But all the time Louis knew that what Edward was most concerned about was the fate of Artois and Flanders, and at last he steered gingerly toward that

---

1. Louis cited the case of the appanage which King John gave to another of his sons, the Duke of Berry. The Duke of Berry left three daughters, but none of them succeeded to the appanage, and though the duke had given the duchy of Auvergne, a part of his appanage, to the daughter who married the Duke of Bourbon, that was done only with the consent of the king, who gave it because, through the marriage, the whole duchy of Bourbon became appanage land and returnable to the crown on failure of male heirs.
2. Louis was also ready to offer a tediously long explanation of how his right to the county of Burgundy was derived from the sale of the county by Count Otto of Burgundy to Philip le Bel when his daughter married Philip's son.

subject. Drawing another treaty from the archives of the past, he announced that the treaty of Arras entitled him to seize Peronne, Montdidier, and Roye, because they were to return to the crown of France in default of male heirs descended from the late Duke Philip. Furthermore, everyone knew, he declared, that the counties of Flanders and Artois and all other lands held by the late Dukes of Burgundy in the kingdom of France were fiefs of the crown of France and that, by the custom of Flanders and Artois, fiefs were forfeited to the feudal lord when homage was not rendered within forty days. When Madame d'Autriche failed to do homage for those lands, he was so anxious to act with reason and justice that he assembled many of the princes and lords of the blood and the members of his great council and the Parliament of Paris to ask their advice, and they all told him that he was bound by his coronation oath to seize the said lands held of him by the house of Burgundy.

Summing up, Louis claimed that the above facts, and also others which it would take too long for him to rehearse, made it clear that he was fully justified in attacking Madame d'Autriche, and, reminding Edward once more that they had sworn to assist each other in case of rebellion or disobedience on the part of their subjects, he expressed his belief that his brother and cousin, the king of England, would not take the part of the daughter of the Duke of Burgundy, but would unite with him, for the sake of the safety of both of them, in putting down her rebellion. All that it was necessary to do to accomplish this easily, he said, was to arrange the division of Madame d'Autriche's lands—both those within the kingdom of France and those without—which had already been spoken of, to decide how the war was to be carried on, and to draw up the agreements in such a way that they would have to be kept and promptly carried out.[1]

Thus spoke the tempter. Before Edward had had time, however, to do more than hear what the French ambassadors desired to say word came that Louis had signed a truce with Maximilian.[2] Although Louis' armies had been so successful at the start, his affairs had not been prospering so well of late, as his alliance with the Swiss had broken down, the Prince of Orange, the nominal head of the troops

---

1. MS. français 4054, ff. 203-210—the original draft, with corrections, of Louis' instructions to the Archbishop of Vienne, Monsieur de la Rocheguyon, and Olivier le Roux. Cf. *Cal. Milanese Papers*, I, 230
2. Legeay, II, 293-294.

he had sent to overrun the duchy of Burgundy, had revolted and gone over to Mary, the towns of Flanders were still resisting, and the nobility of France had been made restless by the execution on 4 August of the Duke of Nemours. With relief, therefore, Louis signed a truce with Maximilian on 28 September and retired to his favourite winter residence in sunny Touraine, Plessis-du-Parc-lès-Tours.

Calais breathed more easily after Louis made his temporary peace with Maximilian and called off his armies.[1] But while there was a lull in the war, there was none in Louis' efforts to ensnare Edward. Although the Archbishop of Vienne, Le Roux, and La Rocheguyon went back to France in a short time, early in October they were replaced at the English court by Charles de Martigny, Bishop of Elne, an ecclesiastic already known to Edward, as on some previous occasion since the signing of the treaty of Amiens he had spent a couple of months in England.[2] The Bishop of Elne soon persuaded Edward to send another embassy to Louis, and the men the king selected for the purpose were Lord Howard, Sir Richard Tunstall, and Thomas Langton. These three ambassadors received their commission on 30 November,[3] and they were on their way to Touraine soon after; but as somewhere *en route* they met Guillaume Restout, and Howard was paid his half-yearly allowance from Louis of six hundred crowns,[4] it is much to be feared that at least one of their number arrived at Louis' door at Plessis-du-Parc-lès-Tours in a frame of mind a little too friendly towards the king with whom they had come to treat.

---

1. The "crew" Hastings had taken over to Calais was reduced in size on 26 September. Warrants for Issues, 18 Edw. IV, 8 Feb.
2. "Interogatoires faicts à Messire Charles de Martigny, Evesque d'Eaulne, Ambassadeur du Roy Louis XI en Angleterre es mois de juillet, aoust, et septembre, 1480," MS. français 18,427, ff. 286-367. (Cited in subsequent notes as "The Trial of the Bishop of Elne.") The bishop stated that Louis sent for him in September, that he found the king at Arras, that fifteen days later he was sent to England, and that, immediately after, the Archbishop of Vienne and the other French ambassadors whom he found at the English court were recalled. See the interrogatory of 2 August. As it was during the last half of September that Louis was at Arras, it must have been October before the bishop reached England. In regard to his earlier journey to England we have no information beyond his statement that Louis sent him thither soon after the treaty with the king of England was signed, and that he remained in England on that occasion two months. He may have accompanied Howard, Cheyne, and Montgomery when they went home in October 1475.
3. Rymer, XII, 50.
4. Howard gave Restout a receipt on 15 December. Edward received his money on 4 January. Restout's account; Signed Bills, file 1513, no. 4929.

Evidently to give his negotiations with Edward's ambassadors the better start, on 23 December Louis ordered that reparations should be made to some English merchants who had been attacked by pirates from the coast of Poitou and Saintonge.[1] Three days later he received Howard, Tunstall, and Langton and listened to what they had to tell him. The king of France, the Englishmen began by saying, has twice sent Monsieur de Vienne and others to propose to the king of England that he should assist him against the daughter of the late Duke Charles of Burgundy and that they should divide between them the lands they conquered; and after the last journey of Monsieur de Vienne and his companions, the king of France had sent in their place the Bishop of Elne to proceed with the negotiations begun by Monsieur de Vienne. But it was not strange that the king of England had taken so long to send his answer to the king of France, as in order to make what he did "firm and stable" he must have the approval of the lords, barons, and others of his realm, and when he consulted them, they raised several objections. To begin with, they wanted an explanation of the "justice of the quarrel" on account of which the war was being waged. Second, they said that, owing to the troubles through which England had passed, it would be difficult to find the money for the war, and they must know how the war was to be conducted and maintained. Third, they pointed out that as most of England's trade was with the countries held by the Duke of Austria and his wife, especially Flanders, and as this trade would cease when the war began, England would suffer much harm. Fourth, they called attention to the difficulty of recovering the goods which English merchants now had in those countries, and which would be seized the moment the war commenced. Fifth, they remarked that no agreement had yet been reached about the division of the possible conquests. And sixth, they said that although there was an "amity" between the king of England and the king of France, that amity was for their lives only, whereas the war, if once begun, might outlast the lifetime of both kings, and England might thus find herself left alone in the war and suffer great loss. In a word, while it was the king of England's intention, Howard, Tunstall, and Langton said, to maintain and observe his amity with the king of France and to keep all the other promises he had made to him, he and his subjects strongly objected

---

1. Tardif, *Monuments historiques*, II, 495.

to plunging into the perils of war without knowing just what they had to depend on.[1]

Edward had not accepted Louis' invitation, but no more had he refused it. Keep on sending ambassadors to me, he seemed to say, and maybe by and by I will do the thing you ask. And Louis must have laughed in sly glee. For what more did he want? Certainly he was not burning to divide Mary of Burgundy's heritage with the king of England.

---

1. "C'est ce que les ambassadeurs d'Angleterre distrent an roy en effect an Plesseys du parc le xxvi[e] jour de decembre l'an mil CCCC lxxvii," MS. français 4054, f. 229. (See Appendix XII).

THE END OF CLARENCE

On 15 January 1478, two little children were married in St Stephen's Chapel at Westminster. The bride was Anne Mowbray, aged six years, the bridegroom Richard, Duke of York, aged four, and their marriage was the result of two years of parental bargaining. Until now, as his negotiations with the kings of France and Scotland and with Ferdinand and Isabella of Spain plainly show, Edward had preferred to look for husbands and wives for his children among the princes and princesses of the reigning houses of Europe rather than among his own subjects, however noble or affluent. For this preference his reasons are obvious, as marriage alliances with other royal houses increased his influence and authority in Europe and, by so doing, tended to give added strength to his dynasty at home. They also served to gratify his personal ambition and that of his queen, which was perhaps greater than his own. Yet great wealth and vast estates in England had their attractions, too, and when, in January 1476, John Mowbray III, Duke of Norfolk, was gathered to his fathers[1] and, for lack of male heirs, all his worldly goods passed to his little daughter Anne, Edward at once resolved to offer the hand of his second son to the young heiress. So eager was the king to lay hold of the Mowbray inheritance that, almost before the Duke of Norfolk had been laid in his grave, he delegated Sir John Say and other members of his council to open negotiations with the Duchess of Norfolk for the marriage he desired.[2]

---

1. According to Sir John Paston, who seems to have been, if not under the duke's very roof at the time, at least nearby, Norfolk died on Tuesday night, 16 January, but according to the inquisition taken in the following year, the duke died on the Tuesday after Epiphany, which would mean 9 January. *Paston Letters*, V, 245; Inquisitions *post mortem*, 17 Edw. IV, no. 58. In the inquisition it is stated that the duke's daughter Anne was four years of age on 10 December preceding his death.
2. Tellers' Roll, Mich. 16 Edw. IV. Paston seems to have hoped that the duchess was *enceinte* at the time of her husband's death. *Paston Letters*, V, 250.

If Edward expected Anne Mowbray's mother to accept his offer on the instant, he was quickly undeceived. The Duchess of Norfolk appreciated to the full the value of her daughter's hand, and she proved a shrewd bargainer. By 12 June 1476, the marriage negotiations had evidently made some progress, as on that day the title of Earl of Nottingham—a title which the late Duke of Norfolk had borne and which had become extinct at his death— was given to the Duke of York;[2] but the duchess's full consent probably was not secured much before 7 February 1477, when the Duke of York was created Duke of Norfolk and Earl Warren and received from his father a grant of "one chamber being in our Receipt above the council chamber of our dearest son, the Prince, to have and to hold .... as his council chamber during his life. "[2] Even when Anne's mother had been brought to terms, the king's difficulties were not over. As Anne Mowbray's great-grandmother had been a sister of the Duke of York's grandmother, a papal dispensation had to be obtained before the marriage could take place, and in all probability it was the slowness of the machinery at Rome, which always needed much lubricating with golden oil, that saved the two babes from wedlock for another year. By the closing days of 1477, however, all the necessary agreements had been signed and all the necessary documents procured from Rome, and as parliament was to meet in the middle of January, it was decided that the marriage should be celebrated at that time, when many of the leading men of the realm would be gathered at Westminster and could lend dignity to the occasion by their presence.

Anne Mowbray was brought to Westminster Palace on 14 January, and the wedding was solemnized on the following morning. With the Earls of Lincoln and Rivers supporting her on either hand and with many other lords and ladies in her train, the little bride was conducted from the queen's chamber, through the king's great chamber and the White Hall, to St Stephen's Chapel, where the walls had been hung with carpets of azure besprinkled with golden fleur-de-lis, and where the king and queen, the Prince of Wales, the Duchess of York, the Princesses Elizabeth, Mary, and

---

1. Close Roll 16 Edw. IV, m. 14; Nicolas, *Hist. Peerage*.
2. Charter Roll 15-22 Edw. IV, m. 12; *Cal. Patent Rolls*, III, 15; Warrants for Issues, 16 Edw. IV, 7 Feb. "Mr. Molyneux" was the Duke of York's chancellor, Andrew Dymock his attorney, and Sir Thomas Grey his chamberlain. Gairdner, *Richard III*, 341; Nicolas, *Wardrobe Accounts of Edw. IV*, 156.

Cecily, and, supposedly, the bridegroom were waiting to receive her under a canopy of cloth of gold. The procession was halted at the chapel door until the papal dispensation was brought forth, but when this had been done by John Gunthorp, dean of the king's chapel, Anne and her attendants were permitted to enter the chapel and the marriage ceremony was performed by the Bishop of Norwich, the king himself giving away the bride. Mass was then celebrated at the high altar, and when the Duke of Gloucester, dipping his hands into golden basins filled with gold and silver coins, had thrown a largess to the spectators, and spices and wines had been passed, "as appertaineth to matrimonial feasts," Gloucester and the Duke of Buckingham led the bride back to the king's great chamber, where the wedding banquet was spread and where "the press was so great," relates one who was present, "that I might not see to write the names of them that served, the abundance of the noble people were so innumerable."[1]

The wedding festivities did not come to end with the banquet in the king's great chamber. Three days later the king made four and twenty new knights of the Bath in honour of his son's marriage, and four days later still there was a great "exercise of arms" at Westminster, the articles for which had been drawn up by the Marquis of Dorset and Earl Rivers, the chief challengers, and proclaimed weeks before in Westminster Hall, at the Standard in Cheap, at Leadenhall, at Grace Church, and at London bridge end.[2] Three kinds of jousts were performed before the tournament was over—"jousts royal," jousts run in "hosting harness," and jousts with swords; and when the little Duchess of York, as "the princess of the feast," distributed the prizes, the A of gold set with a diamond was assigned to Thomas Fiennes, Lord Dacre's second son, as "the best jouster of the joust royal," the E of gold set with a ruby to Richard Haute, as "the best runner in hosting harness," and the M of gold set with an emerald to Robert Clifford, as the one who had "tourneyed best with swords."[3] But to whomsoever the

1. "Narrative of the Marriage of Richard, Duke of York, with Anne of Norfolk, the Matrimonial Feast, and the Grand Justing," a contemporary account of the wedding printed in W. H. Black's *Illustrations of Ancient State and Chivalry* (Roxburghe Club, 1840), 27-40. By what must be a slip of someone's pen, "my Lord of Richmond" is mentioned as one of the guests at the wedding feast. The Countess of Richmond may have been present, but certainly her son was not.
2. A copy of the articles may be found in Harleian MS. 69, ff. 1-2.
3. *Illustrations of Ancient State and Chivalry, ut sup.*

prizes fell, no person had succeeded in drawing more attention to himself on that day than Earl Rivers, who had appeared in the field "horsed and armed in the habit of a white hermit" and bringing with him his hermitage, "walled and covered with black velvet." Among those who had ventured to accept Rivers's challenge was Sir Thomas de Vere, who by this time had been forgiven for his share in what had happened at St Michael's Mount; but defeat was probably that daring nobleman's portion, as not even a De Vere could hope to contend successfully on this kind of a battlefield with "the victorious Earl Rivers." It was only in the presence of the "froward earls" of the Swiss cantons, fighting for their independence and their liberties, that Anthony Woodville's courage forsook him.

To the casual observer nothing could have looked more bright and happy than the court of England at the time of the marriage of the king's second son. Yet every one of the wedding guests knew that, while the wine was flowing in the banquet hall and swords were being broken on the tournament field, a dark cloud was hanging over the house of York, and among those who had waited under the canopy of cloth of gold for the bride's entry into St Stephen's Chapel there must have been at least one person whose heart was very heavy. For while two uncles of the little bridegroom, the Duke of Gloucester and Earl Rivers, had played such conspicuous roles in the festivities, another uncle, who was entitled to play quite as prominent a part as they, had not been so much as bidden to the wedding; and the mother love which had sent the Duchess of York hurrying in dread to Canterbury just before Clarence crossed to Calais to marry Warwick's daughter must have been suffering intensely in these days when that much erring son was lying in the Tower awaiting no one knew what punishment. What passed between Edward and his mother after Clarence's arrest it is not given us to know, but that the Duchess of York pleaded for Clarence's life we may be sure, as no true mother ever failed to plead for the life of a son however sinful. Yet much as Edward loved and revered his mother, any effort the Duchess of York made to save Clarence proved vain. Whether the hint thrown out by the king of France through Olivier Le Roux was based on truth or falsehood, it offered only too good an explanation of Clarence's strange actions, and it sealed his fate. When the duke was ordered to the Tower, it was so well understood that the day of his final reckoning had come that in September a rumour was already

going about on the continent that he had been put to death.[1] But though
Edward may have made up his mind as early as September that Clarence
must die, he had no thought of committing another secret murder in the
Tower. Along with the rumour of the duke's death went another that the
king of England was in fear of an uprising of his people, and this part of
the tale at least might have turned out to be true had Clarence's death
been brought about in any mysterious way. For the duke had his friends
and adherents still, and England, in spite of some experience, had never
acquired a liking for royal murders. In any case, what need was there that
Clarence, who had sinned so openly time and again, should be murdered
as Henry VI had been murdered? Without doubt the duke had violated the
laws of the land, without doubt he had been, if he was not still, a traitor; and
instead of sending Gloucester or some other emissary to the Tower to drive
a dagger into Clarence's heart, Edward could avail himself of a much safer
means of putting his brother out of the way, namely, a bill of attainder.

When parliament convened the day after the marriage of the Duke of
York and Anne Mowbray, the chancellor took for the theme of his address
the fidelity which subjects owe to their king, and when he quoted the
words of St Paul, "Non sine causa rex gladium portat," all understood
his meaning. The Duke of Clarence was about to be called to account for
his sins. Edward himself was the duke's only accuser, and in the bill of
attainder the king charged his brother with a new plot against his throne.
He declared that, although on divers occasions in the past he had been
forced to punish many rebels and traitors, yet after the great victories
which God had sent him he had not only spared "the multitudes in their
fields and assemblies overcome," but had pardoned, as all the world knew,
"the great movers, stirrers, and executors of such heinous treasons." Yet
how had his leniency been repaid? Only, it seemed, by further and more
wicked treason, since he had recently learned of "much higher, much more
malicious, more unnatural and loathly treason" than had been discovered
at any time from his "first reign hitherto." And what made this treason
doubly "heinous, unnatural, and loathly," the king complained, was that
it had been contrived and imagined by one who, of all earthly creatures,
was most in duty bound to love, honour, and thank him—by one, in fact,

---

1. *Cal. Milanese Papers*, I, 230.

whom it "greatly agrudged" his heart to name, to wit, his brother George, Duke of Clarence.

After Clarence's name had been thus reluctantly mentioned, the bill of attainder explained at some length why the king felt himself compelled to take action against him. Though the king had provided for his brother most liberally and had generously forgiven him for what he had done in 1470, the duke had plotted again to disinherit and destroy him and his children "by might to be gotten as well outward as inward." To further his evil ends, the duke had also striven to deprive the king of the affection of his subjects "by many subtle contrived ways." For instance, he had given money and venison to some of his servants and sent them into divers parts of the realm to assemble the king's subjects, "to feast them and cheer them" and make them think that Thomas Burdett had been unjustly put to death. He had also spread a report that the king "wrought by necromancy and used craft to poison his subjects, such as him pleased"; and he had started a story that the king was a bastard. He had induced divers men to swear on the Blessed Sacrament to be true to him and his heirs and had declared to them and others that the king had disinherited him and "intended to consume him in likewise as a candle consumeth in burning"; and he had obtained and secretly preserved an exemplification under the great seal of Henry VI of the agreement between himself and Margaret of Anjou "and other" which provided that, if Henry and his son died without male issue, he and his heirs should rule over England. He had recently sought, through the Abbot of Tewkesbury, one John Tapton, clerk, and one Roger Harewell, to introduce a strange child into his castle of Warwick, who was to be kept there "in likeliness of his son and heir" while his real son was sent to Ireland or Flanders to seek aid against the king; and only the refusal of Tapton and Harewell to deliver his son to the servant sent to fetch him prevented the accomplishment of this design. Finally, he had sent his servants into sundry parts of the kingdom to incite large numbers of the people to be ready at an hour's warning to help him make war on the king.

Formidable indeed was the list of Clarence's offences, and yet, after enumerating them, the king declared that he could still have found it in his heart to forgive his brother had he made "due submission." For nearness of blood, he said, and the tender love he had felt for Clarence in his youth inclined him to mercy. As the duke had shown himself so "incorrigible," however, the safety of the realm demanded his punishment, and the king asked that his brother should be attainted of high treason and be deprived for ever of the name of duke and of all estates and other property which had been granted to him by letters patent.[1]

The end of the sad tale is soon told. A few witnesses were brought in to testify, but they spoke more like accusers of the duke than like witnesses, and though Clarence denied every charge made against him and offered to prove his innocence by the ancient method of wager of battle, no one dared to say a word in his defence.[2] The Commons, under the influence of William Alyngton, who was once more their Speaker, were not long in signifying their approval of the bill of attainder, and on 7 February the Duke of Buckingham was appointed to pass sentence on the accused.[3] The sentence was death. Yet, even when the fatal word had been spoken, Edward could not make up his mind to take the final step, and Clarence remained in the Tower until at last Alyngton took upon himself the responsibility of sending the Duke to his doom. Coming into the House of Lords, the Speaker asked that whatever was going to be done should be done, and on 18 February Clarence's life was extinguished in the Tower.[4] So well did London's great fortress keep its dark secrets that not even the continuator of the Croyland Abbey chronicle, whose narrative is our only strictly contemporary English account of the last years of Edward IV's reign, seems to be quite sure how Clarence died; but the story which reached the ears of Commynes and other continental chroniclers, and which was repeated by later English writers, was that Clarence was drowned in a butt of malmsey wine. One French writer states that it was only the entreaties of his mother which saved the duke from public execution by disembowelment and beheading, while Jean Molinet declares that Clarence was allowed to decide the manner of his death and that he chose to be drowned in a butt of malmsey![5]

---

1. *Rolls of Parl.*, VI, 193-195.
2. *Hist. Croy. Cont.*, 562.
3. Signed Bills, file 1513, no. 4933; *Rolls of Parl.*, VI, 195; *Cal. Patent Rolls*, III, 63.
4. *Hist. Croy. Cont., ut sup.*; Inquisitions *post mortem:*, 18 Edw. IV, no. 46; Fabyan, 666; Kingsford's *London Chron.*, 188.
5. Commynes, I, 59; *Chronique Scandaleuse*, II, 64; Molinet, 377. Olivier de la Marche says (III, 70) that Clarence was drowned "en ung baine, comme l'on disoit." This seems a more likely story.

In whatever manner Clarence met his shameful death, his dead body was treated with the same respect, if not with the same pomp and display, that had been shown to the murdered corpse of Henry VI. "There be assigned certain lords to go with the body of the Duke of Clarence to Tewkesbury, where he shall be buried; the king intends to do right worshipfully for his soul," wrote Thomas Langton to the Prior of Christ Church, Canterbury.[1] But beyond this statement by Langton, all that can be learned about Clarence's funeral is that on 25 February his body was laid beside that of his wife in a vault behind the high altar of Tewkesbury Abbey.[2] Years afterward the bones of the brother of Edward IV and of the daughter of Warwick the Kingmaker were removed to another part of the abbey to make room for those of a Tewkesbury alderman and his family,[3] but pious hands have since restored them to their original tomb, and today they again moulder in peace under the shadow of the abbey's high altar and within a few feet of the resting place of the son of Henry VI, the young prince who is said to have cried in vain to Clarence for protection as he fled from the bloody field of Tewkesbury.

Edward chose to keep most of Clarence's estates in his own hands,[4] and he distributed the duke's offices and titles as he saw fit. Three days before the duke's execution the title of Earl of Salisbury, which Clarence had borne since 1472, was given to Gloucester's son, Edward Plantagenet, and three days after his execution the office of great chamberlain went back to Gloucester himself, who had surrendered it to Clarence in 1471, when the king was trying to make peace between his brothers. The lieutenancy of Ireland, the office to which Clarence had clung so long, was given in July to his namesake, George of Windsor, a third son recently born to the king.[5] Yet it should be added that, though Edward seized Clarence's property, he did not neglect the duke's

---

1. *Christ Church Letters* (Camden Society), 36-37.
2. The Rows Rol, ¶ 59.
3. Blunt, *Tewkesbury Abbey and its Associations* (1898), 85.
4. Ramsay, II, 425.
5. *Cal. Patent Rolls*, III, 67, 118. It is strange that there is no mention of Edward's third son until the lieutenancy of Ireland was given to him on 6 July 1478. By Sandford and others he is called George of Shrewsbury, but Mrs Green (*Princesses of Eng.*, IV, 3) long ago pointed out that his correct name is George of Windsor. For he was born, not at Shrewsbury, but at Windsor, and probably sometime before 15 November 1477, as the king did not go to Windsor at any time between that date and 6 July 1478. Household account book of 17-18 Edw. IV, Accounts, etc., Exchequer K. R., bundle

children. Clarence's son, who had been born at Warwick Castle on 21 February 1475, and to whom Edward himself had stood godfather, was suffered to retain the earldom of Warwick and was committed to the care of one Agnes Stanley,[1] while his daughter Margaret (born at Farleigh Castle on 14 August 1473)[2] seems to have been no less carefully watched over. On 11 January 1482, the king sent an order to the Exchequer for the payment of forty marks to the bearer of his warrant "as well for such clothing and other necessaries as belongen unto our dear and well beloved niece, Margaret, daughter unto our brother, late Duke of Clarence, as for contentation of wages unto such persons as we have commanded to attend upon her"; and in the following November fifty marks more were given to Margaret "as well for her arrayment as for the wages of her servants." Even the rights of the servants of "our late brother of Clarence" were not overlooked. Ten months after the duke's death they were paid £325 19s 3d for their "ordinary and household wages."[3]

"False, fleeting, perjured Clarence" is Shakespeare's now hackneyed characterization of the brother who plotted against Edward IV's throne and ended his days in a butt of malmsey; and though John Ross of Warwick says that Clarence was "a mighty prince, seemly of person and right witty and well visaged, a great alms giver and a great builder," few persons who look upon the plain slab in the pavement of Tewkesbury Abbey which is all that

---

412, no. 9. From the fact that the child was named George, it is probable that he was born before Clarence's attack on Ankarette Twynyho.

1. The Rows Rol, ¶ 60; Tewkesbury chron., Dugdale's *Monasticon*, II, 64; Issue Roll, Easter 19 Edw. IV, 6 July—a payment to Agnes Stanley for attending on the Earl of Warwick "infra ætatem." An annuity was afterwards granted to Agnes Stanley, and another to Marion Chamber, who had been the nurse of Clarence's son. *Cal. Patent Rolls*, III, 191, 199. Nicolas's supposition (*Hist. Peerage*, 501) that Clarence's son did not succeed to the earldom of Warwick until after the death of his grandmother, Anne Beauchamp, seems to be wrong, since the child is called Earl of Warwick not only in the entry on the Issue Roll just cited, but in some grants made by the king in August 1479, and March 1480, and in the wardrobe accounts of 1480, edited by Nicolas himself. *Cal. Patent Rolls*, III, 159, 192; Nicolas, *Wardrobe Accounts of Edw. IV*, 157. Furthermore, the Tewkesbury chronicle, when speaking of the child's birth, says: "Et dictus Edwardus tunc ordinatur comes Warwick per dominum Edwardum regem."

2. Tewkesbury chron., *ut sup.*; The Rows Rol, ¶ 61.

3. Warrants for Issues, 18 Edw. IV, 5 Dec., 21 Edw. IV, 11 Jan., 22 Edw. IV, 16 Nov. For the names of Clarence's servants and the amount due to each one of them, see Exchequer T. R., Council and Privy Seal, file 91, m. 84, 5 Oct. 1478.

4. The Rows Rol, ¶ 59.

marks the duke's grave will feel that his fate was undeserved. Yet it is said that Edward never ceased to regret that he had consented to his brother's death and that all the rest of his life, whenever anyone came to him with a request for a pardon, he exclaimed in bitterness of spirit, "O unhappy brother, for whose deliverance no man asked!"[1]

If Edward lamented his brother's death so bitterly, why, it may be asked, did he sanction, if not seek it? Few even of the king's contemporaries knew the answer to that question. Polydore Vergil, who wrote his history when many of the prominent persons of Edward's reign were still living and who felt enough interest in the circumstances of Clarence's end to make special enquiries about it, states that, while some persons attributed the final and fatal breach between the king and his brother to Clarence's desire to marry the Duchess of Burgundy, the common folk believed that the real reason why George, Duke of Clarence, was put to death was that some soothsayer had told Edward that after him would reign one whose name began with the letter G. And Vergil adds that, although he questioned many of the leading members of Edward's council, not one of them could give him a satisfactory explanation of why Clarence was executed.[2]

Perhaps the only men in Edward's council who could have told Vergil the whole truth were Lord Hastings, who was summoned home from Calais so soon after Olivier le Roux arrived in England, and Robert Stillington, Bishop of Bath and Wells, who was suddenly sent to the Tower a few days after Clarence's dead body was borne out of it;[3] and both Hastings and Stillington had gone to a better world before Vergil came to England. In view, however, of the insinuations of the king of France concerning the schemes of Clarence and the Duchess Margaret, in view of the curious story of Clarence's attempt to spirit his son away to Ireland or Flanders and the statement in the bill of attainder that he had circulated a report that his brother Edward was a bastard, and lastly, in view of the suspicion Edward had entertained that his Burgundian brother-in-law meant to set up a claim to his throne, it is probably a safe guess that Clarence's "heinous, unnatural, and loathly" treason

---

1. Vergil, 681. Cf. *Hist. Croy. Cont.*, 562.
2. Vergil, *ut sup.* John Ross also mentions the story of the soothsayer's prediction in his *Historia Regum Angliæ*, 215.
3. *Stonor Letters and Papers*, II, 42.

consisted in a plan to marry Mary of Burgundy and, after declaring Edward to be of illegitimate birth and without right to reign, to seize the throne with the help of Mary's pretended claim to it and her money and arms.

Why Stillington was imprisoned so soon after Clarence's execution is as much a matter of doubt as the immediate cause of Clarence's punishment. The bishop did not spend many weeks in the Tower, for he ransomed himself, it is said, by paying the king a certain sum of money.[1] According to the pardon which was granted to him on 20 June, the bishop was accused of violating his oath of fidelity by some utterance prejudicial to the king but, on being summoned before the king and certain lords spiritual and temporal, was able to prove his innocence and faithfulness.[2] On the other hand, the story told at a later time was that Stillington had offended Edward by trying to persuade him, through the Duke of Gloucester, to make amends in some way to Lady Eleanor Butler, to whom, "pour en avoir son plaisir," the king had once upon a time, in his presence, made a secret proposal of marriage.[3] But the statement in the bishop's pardon is too vague to be worth much as an explanation, and the story about his effort on behalf of Lady Eleanor Butler must be discarded, as Commynes, who was an eager collector of facts concerning people and events in England, gives his readers distinctly to understand that the story of Edward's pre-contract with Lady Eleanor Butler was not told to Gloucester until after Edward's death, when Stillington, who never forgave Edward for sending him to the Tower, related it to the duke—probably invented it for him—in order to furnish him with ground for declaring Edward's children illegitimate.[4] In all likelihood too close association with Clarence or too much excusing of him was the true cause of Stillington's imprisonment. For it will be remembered that Stillington had been one of the most active workers for the reconciliation of Edward and Clarence before the battle of Barnet.

The Bishop of Bath and Wells was not the only person to whom Clarence's execution caused distress of mind and fear of personal disaster. Whether or not Stillington had been guilty of too much friendship for the fallen duke, there was no manner of doubt that Clarence had regarded the Earl of

---

1. Commynes, II, 64.
2. Rymer, XII, 66; *Cal. Patent Rolls*, III, 102.
3. Gairdner, *Richard III*, 90.
4. Commynes, I, 455, II, 64-65.

Oxford as a sympathizer and possible helper; and Oxford's imprisonment had probably been made more uncomfortable for him after the use which had been made of his name, with or without his knowledge, in the uprising in Cambridgeshire and Huntingdonshire. At all events, Oxford's courage seems to have given out when he heard of Clarence's death, and sometime in the spring or early summer he "leaped the walls" of Hammes Castle and "went to the dike, and into the dike to the chin ... some say to steal away, and some think he would have drowned himself, and so it is deemed."[1] But whatever the unhappy earl was seeking to do, he was pulled out of the dike and taken back to his prison, there to stay as long as Edward IV occupied the throne of England. The attainder of his brother Thomas was reversed by the same parliament that attainted Clarence, and in time his wife was granted a generous annuity,[2] but towards himself there was never any sign of relenting.

Parliament was adjourned, or dissolved, eight days after Clarence's execution.[3] It had been summoned mainly for the purpose of passing the bill of attainder, but it had transacted a small amount of other business as well. It had annulled the verdict against Ankarette Twynyho, repealed—probably in alarm at the use Clarence had tried to make of a document under Henry's seal—all acts of the parliament of Henry VI's readeption, reversed several attainders, including that of Sir Thomas de Vere, re-enacted the sumptuary law of 1463, and prohibited, in the hope of encouraging archery, so necessary to the soldier's training, dice, quoits, football, and "divers new imagined plays." It had also given its sanction to the agreement made by the king with the Duchess of Norfolk prior to the marriage of the Duke of York and Anne Mowbray, and it had taken away from George Neville, son of the late Marquis of Montagu and one-time fiancé of the king's eldest daughter, the title of Duke of Bedford. The excuse given for depriving Montagu's son of his dukedom was that his means were not sufficient to enable him to sustain the dignity, but doubtless the true reason was that the king wanted the dukedom of Bedford for his last born son, George of Windsor.[1]

---

1. *Paston Letters*, VI, 2-3. Paston's letter was written on 25 August 1478, but he speaks of Oxford's leap into the dike as if it had occurred some time before.
2. *Rolls of Parl.*, VI, 176; *Cal. Patent Rolls*, III, 157, 254. Cf. Scofield, *Eng. Hist. Review*, April 1914, pp. 243-244, where, I regret to say, I stated that the Countess of Oxford's annuity was granted on 16 February 1481. In reality it was granted just a year later.
3. Davies *York Records*, 66.

On 1 March Speaker Alyngton received a grant of a hundred pounds from the king in consideration of his "good and laudable services," and a few months later he was made one of the king's councillors and presented with a life grant of the issues of certain lands which had belonged to the Duke of Clarence.[2] But this was slight recompense for the eternal shame the Speaker had earned for himself by the part he had taken in the tragedy of Clarence's death, and he enjoyed his rewards scarcely more than a year, as he died on 16 May 1479.[3]

During the spring Edward obtained a half tenth from the province of Canterbury, and afterwards the province of York also gave him a half tenth and ultimately a second one.[4] From parliament, however, the king had sought no money. Probably he had no desire to test the attitude of the Commons towards him, and fortunately he had no need to do so, as he was now so prosperous that he was not only able to "live upon his own," but to satisfy some of his creditors. As long ago as March 1476, he had effected a settlement with Caniziani, who promised to accept three thousand pounds as full satisfaction for all his claims against him and to restore to him "all assignments, tallies, and patents as appeareth by a bill of record written by Hugh Fenne of his own hand";[5] and now, in the spring of 1478, he succeeded in adjusting matters with his still heavier creditor, the city of London. Edward owed London at this time £12,923 9s 8d, but he cleared off the entire debt by granting the city certain remunerative port and other offices and the reversion of the office of coroner in the city and suburbs, which had been attached heretofore to the chief butlership of England. A few months after making this bargain with the city of London, he also took steps to pay off his smaller creditors.[6]

---

1. *Rolls of Parl.*, VI, 168-192; Ramsay, II, 426, note, 469. Gloucester was granted the custody and marriage of Montagu's son. *Cal. Patent Rolls*, III, 192.
2. Warrants for Issues, 17 Edw. IV, 1 March; Writs of Privy Seal, file 866, no. 4829, 8 July; *Cal. Patent Rolls*, III, 142.
3. Inquisitions *post mortem*, 19 Edw. IV, no. 8.
4. Wilkins, III, 612; Wake, 380; Fine Rolls, 18 Edw. IV, m. 3, and 19 Edw. IV, m. 1 and 2.
5. Warrants for Issues, 16 Edw. IV, 30 March. Caniziani was to be paid one thousand pounds in ready money, one thousand in assignments on the last tenth granted by the clergy, and one thousand "in sufficient and ready payment" at the following Michaelmas. An indorsement on the warrant shows that the first payment was made in Easter term.
6. Exchequer Accounts, Miscellaneous, bundle 516, no. 13—three acquittances given

In accordance with the decision made by parliament in the autumn of 1473, all persons holding accounts against the king which antedated 1 December 1470, had been ordered by proclamation, in February 1474, to bring them to the Exchequer, where, after due proof, they would receive tallies, bills, or letters patent insuring the repayment of their money in twenty yearly instalments.[1] Yet few of the king's creditors seem to have heeded this order, as in the spring of 1475 the Commons complained of delays and that the proclamation had not been duly made in some parts of the kingdom. The time given for the presentation of accounts was then slightly extended,[2] but as at that moment the king needed every penny he had for his expedition to France, those who at last brought in their accounts were put off again. For three years longer the king's promise remained unfulfilled, but he had not forgotten it, and on 20 July 1478, he sent word to the Exchequer that, "for the more near and shorter contentation of our debts proved before the barons of our Exchequer" by force of the act of parliament passed in the thirteenth year of his reign, and "for the pleasure of God and health of our soul," he had given full power to John Morton, Keeper of the Rolls, and William Essex, remembrancer of the Exchequer, to make a settlement with his creditors holding such proofs, and that he wished those creditors to be paid without delay out of "our treasure" and the tenths last granted by the province of Canterbury.[3]

It was not only his debts which disturbed Edward's now thrifty soul. He was troubled also by the knowledge that, owing to the loose way in which his housekeeping affairs were managed, much money was being wasted in his household; and at the same time that he set out to cancel his debts, he made an effort to stop the financial leakages occurring in his ménage. Almost simultaneously with the notice he sent to the Exchequer of what he had directed Morton and Essex to do, he dispatched another warrant to

---

by the mayor and commonalty of London on 21 April; Palgrave, *Cely Papers*, III, 27; Writs of Privy Seal, file 866, 210. 4807; *Cal. Patent Rolls*, III, 303.

1. Close Roll 13 Edw. IV, m. 3 dorso. See also Signed Bills, file 1507, no. 4614.

2. *Rolls of Parl.*, VI, 161-162

3. Warrants for Issues, 18 Edw. IV, 20 July. By command of the treasurer and of William Essex, Thomas Bulkeley, officer of the Receipt, made "divers and many great searches and writings" showing "all manner of annuities, wages, fees, and rewards yearly paid and to be paid at the Receipt" from the first year of Edward's reign. *Ibid.*, 6 Feb. Evidently Edward was bent on a general house-cleaning.

the Chancery in which he stated that, by the advice of his council, he had made "certain ordinances for the stablishing of our household comprised in a book which by our commandment shall be delivered unto you by our trusty and right well beloved clerk and councillor, Master Thomas Langton," and ordered the chancellor to "do put all the said ordinances in writing, sealed under our great seal, and the same so sealed send unto us by our said councillor without delay."[1] The actual book carried to the Chancery by Langton, and also the copy of it which must have been made at the Chancery and sealed as the king had ordered, have disappeared; but a seventeenth century transcript of the ordinances, entitled "Orders and Regulations set down for the Government of the Household of His Majesty, King Edward the Fourth," is still preserved at the Public Record Office,[2] and a careful comparison of it with the famous "Liber Niger Domus Regis Edwardi IV," which was published by the Society of Antiquaries in 1790 and about the genuineness of which there has been some probably uncalled-for discussion, would be of no small interest, at least to the antiquarian. Space prohibits that here, but a few words in regard to the two sets of household ordinances may not come amiss.

The date of the Liber Niger, much of which is avowedly based on very ancient custom, is uncertain, but its contents justify the conclusion that it was drawn up by Edward's order and offered to him for his approval soon after his accession to the throne. Certainly it is older than the ordinances which Langton delivered to the chancellor in July 1478, for the Duke of Clarence is one of the persons credited with having "builded" it. Whatever the gap in time, however, between the Liber Niger and the ordinances of 1478, both reveal the same household organization, with the same offices—the counting-house, the bake-house, the pantry, the cellar, the pitcher-house, the spicery, the confectionery, the chaundlery, the ewery, the lavendry, etc.—and the same officers. Both speak of the bishop confessor, who watched over the king's soul, and of the lord chamberlain, "the chief head of rulers in the king's chamber," as the Liber Niger calls him, whose

---

1. Warrants under the Signet, file 3389, 9 July 1478.
2. Miscellaneous Books, Exchequer L. T. R., no. 206. The book is attested by Sir J. Williamson as being a copy of "a fair Manuscript Book" given to him by Dr Barlow, Provost of Queen's College, Oxford, 1671–1672.

duty it was to look after everything pertaining to the king's "proper royal person, for his proper beds, for his proper board at meal times," and who appointed the carvers and cupbearers and other subordinate officers of the chamber. Both mention also the lord steward, second only to the lord chamberlain in importance, who presided over the court of Marshalsea, or "court of household," sitting "at the board of doom within the household, that is, at the Greencloth in the counting-house," and who on all occasions was the special representative of the king's estate; and both refer to the treasurer and comptroller, the wardens of the household purse and accounts, the cofferers, who kept the accounts and paid the fees, wages, and rewards, and the secretary, with his clerks, who did the king's writing for him and received the necessary parchment, paper, and red wax from the office of the great spicery. In addition to these functionaries, there were the religious officers—the dean of the chapel, who had full charge of all matters concerning the royal chapel, including the assignment of "all the sermons and the persons" and general oversight of the choir and the children of the chapel, famed for the sweetness of their voices, the chaplains, two of whom were always on hand at meal time "to say the day matins mass before the king for graces," and the almoner, or almoners, who controlled the king's charities—and the health officers. The health officers included the doctor of physic, who held consultation with the cook and stood "much in the king's presence at his meals, counselling or answering to the king's grace which diet is best according, and to tell the nature and operations of all the meats," and the master surgeon, who did the bloodletting for all the household and was given the old linen for his "plasters." Finally, there were many petty officers of various sorts, such as minstrels, harbingers, sergeants, marshals, and ushers, knights and squires for the body, sewers or table waiters, clerks of the kitchen, the spicery, and the closet, and, as rulers of the kitchen, three master cooks.

It is not to be wondered at that in a household such as this expenses were very heavy and that abuses crept in despite the strict rules laid down from time to time for its government. The Liber Niger is so precise and minute in its statements that the weary reader feels that by no possibility can any detail have been overlooked or any loophole left open for extravagance or faithlessness on the part of the king's servants. Yet in the preamble of the ordinances of 1478 Edward stated that when, in the month of June of that year, "being right desirous to set within our household a politique, reasonable, and virtuous guiding in every behalf," he called before him the chief officers and clerks of his household and commanded them to make a report in regard to the revenues and expenditures and the rules and orders of his household, "certain enormities and misguidings" were revealed. The expenditures appeared to be in some ways "exceeding and wasteful," in others "wanting or diminute," and the accounts not so "orderly and justly demeaned" as accorded with honour and the good estate of the household. It was for this reason, the king said, that he decided to establish certain ordinances and directions for his household which should be based, not on prodigality, "which neither accordeth with honour, honesty, nor good manner," nor yet on avarice, "which is the worse extremity and a vice more odious and detestable," but on "the two virtues that be most requisite in such guiding and ruling," namely, liberality and justice, "which by philosophers is named of all virtues queen and empress."

Many were the rules, accordingly, that Edward laid down for the guidance of those who handled his money and kept his accounts. For example, he directed that his treasurer and cofferer should always be "two several persons," that no payments should be made except in the counting-house in the presence of the steward and comptroller, or the clerk comptroller at least, and that no officer or servant of the household should buy any "tally, obligation, bill, debenture, or assignment of any creditor," on pain of being put out of his office and the king's service for ever. But still more exact were the king's directions about the feeding of his numerous family, and it is evident that, while some money had been disappearing in the counting-house in improper ways, still more had been running away in the dining hall. For with all his announced intention of basing his ordinances on "liberality," Edward required every member of his household, except in case of sickness or blood-letting, to come to the hall to eat, and though the food provided was abundant, he did not intend that it should be handed out at all hours and without stint. While a "large breakfast" was to be prepared every day for the king, "to the intent that such lords, knights, and esquires, with other awaiting upon his person, shall mow break their fasts with that [that] remaineth of the same," and also one for the queen, "to the same intent," no other breakfasts were to be served, and no "whole beef" cut, except for the king's children or by order of the steward or one of the other household officers.

A loaf of bread for every two persons and a gallon of ale for every four was the allowance at each meal, and wine was served only on special occasions and then sparingly, by the half-pitcherful. The utmost care was also taken to see that no "broken meat" was wasted or carried off. But this was not just for economy's sake, as all such meat that was left in the hall, or that came out of the king's or the queen's chamber, was to be distributed daily to the people who stood at the gates waiting for the king's alms. If any yeoman or groom attempted to "embezzle" a bit of broken meat, or to dispose of it in any way without orders from the almoner, he was to be punished "at least in six days' wages"; and even the more important members of the household, the great officers excepted, were to lose a day's wages if they ventured to give away meat without the almoner's permission. It was also, apparently, to prevent the spiriting away of food that the ushers of the hall were commanded to "keep out of the hall door all men at meal times but such as should come in of duty and strangers such as they can think by their discretions be for the king's honour," and that the porters were ordered to see that "neither messes of meat, nor vessel, nor bottles of wine, nor pots of ale, or other victual, pass the gates without a special commandment of the steward, treasurer, or comptroller."

Edward's ordinances are not confined entirely, however, to the subjects of account keeping and food conservation. They also contain some articles relating to the old source of discontent, the royal prerogative of purveyance. Almost ten years since, in March 1469, Edward had issued a lengthy proclamation in which he had warned his subjects not to heed the demands of any person claiming to be his or the queen's purveyor until such person had exhibited a warrant under the great or the privy seal. He had also confirmed by the same proclamation a statute of 23rd Henry VI which had endeavoured to render the right of purveyance less onerous to the people.[1] But the proclamation of 1469, put forth in very troubled times, had probably remained a dead letter, and now, when the king was attempting a general setting to rights of his household, he again sought to quiet "the great clamour" which the exercise of the right of purveyance ever produced by ordering that only "sober and peaceable men and men of good suffisance and power" should be employed as his purveyors and caterers, and by requiring such agents not only to swear to exercise their office "truly, justly, and equally, without oppression of the poor or favour of the rich," but to have their commission read to the people before taking the goods of any person.

Not the most earnest effort on the part of Edward IV or any other king, however, could make the right of purveyance anything but detestable.[1] It continued to be a curse to the people as long as it endured and, through the ill-will it excited, a constant source of danger to the crown.

---

1. Edward issued another proclamation intended to curb abuses by his purveyors on 16 November 1481. *Ibid.*, f. 170; London Journal 8, f. 260.

THE BISHOP OF ELNE

The king of France had sent Clarence to his grave, but he left all the sorrow and remorse for his deed to Edward. Why should he who had put his own brother to death without a tear weep over the fate of the brother of the king of England? No, if Louis felt any regret, it was only that the poisoned arrow he had shot into Clarence's breast had stopped there. For it was at the Duchess Margaret rather than at Clarence that he had aimed, and Margaret, unfortunately, seemed to have escaped unharmed. The quarrel which Le Roux's insinuations were meant to stir up between Edward and his sister had not come to pass, and to all appearances Clarence's death had done nothing to remove the danger of an alliance between the king of England and Mary and Maximilian. Yet Louis did not lose confidence in his ability to ward off by one artifice or another the alliance which would be such a catastrophe to him. He would need to play his game with skill, however, and the man he chose to handle his cards for him in England was the Bishop of Elne. Charles de Martigny was not as sharp a gamester as Louis himself, but, notwithstanding some superficial weaknesses, he was no dunce, and he succeeded in playing, as later events showed, a fairly good game, though he got no thanks for it.

According to the Bishop of Elne's own statement, Louis had explained to him many times before he sent him to England that what he wanted him to do was to "entertain" the king of England and the English people so that they would not interfere with the war he was waging against the Flemings. And to his task, as he understood it, the bishop stuck manfully, although he did so at the cost of very great discomfort, even, he believed, of very great danger, to himself. For though King Edward seemed to be quite willing to be "entertained," his subjects were not willing, and they made the fact evident by shouting "French dogs"—"qui estoit à dire chiens de France," the bishop afterwards explained to the Parliament of Paris—at the French ambassador and his attendants whenever they set foot outside their door. No wonder the bishop quailed! Yet the jeers of the London populace were not the worst of his troubles, as, almost before he knew it, he found himself fighting, single-handed, against a large embassy from Flanders which was headed by the Marquis de Bade, the Abbot of St Pierre-lès-Gand, Thomas de Plaine, president of Flanders, and Georges de Bar, secretary of Archduke Maximilian, and which seems to have arrived in London in time to enjoy the tournaments held in honour of the marriage of the Duke of York and Anne Mowbray.[2] To make the situation still more trying, in the daily appeals which the Flemish ambassadors made to the king of England and his council, and even to the English parliament, for aid for Mary of Burgundy, they were seconded by two Spanish ambassadors, the Doctor de Lucena and Lope de Valdeniesso, who had also come to England at the beginning of the year, probably to continue the negotiations for the marriage of the Prince of Wales and the Infanta Isabella.[2]

Despite everything he had to contend with, however, the Bishop of Elne enjoyed one great advantage: the heart of the king of England was on his side. Perhaps he enjoyed another advantage also, to wit, the secret help and advice of the Doctor de Lucena, since that gentleman, as we know, had found the money of the king of France very acceptable. At all events, it happened that in a short time the bishop scored what looked like an important victory. Soon after the adjournment of parliament, the Marquis de Bade, the Abbot of St Pierre-lès-Gand, and all their companions went home, taking the Doctor de Lucena and Lope de Valdeniesso with them, and the best news they seem to have carried to Mary of Burgundy and her husband was that Edward would send someone to Flanders to negotiate a new commercial treaty. All that Edward had done, besides holding out this hope, was to confirm

1. The narrative of the marriage ceremonies speaks of ambassadors from France, Scotland, Burgundy, and Germany among the spectators at the tournament. Scotland may be a slip of the pen for Spain.
2. Trial of the Bishop of Elne, interrogatory of 2 August. The bishop described the Spanish ambassadors whom he encountered in London at this time as a prothonotary, who had been sent to England by the king of Spain on several previous occasions, and a knight. An entry on Issue Roll, Easter 18 Edw. IV, 30 June, proves that they were the Doctor de Lucena and Lope de Valdeniesso.

a former treaty of commercial intercourse between England and East and West Friesland and to promise the citizens of Malines the enjoyment of all the commercial privileges granted to the Hanseatic merchants in England as long as Malines remained in the possession of the Duchess Margaret, of whose jointure it was a part and who usually resided there.[1]

Although Edward's secret inclinations had probably had more to do with the disappointment of Mary and Maximilian's hopes of help from England than the artful persuasions of the Bishop of Elne, both Englishmen and Flemings held the bishop responsible for what had occurred and vowed vengeance on him. If they could not undo his work, at least they could make life miserable for him, and that they took delight in doing. The bishop had not spent several months in England without his enemies finding out that he was a rather faint-hearted ecclesiastic, and the account he was afterwards required to give of all that happened while he was in England supplies plenty of evidence of the success and evil joy with which his tormentors played on his sensitive nerves. Twice, the bishop fully believed, the Flemings essayed to poison him, and when they failed in that, they sent a knight of Bruges, one Messire Lancelot, to London to put an end to him by some other means, perhaps a dagger-thrust delivered in some dark street. The bishop was convinced that the only thing which saved him from Messire Lancelot was the friendly warning given to him by one Master Amé de Ville,[2] of whom Messire Lancelot, taking him for an Italian merchant, asked a suspicious number of questions about the bishop's movements and whether he went armed.

As for the English, if they abstained from attempts to poison or stab the object of their hatred, at least they no longer contented themselves with hurling impolite epithets at him. Loudly proclaiming that the bishop was a spy of the king of France, they declared that he deserved to be drowned for having persuaded King Edward to forsake his old friends, the Flemings, whose destruction would mean the destruction of England herself; and at length they grew so clamorous that Edward had some of the noisiest persons

---

1. Rymer, XII, 51; Signed Bills, file 1514, no. 4970; French Roll 18 Edw. IV, m. 5 and 14; Close Roll 18 Edw. IV, m. 1; London Journal 8, f. 186b.
2. "Maistre Amé de Ville, docteur en décret," had been appointed assessor in Roussillon and Cerdagne by Louis XI in 1475. See F. Pasquier, *Un favori de Louis XI, Boffille de Juge, comte de Castres, vice-roi de Roussillon* (Albi, 1914), 12.

among them put under arrest. But even the king's interference on his behalf did not insure peace and safety for the bishop.

One day after that, when he was at Windsor, the people of the village rushed at his servants with the old cry of "French dogs," and, in the general uproar that followed, an archer of the king's household so far forgot his duty as to seize a club and fell one Frenchman to the ground with a blow which left the unlucky man senseless for a couple of hours. The king hastened to send the offending archer to one of the castle's dungeons and would even have had his hand cut off, had not the bishop interfered, saying the king of France would not like it; but the memory of that fierce archer, prompt as his chastisement had been, haunted the poor bishop as long as he stayed in England, and, by his own confession, from that day forth whenever he saw an Englishman draw a bow he was sure the end of his earthly career had come.[1]

While the Bishop of Elne was enduring such agony of mind, Howard, Tunstall, and Langton were still in France, and as by some happy chance several documents which appear to be memoranda of replies made to the three Englishmen by Louis' commissioners, or of bargains proposed to Edward through them, have been preserved, it is possible to follow in more detail than usual the negotiations going on between Edward and Louis at this moment. Those negotiations reveal both how adroitly Louis was leading Edward on and how willing Edward was to appear to be tempted, if he was not actually so.

Upon their arrival at Plessis-du-Parc-lès-Tours, Howard, Tunstall, and Langton had named six obstacles standing in the way of England's participation in the war on Mary of Burgundy: first, the questionableness of "the justice of the quarrel"; second, the expense of the war; third, the loss English merchants would suffer if their trade with Flanders was interrupted; fourth, the difficulty English merchants would find in recovering the goods they had in Burgundy; fifth, division of conquests, and sixth, the fact that the treaty of amity between the kings of France and England was for their lives only. It was the sixth obstacle, seemingly, which was given the first place in the debate that followed. For so insistent was Edward that, before he talked about war with Burgundy, he must have a more permanent treaty with France that the first proposal Howard, Tunstall, and Langton made was that the war should be postponed until a definitive peace had been negotiated

---

1. Trial of the Bishop of Elne, *ut sup.*

between England and France. But Louis declared such a postponement to be quite out of the question, both because he had already made his preparations for war at infinite expense, all of which would be thrown away in case of delay, and because postponement would give his enemies opportunity to strengthen themselves against him; and he proposed in his turn that Edward and he should sign a long truce, say for a hundred years, and that then Edward should declare war at once, leaving the final peace treaty between England and France to be negotiated at leisure. He also suggested that Edward and he might meet personally and talk matters over together.[1]

Howard, Tunstall, and Langton were not in a position to accept Louis' plan outright, but they were not unwilling to consider the substitution of a long truce for a treaty of peace, especially after Louis had said that he would promise that the pension of fifty thousand crowns a year should be paid as long as the truce lasted; and they ultimately took home with them an offer from Louis of a truce for one hundred and one years and a promise that, if this were accepted, the pension should be paid to Edward and his successors during all that time. At the request of the three Englishmen, Louis also promised that he would despatch a messenger to Florence to try to obtain from Lorenzo de Medici or his bank the bond Edward had thus far waited for in vain, and that, should Lorenzo de Medici refuse to furnish the bond, he would then send to Rome for the papal bull which had been named as an alternative for the bond.[2]

The question of a more satisfactory treaty between England and France having been thus disposed of for the moment, one would expect to hear that "the justice of the quarrel," the question which properly ought to have come first, was the next topic of discussion. Yet, probably by Louis' management, it was the much more inviting subject of the division of the possible conquests which was considered next. The English ambassadors called Louis' attention

---

1. Ms. français 4054, ff. 213-215, 219-223. Neither of these documents, the first of which is in French, the second in Latin, bears any date, and the two other documents in this volume of manuscripts (ff. 216-217, in French, and ff. 225-227, in Latin), which will be cited presently, are also undated. It is obvious, however, that they all belong to the same time and that they relate to the messages brought by Howard, Tunstall, and Langton. They are original minutes, with corrections and interpolations, and the two French documents put together correspond pretty closely with the longer Latin one, ff. 219-223.
2. *Ibid.*, ff. 225-226.

to the fact that, by agreeing to any kind of a division, Edward would be virtually withdrawing his claim to the kingdom of France, but Louis glibly replied that this difficulty could be overcome by stating explicitly, when the division was made, that there was to be no impairment of the rights and pretensions of either prince. He claimed, too, that those rights and pretensions would be in no more danger from the proposed partition treaty than they were from the existing treaty of amity. But even if this were so, there were other snags. For while Louis' general proposal was that all lands conquered after England had openly declared war on the daughter of the late Duke of Burgundy and her husband should be held by Edward and himself jointly while the war lasted, and that when the war was over Edward should take all the acquired territories lying outside of the kingdom of France and he himself all lying within the kingdom of France, he made an exception of Lille, Douai, St Omer, and Aire, which, being part of the ancient demesne of the crown of France and of "other quality" than the rest of Flanders, ought, he maintained, to remain in his hands alone; and he also announced distinctly that the duchy and county of Burgundy were not to be included in the partition of territory in any way.

Louis had tried hard to make his offer sound generous, but Edward's ambassadors were quick to see a difficulty. They remarked that Holland, Zealand, and Brabant, which, according to the arrangement Louis proposed, would constitute the king of England's share of the conquests, were a part of the Empire, and that anyone who attacked them would immediately find himself at war not simply with Mary of Burgundy, but also with the Emperor. Nor did the prospect look brighter to them when Louis replied that it was not a war against the rights of the Empire which he was waging, but a war against the daughter of the late Duke Charles of Burgundy; that he had no wish to deprive the Emperor of the rights he had enjoyed during the lives of the dukes of Burgundy, and that, though the fact that the Emperor's son had married "the daughter of Burgundy" might make the war one of personal concern to him, in reality neither the Emperor, as emperor, nor the Empire was affected by it.[1] Then, as this forced into the discussions the too long ignored question of "the justice of the quarrel," Louis repeated his contention that he had a right to conquer the lands of an avowed enemy,

---

1. Cf. a letter Louis wrote to the Emperor in April. *Lettres de Louis XI*, VII, 36.

such as the Duke of Burgundy had been and as his daughter now was, and that his friends and allies ought to give him their aid. He added that, if the Emperor, out of affection for his son or any other relative, caused territories belonging to the Empire to make war on him, it did not follow that he ought not to seek revenge and subjugate those territories if he could, or that his friends ought not to assist him to do so. He even pointed out that the king of England could find a "just quarrel" of his own with Burgundy about territorial matters, since Duke Philip of Burgundy had taken Holland and Zealand from the late (Humphrey) Duke of Gloucester, to whom, and to the king of England of that day, the wife of the Duke of Gloucester, "true lady" of those lands, had given them. This was a fact so well known that the mere "notoriety of the case" was sufficient justification for action on Edward's part.

Having launched into the subject of the justice of his attack on Mary of Burgundy, Louis found much more to say. He had been revolving the matter in his mind and had succeeded in raking up several old accounts against Burgundy. He now announced that, as Duke Charles had never done homage to him for the lands he held in France, he could justly demand restitution of all the rents and other profits which Charles and his daughter had derived from those lands since the death of Philip of Burgundy; and this, he said, would mean a sum of more than eight million gold crowns.[1] Next, he affirmed that he had a right to exact compensation, first, for the damages which he and his subjects had sustained through the war unjustly waged against them—damages amounting in all to not less than twenty million gold crowns—and, second, for the expense to which he had been put by the war, which came to more than ten million gold crowns.[2] Eight million crowns plus twenty million crowns plus ten million crowns made a very large sum of money, and yet even that was not all Louis felt he had reason to demand from Mary of Burgundy. He said that, in as much as Charles had broken the treaty of Arras, he had a right to expect the repayment of all the money—ten thousand crowns and more—which he had paid out for the lands Charles's father had held in pledge (meaning the Somme towns) and for other things. He also declared that he ought to have restitution of more than four million

1. Seven or eight million crowns, according to the French document.
2. In these two cases the figures mentioned in the French document are more than fifteen million crowns and more than six million crowns.

crowns which the Dukes of Burgundy had had in days gone by from the treasury of France, since those dukes, especially Charles, had violated all the agreements by virtue of which they had secured the money, and finally, that those dukes and their heirs ought to be required to give an account of all the money Philip I of Burgundy had received from the revenues of the kingdom of France during the time he had acted as the guardian of Charles VI.[1]

If mere length of argument could convince them, Howard, Tunstall, and Langton ought to have been very sure by this time of "the justice of the quarrel." But even if Louis was beginning to make some impression on their minds, they did not allow themselves to be put off their guard, and they seem to have told him that, if he insisted on having Lille, Douai, St Omer, and Aire left out of the partition treaty, he must promise to assist Edward to get possession of four other towns as an equivalent for these. The towns of Louvain, Brussels, Antwerp, and Malines were then picked out, and the proposal finally made to Edward was that, as soon as these four Brabant towns were in his hands, he should relinquish to Louis the half share in the conquests in Flanders which was to be temporarily allotted to him, while Louis should relinquish to him all right and title not only in the four Brabant towns, but in all the rest of Brabant and in Zealand and Holland. More than that, Howard, Tunstall, and Langton insisted that Louis must bind himself to help Edward to conquer Brabant, Zealand, and Holland by furnishing him with two thousand lances, summer and winter, until the conquest was completed, and with twelve bombards, with the "small artillery" necessary for them, for six months in the year, that is, from May to October inclusive.[2]

---

1. *Ibid.*, ff. 213-215, 216-217, 219-223. In the French document, ff. 216-217, the article relating to Philip I and Charles VI reads as follows: "Item se trouvera en la chambre des comptes que les dues de Bourgogne out eu des roys et de la couronne plus de vj millions d'or tant pour la despense que fit le Roy pour la bataille des flamans [the battle of Roosebek, 1382; où ledit de Bourgogne menna le roy Charles VIe dont il estoit tuteur."
2. *Ibid.*, ff. 225-227. According to Commynes (II, 8-9), Louis told Edward that, if he would come personally and invade Flanders, he would not only let him keep Flanders and Brabant without doing homage to the crown of France, but would, at his own expense, conquer the four largest towns of Brabant for him, pay the wages of ten thousand English soldiers for four months, provide plenty of good artillery, with men and carts to transport it, and keep the enemy occupied elsewhere while the English conquered Flanders. But Louis' offer certainly did not include all this at the start, and that he would ever propose to allow Edward to have Flanders seems incredible.

Four of the difficulties which Howard, Tunstall, and Langton had mentioned when they first came to Plessis-du-Parc-lès-Tours had now been considered and Louis had suggested a way out of each of them. There were two more to be disposed of, however, and they were by no means the least serious ones, as they related to the injury that would be done to England's trade by her entry into the war with Burgundy. But again Louis was ready with what sounded like an attractive offer. Just as he had done once before, in the days of Warwick's supremacy, he held out great inducements to the merchants of England—especially to the cloth merchants, whose hearts were still sore against Burgundy—to transfer their trade from Burgundy to France. As soon as Edward had declared war on Burgundy, he promised, all foreign cloth except that made in England, and all wool or tin except that coming from England, should be excluded from France for the duration of the war; only his own subjects and those of the king of England should be permitted to import cloth, wool, or tin into France, and lastly, all merchandise brought to France by Englishmen should be admitted without payment of customs or other duties. As for the English merchants who had goods in Flanders or other lands now "occupied" by the daughter of the late Duke of Burgundy and her husband, or who had unrecovered debts in those lands, they, Louis said, could be given compensation out of the moveable goods seized in the conquered territories, and when, God granting, the final victory had been won, all the merchants of England would be able to resume their trade relations with Flanders under more favourable conditions than they had enjoyed before.[1]

About the time the negotiations reached this stage, Howard, Tunstall, and Langton received a new commission from Edward. Those who had been appointed by the treaty of Amiens to arbitrate the differences between the kings of England and France had never held a meeting, although the time given them for their labours would expire on 29 August of this year; and one of their number, the Duke of Clarence, was now dead. Hence it had become necessary to make a new agreement, unless this article of the treaty of Amiens was to be suffered to lapse altogether, and by his new commission to his ambassadors Edward empowered them to prolong the time allowed the arbitrators as they might think best. Louis had no objection to signing a new arbitration covenant, and on 7 April the Archbishops of Canterbury and Lyons, the Dukes of Gloucester,

---

1. *Ibid.*, ff. 216-217, 219-223, 225-227

Buckingham, Orleans, and Bourbon, the Bishop of Lincoln, Pierre d'Oriole, chancellor of France, Earl Rivers, and the Count of Dunois were named as arbitrators, with the understanding that they would hold their first meeting in England before Easter, 1479, their second in France before the following Michaelmas, and that they would finish their task by 29 August 1481.[1]

Howard, Tunstall, and Langton had now been in France more than three months, and soon after the arbitration agreement was signed, they took their leave of Louis and set out for home, carrying with them not only Louis' proposals in regard to Burgundy, but ten thousand crowns of Margaret of Anjou's ransom.[2] Yet despite the willingness he had just expressed to continue the pension of fifty thousand crowns for one hundred and one years, Louis was growing a little tired of sending so much money to England, and not only had this instalment of Margaret of Anjou's ransom been due since the preceding Michaelmas, but Guillaume Restout, who had gone over to England again two or three weeks before Howard, Tunstall, and Langton left France, had taken Edward only ten thousand crowns, instead of the twenty-five thousand to which the king was entitled.[3] Did Louis think Edward would pocket the ten thousand crowns and forget that he ought to have more? If so, he did not yet know the king of England. For Edward did not intend to tolerate any delay in the payment of his pension. He had, moreover, another bone to pick with Louis on the core of the Duchess Margaret, who had just been appealing to him most pitifully for a thousand or fifteen hundred archers to protect her, "a poor widow separated from

---

1. Rymer, XII, 52, 61-65; Commynes-Lenglet, III, 536-539; *Lettres de Louis XI*, VII, 31-33.
2. Edward's receipt for this money appears on French Roll 17 Edw. IV, m. 4, immediately after the commission which he had given to Howard, Tunstall, and Langton in November. Rymer, XII, 51, prints it from this source and dates it 3 March, but in reality no date is given on the roll, and neither is the date of payment recorded in the account of the receiver general of France. Legrand coll., MS. français 6982, f. 235 *et seq*. Moreover, Rymer's date looks impossible, as Howard, Tunstall, and Langton certainly did not return home before April.

   Another thing that Langton seems to have brought back from France was a charter, dated Arras, 14 April 1478, by which Louis renewed a grant of wine to Christ Church, Canterbury, made by one of his ancestors. Louis had been received into the fraternity of Christ Church in the preceding year, when he sent what seems to have been his first gift of wine, and his chancellor, Pierre d'Oriole, was honoured in the same way when the charter was received. *Hist. MSS. Com., Report 9*, app., 117; *Christ Church Letters*, xxiv-xxviii.
3. Rymer, XII, 55.

all my kindred and friends," from the king of France, who was doing all in his power to make a beggar of her.[1] Almost before Howard, Tunstall, and Langton had had time to reach home, Edward sent to France, first, his almoner, Thomas Danet, to take up Margaret's cause with Louis, and then John Grauntford, a yeoman of the crown, to demand the fifteen thousand crowns Restout had failed to bring.

The Duchess Margaret had assured her brother that Louis had robbed her of property worth thirty-five hundred marks a year in rents, and that he had also damaged her possessions to the amount of four hundred thousand crowns; and when Danet arrived at the French court, he informed Louis that the duchess would thank him to give back her lands, to compensate her for damages, and to keep his hands off of her other possessions, a list of which she had sent to prevent any plea of ignorance.[2] All that Louis did, however, after he heard Margaret's demands, was to keep Danet waiting a month or longer while he pretended to investigate the duchess's claims, and when, on 23 May, he at last gave the almoner a letter to carry to King Edward, that letter promised nothing. Louis merely told Edward that both he and his chief councillors had listened to all that Danet had been instructed to tell him concerning "certain matters touching my very dear and well beloved cousin, the widow of the late Duke Charles of Burgundy, your sister," and that, though he had replied to Danet, he had decided, in order to inform Edward more fully about his intentions in regard to his sister, to send a member of his council to England shortly with full instructions. "When you have heard him and learned the truth of the matter," wrote Louis, "I have no doubt you will be well content with what I offer and intend to do for your honour and sake. And for the present I will not write more except to say that, if there is anything I can do for you, let me know and I will do it most gladly, so please Our Lord, who, Monsieur my cousin, have you in His very holy keeping."[3]

---

1. Plancher, IV, cDi.
2. *Ibid.*, IV, cDiij-cDiv.
3. *Ibid.*, IV, ccdxxxviij; *Lettres de Louis XI*, VII, 65-67. Through Danet Edward also asked Louis to give a safeconduct to certain Genoese merchants who intended to visit England, but Louis replied that it was the admiral who attended to such matters and also that, as the Genoese were his "subjects," it would be unsuitable for him to offer them a safeconduct. Nevertheless, three days after he wrote the above letter to Edward, Louis directed the admiral of France—"pour ce que nous desirous en toutes choses

But if Louis ventured to hedge about the Duchess Margaret's woes, he did not venture to do so in regard to the fifteen thousand crowns Edward had sent to demand; and Grauntford was soon on his way home with the money. On 6 June, Edward ratified the new arbitration agreement which Howard, Tunstall, and Langton had negotiated, and on the 14th he gave his receipt for the fifteen thousand crowns Grauntford had obtained for him.[1]

Louis' speedy decision to send Edward the rest of his pension may have been due to a warning from the Bishop of Elne that Doctor John Coke had gone over to Flanders in the first days of May.[2] Ostensibly, Coke had been sent only to negotiate a new treaty of commercial intercourse between England and Burgundy, but even this was enough to prove that Edward was not seriously contemplating a rupture with Burgundy. And then who could tell with what other secret missions Coke had been intrusted? So Louis not only found the fifteen thousand crowns for Grauntford, but, as soon as he could, fulfilled the intention he had announced in the letter Danet had taken home by dispatching Master Yves de la Tillaye, advocate of the Chastelet of Paris, to Edward to talk over the affairs of the Duchess Margaret. "Master Yves, my friend," wrote Louis to this emissary, "I know you are a good clerk and a clever man, and they tell me you know well how to behave. I beg you to prove in this matter that you desire to serve me, for there is nothing in which one could do me a greater service. But it is necessary to go promptly, and so I pray you to depart at once, without delay or postponement."[3]

Master Yves carried to England, in addition to his letter of credence and a letter for the Bishop of Elne,[4] full instructions for the bishop and himself. In those instructions Louis told his two envoys to say to Edward that he desired nothing so much as to please him, and that he had more faith in him than in any other prince in the world, but that the Duchess

---

singulièrement complaire à nostredit cousin le roy d'Angleterre plus que a prince qui soit vivant"—to inform all captains, etc., that no Genoese going to England were to be molested or injured. *Lettres de Louis XI*, VII, 75.

1. Rymer, XII, 61, 65. Rymer gives Grauntford's name as Crauford, which is a misreading. Grauntford was paid £20 for his journey to France. Issue Roll, Mich. 18 Edw. IV, 12 Oct.
2. Coke received his commission on 2 May. Rymer, XII, 68. He was paid £40 in advance for his journey to Flanders and 100s for a pursuivant to go with him and carry messages back and forth. Warrants for Issues, 18 Edw. IV, 2 May.
3. *Lettres de Louis XI*, VII, 100-102.
4. *Ibid.*, VII, 97-100.

Margaret had no real cause to complain. To preserve his rights and his crown, Louis maintained, he had been obliged to take up arms against the Duchess Mary and her husband, and while it was true that certain places to which Margaret laid claim had suffered, some of those places were not included in her jointure but had been only recently transferred to her by her stepdaughter, who, as they had reverted to the crown, had no right to dispose of them, while others, such as Oudenarde and Cassel, had brought their troubles upon themselves by their hostility towards him. For of course he could not, as the king of England must see, run the risk of leaving hostile towns behind his advancing army. He went on to state also that his sovereign rights could not be prejudiced by any assignments made by the Duke of Burgundy to his wife for dower, since the sovereign right is superior to all other rights, and that if the places Margaret claimed as hers were disobedient and rebellious, they had to be reduced to obedience. Yet, in spite of all, it was his intention, he declared—it had been his intention even when Doctor Morton first mentioned Margaret's claims to him—that, when all the places in question had submitted to him, she should receive the revenues from them. What was more, notwithstanding the hostility the duchess had displayed towards him since Morton was in France, if she wished to put herself under his protection, and if she would make her towns submit to him, he, who by virtue of his royal dignity was "le vray protecteur de toutes les dames veufves qui veulent habiter en son royaume," would guard and defend her possessions as if they were his very own and, in case anyone did her injury, make good her losses. He would also give her a pension and, in short, treat her in every respect with so much honour and favour that she could not fail to be content.[1]

Louis must have been laughing to himself as he made this offer to serve as the protector of Margaret of York, but nothing was less likely than that the duchess would be deceived by his soft bleatings. She knew the wolf too well. As soon appeared, however, the duchess was in no danger of suffering more losses at present, for scarcely had her brother had time to hear what Master Yves and the Bishop of Elne were to say to him about her, when it was learned that, on 11 July, Louis had concluded a year's truce with Mary

---

1. Plancher, IV, ccclxxxix-cccxcij.

and Maximilian and had promised to restore within a month all the places his armies had taken in the counties of Burgundy and Hainault.[1]

Louis' readiness to sign this truce with Mary and Maximilian was due, first of all, to some discouraging reverses which his armies had met with since the renewal of the war in the spring; but he was probably influenced also by anxiety in regard to what Doctor John Coke might be doing. For Coke had been in Flanders some weeks now, and the day after Louis signed his truce with Mary and Maximilian at Arras, Coke signed at Lille a new treaty of commercial intercourse between England and Burgundy which was identical in most of its articles with the treaty of 1467, except that this time no reservation was made regarding the importation of English cloth into Burgundian territories and the exportation of armour and weapons of war out of Burgundy, and that it was agreed that only "ancient" tolls and other charges should be demanded from the merchants trading back and forth between the two countries. An attempt was made, also, to settle some of the old disagreements between the merchants of the Netherlands and those of the staple of Calais by means of an elaborate set of ordinances.[2]

The publication of the new treaty with Burgundy must have brought great joy to the merchants of England and equally great fear to the king of France that his pensioner, King Edward, was getting out of hand. Indeed, Louis might well feel disturbed, as Edward had evidently been moved to send Coke to Flanders not simply because he wanted to satisfy the merchants of his kingdom, but because he suspected the sincerity of the overtures Louis had been making to him and, furthermore, because he saw great possibilities opening up as a result of an event which had occurred at Bruges just three weeks before the signing of Coke's treaty, namely, the birth of a son to Mary and Maximilian. In anticipation of the happy event at Bruges, Edward, rather curiously, had asked the son of the late Count of St Pol to represent him at the christening,[3] and as soon as he heard that Mary of Burgundy's child was a boy, he began to dwell on the thought of what a fine husband little Philip; as Mary's son was named, would make for one of his daughters. Even the Dauphin of France was hardly

---

1. *Ibid.*, IV, cccxcvj; Commynes-Lenglet, III, 540.

2. Rymer, XII, 67-86. For a discussion of the ordinances mentioned above, see H. E. Malden's introduction to the *Cely Papers*.

3. Molinet, II, 156; *Coll. de Chroniques Belges* (Corpus Chron. Flandriæ), III, 695.

a more desirable *parti*. Nevertheless, Edward had no thought of giving up the Dauphin while he angled for baby Philip, and at the same time that he showed an inclination to hold out the hand of friendship to Mary and Maximilian, he continued without interruption his negotiations with Louis looking to his entry into the war against Burgundy. The Bishop of Elne was still in England, and one French ambassador after another came over to second the bishop's efforts or to make new offers or explanations.

With the offers Louis had made to him through Howard, Tunstall, and Langton Edward found some fault. For one thing, the four Brabant towns which Louis said he would help him seize would be both hard to conquer and hard to keep after they had been conquered, and he proposed that, in place of them, he should be presented with four of the towns Louis had already conquered in Picardy, such, for example, as Boulogne. If Louis would do this, he said, he would then be ready to send English troops to help him.[1] On the other hand, he appeared to be reconciled to the substitution of a longer truce for the treaty of peace between England and France which he had seemed to regard as an indispensable prerequisite to England's entry into the war with Burgundy, though he wanted the one hundred and one years Louis had suggested as a suitable term for the truce to run to be reckoned, not from the day of signature of the new truce, but from the day of the death of the king who happened to die first. Of course Louis was not going to part with any of the towns he had conquered in Picardy, but he saw no objection to Edward's preference in regard to the date from which the one hundred and one years of the truce were to be reckoned, and on 13 July he authorized the Bishop of Elne to alter the reading of the truce as Edward wished and to make a corresponding alteration in the agreement for the payment of the pension of fifty thousand crowns.[2] He seems to have given the bishop to understand, however, that he was not to make use of this authority at once, but to wait until he saw how matters were going to work out.

In August Louis sent the Seigneur de St Pierre to England to repeat his offer to take the Duchess Margaret under his protection. Edward was at Nottingham when St Pierre arrived, but Garter escorted the Frenchman to

---

1. Commynes, II, 9.
2. Rymer, XII, 86.

that town, and when the king returned to Windsor, St Pierre came with him.[1] On 23 August Edward entertained St Pierre at Greenwich, and when, shortly after, Louis' emissary returned home, Tunstall and Langton accompanied him.[2] But though Edward had received St Pierre, whom he had met in France at the time the treaty of Amiens was signed, with all courtesy, either the offer regarding his sister Margaret, which he knew to be sheer nonsense, piqued him or else St Pierre told him that Louis would not give him any towns in Picardy and that excited his anger; for the only reply he seems to have made to Louis was another demand on his pocket-book. On 25 August Edward sent two warrants under his sign manual to the chancellor of England, one for a commission for Tunstall and Langton, "whom we at this time will send unto our cousin of France," the other for "letters of acquittance" to be made "unto our said cousin."[3] The letters of acquittance were a receipt for the last twenty-five thousand crowns which Louis had sent, partly by Restout and partly by Grauntford,[4] and the commission for Tunstall and Langton empowered them to demand of Louis that he should begin at once to pay the Dauphin's fiancée

1. Garter received 13*s* 4*d* for escorting St Pierre to Nottingham. Issue Roll, Easter 18 Edw. IV, 22 May. (Note that again the date on the Issue Roll is misleading, as Edward was at Nottingham at the beginning of August and again a month later, but not on any earlier date in this year.) The French ambassadors were with the king on 16 August, as well as on 23 August, when he entertained them at Greenwich; and on 21 August St Pierre, with the Bishop of Elne, signed the certification that Hastings had received the first half of his pension money for that year. Household Account, 17 and 18 Edw. IV; Restout's account.

2. Tunstall and Langton received £90 in advance for their expenses, and Rougecroix Pursuivant, who went with them, 100*s*. Issue Roll, Easter 18 Edw. IV, 26 August. John Grauntford also received £10 "for shipping of the Lord Saint Pere and other in his company of the parties of France." *Ibid.* See also a document in Warrants for Issues, 18 Edw. IV, which is entitled, "Percelles and Sommes of money paied and deliuered by the kinges high commaundement by John Fitzherbert and other the kinges tellers in his Receipt of the kinges treasure remaignyng in their keping," and a similar account in Exchequer T. R., Council and Privy Seal, file 91, m. 86.

3. Warrants under the Signet, file 1388, 25 August.

4. On Receipt Roll, Easter 18 Edw. IV, no. 931, is recorded, under the date 26 August, the receipt of £2,980 from the king of France by the hands of Restout. But on French Roll 18 Edw. IV, m. 6, is enrolled a receipt from Edward for 25,000 crowns sent by Louis which is dated 19 August, and the quittance which Restout afterwards deposited in Louis' chamber of accounts, and which covered the whole 25,000 crowns despite the fact that only 10,000 crowns of the amount seems actually to have passed through his hands, also bore the date of 19 August. See Restout's account.

the sixty thousand pounds a year he had promised to give her from the time she arrived at the marriageable age.[1]

When Tunstall, Langton, and St Pierre had departed for France, Edward made a journey to Pontefract, and he took with him the Bishop of Elne, although the French ambassador was still such an object of hatred to Englishmen that, after king and bishop had left the city, a crowd of Londoners went four or five times to the bishop's lodgings and terrified his servants by beating on the doors "with big pieces of wood or otherwise," as if they would rob or murder those within.[2] The king did not stay long at Pontefract, however, as he returned to Greenwich at the beginning of October, in time for "our hunting season," when he was fond of spending a little time in Waltham forest. From Greenwich he went to Eltham and there took up his winter quarters, as London was again in the throes of the pestilence.[3]

About the time he came back from Pontefract, Edward had the pleasure of receiving another ten thousand crowns of Margaret of Anjou's ransom which Louis had arranged to pay through Caniziani.[4] But it was some time before he heard anything from Tunstall and Langton, and meanwhile he found other interesting matters to think about, as the Doctor de Lucena was in England again and before the middle of October a messenger arrived from Spain bringing tidings of the birth of a son to Ferdinand and Isabella.[5] Edward gave a reward of twenty pounds to the messenger of Ferdinand and Isabella, but of course he did not overlook the fact that, now that the infanta Isabella was blessed with a brother, she would not be quite so desirable a wife for the heir to his throne. It is possible, however, that he had already come to the conclusion that the negotiations for the Spanish marriage alliance would never come to anything, as he had begun, even before he received the news of the birth of the Spanish heir, to consider the advisability of finding another bride for his son. In that he showed his wisdom, for Louis' agents had been

1. Rymer, XII, 89.
2. Trial of the Bishop of Elne, interrogatory of 2 August.
3. Privy Seals; Household Accounts, 17 and 18, 18 and 19 Edw. IV, Exchequer K. R., bundle 412, nos. 9 and 10; Davies, York Records, 69, 78-79; Warrants for Issues, 18 Edw. IV, 14 Oct. According to Fabyan, 666, the plague did not reach England until late in September. On the continent it had been taking its usual toll of lives for some months past.
4. Rymer, XII, 91; extract from account of Denys Bidon, receiver general, Legrand coll., MS. français 6982, ff. 235 dorso et seq.
5. Rymer, XII, 93 (from Warrants for Issues, 18 Edw. IV, 14 Oct.).

at work in Spain, and it was not long before he heard that Ferdinand and Isabella had accepted a treaty of peace with the king of France. In return for a promise from Louis that he would cease to support the pretensions of Alphonso of Portugal to the throne of Castile, Ferdinand and Isabella had not only made peace with Louis: they had also renounced their alliances with the king of England and the Duchess of Burgundy.[1]

The bride Edward now had in mind for the Prince of Wales was a little maiden to whom he was attracted chiefly because of the large dot that could probably be obtained with her hand. This little maiden was the daughter of the late Galeazzo Sforza, Duke of Milan, who had been murdered in December 1476, and of Louis XI's sister-in-law, Bona of Savoy, who, had Louis and Warwick had their way, would probably have been the consort of Edward himself. But as soon as Edward wrote to Bona of Savoy, who was governing Milan during her son's minority, and applied for her daughter's hand, she, as he might have anticipated, turned to Louis for counsel;[2] and this would probably have ended the matter at once had not Louis made the discovery just then that Edward was receiving offers of another marriage for the Prince of Wales which would be much more threatening to the safety of France than an Anglo-Milanese alliance.

Archduke Maximilian had sent more than one envoy to Edward since the Marquis de Bade and his colleagues went home worsted in their encounter with the Bishop of Elne. One Nicholas Pyngret had apparently come to England twice since then—the first time, perhaps, on some errand connected with the christening of the son of Mary and Maximilian, as on that occasion he is described as a messenger from "the Duke of Ostrych and Burgoyne and the Earl of Saint Poule."[3] And afterwards Maximilian seems to have sent, first, the Seigneur d'Irlain to make anxious inquiry why Edward no longer wore the collar of the Golden Fleece, and then "Ostriche" Herald to tell the king that there would be a chapter of the Order of the Golden Fleece at Brussels in April.[4] But all these envoys merely paved the way for the arrival of still

---

1. Daumet, 123; Legeay, II, 324.
2. *Lettres et négociations de Philippe de Commynes*, III, 38.
3. On occasion Pyngret was given 20 marks. Fitzherbert's account, Warrants for Issues, 18 Edw. IV.
4. Reiffenberg, *Hist. de la Toison d'Or*, 98, 102; Fitzherbert's account, *ut sup.*

another, Stephen van Kelham,[1] who, to the consternation of the Bishop of Elne, came laden with a marriage offer and abundant gifts for King Edward and certain ones "près de sa personne." For it chanced that Maximilian had a sister who lacked a husband, and the Emperor Frederick, being anxious to make suitable provision for his daughter, had taken it into his mind to marry her either to the young Duke of Milan or to the eldest son of the king of England and, to avoid disappointment or because he was unable to decide at once which of the two youths he preferred, to apply for the hands of both.

What Edward thought of the offer Stephen van Kelham brought he kept to himself, but he did not suffer a day to pass without letting the Bishop of Elne hear about the Emperor's proposal. He took pains, too, to make the story as big as he could. He told the bishop that the Emperor not only desired a marriage alliance with his house, but that he wanted him to form an alliance with him against the king of France, and that Maximilian and the estates of Flanders were ready to pay him a pension of sixty thousand crowns a year (which was ten thousand more than Louis was paying him) for a hundred years, to supply him with five or ten thousand soldiers whenever he wanted to set out to conquer France, and to stand by him until the work of conquest was completed.[2] The poor bishop was horrified. Yet what could he do? When the ambassadors of Frederick and Maximilian gave banquets and shouted "Vive Bourgogne!" he gave banquets and shouted "Vive le roi très-chrétien, Duc de Bourgogne!"; but that was not likely to accomplish much, and already the Londoners were saying that the alliance with the Emperor and Maximilian was on the point of being sealed and that some artillery was to be brought down from York—supposedly to be sent across the sea with an English army.[3] With the Londoners the wish may have been father to the thought, but there is no doubt that Edward was pleased by the unexpected offer from the Emperor.

---

1. Edward presented Kelham with a gold collar of his livery. Issue Roll, Mich. 18 Edw. IV, 17 Feb. In the account of the trial of the Bishop of Elne the head of the embassy from Frederick and Maximilian is called the Seigneur de Drolayn. But in the same account Oliver King's name appears as Oliver Guin. The bishop, who was speaking from memory, must have made another slight mistake when he said that the embassy from Frederick and Maximilian came to England "sur le mois de janvier," as a letter written by Cagnola on 28 December shows that the Emperor had asked for the hand of the Prince of Wales before that date.
2. Trial of the Bishop of Elne, interrogatories of 2 and 3 August.
3. *Ibid.*, interrogatory of 4 August.

On 18 December the king not only appointed Montgomery, Coke, and Hugh Bryce to go to Malines, or to any other place where the Duchess Margaret might be staying on 12 January, to attend a diet at which monetary matters and the redress of violations of the truce between England and Burgundy were to be considered, but he signed what amounted to a secret league of friendship with Mary and Maximilian by renewing two articles of the treaty concluded with Charles in 1474, before the expedition to France.[1]

The Bishop of Elne must have given Louis immediate warning of what the Emperor was seeking to obtain from Edward, and evidently Bona of Savoy too informed her brother-in-law of the Emperor's search for a son-in-law, as on 28 December, Cagnola, the Milanese ambassador at the French court, wrote that he felt sure the king of France would rather see the Emperor allied with Milan than with England, though he added that he thought it would be found that the Emperor, who saw what an advantage an alliance with England would be to his son, no longer desired to treat for the hand of the Duke of Milan.[2] But Louis seems to have been less disturbed by what had happened than the Bishop of Elne. At any rate, he determined that, come what might, he was not going to be bullied into, paying Edward any more money than he was paying him at present. Tunstall and Langton had told him, upon their arrival in France with the Seigneur de St Pierre, that the king of England desired above all things to see his daughter married to the Dauphin, and that he wanted the betrothal to take place at once. They had spoken also of the advisability of procuring a dispensation from the Pope so that, in case Elizabeth died, it would be possible for the Dauphin to marry her sister Mary, as the marriage treaty required; and then they had announced that, as Elizabeth was now more than twelve years old, she was entitled to the sixty thousand pounds a year which Louis had promised to pay her from the time she reached the marriageable age. Finally, they had mentioned the Duchess Margaret's affairs and had demanded that Louis should promise the security of all the lands Margaret held by right of dower in the domains of Mary and Maximilian. Yet when, late in December, May de Houllefort, Seigneur de Hamars and bailli of Caen, Antoine de Mortillon,

---

1. Rymer, XII, 95-97. Coke, during his previous embassy to Burgundy, had evidently taken up the matter of the rate of exchange. *Stonor Letters and Papers*, II, 63.
2. *Lettres et négociations de Commynes*, I, 230-231.

and two Benedictine monks, Jacques de Lac and Antoine Raymond,[1] arrived in England with the answer of the king of France, that answer was tantamount to a refusal of every demand Tunstall and Langton had made.

Louis took great care not to make his refusal too abrupt. He softened it by assuring Edward that he too desired nothing more than that the marriage between his son and the Princess Elizabeth should be celebrated as soon as possible, and by saying that he was very willing that the betrothal should take place whenever and however Edward wished. He also agreed that a papal dispensation ought to be obtained which would remove all difficulties should the Princess Mary have to be substituted for her sister, and he promised that, as far as he and the Dauphin were concerned, no step necessary to that end would be omitted. In regard to the payment of the dowry, however, there must, he said, be some misunderstanding. He was most anxious to observe his treaty with the king of England in all respects, and he would gladly pay the dowry when it became due; but surely it was never the intention of any marriage treaty that the dowry, or wedding gift, promised in consideration of the marriage, should be paid before the consummation of the marriage. Such a thing would be so contrary to all law and reason that he could not think the king of England could possibly have understood it so. Certainly as for himself, it had never occurred to him to think of the matter in that way until the last coming of Messire Richard Tunstall and Messire Thomas Langton, and when, to make quite sure that he was not in the wrong, he summoned the Bishop of Evreux, the admiral of France, the Seigneur du Lude, and the Seigneur de St Pierre, the men who had negotiated his treaties with the king of England, and asked them if it was ever understood that the dowry was to be paid before the consummation of the marriage, they assured him, and afterwards declared upon oath before Messire Richard Tunstall and Messire Thomas Langton, that not a word to that effect had ever been uttered and that they had never understood or agreed that the dowry should be so paid. Not content even

---

1. Louis' instructions were addressed to Jean de Hangest, Seigneur de Genlis, to the bailli of Caen, and to the two Benedictine monks; but Antoine de Mortillon must have been substituted afterwards for the Seigneur de Genlis. See Issue Roll, Mich. 18 Edw. IV, 17 Feb., and also Restout's account, from which it appears that Mortillon, with the Bishop of Elne, signed, on 7 February, the certification that Hastings had received his pension. We have proof, too, that the Seigneur de Genlis was in France on 22 January. See *Lettres de Louis XI*, VII, 238.

with this, he had consulted the members of his council and many doctors and great clerks of his kingdom, and by them also he had been told that he was not, and could not be, bound to pay the dowry before the consummation of the marriage—that such a thing would be contrary to all reason.

Whenever a marriage treaty mentioned a dowry or wedding gift, Louis went on to argue, it was always with the tacit understanding that the payment of such dowry or wedding gift was conditional on the consummation of the marriage, and that the clause relating to it would go into effect only after the marriage. Furthermore, according to the custom of France—and in the treaty it was expressly stated that the dowry was to be paid according to the custom of France—no one might demand the dowry until the marriage had taken place, and as the husband was "lord of the dowry" during the marriage, the wife could not claim it until the marriage had been dissolved (by death). Hence it followed that, if the intention in the present case had been that the dowry should be paid before the marriage, the treaty ought to have said so more explicitly. Nor could it be claimed that the wording of the treaty was obscure; for the treaty stated "quod matrimonium contrahetur" between Monsieur the Dauphin and Madame Elizabeth "cum ad annos nubiles pervenerint," and afterwards that the king of France "dotabit" the dowry, "dotabit" being a word, not "de temps present" but "de temps advenir." Also, when the treaty said "quod illa dos assignetur et detur quum primum ad annos nubiles pervenerit,"[1] the word nubility must be interpreted according to the first clause; that is to say, it meant when they both "ad annos nubiles pervenerint." There remained, too, the possibility of Dame Elizabeth's death, which God forbid, before the marriage, or of her becoming a "religieuse," and in either case what a situation would result if the dowry had already been paid!

However, after he had thus expressed his astonishment that Edward should expect him to begin to pay the dowry now, Louis said again that he greatly desired the marriage of his son with the English princess, and added that he was looking forward to having his daughter-in-law with him "for his singular pleasure and consolation," as all who had seen her spoke of her virtues, her beauty, and her accomplishments. More than that, he

---

1. The reading in Rymer's copy of the treaty is "quamprimum ipsa ad annos nubiles pervenerit."

said he realized that he could not hope to find a more exalted marriage for his son, or one which would contribute more to the peace and tranquillity of his kingdom; and then, after throwing in a little praise of Edward's own virtues, in which he included prudence, equity, and loyal affection, he remarked that he was sure the king of England would not want to ask for anything which was not just, honest, and reasonable, and that he would be satisfied with the explanations offered. Finally, he told Edward that if anyone was urging him to demand the payment of the dowry, it was probably with the intent to make trouble between France and England, and he entreated him most affectionately not to listen to such persons, but to preserve his good understanding with his cousin of France, whom he would always find "as good, true, perfect, and loyal a friend as ever one prince was to another."

Louis' answer in regard to the Duchess Margaret was also sugar-coated. His love and consideration for the king of England, he said, made him anxious to treat with favour all whom he loved, and when he refused the overtures made to him by the Duchess Margaret soon after the death of the Duke of Burgundy and also later, he had not supposed that he was doing anything which would displease the king of England. On the other hand, when the king of England himself appealed to him on the duchess's behalf, he resolved to show her as much kindness as he could without interfering with the war he was waging or harming himself or his kingdom. He could not be expected, however, to guarantee the safety of the places which the duchess claimed as hers, as they lay within his enemies' dominions and some of them had even made war on him. Were the circumstances reversed, he would not ask such a favour of the king of England for any places belonging to any kinsman or kinswoman of his own, but would rather assist the king of England with all his power to reduce them to submission; and he felt sure the king of England would wish to do the same by him, as that was the way for true and loyal friends to treat each other, and the way they were bound by their mutual treaties to treat each other. Nevertheless, he repeated the offer he had made through Master Yves de la Tillaye to take Margaret under his protecting wing and then told his ambassadors that, if the king of England still showed dissatisfaction, they might tell him that he would promise not to injure the duchess or her lands and subjects while he was waging war on the Duke of Austria, provided she and her subjects did not injure or make war on him or give shelter to his enemies. But he added a demand for a written assurance from the king of England that he would be absolved from these promises should Margaret or her subjects offend against him in any of these ways.[1]

Edward received Louis' ambassadors at Windsor on 27 December, and they were with him again on 2 and 3 January, when the chancellor, Lord Howard, and other members of the council were present.[2] Nothing, however, could induce the Frenchmen to alter their reply about the payment of the dowry, and when the meaning of Louis' answer was fully grasped, the indignation of Edward's entire council was so great, the Bishop of Elne heard, that they advised the king to break off all relations with the king of France.[3] But Edward thought he saw another way to get even with Louis, and after the matter had simmered for about a fortnight, he commissioned the Bishop of Bath and Wells, Morton, Essex, Rivers, Dudley, Howard, and others to begin negotiations with the Bishop of Elne regarding the change in the duration of the truce which he had asked for and which the bishop was empowered, by the commission Louis had given him on 13 July, to make.[4]

Morton seems to have taken the lead in the negotiations with the Bishop of Elne, and though he was one of Louis' pensioners, and though Guillaume Restout arrived in England on his usual errand soon after the negotiations began,[5] the Master of the Rolls handled Louis' representative without gloves. Every time the bishop ventured to object to the terms proposed

---

1. Régistre de Pierre Doriolle, MS. français 10,187, ff. 193-199; I.egrand coll., MS. français 6987, ff. 391-398 (a not too accurate copy from d'Oriole's Register); MS. Dupuy 751, ff. 129-144 (another copy). For that part of the instructions which relates to the Duchess Margaret, see also Plancher, IV, cccxcv-cccxcvj.
2. Household Accounts, 18-19 Edw. IV, Exchequer K. R., bundle 412, no. 10.
3. Trial of the Bishop of Elne, interrogatory of 23 August.
4. Rymer, XII, 97, 21 Jan. For some reason this commission was issued anew on 8 February. *Ibid.*, 104. Morton was now bishop-elect of Ely, and throughout the account of the trial of the Bishop of Elne he is called the Bishop of "Helin."
5. Howard had received his pension as early as 31 October, but Edward's and Hastings's were paid on 7 February and Montgomery's and Morton's on the following day. See Restout's account, which ends with these payments for Michaelmas, 1478; Signed Bills, file 1516, no. 5058; and French Roll 18 Edw. IV, m. 1. Again the chancellor of England received his money in four instalments, though he gave but two receipts, dated 14 August and 31 October.

to him, Morton and his colleagues told him that the Duke of Austria had offered to help the king of England to conquer France and to pay him sixty thousand crowns a year, giving hostages and towns as security, and that if he, the bishop, did not agree to what was suggested, they would know what to do. The bishop was also informed that, notwithstanding the claim Louis had laid to the title of Duke of Burgundy, the king of England must be permitted to name the Dukes of Burgundy and Brittany among his allies, and, though he tried to protest, it did no good. He was so frightened that he even thought of running away, but after a little calm reflection he realized that would be folly, as it would only drive the king of England into the arms of Mary and Maximilian; and in the end he came to the conclusion that the safest thing he could do was to yield. Telling himself, as he afterwards claimed, that if he was exceeding his powers the king of France would have an excuse for repudiating everything he did, on 13, 14 and 15 February he signed three agreements which Morton had drawn up and which were to be submitted to the kings of England and France for their approval.[1]

The first agreement the Bishop of Elne signed so unwillingly was to the effect that the truce between England and France should endure for one hundred and one years after the death of whichever king, Edward or Louis, died first, and that the arrangement already made for the arbitration of differences should continue in force. The Dukes of Burgundy and Brittany were named among the king of England's allies, and two new clauses were added to the truce, one providing, as Edward had wished, for the safe coming and going of the merchants of Venice, Florence, and Genoa, and one requiring that the truce as now amended should be confirmed within a year by the three estates of France and England, as well as by the two kings themselves, and that both kings should endeavour to obtain a confirmation of it by the Pope also. The bishop had declared that he had no authority to accept these new clauses, but the only reply he got was that, unless he consented to them, the negotiations would end then and there.[2]

---

1. Trial of the Bishop of Elne, interrogatory of 7 August.
2. *Ibid.*, interrogatory of 4 August; Commynes-Lenglet, III, 560-564. As Louis had signed a treaty with Venice in January 1478, it would appear that the objection he had raised to Edward's wish in regard to the merchants of Italy had been removed.

The other documents the bishop signed did not please him any better. One of them was a promise that Louis and his successors would pay to Edward and his successors, at London, fifty thousand crowns a year as long as the truce between England and France continued, and that Louis would send to Edward within eighteen months either the bond of the bank of Medici or the papal bull which he had agreed to give him as security for the payment of this yearly pension. The other was an agreement that the "amity," like the truce, should continue for one hundred and one years after the death of the king who died first.[1] Yet what the bishop objected to was not the extension of the time the treaty of amity and the payment of the pension were to last, but the insertion in these new agreements of the requirement that they should be confirmed not only by the two kings, but by the three estates of their realms and, ultimately, by the Pope.

Perhaps the unhappy bishop hoped that when he had put his signature to these documents he would be allowed to depart in peace. If he did, he very soon discovered his mistake; for then he was informed that, as the pension of fifty thousand crowns a year was being promised for so great a length of time, it was not enough to renew the agreement regarding it which had been signed in 1475. He must also, he was told, go before an apostolic and imperial notary and execute a bond in Louis' name for the payment of the money. In vain he declared that, if such a bond were demanded of Louis, Edward ought to give a bond to keep the truce, as it was for the sake of the truce that the fifty thousand crowns a year were paid. The king of England had given no bond at Amiens, was the reply, and he would give none now. Morton himself drew up the desired bond and insisted that the bishop sign it on the spot. When the bishop refused, quite properly, to sign a document he had not seen, he was allowed to take the bond home with him for consideration, but at the end of two days he was just as much dismayed and just as much puzzled to know what he ought to do as he had been in the beginning. In the meantime he was warned again and again that, if he did not sign the bond, all was over, and at last, on the third day, Morton came to his lodgings and conducted him to the king's council chamber. There, too, he begged hard, saying, as before, that he had no authority to do what

---

1. Rymer, XII, 101-108.

was asked of him; but his excuses were tossed aside, and finally, in despair, he yielded for the second time. On 27 February Morton and Dudley took him to the house of the Preaching Friars, and there, before Walter Bedlow, apostolic and imperial notary, he signed the bond.[1] Nevertheless, his opponents had not got the better of him entirely. He had written to Louis at one time that the English were "grands trompeurs et menteurs," but that he would endeavour to "tromper et mentir comme eux"; and he kept his word, as he managed, when he signed the bond, to add the words, "in quantum vigore commissionis et potestatis sibi commissæ potuit eundem Dominum Ludovicum oneravit," and in that way gave Louis the opportunity to disavow, if he so wished, everything he had done.[2]

The bishop sent his *maître-d'hôtel* to France to tell Louis all about what he had been compelled to do, while Edward sent Oliver King along to present his side of the case.[3] Then all waited for the arrival of Louis' next embassy. But it was not likely to be a long waiting, as at the time the bailli of Caen and his colleagues had gone home—each one of them rejoicing in a fine "ambling horse" Lord Howard had presented to him in King Edward's name—they had promised that the king of France would send another embassy to conclude the arrangements for the marriage of the Dauphin and Dame Elizabeth.[4]

---

1. Trial of the Bishop of Elne, interrogatories of 2 and 7 August; Commynes-Lenglet, III, 564-570.
2. Trial of the Bishop of Elne, interrogatory of 26 August.
3. Trial of the Bishop of Elne, interrogatory of 23 August. King received £40 for this journey to France. Issue Roll, Easter 19 Edw. IV, 7 May.
4. *Lettres de Louis XI*, VII, 325; Issue Roll, Mich. 18 Edw. IV, 17 Feb. The four horses cost Edward £ 13s 4d.

5

LOUIS DELAYS

From the beginning to the end of 1479 England was all but prostrated by the plague, and perhaps this accounts for the fact that the internal history of the kingdom remains almost a blank during that year. The king was careful to stay away from London, but even at Eltham and Sheen he lived in dread, and when, in March, his year-old son, George, Duke of Bedford, died, probably of the dread disease,[1] his physicians seem to have advised a change of diet, as he appealed to the Pope for permission to eat meat, eggs, and food prepared with milk during Lent and on Sunday and other fast days. His Holiness was kind enough not only to grant this dispensation but, as Edward's petition stated that it was customary in England for the king to be attended at table by a large number of his nobles, to extend it, though for the Lenten season only, to any eight persons the king might choose to wait upon him and to two doctors and two cooks;[2] and thanks to, or in spite of, the unusually hearty food he was thus enabled to enjoy on every day of the year, the king's life was spared. But very many of his subjects succumbed. "Much people" fled from London to the country, and the courts were adjourned, first from Easter to Trinity term and then from Trinity to Michaelmas term, and the danger was by no means over even at Michaelmas.[3] At the end of October the king wrote to the chancellor for a *dedimus potestatem* for Elizabeth Shuldeham, lately chosen abbess of the monastery of Barking, as "great mortality" reigned in the monastery and he

---

1. Ramsay, II, 469. One continental chronicler actually says that Prince George died of the plague. *Chron. d'Adrien de But, Coll. de Chroniques Belges inédites*, 538.
2. Vatican Transcripts, portfolio 62. (See Appendix XIII).
3. *Cely Papers*, 16; Close Roll 19 Edw. IV, m. I; Signed Bills, file 1516, no. 5095. Cf. Nicolas's *London Chron.*, 146, and Arnold's *Chron.*, xxxvii. The courts of the city of London were also adjourned. Sharpe, *Cal. Letter Book L*, 164.

did not want her to "come unto us in her person to do her fealty."[1] And as late
as 6 November John Paston, whose brother Walter had died in August while
at home from Oxford for his vacation and their grandmother, Agnes Paston,
soon after, reported a sad state of things in Norfolk. "The people dieth sore
in Norwich," he wrote, "and especially about my house, but my wife and my
women come not out, and flee further we can not; for at Swainsthorpe, since
my departing thence, they have died and been sick nigh in every house of the
town." There was still another death in the Paston family, that of no less a person
than Sir John himself, during the month in which this letter was written, and
it was not until sometime in December that another man of the family, called
to London by business, was able to assure his mother that "thanked be God
the sickness is well ceased here."[2]

About the middle of February, before the Bishop of Elne's *maître-d'hôtel*
reached home to correct false rumours, Louis XI heard that Edward's
subjects were about to revolt and that Edward was going to Wales to quiet
them. But this story appears to have been untrue, as Edward remained at
Sheen. There may have been some momentary restlessness in the west, as it
was avowedly to promote "tranquillity, peace, and the public weal" in Wales
and the marches that, on 8 July, the king conferred on the Prince of Wales the
earldoms of March and Pembroke, after the latter had been surrendered by
William Herbert in exchange for the earldom of Huntingdon.[3] Yet there was
certainly no uprising that could be called a revolt, nor was there probably
any danger of one. For though the execution of Clarence weighed heavily
on Edward's soul, it produced, or at least very largely helped to produce, one
excellent result. England enjoyed more peace at home during the five years
that elapsed between Clarence's death and Edward's own than during any
other part of Edward's reign.

The unusual quiet prevailing in his kingdom during his last years was
naturally grateful to Edward in every way, and not the least of the pleasures he
derived from it was the opportunity it gave him to concentrate his attention
on foreign affairs. Though one of his children, all of whom were still of

---

1. Warrants under the Signet, file 1387, 26 Oct., 19 Edw. IV. Cf. *Cal. Patent Rolls*, III, 169.
2. *Paston Letters*, VI, 25, 32, and Introduction, 306-308.
3. Charter Roll 15-22 Edw. IV, m 10. See also Signed Bills, file 1517, nos. 5103-5104.
   Ramsay, II, 430, speaks of the bestowal of the earldom of Pembroke on the Prince as
   if it occurred in 1478.

tender years, was already married, another betrothed, and another promised, he still had several, including the most important member of the brood, the Prince of Wales, for whom no marriages had yet been arranged, and owing to that fact matrimonial schemes in particular occupied his mind. Not that there was anything unique in Edward's *penchant* for match-making. On the contrary, his neighbours also showed a taste for that species of diplomacy, and the recent matrimonial offer which he had received from the Emperor, and which had so perturbed the mind of the Bishop of Elne, had arrived almost simultaneously with another such offer from the king of Scotland.

James III had had reason to congratulate himself that his proposal of two years ago that his brother Albany should marry the widowed Duchess of Burgundy and his sister Margaret the Duke of Clarence had not been accepted, as since that time not only had Clarence been executed for treason, but Albany too had got himself into trouble and been locked up in Edinburgh Castle. Yet James had not lost his desire to secure an English helpmate for his sister, and towards the close of 1478 Alexander Inglyssh, Dean of Dunkeld, and Lyon King-of-Arms had arrived in England to ask Edward to consent to a marriage between Margaret of Scotland and Earl Rivers. This time Edward was all willingness, and the Bishop of Rochester and Rivers's brother, Sir Edward Woodville, having been empowered, on 14 December, to confer with the Scottish ambassadors, in a short time a marriage contract was drawn up and signed. The bride was to have a dowry of four thousand marks, English money, but as James was too poor actually to pay the money, it was agreed that this sum should be deducted from the yearly payments Edward was making for the Princess Cecily's dowry; and James was to send his sister to England, at his own expense, before 16 May 1479.[1] On 23 January Edward granted a six months' safeconduct for Margaret of Scotland and a retinue of three hundred persons, and when James's envoys returned home to report the success of their mission, Alexander Legh went with them to pay another instalment of Cecily's dowry.[2]

---

1. Rymer, XII, 171 (Rymer has placed this document by mistake under 1482); Signed Bills, file 1528, no. 5660; *Rotuli Scotiæ*, II, 456; *Register of the Great Seal of Scot.*, II, 291-292. Edward gave Inglyssh £40, and Lyon 20 marks. Issue Roll, Mich. 18 Edw. IV, 28 Oct.
2. *Cal. Documents relating to Scot.*, IV, 295, 414-415. The statement of Hume Brown (*Hist. of Scot.*, I, 272) that Edward neglected to make the payment towards Cecily's dowry which was due in 1477 is erroneous. See Rymer, XII, 40, and *Cal. Documents relating to Scot.*, IV, 294.

But though in March, immediately after the arrival of Inglyssh, Lyon, and Legh at Edinburgh, the parliament of Scotland granted James twenty thousand marks to meet the expenses of his sister's marriage,[1] Earl Rivers's bride, when 26 May came, had not reached England—very likely because at that moment James's whole attention was taken up with an effort to drive the Duke of Albany out of Dunbar, whither he had fled after escaping from Edinburgh Castle.[2] James, however, afterwards sent a promise that his sister should be in England before 1 November, and on the strength of this promise Edward, on 22 August, granted another six months' safeconduct for Margaret and her retinue. Edward even laid plans to attend the wedding, which was now expected to take place at Nottingham about the middle of October; and he wrote to the magistrates of York that the sister of the king of Scots would reach their city on 9 October and that they must give her "such loving and hearty cheer as we therefor may have cause to give unto you our right especial thanks."[3] Nevertheless, the bride again failed to arrive, and though it is not easy to suggest an explanation for her non-appearance this time, Edward evidently did not hold James to blame, as his friendly relations with the king of Scots suffered no interruption and in November he granted him a safeconduct—the last of a series of such safeconducts, no one of which was ever used—to enable him to travel through England when he made the pilgrimage he had long contemplated to the shrine of St John at Amiens.[4]

As his hold upon Scotland seemed to be firm enough already, the mishaps, whatever they were, which prevented the marriage of Rivers and Margaret of Scotland probably caused Edward little concern. Rivers may have been disappointed,

---

1. *Acts of Parl. of Scot.*, III, 122.
2. Lesley, *Hist. of Scot.*, 43; Chronicle at end of Wyntoun, Pinkerton, *Hist. of Scot.*, I, 503; *Chron. Scandaleuse*, II, 89.
3. *Rotuli Scotiæ*, II, 457; Davies, *York Records*, 99-100.
4. *Rotuli Scotiæ, ut sup.* Ramsay (and he has been followed by Hume Brown) accuses Edward of having dealings at this time with his former ally, John of the Isles: But the accusation is based solely on an entry on Issue Roll, Easter 19 Edw. IV, 6 July, which indicates that Roos, or Ross, Herald came to England in this year with secret messages and received from Edward a reward of £6 13s 4d; and as a matter of fact the earldom of Ross was no longer held by John of the Isles. It had been annexed to the crown of Scotland in 1476. Moreover, in the Issue Roll entry Ross Herald is distinctly described as a "herald of the king of Scots." Evidently he came as a messenger from James III himself, as we shall find him doing a few months later.

and perhaps Queen Elizabeth too, but to Edward himself the marriage was a matter of small moment. The king was engaged in other matrimonial negotiations at the same time, however, which meant a great deal to him.

It seems to have been early in 1479 that Queen Elizabeth gave birth, at Eltham, to her sixth daughter, Katharine;[1] and in spite of the treaty of peace Ferdinand and Isabella had just signed with the king of France, Edward's thoughts, when he found that he had another daughter to dispose of, flew at once to the Spanish prince whose advent into the world had been announced to him by special messenger in the preceding October. In the latter part of February Bernard de la Forsse made one of his many journeys to Spain,[2] and if he did not present to Ferdinand and Isabella at that time an offer of a marriage between their son and Princess Katharine, certainly when he set out for Spain again in the following August, with Doctor John Coke for a companion, he carried with him such a proposal and, in addition, many yards of scarlet, crimson, and violet cloth to be distributed among divers lords and magnates of Spain whose help it might be well to enlist.[3]

Yet not even the renewed possibility of a marriage alliance with Ferdinand and Isabella could draw Edward's thoughts away for a single moment from the most important of all his matrimonial projects, the marriage of his eldest daughter to the heir to the throne of France; and the ambassadors and other envoys King Louis sent to England with all sorts of offers and excuses scarcely outnumbered those sent by Edward to France. Not that all Edward's emissaries were charged simply and solely with messages regarding the marriage of

---

1. The exact date of Katharine's birth is unknown. She was certainly born before 28 August 1479, when Coke and Bernard de la Forsse received the commission about to be mentioned. On the other hand, it is evident, as Nicolas has pointed out, that she had not been long in the world at that time, as the wardrobe accounts of April-September 1480, speak of nails used "about covering of the font" at her christening. Nicolas, *Wardrobe Accounts of Edw. IV*, xxiv, 122. As the court was at Eltham most of the time from the middle of November till the middle of February 1479, but not during the succeeding months (Privy Seals; Wardrobe Accounts, 18-19 Edw. IV), the queen was probably confined in the winter.
2. Warrants for Issues, 18 Edw. IV, 17 Feb.
3. Rymer, XII, 110; Issue Roll, Easter 19 Edw. IV, 15 June. Arnold Trussell, who figures in the Customs Accounts for Plymouth and Fowey, 12-13 and 16 Edw. IV, both as "Arnold Trussell of Bayonne, alien," and as "Arnold Trussell, dwelling in the city of St Sebastian in the kingdom of Spain," was also sent to Spain with cloth which was to be given to divers lords and magnates of that land. Issue Roll, *ut sup.*

the Princess Elizabeth and the Dauphin. Perhaps even before Oliver King accompanied the Bishop of Elne's *maître-d'hôtel* to France, John Grauntford had gone across the sea again, either to try to hasten the payment of Edward's pension or else to repeat the demand for the payment of Elizabeth's dowry;[1] but John Doget, treasurer of Chichester cathedral, who set out for France, possibly with King, was sent to talk with Louis, not about the dowry or any other matter connected with the marriage treaty, but about a totally different subject.

Since the Pazzi conspiracy and the murder of Giuliano de Medici in April 1478, Italy had been torn by a war in which Pope Sixtus, who had probably instigated the murder and who was backed by Ferdinand of Naples and the republic of Siena, was fighting against a league composed of Florence, Milan, and Venice. At the beginning of this war Lorenzo de Medici had sought the help of the king of France, and Louis, only too pleased to accept Lorenzo's invitation, had at once proceeded to set himself up as the arbiter of Italy's affairs. Yet the war still went on, and when Edward became interested in events in the Italian peninsula through his negotiations with Bona of Savoy and the possibility that someday his son and heir would have an Italian wife, he was suddenly fired with the ambition to make his voice heard also in that faraway land.[2] Already he had sent the Abbot of Abingdon and John Sherwood, archdeacon of Richmond and prothonotary of the Apostolic See, to Rome,[3] and when Doget left England, accompanied by John Giglis, "our Holy Father the Pope's collector," he too was under orders to betake himself to Rome. But Edward could find no real excuse for interfering in Italy except the timeworn one of which Louis himself was making use, namely, Europe's need of confronting the Turk with a united instead of a divided Christendom, and as he could not well attempt such interference without Louis' knowledge and consent, Doget was to go first of all to France to consult with Louis.[1] Oliver King himself, in

---

1. Grauntford received £20 for this journey, as for his earlier one. Issue Roll, Easter 19 Edw. IV, 15 June.
2. If M. Vaesen is correct in assigning to the year 1478 two letters which Louis wrote on 21 September (*Lettres de Louis XI*, VII, 168, 172), the French king was even then seeking to have Italy accept the joint mediation of Edward and himself. But M. Perret (*Relations de la France avec Venise*, II, 387) refers these letters to 1479, and a comparison of their contents with those of a dispatch sent by Cagnola from Tours on 21 September 1479, (*Lettres et négociations de Commynes*, III, 60) seems to prove that he is right.
3. *Cal. Milanese Papers*, I, 232.

fact, had been directed to communicate to Louis the contents of some letters relating to the war in Italy which Edward had received from the Pope and to show him the "instructions" the Pope had sent.[2]

Louis was spending the winter in Touraine again, and when he was warned that more ambassadors from Edward were about to descend on him, he summoned his cleverest councillors to his support. On 6 March he wrote to the chancellor of France that he wanted him to go to see the embassy from England, despite the fact that it was not customary, and to "send for all the good doctors you brought with you to St Quentin for the English matter, for we have much need of them." And when, a few days later, the chancellor, the Count de Castres, and the Seigneur de St Pierre went to meet the Englishmen at Tours,[3] they soon heard from Oliver King all that Edward had directed him to tell Louis about the messages from the Pope. More than that, King told them that Edward hoped the king of France would send to England as soon as possible some persons who were versed in monetary matters to hold the long-postponed monetary diet, and that he also wanted Louis to permit Maximilian to be represented at the diet. Edward wanted even more than this—much more. He wanted the honour of mediating between France and Burgundy. Maximilian, whom he had evidently sounded on the subject, seemed to be willing to let him make an attempt at mediation, and if Louis too would give his consent, how great would be the gain to Christendom at this time when it was so necessary that all Christian nations should join forces against the Turk! If it should turn out that the mediator was able to procure two pensions for himself, and also the marriage of his younger daughter to the son of Mary and Maximilian in addition to the marriage of his eldest daughter to the Dauphin of France, that would detract nothing, in his eyes, from the benefit to all the western world.[4]

---

1. Warrants for Issues, 18 Edw. IV, 8 and 10 Feb. Doget was going "in our message into France and unto Rome and other places," Giglis "to do errands as well unto the same our Holy Father as in divers other places."
2. See in MS. français 4054, f. 244 *et seq.*, a minute, with corrections, of some very lengthy instructions which Louis drew up for some unnamed ambassadors going to England. Although these instructions are without date, the references they contain to Oliver King and the affairs of Italy prove that they belong to 1479.
3. *Lettres de Louis XI*, VII, 268-269, 274.
4. The instructions given by Maximilian to the Duchess Margaret when she went to England in 1480 sound as if he thought Edward was hoping for both marriages and would get two pensions if he could.

Unfortunately Louis' answer about Maximilian was prompt and emphatic. He showed his gratitude for Edward's frankness in regard to the Pope's messages by telling King all he knew about the affairs of Italy, and by explaining how his own interest in them had grown out of the ancient alliance between the Florentines and the house of France and out of his friendship with Lorenzo de Medici. He said also that he was ready and willing to send suitable persons to England before 1 September to hold the monetary conference with Edward's commissioners. But with the Duke of Austria, he declared, he would hold no communication on any subject whatever, for the duke was his enemy.[1]

Louis had his reasons for welcoming instead of resenting Edward's wish to dabble in the affairs of Italy. For one thing, he was glad to humour Edward when he could, as that helped to pacify him; in the second place, it served his purpose to have the world think that he and the king of England were hand and glove. "He considers that this brings him great reputation and is a thing which keeps his enemies cast down."[2] And if he was anxious to have the world think that Edward and he were very good friends, what could serve such an end better than the sight of Edward and himself working side by side at Rome? Louis probably felt, too, that Edward would have little opportunity to do harm in Italy, as his own control of the situation there was sufficiently complete to enable him to restrain and, if necessary, circumvent him. When it came to Burgundy, however, the whole case was different. The prime object of Louis' strategy had been to keep Edward and Maximilian as far apart as possible, and he had not the slightest intention of abandoning that policy.

In a long and interesting letter which Cagnola and another Milanese envoy, Carolo Visconti, wrote to Bona of Savoy from France on 14 March, they told her that the Count de Castres had informed them on behalf of the king of France that ambassadors had come from the king of England and had had audience of his Majesty. Some of these ambassadors had come, they said, "about the dowry which they desire his Majesty to make up for the daughter of the king of England, promised at another time to my lord the Dauphin, according to the arrangements," and the king had referred them to his council to examine their claims. One of them, on the other hand, had come

---

1. MS. français 4054, *ut sup*.
2. *Cal. Milanese Papers*, I, 233.

to communicate to his Majesty the views of the king of England: firstly, that he would like his Majesty to remain in concord with Duke Maximilian, and that his Majesty would allow him to interpose to settle their differences. He also thought he would like to send to the Pope and exhort him to pacify Italy, owing to the great perils which his Majesty perceives for the Christian religion, when the Turk is at the gates of Italy and so powerful, as everyone knows. If the Pope should fall in with this, that king is disposed to follow the advice and opinion of his Majesty.

But it seemed to the king of France, the writers continued, that the English ambassadors were not very well informed regarding the justification for the league which had been formed against the Pope, and so he had asked them to go to the Englishmen and try to make them see that it was the opponents of the league who were in the wrong, and that, "if it rested with the league alone, peace would be made." Consequently, accompanied by the Count de Castres and the Seigneur de St Pierre, the two Milanese had visited Edward's ambassadors and, after making the explanations the king of France had suggested and stating that the league and the king of France, to whom the league had referred everything, had already sent ambassadors to the Pope to conclude peace, they had told the Englishmen that they were "greatly delighted that their king had also deigned to offer his interposition, especially as it was done in full accord with the king here, as we were given to understand." Whereupon the Englishmen had made a very gracious reply and one of them, "who is a doctor" and who had been commissioned to go to the Pope and advise him to make peace, said he would hurry on to Rome as soon as he had talked the matter over with the king of France, with whom his king had a thorough understanding and a real friendship.[1]

Two days after Cagnola and Visconti wrote this letter, the king of France appointed Louis Toustain, one of the secretaries of his chancery, to go with Doget to Rome and instructed him to tell everybody he met that the kings of France and England were one in their wishes and plans and were determined to do everything possible to restore peace to Italy.[2] And as Cagnola stated in another letter written on the day Toustain received his commission that the

---

1. *Cal. Milanese Papers*, I, 230-232.
2. *Ibid.*, I, 232-235; *Lettres de Louis XI*, VII, 274-275; Commynes-Lenglet, IV, 240-241. The statement made, in a note, by the editor of the *Calendar of the Milanese Papers* that Langton went to Rome with Toustain is incorrect.

French and English ambassadors would start for Italy the next day or the day after, Doget and Louis' emissary were probably well on their way to Rome when two more English ambassadors—Tunstall and Langton again, who had evidently started for France with Doget but had been recalled, probably to be given further instructions[1]—arrived in Touraine.

The Count de Castres was waiting to receive the new arrivals, and, to judge from a memorandum made by the count of what he learned from Langton, it would appear that at least one subject of Edward IV was well trained in the diplomatic art of colouring the truth to suit the occasion. For after telling the count that the king of England was well aware that some Flemish ambassadors were coming to France, Langton remarked that those ambassadors would no doubt speak humbly, as the king of England had refused to grant the Flemings what they wanted. Then he said that the reason for his coming to France was to ask the king of France to send the promised embassy to conclude the arrangements for the marriage of the Dauphin and Princess Elizabeth, and he declared that never had the king and kingdom of England been so favourably inclined towards an alliance with the king of France as they were at the present moment. He told "merveilles," too, about Lord Hastings's friendly feeling for the king of France, declared that King Edward wished ill to all who spoke ill of the king of France and were opposed to peace with him, and finally, crossing his hands on his breast, swore solemnly that he himself was a "bon serviteur" of the king of France.

When the Count de Castres, feeling a little sceptical about all this, reminded Langton that there were English soldiers in the armies of Mary and Maximilian, Edward's ambassador offered to prove that, before those soldiers left England, they had been ordered to fight the men of Gueldres and such persons but had been strictly forbidden to make war on the king of France or his subjects. And when the count informed him that Englishmen had been killed and captured in Picardy in the very act of making war on the subjects of the king of France, he answered that King Edward had rejoiced at the fate of those men, because they had been disobedient and violated his commands, and that, had they lived to return home, they would have been severely punished. On being asked why the king of England had been equipping an army, he replied—apparently

---

1. Langton told the Count de Castres that he put to sea on the vigil "de la Nostre Dame de mars," which I take to mean 24 March, the day before the feast of the Annunciation.

lying unblushingly—that the army was going to Scotland.[1] He hastened to say also that King Edward was anxious to find out, before he launched into war, just how he stood with the king of France, so that he might know how to reply to the requests which were coming to him from many quarters. For King Edward preferred, he said, an alliance with the king of France and the proposed marriage to all the other alliances in the world.

One statement made by Langton must have caused his interrogator not a little surprise. He had not come, he said, to ask for money. He did express astonishment, however, that the king of France did not send more money to King Edward, seeing that the king's man had now been in France some time waiting for it and that this delay gave the enemies of the king of France a chance to hinder the peace and to win the king of England away from it. Lastly, as a hint to Louis that the enemies of France were not napping, he offered the information that the Prince of Orange had gone to Brittany to make all the trouble he could.[2]

But not even Langton, quick-witted diplomat though he was, could bring Louis to alter his decision about the dowry. "The English ambassadors here will leave in two or three days," wrote Cagnola on 16 April,

> being dispatched about their embassies, though not altogether as they wish. In the first place, with regard to their request for the dowry to be made up for the king's daughter promised to my lord the Dauphin, as I have reported before, the Most Christian King refers the question to his council, so that he may decide *quid juris*, because there was a point of right. It was ultimately decided that his Majesty is not bound to make up any dowry at present, and so he answered the ambassadors to that effect. However, he gave them a thousand fair words, as well as hopes, although, from what I understand, the king is firmly resolved that the marriage shall not take place, and so he temporizes until such time as he shall have worked out his plans.

Cagnola understood that Tunstall and Langton also mentioned again King Edward's desire to mediate between the king of France and Archduke

---

1. There is nothing to prove that Edward had been preparing an army of any size in the spring of 1479, and certainly he was not quarrelling with James III at this time. If he was sending troops to the northern border, it must have been to punish some outrages which followed upon the escape of the Duke of Albany to Dunbar and for which Albany, not James, was responsible. See *Acts of Parl. of Scot.*, II, 125-129.
2. *Lettres de Louis XI*, VII, 325-327.

Maximilian. But when it came to that subject, Louis did not offer so much as "a thousand fair words." He was quite polite, but he told Tunstall and Langton bluntly that he did not care to have Edward interfere. So the Englishmen had to get such consolation as they could out of the friendly interest Louis pretended to feel in Edward's marriage negotiations with Bona of Savoy. Yet in that matter, too, as Cagnola said in his letter, which was addressed to Bona and her son, the Most Christian King was insincere. Those who were in Louis' confidence had told Cagnola that the chief difficulty in the way of the marriage would be the large amount of money the king of England would want

> for the dowry and for presents, as they say he knows that you have a great treasure, and he proposes in this way to obtain a good share of it, as being one who in any ease tends to accumulate treasure. They presuppose that your Excellencies will not humour this appetite of his, and that will be the way to create great difficulties in this question and spin it out indefinitely, because they say that the king of England does not desire to make this marriage alliance for any other purpose than to obtain a great quantity of money from your Excellencies.[1]

Louis' continued denial of his obligation to begin to pay Princess Elizabeth's dowry and his flat refusal to allow Edward to mediate between him and Maximilian were not the only indications he gave of a determination to stand his ground against Edward's ever increasing demands. When the Bishop of Elne's *maître d'hôtel* laid before him the agreements the bishop had signed under duress, he had given one look at them and vowed that never would he ratify them. The bishop himself had advised him to send an embassy to Edward to dispute the agreements, and that advice he decided to act upon forthwith. He told the *maître d'hôtel* that he would dispatch the Abbé de la Grace to England,[2] and in anticipation of the departure of the

---

1. *Cal. Milanese Papers*, I, 235-236; *Lettres et négociations de Commynes*, I, 241.
2. Trial of the Bishop of Elne, interrogatories of 23 and 26 August. The person Louis proposed to send to England was probably the Abbot of La Grace-Dieu, a Cistercian abbey in the diocese of La Rochelle. The undated letter from Louis to the Bishop of Elne which is printed in *Lettres de Louis XI*, VIII, 199, would seem to belong to this time, not to the year 1480, as M. Vaesen thought. The secretary referred to in that letter was probably Oliver King.

abbot and those who should be chosen to go with him, he drew up very lengthy and explicit instructions for their use.

After referring to the messages brought by Oliver King and the replies which had been made to them, Louis' ambassadors were to say for him that he had learned from the letters of the Bishop of Elne, and from other sources, the desire of the king of England for the preservation of the treaties signed at Amiens in August 1475, and for their continuance for a hundred years after the demise of the king who died first, and that for this proof of the king of England's affection he wished to thank him very warmly. Indeed, there was nothing in the world, Louis declared once more, which could possibly give him so much happiness as the continuance of this "bonne amour" and the strengthening of it by the marriage of Madame Elizabeth with the Dauphin; and to prove that he meant to keep all the treaties he had signed with his cousin of England, as well regarding the marriage, which had already been delayed too long to please him, as regarding the continuation of the truce and amity, the arbitration covenant, and the payment of the fifty thousand crowns a year, he was quite ready to consent to the prolongation of those treaties for a hundred years in the form given them at Amiens, and also to provide guarantees which ought to be satisfactory to the king of England. But in the documents sent to him by the Bishop of Elne there were some things which would injure him greatly without benefiting the king of England and which, furthermore, were directly opposed to the intention of the treaties between him and his cousin of England and even destructive of their main purpose. For this reason he wished, before going farther, to make matters quite clear between his said cousin and himself.

To begin with, Louis said, in the renewal of the truce for a hundred years as agreed to by the Bishop of Elne, the king of England had named the Duke of Burgundy among his allies, although the only Duke of Burgundy at the present time was the king of France himself, to whom the duchy of Burgundy had reverted at the death of the late Duke Charles without male heirs, and whose right to it the king of England was bound by his treaties with him to support. If any other person than the king of France was intended by "the Duke of Burgundy," then for the king of France to accept the new truce would amount to an admission by him that someone other than himself was duke of Burgundy; and that would be very detrimental to him. Particularly would it be to his detriment if by "the Duke of Burgundy" was meant Duke

Maximilian of Austria, as in that case his acceptance of the truce would be equivalent to a recognition by him of the unjust claim Maximilian had advanced to the duchy of Burgundy. On the other hand, the king of England could not include Duke Maximilian in the truce under any other name than that of Duke of Burgundy; for, as the duke was not included in the original truce, he could not be included in the prolongation of it. No more could he be included in it as the heir of the late Duke Charles, whose daughter he had married: first, because the conditions under which Charles had been included did not apply to his successors; second, because, although Charles had been given three months in which to declare his wish to be included in the original truce, he had never in his life made such a declaration, and therefore he never had been included in it and his heirs could not be; third, because Duke Maximilian was a declared enemy of the king of France, retaining by violence lands belonging to the kingdom of France, and the treaties between the kings of France and England bound them to assist each other against just such offenders.

The king of England should remember, too, Louis argued further, that in all their previous negotiations with each other Duke Maximilian had always been spoken of as the enemy of both of them. Also the king of England knew that the king of France had refused many times to sign a long truce with Maximilian because it was not to his interest to do so, and if the king of England now insisted on including the duke in the hundred years' truce, the duke would in that way secure what he had thus far sought in vain, and it would be possible for him to keep the truce when he wanted to and to break it when he wanted to. What was more, the homage and fidelity which the duke owed to the king of France for the county of Flanders and other lands in the kingdom of France would remain in abeyance for the whole hundred years of the truce and would be very difficult to recover afterwards. Lastly, the duke would be left in possession of Lille, Douai, Orchie, and many other places belonging to the demesne of the king and crown of France.

Louis also insisted that it was unreasonable for the king of England to include the Duke of Brittany in the truce. For that duke, he claimed, was his subject, owing homage to the kings of France for his duchy and subject to the jurisdiction of the Parliament of Paris, and to include him in the truce would be, in effect, to exempt him from that jurisdiction and to imply that he was not his, Louis', subject. It was true the duke had been included in the truce signed at Amiens, but the situation was different then, as at that time the duke was at war with the king of France, whereas since then he had submitted and had sworn to serve the king of France against all men. Moreover, if the present duke were included in the truce and it should happen later that one of his successors refused homage to the king of France or obedience to his court, the king of France would be unable to use force against him, as right demanded, and so would practically lose his sovereignty over him. If this state of disobedience continued for a hundred years, the very memory of the rights of the king and crown of France would be lost and it would be necessary to wage a new war to recover them. Finally, Louis wound up by declaring, as he had done similarly in the case of Maximilian, that by including the Duke of Brittany among his allies the king of England was breaking the treaties signed at Amiens.

Louis had something to say also about the bond for the payment of the pension of fifty thousand crowns which the Bishop of Elne had been forced to sign. He was quite willing to go on paying the money, and he expected his successors to pay it, but in the documents sent to him by the Bishop of Elne there were some clauses and conditions which did not appear in the agreement made at Amiens, which were a very heavy charge on him, and which would displease his people. He would like to point out these things to his cousin of England, not to spoil or alter the agreement in any way— for he meant to pay every penny of the money—but merely to request his said cousin to be content with the honest and reasonable guarantees given at Amiens. In the first place, he said, the Bishop of Elne had given two bonds for the same thing—one which he signed and sealed with his seal on 14 February and one which was signed in the presence of an Apostolic and imperial notary at the house of the Preaching Friars at London on 27 February—and that there should be two bonds for the same thing was certainly strange and unreasonable. In the second place, it was neither proper nor customary for great princes to be bound by such instruments as these, as their letters, sealed with their seals, or merely signed by their hands, were sufficiently authoritative; and while he was willing to abide by the bond he had given at Amiens, for him, who was "empereur en son royaume" and recognised no sovereign, to confirm a bond signed before an imperial notary would do injury to the authority and sovereignty of the kingdom and crown of France, and never would the estates of France permit it. In the third place, the bond in question would subject him and his successors, his kingdom and his subjects, to the jurisdiction and coercion not only of the Pope and the Apostolic Chamber, but of all secular courts, which would mean subjection to the jurisdiction and coercion of the court of the Emperor; and such a thing he could not accept even if he wished. Nor would his kingdom ever consent to it.

This was not by any means all that Louis had to say against the bond. But the rest of his tedious arguments need not be rehearsed, for when he had had his say, he told his ambassadors that, if the king of England could not be persuaded to renounce his demands, they might tell him that the king of France would accept the bond the Bishop of Elne had given, with all its pains and penalties, provided the king of England would bind himself to keep the truce, for the sake of which the fifty thousand crowns a year were paid to him, under the same pains and penalties. Louis also hoped that Edward would send an embassy to France to settle all moot-points, and his final order to his ambassadors was that when they saw a good chance to introduce the subject of the marriage, they should do so. After requesting the king of England to let them see "Madame la Daulphine" in order to offer her the "très affecteuses recommandacions" of the king and queen of France and of Monsieur the Dauphin, they were to repeat again that there was nothing in the world the king of France desired so much as the consummation of the marriage of the Dauphin and Dame Elizabeth, whom he already regarded as his daughter, and add that he had charged them to inquire about having the princess sent to France at his expense.[1]

Yet though Louis drew up his instructions for his ambassadors in such detail, and though the Bishop of Elne was waiting anxiously, the Abbé de la Grace never went to England. Louis sent two other envoys across the sea before the summer was over, but neither of them, apparently, was told to raise objections to the agreements the Bishop of Elne had signed. The Seigneur de St Pierre's mission seems to have been to persuade Edward of the folly of accepting the marriage alliance which the Emperor and Maximilian had offered him. The second envoy, Pierre Jouvelin, *correcteur* of the chamber of accounts,[1] probably came to represent Louis at the

---

1. MS. français 4054, f. 244 *et seq.*

monetary conference, which appears to have taken place before the end of the year and to have borne good fruit, as on 27 January 1480, Louis sealed some orders fixing the values to be given to English coins in France and on 12 May following Edward issued similar orders regarding the values to be given to French coins in England.[2] Evidently Louis had decided, on second thought, to keep his temper and to avoid taking any definite action for the present about the Bishop of Elne's agreements. Thus valuable time would be gained during which Edward's own temper might cool down and his demands be modified. So, while relations between the kings of France and England were somewhat ticklish, there was no open quarrel between them; and in Italy they even succeeded in acting as friends and partners in a way to edify the world.

On 17 April Edward issued a formal commission to the Abbot of Abingdon, Sherwood, Giglis, and Doget to represent him in the negotiations at Rome,[3] but he was soon to find out that the task he had undertaken was much more difficult and complicated than he had realized. For the Emperor and Maximilian, feeling that it was the place of the head of the Holy Roman Empire, not of the kings of France and England, to mediate between the warring factions in Italy, tried to thrust their fingers into the pie, while the Pope, discovering that there was division in the camp of the would-be peacemakers, declared it to be out of keeping with the dignity of the Apostolic See to submit the affairs of the papacy to the mediation of anyone. After some weeks of fruitless talking, Sixtus seemed to be brought to his senses by an announcement from the ambassadors of the league and of the kings of France and England that they would leave Rome unless he gave a definite reply within eight days, and on 2 June he declared his willingness to permit the two kings to settle the troubles of Italy. But he coupled with his surrender a stipulation that the two kings should accept the aid of a legate, whom he would send to France, and that, in case of disagreement, the Emperor and Maximilian—the latter of whom, to Louis'

---

1. Rougecroix Herald was paid £6 for the passage of Peter Joubelyn, ambassador of the king of France, from Dover to Boulogne. Issue Roll, Easter 19 Edw. IV, 15 June. For some account of Jouvelin, see *Lettres de Louis XI*, VI, 178, note 2.
2. Rymer, XII, 115.
3. *Ibid.*, XII, 108.

wrath, he persisted in calling Duke of Burgundy—should also be invited to act as assistants.[1]

Perhaps there would have been little hope under any circumstances that the kings of France and England would succeed in adjusting the quarrels of Italy; for as Commynes remarked to Visconti,

> notwithstanding the great friendship which seems to exist between his Majesty and the king of England, and although they have sent their ambassadors together, they will never be able to agree on a single question, as that which is done for the one is to the prejudice of the other and the friend of one is necessarily the enemy of the other.

But when a papal legate was added to the mediators, the hope of a swift and happy ending of the negotiations was slight indeed, and Commynes' prediction was that "they will never finish in our time." As for Louis, not only did he look for delay in consequence of the legate's presence, but he feared that the legate would seek to make trouble between him and Edward; and what with this fear and what with his disgust at Sixtus's insistence on giving the Emperor and Maximilian a hand in the proposed mediation, he felt inclined to disavow altogether what his ambassadors had done in Italy.[2] All that he did at the moment, however, was to make sure that his neighbours heard about the excellent understanding which existed between the king of England and himself. On 4 July he wrote to the magistrates of Lucerne to announce that his conquest of the county of Burgundy was now complete, that his arms had also been successful in Picardy, and that, as the king of England had agreed to an extension of his truce with him for one hundred years after the death of either of them, neither Edward IV nor his successors could ever again give aid or favour to the Duke of Burgundy.[3]

The magistrates of Lucerne may have believed everything Louis told them, but if they did, they showed their ignorance and gullibility. For in reality neither Edward nor Louis had yet ratified the proposed hundred years'

---

1. *Cal. Milanese Papers*, I, 237-242; Commynes-Lenglet, IV, 241-251; *Lettres et négociations de Commynes*, I, 254; Perret, II, 176-178.
2. *Lettres et négociations de Commynes*, I, 261, 268. By this time Venice had decided to accept the Pope's terms, although the doge and senate expressed doubt, in a letter which they sent to Edward on 8 June, about Sixtus's having any real intention of accepting mediation. *Cal. Venetian Papers*, I, 139.
3. *Lettres de Louis XI*, VIII, 48.

truce between France and England, and, notwithstanding his co-operation with Louis in Italy, Edward seemed to be drawing nearer and nearer to an alliance with Mary and Maximilian. It is said that in June the Flemings found on a captured French ship some gifts Louis was dispatching to Lord Howard along with a letter exhorting that friendly nobleman to arrange for the sending of ten thousand English soldiers to help him in Flanders, and that this discovery led Edward to arrest Howard and eleven of his friends.[1] But if this story is true, Howard's disgrace was of very short duration and Mary and Maximilian were sufficiently reassured by his arrest, as on 18 July they promised that for three years they would refrain from betrothing their son to anyone except Edward's daughter Anne, while on 16 August Edward promised not to betroth Anne to anyone except Philip.[2] Nor was this all. On 7 August Maximilian defeated Louis' army at Guinegate, and although Louis may have known nothing about the Anglo-Burgundian betrothal compact, he did know that under the ducal standard had fought, and fought ardently, some three hundred or more English auxiliaries.[3]

The disaster at Guinegate was a rude shock to Louis, who was not used to defeat and whose health had been considerably shaken by a stroke of apoplexy suffered in the spring. In fact, his discouragement was so great that he resolved to make peace with Maximilian as soon as he could do so advantageously. It even affected his policy in Italy, and he dispatched a letter to Bona of Savoy telling her that he had decided to accept the Pope's proposal in regard to mediation. But this letter had scarcely started on its way to Milan when a messenger arrived from Rome with the announcement that Sixtus had rejected absolutely the provisional agreement which had been offered for his approval, and that he now proposed that his legate and the king of France should do all the mediating between him and the league, without any help

---

1. Kervyn de Lettenhove, *Hist. de Flandre* (Brussels, 1847-1855), V, 314.
2. Rymer, XII, 110. The negotiations which ended in these mutual promises were probably conducted for Edward by William Slefeld, who received £20 for an embassy to Flanders about this time. Issue Roll, Easter 19 Edw. IV, 6 July. As we shall see, Slefeld had a hand in the subsequent negotiations regarding the marriage of Philip and Anne.
3. Commynes, II, 34; Molinet, II, 204, 209. Commynes gives the name of the captain of these English soldiers as Thomas Auriguen and says he was a knight who had served under Charles the Bold. Molinet writes the name "Thomas d'Orican." Probably the person meant was Sir Thomas Everingham, whose name, in another instance, is spelled "Deuringhem." See Commynes-Lenglet, III, 578.

from the king of England.[1] What doubt was there now that Sixtus was bent on sowing discord between the kings of France and England? However, if that was what His Holiness was aiming at, he failed to accomplish his purpose. Early in September Pierre le Roy, "magister monete de Rouen"—taking the place of Guillaume Restout, who had made his last journey to England— arrived in London with Edward's pension;[2] and when the Seigneur de St Pierre returned home in the first days of October, accompanied by Louis de Bretaylle, he carried to Louis a letter in which Edward said that, as he did not want to ally himself with the enemies of his cousin of France, he had decided to consent to the marriage of his son with the sister of the Duke of Milan and expressed his wish to have Louis conduct the marriage negotiations for him.[3]

Now it happened that Louis was only too glad to grant Edward's request for help in his marriage negotiations with Bona of Savoy, not only because if the Prince of Wales married Bona of Savoy's daughter he could not marry Maximilian's sister, but because Louis had heard that Bona was thinking of affiancing her daughter to the son of Alphonso of Aragon, Duke of Calabria, an alliance which was not at all to his fancy. So he told Louis de Bretaylle that he would do his best for Edward, and on 13 October he wrote to Bona urging her to accept the king of England's offer. Seeing how very close are the commercial relations between Genoa and England, Louis argued in this letter, no surer means of re-establishing Milan's power over Genoa could be found than an alliance between Milan and England; and he added that

---

1. Commynes, II, 36-37, note 3; *Lettres de Louis XI*, VIII, 62-64; *Lettres et négociations de Commynes*, I, 286-288.
2. Rymer, XII, 111; Tellers' Roll, Easter 20 Edw. IV.
3. See the letter which Louis wrote to Bona of Savoy on 13 October encouraging her to accept the English marriage. *Lettres de Louis XI*, VIII, 278. Both M. Vaesen and M. Perret (II, 201, note) have referred this letter to the year 1480, but there are three reasons, one positive and two negative, for believing that it belongs, not to 1480, but to 1479. In the first place, it fits in with the last articles of some instructions which Louis gave to the Bishop of Elne and others on 10 February 1480 (see later). In the second place, it is very unlikely that Edward would have asked Louis in October 1480, to negotiate a marriage for the Prince of Wales, as by that time Louis was so angry with him for having furnished more archers to Maximilian that there was some prospect of war between France and England. In the third place, in October 1480, it was certainly known at Venice, and in all probability at Milan also, that the Prince of Wales's hand had been offered to Anne of Brittany.

the English marriage would also insure his own friendship with the king of England and his son for ever and that Bona need feel no fear that war would break out between France and England during her daughter's lifetime, as he had already made a truce with the English for one hundred and one years.[1]

Louis seems to have sent an embassy to Bona as well as this letter; for in February 1480, some French ambassadors who were about to go to England were instructed to tell Edward that such an embassy had been sent and that, had it not been for events which had occurred in Milan,[2] the marriage Edward sought would have been secured already, as the Duchess of Milan had written to the king of France many times that she would follow his wishes in the matter. When this embassy returned from Italy, Edward was to be told, he should hear what word they brought, and then he could send some ambassadors of his own to Milan to conclude the negotiations. And in the meantime he might be sure that the king of France would do, as he had assured Louis de Bretaylle, as much to promote the marriage as if the Prince of Wales were his own son.[3]

In the following month, however, the war in Italy was ended by the signing of a treaty of peace between Ferdinand of Naples and Lorenzo de Medici which Louis had been instrumental in negotiating,[4] and from that day on nothing more is heard about a marriage between the Prince of Wales and the daughter of Bona of Savoy. On 10 February 1480, Hercules d'Este, Duke of Ferrara, was created a knight of the Garter, and in the following autumn some ambassadors came to England to receive the Garter and the mantle of the Order for the duke and to bestow some mirrors and other gifts pleasing to ladies upon Queen Elizabeth and her daughters.[5] But except for the conferring of this honour on the head of one of the lesser Italian states and a slight interest which he continued to manifest at times in the plans of the Holy See to withstand the Turks, there is nothing to show that after 1479 Edward IV ever again essayed to dip into the affairs of Italy or to form any

---

1. *Lettres de Louis XI, ut sup.*
2. Louis refers to the overthrow of Cico Simonetta, who had been all-powerful in Bona's government, by Ludovico il Moro, her brother-in-law. This occurred in September 1479.
3. See the instructions given to the Bishop of Elne, etc., on 10 February 1480. *Lettres de Louis XI*, VIII, 356-357.
4. Perret, II, 193.
5. Beltz; Commynes-Lenglet, IV, 10; Nicolas, *Wardrobe Accounts of Edw. IV*, 124.

alliances in that peninsula. His loss of interest in Italy was due largely, no doubt, to the fact that he soon found another fiancée for his son who pleased him better than the sister of the Duke of Milan; but it also grew out of the fact that his relations with the king of France, whose influence in Italy must always outweigh his own, grew daily more unfriendly.

6

A VISIT FROM THE DUCHESS MARGARET

That the collapse of their joint enterprise in Italy did not cause trouble between the kings of France and England was the more remarkable because their negotiations regarding that enterprise had gone hand in hand with other negotiations which were ever threatening to end in a rupture if not in war. When Doget was sent in the spring of 1479 to consult Louis about what was to be done at Rome, other envoys who accompanied him had been commissioned to negotiate with the French king about the Bishop of Elne's agreements, about the payment of Princess Elizabeth's dowry, and about the very delicate subject of mediation between France and Burgundy. And when, in the following October, the Seigneur de St Pierre was returning home and Edward wrote the letter in which he intimated that, for love of his cousin of France, he would content himself with the Milanese marriage alliance instead of accepting the marriage proposed to him by the Emperor and Maximilian, and which is the last echo of the joint Italian venture of the two kings, Louis de Bretaylle went with St Pierre to France, not simply to receive Louis' reply about the Milanese marriage, but to press again Edward's offer of mediation and his demand in regard to the dowry.[1] After the battle of Guinegate, Edward may have thought that Louis would be only too glad to avail himself of his offer of mediation, but if such was his hope, it proved to be a false one. On the other hand, Louis did show a little inclination to relent in regard to the payment of the dowry; for though he made Louis de Bretaylle no promises, about 26 November 1479, he dispatched another embassy to England to suggest a compromise.

Commynes says that Louis was careful to choose different men for every embassy he sent to England, so that if Edward complained because some

---

1. *Lettres et négociations de Commynes*, III, 69; *Lettres de Louis XI*, VIII, 356.

promise made by one set of ambassadors had not been kept, the next set could plead ignorance of the whole matter.[1] And the facts seem to bear out Commynes' statement, as among the many French ambassadors—the Archbishop of Vienne, the Bishop of Elne, Olivier Guérin, Olivier le Roux, Yves de la Tillaye, the Seigneur de St Pierre, May de Houllefort, Antoine de Mortillon, and others—who had come to England since the death of Charles the Bold, there was scarcely one who had come more than once. The ambassadors who now arrived were no exception to the rule, for they were Guyot du Chesnay, Louis' *maître d'hôtel*, and Louis Garnier, master of requests and mayor of Poitiers, and, so far as we know, neither of them had ever before visited the English court. Their stay in England was not a long one, however; for while they had been instructed to offer Edward ten thousand, or, if necessary, fifteen, twenty, or even twenty-five thousand crowns a year towards the maintenance of Princess Elizabeth until her marriage with the Dauphin could be solemnized, at the very first hint of what they intended to propose Edward seems to have expressed himself so forcibly that they were given no chance even to raise their first bid.[2] Silenced, they turned about and went home, and the Bishop of Elne appears to have gathered up his effects and gone with them.[3]

Edward's patience with Louis was now rapidly breaking down. Nearly a year had elapsed since the Bishop of Elne signed the agreements with him about the truce and the pension, and yet Louis had not ratified them. It was more than a year, too, since he had first informed Louis that the Dauphin's future wife was now entitled to receive the sixty thousand pounds a year which had been promised to her, and yet he had no assurance that the money was going to be paid. Rather he had reason to think that Louis would never pay the dowry unless he compelled him to do so. Consequently, soon after Guyot du Chesnay and Louis Garnier had slunk away and the Bishop of Elne too had disappeared from the scene, Edward made up his mind to take

---

1. Commynes, II, 7.
2. Régistre de Pierre Doriolle, MS. français 30,387, ff. 210-211. See also Legrand coll., MS. français 6986, ff. 523-525, and compare Legeay, II, 362. As late as July 1480, Louis was offering Elizabeth only fifteen thousand crowns a year. See later.
3. The bishop afterwards stated that the second time he was sent to England he spent twenty-six months there. Therefore, if he reached England in October 1476, as his story indicates, he must have gone home in December 1479.

the aggressive, and he sent Louis de Bretaylle to France once more, together with the chancellor of the Prince of Wales[1] and Sir James Radcliff, a man who had become something of a royal favourite.[2]

The three English ambassadors reached Touraine in the early part of January, and while some of the wisest gossips in Louis' entourage were sure they had come to talk about the marriage alliance, others, also likely to be well informed, thought they had instructions to warn Louis that he must not make war on the Duke of Brittany, as he had been threatening to do, because the duke was a friend of the king of England. "We have not heard what reply the king here will make to this," wrote Cagnola and Visconti on 16 January, adding a word about how important, on account of the geographical location of Brittany, the Duke of Brittany's friendship would be to the king of England should he decide to invade France again. But if Edward told Louis that he must not harm his friend Francis, the marriage and the payment of the dowry were certainly the first objects of his solicitude, and a fortnight later the two Milanese ambassadors wrote that the Englishmen were still pressing "in and out of season for the conclusion of the marriage." At the same time Cagnola reported, in a separate letter, that all that the king of France was trying to do was to keep the king of England "in a good temper by fair words while he delays the business until he has accomplished his own plans by exterminating this Duke Maximilian and the Flemings." Yet the writer was wise enough to doubt "whether the king of England does not quite well see through this plan," and was of the opinion that it was because he saw through it that Edward had sent his ambassadors to press the question of the marriage.[3]

It was almost the middle of February before the English ambassadors left Touraine, and even then they had received no definite answer to their questions. However, Louis sent some more ambassadors to England in their company, and also a tender letter to King Edward. After telling Edward that he loved and trusted him more than any other prince in the world, Louis begged him to believe that he had the extension of the truce of one hundred

---

1. Probably Thomas Millyng, Bishop of Hereford, who six years before, when he was Abbot of Westminster, had been the Prince's chancellor. *Cal. Patent Rolls*, II, 366.
2. In November 1479, Paston speaks of Radcliff as one of those who "wait most upon the king and lie nightly in his chamber." *Paston Letters*, VI, 29.
3. *Cal. Milanese Papers*, I, 243-244.

years and the other matters about which they had been negotiating "as much at heart as anything in the world" and assured him, as he said he had already assured the chancellor of Monsieur the Prince of Wales, Messire James Radcliff, and Louis de Bretaylle, that there would be no failure on his part. Louis also expressed his wish to do anything for his cousin of England that was in his power, and ended by praying to the Blessed Son of God to have his cousin in His holy keeping.[1]

The chief of the French embassy which accompanied Edward's ambassadors home was the Bishop of Elne; but the bishop had with him as colleagues two more newcomers to England, namely, Louis' chamberlain, Jean, Baron de Castelnau, and Master Thibaud Baillet, master of requests. And of the two sets of instructions with which Louis had provided his ambassadors, the longer one was identical with the instructions prepared some months before for the use of the Abbé de la Grace, except that the articles reciting the reply made to Oliver King and those relating to the marriage of the Dauphin and Princess Elizabeth had been omitted,[2] while the briefer set was for the most part merely a summary of the longer one. In the briefer set, however, Louis had made a few important additions. In the first place, he had directed his ambassadors to persuade Edward, if possible, to permit the extension of the truce and the promise of the pension to be incorporated in one "letter";[3] but if they could not accomplish this (which would be equivalent to an admission by Edward that the payment of the pension should be dependent on the keeping of the truce), they were to say that they would be glad to report to the king of France any proposals the king of England wished to make to them, and that they did not doubt the king of France would do whatever he could in honour to please the king of England and to maintain the treaties between them. In the second place, through this embassy Louis delivered the final message, which has already been mentioned, about the proposed marriage between

---

1. *Lettres de Louis XI*, VII, 252-253. Notice that this letter, which was written on 10 February, has been misplaced in the edition of Louis' letters. Cf. *Ibid.*, VIII, 138-139.
2. Compare the already cited instructions in MS. français 4054, f. 244, with those which are printed (with occasional slight inaccuracies) from Régistre de Pierre Doriolle by Morice, III, 354-368. The articles relating to Burgundy are also printed in Plancher, IV, 393-395.
3. A copy of the proposed document may be found in Régistre de Pierre Doriolle, ff. 234 dorso—239. See also Legrand coll., MS. français 6987, ff. 47-50.

the Prince of Wales and the sister of the Duke of Milan. And in the third place, he prepared his ambassadors to meet the question of the payment of the dowry. Possibly the subject of the dowry would not be brought up by Edward's negotiators at all, and apparently the Frenchmen were not to refer to it if the Englishmen did not. But if the subject were mentioned, Louis' ambassadors were to declare once more that there was nothing in the world he desired so much as to see the marriage of his son and Princess Elizabeth become an accomplished fact and then to say, as the Abbé de la Grace would have said if he had gone to England, that they were charged to consult with King Edward about the time, place, and manner in which the king of France might convey his son's bride to his kingdom at his own expense. They were also empowered to promise that, when the day was agreed upon, the king of France would send a delegation of princes and other noble persons to perform the betrothal, to give all the required guarantees, and to bring the princess to France; and if the king of England objected to sending his daughter to France so soon, he was to be informed that the king of France would very gladly contribute towards her maintenance in England until time for her to be sent to France for her marriage. And this time Louis was prepared to offer twenty thousand crowns.[1]

In addition to the instructions given to all three of his ambassadors, Louis had supplied the Bishop of Elne with a few which were exclusively for his own use and which were concerned with Edward's offer to serve as a mediator between the rulers of France and Burgundy.[2] That offer was to be declined as before, but, as if he took it for granted that the king of England's opposition to the war against Burgundy arose from nothing except fear of injury to English merchants and to his sister Margaret, Louis had given the bishop two commissions. By the first of these commissions he authorized the bishop to say that if, by the grace of God, he succeeded in reducing to obedience the lands now held by the Duke of Austria and his wife, he would allow all subjects of the king of England, except those found to be making war against him, to retain any merchandise or other property they might own in those lands. By the second he empowered the bishop to promise that he would permit the Duchess Margaret to enjoy all her dower lands and

---

1. *Lettres de Louis XI*, VIII, 349-357 (from Régistre de Pierre Doriolle). These instructions, like Louis' letter to Edward, are dated Plessis-du-Parc, 10 February.
2. *Ibid.*, VIII, 194.

revenues in the conquered territories, provided she did not make war on him, his lands, or subjects, and also that he would assign to her, "en bons lieux et convenables," as much revenue as she might have lost as a result of the war.[1]

When Louis' ambassadors reached London, about the end of February, they were given lodgings at Master Sutton's place,"[2] but they found that King Edward was at Greenwich and that he was in no hurry to see them. Day after day passed and they were not summoned to an audience. Edward may have guessed that they had brought him an unsatisfactory message and decided on that account to let them wait awhile; but he had a still better reason for not extending a cordial hand of welcome to the envoys of the king of France. This reason was that he had suddenly found himself in danger of a quarrel with Scotland for which he strongly suspected he had his cousin of France to thank.

Edward's relations with James III had certainly remained amicable up to the end of November 1479. But recently the Scots had been committing serious breaches of the truce, and evidently someone had given Edward warning that, under the guise of a friendly attempt to effect a reconciliation between the Duke of Albany, who was now in France, and James III, Louis was trying to induce James to break off his alliance with England and send an army across the border.[3] Edward's suspicions increased when James, on being asked to make reparation for what his subjects had done, sent Ross Herald to England with a letter laying all the blame for the breach of the truce at the door of the English themselves; and to show James that he would put up with no dilly-dallying or subterfuges, Edward dispatched some guns and gunners to Norham Castle and made a sudden demand that the Prince of Scotland should be given into his custody as a guarantee that he would marry Princess Cecily. Thereupon James proposed to send some ambassadors to London to talk matters over, but Edward, without waiting for James's envoys, hurried off an embassy of his own to Edinburgh.

Edward put at the head of his embassy to Scotland Alexander Legh, who, had all been going well, would have been starting for Edinburgh about this

---

1. 'Régistre de Pierre Doriolle, ff. 239-240. Cf. Legrand coll., MS. français 6987, f. 62.
2. Nicolas, *Wardrobe Accounts of Edw. IV*, 121.
3. See a letter written by a Breton spy in June 1480. Commynes-Lenglet, IV, 7. Cf. Hume Brown, I, 273.

time with another payment towards Cecily's dowry; and his first charge to his envoys was to inquire whether the ambassadors James thought of sending to him would be prepared to hand over the Prince of Scotland and to make the reparation for the breaches of the truce for which he had asked. If they were told that the Scottish ambassadors were not going to be authorized to do these things, they were to announce without further ado that, in as much as, contrary to the truce and the marriage treaty, in consideration of which he had received large sums of English money, James had caused his subjects to murder the king of England's subjects "without cause or summonition, against all honour, law of arms, and good conscience," the king of England, upon the advice of his council and with the consent of his kingdom, had determined to make "rigorous and cruel war" against him. They were also to say, by way of further justification for this declaration of war, that Berwick, Coldingham, Roxburgh, and divers other places now occupied by the king of Scots belonged by right to the king of England, that the king of Scots had not done homage to the king of England as it was his duty to do and as his progenitors had done in times gone by, and finally, that the Earl of Douglas, who had been unjustly deprived of his inheritance by the king of Scots, had appealed to the king of England as sovereign lord of Scotland and that the king of England intended to "see him restored according to his right and good conscience." Yet at the same time Edward told his ambassadors that, if James would not make all these things right, he would content himself, in order to avoid "the effusion of Christian blood," with the surrender of Berwick and the deliverance of James's son into his hands. He wanted the Prince of Scotland to be handed over to the Earl of Northumberland "within England's ground" before the last day of May.[1]

As a party of ambassadors did not usually travel to Edinburgh and back very rapidly, and as it was also not to be expected that King James would be ready to give an immediate answer to Edward's sharp communication, the Bishop of Elne, the Baron de Castelnau, and Master Baillet were in danger of having to twirl their thumbs in the chilly air of London for some time

---

1. *Cal. Documents relating to Scot.*, IV, 412-414. Cf. *Ibid.*, xxxvi, where the editor says that these instructions, though placed under the year 1476, probably belong to the autumn of 1479. Certainly their date must be later than 23 November 1479, when Edward granted James the already mentioned safeconduct for his pilgrimage to Amiens, and earlier than 12 May 1480, when the first step preparatory to war was taken.

to come. But luckily for them Pierre Le Roy arrived in the English capital just after the middle of March, and his coming had a warming effect. On 20 March Louis' ambassadors had what seems to have been their first audience with the king and his council at Greenwich,[1] and the very next day Le Roy paid Edward thirty-five thousand crowns—twenty-five thousand crowns of pension money, due since Michaelmas, and the final ten thousand crowns of Margaret of Anjou's ransom. Later the bond Louis had given for the payment of Margaret's ransom was surrendered to the French ambassadors.[2]

Yet even after Pierre le Roy had emptied his money-bags into the king of England's capacious pocket, Louis' ambassadors found London a not very pleasant abiding-place. Absence had not softened the hearts of Edward's subjects towards "the Bishop of France," as they had dubbed the chief of the French ambassadors, and again the poor Bishop of Elne's knees shook under him when he heard of the stories that were being told in the country places around London. For one of these stories was that the king had clapped him into the Tower and was going to drown him, and another that he had already been decapitated and sent back to France![3] Nevertheless, Edward neither drowned nor beheaded the Bishop of Elne, well as the bishop may have deserved either of those fates. After receiving the French ambassadors at Greenwich, the king merely left them to their own devices again while he waited for further news from Scotland and dispatched the clerk of his council, William Lacy, to Louis to ask once more for permission to mediate between Louis and Maximilian.[4]

---

1. Household Accounts, 19-20 Edw. IV, Accounts, etc. (Exchequer K. R.), bundle 412, no. 10.
2. Rymer, XII, 112; Palgrave, *Cely Papers*, III, 24. Rymer prints Edward's receipts from French Roll 20 Edw. IV, m. 14, and on the same membrane of that roll will be found another receipt, also dated 21 March, for the ten thousand crowns of Margaret's ransom. In this case, however, the receipt is made out to "Dionysius de Biden," Louis' receiver general. Cf. an account of Denys Bidon, Legrand coll., MS. français 6982, ff. 235 dorso—237 dorso. On 6 June 1480, Edward gave a warrant for the payment of the expenses of "Piers le Roy, argenter of Roane, late coming toward us from our Cousin of France and of late departing from us toward the same parties, that is to wit in the month of May last past." Exchequer T. R., Council and Privy Seal, file 92, m. 34.
3. Trial of the Bishop of Elne, interrogatory of 2 August.
4. *Lettres de Louis XI*, VIII, 187-188, 193-194. Lacy afterwards received £13 9s 7d for his expenses while in France. Warrants for Issues, 20 Edw. IV, 17 June. He had been sent to Maximilian in 1478, and after the present journey to France he seems to have gone to Denmark. Fitzherbert's account, Warrants for Issues, 18 Edw. IV; Rymer, XII, 121.

When at last there was further news from Scotland, it was by no means agreeable. In fact, it was so disquieting that on 12 May the Duke of Gloucester was appointed the king's lieutenant in the north and authorized to call out the men of the marches and the adjoining counties. Steps were also taken to get a fleet in readiness and to send to Norham the artillery usually kept at Nottingham Castle, and ultimately commissions of array were dispatched to Yorkshire, Northumberland, Westmoreland, and Cumberland. Of special significance was it, too, that Lord Hastings was ordered to go and look after Calais. For it was the French, not the Scots, who were feared at Calais.[1] But though Edward's suspicion that it was Louis who was turning the wheels in Scotland was confirmed by all he heard and he felt he must prepare for every emergency, he did not think of handling Louis in the rough way in which he had handled James III. No ultimatum was sent to France, but on the day on which Gloucester was made his brother's lieutenant, Howard and Langton were commissioned to go home with Louis' ambassadors to back up Lacy's efforts to win Louis to the idea of mediation between him and Maximilian, and also to demand once again the ratification of the Bishop of Elne's agreements and the immediate beginning of the payment of Princess Elizabeth's dowry.[2]

Two days later the French ambassadors were again received by the king at Greenwich,[3] and Edward, who was not above enjoying a little fun of his own at the Bishop of Elne's expense, drew the timorous bishop aside and asked him if it were true, as Rougecroix had reported on returning recently from France, that when he reached home King Louis would cut off his head. The bishop replied with dignity that those who told such a tale were "mauvaises gens" who wanted to destroy the alliance between the kings of France and England, and that he was sure the king of France, far from beheading him, would reward him for what he had done. And when Edward urged him not to take any risks and promised to provide for him if he would stay in England, he declared again that he had no fear and added tartly that, when he wanted

---

1. Rymer, XII, 115; *Cal. Patent Rolls*, III, 205. 213-214; Tellers' Roll, Easter 20 Edw. IV, no. 57.
2. Rymer, XII, 113. The king gave Howard nine yards of black velvet, perhaps to help to equip him for his journey to France. Nicolas, *Wardrobe Accounts of Edw. IV*, 156.
3. Household Accounts, 19-20 Edw. IV, *ut sup.*

to fly from France, he would fly to some place other than England. The king took this retort good-naturedly, and he afterwards sent the comptroller of his household to the bishop to offer him two thousand crowns for his expenses; but the bishop dared not take the money, as Louis had already found fault with him for accepting, at the end of his former sojourn in England, a couple of basins and a little cup of silver gilt which, according to report—though the bishop declared it was not true—contained two thousand nobles. The only remembrance the bishop could be prevailed upon to accept this time was a hackney. And it was well for him that he refused to take more, as the day came when he was very glad to be able to say that the only gifts he had ever received from the king of England were the two basins and the little cup of silver gilt, three hobbies, two of which he afterwards presented to the king of France, and this hackney. One of the members of the bishop's suite, Pierre de Vaux, showed less self-restraint, for he accepted from the king of England a licence to import and export, without paying customs or subsidy, as much merchandise, "not staple ware, unless than it be pewter made in vessel for his household," as would amount to the sum of six hundred pounds sterling.[1] But Vaux could offer a good excuse for himself, as he had been robbed in England of a handsome chain, diamonds, and other articles of value, and when Edward had sent Lord Howard to offer him a thousand crowns as compensation for his losses, the Bishop of Elne had advised him not to take the money for fear the king of France would be displeased.[2]

Edward sent Louis' three ambassadors home in the *Grace Dieu* and provided a tun of wine to help them forget the woes of seasickness, while Howard and Langton, with their suites, seem to have made the crossing from Dover to Calais in other ships supplied by one John Barker.[3] Altogether it was quite a large party that arrived at Calais and travelled thence to Boulogne and

---

1. Writs of Privy Seal, file 872, no. 5140, 13 May 1480. Cf. *Lettres de rois, reines, etc., des cours de France et d'Angleterre*, II, 497.
2. Trial of the Bishop of Elne, interrogatory of 7 August. No doubt this Pierre de Vaux is identical with "Pierre de Vraulx of Montpelier in Gascoignyne" from whom £338 15s 6d worth of velvets, satins, damasks, and other silks were bought in this year for Edward's wardrobe. Nicolas, *Wardrobe Accounts of Edw. IV*, 115.
3. Warrants for Issues, 20 Edw. IV, 17 July—an account rendered by John Fitzherbert and other tellers of the Receipt and sent back by the king to the Exchequer; Tellers' Roll, Easter 20 Edw. IV, no. 57; Tellers' account, Exchequer T. R., Council and Privy Seal, file 92, m. 14.

finally to Paris; for Richard Martyn and John Grauntford, as well as Howard and Langton, were making a journey to France,[1] and, in addition to all the attendants and servants of the ambassadors, both French and English, room had to be found for some valuable animals, including not only the Bishop of Elne's new hackney, but two dogs which Grauntford was taking to Louis as a gift from the king of England[2] and some other horses and dogs which were also going to Louis as a gift from Lord Hastings. "You may be sure, Sire," Hastings had written on 17 May, after acknowledging the receipt of some letters from Louis which the Bishop of Elne had brought him, "that I shall ever be ready to render you all the service I can, as I have sent you word by Monsieur d'Elne, Monsieur Castelnau, and Master Thibaud le Baillet, and also by Monsieur de Howard, who is your very good servant. And by them you will be told about everything. Sire, I have been so bold, on the advice of Monsieur d'Elne, as to send you by the bearer of these some greyhounds, and also a hobby and a hackney, which go quite gently; and if there is anything else you wish to ask of me, you will ever find me ready to serve you."[3]

Louis came to Paris to meet Edward's ambassadors and feasted them there most royally on 3 June. But so anxious was he that no one should find out what they had come to say to him that, to make quite sure there were no listeners at the keyhole, he sent nearly every living person out of the palace before he closeted himself with them.[4] So all that Visconti could write home was that some English ambassadors had arrived and that the king of France had received them with great honour and was defraying their expenses. It was conjectured, however, that the Englishmen had come "about this business of the Flemings, because the king of England wants to be the arbiter of those disputes," and that "the king here does not desire that at all."[5] All of which was true. For though we are not so fortunate as to have any record of

---

1. Tellers' Roll, *ut sup.*
2. Douet-d'Arcq, *Comptes de l'hôtel des rois de France aux XIVe et XVe siecles* (Paris, 1865), 378. The name of the man who brought the dogs to Louis is given as Craffort, but no doubt the person meant was Grauntford, who was paid £20 for making another journey to France about this time. Tellers' Roll, *ut sup.*
3. Legrand coll., MS. français 6987, f. 140; Barante, *Histoire des Ducs de Bourgogne* (Paris, 1837-1838), XI, 340.
4. Letter of the Breton spy, Commynes-Lenglet, IV, 6; *Chron. Scandaleuse*, II, 95.
5. *Cal. Milanese Papers*, I, 244.

what passed between Louis and Howard and Langton at this time, there is in existence a draft of a letter which Louis wrote, or planned to write, to Edward after Lacy's arrival in France and in which he set forth at length his objections to Edward's wish to mediate between him and Maximilian. Though there was no prince under the heavens, Louis declared in this letter, to whom he would so willingly trust his affairs as to the king of England, he was sure that, when it came to the question of his differences with the Duke of Austria, the king of England would not want to take the responsibility of arbitration if he understood the whole situation. For if you decided in my favour, Louis told Edward in effect, your whole people would be angry, a result I should regret with all my heart, whereas if you set out to please your people, you would have to deprive me of my rights, a result I am sure you would deplore. He also explained once more his right to the lands claimed by the Duke of Austria and his wife and remarked that if the Duke of Austria desired peace, he should come forward with a reasonable offer. He would be very glad, he declared, to listen to such an offer, and he thought it astonishing that the duke had not made an offer before seeking to employ the kind services of the king of England. Finally, he called upon God to be his witness that he had always desired peace with all his heart and that it was not he, but the Duke of Austria and his wife, who had commenced the war; and he argued that it was a very strange thing that, at this time when the Catholic Faith was in danger from the Turks, the father of the Duke of Austria, who, as he enjoyed the imperial dignity, ought to be especially solicitous for the defence of the Faith, should have incited his son to make war on the Most Christian house of France. If the Emperor desires peace among the princes of Europe, he exclaimed, let him see that his own son repairs the wrongs he has done me, leaving me to enjoy in peace the lands which belong to me and rendering the obedience he owes to me and to the crown of France.[1]

But while Howard and Langton undoubtedly proposed to Louis once more that he should allow their king to adjust his quarrels with Maximilian, they spoke also of the Bishop of Elne's agreements and of the dowry, and when it came to those matters, Louis had to draw even more heavily on his ingenuity to find an answer. He was quite aware, too, that he had need to tread softly. For if his spies had not sent him word that

---

1. *Lettres de Louis XI*, VIII, 193-199.

Jacques de la Villéon had gone to England and that negotiations were on foot for a marriage between the Prince of Wales and the Duke of Brittany's daughter, Anne, who, as Francis had no sons, would probably inherit his duchy, at least he had heard something which made him fear that Edward and Francis had formed some kind of a league and that Edward had thoughts of attempting another invasion of France, this time by way of Poitou and Anjou. So, in order to relieve his father's difficulties and furnish a little time to find out what the king of England was about, the Dauphin was seized with an illness so dangerous that all talk of his marriage had to be postponed; and in the meantime the Seigneur de St Pierre was sent to England again with instructions to travel by way of Calais and to have one or two of his men fall ill there in order that they might stay behind and report if any messengers crossed from England to Flanders or from Flanders to England. Then, after distributing a thousand marks' worth of silver vessels among the English ambassadors, Louis took himself away from Paris, leaving Lord Howard to wander up and down the streets of that attractive city and wait for St Pierre's return.[1]

St Pierre's sick man or men at Calais must have had some interesting news to report in a very short time, as on 11 June the king of England received at Greenwich two ambassadors from Mary and Maximilian, Jean Gros, treasurer of the Order of the Golden Fleece, and Jean de Lannoy, Abbot of St Bertin, who was soon to become chancellor of the same Order. Edward divided between these two visitors a dozen bowls and two standing cups of silver gilt, while to Gros he gave also two pots of silver, parcel gilt, and, what was of much greater consequence, a licence to export from England every year as long as he lived one hundred oxen and five hundred sheep without paying customs or subsidy.[2] But the king's gifts were hardly excessive, in view of the fact that the recipients of them represented the magnificent Order of the Golden Fleece, to which he belonged, and that they had brought him the glad tidings that his sister Margaret proposed to pay him a visit. Vexed and troubled by the snail-like progress which Maximilian's negotiations with

---

1. Commynes-Lenglet, IV, 6-9.
2. Household Accounts, *ut sup.*; Warrants for Issues, 20 Edw. IV, 14 June; Tellers' Roll, Mich. 20 Edw. IV; Writs of Privy Seal, file 873, no. 5195; *Cal. Patent Rolls*, III, 212; Reiffenberg, *Hist. de l'Ordre de la Toison d'Or*, 106.

her brother were making, Margaret had conceived the idea that she could do something to hasten them, and when she offered to go to England and bring her personal influence to bear on Edward, Maximilian gladly gave his consent—the more gladly, perhaps, if any hint had reached him of a story picked up by a Breton spy in France at this moment. This story was that the Pope's nephew, Giulio della Rovere, Cardinal of St Peter *ad Vincula*, who was about to visit the court of France in the interest of the struggle against the Turks, intended to go on to Flanders and make the Duchess Margaret a secret offer from Louis of a splendid marriage and other great benefits if she would do something the spy did not learn what—in return.[1]

When Edward heard that Margaret wished to visit her old home, he sent Sir Thomas Montgomery and William Slefeld post haste to Flanders, apparently for the double purpose of assuring his sister that he would be glad to see her and of conveying to Mary and Maximilian some further messages about the betrothal of their son to his daughter Anne and the terms of the alliance which was to accompany the betrothal.[2] At the same time he hurried to fit up "the Coldharbour," a house in Thames Street, London, which had once belonged to the Earl of Salisbury, for Margaret's occupancy and to send an escort, consisting of Sir Edward Woodville, Sir James Radcliff, and some other members of his household, all resplendent in fine new jackets of purple and blue velvet, to Calais to bring the duchess across the sea in one of his own ships, the *Falcon*, which was under the command of that trusty captain, William Fetherston, and was manned by one hundred and forty mariners and five hundred armed soldiers.[3] Margaret left Bruges on 24 June[4] accompanied by the Seigneur d'Irlain, the gentleman who had gone to England two years before to inquire why Edward had ceased to wear the collar of the Golden Fleece, and Thomas de Plaine, who had been a member of the embassy sent to England by Mary and Maximilian early in 1478 and there so ignominiously routed by the Bishop of Elne. Soon after she crossed

---

1. Commynes-Lenglet, *ut sup.*
2. Slefeld received £20 for this embassy to Burgundy. Tellers' Roll, Easter 20 Edw. IV.
3. Nicolas, *Wardrobe Accounts of Edw. IV*, 126, 141-145, 163-165, 241; Warrants for Issues, 21 Edw. IV, 12 Jan.—an account of John Barker, collector of the port of Sandwich; Tellers' accounts in Warrants for Issues, 20 Edw. IV, 17 July, and Exchequer T. R., Council and Privy Seal, file 92, m. 24; Tellers' Roll, Easter 20 Edw. IV.
4. Gilliodts-van-Severen, VI, 202.

from Calais to Dover and thence proceeded to Gravesend, where she was met and welcomed by Sir John Weston, Prior of St John's, and others whom Edward had sent to conduct her to Greenwich—in the royal barge, no doubt, as the master and twenty-four bargemen had been fitted out, against her coming, with new jackets of blue and murrey garnished with roses.[1]

Cordial as was the reception her brother accorded her, the task which Margaret had taken upon herself turned out to be no light one. Maximilian was in pressing need of more soldiers, and the first thing the duchess was asked to do was to solicit for him a loan of the services of two thousand English archers, the money for whose wages, Edward was to be told, lay ready and waiting. But in addition to that she was to proceed with the negotiations for a treaty of alliance and, if possible, secure a lowering of Edward's demands. These were truly staggering, as he had been arguing that since, by allying himself with Burgundy, he would lose the money the king of France was paying him, and also the marriage of his eldest daughter with the Dauphin, Maximilian ought to be willing to replace the lost pension and to forego altogether the dowry of two hundred thousand crowns which he had been hoping to get with Anne. What Maximilian maintained on his side was that for Edward to give his daughter no dowry whatever would be a strange and unreasonable proceeding, and, realizing that he could not hope to avoid paying Edward a pension of some amount, he suggested that for the first two years the king should excuse him from the payment of whatever pension was agreed on and that the whole sum thus remitted should be regarded as Anne's dot. At the same time the duke wanted it to be fully understood that, if it should happen that the marriage of Princess Elizabeth and the Dauphin took place in spite of all, Edward must provide Anne with a dowry, if not of two hundred thousand crowns, at least of some goodly sum.

As for the amount of the pension or "recompense" Edward expected Maximilian to promise him, Montgomery and Slefeld had said that the king thought he ought to have fifty thousand crowns a year. But had he not declared on several occasions, Margaret was to remind him, that he would be content with less from Maximilian than he was receiving from Louis?

---

1. *Cely Papers*, 36; Nicolas, *Wardrobe Accounts*, 166; Household Accounts, *ut sup.*

And surely that was no more than right, seeing that he would be much
surer of his money when it came from Maximilian than when it came from
Louis, as it was evident that the French king would continue to make the
payments he was now making only so long as his war with Maximilian
lasted. Edward should remember, too, that he would gain in another
way by exchanging his alliance with Louis for one with Maximilian; for
by doing so he would set himself free to pursue his claim to the crown
of France, a claim which, with Maximilian's aid, he could easily enforce.
All things considered, therefore, Maximilian thought Edward might well
be satisfied if he paid him forty thousand crowns a year. That much the
duke was prepared to pay, and as security he and his wife, and, if need
be, the estates of their dominions also, would give a bond confirmed by
the Pope. But again the duke wanted it to be clearly understood that he
gave this promise only because Edward said that, by allying himself with
him, he would lose what the king of France was paying him, and that if it
should turn out that this loss did not occur, Edward was not to look for
any pension whatever from him, as Edward had always told him he would
not expect a pension from him unless he lost his pension from the king
of France. And finally, Maximilian expressed the hope that in any case
Edward would excuse him, inasmuch as his expenses were so heavy, from
paying the pension the first year.

Referring to the treaty of alliance which was to accompany the marriage
treaty, Maximilian suggested that it would be suitable to renew the treaty
signed at the time the marriage between the late Duke Charles and King
Edward's sister was in contemplation. But he had told his ambassadors that,
if Edward was not pleased with this and still preferred to try to negotiate a
peace or truce between him and Louis, then Edward ought to demand that
Louis should restore to Maximilian all that belonged to him and threaten,
if this was not done, to help him recover what had been taken from him.
Should it prove that a truce for five or six years was the most that could be
arranged with Louis and restitution of all the territories he had seized was
unobtainable, Edward ought to require Louis to restore at least the counties
of Artois and Burgundy. On the other hand, if the attempt at mediation
failed completely, or if a peace or truce was signed and Louis afterwards
violated it, then, Maximilian thought, Edward ought to be willing to assist
him against Louis with five thousand men at the least and to advance a

loan for the wages of these soldiers for three or four months. The duke was particularly anxious to have this loan, for he thought it would make a great impression both on his subjects and on his enemies, who would suppose it to be a gift and therefore would be unable to say, as they would if he himself paid the English soldiers, that his alliance with the king of England would last only as long as his money held out.

There were three other matters about which Maximilian had charged Margaret to speak to Edward. First, should Edward express a wish to invade France again, he wanted to hear what bargain the king had to offer him. Second, if a treaty should be arranged between him and Louis by Edward's instrumentality, he wanted the Count of St Pol to be included in it and provision made for the count's recovery of all the lands which had once belonged to his father. Third, he wanted the English merchants who used to attend the fair at Bergen-op-Zoom but who of late had objected to coming to it unless he made certain concessions necessarily meaning a diminution of his tolls from the fair, to renounce their demands.[1]

On 16 July there was a meeting of Edward's council at Greenwich, probably to consider Maximilian's proposals, and on the 20th the king gave a banquet in honour of his mother and his sister.[2] But as yet the only news Margaret was able to send home was that Sir Thomas Montgomery had come to her and her fellow ambassadors with a request that they would obtain fuller powers and instructions to treat regarding a possible descent by the king of England on France. Immediately upon receipt of this message, which suggested so many possibilities, Maximilian dispatched Michel de Berghes to England with the desired instructions, and, though he reproached his ambassadors for not having secured, the minute an invasion of France was mentioned, a statement of Edward's intentions and of what he would expect from him, he hastened to offer the king "la faveur de ses pays" and to promise all the assistance it was in his power to give. In fact, the duke wanted a bargain made forthwith, though he did not forget to warn Edward that he must not expect from him both a pension and assistance to conquer France, and also that the invasion of France would

---

1. Commynes-Lenglet, III, 577-583.
2. Household Accounts, *ut sup*. On 23 July Edward sent Margaret "one pipe of our wine of the price of 36s 8d." Exchequer Accounts, Butlerage, bundle 82, no. 18.

be too late to do him much good unless it were made in the summer of the coming year.

Yet, pleased as he was at the prospect of another English invasion of France, what Maximilian was most anxious to know just now was whether Edward was going to let him have the troops he needed so badly. It was his hope that Michel de Berghes would be able to bring fifteen hundred archers home with him, and he charged his envoy to find out, as he passed through Bruges, when the wage money could be sent to Calais, so that on reaching England he could say that a month's pay would be waiting at Calais. He told him further to procure two or three hundred crowns in cash to pay for the passage of the archers, if he found it necessary to do that in order to satisfy them.[1]

Michel de Berghes arrived in London before the end of July. But so did Lord Howard and Pierre le Roy. For as soon as he learned that the Duchess Margaret was on her way to England, Louis knew he must bestir himself, and he immediately started Le Roy off for London with Edward's pension. He also indited another honeyed letter to Edward, announcing his intention to send another embassy to him, and ordered the Count de Castres to try to strike a bargain with Howard and Langton by offering again to pay Edward's daughter fifteen thousand crowns a year until her marriage with the Dauphin.[2] On 27 July Margaret wrote to Maximilian that Lord Howard had just returned from France with her brother's pension for Easter term last past,[3] and that Edward himself had come to her and told her that, according to Howard, Louis was prepared to agree to a hundred years' extension of his truce with England, to promise the payment of the pension of fifty thousand crowns during all that time, to give all the guarantees Edward desired for the marriage of the Dauphin and Madame Elizabeth, and to do even greater things, all on one condition, which was that Edward would consent to leave the Dukes of Burgundy and Brittany out of the truce. Howard had also said

---

1. Commyttes-Lenglet, III, 584-587.

2. *Lettres de Louis XI*, VIII, 229-231.

3. It was not Howard but Pierre le Roy who brought the pension, and it was on the very day on which Margaret wrote her letter that Edward gave Le Roy his receipt. Rymer, XII, 123. The king also gave the "Argenter of France" twelve yards of scarlet, and John Shylton, groom of the chamber, was paid 100*s* for the shipping expenses of the "magister monete de Rouen," going home to France. Nicolas, *Wardrobe Accounts of Edw. IV*, 160; Tellers' Roll, Easter 20 Edw. IV.

that Louis would spend half of the yearly revenues of his kingdom on gifts rather than fail to accomplish his purpose and that, in case the embassy he was about to send to England did not secure what he wanted, he would do his utmost to obtain a treaty with Maximilian by which he could separate the duke from England and Brittany. And yet, in spite of all this, Margaret was able to tell Maximilian that her brother seemed to be more and more inclined to enter into an alliance with him against the king of France, and that when Howard stated that Louis was getting an army ready with which to lay siege to St Omer or Aire, Edward had declared that, if Louis did such a thing as that, he would go and raise the siege himself and had told her to send word to that effect to Maximilian and the towns concerned. What was better still, the two thousand English archers Maximilian wanted were being made ready, Margaret said, and Edward was willing to advance ten thousand crowns for their wages on receipt of an "obligation de nous tous ensemble" that the money would be repaid before Christmas.[1]

Louis' large talk and his twenty-five thousand crowns notwithstanding, Margaret was indeed making headway; for on 1 August Edward, as well as Mary and Maximilian, confirmed the entire treaty of perpetual friendship which Edward and Charles had signed on 25 July 1474, and two articles of which had already been renewed in December 1478. On the same day Edward also empowered Gloucester, Montgomery, and others to make an agreement with Margaret and Maximilian's other ambassadors, to whom had now been added Pierre Puissant, one of Maximilian's secretaries, for the marriage of Philip and Anne; and two days later he promised to supply Mary and Maximilian with, not two, but six thousand archers to be employed in their war with the king of France.[2] On one point, however, the king was inflexible. Maximilian must pay him the same pension that Louis was now paying him. With nothing less than that would he be satisfied. And Maximilian, when he heard how many archers Edward had promised him, yielded. The duke succeeded in giving to the pledge made by Mary and himself on 5 August the form he wished, as it read that if Edward, *in consequence* of the assistance he granted them, lost the fifty thousand crowns a year which the king of France was now paying to him and found

1. Commynes-Lenglet, III, 576-577.
2. Rymer, XII, 123-127; Signed Bills, file 1518, no. 5170.

himself at war with that king, they would make good his loss. On the other hand, Mary and Maximilian had to promise that they would pay Edward the first twenty-five thousand crowns of his pension, in addition to any arrears Louis might have failed to pay, within six months after Louis' payments stopped, and also that Edward should receive within two years bonds given by the three estates of Flanders, Brabant, Holland, and Zealand, as well as bonds given by Mary and Maximilian and confirmed by the Pope.

On the same day on which Mary and Maximilian agreed to pay Edward fifty thousand crowns a year, the treaty concerning the marriage of Philip and Anne was sealed. It stipulated that Edward should give his daughter a dowry of one hundred thousand crowns—one half of the amount to be paid within a month, the other half within two years after the marriage—and that Mary and Maximilian should pay her, from the time she was twelve years old, six thousand crowns a year, assign to her, when the marriage was celebrated, lands, rents, etc., worth two thousand Flemish pounds a year, and pay all the expenses of her journey from England. Yet Edward had not made as much of a concession in the matter of the dowry as would appear at first glance, as a few days after the marriage treaty was sealed two supplementary treaties were signed which modified the bargain substantially. One of these treaties provided that if Anne consented to marry Philip, when both of them reached the marriageable age, and did not change her mind later, she was to receive from Mary and Maximilian lands, rents, etc., of the yearly value of eight thousand pounds Artoises, whereas if she refused to marry Philip, Edward must pay the disappointed bridegroom forty thousand pounds Artoises within two years. By the other treaty Edward released Mary and Maximilian from the payment of his pension for the first year, while Mary and Maximilian made a much larger sacrifice, as they released Edward altogether from the payment of Anne's dowry.[1]

Mary and Maximilian had had to give up much, and their only immediate reward was fifteen hundred archers, instead of the two thousand Margaret had said were coming, and thirty men-at-arms. Margaret signed a contract with the captains, Sir John Middleton, Sir Thomas Everingham, and Sir

1. Rymer, XII, 127-135.

John Dichefeld, on 8 August, and Middleton's and Dichefeld's men were to be ready at Dover, and Everingham's at Hull, by the 28th.[1] But Edward also gave, on 14 August, a very important secret promise, which was that if Louis continued to decline his offer of mediation and refused to make a truce with Maximilian before Easter, or if Louis consented to mediation and afterwards violated the peace arranged, he would declare openly for Maximilian.[2]

When Michel de Berghes returned to Flanders, he carried a letter from Margaret saying that the king of England would soon send an embassy to France on Maximilian's behalf. And, indeed, Langton and the Prior of St John's, who was substituted for Howard this time because the question of relief for the island of Rhodes, the headquarters of the knights of St John, now undergoing attack by the Turks, was one of the matters to be discussed with Louis, were very soon on their way to France.[3] As soon as they reached the French court, however, and before they had a chance to speak to Louis about Rhodes, about the marriage of the Dauphin and Princess Elizabeth, the performance of which they had been told to demand, or about a truce between France and Burgundy, the English ambassadors learned to their amazement that Louis had succeeded in making good his threat to secure a separate treaty with Maximilian. In Margaret's absence, and without any warning to her, Maximilian had entered into negotiations with Louis which terminated, on 21 August, in a seven months' truce and an agreement that plenipotentiaries, or even Louis and Maximilian themselves, should meet on 15 October to treat for a lasting peace. Maximilian had asked to have the king of England and the Duke of Brittany made conservators of the truce, but all that he had been granted was the right to name the king and the duke among his allies.[4]

That a truce between Louis and Maximilian had been signed was not the only disturbing discovery Langton and Weston made on reaching France.

---

1. Commynes-Lenglet, III, 587-589. Dichefeld was captain and governor of Guernsey. *Cal. Patent Rolls*, III, 74. Everingham had served in France during the Earl of Shrewsbury's last disastrous campaign. Basin, I, 265.
2. Rymer, XII, 133.
3. Margaret's letter of 14 September, Commynes-Lenglet, III, 603-608; Rymer, XII, 135; *Cely Papers*, 37-38; Warrants for Issues, 21 Edw. IV, 12 Jan.
4. Commynes-Lenglet, III, 589-595. Cf. the letter which Edward wrote to Maximilian on 21 February. *Ibid.*, 609. The truce between Louis and Maximilian was for three months only, but later, if the peace negotiations came to naught, it was to be extended to 27 March 1481.

They learned also that for more than a month past the Bishop of Elne had been under trial before the Parliament of Paris for malfeasance during his embassy to England—with what intent on Louis' part it was easy to divine. The bishop's trial lasted from 31 July to 2 September, and, farce though it was, the defendant was subjected to a searching examination and put up a very pitiful plea for himself. All the indignities he had suffered and all the death-traps he had so narrowly escaped in England the bishop described in full detail; and over and over again he asserted that all that he had done while he was there he had been compelled to do to save his life and to prevent what he had been sent to England to prevent, namely, an alliance between the king of England and the Duke of Austria. He admitted that he had exceeded his authority in allowing the king of England to include the Dukes of Burgundy and Brittany in the truce, but he declared that only by that means did he avoid a rupture of the negotiations at a critical moment. And when he was told that a rupture of the negotiations would have been preferable to what he had done, since, if the Dukes of Burgundy and Brittany were included in the truce, the king of France would have to lay down his arms and wait a hundred years before he could force those dukes to render the obedience and homage they owed to him, he replied that, in the hope that in the meantime the king of France would secure what he was fighting for, he had managed without making any use of his commission to keep the English idle for months. At length, however, he discovered that the Emperor and the Duke of Austria had offered the king of England an alliance, and when the king of England threatened to follow the advice of his council and accept the offer, he decided that the best thing for him to do was to yield to the demands of the English, especially as he knew that if he overstepped his authority, the king of France could easily disavow his acts.

An attempt was made to extract from the bishop a confession that he had been bribed by the king of England and had taken an oath to him as his sovereign lord, but he made a spirited denial. Never had he taken such an oath, he declared; and though he acknowledged that he had accepted from King Edward a few small presents, the much more valuable gifts which had been pressed upon him, including a very costly salt-cellar of gold set with precious stones, he had refused to take for fear of displeasing the king of France.

Nor would he admit that he had made any gifts of value to the king of England or his lords. Some boar-spears and axes which the king of France had sent to him he had distributed, and also about twenty-four swords and some leather brodekins for which he had sent to his bishopric; but that was all. When questioned about some silver vessels he had caused to be made and later had sold to the king of England and some of the English lords,[1] he averred not only that the sale was an entirely innocent affair, but that he had lost money by it, since for the silver which cost him eleven francs and a quarter in France he received only ten francs and a half when he made it into plate and sold it in England. In spite of this statement he was required to give a full description of the vessels he had thus sold, and the instant he said there were roses among the decorations the court pricked up its ears and reminded him sharply that the rose was the device of the king of England. Fortunately, however, he was able to say that the rose appeared but once, in the customary way on the cover of a cup, and with that the court allowed itself to be satisfied. For the king of France did not really distrust the ambassador he had kept in England so long, and when the bishop had been thoroughly examined about all his acts, great and small, no judgment was pronounced against him. He neither lost his bishopric nor, as King Edward had mischievously suggested that he might, his head.[2]

It is not likely that the news that the Bishop of Elne was being called to account for what he had done in England caused much surprise at the English court, as it was already plain that Louis did not intend to accept the bishop's agreements if he could find any escape. On the other hand, the news of Maximilian's treaty with Louis was a great and very unpleasant surprise not only to Edward but to his sister, who, in the belief that her work in England was done, was on the point of starting for home when she received a copy of the truce sent for her information by Maximilian himself. Though the duke had acted without consulting her, Margaret had to call up her self-control and explain and apologize for him as best she could, since otherwise Edward would probably renounce all the treaties she had worked so hard to get him to sign and recall the archers, whose departure

---

1. Edward bought from the bishop two pots of silver partly gilt, twelve cups or bowls, and two other pieces of plate, and for all these the bishop received £114 13s 1d ob. Issue Roll, Mich. 18 Edw. IV, 12 Oct.
2. Trial of the Bishop of Elne. Cf. Legeay, II, 397-398.

had been delayed somewhat but who were now about to take ship. To make the situation still harder for the duchess, in the possession of some Scots who had just been arrested in England had been found some letters of very friendly tone which Maximilian and the city of Bruges were sending to the king of Scotland in reply to an inquiry from James about the kind of treatment Scottish merchants residing in Flanders were likely to receive now that Scotland was at war with England. As the Duke of Gloucester was at this very time leading a band of Yorkshiremen across the border to take revenge for the burning of Bamburgh by the Earl of Angus during a raid,[1] and one of Margaret's colleagues, Thomas de Plaine, had just gone home to tell Maximilian how Edward wished him to act with reference to the Scots, nothing more unfortunate could have happened at this critical moment than the discovery of these letters.

Poor Margaret was almost at her wits' end. Maximilian had written to her to tell Edward that, as soon as Michel de Berghes brought him word that the king of England was going to send an embassy to France on his behalf, he had sent orders to his negotiators at Douai not to agree to the proposed meeting of French and Burgundian ambassadors on 15 October, but that his orders had arrived too late. It was now his hope, therefore, that the king of England would either make other arrangements for peace negotiations between him and Louis or else consent to send representatives to the October meeting. This was a weak excuse for what had happened, and there was little hope that Edward would be satisfied with it; but Margaret did her best, and although she found Edward's councillors even harder to placate than Edward himself, in the end she won more than she had reason to expect. For Edward actually gave his approval to the October meeting and promised to send Langton orders to proceed according to the instructions which had been given to him before he left England. That is, Langton was to demand that Louis should permit the king of England to arbitrate his differences with Maximilian, and, in case Louis replied that there was to be a peace conference on 15 October was to insist that King Edward should be allowed to arbitrate if the October meeting miscarried. Edward also promised Margaret that he would abide

---

1. Chronicle at end of Wyntoun, Pinkerton, *Hist. of Scotland*, I, 503; *Plumpton Correspondence*, 40; Davies, *York Records*, 106-107. Gloucester's expedition was soon over, as he was at Sheriff Hutton in October. *York Records*, 208.

by the treaties with Maximilian which he had already signed, provided the duke also signed them within the time appointed and took no further steps towards peace with the king of France without his advice and consent.[1]

Now at last Margaret felt that she could go home. Her brother had already presented her with ten hobbies and palfreys and filled her pockets with parchments which licensed her, regardless of the harm that might result to English breeders, to export from England thousands of oxen, sheep, and rams, as well as several hundred sacks of wool, all without paying any customs or subsidy; and as she was about to take her departure, he bestowed on her a gorgeous pillion of blue and purple cloth of gold with fringe of "Venice gold" and announced that he would go with her as far as the seaside.[2] On 13 September London, whose offering to her had been a hundred pounds in money,[3] saw the duchess set out on her homeward journey seated on her new pillion and with the king riding by her side, and as her hobby trotted along through the smiling Kentish countryside on the way to Dover, Margaret of York had good reason to feel triumphant. For not only had she induced her brother to sign a whole sheaf of treaties with Maximilian, but she was carrying home with her a pretty engagement ring which her niece Anne was sending to her stepdaughter's son in exchange for another ring, set with diamonds and pearls. This with a gold chain to be used when the little fiancée chose to hang the ring upon her neck, Margaret herself had purchased for Philip (with sixty pounds taken out of the loan of ten thousand crowns Edward was making to Maximilian) and presented to Anne in the presence of her father and mother.[4]

But alas! even now Margaret's worries were not over. At Rochester she was met by a messenger bringing another letter from Maximilian in which the duke told her that Louis had now proposed a personal meeting to arrange a peace and asked her to make this fact known to Edward and invite him to be present at the meeting. The duchess at once held anxious consultation with

---

1. See Margaret's letter of 14 September.
2. Nicolas, *Wardrobe Accounts of Edw. IV*, 225, 253. 163; Rymer, XII, 237; *Cal. Patent Rolls*, III, 236; French Roll 20 Edw. IV, m. 2, 5, 6. Signed Bills, file 1518, nos. 5164, 5165, 5189.
3. London Journal 8, f. 232. Edward used "right large language" because the Archbishop of Canterbury failed to make a gift to Margaret. *Christ Church Letters*, 19.
4. Margaret's letter of 14 September.

her colleagues, and they all agreed that it would be unsafe to tell Edward what Maximilian had written until after he had dispatched the letters he had promised to write to Maximilian and Langton. This decision Margaret communicated to Maximilian in a letter which she wrote to him from Rochester and which was not a little admonitory in tone. She told the duke about the engagement ring she was bringing, that Everingham and seven hundred and fifty archers had already sailed, after she had paid them six weeks' wages out of Edward's loan of ten thousand crowns, and that Middleton and Dichefeld and the other seven hundred and fifty archers were ready to follow them;[1] but at the same time she gave the duke warning, as did also the Abbot of St Bertin, the Seigneur d'Irlain, and Jean Gros in a letter written three days later to the duke's chancellor,[2] that it was high time he sent Edward an explanation of his friendly attitude towards the king of Scotland. She informed him, too, that it behooved him to treat the English archers well, as Edward had remarked on one occasion when the duke sent back three or four hundred English archers who had been in his service that, if Maximilian could not maintain that small band, the outlook for a larger one certainly was not good, and she had had to explain that the men had been sent home because they had robbed and pillaged until the duke's subjects could bear it no longer.[3]

Margaret wrote that, on leaving Rochester, she and the king were to be entertained by Earl Rivers at his Kentish estate, that after this they would go to Canterbury to spend Sunday, and that on Monday they would proceed to Dover, whence she would sail for home as soon as the ships were ready and the weather favourable. But for some reason Friday, 22 September, found the whole party still at Canterbury. Meanwhile, however, Edward had written two letters to Maximilian which prove that Margaret had made good use of the extra days. For in the first letter the king not only thanked the duke for inviting him to be present if there was a personal meeting between the duke and the king of France, but expressed his hope that the meeting would be fruitful and

---

1. Some of the archers landed at Calais, some at Sluys, and all were used by Maximilian in the campaign he was carrying on in Gueldres. Gilliodts-van-Severen, VI, 203.
2. Commynes-Lenglet, III, 608.
3. Margaret's letter of 14 September. Maximilian probably changed his attitude towards James III as a result of Margaret's remonstrance, for before the end of October Scottish ships of war were seizing Englishmen and Flemings indiscriminately. Commynes-Lenglet, IV, 10.

asked that it might be held where he could easily attend it. Further, he said he
had instructed some ambassadors he was sending to Flanders to accompany
the duke or his ambassadors to the October peace conference and, best of
all, announced that he accepted the duke's explanation of how he happened
to sign a truce with the king of France without consulting him and therefore
would stand by all the agreements he had made with his sister. The king's
second letter was primarily a letter of credence for Sir Thomas Montgomery,
who, with William Slefeld and John Coke, made up the embassy he was
sending with Margaret; but in it he also gave expression to the grief he felt
at parting with his sister, begged Maximilian, "pour l'amour et contentement
de moy, des miens, et d'autres de mon sang," to ratify the treaties she was
carrying home, and with his own hand added: "Cousin, je vous requiere
d'avoir au cœur cette matière pour l'amour de moy, vostre bon cousin."[1]

At last the *Falcon* carried Margaret back to Calais,[2] and there she received
still another letter from Maximilian. But this time the duke did not write
about his negotiations with Louis. Not knowing that the duchess had left
England, he wanted her to consult with her brother about what attitude he
ought to take towards the Cardinal of St Peter *ad Vincula*, who had now
arrived at Peronne. As it was too late for her to speak with Edward about
this or any other matter, Margaret sent Maximilian's letter to England by a
messenger, and from Calais she proceeded to Malines.[3]

Margaret's messenger must have reached London in a few days, but very soon
after his arrival an envoy from Louis also appeared there. Although Margaret
had gone home, she had left an ally behind her in the person of Jacques de la
Villéon, who had been in London when she came and who remained there after
she departed. As Maximilian, like Charles before him, looked upon the Duke
of Brittany as his natural ally against the king of France, he had been taking a
benevolent interest in the negotiations which La Villéon had been conducting

---

1. Commynes-Lenglet, III, 609-610; Rymer, XII, 139.
2. Tellers' account, Exchequer T. R., Council and Privy Seal, file 92, m. 24.
3. Margaret's letter of 3 October, Commynes-Lenglet, III, 614; *Ibid.*, IV, 11. Edward advised
   Maximilian to receive the Cardinal of St Peter *ad Vincula* but asked him not to sign
   any agreement with the Pope's emissary without giving him warning, "car je repute
   pour le present le bien de nous deux comme un seul bien." Nevertheless, Maximilian,
   who suspected that the cardinal represented the king of France rather than the Pope,
   refused to allow him to enter his presence. *Ibid.*, III, 616.

for the marriage of the Prince of Wales and Anne of Brittany and had authorized an ambassador he sent to Venice at the beginning of September to state not only that his son was going to marry the king of England's daughter, but that the king of England's eldest son was going to marry the Duke of Brittany's daughter.[1] This was anticipating the truth a little, but La Villéon had been making progress, and Louis, who was aware of the fact, resolved to let Edward know that he knew what was going on. To this end on 18 October Jean le Fèvre, one of Louis' secretaries, arrived in London with a contribution to King Edward's natural history museum which consisted of a boar's tusk, "the largest that ever was seen," and the dried head of a strange animal resembling a roebuck.

If the full meaning of Louis' gift was not evident at once, it was made so when, the day after Le Fèvre's advent, Chester Herald, who had gone to France with Langton and the Prior of St John's, returned home. For Chester drew a lively picture of Louis' state of mind. Louis was "wonderfully displeased," he said, because English archers had been sent to Maximilian, and he had spit out the remark that the reason the Duchess Margaret had refused his offers was that she hated him for not having helped the Duke of Clarence when he was conspiring against the king of England. Louis had also sent word to Langton and Weston that they might as well go home if they wanted to, for they would get no other reply from him than the one he had already given them. So, take it all in all, Chester thought Louis was a very angry man, too angry a man, indeed, ever to send money to England again; and furthermore, he had heard it said at the French court that Louis was going to make peace with the Duke of Austria no matter what it cost him. In fact, it seemed to Chester that Louis must already have an understanding with Maximilian and some of his chief councillors, as one day when he was present Louis had displayed before the Prior of St John's eyes some letters which the king of England had written to the Duke of Austria and the Duchess Margaret.[2]

But while Chester had some ground for thinking there was an understanding between Louis and Maximilian, that understanding was a

---

1. *Cal. Venetian Papers*, I, 141.
2. Letter from Étienne Frizon to Jean Gros, Commynes-Lenglet, IV, 9-10. Frizon, in spite of his name, seems to have been a subject of the king of England, and he may be identical with Master Stephen Fryon, who was made one of Edward's secretaries in September of this year. *Cal. Patent Rolls*, III, 221.

very poor one, as was shown by the fact that the peace conference set for 15 October failed to take place. For this failure Louis himself was chiefly to blame, as when he found that Maximilian had promised Edward that he might be represented at the meeting, he raised violent objections and declared that the English wanted war and would therefore do all they could to obstruct the negotiations. He also found fault, for one reason or another, with every meeting place that was suggested. A month after the date set for the conference George Cely wrote from Calais that the Duchess Margaret was coming to St Omer and that the French ambassadors would "lie at Thérouanne three weeks hence," though he added that he did not know "what world we shall have," as some of Maximilian's councillors were for war and some for peace and the king of France had "furnished his garrisons upon the fronts." But, as it proved, Louis would not hear of sending his ambassadors to Thérouanne, as that place was so near Calais that the English might seize them and hold them as hostages. Moreover, if the Duchess Margaret was going to be hovering around, it was silly, Louis thought, to expect anything to come out of the negotiations.[1]

Langton and Weston, returning from France, arrived at Eltham on 11 November, and they were just in time for the prior to pass the spice plate at the christening of a seventh royal princess, born the day before,[2] who was called Bridget and whose fate it was to be to take the veil, like the Irish saint whose name she bore, and to spend the greater part of her not very long life in a nunnery at Dartford. There was all the usual pomp and display at the christening, with a stately procession composed of knights, esquires, and "other honest persons" to the number of a hundred, all carrying lighted torches, and, following after, Lord Maltravers with the basin in his hands and "a towel about his neck," the Earl of Northumberland with a taper not yet lighted, the Earl of Lincoln with salt, and finally, under a canopy, Lady Maltravers, with "a rich chrisom pinned over her left breast," and the Countess of Richmond, now Lord Stanley's wife, who, with the assistance of the Marquis of Dorset, carried the child. The Bishop of Chichester officiated at the font, the baby's grandmother, the Duchess of York, her eldest sister, Princess Elizabeth, and the Bishop of Winchester were her sponsors, and

---

1. *Lettres de Louis XI*, VIII, 295-297, 301, 308; *Cely Papers*, 48-49.
2. *Cely Papers*, 46.

when she was taken back to her mother's chamber, the "great gifts" her godparents had given her were carried before her.[1]

But though Langton and Weston arrived at so happy a moment, it was not cheerful news they brought to the king. They had left France in a mood far from pleasant, and George Cely, who had seen them as they passed through Calais, begged his father to write to him whether the king "purposeth to have war with France or no." It was not likely, however, that Edward, who already had one war on his hands (Louis had seen to that) would seek another, and Cely's brother replied hopefully, on 22 November, that he thought there was no probability of war between England and France, that an embassy was going to France shortly, and that a council meeting was beginning at Westminster that day.[1]

It is doubtful if Edward actually sent an embassy to Louis at the end of 1480, and it is certain that he had called his councillors together not to consult them about a possible war with France, but about what was to be done to chastise the Scots. Yet, while his hands were tied by the Scots, Edward did not suffer the possible consequences of Louis' anger to alter the course he had already chosen. By this time Michel de Partenay had arrived in London with a commission for La Villéon and himself to treat through the king of England for an alliance between Brittany and Burgundy of whatever nature the king might choose,[3] and this so pleased Edward that on 1 December he empowered John Russell, who was now Bishop of Lincoln, and others to sign the treaty for the marriage of the Prince of Wales and Anne of Brittany with a clause providing that, in case of Anne's death, the Prince should marry her sister Isabella.[4] If the marriage treaty was not sealed on the spot, at least a treaty of alliance must have been; for though no copy of such a treaty has come to light, in a warrant which he sent to the chancery a few weeks later Edward spoke of the "league, amity, and confederation late made betwixt us and our right dear cousin, Francis, Duke of Brittany," and ordered proclamation to be made that the merchants of Brittany were

---

1. Madden, *Gentlemen's Mag.*, Jan., 1831; More, *Hist. of Richard III*, 1. Bridget, who seems to have been a sickly child, became a nun sometime between 1486 and 1492 and died, apparently, before 1513. Green, *Princesses of Eng.*, IV, 46-48.
2. *Cely Papers*, 49, 50.
3. Legrand coll., MS. français 6987, f. 295. Francis's commission was given on 28 October.
4. Signed Bills, file 1519, no. 5212.

to be accorded the same treatment in England in regard to the payment of customs and subsidies as the merchants of Spain.[1]

As the year was drawing to a close Jacques de la Villéon left England. But, instead of going home, he went to Flanders, and he carried with him a letter in which Edward urged Mary and Maximilian to seize the opportunity to form an alliance with the Duke of Brittany and expressed his readiness to help the matter on. So uncertain did the king feel, however, since his recent experience with Maximilian, about the turn events might take that he informed Mary and Maximilian that, if they signed a truce or treaty of peace with the king of France, he and Francis wanted to be included in it, and that Francis wanted assurances from them that he would be so included.[2]

---

1. *Ibid.*, file 1519, no. 5237, 23 Feb., 1481.
2. Commynes-Lenglet, IV, 19.

7

WAR WITH SCOTLAND

Louis XI had felt grave misgivings when he discovered that both Margaret of York and Jacques de la Villéon were in London. And no wonder, since all signs went to show that he was fast losing his hold on the king of England and that, unless he succeeded in regaining that hold or in bringing strong pressure to bear on Edward in some other way, he would be confronted at no distant day with a fresh linking together of England, Burgundy, and Brittany against him. Fear of such a combination of his neighbours had haunted Louis almost from his accession; it was such a league that had threatened the overturn of his throne in 1475 and that had compelled him to make great sacrifices to save himself; and if such a league were now formed a new, all the dangers from which he had escaped so narrowly six years before would loom up afresh. Louis, however, was by no means in despair, for while his enemies had been taking counsel with one another, he had been taking counsel with himself to excellent effect. The day had gone by when he could hope, with a small expenditure of money and effort, to excite a new outbreak of civil war in England, but with practically no difficulty he had contrived to bring about a conflict between England and Scotland which, while it lasted, would force Edward to waste his strength in the northern marches of his kingdom, and his continental friends, whoever they might be, to struggle along with little or no help from him. Although Maximilian had given warning that the invasion of France must take place the very next summer if he was to reap much benefit from it, neither to preserve Burgundy from destruction nor to gratify his own ambition to wear the crown of France could Edward take another army across the sea while the Scots were threatening to push beyond his border. Not until he was sure of peace with Scotland had he dared to think of invading France with Charles's help, and not until he had won the war he had now begun with James III could he think of assailing France with Maximilian's help. Yet, from the vigorous preparations he was making, it was evident that Edward had hope of settling his account with James very speedily, and if in the meantime he should arrive at a satisfactory agreement with Maximilian, there was still the danger that, as soon as the Scots had been repressed, he would turn his arms against the man whom he rightly believed to be responsible for the offences they had committed against him.

During the council meeting at Westminster in November, it had been decided that the king ought to go north in person to assist Gloucester, whose raid into Scotland in revenge for the burning of Bamburgh was over before that time and who was now engaged in repairing the walls of Carlisle' and in taking other measures to strengthen the border defences. Soon after the council meeting, consequently, the exportation of all grains from the kingdom was prohibited by proclamation and commissions were sent out for the requisitioning of thousands of quarters of wheat and other supplies needed by an army. Orders were also given for the arresting of ships and mariners,[2] and the king bought outright at least four splendid ships—the *Mary Howard*, purchased from Lord Howard, the *Holy Ghost* of Portugal, the *Marie* of Bilbao, and the *Trinity* of Eu[3]—to swell the size of the fleet which would have to perform the double task of harrying the coasts of Scotland and of guarding those of England not only against the Scots, but also against the more formidable French. Lord Howard was to be captain of the entire fleet, with three thousand men, reckoning both "landmen and mariners," under his command, and his indenture bound him to serve for sixteen weeks, from the middle of May till the last day of August, "toward the parties of Scotland"

---

1. Tellers' Roll, Mich. 20 Edw. IV.
2. Writs of Privy Seal, file 875, no. 5264—a licence granted on 13 January 1481, to two Norwich men to export 800 quarters of barley although it had been proclaimed that no manner of grains were to be conveyed out of the realm; *Cal. Patent Rolls*, III, 240, 249-250, 264, 268.
3. Tellers' Roll, *ut sup.*; Tellers' account, Exchequer T. R., Council and Privy Seal, file 92, M. 26; *Cal. Patent Rolls*, III, 282. The *Holy Ghost* of Portugal I take to be identical with the *Kervel* of *Portyngale* mentioned in the Household Books of the Duke of Norfolk and *le Great Portingale* referred to in *Cal. Patent Rolls*, III, 240. The *Trinity* of Eu must be the same as the *Kervel* of *Ewe* of the Norfolk Household Books and of Accounts, etc. (Exchequer K.R.), bundle 329, no. 2. See also Nichols, *Grants of King Edward the Fifth*, 67.
4. *Household Books of the Duke of Norfolk*, 9, 274. The wages were to be 15*d* a week for each man, with 12*d* ob. for food, and Howard was paid £5,500 in advance in two instalments. Tellers' Roll and Accounts, etc., *ut sup*.

or wherever the king might direct.[4] The *Grace Dieu*, carrying five hundred men and commanded by Avery Cornburgh, and the *Carican* of St Michael's Mount fame, with two hundred men, were the largest of the seven ships which were detailed to "keep the narrow sea," while the *Mary Howard* and the *Holy Ghost* of Portugal, each with four hundred men, and the *Antony* were to head the somewhat larger fleet which was to sail northward.[1]

But when he came to lay plans for the invasion of Scotland, Edward was met by the same old difficulty that had troubled him during all his earlier wars. His financial affairs were in a far better condition now than they had been when he conducted his early campaigns against his rebels in the north and their Scottish allies, but under no circumstances could he hope to carry on a war of any length without direct assistance from his people. At the same time, remembering the humiliating struggle it had cost him to win from the cautious Commons the money he wanted for his expedition to France, popular as that expedition had been, and the indignation his subjects had so openly expressed when it was found that the money finally conceded to him had been spent in vain, he shrank from summoning parliament to ask for a war grant. So once more he tried a benevolence. Only a sample, one may be sure, of many royal letters sent out at this time was the one in which the king solicited from the city of Salisbury such aid towards the expenses of the war with Scotland that "God and we may be pleased." Although for the "perfecter establishment" of the long truce which he had negotiated with Scotland, Edward explained, he had agreed to give one of his daughters in marriage to the son and heir "of him that now pretendeth him to be king there" and, in expectation of this marriage, had paid James III large sums of money each year, James had been faithless enough to levy war on him in order to "dilate his marches far within ours"; and as the successful raid made by the Duke of Gloucester and the Earl of Northumberland into Scotland at the end of the summer had evidently been insufficient, he had determined, on the advice of the lords assembled in the great council held at Westminster in November, to proceed in person

---

1. *Household Books of the Duke of Norfolk*, 3, Robert Michelson, who had been "lodesman" of the *Antony* when that ship brought Edward home in 1471, was now master of the *Mary Howard*. *Ibid.*, 243; *Cal. Patent Rolls*, III, 240. Lord Cobham served under Howard in the *George Cobham*.

against James and win such a victory over the Scots that fear of them would be banished for many years to come.[1]

Salisbury sent the king only a hundred pounds in response to his long letter, but Canterbury gave him twice that amount, and the city of London presented him with five thousand marks *ex benevolencia*. Other cities and towns must have done their part also, and the commissioners of benevolence appointed to gather money in the counties returned considerable sums to the Exchequer, those of the county of Norfolk, for example, sending in £387 15s 3d at one time and at another £751 11s 3d. Added to this, the clergy of the province of Canterbury granted a tenth for the defence of the kingdom.[2] Nevertheless, Edward found that the benevolence was not going to provide him with enough money to meet the expenses of the war, and he finally ventured upon a very dangerous step. He called for the payment of the three quarters of a fifteenth and tenth which he had remitted to his subjects after his return from France in 1475. He had the wisdom, however, to grant an exemption from this tax to at least two of the northern counties. The county of Lancaster he excused from the payment of its share of the three quarters of a fifteenth and tenth on the ground that its people had undertaken "of their free will" to find him a thousand archers to resist "his old enemy, the king of Scots," and the county and city of York were excused in consideration of what they had done during the past year and "this year trusted to be done" in withstanding the same foe.[1]

Long before Edward's preparations for war had advanced to this point, James III, who had probably been encouraged by the king of France to think that Edward had sunk into such a state of lethargy that he would bear anything rather than fight, had taken alarm and had begun to manifest an inclination to back down. One of the Celys, writing towards the end of January 1481,

---

1. Hatcher, *Old and New Sarum*, 198-200.
2. *Ibid.*; Hist. MSS. Com., *Report 9*, app., 144; London Journal 8, ff. 236b-244; Sharpe, *Cal. Letter Book L*, 175; Tellers' Roll, Mich. 20 Edw. IV; Wilkins, III, 612; Wake, 381; Fine Roll 21 Edw. IV, m. 1-2. Both Fabyan and Kingsford's *London Chronicle* state that the money given by London was repaid in the following year.
3. Signed Bills, file 1520, no. 5267, file 1528, no. 5411. The first of these bills was delivered to the chancellor on 20 June, 21 Edw. IV. The second one is without date, but its close resemblance to the first leaves no doubt that it belongs to the same time. Compare the first one with the king's commission to Lord Stanley to retain the thousand men the county of Lancaster had promised to furnish and two thousand other men from the same county. *Ibid.*, file 1528, no. 5268, 20 June 21 Edw. IV.

speaks of the active preparations for war which were going on in London but closes his story with the tidings that some ambassadors had arrived from Scotland, "and the king would not let them come no nearer, but sent their offer to Newcastle."[1] The rejected embassy consisted of a herald and a pursuivant, and if one may believe what the Scottish historian Lesley says, it was sent at the desire of the king of France to make three demands, namely, that Edward should desist from giving aid to the Duke of Burgundy, that he should give redress for violations of his truce with Scotland, and that he should "restore the Duke of Albany." If Edward proved intractable, he was to be told that James, "by reason he was confederate with France," would not merely seek revenge for his own injuries, but would give assistance to the French.[2] But there is at least one flaw in this story. The Duke of Albany was not in England at this time, but in France. It seems improbable also that Louis would have permitted, much less inspired, James thus to divulge the secret of his intrigues with him; and there is the further fact that the parliament of Scotland afterwards stated that James's "will, mind, and intention" were against war with the English and that he sent the herald and pursuivant to England, not with any such war-provoking message as Lesley relates, but, on the contrary, to offer redress for all breaches of the truce which had been committed by his subjects, provided similar redress was granted by Edward.[3] Whatever their errand, James's envoys made their journey wholly in vain, and so little did Louis succeed, through James's agency or by any other means, in interrupting the negotiations going on between England and Burgundy that, about the middle of February, Edward welcomed another embassy from Maximilian.[4]

This time Maximilian had chosen for his chief ambassador the Prince of Orange; the prince's associates were Philip de Croy, Count of Chimay, the Abbot of St Bertin, who had left England so recently with the Duchess Margaret, Pierre Bogart, prothonotary of the Apostolic See and Dean of St Donas, Bruges, and a secretary named Antoine de Branges. Edward sent

---

1. *Cely Papers*, 55.
2. Lesley, 44.
3. *Acts of Parl. of Scotland*, II, 138.
4. Maximilian's instructions to his ambassadors were drawn up on 29 January, but as a letter which Mary of Burgundy sent by them to the Duke of Brittany (Commynes-Lenglet, IV, 30) was written on 13 February, it would appear that they did not leave home until after that date.

the barge of the Prince of Wales to Gravesend to bring these distinguished visitors to London, and he seems to have defrayed the expenses of the Prince of Orange, if not those of all the ambassadors, during their stay in England.[1] Unhappily, however, he found the messages the prince had brought rather disconcerting. While Maximilian had told his ambassadors to say that he and his wife had ratified the treaties and agreements negotiated by the Duchess Margaret and had delivered the documents to Montgomery, Coke, and Slefeld, he followed up this pleasing announcement with a demand for the fulfilment of Edward's promise to declare for him in case Louis refused to make peace with him before Easter. In explanation of this demand, Maximilian stated that it was obvious that Louis would never agree to any reasonable terms of peace, and he maintained that Louis' hostile attitude towards him was due in large measure to the fact that he and his wife had allied themselves with the king of England. If Edward wished to send another embassy to France to make one more effort to bring Louis to reason, the duke had no objection, but he still wanted his ally to prepare to invade France in the coming summer. The time was most favourable for such an undertaking, the duke affirmed, as Louis' subjects were so burdened with taxes that they would welcome the restoration of English rule in France, the advantages of which they had never forgotten. Nor would there be any difficulty, he thought, in securing the support of the great lords of France. And therefore, as he himself would help to the limit of his power and the assistance of Brittany could also be counted on, Edward would undoubtedly find himself in a very short time in possession of the crown of France, or at least of a large part of that kingdom. From first to last, however, Maximilian urged that the attack on Louis must be made this very summer, as he would be in no position later on, if meanwhile he had to continue bearing the burden of the war alone, to give the assistance he could give now.

Since he knew that Edward was already at war with Scotland, and also that at best the king could not raise and equip on a few weeks' notice such an army as it would be necessary for him to have if he set out to invade France again, Maximilian must have been conscious that he was asking for the impossible. But quite unexpected things sometimes happen in this world, and the duke had told his ambassadors just what they were to say

---

1. Tellers' Roll, Mich. 20 Edw. IV.

in case Edward showed a disposition to talk about invading France. A joint declaration of war against Louis and a mutual promise not to make a separate peace with him were Maximilian's first suggestions, and he proposed that he himself should put at least ten or twelve thousand men into the field and that Edward should do the same. If Edward chose to begin by landing in Calais and conquering Boulogne and Montreuil, the duke and his wife were ready to assist him and to transfer their rights over those towns to him, provided he would assist them to recover the territory which Louis had seized in Artois, a recovery that would be easily accomplished, as the people of Artois were eager to return to their natural lord. If Edward wished, later on, to march into Champagne to conquer it and to assume the crown of France at Rheims, Maximilian was prepared to accompany him with his entire army, and when the campaign was over, the newly crowned king could requite his ally by helping him to recover the adjoining county of Burgundy, where again the desire of the people to return to their natural lord would facilitate the work of conquest. Or, in case Edward objected to this plan, because Champagne was too distant or for any other reason, Maximilian was willing to help the king conquer Normandy or any other part of France equal in size to the county of Burgundy, if he was rewarded with assistance to recover that county; and if it proved necessary to offer still more inducements, the duke would promise to surrender to Edward all the rights he and his wife had in the county of Ponthieu and the towns of the Somme, though he hoped he would be permitted to keep Peronne, Montdidier, and Roye. He was ready, too, in spite of the fact that the territories which were to be conquered for his benefit were of small moment in comparison with the kingdom of France, which was to be Edward's reward, and could be much more quickly overrun, to bind himself not to withdraw from the war when he had regained what belonged to him, but to continue his assistance with five or six thousand men until the conquest of France was completed. The wages of these five or six thousand men Edward would have to pay himself, however, and Maximilian also wanted permission to use for the expenses of the war and the payment of his troops the pension of fifty thousand crowns a year which he was to give Edward; or at the least he wanted an agreement that the payment of the pension was to end as soon as Edward, with his aid, had made sufficient conquests in France to provide him with yearly revenues equal in amount to the pension.

Yet while he talked about an invasion of France, now, just as when the Duchess Margaret had gone over to England, the most Maximilian really counted on securing from Edward was some archers, although this time he made bold to ask the king not only to supply the men, but to pay their wages. He must have succour of some sort this very year, he urged continually, unless he was to succumb and make terms with Louis; and he gave Edward to understand that if he refused, on account of his war with Scotland or for any other cause, to attempt an invasion of France, or if he wished to postpone the invasion for a year, he must at least live up to the promise he had given to Margaret by sending three or four thousand archers at his own expense to help carry on the war. The duke coupled with this warning of what he might be driven to do if no help were given him the information that Louis had requested him to send an envoy to him, and that he had promised to do so. He took pains, it is true, to add that he had made this promise on the advice both of the Duchess Margaret and of Montgomery, Coke, and Slefeld, who thought that in this way he might ward off any sudden renewal of Louis' attacks and at the same time find out what Louis' intentions were, and also that he was still resolved to make no treaty with the French king without the consent of the king of England, whom he regarded as "son père" and according to whose wishes he desired to regulate all his affairs. But it ought to have been plain to Edward that Maximilian's courage was failing him and that, if he did not answer his cry for help very soon by declaring war on France or at least by sending him substantial support, the duke would accept the first good offer Louis made.

Still there was no question that Maximilian very much preferred an alliance with England to an unsatisfactory and humiliating peace with the king of France. He would not knuckle under to Louis if he saw any hope of avoiding it, and with Edward's wishes on one point he was more than glad to comply. He was eager to enter into an alliance with the Duke of Brittany, and he was just as willing as Francis was to leave the negotiation of the alliance to Edward. But here again the Duke revealed how great was the strain of anxiety he was living under. For when he had thanked Edward with all his heart for the kind interest he had shown in the matter of an alliance between Francis and himself, he began to beg that, as soon as the alliance was signed, Edward and Francis would unite in requiring Louis to agree to a peace and a just settlement with him and in threatening to give him all the help in their power should this demand be refused. More than that, he sent word to Jacques de la Villéon and Michel de Partenay, the former of whom had now returned to London from Flanders and, with Partenay, was lingering there, partly to put the finishing touches to the negotiations for the marriage of the Prince of Wales and Anne of Brittany and partly to conclude the alliance between Francis and Maximilian, that Francis must send him aid immediately in order to relieve him from the necessity of making a peace with Louis which would render their alliance fruitless; and one or two of his ambassadors were under orders to go to Brittany to labour with Francis directly.[1] Should Edward agree to invade France this year, Maximilian wanted Francis to march into Normandy or Poitou or to send ships to assist in ravaging their coasts; and if the invasion of France did not take place this year, he wanted the duke to give him some money, say a hundred, or at least sixty, thousand crowns. Granted this, he would promise, as Francis had asked him to do, not to make peace with Louis without Francis's consent or without securing his inclusion in it.

In addition to the urging of Maximilian's need of help against Louis and the negotiation of an alliance between the duke and Francis of Brittany, the Prince of Orange had been charged with two lesser matters. Edward had been careless enough to let the pension which he had granted to the Seigneur de la Gruthuyse when his memory of that gentleman's many courtesies to him was still fresh to fall into arrears, and Maximilian had instructed his ambassadors to bring the matter to the king's attention and help Gruthuyse obtain the money that was owing to him. Second, the question of a staple for Newcastle wool needed to be settled. The agreement concerning such a staple which had been signed at the close of the year 1476 had apparently never been carried out, on account of the death of Charles the Bold so soon after, and although Montgomery, Coke, and Slefeld had been told to mention the subject to Maximilian, they had been put off with a promise that the ambassadors the duke was about to send to England should have full powers to make a new agreement. Accordingly, the Prince of Orange had brought with him a copy of the articles drawn up before Charles's

---

1. Commynes-Lenglet, IV, 30.

death and authority to conclude a new agreement on similar terms. But in regard to the two points which had been left "in suspense" when the former agreement was made, that is, the demand of the Newcastle merchants that they should be excused from paying tolls and from compensating certain of Maximilian's subjects for injuries for which they were held responsible, Maximilian was reluctant to make any engagements. There was no reason, he thought, why Newcastle wool should enjoy more privileges than other English merchandise coming into his domains every day, or than the wools of Spain and Scotland, which were equally good and yet were not exempt from the payment of tolls; and while, to please the king of England, he would grant the Newcastle wool merchants a six years' safeconduct, he hoped the king would see to it that those merchants gave his injured subjects the compensation they had so long sought from them in vain.[1]

Except for Maximilian's admission that he was going to dispatch an envoy to Louis and his obstinacy about the payment of tolls by the Newcastle merchants, there seems to have been nothing in the Prince of Orange's instructions which could cause Edward offence. And to the duke's decision to send an envoy to Louis Edward ought not to have taken exception, since the duke explained so carefully that he was acting on the advice of the Duchess Margaret and of Edward's own ambassadors. It appears, moreover, that Edward had suggested that it might be well for the duke to make a year's truce with Louis,[2] while the most Maximilian eventually did was to prolong the existing truce till the end of June.[3] But Edward's ire was aroused against the Members of Flanders, who were probably responsible for the disappointment of the Newcastle merchants, and for this reason, or because he had a suspicion that Maximilian was playing fast and loose with him, he dispatched Langton to France with some message not of a nature to please Maximilian and then, about the middle of March, turned his back on the duke's ambassadors and withdrew to Greenwich.[4] Letters which sounded

---

1. *Ibid.*, IV, 10-19.
2. See the letter Maximilian wrote to his ambassadors in England on 16 April. *Ibid.*, IV, 32-35.
3. See the first article of the instructions given by Maximilian to some ambassadors he sent to Louis in March 1482. *Ibid.*, IV, 71. Cf. *Lettres de Louis XI*, IX, 43-44.
4. The king seems to have been at Greenwich from 14 to 24 March, but at the Tower from 28 to 30 March. Privy Seals.

promising, if they were not actually so, were soon received from Flanders,[1] however, and, thanks in part to them and in part to the friendly offices of La Villéon and Partenay, the king was shortly persuaded to return to the city, and on 1 April Maximilian's ambassadors sent home a pleased and happy letter. The chancellor of England had informed them in the presence of the king's council, they said, that, the war with Scotland permitting, King Edward would either make a descent on France this very year or send troops to Maximilian's support. Another ambassador had already followed Langton to France[2] to speak more openly in the duke's behalf, and Edward had declared that before Easter he would send a third messenger, with "le feu en la main," if Louis did not do justice to Maximilian.

Maximilian naturally felt elated when he received this encouraging epistle from his ambassadors, and in a commendatory letter which he wrote to them on 16 April he declared that he would be guided in all his acts by the advice of the king of England and the Duke of Brittany, and that he was getting everything ready so that, with the help of the king and the duke he could strike the moment his truce with the king of France expired. Gueldres, he wished Edward and Francis to know, seemed to be on the point of submitting to him, and, with that incubus removed, he would be able to give his entire attention to Louis. Another piece of very good news was that some ambassadors from the princes of the Empire who were returning from France had brought word to Bruges that, throughout their audience with Louis, he had remained seated in a chair, and that he looked as if he had been very ill.[3] Who knew but what Death would prove to be Burgundy's best ally? But, for that matter, Life itself now seemed to be on Maximilian's side, as, on the very day he wrote his letter to his ambassadors in London, those ambassadors concluded his treaty of alliance with the Duke of Brittany, and

---

1. On 22 March the Count de Chimay wrote from London to the bailli of Ghent acknowledging the receipt on that day of important letters from him and saying, after thanking him for having written so promptly, that he had sent his letters to the king "qui en a faict grant estime, et croy quelles profitteront de beaucop, et vous en est tenu monseigneur le duc, ceulx de Gand et le pays de Flandres." *Mémoires de Jean de Dadizeele* (Société d'Emulation de Bruges, 1850), 116.
2. Probably Robert Nyter, who received £13 6*s* 8*d* for making a journey to France. Tellers' Roll, Mich. 20 Edw. IV.
3. Maximilian's letter of 16 April.

in one article of that treaty Francis promised to pay four months' wages to two thousand of the five or six thousand English archers which Edward was to let Maximilian have.[1]

Francis, indeed, was now committed not only to an alliance with Burgundy but to a much closer one with England, as at this moment La Villéon also brought to a happy termination the negotiations for the marriage of the Prince of Wales and Anne of Brittany. The marriage treaty was ratified by Edward on 10 May, by Francis on 22 June,[2] and its leading provisions were that the Prince of Wales should marry Anne as soon as she reached the age of twelve (which meant in eight years) or, in case of her death, her sister Isabella; that in case of the Prince of Wales's death, the oldest living and unmarried son of the king of England should be the bridegroom, if the difference in age between him and the bride was not too great, and that if a son should be born to the Duke of Brittany at any time, that son should marry a daughter of the king of England, if the king had one who was of suitable age and still unmarried. If the king had no such daughter, the duke must seek his advice and consent before arranging any other marriage for his son. The dowry of Anne or her sister was to be a hundred thousand crowns, if the bride was still heiress to the duchy of Brittany at the time of her marriage, but twice that amount if a son had been born to the duke meanwhile; and the duke must meet the cost of his daughter's journey to Salisbury or London for her wedding. If the Prince of Wales should die before ascending the throne, Edward must give his son's widow twenty thousand crowns, English, a year. Lastly, if Louis XI or any of his successors, or any person at the instigation of Louis or his successors, should invade the duchy of Brittany, Edward must, at his own expense, supply the duke with three thousand archers for three months, and with others up to the number of four thousand at the duke's expense, if the duke needed further aid, while Francis was required to assist Edward with three thousand archers for three months should the king undertake to invade France.

When the Prince of Orange left England, a few points in the arrangements between Maximilian and Edward were still unsettled, as Edward insisted that, before he engaged to invade France, Maximilian must bind not only himself

---

1. Commynes-Lenglet, IV, 35-37.
2. Morice, III, 394; Rymer, XII, 142.

but also his heirs to help him and his heirs, that the duke must promise to give him a new bond for the payment of his pension every time he fulfilled the conditions of the bond (by furnishing the duke with troops), and that the three estates of the duke's dominions must confirm this bond within six months instead of two years, the time mentioned in the agreement made with the Duchess Margaret.[1] But these were comparatively small matters, and, all things considered, Maximilian was justified in thinking that he was now sure of the support of the king of England and the Duke of Brittany in his struggle with Louis. Yet, as far as aid from Edward was concerned, there were still two chances of disappointment. The war with Scotland might prove to be all the king could manage, or, if he overcame that difficulty, Louis might succeed in buying him off. There was no doubt that Louis was already looking over his weapons with a view to using them wherever and however self-defence dictated, and almost avowedly now the French and the Scots were fighting one battle. A couple of days after Edward ratified his marriage treaty with the Duke of Brittany, two French ships were captured off Calais in the act of chasing an English one, and the story ran that there were "Scots amongst them." The many possibilities this suggested were so serious that Lord Hastings was at once ordered to exclude all strangers from Calais, and persons who had houses without the gates were warned to remove them into the town if they did not want them to be "plucked shortly down or else burned."[2]

It may have been a desire to find out what was going on in Calais that brought the two French ships too near for safety. For by this time Edward's preparations for his "voyage into Scotland" were well advanced, and on the very day on which the French ships were captured the well-filled military storehouses of Calais were rendering up to one William Comersale, captain of the *Michael of the Tower*, a number of large guns, including the *Great Edward*

---

1. See the instructions given by Maximilian to the ambassadors he sent to England some months later. Commynes-Lenglet, IV, 20-21.
2. *Cely Papers*, 57-58; Exchequer T. R., Council and Privy Seal, file 92, m. 57.
3. Exchequer Accounts, France, bundle 298, no. 13. This is a paper book in which are recorded matters concerning Calais and Guines. The entries from which the above facts are drawn are dated 12 May 21 Edw. IV. A "last of gunpowder for my Lord Howard" is also mentioned, and another for Avery Cornburgh. Comersale is not described in the book as captain of the *Michael of the Tower*, but see Accounts, etc. (Exchequer K. R.), bundle 329, no. 2, where record is made of a payment to him for the wages and food of ninety men in his ship.

of Calais, the *Great Brazen Gun*, the *Messenger*, the *Fowler of Chester*, and the *Little Edward*, as well as a potgun of brass, another of iron, a hundred hakeguns of brass, a hundred and fifty handguns of brass, and much other "stuff and habiliments of war."[3] The *Michael of the Tower* was one of the ships destined to sail with Lord Howard along the eastern coast towards Scotland, and on 14 May Sir Thomas Fulford received a commission from the king for the keeping of the western seas with power to take ships, mariners, and supplies "for our reasonable money." Fulford seems to have sailed shortly after, with three hundred armed men, for the west coast of Scotland,[1] and England was soon to ring with the echo of Lord Howard's exploits on James's eastern shores. The king and the Prince of Wales went to Sandwich about the middle of May,[2] apparently to review and wish godspeed to Howard's fleet, and not long after that nobleman, sailing audaciously into the Firth of Forth, carried off eight of the largest ships lying in the harbours of Leith, Kinghorn, and Pettenween and destroyed all the smaller ones. He even effected a landing at Blackness, where he burned the town and another large ship.[3]

Howard's stinging blow could hardly fail to have a subduing effect on the Scots, and, to add emphasis to it, Edward now sent James's curtly received ambassadors back to Edinburgh without having once admitted them to his presence or given them an answer "either in word or writ."[4] But even if James had wished to make peace after receiving so hard a lesson in what it meant to quarrel with his nearest neighbour, he would have had no chance to do so, as Edward was determined to fight and even, according to a letter in which he explained to Pope Sixtus how the perfidious behaviour of the Scots

---

1. See Warrants under the Signet, file 1390, 14 May 21 Edw. IV, and in Accounts, etc. (Exchequer K. R.), *ut sup.* the record of a payment of £171 17s 6d to one William Castelton for the wages of three hundred men of war retained by the king to serve upon the sea on the west coast of Scotland.

2. Privy Seals. They stopped at Canterbury, and as this was the Prince's first visit to that city, the citizens presented him with a box of silver gilt containing twenty pounds in money. Hist. MSS. Com., *Report 9*, app. 144-145.

3. Lesley, 44. Because Lesley connects the death of the Bishop of Aberdeen, which occurred on 14 April 1481, with the rupture between Edward and James and mentions it immediately after his account of the destruction wrought by the English fleet, it has been thought that Howard made his attack on the coast of Scotland in April. See Ramsay, II, 439, and Hume Brown, I, 271. But this is certainly incorrect. Howard bade farewell to his wife at Harwich on 20 May. *Household Books of the Duke of Norfolk*, 98.

4. Lesley, *ut sup.*; *Acts of Parl. of Scotland*, II, 138.

prevented him from lending to the defence of the Faith the support he would so gladly give, to command his army in person.[1] Gloucester evidently had a formidable force in the north already,[2] but Edward was to bring him a yet larger one gathered from all parts of the kingdom. Not many facts regarding the composition and leaders of the army raised to invade Scotland in 1481 can be picked up, but we know that the city of York was represented in its ranks, that Lord Stanley led a body of three thousand Lancashiremen—the thousand archers who had won for Lancashire exemption from the payment of its share of the three quarters of a fifteenth and tenth and two thousand other men retained at the king's wages—that the Marquis of Dorset brought six hundred Warwickshire men who were to receive sixpence a day from the king, and that Earl Rivers commanded a thousand men from some other county.[3]

In addition to his army and his fleet, Edward had another weapon up his sleeve. In other days he had found Scotsmen who were not opposed to helping him, and he hoped to find more helpful Scotsmen now. Already, in the winter or spring, the Earl of Douglas had been sent north "upon the king's message," and behind Douglas had followed two other expatriated Scots, Richard Holland, clerk, and Patrick Holyburton, or Haliburton, chaplain.[4] Something of the nature of Douglas's errand in the north may be gathered from the fact that in August he and Gloucester were empowered to promise security and gifts of land, etc., to any Scots who wished to come into England,[5] while Haliburton, it seems, went to see Edward's quondam ally, the Lord of the Isles. But however many of James's subjects Gloucester and Douglas may have enticed across the border, the Lord of the Isles disappointed the hopes of his former friend. Although at first he may have shown some inclination to betray his country again, as in June Edward authorized Haliburton, one Henry Pole, a captain of the fleet, and the mayor of Cragfergus to treat with

---

1. *Cal. Venetian Papers*, I, 142-143.
2. As much as £10,000 was sent to him at one time for the wages of his men. Accounts, etc. (Exchequer K. R.), bundle 329, no. 2.
3. Davies, *York Records*, 108 *et seq.*; Signed Bills, file 1520, no. 5268; Accounts etc. (Exchequer K. R.), *ut sup.*; Warrants under the Signet, file 1390, 11 June.
4. Tellers' Roll, Mich. 20 Edw. IV; Tellers' account, Exchequer T. R., Council and Privy Seal, file 92, m. 26. On Holland and Haliburton, see *Acts of Parl. of Scotland*, II, 139, and *Exch. Rolls of Scot.*, IX, 211.
5. Signed Bills, file 1520, no. 5273; *Cal. Documents relating to Scotland*, IV, 300.

him and Donald Gorne for a league and amity, what he did in the end was to go, "with a great company," to join King James's army.[1]

On 22 June Edward ordered the adjournment of the courts until Michaelmas, giving as his reason the need of resisting the Scots.[2] But he was not yet ready to go north, and on 10 July he invited the mayor and aldermen and a few other leading Londoners to a hunting party in Waltham forest which the city chroniclers delight to tell about. The king displayed on this happy occasion all his old-time *bonhomie*. When his guests arrived at the "pleasant lodge of green boughs" where the tables had been spread, he refused to go to his own dinner until they had been served; and after the day's sport, during which many deer were killed, not only were the mayor and the whole company made glad with gifts of generous amounts of venison, but the king sent to the mayoress and the other ladies two harts, six bucks, and a tun of wine "to make them merry with," which they proceeded to do in the Drapers' Hall.[3] Sir Thomas More, speaking of the pleasure Edward gave by this gay hunting party, remarks that nothing the king had done for many a day "gat him either more hearts or more hearty favour among the common people, which oftentimes more esteem and take for greater kindness a little courtesy than a great benefit."[4] Yet evidently the Londoners, though flattered and pleased, were not without a suspicion that the king had a canny reason for his graciousness. "The cause of which bounty thus showed by the king," remarks Fabyan," was, as most men took it, for that the mayor was a merchant of wondrous adventures into many and sundry countries, by reason whereof the king had yearly of him notable sums of money for his customs, beside other pleasures that he showed to the king before times."[5] So most of the king's guests had probably paid heavily in advance for the "well-seasoned meat" and the bountiful wines which were set before them, and very likely they found it necessary to pay again when the feast was over. For why the king was still in London on 10 July, instead of on his way north, it is hard to see, unless he was finding his money campaign a more serious undertaking than the military one Gloucester was conducting. Luckily, however, Gloucester was able to hold

---

1. Rymer, XII, 140; Lesley, 45.
2. Rymer, XII, 141.
3. Kingsford's *London Chron.*, 189; Privy Seals.
4. More, *Hist. of Richard III*, 3.
5. Fabyan, 667.

his own, although not to advance into Scotland, without the king's help, and Howard's fleet, and perhaps Milord's also, kept the Scots pretty well frightened. Early in July Edward wrote to Howard that he was sending Sir John Elryngton, the treasurer of his household, to Newcastle to see that the ships which had been sent north with supplies were put in order to go with the fleet "to brenne the Leith and other villages along the Scottish sea," and not long after Howard appeared in the Firth of Forth again, though this time, as his enemies were on the lookout for him, he was able to do little or no damage.[1]

Another thing which may have helped to detain Edward in London was the still unfinished state of his negotiations with Maximilian. Louis XI's summons to a better world did not come as soon as some persons had evidently been hoping it would, and some time before 1 July Maximilian, because there seemed to be nothing else to do, prolonged his truce with him once more, this time for a year.[2] There was even renewed talk of a peace conference, at St Quentin. Nevertheless, Maximilian's desire to see an English army land in France was undiminished, and Pierre Puissant soon arrived in London to say that the duke wished to send another embassy to continue the negotiations already begun. But though Edward was glad to go on with the negotiations, he advised delay partly on the ground that his councillors had dispersed and partly because he thought he might be able to go over to Calais about Michaelmas and talk with Maximilian in person, if the duke could meet him there at that time; and Maximilian, who was delighted at the prospect of a personal interview with the king of England, sent Puissant back to England immediately after he reached home to tell Edward that he would gladly go to Calais to meet him.[3]

Would Maximilian have been quite so affable if he had known that even at this moment Edward was receiving advances from Louis with evident signs of pleasure? Hearing that a journey he had made to Normandy in June had started

---

1. *Household Books of the Duke of Norfolk*, 274; Lesley, 45. Howard's second appearance in the Firth must have occurred before the middle of August, as he seems to have returned to Harwich by 17 August. Lesley, it is true, speaks as if Howard's second raid occurred after James had disbanded his army, but he does not always stick to the correct sequence of events.

2. Commynes-Lenglet, IV, 71-72.

3. See the instructions Maximilian gave to Puissant, probably in August, and also a little later. Commynes-Lenglet, IV, 38-40. Many of the valuable documents printed by Lenglet are not given in chronological order, and it takes careful study to determine the proper sequence.

in England the old story that he was planning to attack Calais, Louis wrote to Lord Hastings to explain the innocent reason for his visit to Normandy and to request him to assure Edward that he had never thought of touching so much as "the least village of the land of Calais."[1] And Edward, though he had every reason to discount this message of goodwill, pretended to accept it at its face value and sent to France, if not an embassy, at least Hastings Pursuivant with a couple of horses which were taken from his stables at Windsor and which in all probability were intended as a gratuitous addition to Louis' stud.[2] And how quick Louis was to reward him! On 14 August Pierre le Roy appeared in London again, after a whole year's absence, and presented his English Majesty with twenty-five thousand crowns, the Easter instalment of his pension.[3]

Even when September came, Edward did not go north. Instead, he made a stay of a fortnight or more at Woodstock, whence, at the invitation of the Bishop of Winchester, he went over to Oxford to inspect Magdalen College, the magnificent new college of the bishop's foundation.[4] In the meantime Pierre Puissant arrived once more, bringing word that Maximilian was holding himself in readiness to go to Calais and also that the princes of the Empire, anxious to see peace restored between France and Burgundy, had suggested the holding of a conference at Metz on the first Monday in December, but that Maximilian, though he thought he ought to send ambassadors to this conference, since the king of France was going to do so, would keep his promise to make no treaty with Louis without first consulting Edward.[5] But Edward could not go to Calais. If he went anywhere, he must join his army on the Scottish border, according to his announced intention, and sometime after 22 September he did actually start for the north, though only to stop half way, just as he had done on so many similar occasions in the early years of his reign. He remained at Nottingham Castle from 1 October

---

1. *Lettres de Louis XI*, IX, 52.
2. Account Book of John Cheyne, master of the horse, 21-22 Edw. IV, Exchequer Accounts, Equitium Regis, bundle 107, no. 15. Lord Howard sent a "gray nag" to Louis somewhat later. *Household Books of the Duke of Norfolk*, 181. According to the *Chronique Scandaleuse*, II, 105-106, Louis received an embassy from Edward at this time. But probably Hastings Pursuivant was the only ambassador.
3. For Edward's receipt, see French Roll 21 Edw. IV, m. 9. Rymer prints it (XII, 145) but gives the date incorrectly as 24 August.
4. Chandler, *Life of Wayneflete*, 150-152.
5. Commynes-Lenglet, IV, 39-40.

until about the 20th, and then returned, by way of Fotheringhay, to London.[1]

In a long letter written to Sixtus IV a year later, Edward stated that it was "adverse turmoil" which prevented him from leading his army into Scotland;[2] and as such a confession cannot have been pleasant to make, we may believe that he spoke the truth. His attempt to exact payment of the three quarters of a fifteenth and tenth reluctantly renounced in 1475, added to a very bad harvest which caused a terrible dearth of corn in the following winter, had apparently tried the patience of his subjects too far, and he found it necessary to look after the safety of his own throne instead of trying to overthrow that of his neighbour James. He had some ground, however, for believing that he had extracted the fangs of his enemy by other means than fighting, as while he was at Nottingham, he had renewed the treaty signed with Louis on 21 July 1477, that is, the treaty insuring the continuance of the truce between England and France as long as both he and Louis lived and for one year after the death of whichever one of them should die first.[3] Louis had already signed his renewal of this treaty on 28 September, and from that day forth, though James III wrote many a letter to the French king asking for aid against their common foe, the English, he "got nane answer."[4]

The renewal of the treaty of 1477, which Louis had evidently paid for with a promise to have nothing more to do with the Scots, was as good as a renunciation on Edward's part of the agreements he had forced the Bishop of Elne to sign. But Edward did not offer any renunciation of the other demands he had been making of Louis, and though Louis may have avoided giving any promise about Princess Elizabeth's dowry, at least he seems to have given fresh assurances that the Dauphin would marry her.[5] Louis had had another stroke of apoplexy in September, and he was now living in terror

---

1. Privy Seals. On 20 October, at Nottingham, a gray gelding, a present from the Duke of Gloucester, was added to the number of the king's horses. Exchequer Accounts, Equitium Regis, *ut sup*. This may mean that Gloucester came to meet his brother at Nottingham.
2. *Cal. Venetian Papers*, I, 145.
3. Warrants under the Signet, file 1390, 19 Oct. 21 Edw. IV; French Roll 21 Edw. IV, m. 12-13. It is singular that everyone seems to have overlooked the fact that Rymer (XII, 46) has printed the treaty of 21 July 1477, from this renewal of it by Edward in 1481. Even Hardy, when preparing his syllabus of the *Foedera*, slipped into the error of placing the document under the date of 25 October 1477, instead of 25 October 1481.
4. Palgrave, *Cely Papers*, III, 32; *Acts of Parl. of Scotland*, II, 140.
5. Commynes, II, 57.

of death; but let no one think for a moment that his preparations for the final trumpet-call included a purging of his soul of evil intentions towards his neighbours. At the beginning of November, while he was recuperating under Philip de Commynes' roof, he wrote to one of his councillors that he had had word from Normandy that the English army was "broken for this year," and, after giving this welcome piece of news, remarked sweetly that he intended to spend his time killing wild boars until he could kill Englishmen instead.[1]

Although Edward went back to London without reaching the scene of the fighting, Gloucester, still assisted by the Earl of Northumberland, continued to wage a vigorous war against the Scots, and on 29 October the clergy of the northern province, following the example set by the convocation of Canterbury in the spring, granted a tenth for the defence of the kingdom.[2] Nevertheless, the great invasion of Scotland had to be postponed until another year. Berwick was besieged by land and sea all winter long, but it was not captured, and on the whole the Scots came out of the year's fighting with quite as many victories to their credit as the English, if again we may accept the testimony of Lesley, who says that "the borderers of Scotland invaded the marches of England and took away many preys of goods and destroyed many towns and led many persons in Scotland."[3] King James himself seems to have boasted, in letters sent to Rome and elsewhere, that, in addition to destroying some of the English border strongholds, he had put to flight an army of two hundred thousand men.[4] Yet the real truth seems to be that James not only did not put to flight two hundred thousand Englishmen, but that he allowed himself to be cheated out of a great opportunity. To judge from all accounts, he had assembled a powerful army, and if it was true that Edward's subjects were showing signs of rebellion, a sudden dash across the border might have carried him through Gloucester's lines and enabled him to raise the siege of Berwick and perhaps play havoc in the northern counties of England. But no such dash did James make. On the contrary, he tamely disbanded his army, and the story subsequently told to the Scottish parliament was that, "at the request and monitions of our Holy Father the

1. *Lettres de Louis XI*, IX, 89.
2. Wilkins, III, 614; Wake, 381; Fine Roll 21 Edw. IV, m. 3.
3. Lesley, 45.
4. See Edward's letter to Sixtus already cited.

Pope's bulls, shown to him in the time," he "scaled his great host in hope and trust that his enemies should have been in likewise obedient to our Holy Father."[1] Lesley's tale is that the Pope's bull commanded James, on pain of interdiction, to stop fighting, so that all Christian princes could prepare a great army with which to put down the Turks, that the bull was "sent from a cardinal legate being resident in England for the time" and brought by one of Edward's own messengers, and that after James had thus been persuaded to lay down his arms, Edward shamelessly sent his fleet against the firth of Inchkeith, where he was repulsed, as he deserved to be.[2]

There is no English account of the events of the war between England and Scotland during the year 1481 with which the Scottish one can be compared and tested, and the English records, which are more than usually scanty for that year, throw not a particle of light on the reason for James's strange action. Unless new facts come to light to disprove Lesley's story, we must conclude that Sixtus, led to believe, by the letter Edward had written to him in May, that the king of England would actually "turn his whole might to the assistance of the Roman church" if only his hands were not bound by the war he was carrying on with Scotland, tried to restore peace between the English and the Scots, and that Edward deliberately availed himself of the Pope's interference to, trap the too trusting James. Yet Sixtus cannot have held Edward guilty of any grave fault, for in the following spring he sent him a sword and a cap of maintenance which were presented with much ceremony on St George's Day.[3] It is also to be noted that in another letter concerning Scotland which Edward wrote to Sixtus in the summer of 1482 and in which he reviewed briefly the events of the previous year, he makes no reference to any attempt by the Pope to end the war between him and his neighbours. Much less does he offer any excuse for any failure on his part to keep faith either with James or with Sixtus himself.[4]

After the king's return from the north, a report appears to have gone abroad that parliament was to be summoned.[5] But if Edward really contemplated calling a parliament, he soon changed his mind. The war with

---

1. *Acts of Parl. of Scotland*, II, 138.
2. Lesley, *ut sup.*
3. Beltz, lxxiii-lxxiv. Cf. Ross, *Hist. Regum Angliæ*, 211.
4. *Cal. Venetian Papers, ut sup.*
5. *Cely Papers*, 81.

Scotland was not going so well that it would be a pleasure for him to meet the Lords and Commons, and even at the risk of more "adverse turmoil," he preferred to go on raising the money he needed by illegal shifts. However, if the king did not come riding to Westminster to open parliament, there was a spectacle of a different sort for the people of London to gaze upon, to wit, the funeral of the little maiden who, less than three years ago, had been married with so much pomp and splendour to the king's second son. "My young lady of York" died some time before 26 November,[1] and the king, who had one reason, if no more, to feel grief at the death of his little daughter-in-law, as the great estates she had inherited now passed out of his own control into that of the Howard and Berkeley families, sent three barges to Gravesend to escort her body to Westminster Abbey. The interment took place in the chapel of St Erasmus, and as it cost the king £215 16s 10d, there must have been almost as much display at Anne Mowbray's burial as at her wedding.[2]

---

1. *Cely Papers*, 79.
2. Dugdale, I, 531; Tellers' Roll, Mich. 22 Edw. IV; Warrants for Issues, 22 Edw. IV, 21 Jan. During the parliament held in the last months of Edward's reign, Viscount Berkeley was induced to surrender his claims on the Mowbray estates to the Duke of York, but they were to return to him in case both the duke and his father, the king, died without male issue, as they soon did. *Rolls of Parl.*, VI, 205-206.

8

GLOUCESTER INVADES SCOTLAND

About the time of Anne Mowbray's funeral, Edward went to Southampton and Winchester to make a stay of some length, which may have been occasioned by local disturbances in that neighbourhood.[1] Then he returned to Windsor to keep "a royal Christmas" and to distribute his usual "year's gifts," which consisted on this occasion of a cup of gold, a cross of gold set with diamonds, four rings with "tables" of diamonds, "a square salt with a covering," a pair of large gilt flagons, more than a dozen gilt bowls, two large pots, and twenty-three standing cups.[2] Almost before the Christmas festivities were over, however, he was obliged to turn his attention to very serious matters, as embassies from Burgundy and France arrived almost simultaneously and the uncomfortable problem of how he was to satisfy Maximilian and yet avoid a rupture with Louis confronted him once more.

Doctor Morton was at the French court at this time negotiating about certain "difficulties,"[3] and it was probably to reply to some of the questions he had raised that the present embassy from the French king came, though just who the ambassadors were and just what instructions Louis had given them it is impossible to say. All that can be stated with certainty is that the Frenchmen completed their mission some time before the end of January and then went home in two "passengers of Dover," which Edward ordered to transport them to Boulogne and which were convoyed by a third ship full of armed soldiers.[4] But it cannot have been an unpleasant message that

1. Privy Seals; *Cal. Patent Rolls*, III, 263—a commission to the Marquis of Dorset and others to inquire into escapes of felons, etc., in the county of Southampton.
2. Stow, 433; Warrants for Issues, 21 Edw. IV, 4 Feb.
3. *Lettres de Louis XI*, IX, 139-140.
4. Tellers' Roll, Easter 22 Edw. IV.

Edward received from Louis, as outward harmony had reigned between the two kings since Pierre le Roy's visit to London in August and as Louis made known on 27 January that, at the request of his very dear and very beloved brother and cousin, the king of England, he had granted his said brother and cousin the privilege of purchasing in the city and port of Rouen, through his servant, William Lanarroc, fifty tuns of wine for the use of his household and of exporting the same to England without paying customs.[1]

Just because he was on such good terms with Louis, Edward found it anything but easy and comfortable to meet Maximilian's ambassadors. He had never confessed to the duke that he had renewed his long truce with Louis, but Maximilian had heard enough from some source to excite his suspicion, and although the nominal errand of the Burgundian ambassadors who reached England in the early days of January, and who must have met and glared at Louis' ambassadors in the streets of London, was to convey Maximilian's answer to the new demands Edward had made through the Prince of Orange regarding the projected invasion of France and the bond for the payment of the pension he was to receive from the duke, their real one was to find out just how matters stood between the kings of England and France.[2] Even now, however, though he feared the worst, and feared it more every day, poor Maximilian could not bring himself to believe that Edward was only cheating him with promises and that all hope of the alliance with England which he so longed for was actually dead. The instructions the duke had given to his ambassadors—the Count of Chimay, who had been in England with the Prince of Orange and who was to go on to Brittany when he had completed the negotiations with Edward, Guy de Rochefort, Seigneur de Labergement, and Antoine de Branges, another former companion of the Prince of Orange—show that, while his heart was sick with hope deferred,

---

1. Legrand coll., MS. français 6989, f. 3. William Lanarroc may probably be identified with William Lanerolz, mentioned in the letter Edward wrote to Louis on 17 May. See later.

2. Maximilian's instructions to his ambassadors are to be found in Commynes-Lenglet, IV, 20-25. They are not dated, but the references they contain to the conference with the princes of the Empire at Metz and to Maximilian's intention to send the Cardinal of Tournai to Rome, coupled with the letter Edward wrote to the Pope on 12 January about the cardinal, fix their date as the very end of December or the very beginning of January. It may be added that some special instructions given to the Count of Chimay (Commynes-Lenglet, IV, 25-30), who was to proceed from England to Brittany, contain a reference to "feu François Monsieur," the second son of Mary and Maximilian, who died on 26 December 1481.

he was still eager to offer concessions, if by so doing anything could be gained. To promise that the bond for the payment of the pension of fifty thousand crowns should be renewed each time the conditions were fulfilled by the king of England seemed to him supererogatory, but since King Edward desired such a promise, he would give it. He would also, in spite of the fact that no such requirement had been mentioned in the beginning, bind his heirs as well as himself to support Edward and his heirs if Edward commenced an invasion of France, although he insisted that he must not be asked to commit himself to that extent until Edward had won the crown of France and had brought across the sea an army capable of conquering the kingdom. Only when it came to Edward's demand that the estates of his dominions should confirm the agreement concerning the pension within six months did the duke stiffen perceptibly. That he dared not promise. Yet he said that, God helping him, he would arrange to have the confirmation given within two years, the time named in the treaty; and while he begged Edward to be content with this, he threw out the suggestion that if the king would give him some assistance, that is, some recognizable assistance, his subjects might be more willing to grant the confirmation immediately.

Maximilian did not leave any doubt about the kind of help he hoped the king of England would see that it was wise to give him. For again he urged with all the earnestness he was capable of that France must be invaded, not sometime in the distant future, but this very year, and also that Edward must not fail to send him the five or six thousand men he had promised to let him have in case he needed them. And if the worst had happened, if his ambassadors found that the dreadful report that the king of England had signed a new truce with the king of France was really true, they were to point out to Edward that such a truce meant his, Maximilian's, "totale ruine et destruction." In addition, they were to remind the king of all the promises he had made and all the hopes which Maximilian and his people had built on them, to entreat him to have some consideration for the necessities of one who had placed all his trust in him and had looked upon him as a father, and to admonish him that any promises he had received from the king of France would be worthless if he let Maximilian perish or be forced into an agreement with Louis. The duke's ambassadors were also charged not to fail to find out just what were the terms of the new truce between the kings of England and France, if such a truce there was; and if Edward began to talk to them about the truce, they were to tell him that their instructions did not cover that subject, as their duke had no definite information about the truce and could not believe that the king of England would agree to such a thing without his knowledge, and then to beg him to take no further steps concerning it until their duke had had time to consider the matter and to let him know his decision.

The harassed duke realized, however, that neither reproaches nor warnings from him would avail anything if Edward had really signed a new truce with Louis. If such a truce existed, the most he could hope for was that it would still be Edward's pleasure to act the part of mediator between him and Louis. Even for that help he would be very thankful now, especially as the recent conference at Metz, as he sent word to Edward, had come to naught through the non-appearance of Louis' representatives. If the subject of mediation was mentioned, therefore, Maximilian wanted his ambassadors to inform the king of England that, if Louis would restore to him the county of Burgundy and what he had robbed him of in Artois, he would agree to place all other matters of dispute between them "en connoisance," so that a truce or peace might be arranged. Finally, almost humbly he asked for a small favour. It was a painful memory to him that three years ago Italy had seen Edward acting in concert with Louis and in more or less opposition to him and his imperial father, and in the hope of wiping out the impression which might have remained in the minds of those who had seen only the outside of things at that time, that the king of England was in alliance with the king of France against him, he entreated Edward to intrust to the Cardinal of Tournai, whom he was about to send to Rome, any business he might have at the papal court. He hoped that the Duke of Brittany also would make use of the cardinal's services[1] and thus lead the world to conclude not only that it was a mistake to suppose that the kings of France and England were in league, but that the old alliance of England, Burgundy, and Brittany had come to life again. It was a mere straw, but what did Maximilian have to cling to in these days except straws?

And yet the duke had one good card in his hand, and he played it with some skill. The king of Scotland, he gave Edward to understand, had recently sent an ambassador, a bishop, to him with an offer of a close alliance and a

---

1. Commynes-Lenglet, IV, 30.

request for some bombards and other engines of war, but, out of the singular love he bore to the king of England, whom he knew to be at war with the king of Scotland, he had not only resisted all the inducements the bishop had held out to him, but had expressed a wish to do anything he could to restore peace between England and Scotland. Of course there was danger that Edward would recall how he had had to take his friend Maximilian to task not so very long ago for being too friendly with the ruler of Scotland, but, even if he did, he was not likely to overlook the fact that England would be placed in a very uncomfortable position if by anything he did or left undone Maximilian should be led to enter into a league with James III. An alliance between Burgundy and Scotland which was hostile to England would be no less of a disaster than the alliance between France and Scotland which had been for so long a period one of England's worst trials. For Edward personally it would be even more unfortunate, as it would condemn in the eyes of his people his whole foreign policy.

Edward was, indeed, in a predicament, and for the moment he did nothing except to try in every way to conceal from Maximilian's ambassadors the true state of his relations with Louis and to seize upon the easy means which the duke's request concerning the Cardinal of Tournai gave him to prove his friendship for Burgundy. On 12 January he wrote a letter to the Pope in which he said he loved the Cardinal of Tournai both for his virtues and for the services he had rendered him, especially at the time of the marriage of his sister to the late Duke Charles, and that he desired to intrust to him all his own and his subjects' interests at Rome.[1] Yet sooner or later Maximilian had to be given an answer of some sort, and in February Montgomery and Coke were sent to Flanders, not to say that the king of England still hoped to invade France, for that was too palpably untrue, but to suggest that probably the best thing Maximilian could do was to accept another truce with Louis. Edward offered his aid in obtaining such a truce and repeated his old promise of help in case Louis refused to make a just settlement. He also sent Langton to France, perhaps to make an honest attempt to mitigate Maximilian's woes.[2] But the duke found all this rather cold comfort.

---

1. *Cal. Venetian Papers*, I, 144.
2. Tellers' Roll, Easter 22 Edw. IV; Commynes-Lenglet, IV, 40-43. Coke cannot have remained in Flanders long, as he helped to negotiate the treaty with Guipuscoa early in March. Langton went to France in February.

Other foreign envoys besides those from France and Burgundy came to the English court in the first months of 1482. During the past summer Bernard de la Forsse and Arnold Trussell had gone to Guipuscoa with a commission to treat for a new treaty of mercantile intercourse with that province and for the redress of past breaches of the truce;[1] and now Sebastian de Olacabal and other Guipuscoans arrived to sign the treaty. On 9 March, after Olacabal had been promised ten pounds a year from the customs collected in the port of London as long as the peace between the kings of England and Castile endured, the treaty was sealed; and a few days later, probably in Olacabal's company, Bernard de la Forsse, Trussell, and Henry Aynesworth, one of the men who had helped to draw up the treaty, set out for the court of Ferdinand and Isabella.[2] These three ambassadors were to renew the negotiations for the marriage of Princess Katharine and John, son of Ferdinand and Isabella, and to smooth their way Edward placed in Trussell's hands a thousand pounds in money "to be employed within the realm of Spain according to our commandment" and "three whole cloths of scarlet and two cloths of green" which were to be bestowed on "the constable and other lords of Spain."[3]

But if Edward still hankered, as it seems he did, for a marriage alliance with Ferdinand and Isabella, it was not for the old reason. He no longer cherished any dreams of invading Guienne with the help of allies from beyond the Pyrenees, and when his three ambassadors had departed for Spain with his thousand pounds and his cloths of scarlet and green, he turned to greet that ever welcome visitor, Pierre le Roy. On 16 March he received from Le Roy Louis' usual dole of twenty-five thousand crowns, and soon after the "argentier of Rouen," like the French ambassadors who had gone home in January, was carefully conducted across the sea to Boulogne.[4] Perchance Le Roy had as a fellow traveller on his homeward journey

---

1. Rymer, XII, 150. They seem to have taken with them, as a peace offering, grants of annuities of twenty pounds each to the grand pretor of Guipuscoa and the provost of the town of San Sebastian. French Roll 21 Edw. IV, m. 15.
2. Rymer, XII, 346, 147, 148-153; *Cal. Patent Rolls*, III, 258.
3. Warrants for Issues, 22 Edw. IV, 6 and 10 March. The marriage of Katharine and John never took place. In 1495 Katharine married Sir William Courtenay, afterwards Earl of Devonshire. She lived until 1527. Sandford; Nicolas, *Wardrobe Accounts of Edw. IV*, xxiv-xxix.
4. Rymer, XII, 153; Tellers' Roll, *ut sup*.

Hastings Pursuivant, who, also on 16 March, again received into his care two horses from the royal stables—sorrel ones this time—which he was to take to France and present to someone whose name is not recorded but who was probably the head of the house of Valois.[1]

If the Count of Chimay and his colleagues had built any hopes on the fact that Edward had sent Langton to France, those hopes must have been rudely shaken if they were still in London when Pierre le Roy arrived there, and if they knew for what purpose the Frenchman had come. And even if they had left the English capital before Le Roy's arrival, Pierre Puissant must have been there, as sometime in March Maximilian, depressed by the lukewarmness of the encouragement Montgomery and Coke had brought him but still unwilling to give up, sent this faithful servant to deliver—or to tell the Count of Chimay, if he had not already gone to Brittany, to deliver—one more message to Edward.[2]

To Edward's suggestion that he should accept a truce with Louis, Maximilian now replied that it would be to the advantage neither of himself nor of his people for him to make another truce with the French king. Yet, since the king of England, whose advice he esteemed so highly, recommended such a truce, he would accept one of three or four years' duration if Edward could arrange it on certain terms; that is, if it was "marchande et communicative," if the subjects of both signatories were permitted to keep their property without swearing allegiance to the prince in control, if all troops, with the exception of some guards of foot soldiers, were withdrawn from the frontiers, and lastly, if Edward himself was made conservator of the truce and promised, in case the truce was broken, to aid the injured party, which, it went without saying, would be Maximilian. But even after telling Edward this, the duke went on repeating in a mechanical sort of way his old plea that France ought to be invaded and Louis punished, and his old entreaty that Edward would give him assistance openly and in his own name. As Louis' army was ready for action and might attack him before a truce could be negotiated, he thought the least Edward could do was to send him immediately enough money for the wages of three thousand

1. Exchequer Accounts, Equitium Regis, bundle 107, no. 15.
2. Maximilian's instructions to Puissant on this occasion may be found in Commynes-Lenglet, IV, 40-42. Again they are undated, but the reference to the peace conference about to take place at Arras proves that they belong to March 1482. Cf. Maximilian's instructions to his ambassadors going to Arras. *Ibid.*, IV, 71.

soldiers for three months. And as, even if a truce with Louis were arranged, he would have to maintain garrisons on his frontiers, he also thought Edward ought to help him to pay those garrisons and to compensate his subjects in the territories Louis had seized. He had to make the usual confession that he was negotiating, or about to negotiate, with Louis. Once more a peace conference had been proposed, to be held at Arras this time, and he had decided to send representatives to it. It was not, however, by choice that he was doing this, but in part to keep Louis' army from descending on him and in part because he was afraid the burghers of Ghent, who were trying to open peace negotiations with the French king on their own account, would do something to his prejudice. And nothing, he declared, should be done without Edward's knowledge.

Maximilian scarcely owed Edward an apology for contemplating further direct negotiations with Louis. Even if Edward had not signed a new truce with Louis, as rumour said, he had been given more than due warning of what Maximilian would be compelled to do if his friends did not succour him, and yet, in the face of that, the king had practically told the Count of Chimay that Maximilian must not count on aid from him at present. It was his desire, Edward had assured the count, to keep his engagements with the Duke of Austria, but as his war with Scotland made it impossible for him either to invade France or to send the duke the troops he had promised him, he was still of the opinion that the wisest thing the duke could do was to make a truce, "marchande et communicative," with the French king for a couple of years or so and then wait for Louis' death, which was evidently going to occur soon. Only two promises had the count been able to secure. If Louis declined to sign a truce and invaded Maximilian's territories, or if he signed a truce and afterwards broke it, then Edward would send the duke the five thousand soldiers he had engaged to let him have: and if Louis agreed to a truce, as Edward thought he would, Edward would give the duke some money every year while the truce lasted to help satisfy—in other words, to help preserve the loyalty—of Maximilian's subjects in the lands now occupied by Louis. But the exact sum he would give the king was not prepared to state, as that would be determined by the condition of his affairs at the time and also by what was done by the Duke of Brittany, who, it seemed to him, ought to be willing to do more for Maximilian than he did, since Francis's interests too were at stake and he was not burdened with any war. Lastly, the king had told the count that, as he would like to give his sister the honour and satisfaction of concluding negotiations in which she had had a hand from the beginning, he would send some ambassadors to Maximilian and the Duchess Margaret who should accompany the count when he went home after his return from Brittany.[1]

But what were such promises from Edward worth? They had scarcely been given when, on the last day of March, a French embassy, headed by Étienne Pascual, one of Louis' councillors, reached London to be "worshipfully received with the mayor and all the crafts" of the city and to spend more than two months in lodgings provided for them at the Wardrobe.[2] Of course it was possible that Edward's reason for receiving Louis' ambassadors so cordially was that their coming afforded him a good opportunity to plead Maximilian's cause, but unfortunately, even if that were the case, no gains accrued to the duke. Moreover, as if his cup of sorrow were not already quite too full, at this moment Fate dealt the duke a terrible blow. On 27 March Mary of Burgundy died from the effects of a fall from her horse, and, in addition to his grief at the loss of his wife, the duke had the humiliation of finding himself practically in the power of the Flemings, who had never liked him and who now gave free expression to their hostility. Coke, who appears to have been at the Burgundian court when Mary's death occurred, hurried home, probably to seek advice; but when he returned, at the end of April,[3] he brought the bereaved duke no aid, and the estates of Flanders, declaring that Maximilian was unfit to direct the affairs of his children, handed his son and daughter over to the custody of the citizens of Ghent, who at once fulfilled his fears by opening communication with Louis in an effort to secure a treaty of peace for their young charges.[4]

The burghers of Ghent may not have been guided by the highest motives, for Louis had plenty of pensioners among them; but, after all, was not the course they were taking the only wise one? Was not a treaty of peace with the king of France the only possible solution of Burgundy's difficulties? Single-handed, Maximilian would never be a match for Louis, and to go on

---

1. Commynes-Lenglet, III, 616-617.

2. *Cely Papers*, 90; *Lettres de Louis XI*, VII, 127, note; Tellers' Roll, Easter 22 Edw. IV.

3. On 26 April Edward ordered that £40 should be paid to Coke because he was sending him on an embassy to the Duke of Austria. Warrants for Issues, 22 Edw. IV, 26 April.

4. Legeay, II, 442; *Lettres de Louis XI*, IX, 221-223.

looking for help from England, the only source from which efficient help could come, was evidently sheer folly. Even if Edward had not sold himself to Louis again, as there was so much reason to think, his war with Scotland, by his own confession, tied his hands.

During the latter part of the winter Edward had spent a good deal of time at the Tower,[1] where he was occupied with all the details of army equipment. "The great new gun of brass" was "shot at Mile End that was made in the Tower and it burst all to pieces" was the sad news reported by Richard Cely one day at the end of March,[2] But the destruction of one of his new guns was as nothing compared with the king's financial worries. Considerable sums of money were still coming in from the benevolence, but in February ten thousand marks had to be sent to the Duke of Gloucester for the defence of the West march and £456 13s 4d to the Earl of Northumberland, the residue of two thousand marks which the earl had been assigned for the defence of the east and middle marches; and as many other calls for large amounts of money were inevitable, the benevolence had to be pieced out with loans.[3] The question of where the necessary food for the army was to come from was also a very serious one, as the bad harvest of the preceding summer had produced an appalling scarcity of all kinds of grain, a scarcity from which not only England but her enemy, Scotland, and nearly the whole of western Europe was suffering in about equal measure.[4] On 21 February Gloucester was authorized to purchase two thousand quarters of wheat and a thousand quarters of barley, rye, oats, mixtelyn, beans, and peas for the victualling of the west marches in any place or places in England, Wales, or Ireland,[5] but he must have had to look long and pay a large price for what he wanted. In Ireland he would certainly find little or nothing in the way of such supplies, both because the necessaries of life were running so short there

---

1. Privy Seals.
2. *Cely Papers*, 88.
3. Warrants for Issues, 21 Edw. IV, 20 Feb. (two warrants of the same date); Tellers' and Receipt Rolls, Easter and Mich., 22 Edw. IV.
4. Chron. printed in Pinkerton, *Hist. of Scotland*, I, 503; *Chronique Scandaleuse*, II, 111-112. There was also a scarcity of wine in Europe, as the intense cold of the winter of 1480-1481 had killed most of the vines in France and Germany. *Chron. Scandaleuse*, II, 104-105; Basin (who makes a mistake in the year), III, 60.
5. Writs of Privy Seal, file 880, no. 5513. Cf. *Cal. Patent Rolls*, III, 254.

that in March Cork and Waterford were granted permission to buy wheat, beans, peas, and malt in south-western England and the Welsh marches, and because a commission had already been issued to the Earl of Kildare and others to take ten thousand quarters of wheat in Ireland for the army.[1] And in England wheat was worth more than twelve shillings a quarter and other corn was equally "dear."[2]

There are some indications that to the king's anxieties during the winter was added the fear of more "adverse turmoil." In Northumberland and Yorkshire there must have been disturbances of some sort, as at the beginning of March Gloucester was empowered to grant the royal pardon to any persons in the lordship and liberty of Tyndale who would submit to the king before St John's Day and was also given, together with the Earl of Northumberland and others, a commission of oyer and terminer in the county of York. We learn, too, that in the city of York certain persons who had offended by ringing the common bell, perhaps to call their fellow malcontents together, were imprisoned by the city's officers until orders should be received from "the right high and mighty prince, the Duke of Gloucester." That conditions were far from satisfactory in the duchy of Lancaster as well is shown by a decision by the council of the duchy on 4 May that the "great strifes, variances, controversies, and debates" which had long continued in the duchy without punishment could be remedied "by no person but only by the king himself, if it would like his Grace to come into those parties."[3] Lastly, in the summer one Piers Fillow obtained a licence from the king to export two thousand weyes of beans and as many pipes of beer without paying duties because he had "opened certain treason committed against us by certain persons, in the proving whereof he hath sustained great charges and costs."[4]

However, if Edward had much to contend with, one piece of good luck came his way. About the end of April a very valuable recruit joined his ranks. It was now almost three years since James III's brother, the Duke of Albany, had fled to France, where Louis not only had made him welcome, but had provided him with a wife, Anne de la Tour, daughter of the Count

---

1. French Roll 22 Edw. IV, m. 18, 19; Signed Bills, file 1520, no. 5298.
2. Nicolas's *London Chron.*, 147; *Cely Papers*, 128.
3. Signed Bills, file 1521, no. 5315; *Cal. Patent Rolls*, III, 343; Davies, *York Records*, 126; *Duchy of Lancaster, Entry Books of Decrees and Orders*, Vol. I, 62.
4. Warrants under the Signet, file 1391, 20 July 22 Edw. IV.

of Boulogne and Auvergne. But since the failure of his effort to restore
peace between Albany and James—the effort under cloak of which he had
worked to bring about the present rupture between the kings of England
and Scotland—Louis had apparently given Albany little thought, and it may
have been a part of the bargain he had made with Edward at the time of the
renewal of their truce in the autumn of 1481 that Edward should be at liberty
to try to draw Albany into his service. At all events, Edward dispatched
a "secret person" to France to interview Albany, and he offered the duke,
together with a six months' safeconduct for himself and twenty attendants,[1] a
promise that he should be recognized as king of Scotland if he would aid in
driving James from his throne. With unhesitating alacrity Albany accepted
this offer, and very soon, no doubt with the connivance, if not with the frank
consent, of Louis, whose ambassadors were still imbibing Edward's wine at
the Wardrobe and continued to do so until sometime in June,[2] he was *en
route* to Southampton in a Scottish carvel called the *Michael*. Edward gave
Sir John Cheyne, his master of the horse, the task of welcoming Albany upon
his arrival, and on 25 April "Bayard Kyldare," a recent present to the king
from the Earl of Kildare and now destined to be the king's first gift to his new
ally, was led out of the royal stables to make the journey to Southampton
along with twenty other horses of less noble lineage which Sir John had
hired for the use of Albany's attendants.[3]

Sir John Cheyne was not the only person who was waiting at Southampton
to do honour to the Duke of Albany when the Michael brought him safely
into port, as a number of the "gentlemen of the country" also hastened
thither to pay their respects to the brother of the king of Scotland. Nor was
Bayard Kyldare the only gift presented when the duke had landed. For a
reward of a hundred pounds was divided among the soldiers and mariners
of the *Michael*, with such happy effect on her master, James Douglas, that
he immediately engaged to serve the king of England at sea for eight weeks
with one hundred soldiers. But there is never a rose without some thorns,

---

1. Warrants for Issues, 22 Edw. IV, 10 Nov., with schedule enclosed; Signed Bills, file
1521, no. 5345.
2. One John Frysley was paid £26 13s 4d for the travelling expenses of the French
ambassadors going from London to Dover in the month of June. Tellers' Roll, Easter
22 Edw. IV.
3. Exchequer Accounts, Equitium Regis, bundle 107, no. 15.

and not only did the king of England have to pay for the return of thirty-two of the *Michael's* mariners to Normandy, but he had to give forty shillings to a couple of Spanish merchants who had been robbed by Albany's servants. These, however, were mere trifles. No matter how many mariners had to be shipped back to France or how many outraged merchants had to be appeased with small gifts, Albany was a more than welcome guest, and by 2 May he was in London, residing in the house in Thames Street which Margaret of York had occupied during her visit to England two years before.[1]

Why the Duke of Albany had come to England everyone knew or could guess, and on 10 May a royal proclamation ordered every man who had indented to go with the king to Scotland to be ready to do so on fourteen days' notice.[2] It was now expected that the king would proceed to the north on the Tuesday in Whitsunday week, but instead he started out in the middle of May for Dover, where a fleet with which Robert Radcliff was expected to emulate the gallant deeds performed by Lord Howard in the preceding summer was probably being assembled; and on the 17th, while he was stopping at Canterbury, he indited a brief letter to the king of France. "Monsieur my Cousin," wrote Edward, "I recommend me to you as much as I may. I have given orders to my faithful servant, William Lanerolz, who is at present over there, to ask you for the payment which is due to me for the term of Easter last past; and I pray you, Monsieur my Cousin, please to send it with all good diligence possible, letting me know if there is anything I can do for you, as I should do it most willingly, with the help of Our Lord, who, Monsieur my Cousin, have you ever in His very holy keeping. Written at Canterbury, the 17th day of May. Your good cousin, Edward R."[3]

But what Edward wanted from Louis at this moment was not so much his twenty-five thousand crowns, though he wanted them badly enough,

---

1. For the above details concerning Albany's arrival, see Tellers' Roll, Easter 22 Edw. IV (many of the entries in this roll relating to Albany are printed in *Cal. Documents relating to Scotland*, IV, 301); Warrants for Issues, 22 Edw. IV, 11 Oct., with a schedule of payments made by the collectors of the port of Southampton; and Rymer, XII, 154 (from Warrants for Issues, 22 Edw. IV, 9 May).

2. *Cal. Patent Rolls*, III, 320. Cf. *Stonor Letters and Papers*, II, 146. The proclamation also prohibited the shipping of wheat and other grains out of the realm.

3. MS. français 4054, f. 204 (the original letter, in French). The year to which this letter belongs is determined by the king's itinerary. Cf. Hist. MSS. Com., *Report 9*, app., 136-137.

as a little reassuring. Although Louis had renewed his truce with him and had permitted, probably even encouraged, the Duke of Albany to come over to England, Edward could not get rid of the feeling that Calais was not altogether safe. Deaf to all warnings of danger and appeals of honour, he had sat with folded hands and all but silent lips while Louis pushed his conquests nearer and nearer to Calais, and now, when he needed to concentrate all his thoughts on Scotland, he was reaping the fruits of his folly in trouble of mind. It was less than a year since Louis had declared to him that he would not touch "the least village" of Calais and since his new truce with Louis had been signed, but the precautionary measures he now felt it necessary to take at Calais included not only the repairing of the fortifications, but the "drowning of much land" near the town;[2] and some onlookers not unnaturally drew the conclusion that he was anticipating war with someone besides the Scots. "Our mother longs for you," wrote Richard Cely on 23 May to his brother, who was then in Calais. "William Cely wrote that we be like to have war with France and that makes her feard."[2]

Edward's sojourn at Dover was very brief, as he returned to the Tower on the 23rd, and too hurriedly, apparently, to stop at Greenwich, although there, on that very day, his daughter Mary was breathing her last. It was Mary who was to have married the Dauphin of France in case of her sister Elizabeth's death, and a still brighter prospect of matrimony had been held out to her a year since by the offer of the hand of the young king of Denmark, Frederick I. Yet now, although she was only fifteen years of age, death had come to claim her. Wrapped in cerecloth and enclosed in a leaden coffin, her body was carried to Windsor, where, under the pavement of St George's Chapel, she found her resting place close by that of her baby brother, George of Windsor.[3] Her oldest brother, the Prince of Wales, was the chief mourner at her funeral, as neither her father nor her mother was at Windsor on that day. But not many months were to pass before one of Mary's parents joined her in the silence of the tomb, and even at this moment, as if some warning bell

---

1. Writs of Privy Seal, file 879, no. 5492, 10 Feb.; *Letters, etc., Illustrative of Reigns of Rich. III and Hen. VII*, I, 14-15.
2. *Cely Papers*, 105.
3. Green, *Princesses of Eng.*, III, 401-403. Some items of expense connected with Mary's funeral may be found in Tellers' Rolls, Easter and Mich., 22 Edw. IV.

had sounded, a royal sepulchre, so ponderous that its weight broke the crane which attempted to lift it,[1] was being set up in the church above her grave.

It was not heartlessness that kept the king away from the deathbed and funeral of his daughter. On the day of her burial, 29 May, he and the Duke of Albany were hurrying to the north of England,[2] where already Gloucester had taken advantage of the coming of spring to begin a fresh attack on the Scots. Two weeks since the magistrates of York had been informed that "the right high and mighty prince, the Duke of Gloucester, by the grace of God intendeth privily in his own person to enter Scotland upon Wednesday next coming after this present date in subduing the king's great enemy, the king of Scots, and his adherents"; and the eighty men sent to the duke by York rode with him as far as Dumfries and helped him to burn not only that town but many another besides.[3] Very soon, however, the duke returned from his successful raid, and in the early days of June he went down to Fotheringhay to meet his brother and the Duke of Albany.

Edward had postponed making any definite contract with Albany until he could take counsel with Gloucester, but, as it proved, the one brother was not more delighted than the other to welcome the duke as a colleague, and on 11 June a carefully drawn up agreement with Albany was signed. Albany now assumed the title of "Alexander, king of Scotland," and Edward bound himself and his heirs to assist the said Alexander "to the getting and rejoicing" of the crown of Scotland and to defend him and his heirs against James III. Edward demanded full pay for his aid, however, as the new king of Scotland had to acknowledge the right of the kings of England to Berwick, which Gloucester was still besieging, Liddesdale, Eskdale, Ewesdale, and Annandale, with the castle of Lochmaben, and to give several other promises. These promises were: first, that, unless he was granted an extension of time, he would, within six months after he gained possession of the crown and the "more part" of Scotland, do homage and fealty to the king of England; second, that within fourteen days after he had entered Edinburgh, or as soon

---

1. Tellers' Roll, Easter 22 Edw. IV; Devon, *Issues of Exchequer*, 502.
2. The king was at Royston on 30 May, at Cambridge on the following day, and he reached Fotheringhay on or before 3 June. Privy Seals.
3. Davies, *York Records*, 127-128, 174; *Cal. Documents relating to Scot.*, IV, 306; Malden, An Unedited Cely Letter of 1482, *Trans. Royal Hist. Society*, Series III, Vol. 3, pp. 159-165.

thereafter as the members of the king of England's council who were with him deemed possible, he would deliver, or at least do his utmost to deliver, Berwick to the king of England; third, that he would break off Scotland's alliance with France and that neither he nor his heirs would ever again enter into any alliance which was hostile to the king of England or his heirs; and fourth, that, if he could "make himself clear from all other women according to the laws of Christian Church" within a year or sooner, he would marry his nephew's one-time fiancée, the Princess Cecily, now a lovely girl of thirteen years,[1] and that, if he could not "so clear him," he would at least arrange no marriage for his son and heir, should he ever have one, except according to the king of England's wishes and "unto some lady of his blood such as they both can be agreeable unto."[2]

As soon as he had signed this compact with Albany and had presented the duke with three coursers and a hundred marks for his expenses, Edward renewed his commission to Gloucester as his lieutenant and then turned around and started back to London.[3] The state of his health probably made it unwise, if not impossible, for him to try to share in the hardships of the coming campaign. But there was much valuable help he could give even when he was far away, and he was soon issuing orders for the sending of money to Gloucester to pay for the transportation of the ordnance and for the purchasing of arrows and draught horses.[4] Furthermore, so determined was Edward to keep in close touch with his army and to direct its movements as far as he could do so from a distance that, borrowing an idea from Louis XI, who, as far back as 1464, had established a system of couriers in France,[5] he appointed ten men "to do us service in our messages between us and our brother, the Duke of Gloucester," in other words, to carry letters back and forth between London and Berwick. As the distance by road from London to Berwick is three hundred and thirty-five miles, each of these ten men must

---

1. "Not so fortunate as fair," says Sir Thomas More of Cecily. The Croyland chronicler speaks of Edward's daughters as all beautiful, and they ought to have been beautiful, as their father and mother were both celebrated for their good looks.

2. Rymer, XII, 156.

3. *Ibid.*, XII, 157; Tellers' Roll, Easter 22 Edw. IV; Exchequer Accounts, Equitium Regis, *ut sup.*

4. Rymer, XII, 158.

5. Ordonnances des rois de France, XXI, 347, note.

have had a course of thirty miles or more to cover, and each received wages of twelve pence a day for ninety-five days, that is, from 4 July to 12 October.[1] At the end of that time, when "our wars against the Scots" were presumably well over, the men were apparently dismissed and this "first attempt at a postal system in England" came to an end—only to be revived, however, a few months later for a different purpose by Gloucester, then become King Richard III, who had had so good a chance to test its value.[2]

Soon after his return from the north, Edward went to Dover again, reaching there on 9 July; and as Radcliff's appointment as captain of the fleet passed the great seal on 8 July, it may be assumed that again, as in the preceding year, the king desired to take a personal farewell of his ships.[3] Those ships were to see far harder service this season, as the Scots, having learned their lesson, were no longer staying in their snug harbours waiting to be victimized. James and his subjects had been preparing themselves to fight on sea as well as on land, and already they were giving proof of their daring. "Robert Eryke was chased with Scots between Calais and Dover," Richard Cely had written on 23 June; "they escaped narrow."[4] Even in western waters, where Sir Thomas Fulford had probably had much his own way the summer before, the situation was wholly different now. Two hundred marks were sent to Gloucester during the summer for the wages of "divers men at war upon the western sea proceeding against the Scots, according to the discretion of the said duke"; but there is no record of any damage which the duke's fleet inflicted on the enemy, and as, on 10 July, a warship of the Scots, the *Kateryn*

---

1. Warrants for Issues, 22 Edw. IV, 25 Oct.; Tellers' Roll, Mich. 22 Edw. IV—a record of the payment of £8 5s to five of the men named in the king's warrant, who are described as messengers remaining on the way between the town of Berwick and the city of London to carry the king's letters to the Duke of Gloucester. According to the Croyland chronicle, the distance each man was to travel was only twenty miles. But the writer is speaking of the courier system as used by Richard III, who may have discovered during the campaign of 1482 that thirty miles and more was too long a course for one man.
2. Stubbs, III, 224; *Hist. Croy. Cont.*, 571.
3. Privy Seals; Rymer, XII, 159; *Cal. Patent Rolls*, III, 307. Radcliff had at least one Breton ship in his fleet, the *Magdalene* of Saint Pol de Léon, Writs of Privy Seal, file 884, no. 5721—a licence to Nicholas Bozek, a subject of the Duke of Brittany and master of the *Magdalene*, to export 200 quarters of beans because he had served in the said ship against the Scots and had afterwards been robbed by them of such merchandise as his ship contained. Cf. *Ibid.*, 110. 5722.
4. *Cely Papers*, 106.

of Edinburgh, was captured off the coast of Devonshire by one Richard Cruse and one Robert Symondes, who went out in pursuit of it with a couple of Barnstaple boats, there is reason to conclude that Gloucester's men at war proved inadequate even as a police force.[1]

While Edward was at Dover, Lord Hastings probably came over from Calais to get orders and advice from him, as one of the Celys had written not long before that the king was expected at Dover and that "my lord chamberlain looketh alway when he shall be sent for."[2] Certainly Pierre Puissant was one of the king's visitors at Dover, and while Hastings's report of conditions across the way was so little reassuring that an order was given for the raising of a thousand archers in Kent to be sent to reinforce the garrison at Calais,[3] Puissant brought the usual plaintive appeal from Maximilian.

Although Edward had promised to send some ambassadors to Maximilian and the Duchess Margaret when the Count of Chimay came back from Brittany, the count had apparently been forced to go home without the promised embassy[4] and, more than that, with the knowledge that the ambassadors of the king of France were outstaying him in London. Nevertheless, Maximilian could not keep from hoping, when he discovered the king of England was at Dover, that Edward intended, or might be persuaded, to come to Calais and that he could meet him there, as had been proposed, to his delight, in the preceding autumn; and the prime object of Puissant's sudden journey to Dover was to ascertain, "par bon et secret moyen et comme de soy-mesme," for how long a time Edward was to be there, whether he wanted Maximilian to come to meet him, and if so, if it would be his pleasure to cross to Calais.

As there was no certainty about the Calais meeting, however, Maximilian's messenger carried other instructions also—not to mention letters of thanks and promises of reward to certain Englishmen who had been particularly friendly and a special message of gratitude to Lord Hastings for the kind

---

1. Tellers' Roll, *ut sup.*; Devon, *Issues of Exchequer*, 504; Warrants for Issues, 22 Edw. IV, 28 Aug.
2. *Cely Papers*, 107.
3. *Cal. Patent Rolls*, III, 322. The interesting document printed by Gairdner, *Richard III*, App. II, as an illustration of the unpopularity of the Woodvilles seems to show that Hastings was having all he could do to keep even his colleagues at Calais under control.
4. A grant which Edward made to the count on 3 June of the privilege of exporting two hundred oxen to Flanders may have been a parting gift. Writs of Privy Seal, file 881, no. 5599. In this writ the count is carelessly described as the Count de Croy.

reception and good advice he had given to the Count of Chimay. The duke was desirous that Edward should know that he was not unappreciative of the promise he had received from him, first through Montgomery and Coke and afterwards through the Count of Chimay, that he should have aid if neither a treaty of peace nor a satisfactory truce could be obtained from the king of France. Of this promise he had informed the estates of his dominions and, furthermore, as Montgomery and Coke were aware, the Count of Chimay had given great pleasure to the Members of Flanders, as he was passing through Bruges, by telling them of the king of England's wish to protect Maximilian's possessions and to secure a peace or truce "marchande" for them from the king of France. But verbal promises, the duke felt, were not enough, and Puissant was to ask Edward to send "letters close," especially to the estates of Brabant and Hainault and to the Members of Flanders, expressing his affectionate interest in the welfare of the duke and his dominions, and to inquire at the same time whether there was not some word from Doctor Langton which gave hope of peace, or at least of a suspension of arms for three or four months so that the crops could be harvested. There was also a change in the situation about which Edward ought to know. Since the departure of Montgomery and Coke from Maximilian's court and the return home of the Count of Chimay, the Members of Flanders, in their great desire for peace, had sent an embassy to the king of France. Maximilian had been assured that this embassy would endeavour to obtain the most advantageous treaty possible, but if a wholesome fear of the king of England could be instilled into the mind of the king of France, no doubt he would grant better terms. Finally, Master Pierre was to make the so often repeated plea for men and money.[1]

But if Puissant succeeded in getting a few more vague promises from Edward, that was all he did get, and the king neither went to Calais nor invited Maximilian to meet him elsewhere. By 22 July Edward was back at the Tower,[2] and very soon after William Cely was writing tidings from Calais which show not only to what a state of helplessness and hopelessness Maximilian was now reduced, but how nearly his misfortunes touched the safety of Calais. "It is so that the

---

1. Commynes-Lenglet, IV, 42-44.
2. Privy Seals.
3. 28 July. *Chron. Scandaleuse*, II, 117, note.

town of Aire is given up to the Frenchmen,[3] and another castle within a Dutch mile of St Omer, by the means of treason . . . and the Frenchmen purposeth to be at Gravelines, and they be not letted, within this two days and less; and there comes every day from St Omer to my lord chamberlain [petition for] help and rescue out of England, and my lord hath promised them that they shall lack no men nor victual, wherefore we look after here that there shall come a fellowship out of England shortly." Nor did the news grow better as the days passed. Although on 3 August Cely wrote that Maximilian was at Ypres "with a great host" and that it was said that, after victualling and garrisoning the town of Aire, the French had returned home, ten days later his news was that the French were gathering on the borders in daily increasing numbers and that, though according to rumour the Duke of Burgundy was "on this side Ypres with a great host of men and should have been at St Omer or this time," nothing had yet been heard from him and some persons said he had "gone back again." It turned out that the duke had gone back to Bruges, and one Hobener who was in Bruges a few days later saw him depart "but with ten horse into Zealand."

> For they of Ghent and of Bruges will not grant him such things as he asketh, for the duke asketh no thing of them but money, and he will take such men with him to go upon the Frenchmen as pleased him; but the Ghenteners and they of Bruges will not give him no money without he take such men as they will assign him, for the which he departed into Zealand; but I understand the Frenchmen lieth still in garrisons upon the marches and increase daily with new men out of high France.[1]

And still the king of England sent no help. Edward was blind indeed if he did not see that Maximilian could not possibly hold out much longer. Yet he made no move. His war with Scotland gave him an entirely plausible excuse for withholding help from Maximilian, but it is to be feared that Louis' money also influenced him. For on 25 August Pierre le Roy brought him the twenty-five thousand crowns he had asked for in May.[2] Moreover, had the war with Scotland been all that prevented Maximilian from receiving the aid he so desperately needed, the situation might yet have been saved, as before the middle of August Gloucester had won successes which caused the lieutenant

---

1. *Cely Papers*, 108, 109, 112, 115.
2. Rymer, XII, 123.

of Calais to give orders for a general procession, a firing of the guns, and "at night bonfires to be made at every man's door as was on midsummer night."[1]

After parting from Edward at Fotheringhay, Gloucester and Albany had gone to York, where the citizens received them in their best array and where the Earl of Northumberland came to meet them. Yet it was 15 July before another band of men furnished by York marched away towards the border,[2] and if Gloucester and Albany had set out before these men, it was not long before. Gloucester now had under his command an unusually powerful army, including at least twenty thousand men retained at the king's wages;[3] but James III had also been raising large forces, which he was not likely to disband this time without a fight, and early in the spring the Scottish parliament had tried to provide for the defence of the kingdom by issuing orders for the strengthening of the garrisons in the border strongholds, for the establishment of a courier service to carry warnings of danger to the farthest parts of the realm, for the offering of rewards for the killing or capture of the Earl of Douglas and any traitor with him, and for the sending of an embassy, since letters had been ignored, to the king of France and the Parliament of Paris to ask for aid.[4] However, all efforts made by James and the Scottish parliament to put Scotland in a state of defence were rendered vain by an unfortunate breach between James and his nobles. James, who was possessed of no strength of character, had gathered unto himself a number of lowborn favourites whom the lords of Scotland detested and whom they held responsible for the exile of the Duke of Albany and the death of the king's other brother, the Earl of Mar; and when the king was so foolish as to take his hated favourites with him, as he

---

1. *Cely Papers*, 113.
2. Davies, *York Records*, 130-131.
3. "A number unheard of on record evidence," says Ramsay, II, 442, who adds, citing Tellers' Roll, Easter 22 Edw. IV: "Edward assigned a sum of £6,092 for the wages of this force: at the established rate of 6*d* a day, £6,000 would keep 20,000 men for just twelve days; not enough to take them to the border and back again." Sir James seems to have overlooked the fact that the entry mentioning this sum (£6,092 9*s*, to be exact) says distinctly that it was assigned to Sir John Elryngton, treasurer of war, "towards the wages of divers men retained by him for the war against the Scots for the space of fourteen days," and that another entry mentions £7,000 assigned to Elryngton for the wages of 20,000 men retained for the said war "for the space of other fourteen days immediately following the aforesaid fourteen days."
4. *Acts of Parl. of Scotland*, II, 138-140. Cf. Lesley, 47.

set out, after the middle of July, at the head of his army to meet the expected English invasion, the wrath of the nobles boiled over. James had gone only as far as Lauder when the Earl of Angus and some of the other lords presented themselves before him, told him what they thought of his manner of ruling the kingdom, hanged several of his favourites on the bridge, and then hurried him back to Edinburgh. On 22 July James III re-entered Edinburgh Castle, the bolts were shot, and he remained in the "firm keeping" of Lord Darnley.[1]

The lords of Scotland had administered punishment to their weak and foolish sovereign, and as some or all of them were kindly disposed towards, if not actually in league with, the Duke of Albany, perhaps they cared little that they had placed their country at the mercy of the great English army already pressing against her border. They stationed a part of James's troops at Haddington, but that was all they did to oppose the English, and as soon as the news of what had occurred at Lauder reached Berwick, Gloucester, Albany, and Northumberland, leaving a small force to continue the siege of the castle of Berwick (the town had been taken by this time), started for Edinburgh. Burning town after town and spreading general terror through the countryside, the English host swept on until it arrived before the Scottish capital, and inasmuch as there was no one—least of all King James—who could offer any effectual resistance, Gloucester, without the firing of a gun or the shooting of an arrow, took possession of the city in the name of Edward IV. Then Garter King-of-Arms was sent to proclaim at the market cross that James must keep the promises he had formerly given to the king of England, that he must make amends before 1 August for all violations of the truce with England of which he and his subjects had been guilty, and that he must restore his brother Albany to all his rights, or take the consequences, which would be the destruction of himself and his kingdom.[2]

When Edinburgh had been cowed, Gloucester set out to deal with the forces at Haddington. But again he found no need to fight, as on 2 August the Scottish lords sent to ask for a treaty of peace and the renewal of the

---

1. Chron. printed in Pinkerton, I, 503-504; Lesley, 48-49. Lesley says James was put in the Earl of Athol's custody, but Darnley seems to have been the immediate custodian. See Hist. MSS. Com., *Report 3*. app., 390.
2. Hall, 332-333; Nicolas's *London Chron.*, 147. Hall's account of the events in Scotland is apparently based on documentary authority. He seems to draw his facts partly from the documents which Rymer has printed in the *Fœdera* and partly from others, as, for example, the proclamation made at the market cross, which have now disappeared.

old agreement for the marriage of James's son and Cecily of York. Not being vested with authority to make peace on such terms, and knowing, too, that Albany was now pledged, after a fashion, to marry Cecily, the duke greeted this request of the lords with the cool remark that he did not know his brother's mind about the former marriage treaty. No uncertainty regarding his brother's wishes, however, prevented him from announcing on the spot that, if the Scottish lords desired peace, they would have to pay back all the money which had been sent to James for Cecily's dowry and also promise to surrender Berwick Castle or, if that was beyond their power, to abstain from interfering with the siege now being conducted against it.[1]

The only surprise is that Gloucester did not demand much more, even the abdication of James in favour of Albany. But he had discovered before now that James's subjects were not at all disposed to rally around Albany,[2] and very likely he knew also that the duke had already been approached by some of the Scottish lords and had been found to be not unwilling to renounce his pretensions to the throne if the lords would assure him of the restoration of his estates. Indeed, on the very day on which Gloucester was asked for peace and the renewal of the former marriage treaty, the Archbishop of St Andrews, the Bishop of Dunkeld, Lord Avondale, chancellor of Scotland, and the Earl of Argyle signed and sealed, at Edinburgh, an agreement whereby they bound themselves to secure for Albany a grant from James, ratified by the parliament of Scotland, of all the lands and offices belonging to him at the time of his "last parting forth of the realm of Scotland" and a full pardon for all his offences—not even omitting his "aspiring and tending to the throne"— provided only that he would swear to keep his "true faith and allegiance" to James and his "faith, loyalty, and bond" to the lords of the realm.[3]

Far from displaying any resentment when he found that Albany was inclined to make this bargain with the Scottish lords, Gloucester seems to have sanctioned, perhaps even urged, the duke to accept the terms offered to him. Nor does Edward's brother appear to have demanded from his recent comrade in arms any guarantee of loyalty to his English friends beyond the signing of a written declaration, which was drawn up on 3 August, that he

---

1. Hall, *ut sup.*
2. Vergil, 682.
3. Rymer, XII, 160. Cf. Hall, who gives an accurate epitome of the document.

would keep the promises he had made to the king of England.[1] The next day, moreover, Gloucester himself accepted an offer which, though it fell far short of his dreams, enabled him to withdraw gracefully from a hostile land into which he had penetrated rather too far for safety. On 4 August the provost, merchants, burgesses, and commonalty of Edinburgh gave a solemn promise, in the presence of Gloucester, Albany, Northumberland, the Earl of Argyle, the Bishop of Dunkeld, and others, that, if it was still the wish of the king of England that his daughter should marry King James's son, the marriage should be performed, while, on the other hand, if the king of England sent word before All Hallows' Day that he did not desire the marriage, all the money he had paid for Cecily's dowry should be refunded in yearly instalments paid in the same manner in which he had paid the money to James.[2] Then, when a promise had been added that James's sister Margaret should be sent to England before 1 November for her long postponed marriage to Earl Rivers, Gloucester, probably no less thankful for what he had escaped than for what he had gained, hastened back to Berwick.

Up to the present moment Berwick Castle had held out successfully against all attacks. But, deprived of all hope of succour, it must surrender soon, and, no longer feeling any need for the great army that had followed him to Edinburgh, Gloucester seems to have distributed suitable rewards among his troops and then, on 11 August, dismissed all but seventeen hundred of them.[3] Scarcely had he taken this step, however, when it began to look as if he had congratulated himself too soon, for the Scottish lords commenced, as soon as he was out of sight, to try to force Albany to renounce his alliance with the king of England. Although Albany resisted secretly, if not openly, the lords called for troops to raise the siege of Berwick and dragged the duke along with them as far as the Lammermuirs. Yet luckily, even with only seventeen hundred men, Gloucester was still overawing, and in the end the Scottish lords tried nothing more dangerous than a little more bargaining. They offered to raze the walls of Berwick Castle if Gloucester would raze the walls of the town, or to suffer the duke to establish an English garrison in the

---

1. Hall, 334. Here again the chronicler seems to derive his facts from the document itself.
2. Rymer, XII, 161. Cf. Hall, 335-336, who confuses his narrative by quoting this document after his account of the surrender of Berwick Castle.
3. Tellers' Roll, Easter 22 Edw. IV; Devon, *Issues of Exchequer*, 502.

town while they kept a Scottish one in the castle. Gloucester, however, would hear of nothing short of complete surrender, and complete surrender he finally got, on 24 August, without making any concessions on England's side, apparently, except a truce on land and sea from 8 September till 4 November. The brave defenders of Berwick Castle were then permitted to march out "bag and baggages," an English garrison marched in, and the town and castle which Margaret of Anjou had sold to Scotland in the brief interval between Edward IV's seizure of her husband's throne and his coronation became once more a part of England.[1]

Two days before the fall of Berwick Castle, Edward had granted a safeconduct—not the first of its kind—to Margaret of Scotland so that she might come to England to marry Earl Rivers;[2] and so swiftly did the king's couriers carry to him the news of Gloucester's final victory that as early as 25 August he had the pleasure of rehearsing, in a long letter hastily written to the Pope, the whole story of his brother's triumphant march through Scotland. Though the king of Scotland and his chief lords had shut themselves up in the castle of Edinburgh without trying to resist, Edward told Sixtus, the English soldiers, partly out of noble compassion and partly because the Duke of Albany was anxious not to spoil his welcome home,[3] refrained from burning the city and murdering the inhabitants; and the great achievement of the expedition was the capture, first, of the strongly walled town, and afterwards of the castle of Berwick. "It now remains for your Holiness," the king continued, "to complete the work by monitions; for we would that these two nations should be as united in heart and soul as they are by neighbourhood, soil, and language." And he closed his letter with an expression of his hope that, as the Duke of Albany's influence was now supreme in Scotland, the Scots would be more careful hereafter about observing their treaties with him.[4]

According to the Croyland Abbey chronicle, Edward was far from satisfied with what Gloucester had accomplished for him in Scotland and felt much vexation of spirit because so little had been gained in return for the great sums

---

1. Hall, 334-335; Lesley, 49-50.
2. Rymer, XII, 162.
3. Cf. Hall, 332.
4. *Cal. Venetian Papers*, I, 145-146.

of money which had been expended on the expedition.[1] Yet the king's letter to the Pope sounds exultant enough, and though the spectacular entry into Edinburgh had proved but a momentary victory, the conquest of Berwick gave back to his crown a very precious jewel whose loss he had mourned for more than a score of years. Even the Croyland chronicler admits, indeed, that the recovery of Berwick assuaged to some degree Edward's disappointment touching the results of Gloucester's great effort; and the great pains immediately taken to strengthen and protect the town and castle show plainly that the king was determined not to be robbed of them again. The captaincy of Berwick fell to the Earl of Northumberland, as he already held the wardenship of the east march, to which the captaincy of Berwick had been wont to be attached, and Edward immediately empowered John Elryngton, treasurer of war, Alexander Legh, who had been made comptroller of Berwick the day the castle surrendered,[2] and four other men to receive the earl's bond, to promise him a garrison of a thousand soldiers at the king's wages, to advise with him concerning the defences of the town and castle, and to take all other steps which might be necessary for the safe keeping of the newly recovered treasure.[3] Four hundred and thirty-five pounds a month was the amount ultimately allowed to Northumberland for the custody of Berwick, and Alexander Legh paid out five hundred pounds for repairs in the town and castle.[4]

---

1. *Hist. Croy. Cont.*, 563. Ramsay thinks that "a certain distrust of Gloucester on the part of the king may be traced in the fact that in November the constable's staff was taken from him and the office put into commission." (Cf. *Cal. Patent Rolls*, III, 317.) But it appears that in reality Gloucester was not deprived of the constableship, for in the charter creating Francis, Lord Lovel, Viscount Lovel on 4 January 1483, the duke, who was one of the witnesses, is described as constable of England. Charter Roll 15-22 Edw. IV, m. 1. Everything else goes to show, moreover, that Gloucester was in high favour with his brother during the last months of the king's reign, that his influence, in fact, was paramount.

2. *Cal. Patent Rolls*, III, 333.

3. Signed Bills, file 1527, no. 5463. The charters of Berwick were confirmed by Edward on 18 February 1483. *Rotuli Scotiæ*, II, 458-460.

4. Tellers' Roll, Mich. 22 Edw. IV; Ramsay, II, 447. The Croyland chronicler, who denounces the war with Scotland as an expensive and fruitless affair, complains that the keeping of Berwick cost £30,000 a year. The £435 a month allowed to the Earl of Northumberland would mean only £5,220 a year, but in addition to that the king had to pay the garrison and for the victualling of the town and castle. In November Edward appointed Thomas Eldreton, clerk of the lardery of his household, to purchase for ready money in the counties of Lincoln, Norfolk, and Suffolk 1000 quarters of wheat, 500 quarters of malt, 500 quarters of barley, 300 quarters of beans, 20 lasts of herring, and 40 weyes of cheese for the victualling of Berwick. Warrants under the Signet, file 3379, 13 November.

9

THE TREATY OF ARRAS AND THE DEATH OF EDWARD

While Gloucester was marching to Edinburgh and back again, a very noble guest from the East, Andrew Palæologus, nephew of the heroic Emperor Constantine XIII, who had lost his life when Constantinople was captured by the Turks, was being entertained in London by the king. "The Prince of Constantinople," as Palæologus is designated in the English records, spent a number of months in England, for he seems to have arrived by the end of July 1482, if not earlier, and to have stayed until the end of November, if not later; and during the whole of his visit Edward gave him twenty pounds a month for his expenses.[1] It would be a natural assumption that the prince came to England in the hope of obtaining aid against the Turks, but there is no actual evidence that his visit had any political significance, and it may be that curiosity was all that brought him to London. On the other hand, a group of strangers, not of princely rank, who reached the English capital while Palæologus was there, had a definite and interesting errand.

Of the wider and more adventurous life into which England was soon to plunge, and which was to make so great a change in her interests and her history, there had already been a slight foreshadowing in a voyage upon which two ships of Bristol had set out in the summer of 1480 in the hope of finding Brazil, a mysterious country supposed to be an island and to lie somewhere between the western coast of Ireland and the eastern coast of Asia. But, near though it was, the time had not yet come when English mariners were to find their way to the shores

---

1. Two payments to the prince of £20 each are entered on Tellers' Roll, Easter 22 Edw. IV, indicating that before Michaelmas he had been in England at least two months, while another, entered on Tellers' Roll, Mich. 22 Edw. IV, is distinctly stated to be for his expenses in the month of November. The prince seems to have received a reward of 200 marks as well. *Ibid.*

of the Americas, and the Bristol ships came home with only disappointment to report.[1] There were other distant lands, however, lands less mythical than Brazil, which were also believed to contain fabulous wealth for the merchant who had the hardihood to embark on long and perilous voyages, and early in 1481 some enterprising Englishmen were seized with a desire to sail to the coast of Africa. The plan met with the king's approval, and in February of that year Edward wrote a letter to the Pope in which he stated that he willingly permitted his subjects to voyage to any part of Africa and asked, on the plea that it was to the advantage of the Christian faith that "wealth and other things precious from their material excellence should be drawn into its power from the hands of the infidels," that the Pope would sanction the proposed expedition.[2] Yet it is doubtful if the daring Englishmen ever left home, since nothing more is heard of their enterprise, and when, in the summer of 1482, two other subjects of Edward IV began, at the suggestion of the Duke of Medina Sidonia, to fit out a fleet to sail to the coast of Guinea, it was discovered that the sanction of someone besides the Pope would be required. For in 1479 Alphonso V of Portugal had signed a treaty with Ferdinand of Aragon whereby he gave up all right to the Canary Isles in exchange for undisputed possession of Guinea, and when it became known in Portugal that an English expedition was about to sail for Guinea, Alphonso's successor, John II, hastened to enter a protest. The story is related in a passage of the works of Garcia de Resende which Hackluyt has translated thus:

"The king (John II) sent as ambassadors from the town of Monte-major to King Edward the Fourth of England Ruy de Sousa, a principal person and a man of great wisdom and estimation, and in whom the king reposed great trust with Doctor John d'Elvas, and Ferdinand de Pina as secretary. And they made their voyage by sea very honourably, being very well accompanied. These men were sent on behalf of their king to confirm the ancient leagues with England, wherein it was conditioned that the new king of the one and of the other kingdom should be bound to send to confirm the old leagues. And likewise they had order to show and make him acquainted with the title which the king held in the seigniory of Guinea, to the intent that after the king of England had seen the same he should give charge through all his kingdoms that no man should arm or set forth ships to Guinea: and also to request him that it would please him to give commandment

---

1. Worcester's *Itinerarium*, 267-268, cited by H. P. Biggar, *The Voyages of the Cabots and of the Corte-Reals to North America and Greenland* (Paris, 1903). 40.

2. *Cal. Venetian Papers*, I, 142.

to dissolve a certain fleet which one John Tintam and one William Fabian, Englishmen, were making by commandment of the Duke of Medina Sidonia to go to the aforesaid parts of Guinea. With which ambassage the king of England seemed to be very well pleased, and they were received of him with very great honour, and he condescended unto all that the ambassadors required of him, at whose hands they received authentical writings of the diligence which they had performed, with publication thereof by the heralds; and also provisos of those confirmations which were necessary. And having dispatched all things well, and with the king's good will, they returned home into their country."[1]

What the men of Monte-major brought to the king of England was a confirmation of the ancient treaties between England and Portugal which John II had signed and sealed at Monte-major on 8 February 1482; and when they went home, they carried with them Edward's confirmation of the same treaties given under England's great seal on 13 September.[2]

During the first week of October, Edward made a pilgrimage to Our Lady of Walsingham and stopped on the way at Norwich, where he received a gift of fifty marks of gold from the city.[3] But the cares of state pursued him even to Our Lady's shrine, for while he was at Walsingham, Patrick Haliburton and one Hugh Iver brought him certain writings touching Scotland, sent by his council, which caused him to hurry back to London. He reached Eltham about 10 October, and a week later he was at the Tower holding daily counsel with "his lords."[4]

About Michaelmas James III was forcibly released from Edinburgh Castle by the Duke of Albany himself, and from that day forth the two brothers seemed to live together in harmony and even the closest affection. In reality, however, there was no more sincerity in the reconciliation between James and Albany than there had been in the reconciliation once patched up between Edward IV and the Duke of Clarence. Albany, like Clarence, made a pretence of submission and loyalty, but, also like Clarence, he went on coveting his brother's crown; and it may have been an intimation from Albany that he was ready to rebel against James again which Haliburton and Iver had brought to Edward at Walsingham.

---

1. *Hakluytus Posthumus: or Purchas His Pilgrimes* (Glasgow, 1905), VI, 122-124. I am indebted to my friend Miss Frances Davenport for calling my attention to this interesting extract.
2. Rymer, XII, 245, 163.
3. *Records of City of Norwich*, II, 102-203.
4. Tellers' Roll, Easter 22 Edw. IV; Privy Seals; *Cely Papers*, 128.

At all events, perhaps because James's throne was so obviously unstable or perhaps because Gloucester, having had a taste of military success, desired a renewal of the war with Scotland, Edward made up his mind that he did not care to have his daughter marry James's son, and as soon as he got back to London, he sent Garter to Edinburgh to tell James that he preferred to have the dowry money refunded. He had been given till All Hallows' Day to let the Scots know his decision in regard to the marriage, and it was not until 27 October that Garter appeared at Edinburgh and informed the magistrates of the city that the king of England had decided for divers reasons "to refuse the accomplishing of the said marriage and to have the repayment of all such sums of money as by occasion [of] the same betrusted marriage his Highness hath paid." James could hardly fail to be offended by such a message, but if he did take offence, he thought it safer to hide the fact, and two days later he told Garter politely that "your king's writing is right welcome unto us" and that he trusted "to God that at the day of payment of the money your king's grace shall be so contented that he shall hold him pleased."[1]

If Edward's wish for a marriage between his daughter and James's son had faded away, so naturally had his wish for a marriage between his wife's brother and James's sister; and probably Garter also made known at Edinburgh that Earl Rivers was no longer an applicant for the Princess Margaret's hand. At any rate, Margaret once more failed to make use of the safeconduct Edward had granted to her, and the subject of her marriage to Rivers was never again revived. There were other good reasons, however, besides those of state for breaking off the proposed union between Rivers and Margaret of Scotland, for Margaret's character, it had now been learned, was by no means above reproach.[2]

Edward evidently took pleasure in snubbing James III, and when the brief truce which Gloucester had granted at the time Berwick Castle capitulated came to an end, he seems to have shown no desire to sign a more lasting treaty with the Scots. But possibly he would not have thrown away so carelessly his chance to renew his alliance with James if he had known what was about to happen in another part of Europe.

Lord Hastings had been summoned to London to attend the council meetings at the Tower, "and there was at Dover to him five hundred men all in white gowns to bring him home."[3] How great was his call to consult with

1. Rymer, XII, 164-569.
2. *Exchequer Rolls of Scot.*, VIII, lxii-lxiii.
3. *Cely Papers*, 129.

the lieutenant of Calais Edward may not have realized at the moment, but Hastings had not been in London very long before the king discovered that he was face to face with a situation which gave him more reason than ever to be concerned about the safety of Calais.

Louis XI certainly had not anticipated, when he turned a deaf ear to James III's appeals for aid and permitted the Duke of Albany to go over to England to co-operate with Edward, that the Scottish lords would rise in rebellion at the most critical moment and thus make it possible for Gloucester to march into the Scottish capital. He had counted on the war between England and Scotland to keep Edward from helping Maximilian, and had he foreseen that James would collapse so quickly, he would have kept Albany in France and broken any promise he had made to Edward to have nothing more to do with the Scots. But Gloucester had entered Edinburgh before Louis was aware of the danger, and though the results to Scotland were less serious than might have been expected in view of the completeness of James's overthrow, Louis saw at once that he could no longer rely on the Scots to prevent Edward from interfering in Burgundy. He looked about in haste, consequently, for some other means of staying Edward's hand, and the choice he made was characteristic of the man. He resolved to publish the renewal of his truce with Edward, the existence of which Maximilian more than half suspected but which Edward had never been honest enough to acknowledge, and on 29 September he gave orders for proclamation to be made throughout Guienne that the truce which he had formerly made with the king of England, and which was to endure during their lives and for a year after the death of the one who died first, had been continued on the same terms as before.[1]

Louis' announcement cannot have caused Maximilian much surprise, but, surprise or no surprise, it filled the duke with wrath and dismay and thus accomplished the purpose for which it was intended. Yet it may be doubted if Maximilian's consternation was as great as that of the king of England. For Edward thought with alarm not only of the bad effect Louis' revelation was

---

1. The proclamation was not actually made at Bayonne until 20 October. *Régistres Gascons*, edited by MM. Bernadou, Ythurbide, and Ducéré (Bayonne, 1896), I, 132, 133-134; Gairdner, *Eng. Hist. Review*, July 1897, pp. 521-523. Apparently even Dr Gairdner's careful eye overlooked the fact that the truce between Edward and Louis had really been renewed in the autumn of 1481. Louis by no means "smoothed matters with Edward" by a new treaty just before signing the treaty of Arras with Maximilian.

sure to have on Maximilian, but of what his own subjects might think and do when they heard of it.[1] The secret being out, however, and denial impossible, the king seems to have decided that his best policy was to put a bold face on the matter, lay the blame as far as possible on Louis, and then give his subjects something else to think about. So, relying on his popularity among his people, which no iniquities on his part seemed to lessen permanently, or on the good impression he hoped the recent recovery of Berwick had made, to save him from the worst consequences of what he had done, on 15 November he issued writs for a parliament.[2] And in the meantime he struggled hard to find some way to ward off the disaster he knew must be impending in Burgundy. Sir Thomas Montgomery and Sir Thomas Vaughan, accompanied by Francis Dupon, a secretary of the Duke of Brittany who had been in England for some months past, were sent to Maximilian and a messenger to the Duchess Margaret, and finally, about 1December, Langton was dispatched on one more embassy to Louis.[3]

No matter how frantically he tried, however, Edward could not prevent the inevitable results of his own folly and wrong-doing. Only one thing could have saved him, namely, the longed-for death of Louis, and that Heaven did not vouchsafe. Langton seems to have returned home very soon after he reached France, probably to give warning of what was coming and of his own powerlessness to check it, and when he was sent back to France almost immediately after, Lord Howard and other ambassadors appear to have gone with him.[4] But even Howard could do nothing. Louis was gracious enough to pay Langton nine hundred and eighty livres, a sum which was probably

---

1. Commynes, II, 63.
2. *Reports touching Dignity of a Peer*, IV, 984-988. Sir Thomas More says that "no prince of this land attaining the crown by battle" was ever so much beloved by "the substance of the people" as Edward, "nor he himself so specially in any part of his life as at the time of his death."
3. Tellers' Roll, Mich. 22 Edw. IV; Warrants for Issues, 22 Edw. IV, 1 Dec. Francis Dupon had been given a reward of £13 6s 8d in Easter term. Tellers' Roll, Easter 22 Edw. IV. He had been in England at least twice before, first in 1475, in company with the Procurator of Rennes (Warrants for Issues, 15 Edw. IV, 7 July), and afterwards in the summer of 1481, when, on 21 June, Edward granted him a licence to export 300 quarters of corn to Brittany, Flanders, or Spain. Exchequer T. R., Council and Privy Seal, file 92, m. 43.
4. John Barker, late collector of customs and subsidies in the port of Sandwich, was paid £30 for the passage of Howard, Langton, and other ambassadors to France. Tellers' Roll, Mich. 22 Edw. IV.

intended for the expenses of all Edward's ambassadors during their stay in France,[1] but he had no wish to undo what he had done, even had that been possible; and meanwhile his negotiations with Maximilian, whose courage was now entirely gone, were proceeding apace.

Edward spent Christmas at Westminster Palace, and though his heart must have been full of dread and deep misgivings, he took pains to keep up appearances. He astonished all beholders by the variety and costliness of the clothes he wore, and if he was growing old, as men of forty did in those days, and "with over liberal diet somewhat corpulent and burly," he was still remarkably handsome, and the Croyland chronicler records that the robes of the latest style, with padded shoulders and long full sleeves lined with handsome furs, in which the king arrayed himself gave him a very distinguished air.[2] But all too soon came the dreaded news from Flanders; and it was even worse news than Edward had looked for. On 23 December, Louis and Maximilian signed the famous treaty of Arras by which they mutually agreed not only that all the rancour, hate, and ill-will which they had cherished against each other so long should be forgotten, but that Maximilian's daughter should marry the Dauphin of France as soon as she was of marriageable age, that she should be placed in Louis' care at once, and that the counties of Artois and Burgundy should be regarded as her marriage portion. Maximilian stipulated that the territories to which he thus practically relinquished his children's right should revert to his son Philip and his heirs if his daughter's heirs failed, and to this Louis gave his consent; but when the duke also asked for the inclusion of the king of England in the treaty of peace, Louis refused, saying that he already had a truce with the English and that the present treaty "ne leur touche de rien"![3]

It was Howard who brought Edward a full account of the treaty of Arras, as well as the information that some Flemish ambassadors who had been with the king of France at Plessis-du-Parc, and who had also seen the Dauphin at Amboise, had gone home with Louis' ratification of the treaty in their pockets.[4] Nothing could have happened which would have been

---

1. *Lettres de Louis XI*, VIII, 229, note.

2. *Hist. Croy. Cont.*, 563; More, *Hist. of Richard III*, 2. According to Stow, Edward celebrated his last Christmas at Eltham.

3. Commynes-Lenglet, IV, 95, *et seq.*

4. Hall, 388. Hall says that Howard also reported that he had seen Maximilian's daughter brought to Amboise and espoused to the Dauphin. But as a matter of fact the little princess

more disastrous or more mortifying than this complete triumph of Louis over Maximilian and his cool ignoring of his repeated promises that the Dauphin should marry Elizabeth of York; and as he listened to Howard's story, the scales dropped from Edward's eyes for ever. Now at last he saw how blind and heedless he had been and how completely he had allowed Louis to trick him. With what eagerness would he now have snatched at a proposal from Maximilian for a joint invasion of France! How gladly would he have whetted his sword and plunged it to the hilt in Louis' breast! But the day when he might have done these things had passed never to return, and as he stood viewing the ruins of his impossible foreign policy—impossible because it was conceived, as he knew so well, in opposition to his people's wishes and best interests—he must have blushed with shame. Nor was there anything he could do to rectify his blunder or redeem his fame. He had made his bed and he, and England too, must lie in it. Yet his brother Gloucester may have tried to persuade him that further victories over the Scots would be in some sort a revenge on Louis, since they would prevent a revival of the old alliance between Scotland and France, which was the next disaster England might anticipate. There was even a possibility that they would open a way to secure from Scotland the help to invade France and punish Louis which could no longer be hoped for from Burgundy. Gloucester may have argued also that to win victories in the field—in any field—was the quickest and surest way to remove the danger of a popular outbreak in England when the full meaning of the treaty of Arras was comprehended. At all events, the last months of Edward's life were devoted to preparations for a new war against the Scots.

A Scottish parliament which assembled at Edinburgh in December made the Duke of Albany lieutenant general of his brother's kingdom. It decided further that peace should be sought with England, if it could be obtained with honour, and that a herald should be sent to arrange for a meeting of commissioners to redress the daily occurring "attemptates" on the border and to renew the proposal which Edward had so recently rejected for the fulfilment of the former marriage treaty. But the prospect that Edward and Gloucester would listen to peace proposals was so slight that the Scottish

---

was not handed over to Louis until after Edward's death. Louis did accompany the Flemish ambassadors to Amboise, however, to see the Dauphin. *Chronique Scandaleuse*, II, 126-128.

parliament also called upon James to make himself ready "with all his extreme power for war of England and for the defence of his realm both by sea and land, and also for invasion of his enemies";[1] and Albany, who had probably been made lieutenant general in the belief that he would be more successful than James in negotiating with the English, betrayed the trust put in him. Before the end of the year Albany withdrew from Edinburgh to Dunbar Castle, apparently because he could conspire with the English more easily and safely from there, and about 10 January the king of England sent to him "our trusty and well beloved chaplain, Master Patrick Haliburton."[2] Other agents of Edward and Gloucester, however, had apparently visited Albany before Haliburton set out for Dunbar, as the duke's decision must have been fully made by 12 January, when he empowered three of his friends, the Earl of Angus, Lord Gray, and Sir James Liddell, to treat with the king of England on the basis of the agreements signed at Fotheringhay in June 1482.[3]

On 20 January Edward was at Westminster to open the parliament. "Dominus illuminatio mea et salus mea" was the text of the chancellor's address, and though there is no record of his words, from what the Croyland chronicler has written and from what was afterwards done, it appears that Rotherham denounced Louis of France for his wicked deceitfulness and gave the Commons to understand that they were expected to make a grant for the defence of the realm. There does not seem to have been any talk, however, of making war directly on France—not even when fresh excitement was caused by the discovery that someone had "counterfeited" the keys of Calais.[4] It was to fight the Scots that money was wanted, and the king's wish seems to have been to keep the thoughts of Englishmen turned as much as possible in the direction of the kingdom of James III.

For their Speaker the Commons selected John Wode, a man who seems to have been a special friend of the Duke of Gloucester, as he was made treasurer of England after Edward's death and reappointed to that office when Gloucester seized the crown;[5] and the most noteworthy act of the

---

1. *Acts of Parl. of Scotland*, II, 143-144.
2. Warrants for Issues, 22 Edw. IV, 10 Jan. Cf. Tellers' Roll, Mich. 22 Edw. IV.
3. Rymer, XII, 172.
4. Nicolas's *London Chron.*, 147.
5. *Cal. Patent Rolls*, III, 349, 361.

session was the recognition and requital of Gloucester's services in the war with Scotland. The duke was rewarded not specifically as the conqueror of Berwick, but as the warden of the west march, where he had lately subdued "by his manifold and diligent labours and devoirs" thirty miles and more of the border lands of Scotland. "Divers parcels" of the lands subdued by him, it was stated, he had brought under the obeissance of the king of England, and much more of them "he intendeth, and with God's grace is like, to get and subdue hereafter."

It was not only past services, therefore, but prospective ones also for which the king's brother was to receive thanks and recompense, and the reward Edward had rashly promised him, and to which parliament now unmurmuringly gave its consent, was one that never ought to have been granted. For the duke and his heirs male were made permanent possessors of the wardenship of the west marches, of the city and castle of Carlisle, and of all other crown "possessions and hereditaments whatsoever they be" in the county of Cumberland, with the right to appoint the sheriff and escheator in that county. Even that was not all. Permission was also given to the duke and his heirs to hold in fee simple, with palatine rights similar to those enjoyed by the Bishop of Durham in his bishopric, all lands which by God's help they might acquire from the Scots in Liddesdale, Eskdale, Ewesdale, Annandale, Wachopedale, Clydesdale, and the west marches of Scotland.[1] In other words, by this pernicious grant Gloucester and his descendants were made the perpetual guardians of England against Scotland in the west marches and rulers over an hereditary principality which was to be carved partly out of England and partly out of Scotland and which, though subject to the English crown, was to be endowed with a degree of independence that would cause it to be a constant danger to the occupant of the throne. That a grant so extravagant and ill-advised was tolerated by parliament must mean that that body was at the moment completely under Gloucester's thumb, and that Edward himself was willing to consent to it can only be explained by the supposition that the shock of the treaty of Arras and the fatal illness now fast creeping upon him had so weakened his judgment and understanding that he did not realize what he was doing.

The Duke of Albany's envoys arrived in London not many days after

---

1. *Rolls of Parl.*, VI, 204-205.

parliament convened, as they had the honour of accompanying the king and queen in a procession from St Stephen's Chapel into Westminster Hall on Candlemas Day;[2] and, the warmth of their reception being assured, their work was soon accomplished. When, on 9 February, Edward authorized the Earl of Northumberland, Lord Scrope, and Sir William Parre to treat with the three Scots, an understanding was already practically reached, and the treaty of alliance signed at Westminster Palace two days later decreed that henceforth "good amity, love, favour, and friendly intelligence" should exist between King Edward and the Duke of Albany and that each should help the other to uphold and increase his estate against all persons. There was also to be a truce for a year "by land and fresh waters" between the "subjects, lovers, and wellwillers" of the two princes, and Albany was to notify the English wardens of the marches before 1st March which Scots were his subjects, lovers, and wellwillers and which were not. As breaches of the truce were sure to occur, it was also agreed that in case of such breaches restitution and amends should be made to the injured parties out of the goods of the offenders, and that the Earl of Northumberland and the Earl of Angus should see to the execution of this arrangement in the east and middle marches, the Duke of Gloucester and Albany himself in the west march.

Of greater interest than these general provisions of the treaty with Albany are the specific engagements made by the duke. They disclose not simply that he was again angling for his brother's throne, but that Edward's ulterior purpose in encouraging and supporting his pretensions was the procurement of aid against France. For the duke was required to work daily for the conquest "to his proper use" of the crown of Scotland in order that he and all his friends among the Scottish nobles might render the king of England and his heirs "great and mighty service against the occupiers of the crown of France." He must not only keep the agreement he had made at Fotheringhay the year before to break off the league between Scotland and France and never renew it, but he and his heirs must serve the king of England, whenever called upon, against the "occupiers of the crown of France" with all their power and at their own expense "unto the final conquest of the realm of France unto the obeissance of the king of England."

---

1. Stow, 434. Edward paid Sir James Liddell £40 and one of Gloucester's servants who had conducted Liddell to London 40s. Tellers' Roll, Mich. 22 Edw. IV.

The duke also promised Edward undisputed possession of Berwick and that, "being king and at freedom of marriage," he would, as he had also agreed at Fotheringhay, take one of Edward's daughters to wife. Lastly, he promised the full restoration of the lands and rights of the Earl of Douglas, who, a few days later, received letters of protection under the great seal of England and was recognized by Edward as "a free Scottish man unbounden for to take part and serve the high and mighty prince, Alexander, Duke of Albany, in his wars."[1] In return for all this Edward was expected to help Albany obtain the crown of Scotland and, to that end, was to notify the Duke of Gloucester and the Earl of Northumberland, wardens of the marches, that they must be ready at all times to send the duke aid to the extent of three thousand archers, paid by Edward, for six weeks' service. If there should "hap a great day of rescue of the duke, or any other necessary defence for him to be appointed," then Edward must see that the duke was "assisted and helped by such a notable army, joined to his friends, as, with God's grace, shall suffice. "[2]

Douglas probably started for the north as soon as he secured his letters of protection from Edward, and as he did so parliament was adjourned. The session had lasted less than a month, but both Edward and Gloucester had obtained what they were seeking, as not only had Gloucester received his extraordinary reward, but the Commons had granted the king a fifteenth and tenth "for the hasty and necessary defence" of the realm. The Commons did even more. Three days later, 18 February, they announced, after praising the services which the Duke of Gloucester, the Earl of Northumberland, Lord Stanley, and certain other barons and knights had performed in the war with Scotland, that, with the assent of the Lords, they had granted for the defence of the realm a tax on aliens. Again, however, as when two years before Edward had levied the three-quarters of a fifteenth and tenth he had seen fit to renounce after his return from France, special consideration was shown to some of the northern counties. At Gloucester's own suggestion, the counties of York, Cumberland, Northumberland, and Westmoreland and the cities of York and Kingston-on-Hull were exempted from the payment of the fifteenth and tenth on account of the labour and expense they had already

---

1. Warrants under the Signet, file 1391, 13 Feb. 22 Edw. IV; Rymer, XII, 176.
2. Rymer, XII, 173-176.

sustained in the Scottish war. There were also special exemptions in the case
of the tax on aliens, as the Commons themselves exempted the merchants
of Spain, Brittany, and the Hanse towns, while Edward added those of Italy,
who in December had secured from him another renewal for ten years of
their exemption from the tax on aliens granted by the parliament of 1453.[1]

The chief concession the king had to make before he obtained the fifteenth
and tenth was an act which was intended to insure to his "poor liege people"
proper payment for the goods taken from them by the royal purveyors. This
act provided for, first, the setting aside of eleven thousand pounds a year out
of the customs and subsidies collected in the chief ports of the kingdom, out
of the revenues of certain offices, the profits of ulnage, etc., for the expenses
of the royal household,[2] and second, for the resumption of all grants which
the king had made out of the customs and subsidies and out of the issues and
profits of ulnage. But there were some other fruits of the session, including
an act which sought to encourage a flow of new inhabitants to "poor and
desolate" Berwick by requiring all trade with Scotland, except what passed
through Carlisle and the west march, to be carried on through that town,
and by establishing the right of its freemen to a monopoly of the sale of
salmon caught in the Tweed. The statute of 1463 prohibiting the importation
of wrought silks was also re-enacted for a period of four years, and among
several new statutes was one which is suggestive of the great war between
man and machinery that was to loom so large in later English history. This
new statute forbade the use of fulling mills for two years on the ground that

> there is a subtle mean found now of late by reason of a fulling mill whereby
> more caps may be fulled and thicked in one day than by the might and strength
> of four score men by hand and foot may be fulled and thicked in the same day.

The caps fulled by the mills were declared to be of poorer quality than those
fulled by hand, but the real rub was not there, but in the fact that men were
in danger of losing their employment.[3]

---

1. *Rolls of Parl.*, VI, 197-198; *Cal. Patent Rolls*, III, 339, 342; Signed Bills, file 1523, no. 5405.
2. This is two thousand pounds less than the amount estimated in the Liber Niger to be
   necessary for the household. *Ordinances of the Royal Household*, 21.
3. *Rolls of Parl.*, VI, 198-202, 222-225; Statutes 22 Edw. IV, c. 3, 5, 8. Speaker Wode was
   paid £100 for his services during this parliament, which was the same amount that
   Alyngton had received at the end of the preceding one. Tellers' Roll, Mich. 22 Edw.
   IV; Devon, *Issues of Exchequer*, 505.

Edward was probably hoping to secure money from convocation as well as from parliament, as the Archbishop of Canterbury was asked, while parliament was in session, to call his clergy together. But the archbishop, when sending out his summons, chose 18 April as the date for the meeting of convocation, and before that day arrived the cares of this world had ceased to trouble Edward IV.[1] Perhaps little more was Edward destined to receive of a loan of two thousand pounds which the city of London agreed, on 22 February, to let him have, as some of the aldermen, each one of whom was expected to contribute fifty marks, and some of the eighty commoners who were called on to give fifteen pounds apiece, rebelled. The king demanded that the names of the contumacious ones should be sent to him, but unless the ungenerous aldermen and commoners repented very speedily, Edward never saw their money.[2]

On 20 February Edward wrote a letter to the Duke of Brittany which shows what his mind was dwelling on in these days when he was already walking in the valley of the shadow of death. Though Maximilian had made peace with Louis, Edward was evidently clinging to the vain hope that he could keep Francis II from surrendering to the enemy in the same way; for in his letter he offered to send the duke, at his own expense, four thousand archers for three months' service and have them ready at Plymouth or Dartmouth within a month at most after the duke called for them.[3] He promised also that if Francis desired to have still more men and was prepared to pay their wages, he should have them as well. It is a curious and interesting fact, however, that, a few days after he wrote this letter to Francis, Edward dispatched Garter "into the parties of France on certain our messages to be done there."[4]

Was Garter sent to revile and defy Louis, or to seek a reconciliation with him? If it was to defy him, the flourish was a meaningless one and must have called a mocking smile to Louis' cruel lips. For though Edward may have been trying to believe that he would yet get his revenge, Louis knew that, in order to invade France, the king of England would have to find far more help

---

1. Close Roll 22-23 Edw. IV, m. 9 dorso; *Reports touching Dignity of a Peer*, IV, 988; Wake, 381.
2. London Journal 9, f. 14-14b; Sharpe, I, 319.
3. Morice, III, 426; Dupuy, I, 410-411.
4. Warrants for Issues, 22 Edw. IV, 24 Feb.; Tellers' Roll, Mich. 22 Edw. IV.

than he could ever hope to receive from the Duke of Brittany, or even from a king of Scotland elevated to the throne by English arms. And as for Scotland, in a few days it was to be made evident again that the Duke of Albany was a very weak reed for anyone to lean on, as on 19 March the duke, still at Dunbar Castle, signed an agreement with James III which contained, among other strange articles revealing the weakness of both brothers, a promise by James to forgive Albany's transgressions and receive him into favour again and one by Albany to surrender his office of lieutenant general and never to come within six miles of James without a special licence. So lightly did Albany's pledges to the king of England rest on his mind and his conscience that he also promised to renounce his treasonable compact with him. To be sure, he undertook to obtain a treaty of peace with England and the marriage of James's son with Cecily of York, but that was by no means what Edward had bargained for.[1]

More than likely, however, Edward never knew of Albany's fresh defection. And it is doubtful if even Gloucester had heard of it before he was called to London by an event which opened up another channel for his over-leaping ambition and made the new campaign he had planned to carry on against the Scots appear a secondary matter.

In the middle of March Edward went to Windsor, but about the 25th he returned to Westminster Palace, and there, a few days later, he was seized with a sudden illness which from the first was so alarming that on 6 April word reached the city of York that he was dead and a dirge was sung in the Minster.[2] In reality the king's strength held out long enough to enable him to add a few codicils to his will,[3] to charge his executors to see that his debts were duly paid, and even to make an attempt to end the hostility which had existed for so long between Lord Hastings and the Woodvilles and which,

---

1. *Acts of Parl. of Scot.*, index, p. 31; *Exchequer Rolls of Scot.*, IX, xlix-lii.

2. Privy Seals; *Hist. Croy. Cont.*, 563-564; Davies, *York Records*, 142-143. According to the Croyland chronicler, Edward's last illness began about Easter, which in this year fell on 30 March.

3. Not the will, apparently, which he had made before his expedition to France, but one of more recent date. Cf. the will of 1475, as printed in *Excerpta Historica*, with the extracts from the Lambeth Registers quoted in *Royal Wills* (Society of Antiquaries, 1780), 345-348. See also Dr Gairdner's remarks on this subject, *Richard III*, 44. In the will of 1475 Queen Elizabeth's name heads the list of executors, while in the later one her name does not appear in the list at all.

though he himself had been able to hold it in check, might prove a grave danger when his restraining hand was removed and the sceptre passed to his young and inexperienced son. No thought of asking Queen Elizabeth to use her influence in the cause of peace, though she had been in no merely nominal sense the head of the Woodville faction, seems to have entered Edward's mind; and he could not call Earl Rivers to his bedside, as the earl was at Ludlow with the Prince of Wales. But he sent for Hastings, for whom his affection was so great that, in order to keep him near even in death, he had offered him a burial place in St George's Chapel,[1] and for the Marquis of Dorset, with some of the friends of each, and with almost his last breath he pleaded with these two men to lay aside their quarrels for the sake of his young children. So earnestly did he speak that at length they grasped each other by the hand and vowed mutual forgiveness.[2] Then, feeling that he had removed the most serious trouble his heir was likely to encounter, and resting in the hope that any other difficulties time might bring would be successfully overcome by his brother Gloucester, whose faithfulness he had never had occasion to question and whom he had probably named in his will as the protector of his son and the kingdom,[3] Edward IV closed his eyes in peace and, on 9 April 1483, rendered up his spirit.

There is some uncertainty about the nature of the disease which terminated Edward's life. Hall maintains that the ague the king had brought home with him from France in 1475 "suddenly turned into an incurable quarten";[4] but it is more probable that apoplexy[5] or acute indigestion induced by a "superfluous surfeit," to use Hall's words again, was the immediate cause of death. Indeed, a contemporary French historian, Thomas Basin, says definitely that it was a too hearty dinner of fruits and vegetables on Good Friday which brought the end.[6] On the other hand, Phillip de Commynes declares that what really killed the king of England was the treaty of Arras. This statement can scarcely be accepted literally, but it is at least easy to believe that anger and chagrin may have hastened the end of a life which

---

1. See Hastings's will, *Testamenta Vetusta*, I, 368.
2. More, *Hist. of Richard III*, 8-12; *Hist. Croy. Cont.*, 564.
3. Vergil, 685. Cf. Gairdner, *Richard III*, 44, 55.
4. Hall, 338.
5. Commynes, II, 63, 91; *Chronique Scandaleuse*, II, 130-131.
6. Basin, III, 133-134.

had been not too well lived. Had Death delayed his work three weeks longer, Edward would have been forty-one years old. It was an early age for a man to die, even then when the average life was considerably shorter than it is today; but for libertinism and high living, to both of which, there is no doubt, Edward was much given, even the strongest constitution must sooner or later pay the price. The Croyland chronicler reports with pious satisfaction that those who stood by the deathbed testified that the king died truly repentant for all his sins, but while he expresses the Christian hope that a godly end saved the king's soul, he adds with amusing frankness that perhaps it was well that the death summons came too swiftly to leave the penitent time for a change of heart.

When the king's spirit had flown, his lifeless body was "laid upon a board all naked, saving he was covered from the navel to the knees," and in this manner it "lay openly" for ten or twelve hours, during which all the lords spiritual and temporal gathered in London or the neighbourhood, and also the mayor and aldermen of the city, came to look upon it. Afterwards the body was "cered," and the following morning it was removed to St Stephen's Chapel, where, when the masses of Our Lady, the Trinity, and the Requiem had been sung, it was left to lie in state for eight days. On each of the eight days a solemn mass was sung by a bishop and offerings were made, and each night careful watch was kept. When the lying in state was finally over, the body was placed upon a bier, covered with a large black cloth of gold with a cross of white cloth of gold, and borne into the Abbey by fifteen knights and esquires for the body. Ten bishops and two abbots led the procession into the Abbey; in front of the bier, among the officers of arms, walked Lord Howard, with the dead king's banner; four knights supported the canopy of "cloth imperial fringed with gold and blue silk," four others bore aloft the banners of the Trinity, Our Lady, St George, and St Edward, and many lords followed or walked beside the bier, "laying their hands thereto." The usual "hearse" was waiting in the Abbey, and also the usual image "a personage like to the similitude of the king in habit royal, crowned with the very crown on his head, holding in that one hand a sceptre and in that other hand a ball of silver and gilt with a cross-pate." And when, on the following day, after a final service at which the Archbishop of York officiated and during which offerings were made by the mayor and aldermen of London, the judges, and the barons of the Exchequer, as well as by the lords and bishops, the funeral procession started for Windsor, this "personage" was placed, with the corpse, on the chariot. The chariot was hung with black velvet and drawn by six coursers with trappings of the same sombre material, and "upon the fore-horse and the thill-horse sat two chariot men, and on the four other horses sat four henchmen," while on either side "went divers knights and esquires for the body and other, some laying their hands to the draught and some leading the horses . . . . And the Lord Howard, the king's bannerer, rode next before the fore-horse, bearing the king's banner upon a courser trapped with black velvet with divers scutcheons of the king's arms, with his mourning hood upon his head."

The slow journey from Charing Cross, at which point the chariot was "censed" and the lords "took their horse," to Windsor was broken at Sion nunnery, where Edward's niece, Anne de la Pole was a nun;[1] and "the corpse and the personage" rested overnight in the choir of the nuns' church. The next day, when Eton was reached, the Bishops of Lincoln and Ely and the members of Eton College censed the corpse; and at the gate of Windsor Castle the Archbishop of York, the Bishops of Winchester, Norwich, Durham, and Rochester and the canons of St George's Chapel met the cortège and, after the corpse had been censed once more, led the way to the beautiful but still unfinished chapel, where a "marvellous well wrought hearse" was in readiness, as well as the massive marble tomb which, in anticipation of this day, Edward had caused to be erected on the north side of the altar not many months before. That night a "great watch" was kept by lords, knights, and others, and the next morning took place the final rites, when the Mass of Our Lady was sung by the Bishop of Durham, the Mass of the Trinity by the Bishop of Lincoln, and the Requiem by the Archbishop of York. When the time for the offerings came, the shield was offered by Lord Maltravers and Viscount Berkeley, "a rich sword which had been sent from the Pope"—no doubt the one Sixtus IV had presented to the king on St George's Day in the preceding year—by Sir John and Sir Thomas Bourchier, "the king's aunt's sons," and the helmet by Lords Stanley and Hastings; and then Sir William Parre, arrayed in full armour, save that his head was bare, and holding in his hand an axe, "poll downward," rode up to the choir door and, after alighting,

---

1. Dugdale, II, 190. Though the nunnery of Sion was a Lancastrian foundation, Edward had bestowed a number of favours on it. See *Cal. Patent Rolls*, I, 56, 97, 144, 216.

was escorted into the church to make his offering as "the man of arms." Next followed the general offerings, those of the lords consisting of the usual cloths of gold; and when at last the body of Edward IV was laid in the tomb, the great officers of his household, the steward, the chamberlain, the treasurer, and the comptroller, threw their staves into the grave "in token of being men without a master and out of their offices," and afterwards all the heralds did likewise with their coats of arms. Then straightaway the heralds were given other coats of arms of the kings of England, and when they had put them on, they all cried, "'Le roy est vif! Le roy est vif! Le roy est vif!' praying to God and saying Paternoster and Ave Maria for the defunct."[1]

---

1. *Letters, etc., Illustrative of Reigns of Rich. III and Hen. VII,* I, xvii, 1-10; *Archæologia,* I, 350-357. Edward's gilt coat of mail, covered with crimson velvet embroidered with the arms of England and France in gold, pearls, and rubies, and also a banner of the royal arms, remained hanging over his tomb until 23 October 1642, when they were taken down by the parliamentary soldiers. Ashmole, *Hist. and Antiquities of Berkshire* (Reading, 1736), 295; Beltz, lxxiv.

BOOK VI

MISCELLANEA

1

EDWARD'S RELATIONS WITH HIS COUNCIL, WITH PARLIAMENT, AND WITH THE CHURCH

Students of English constitutional history have shown a tendency to regard the reign of Edward IV as of little consequence, except in so far as it was a preparation for the coining of the Tudor autocrats. Nor is this very surprising, since the twenty-two years during which Edward wore the crown are certainly not memorable for any striking constitutional innovations or developments. When the house of Lancaster gave place to the house of York in 1461, the shire courts, over which presided the sheriffs appointed by the crown and through which most of the work of local government was carried on, were already centuries old; the great financial and judicial organs of the central government, the Exchequer and the courts of King's Bench, Common Pleas, and Exchequer, had long since emerged from that nebulous body of Norman days, the Curia Regis, and the itinerant justices, whose office welded local and central governments together, had been going their rounds since the days of Henry II. The legislative body of the kingdom had also taken on its final form long before Edward of York seized the throne. It was more than a century and a half since the meeting of "the Model Parliament," and by this time England had grown accustomed to seeing knights of the shire and well-to-do burgesses reluctantly wending their way to Westminster, along with the nobles and great prelates of the land, to vote supplies to the crown. Even the electoral franchise in the counties had recently been determined by an act of parliament of the year 1430, which decreed that only men owning a freehold worth forty shillings a year should have the right to vote in the shire courts for the knights of the shire who were to represent them in parliament. And yet, even if no new institutions came into existence while Edward was king and no old ones underwent vital changes, his reign is not devoid of all interest for the constitutional historian. For the institutions which were the outcome of centuries of growth were put to a hard test in his day, and both their weakness and their strength were made manifest in a way that had its lessons for the kings who came after him, and also for the people over whom those kings ruled.

Edward was not by instinct either a despot or a tyrant. On the contrary, there is good reason to believe that he ascended the throne with a keen sense of the responsibilities of his high office and a genuine desire to be, as he told his first parliament, "as good and gracious sovereign lord as ever was any of my noble progenitors to their subjects and liegemen." Unluckily, however, he had grown to manhood in the midst of civil war and been raised to the throne by the sword. Unluckily, too, he came into possession of a royal prerogative of ill-defined limits, of a kingdom whose whole constitution was somewhat vague and formless and whose people, in spite of the remarkable strides they had already made towards political liberty, were still as a whole very far from possessing the political wisdom and alert national consciousness which they were to display in after years. How could it be expected under such conditions that, even should his good intentions persist to the end, Edward would not sometimes offend against the rights and liberties of his subjects? And unfortunately, as the years passed, not only did the experiences of bitter reality tend to weaken the king's youthful goodwill and resolutions, but selfish and evil influences were brought to bear on him which after a time seemed to cause his nature to undergo a sad alteration.

Nothing illustrates better the breakdown of Edward's good intentions than the change which took place in his attitude towards the administration of justice. That he made an earnest effort at the start to see that the law was properly administered in his kingdom there is no doubt. He even took the trouble on several occasions to sit in person in the court of King's Bench, where theoretically the sovereign was always present but where in reality he had not been seen for many a day. Repeatedly, too, he announced his determination to be just and impartial towards all his subjects. But as the wearer of the crown, he enjoyed the dangerous right to appoint and remove the officers of the law, and though this right had been less often abused than might easily have happened in a period of constantly recurring civil disturbances, the day came when Edward disgraced himself by dismissing a man whom he should have rewarded, not punished, for the fearless stand he had taken on behalf of justice and right. Chief Justice Markham's only offence consisted in charging the jury to bring in a less severe verdict against

Sir Thomas Cook than was desired by those who had brought about Cook's arrest, but for that fault, and that fault only, he lost his office. Again, the trial of Burdett, Stacy, and Blake in 1477 is painful evidence not only of how far it lay within the power of the king to control the courts and to pervert justice to serve his own ends, but also of how completely Edward had forgotten by that time the good resolutions of his early days. And evidently it was not merely in such important cases as that of Burdett, Stacy, and Blake that Edward stooped to interfere. Two brief entries which occur in an account presented by the tellers of the Exchequer in 1481 speak for themselves:

> "Paid to John Wideslade for his labour in making of a return of a verdite[1] which passed with the king in Devonshire against Philip Atwell and other —vjs. viijd.
>
> Also paid to John Tailour for part of his reward for labouring of the jury which gave the foresaid verdite and caused them to pass—xxvjs viijd. "[2]

Finally, it can never be forgotten that Edward IV was the king who extended the jurisdiction of the court of high constable to include cases of high treason and let loose upon England the savagery of John Tiptoft, Earl of Worcester, or that to his reign belong "the first authoritative proofs" of the use of torture in England, in the cases of Cornelius and Hawkins.[3]

Another instrument of government which Edward bent to his will was his council. England had suffered much in the days of Henry VI, but the English people had been just enough to lay the blame where it belonged, which was at the door of Henry's councillors. Not only during the years of Henry's minority, but during his sickly manhood as well, it was the council, not the king, that had wielded the powers of kingship. But for such evils as existed in the reign of Henry's successor it was impossible to blame the council, since, although to certain members of his council, whose advice was too often none of the best, Edward may have been at times too prone to listen, his council, as a body, did not dictate to him, but bowed to his dictates. What better proof of this could be asked for than William Monypenny's reports to Louis XI of the council meetings held in the early months of 1468 when,

---

1. Verdict.
2. Tellers' Account, Exchequer T. R., Council and Privy Seal, file 92, m. 26.
3. Stubbs, III, 282.

although Warwick was bringing all his great influence to bear against the Burgundian alliance, and Monypenny himself had done everything he could think of to guide the minds of Edward's advisers in the desired direction, the king made his decision to suit himself?

In spite of the almost complete lack of council records of Edward's reign, there is plenty of evidence that the council met frequently while he was king, and that the meetings were ordinarily held in the Star Chamber at Westminster.[1] The chancellor, treasurer, and keeper of the privy seal were all *ex officio* members of the council and necessarily constant attendants at its meetings, and doubtless they often pressed their advice on the king and at times succeeded in exercising a guiding and restraining influence over him. Yet, after all, these officers were appointees of their royal master, and if they ventured to oppose him too far, as George Neville found out to his sorrow, dismissal was the penalty. The Archbishop of Canterbury, who by virtue of his office was the first constitutional adviser of the crown,[2] was also a pretty faithful attendant at the council meetings, and his opinion must have carried much weight in its deliberations. But Thomas Bourchier was so much of a courtier, and also so strong a partisan of the house of York, that he was not likely to set up his will against the king's. Nor were the other prelates who attended Edward's council meetings from time to time more likely to give him trouble by their opposition. To follow the proceedings of convocation during Edward's reign is to become convinced that the whole body of the clergy was well under the king's control.

It was only from the temporal lords of his council, therefore, that Edward need fear any formidable attempt to force unwelcome advice upon him, and, as it happened, the most important temporal lords were seldom seen in his council chamber. Warwick, for example, the most powerful and self-asserting of all the temporal lords, was too busy in the north and at Calais, where there was a special council to look after the king's affairs, to spend much time in the Star Chamber. And probably Lord Fauconberg (afterwards Earl of Kent),

1. For proof that the Star Chamber was the usual meeting place of the council at this period, see Warrants of the Council, file 1547; Signed Bills, file 1499, no. 4213, file 1508, no. 4671; and payments for fuel, etc., for the "camera consilii regis stellata," for example, in Tellers' Roll, 4 Edw. IV, and Issue Roll, Easter 9 Edw. IV, 28 April. Cf. Scofield, *A Study of the Court of Star Chamber*, 3.
2. Stubbs, III, 303.

who was made a salaried member of the council immediately after Edward's accession,[1] had almost as little time as Warwick himself to spare for council meetings. The same must have been true of the Earl of Worcester, who was appointed a member of the council on 1 November 1461;[2] for, except during his two terms as treasurer of England, Worcester was generally engaged on business for the king in remote parts of the kingdom. Some other lords, such as the Earls of Essex and Rivers, both of whom, like Worcester, served their turns as treasurer, Lord Wenlock, who probably became a member of the council when Fauconberg did,[3] and Lords Dacre, Scales, Ferrers, Hastings, Cromwell, Mountjoy, Duras, Howard, Grey, Beauchamp, and Dynham, also appeared occasionally at Edward's council table. But side by side with these noblemen sat a good many lesser men, such as the Dean of St Severin's, the Dean of St Paul's, Sir John Say, Sir John Fogge, Thomas Colt, Thomas Kent, and William Notyngham, who, having no duties in distant parts of the country, were able to attend the council meetings much more frequently than their noble colleagues; and on the subserviency of these men Edward could count with certainty. It was the predominance of these lesser men, in fact, which made the council so pliable a tool in Edward's hands and explains the jealousy and distrust it excited in the breasts of the great lords. When Warwick and Clarence rose in revolt and sought in their manifesto of 12 July 1469, to draw a parallel between Edward and three of the most unfortunate of his predecessors, Edward II, Richard II, and Henry VI, one of the charges they brought against him was that he had "estranged the true lords of his blood from his secret council." And when Sir John Fortescue, probably after he himself had become one of Edward's councillors, wrote his treatise on the Governance of England, the ideal council he tried to portray was very different from the one of which he was a member. For what the great jurist recommended was a council composed of, first, twelve spiritual and twelve temporal men, "of the wisest and best disposed men that can be found in all the parties of this land," who should take an oath to accept no fee or reward from anyone save the king and who could be removed only with the consent of the majority of their fellow

---

1. See above, Vol. 1, p. 159.
2. See above, Vol. 1, p. 217.
3. As early as 8 August 1461, Wenlock is described as a councillor of the king. See his commission to treat with the Duke of Burgundy, French Roll 1 Edw. IV, m. 24.

councillors, and second, four spiritual and four temporal lords who should be chosen anew each year. Fortescue thought that all members of the council should be paid for their services, but the spiritual men less than the laymen, "because they shall not need to keep an household in their country while they been absent, as the temporal men must needs do for their wives and children"; and over-all he would have set, as presiding officer, a chief councillor chosen by the king from among the twenty-four and holding office at the king's pleasure.[1]

But if Edward really shut the true lords of his blood out of his secret council, at least he frequently consulted "the lords spiritual and temporal of this our land assembled in our great council," to quote his own description of what is known as the *magnum concilium*.[2] The latest historian of the council believes that, after the fourteenth century, the meetings of the great council were generally merely expanded sessions of the privy council, and that in both organization and functions there was only one council.[3] Yet even if this be granted, it must still be acknowledged that the distinction between the privy council and the great council was a very real one and fully appreciated by the king's subjects. The privy council sat day after day at Westminster, weighing and deciding a large variety of matters such as would naturally be laid before the king's advisers and also attending to a certain amount of judicial business,[4] while the great council met only when it was specially summoned, and was summoned only when very grave questions of state were up for consideration. For to require the chief men of the land to come to Westminster or Reading or Canterbury, or such other place as the king might designate, to give their sovereign the benefit of their advice was no light matter. Yet serious undertaking though it was to call a great council, writs of privy seal summoned the lords spiritual and temporal to Edward's assistance on a good many occasions of which we have knowledge, and probably on a good many more which we hear nothing about.

---

1. *Governance of Eng.*, 145-147. Cf. Stubbs, III, 251-252.
2. Edward's letter to the city of Salisbury, 27 February 1481. Hatcher, *Old and New Sarum*, 198-200.
3. Baldwin, *The King's Council in England during the Middle Ages*, 107-108.
4. Prof. Baldwin thinks that the paucity of council records for the first part of Edward's reign indicates a reduction of the judicial activities of the council. But the part which the council took in Edward's controversy with the Hanseatic merchants is enough to prove that its judicial labours did not cease, however slight may be the evidence of it which we now possess.

For example, it seems to have been a great council which gathered at Stamford in August 1464, to consider the state of the currency, and also at Reading in the following month when the same subject was discussed and when Edward made the announcement of his marriage. And according to William of Worcester, it was at a *magnum concilium* held at Westminster in December of the same year that provision was made for the new queen's expenses. It was with the consent of such a council, too, that on 1 July 1467, the Bishop of Ely received the commission to treat with the king of Castile which resulted in the signing of the treaty of alliance between England and Castile five days later and Edward's promise that neither he nor his successors would ever press the hereditary claim to the crown of Castile belonging to him by virtue of his descent from Constance of Castile. Parliament was prorogued on the very day the Bishop of Ely was given this important commission, and it is evident that the king had seized the opportunity afforded by the presence of so many noblemen in the capital to obtain special advice and approval regarding a matter which was too weighty to be decided at an ordinary council meeting and yet could not properly be laid before parliament. For the bishop's commission was given under the great seal and sign manual at Westminster Palace in the presence of the Archbishop of Canterbury, the Bishop of Bath and Wells, chancellor of England, the Bishops of Norwich, Lincoln, and Durham, the Dukes of Clarence and Suffolk, the Earls of Arundel, Essex, and Kent, Earl Rivers, treasurer of England, Lords Audley, Dudley, Cromwell, and Hastings, and many other *proceres* and *magnates* of the realm, besides Master Henry Sharp, canon of London, king's notary.[1] Certainly in this instance at least the great council seems to answer well to Bishop Stubbs's description of it as an "extra-parliamentary session of the House of Lords."[2]

According to William of Worcester once more, it was before the *magnum concilium* that Margaret of York came on 1 October 1467, and agreed to marry Charles the Bold. And it must have been with the consent of the same council that the statute prohibiting the importation of Burgundian merchandise had been revoked two days before. Again, it must have been such a council meeting which Warwick was persuaded to attend in January

---

1. French Roll 7 Edw. IV, m. 16; Rymer, XI, 588.
2. Stubbs, III, 262.

1468, and at which the king chose, because the lords of his council were "then present more plener in number," as the chancellor stated in his address to parliament a few months later, to set forth "by his own mouth" the subject of the Burgundian marriage, and also his wish to recover the crown of France.[1] When the storm had burst over Edward's head and Warwick, after holding him captive for several weeks, allowed him to return to London in October 1469, all the peers of the realm were summoned to a great council meeting whose sittings in the Parliament Chamber began early in November and did not end until 10 February or later. And in June 1470, after Warwick and Clarence had fled to France, Edward held another *magnum concilium* at Canterbury which lasted two days and which was attended by the Bishops of Ely, Rochester, Bangor, Durham, and Carlisle, the Marquis of Montagu, the Earls of Northumberland, Essex, Worcester, and Rivers, Lords Maltravers, Cromwell, Abergavenny, Say, and "many other barons and knights."[2] In February 1478, eighty-five of the great men of England, if all came who had been summoned by the king's letters of privy seal, assembled at Westminster to consider the situation which had been produced by the death of Charles the Bold; on 15 November 1479, a great council assembled at Guildford;[3] and in November 1480, there was another meeting of "our great council" at Westminster to decide what should be done to punish the Scots. Finally, the meetings of the "lords of the council" held at the Tower in October 1482, were evidently much more than ordinary council meetings, as the king himself returned from Norfolk in order to be present at them and Lord Hastings was summoned from Calais to attend them.

　　Although Edward's council incurred dislike and distrust, as the complaint of Warwick and Clarence shows, it is a striking fact that at no time during his reign did parliament make any such effort to control the council as it had made in Richard II's reign and again in the reigns of Henry IV and Henry VI, and that even Fortescue, when delineating his model council, did not go so far as to suggest that the king's councillors ought to receive their appointment from parliament.[4] This failure of parliament to make

---

1. *Rolls of Parl.*, V, 623.
2. *Chron. of John Stone*, 113-114.
3. *Christ Church Letters*, 32. The fact that the king was at Guildford in November 1479, makes it more than probable that the letter cited belongs to that year.
4. Fortescue's plan would apparently have increased the influence of the council over

any attempt to interfere with Edward's council is doubly worthy of remark, because it is traceable not merely to increased strength on the part of the crown, but to increased weakness on the part of parliament.

Even the Lancastrian kings, who owed to parliament their right to reign and who were forced by their financial necessities to call upon their subjects continually for help, had not always observed the rule of annual parliaments. And under Edward IV, who, though he sought parliamentary recognition of his title to the throne, would have asserted that he did so without any real need, and who, despite the fact that he undertook to renew the war in France and afterwards sent armies against Scotland, was in general free from the financial strain of foreign wars, that rule was entirely disregarded. Only seven times in all did Edward issue writs of summons to a parliament, and as the writs issued in August 1469, were afterwards recalled, only six parliaments actually met during his reign. The first of these parliaments, which met in November 1461, sat about seven weeks, and when it reassembled in May 1462, was immediately dissolved. The second one had a considerably longer life, as it met for the first time on 29 April 1463, and was not dissolved until sometime in the early part of 1465; but, owing to the disturbances in the kingdom, four times during its existence it reassembled only to be at once prorogued, and it was probably actually in session only about three months all told. The third parliament Edward summoned lived just a year, from June 1467, to June 1468, and during that time it sat between seven and eight weeks; but it too reassembled on one occasion only to be prorogued, not on account of a civil upheaval this time, but because the king was not quite ready to announce the results of his negotiations with Burgundy. On the other hand, Edward's fourth parliament was the longest one England had known up to that time, as it met for the first time on 6 October 1472, and was not dissolved until 14 March 1475; and during the two years and a half of its existence there were six sessions of some length. After his return from France, however, Edward waited more than two years before he called another parliament, and the one which met on 16 January 1478,

---

parliament rather than the influence of parliament over the council; for the council was to deliberate upon how the laws "may be amended in such things as they need reformation in; where through the parliaments shall mowe do more good in a month to the mending of the law than they shall mowe do in a year if the amending thereof be not debated and by such council riped to their hands."

sat only until the following 26 February and did little save pass the bill for Clarence's attainder. And after the parliament of 1478 came a gap of no less than five years, as Edward's sixth and last parliament was not opened until 20 January 1483. It was adjourned a month later, and soon after its existence was terminated by the king's death.

The story of what happened in Edward's parliaments has already been told at considerable length, but a little more emphasis may well be laid on a few facts concerning them, and particularly on Edward's relations with them. First of all attention may be called to the significance of what occurred in connection with John Paston's election to parliament in 1461. Paston's election was attended with much quarrelling and even a show of force, and Edward, when he was told of this, summoned both Paston and the sheriff of Norfolk, Sir John Howard, before him. Paston, however, delayed his coming, and this so angered the king that he exclaimed: "We have sent two privy seals to Paston by two yeomen of our chamber and he disobeyeth them; but we will send him another tomorrow, and by God's mercy if he come not then he shall die for it. We will make all other men beware by him how they shall disobey our writing." Accordingly, when Paston at last put in an appearance, he was sent to the Fleet prison, and there he languished until the king, deciding, after investigation, that Howard was the man who deserved punishment, sent that gentleman to take Paston's place, appointed a knight of his own household sheriff of Norfolk, and gave the people of the county to understand that he intended to have his laws kept.[1]

Edward's quick, strong handling of the disputed election in Norfolk was a promptly given warning that the new hand at the helm was a forceful one and that it was going to compel respect for the laws. It is impossible, also, to read the speech which the new king made to the Commons at the close of his first parliament without feeling convinced that he began his reign with every intention of living on the best of terms with the representatives of his people. Who knows, therefore, but what, had circumstances been less unfavourable, Edward IV might have been by his own choice as truly a "constitutional king" as any of his Lancastrian predecessors had been? But he was young and inexperienced and, what was worse, he had acquired with the

---

1. *Paston Letters*, III, 302-303, 313-314. Howard obtained a pardon on 6 February 1462. Pardon Roll 1-6 Edw, IV, m. 43.

crown many enemies and heavy debts. This made the task lying before him a herculean one for which he would need the help to restore law and order and to straighten out the finances of his kingdom which it was the duty of parliament to give him, just as much as he would need the help to overcome his enemies and reunite the kingdom which Warwick and his kinsmen stood ready to furnish. But unluckily parliament, to its shame, showed little inclination to do its part. Although the long and flattering speech which the Speaker of Edward's first parliament took the liberty of addressing to him ended with a plain intimation that he would be expected to keep the kingdom in better order than Henry VI had done, no steps were taken— with the exception that ample provision seemed to be made for the king's personal and household expenses by the forfeitures following upon the attainder of the Lancastrians, by the act of resumption, and by the addition of the duchy of Lancaster to the crown estates—to set the general finances of the kingdom in order or to meet the extraordinary expenses made inevitable by the still unpacified condition of a large part of the country. And although a statute transferring to the justices of the peace the criminal jurisdiction which the sheriffs had hitherto exercised in their tourns, and shamelessly abused, probably helped to some extent to secure a better administration of the law, that measure too fell far short of what the situation called for. Yet this was all that Edward's first parliament did to assist him to solve his problems—unless account be taken of the promise given to him by the lords spiritual and temporal in the parliament chamber that they would observe his new ordinance against maintenance and the giving of liveries. And alas! William Huse afterwards declared, probably with this very promise in mind, that, while he was Edward's attorney, he saw all the lords swear to obey the statutes relating to maintenance and the giving of liveries and then, an hour later, in the Star Chamber, make retainments and in other ways directly violate their oath.[1]

When Edward, within a year after the dissolution of his first parliament, summoned his second one, he showed a still keener interest in the conduct of the elections than he had shown before. He made a great effort in at least two counties, and apparently in all, to see that only men of "reputation"

---

1. Year Book, 1 Hen. VII, no. 3.

were present when the elections took place; and because his effort failed, he postponed the parliament and issued a proclamation commanding that only forty shilling freeholders, that is to say, only properly qualified electors, should assemble in the county courts to elect the knights of the shire, and that they should come "in peaceable manner." It was too much to hope that this proclamation would be obeyed to the letter, but at any rate the new House of Commons was probably filled with the king's friends, and the Speaker chosen to preside over the Commons, John Say, was a member of the king's council.

Say presided over the House of Commons not only during the parliament of 1463-1465, but also during that of 1467-1468, and it is therefore not surprising to find that both of these parliaments were disposed to be generous to the king. Edward's troubles, though still serious, were certainly not greater in 1463 than they had been in 1461, yet, while his first parliament had made him no direct grant of money, his second one voted him an aid of £37,000, a sum which exceeded by £6,000 the fifteenth and tenth usually granted by the Commons, when they saw fit to grant anything. It is true that this novel form of grant caused such a popular outcry that the king had to renounce the extra £6,000 and promise that the remaining £31,000 should be raised in the old orthodox way, after the manner of a fifteenth and tenth; but when this same parliament reassembled more than a year later, it passed a fresh act of resumption and, with doubtful wisdom, as it thereby sacrificed one valuable hold on the crown, made the king a life grant of tunnage and poundage and the subsidy on wool similar to the one which had been made to Henry V upon his triumphant return from France and afterwards, in 1453, to Henry VI. And the parliament of 1467-1468, pleased by the king's announcement that he intended to live henceforth "upon my own" and not to ask his subjects for money except when their welfare or the safety of the country was at stake, presented him, during its first session, with still another act of resumption and, during its second, though in the meantime he had taken the unpopular step of revoking the acts which kept Burgundian products out of England, was led by his declaration of his purpose to "go over the sea into France" to give him two whole fifteenths and tenths for the defence of the realm, which meant, in this instance, for the overthrow of Louis XI and the recovery of England's lost possessions over sea.

Certainly the Commons had served the king well while Say was their Speaker. But what had the English people profited by Edward's second and third parliaments? They had gained many statutes concerned with wool, cloth, and other commodities, an act regulating the wearing apparel of men and women, another prohibiting any man or beast, save only soldiers and merchants with their merchandise, to sail to or from any port in Kent except Dover when passage and ships were to be had there, another which confirmed all previous statutes and ordinances against the giving of liveries and which was apparently as ineffectual as its predecessors, since both in 1472 and in 1483 the Commons requested that the same statutes should be proclaimed again,[1] another which was intended to save jurors in the county of Middlesex from annoying delays, and lastly, one which extended a pardon to all sheriffs who, during the first three troubled years of Edward's reign, had exercised their office for more than the legal term. But that was all. Not a single law of lasting value had been passed or, so far as is known, even proposed.

Nor did Edward's later parliaments leave any more valuable legacy to posterity. Both during the parliament of 1472-1475 and during the brief one of 1478, William Alyngton[2] occupied the position which Say had held in the two preceding ones; and though Alyngton was not, like Say, a member of the king's council when he was first chosen Speaker,[3] he became one eventually, as he not only served as a member of the council in England during the expedition to France but later, after he had rendered the unpleasant service of asking that Clarence's execution should be hastened, was appointed one of the king's permanent councillors. To judge from what came to pass while he held the speakership, Alyngton was an even more useful tool in Edward's hands than Say had been; for during the parliament of 1472-1475 grant after grant was made for the expedition to France, in spite of the fact that many persons suspected the king had no intention of leaving England, and during

---

1. *Rolls of Parl.*, VI, 8, 198. The city of London did what it could to check the giving of liveries by decreeing on 27 September 1467, that no freeman or officer of the city should take or use the livery of any lord or other magnate on penalty of losing his freedom and his office. London Letter Book L, f. 53.
2. Son of the William Alyngton who had been Speaker in 1429.
3. It will be remembered, however, that he was made a member of the council of the Prince of Wales in 1473, shortly before the Prince was sent to reside at Ludlow.

that of 1478 Clarence was attainted and other less weighty things were done to please the king. Nevertheless, Edward resented deeply the cautious and grudging way in which the grants for his French expedition were made, and when he found it necessary, after his return home, to renounce a part of the last grant he had received, he tried to cast the blame for the failure of the expedition on his people by claiming that he had not been provided with enough money.

So bitter was the taste left in Edward's mouth by the parliament of 1472-1475 that he resolved to rule henceforth without parliament, and so low had parliament sunk that he almost succeeded in keeping his resolution. Only his wish to secure Clarence's attainder induced him to summon the parliament of 1478; and only the prolongation of the war with Scotland, which had already been going on for two years, and the frightful news of the treaty of Arras drove him, five years later, to face the representatives of his people for what turned out to be the last time. Yet, even in his last parliament, Edward, or perhaps his brother Gloucester, was able to place a friend in the Speaker's chair. For John Wode had been victualler of Calais in the early part of Edward's reign, master of the ordnance from 1463 to 1477, and of late years under-treasurer of England. It is evident, consequently, that the king had succeeded again in filling the House of Commons with submissive men, and, instead of receiving the rebuke he richly deserved, he was given a fifteenth and tenth, as well as a tax on aliens, for the defence of the realm and his strange grant to Gloucester was meekly confirmed, while the only important concession he had to make in return was to consent to a limitation of the amount he might take from the crown revenues for his household expenses.

How did it happen that parliament failed so conspicuously during Edward's reign to wrest any new and lasting concessions from the crown or to make any noteworthy additions to the laws of England? The answer is not far to seek. It is to be found partly in the influence the king was able to exert by guiding the elections and by bringing into play his consciously cultivated popularity, but chiefly in conditions within parliament itself. The special right of the lords of the realm to advise the crown no one disputed, and, had they been asked, the members of the House of Lords would have asserted, with astonishment at the raising of the question, that of course they constituted the most important branch of the legislature. In reality, however, the preponderant strength had passed from the Lords to their less haughty and showy colleagues, the Commons, who owed their right to advise the king not to the chance of noble birth or to the holding of some high ecclesiastical office, but to the choice of their neighbours in the county or of their fellow citizens in the borough. For the House of Lords represented, first, a spiritual nobility which, through the growth of a new and more independent religious thought, was losing its hold upon the people and second, a temporal nobility which was being steadily weakened by the numerous deaths and attainders resulting from a long-continued civil war; while the House of Commons represented the larger freeholder, the well-to-do yeoman of the counties and the middle-class Englishman of the towns, who, thanks to his growing wealth and intelligence, had become the real backbone of the nation. But in Edward's day the Commons did not yet realize how strong they were or understand the full significance of the powers and privileges they had won under the Lancastrian kings; and their half-awakened state, added to their preoccupation with questions of industry and commerce, made it possible for the king to lead them in most things to do what he wished.

There is one fact, however, which should always be kept in mind. Edward's control over parliament never reached the point where he could dare to forget to be conciliatory, and the "poor Commons" never became too weak to keep a firm grip on the purse-strings. So difficult did Edward find it to persuade the Commons to grant him money that he usually tried to obtain what he wanted without their help; and for the student of constitutional history perhaps the chief interest of his reign attaches to the devices he employed to extract money from his subjects without the aid or authority of parliament. But as so much has already been said in the foregoing pages about the king's forced loans and benevolences, the subject may be passed over here without further comment, though it may be well to add that, while to demand *gifts* to the crown, which was what Edward did when he called for a benevolence, seems to have been a new departure,[1] it would probably

---

1. Benevolences are described in Statute 1 Richard III c. 2, as "a new imposition," but Stubbs says (III, 281) that, while they were looked upon as something new, they were perhaps only a "resuscitated form of some of the worst measures of Edward II and Richard II." Strange to say, however, Stubbs seems to make no distinction between forced loans and benevolences. The assertion in Richard's statute that the benevolences had compelled many men "to break up their households and to live in great penury and wretchedness" may be dismissed as an exaggeration.

be hard to distinguish between Edward's method of raising loans and that employed at times by the Lancastrian kings, as, for example, when the Earl of Wiltshire, with the sanction of the king's council, called for loans to resist the expected Yorkist invasion and "taxed the sum what every man should leave."

The most remarkable financial feat Edward ever accomplished was the waging of war on Scotland for nearly two years without a grant from parliament for the purpose, and it may not be amiss to recall in a few words how he succeeded in doing this. During the first year of the war, when neither the English nor the Scots essayed anything more serious than short raids across the border, Edward threw the burden of the war on the northern counties by issuing commissions of array for Yorkshire, Northumberland, Westmoreland, and Cumberland. He had no legal right to demand that any county should raise men for service outside of the county limits except in case of invasion by "strange enemies," but it was easy, especially after the Earl of Angus had burned Bamburgh, to represent that the kingdom was in danger of invasion; and the northern counties, long sufferers at the hands of the Scots, seem to have accepted the burden laid upon them as belonging to the proper order of things. In 1481, however, when the war assumed larger proportions and he proposed to take a personal share in the fighting, Edward did not repeat the commissions of array. Instead, he obtained a tenth from convocation, called for a benevolence, which was probably paid in most cases with ready money but by the city of York with six score armed men[2] and by the county of Lancaster with a thousand archers, and finally, daringly demanded the payment of the three quarters of a fifteenth and tenth which he had remitted after he came home from France. The result of these high-handed measures seems to have been just what one would expect, namely, "adverse turmoil," and in consequence no invasion of Scotland was possible that year. But much money had evidently been collected for the

---

1. Statute 4 Hen. IV, c. 13.
2. York seems to have granted the king the same "benevolence" in two succeeding years, and this was in addition to the eighty men sent to the Duke of Gloucester in May 1482. Davies, *York Records*, 112, 130. Probably the king also raised quite a little money through an order of the council of the duchy of Lancaster, issued on 27 October 1480, for the levying of fines for respite of knight's service upon all tenants of the duchy in the county of Lincoln who held by that service. *Duchy of Lancaster, Books of Decrees and Orders*, Vol. I, p. 42.

war, for the next year, though still no parliament had been summoned, at least twenty thousand soldiers receiving wages from the king marched with Gloucester to Edinburgh. That Edward was able to send twenty thousand paid soldiers into a neighbouring country without the help of parliament is a fact which seems more remarkable the longer one contemplates it. It may even be considered the most remarkable fact of the king's career—unless exception be made of his success in persuading parliament, a few months later, to forgive his sins and make him the grant he had put off asking for as long as he possibly could.

Next in interest to Edward's relations with parliament are his relations with the Church. He and Warwick returned to England from Calais in 1460 under the aegis, so to speak, of a papal legate, and unquestionably this fact was of considerable help to them in the days that followed. But it was probably very lucky for Edward and for England that Margaret of Anjou so soon compassed Coppini's downfall, as the legate's disgrace and recall severed a bond which ultimately must have proved awkward, if not actually dangerous. Coppini's conceit may have led him to overrate his contribution to the success of the house of York, but there is no doubt that he had a considerable claim on the gratitude of Edward and Warwick; and had he obtained from Pius II the ready support he and his Yorkist friends looked for and been able to accept the English bishopric the grateful Yorkists were willing to bestow on him, so excellent an opportunity for papal interference in England would have been opened up that, later on, Edward would almost inevitably have found himself involved in relations with Rome which were inconsistent with, and imperilling to, the independent attitude so remarkably maintained by the English church in the past. As it was, Coppini ended his days far from England, and when Pius proposed to exact a tenth from the English clergy for the support of his crusade, Edward, though, as a Christian prince, professing sympathy with the Pope's enterprise, refused to allow the papal bulls to be brought into his kingdom. In the end the king suffered the clergy to grant a subsidy of sixpence in the pound, but the money was to be paid into his hands instead of directly into the Pope's, and in his hands much if not all of it actually remained.

With Pius's successor, Paul II, Edward's relations were not altogether happy, as Paul allowed himself to become more or less mixed up in Warwick's treasonable schemes. Of the inclination of papal legates to stick a finger into the internal affairs of the countries to which they were accredited Edward had already had a sample in Coppini's case, and it will be recalled that the too great intimacy of one of Paul's legates with the Archbishop of York helped to bring the Nevilles under suspicion. Put on his guard, Edward succeeded temporarily in counteracting Warwick's influence at Rome, and Paul not only declined to grant the dispensation for the marriage of Clarence and Warwick's daughter, but sent the cardinal's hat, so much desired by the Archbishop of York, to the Archbishop of Canterbury instead. Afterwards Warwick so far triumphed that the marriage dispensation was granted, but as Paul died a few months after Warwick fell at Barnet, Edward escaped the need of further intercourse with him, and such differences as he had with the next occupant of the papal throne, Sixtus IV, do not seem to have been very serious, or at any rate to have left any permanent ill-feeling.

In December 1474, Sixtus wrote a complaining letter to Edward asking why he received no money in spite of the fact that his collector had been in England many months; and in May 1476, he sent two still more indignant epistles demanding the release of his nuncio and two other men whose imprisonment had been sought and secured by certain false accusers in England jealous of them and of the Holy See. It became evident later, however, that Edward too could write testy letters. On some occasion, perhaps in 1474 when he went to Italy on his embassy to the king of Naples, the Abbot of Abingdon had been directed to go to Rome and inform the Pope that the monastery of Westminster was suffering serious injury because of an unusually frequent change of abbots, and to beg that some remedy might be found; and because Sixtus paid no heed, Edward got a little out of patience and finally, on 23 May 1478, wrote to remind His Holiness of the frequent letters he had written to him on behalf of this ancient and holy monastery and to repeat his request that something should be done for its relief. Owing to its poverty, the monastery could not complete its church, the king said, and as this poverty was due, he declared, not simply to the disastrous times and the inundations which had destroyed many of the monastery's possessions, but to the large sums of money which had been spent at Rome for the confirmation of its abbots, he asked that hereafter the papal confirmation might be dispensed with when a new abbot was elected. When thus reprimanded, Sixtus woke up, and in a few months it was agreed that the monastery of Westminster should pay a hundred florins a year to the Holy See and that the Pope should excuse the abbots of the monastery from coming to Rome for their confirmation.[1]

Much more exciting were the exchanges between Edward and Sixtus a year later, when Edward's attempt to take a hand in the affairs of the Italian peninsula brought him into contact with the papacy in a novel way. But that long story has already been related, and, interesting as the episode was, it was soon over and apparently forgotten. When, in the spring of 1480, Sixtus authorized John Kendall, "turcoplerius of Rhodes," to grant indulgences as a means of raising recruits for the defence of the island of Rhodes, Edward not only permitted Caxton to print the indulgences at his Westminster press, but, upon the petition of the Grand Master of the knights of St John and the convent of Rhodes, took the Grand Master and the convent under his protection. In the following year John Giglis, the papal collector, was also allowed to seek aid in England against the Turks, and again Caxton printed the indulgences.[2] It will be remembered, too, that when the Prior of St John's was sent to France in August 1480, it was in part that he might talk with Louis XI about the defence of Rhodes. Yet neither the English king nor the English church displayed much desire to make sacrifices for the safety of Christendom; for when, in January 1481, Weston was summoned to Rhodes by the Grand Master, Edward refused to let him go, and when, in the following April, Giglis went before convocation and asked in the Pope's name for an aid for the war against the Turks, the clergy managed to avoid giving a definite answer.[3] After all, however, Edward neither wished to offend Sixtus nor to let it appear that he was indifferent to the danger threatening the Christian world, and ultimately—though this was not until late in the summer, before which time Mohammed II had died and the situation in the East had taken a turn for the better—he suffered Weston to set out for the East with John Kendall and a few other companions.[4] He even intrusted

1. Martène and Durand, II, 1476-1477, 1537-1538; *Cal. Venetian Papers*, I, 138-139; Dugdale, *Monasticon*, I, 276; *Hist. MSS. Com., Report 4*, app., 171.
2. Rymer, XII, 112; Blades, *Caxton* (condensed edit.), 222, 254-255; Signed Bills, file 1517, nos. 5146-5147; *Cal. Patent Rolls*, III, 193-194. Cf. Hist. MSS. Com., *Report 6*, app., 330.
3. *Cely Papers*, 55; Wilkins, III, 612-613; Wake, 381.
4. *Cely Papers*, 60, 63-66; Malden, An Unedited Cely Letter of 1482, *Trans. Royal Hist. Society*, Series III, Vol. 3, 159-165. When the prior reached Rome, the Pope wished for

Weston with some complimentary letters to the Grand Master, and on 20 May he wrote the letter to Sixtus in which he explained that, great as was his desire to assist in quelling the Turks, the perfidious behaviour of his neighbours, the Scots, which had driven him to assert the ancient right of the kings of England over Scotland and to prepare to lead an army against that kingdom, tied his hands. The king ventured, after making this excuse for himself, to suggest that His Holiness would do well to admonish James III "to mend his malicious ways;" and if it is true that it was Sixtus's bulls which caused James to disband his troops, those bulls were probably issued upon receipt of this letter and in the hope that, when peace was restored between England and Scotland, Edward would hasten to prove his gratitude to God and the Holy See by sending an army against the infidels.

With the prelates of the English church Edward's associations were at all times of the closest. The open support which he had received from the Archbishop of Canterbury and his clergy when he was seeking to obtain the throne had been of immeasurable assistance to him, and this made it all the more fitting that Thomas Bourchier should place the crown on his head and should wield great influence in his council chamber. It was always to the hands of an ecclesiastic, moreover, that Edward intrusted the great seal. His first chancellor was George Neville, Bishop of Exeter and afterwards Archbishop of York, his second Robert Stillington, Bishop of Bath and Wells, his third Lawrence Booth, Bishop of Durham, and his fourth Thomas Rotherham, Bishop of Lincoln and later Archbishop of York. His keepers of the privy seal, Stillington, Rotherham, and Russell, were also ecclesiastics. And it is doubly interesting to remember these facts on account of the heavy demands Edward made upon the clergy. For these officers of the crown, members of the clerical body though they were, must have lent their approval when, year after year, the king sought money from convocation instead of from parliament. More than that, their influence probably accounts largely

---

some reason to send him home again, but Weston asked to be allowed to continue his journey and Sixtus finally sent him on his way "as his ambassador with matters of great importance." *Cely Papers*, 69. Yet in the following March one of the Celys speaks of having received letters from Weston written at Naples, and it seems that the prior did not actually arrive in Rhodes until the summer of 1482. *Ibid.*, 88; Malden, *ut sup*. The complimentary letters which, according to Malden, Weston delivered to the Grand Master, were probably the letters of protection which Edward had granted in April 1480.

for the meekness with which the king's constant requests were granted, since what the two archbishops had sanctioned in the king's council the clergy of their provinces were not likely to oppose in convocation. The consent of Archbishop Bourchier must have been given even to a "voluntary subsidy" which Edward levied in the province of Canterbury in the spring of 1462,[1] and doubtless this explains why that extraordinary and illegal demand was not resisted. It is true that the clergy joined in the chorus of grumblers in the following year, when a subsidy was required of the stipendiary priests, whose poverty usually saved them from such taxation, and the campaign against the Scots, for which the money was asked, ended, as it seemed to the king's subjects, in failure. But this is the only instance of audible complaint by English churchmen against Edward IV; and it is surely to their credit that the one time they raised their voice against the king was when he extended his exactions to the poorest members of their body. Even when the king asked for a loan or a benevolence and, with seeming forgetfulness of all that convocation had done for him, turned confidently to the bishops, abbots, and priors of his kingdom, hands were dipped unremonstratingly, if not cheerfully, into church chests and the expected contributions brought forth.[2]

The king's financial burdens were not the only ones the clergy were asked to share with him. Not even from military service were the clergy exempted. A letter Edward sent to the Archbishop of York, as he was returning to London after the battle of Towton, not only summoned the archbishop to London, where his services were wanted at the coronation, but charged him to announce that all his clergy must be ready to go forth "in most defensible wise" to resist the Scots, and to send the names of those who would act as his deputies during his absence to Lords Fauconberg and Montagu, so that those lords could call his clergy to their aid in case of need. And two years later the same archbishop was directed to send his clergy to Durham to give help against the Scots.[3]

All things considered, therefore, the charter of 2 November 1462, by which Edward confirmed the much cherished and too often abused privilege of clerks to be tried in the ecclesiastical courts was small return for what

---

1. Scofield, *Eng. Hist. Review*, Jan., 1908, p. 85.
2. On the subject of Edward's retention of ecclesiastical temporalities, see above, vol. II, p. 160, note 3.
3. Raine, *Priory of Hexham*, I, app., C, Cvii-Cviii.

he required of the clergy of his kingdom. And yet there is no doubt that, while he took much money from the clergy, and while he fell far below his predecessor's standard of piety, Edward, according to his lights, was a loyal son of the Church. He proved his loyalty, if in no other way, by the efforts he made to stamp out heresy. The Croyland chronicler gives Edward the credit of being a very stern enemy to heretics, and abundant facts can be found to support his statement.

Although the Lollards, having ceased to find friends and supporters among the nobility, were no longer a political danger, and although the people in general unquestionably looked upon Lollardy as heresy, and heresy as a crime which it was the duty both of Church and of State to punish, the seed sown by Wycliffe was not entirely dead, and there were still Lollards in England. But the responsibility for the heresies which cropped up during Edward's reign probably lay less at Wycliffe's door than at that of a more recent reformer, Reginald Pecock, Bishop of Chichester, who had attacked the Lollards in his famous work, "The Repressor of Over Much Blaming of the Clergy," only to find himself condemned as a heretic. For while the popular mind made little distinction between one kind of heresy and another, it is evident that Edward traced such religious disaffection as he had to contend with rather to the writings of Pecock, who was still living, as a prisoner, during the first years of his reign, than to Wycliffe, who had been dead for nearly a century.

That Edward found time, even in the years when he was completing the conquest of his kingdom, to take an interest in the chastisement of heretics is indicated by what is told in a petition for a writ of *certiorari* which was addressed to George Neville while he was chancellor and still Bishop of Exeter. The petitioner, whose name is Thomas Wykes, states that, after certain persons of Risborough (in Buckinghamshire) had been "detect of heresy," the king sent a special commandment to the mayor and bailiff of Wycombe to assist the Bishop of Lincoln and his officers "in execution of their office in that behalf," but that, in spite of this, a great crowd of rioters came to carry off the heretics, and because he, Wykes, joined with some of his neighbours to help the bishop's officers, according to the king's commandment, two of the rioters had brought suit against him in the honour of Wallingford for trespass and had seized one of his horses for security.[1] What were the particular doctrines of the heretics of Risborough this petition does not reveal, but very likely one James Wyllys who was tried before the Bishop of Lincoln in 1462 and afterwards burned[2] was one of the Risborough offenders.

Fortunately much fuller information is obtainable concerning "a great schism between friars and priests" which broke out in London about Michaelmas, 1464, and which led to accusations of heresy. In this case the trouble originated, according to Gregory, with one Harry Parker, a White Friar and the son of a London skinner, who stirred up a hornet's nest by preaching the virtue of poverty, criticising with special severity the holders of great benefices, and declaring that Christ and His Apostles "had no thing in proper but all in common," that, in fact, Christ was a beggar. The idea that the Church ought to give up its wealth had had advocates in England before, and the friar's bold attack and socialistic doctrine led to an exchange of sermons at Paul's Cross, where Thomas Halden and John Mylverton, provincial of the White Friars and prior of their house in Fleet Street, defended the thesis that Christ was a beggar, while William Ive, Master of Whittington College, and Edward Story, at this time parson of Allhallows the More but soon to become Bishop of Carlisle, maintained that, though Christ was poor, he did not beg and that it was blasphemy to speak of him as a beggar. When the doctors openly disagreed, the minds of ordinary men naturally got into sad confusion, and though some persons turned against their curates, declaring that it was their duty to live by alms, as Christ had done, others turned against the friars. After a time an effort was made to restore peace by means of a debate between Halden and a Grey Friar, which was held in the presence of many great doctors and clerks, but the result was not happy, as Halden "yode so far" that Master John Alcock cited him to appear before the Archbishop of Canterbury and, when the friar replied that he would not obey the citation, as friars were exempt from the jurisdiction of bishops except in case of heresy, promptly brought an accusation of heresy against him. Halden was then brought before Doctor Thomas Wynterbourne, the Archbishop of Canterbury's officer, but though many worthy doctors testified against him, he "leaned ever unto his privilege"; and in the end the

---

1. Early Chancery Proceedings, bundle 27, no. 394.
2. Thornley, *England under the Yorkists*, 192-194 (translation from Lincoln Episcopal Registers, Chedworth, f. 57b.).

Bishop of London, in whose diocese the controversy had taken birth, was called upon to deal with the matter. At this juncture, however, Halden and Mylverton fled to Rome, and when the chancellor of England, who had taken sides against the friars, heard of their flight, he sent the friar who had started all the trouble to prison. Afterwards, when brought before the Bishop of London, Parker abjured, admitting not only that Christ was lord of all things, but that he and his followers had said that Christ begged in order to cause men to regard the order of friars as the "most perfectest of all orders"; but so much harm had been done in the meantime that in a little while a Black Friar was preaching the same heresy, and he too had to be brought before the Bishop of London and made to "revoke." After that Master William Ive was sent to Paul's Cross to pronounce a curse upon Halden and Mylverton for their contumacy, and it was hoped that now at last the trouble was over. But Ive foolishly kept the subject alive by disputations in the cathedral school of St Paul's, and eventually, after an English friar at Rome had written a treatise concerning the begging of Christ which had a wide sale and some copies of which reached England, the Holy See became agitated. The Pope sent to the Archbishop of Canterbury and the Bishop of London for a written account of the whole controversy, and a statement, drawn up by Doctor Ive and signed by nine doctors and bachelors of divinity, was accordingly dispatched to him, along with letters from King Edward himself, who, as he had been much annoyed by all the wrangling the friars had caused, asked the Pope to chastise the offenders. Finally, the friar at Rome who had written the treatise was examined before the cardinals, found guilty of many errors, and imprisoned in the Castle of St Angelo, while the Pope sent a bull to England announcing that, according to a decision long since made, it was heresy to hold that Christ had publicly begged.[1]

Perhaps the trouble this prolonged dispute in regard to the begging of Christ had caused him made Edward resolve that a very conspicuous example should be made of the next heretic who dared to raise his head in London; for in the seventh year of the king's reign one William Balowe was burned on Tower Hill for having "despised the sacrament of the altar." The poor man was kept in prison a long time, but to the end he refused to make confession, declaring that "no priest had no more power to hear confession than Jack Hare"; and

---

1. Gregory, 228-232; *Three Fif. Cent. Chron.*, 180-181.

even at the stake, when he was again laboured with for his soul's salvation, the only reply he deigned to make was: "Bah! bah! bah! What meaneth this priest? This I wot well, that on Good Friday ye make many gods to be put in the sepulchre, but at Easter Day they cannot arise themself, but that ye must lift them up and bear them forth, or else they will lie still in their graves."[1]

Balowe's tragic death may have given a wholesome fright to other heretics, but it did not save the Church from vexations of another sort. In the very year he was burned so many of the London churches were robbed of their jewels, and especially of their sacramental vessels, that "sad men deemed that there had been some fellowship of heretics associate together."[2] So intense was the indignation caused by the robberies that the House of Commons, attributing them to "Lollards and heretics," petitioned that the stealing of any "cup, pix, or any other thing wherein the Blessed Sacrament hath or shall be put or closed" should be held to be high treason, and that any person convicted of such robbery should be burned.[3] Fortunately, however, the king was not ready to give his assent to such a law, and in a short time it was discovered that the thefts had been committed, not by heretics, but by ordinary hungry sinners. It must have been a relief to the king and to all worthy Christians when one of the thieves, a coppersmith, shocked one of his fellow culprits, a locksmith, into confession by exclaiming one evening, as they sat at supper together, "I would have a more dainty morsel of meat, for I am weary of capon, coney, and chickens, and such small meats: and I marvel I have eat nine gods at my supper that were in the boxes." The story ends with the hanging at Tyburn of the coppersmith, the locksmith, and two of their confederates, after Master William Ive had helped, in so far as he could, to lead their wicked souls heavenward.[4]

Although the excitement caused by the robbing of the churches died down after the perpetrators had been punished, both the king and the officers of the Church continued to keep a watchful eye out for heretics. In March 1468, the Archbishop of Canterbury sent a notorious but very contrite heretic to Canterbury to complete his penance, which he did, first, by walking before the

---

1. Gregory, 233-234.
2. *Ibid.*
3. *Rolls of Parl.*, V, 632-633.
4. Gregory, 234-235.

procession on Passion Sunday clothed in his shirt and breeches and carrying a bundle of faggots on his back and, second, by listening in silent shame while Doctor William Selling denounced his heresies in a sermon preached to the monks of Christ Church and a great throng of people.[1] And in 1473 or 1474 another fire was lighted on Tower Hill to destroy a Lollard named John Goose, who displayed the traditional courage of the Christian martyr by remarking coolly to those who looked on while he ate, with evident enjoyment, his last meal, "I eat now a good and competent dinner, for I shall pass a little sharp shower or I go to supper," and, when he had finished, begging the sheriff to lead him quickly to his execution.[2] Goose may have been the king's own discovery. For so eager a heretic hunter had Edward become by this time that, while he was journeying from place to place in the winter of 1474-1475 in search of money for his expedition to France, he also turned his personal attention to the ferreting out of unbelief. So much credit does a letter addressed to Edward at this time by the University of Oxford give him for braving the discomforts of winter travel for the good of the Faith, that one might conclude, were there no evidence to the contrary, that his sole purpose in going from town to town was to hunt down heretics, And so anxious was Oxford to further the king's good work that, in response to a letter from him, all the writings of Wycliffe and Pecock which could be found in the University after a careful search were committed to the flames and a promise given that, if any more such writings came to light, they too should be burned.[3]

Yet earnestly as the king pursued heretics, and horrible as were the sufferings of those who died at the stake, heresy was not crushed out. Rather it would seem that the second burning on Tower Hill caused a recrudescence of the disease it was meant to cure. For on 7 December 1475, a large commission, headed by the Dukes of Clarence and Gloucester, was appointed to inquire into certain treasons, Lollardies, heresies, and errors in Dorset and Wiltshire.[4] And probably these two counties were not the only infected districts, since, in the following February, the king went to the length of appealing to Sixtus IV to authorize proceedings against the owners of heretical books, especially the books and treatises of Reginald Pecock.

---

1. *Chron. of John Stone*, 108.
2. Fabyan, 663-664. Cf. Kingsford's *London Chron.*, 186.
3. *Epistolæ Academicæ Oxon*, II, 411-413.
4. *Cal. Patent Rolls*, II, 573.

Edward told the Pope that, before his accession to the throne, proceedings against Pecock had been begun and Pius II had been consulted about the taking of more severe measures, but that, though Paul II afterwards sent some letters regarding the matter, the civil war in England and Paul's death had brought the proceedings to a standstill. Meanwhile, he said, Pecock's writings had multiplied to such an extent in England that

> not only the laity but churchmen and scholastic graduates scarcely studied anything else, so that the pestiferous virus circulated in many human breasts and ere long would have spread immensely had not the Almighty revealed the confessions of certain penitents for the easier dispersion of the remaining followers of that sect.[1]

The king closed his letter with a promise to do all he could to expel "all novelties and condemned dogmas of this sort" from his kingdom and the assurance that he had already begun the good work. And he was certainly deserving of the papal benediction, for, before the year was done, there was another public burning of the works of Wycliffe and Pecock at Oxford[2] and "an heretic called Abraham" was captured and several persons whom the said Abraham accused of heresy were made to do penance at St Paul's.[3] The history of heresy in England during the final years of Edward's reign is unchronicled, but on 22 February 1480, three more church robbers were drawn to Tower Hill to be hanged and burned and two other men, their accomplices, were "pressed to death."[4]

The name of the London heretic captured in 1476 has a Hebrew sound, and we might expect to hear that Abraham was an inmate of the House of Converts, which was founded by Henry III as a home for converted Jews and which had been duly maintained by his successors even after the expulsion of the Jews from England in 1290. But there is no trace of Abraham in the accounts of the keeper of the House of Converts, and, to judge from the same accounts, if the king who searched his kingdom over for Christian heretics also laboured to convert the few Jews left in England, he found those unfortunate beings quite as hard to subdue as the followers of Wycliffe and

---

1. *Cal. Venetian Papers*, I, 134-135.
2. The burning took place at Carfax. Bryan Twyne, *Antiquitatis Academiæ Oxoniensis Apologia* (Oxford, 1608), 322.
3. Nicolas's *London Chron.*, 145-146.
4. Stow, 432; Kingsford's *London Chron.*, 188; Fabyan, 666.

Pecock. For at no time during Edward's reign were there more than three christianized Jews in residence at the House of Converts. Martin, son of Henry Wodstok, John Seyt, and Edward of Westminster, who was evidently so called because he had been baptized at Westminster on 10 January 1462, were the only occupants of the house for several years. Then the son of Henry Wodstok disappears, giving place to Edward Brandon, who afterwards disappears in his turn, giving place to Edward Beauchamp.[1] Yet, if the king's Jewish converts were few, it is evident from the number of Edwards in the list that they usually honoured their royal benefactor by accepting his name; and it is interesting to remember in this connection that Perkin Warbeck, who afterwards pretended to be the younger son of Edward IV, is said to have been brought up by a baptized Jew who was Edward's godson.[2] It is also interesting to find that Edward planned to do more for one of his converts and namesakes than to give him a home in the House of Converts. The name of Edward Beauchamp appears only in the last extant account rendered by the keeper of the House of Converts during Edward's reign, an account running from 9 January 1481, to 9 January 1482, and on 14 April 1481, the king granted John de Bardi of Florence permission to export nineteen sacks of wool in recognition of his services in certain matters and because he had undertaken to pay the value of fifty pounds for the exhibition of Edward Beauchamp at the schools of Bologna or Padua.[3] However, young Beauchamp's hope of an education in foreign universities seems to have been quashed by his royal godfather's death; for he continued to be an inmate of the House of Converts, though he changed his name to Richard in honour of the new king and after the battle of Bosworth changed it back again to Edward![4]

Another way in which Edward's devotion to the Church manifested itself was in goodwill towards the monasteries, a goodwill of which his correspondence with Sixtus IV about the monastery of Westminster is an illustration. The king might well be kind to the wealthy religious orders and their great monasteries, inasmuch as they contributed so generously to his loans and benevolences, but to his credit be it said that he was also mindful of the welfare of the mendicant

---

1. Exchequer Accounts, Jews, bundle 252, nos. 24-30; bundle 253, nos. 1-3. Martin, son of Henry Wodstok, lived in the House of Converts no less than fifty-five years. See an article on the Domus Conversorum by Rev. Michael Adler, *Trans. Jewish Hist. Soc.*, 1899-1901.
2. *Memorials of Henry VII* (Rolls Series), 65-66.
3. French Roll 21 Edw. IV, m. 15. See also Warrants under the Signet. file 1390.
4. Adler, *ut sup.*

orders, from whom no such contributions could be looked for. A few months after his accession he took pains to confirm a grant of fifty marks a year which had been made to the Friars Minor of Oxford by Edward I to sustain the doctrine of the Catholic Faith in the University, and in 1463 he renewed similar grants to the Friars Preachers of Oxford and to the Friars Minors and Friars Preachers of the University of Cambridge. He also renewed, early in his reign, an annuity of twenty pounds which the provincial chapter of the Friars Preachers had received from Edward III for the celebration of the anniversary of Queen Philippa, and one of four tuns of wine which was enjoyed by the Friars Preachers of Chiltern Langley; and in 1466 he renewed one of twenty pounds to the Friars Preachers of London.[1] Much more important than these small favours, however, was the welcome he extended, about the year 1481, to some Observant Franciscans, the first of these reformers of the order of St Francis who had ever come to England. To these friars he assigned as a temporary home a chantry and chapel of the Holy Cross at Greenwich, and it was in special recognition of this act of kindness that Sixtus IV sent him, in the spring of 1482, the sword and cap of maintenance of which mention has already been made.[2]

To some of the monasteries of England Edward was probably indebted for things more precious than money. For instance, at the beginning of his reign, when the northern part of England still belonged to Henry VI rather than to him, he may have had some cause to feel particularly grateful to the abbot and convent of Alnwick, as he gave orders that a hundred pounds should be paid to them to compensate them for the losses of cattle, foodstuffs, etc., which they had sustained during the siege of Alnwick.[3] And three years later he granted a like sum to the prior and convent of Tynemouth because, by his command, they had "kept the said place to their great costs, jeopardies, and charges from the danger and assaults of our enemies, traitors and rebels."[4] On the other hand, it will be remembered that when the abbot of the great Cistercian monastery of Fountains dared to resist after the battle of Towton, he was carried to London and placed under bond. And apparently only a few weeks later an ex-abbot of another Cistercian monastery also arrived in London as a prisoner. The convent of St Mary, Furness, was situated in the

---

1. *Cal. Patent Rolls*, I, 71, 156, 192, 260, 267, 286, 524; Issue Roll, Mich. 1 Edw. IV, 3 Oct.
2. Ross, *Hist. Regum Angliæ*, 211.
3. Issue Roll, Mich. 2 Edw. IV, 23 March.
4. Warrants for Issues, 5 Edw. IV, 27 March.

duchy of Lancaster, and if it is true that Henry VI found shelter for a time under its roof, he must have had reason to believe that the monks were his friends. But the Abbot of Furness was of other clay than his courageous brother of Fountains, for instead of making display of his loyalty to the house of Lancaster, he seems to have courted the goodwill of the Earl of Warwick and Lord Montagu, when they appeared at his door and demanded his submission, and to have been rewarded with their aid in a little affair of his own. Nothing is known about the man who was abbot of Furness at the close of Henry VI's reign except that his name was John Thornour and that he was elected abbot in 1443, or about his successor in office except that his given name was Lawrence and that he became abbot sometime before 25 November 1461.[1] For this reason, if for no other, the following petition, which Edward IV received and sent to the chancellor of England on 17 September 1462, may well be allowed, in spite of its length, to tell its story in its own quaint way:

> To the king our liege lord. Humbly beseecheth your most noble and abundant grace your poor orator, John Thornour, late Abbot of Furness, that it may please your Highness to have in your most gracious consideration and understanding how your said orator, for great age and divers other causes moving him thereto, resigned his abbacy to the Abbot of Furness that now is; whereupon the said abbot, upon the same resignation to him so made, granted unto your said suppliant under the convent seal, term of his life, an office called the master office of Furness Fell, the value of £50, to him two priests, seven bailiffs, and other divers servants, with great reparations, pertaining to the said house and office, so that truly the said £50 will not suffice to uphold the said charges without other purveyance; whereupon the said abbot, within a month after the said resignation, sent after your said orator and grievously, with strange and unlawful means, desired him to release yearly £30 of the said £50, which in no wise he might so do, and to bear the great charges and the costs aforesaid. And so the said abbot, moved with great impatience and strange will, said that he should expend all the revenues of his house one year but he had his intent and will of that his unreasonable desire, saying that your said orator should have nothing of the said £50 to live with, the which is against all manner of right, law, and conscience, so that through his ungodly disposition he made such wrongful and sinister informations, as God knoweth, to the lords of Warwick and Montagu as your said orator by means thereof was committed by your writ into your Tower of London, where he hath

---

1. T. A. Beck, *Hist. and Antiquities of the Abbey of Furness* (London, 1844), 296-297.

continued as prisoner with full great sickness and unheart's-ease sith Simon and Jude Day the first year of your most noble reign, and is a man of the age of sixty years and more. And, saving the reverence of your most high and excellent nobley, among other sickness he is often times vexed with the gout, and hath nothing to help himself with but as his full worshipful Master Robert Mallory, lieutenant of your said Tower, succoureth him with meat and drink, which he is not bound so to do, but of his own charity, free will, and gentleness doth it. And for [as much as] your said suppliant without your gracious aid and help, what for default and for his great disease and sickness that he hath, in the cold time of the year now coming is like utterly to be mischieved and undone without your most gracious help and succour; for his said abbot hath taken away all the said £50 from him; wherefore please it your most abundant grace the premises graciously to consider and how that your said orator standeth under the obedience of his said abbot and is not personable to sue him at the common law, [so] that it [may] please your said Highness to have pity and compassion upon your said beseecher so as he shall now have release of this his imprisonment and to be at large and at freedom, where he may, according to his acquittal and duty, pray Almighty God and His Blessed Mother for the preservation and keeping of your most prosperous and royal estate and the souls of your most noble progenitors, and that at the reverence of Our Blessed Saviour and in the way of charity.[1]

So much has been written, though not always in a temperate and impartial spirit, regarding conditions in the English monasteries in the period immediately preceding the Reformation that the subject is one to be avoided. But it is impossible to resist the temptation to add to this account of a controversy in Furness Abbey two other short stories which reveal the determined, not to say bellicose, disposition of some of the heads of religious houses with whom Edward IV had to cope. They will fittingly close this chapter.

In April 1473, one Dan John Marlowe was elected, by royal consent, Abbot of St Saviour, Bermondsey, one of the Cluniac monasteries which had been in the hands of the kings of England since the suppression of the alien priories in the reign of Henry V, and immediately after his election was confirmed by the commissaries of Dan William Brekenok, Prior of the house of Ste. Marie, Charité-sur-Loire, in France, to which the monastery of Bermondsey was subject.[2] But some years later Brekenok ceased to be Prior

---

1. Signed Bills, file 1491, no. 3831.
2. *Cal. Patent Rolls*, II, 387-388, 390. Marlowe was Abbot of Bermondsey from 1473 to 1516. Dugdale, *Monasticon*, V, 92.

of Ste. Marie, Charité, and after he had served for a time as the vicar-general in England of his successor at Ste. Marie, on 6 August 1480, he was appointed Prior of St Andrew, Northampton, another English Cluniac monastery, and at the same time procurator general of the Prior of Ste. Marie in England.[1] The monastery of St Andrew had not always been distinguished by the perfect propriety of its inmates, for at one time, shortly before Marlowe received his appointment to Bermondsey, the king had ordered the arrest of some of its monks who had put off their habit and spurned the authority of their superiors.[2] But Brekenok either decided that his own stables had been sufficiently cleaned or that there were others which were in greater need of attention, for upon becoming procurator general, he hastened to inspect the abbey of Bermondsey. There he discovered what he was pleased to describe as "great ruin and decay, as well of the said monastery as of religion within the same," and he at once cited Abbot Marlowe to appear before him in the chapter house on a certain day. This order, however, the abbot contemptuously ignored, and as the procurator could not allow such disregard for his authority to pass, he "descended again to the said monastery of Bermondsey." But this time Marlowe was ready for him. When the procurator general entered the church, the abbot, with Master John Coke, doctor of laws, and a great multitude of lay people, "took him and pulled him from his doctors, notaries, and other his learned counsel and had him to secret prison," whence the unlucky man afterwards dispatched a petition for a writ of subpœna, declaring that his captors intended to murder him "or otherwise mischief him contrary to the law and all good conscience."[3]

A much more important person than either Dan John Marlowe or Dan William Brekenok was the abbot who figures in our second story. And in this case the object of the abbatial wrath was not an intruding superior officer, but a woman. But here again the original document tells the story best.

Right worshipful and, as I trust, my very good lady," wrote John Selwood, Abbot of Glastonbury, to the widow of Lord Wenlock,[4] "considering the true

---

1. *Cal. Patent Rolls*, III, 156, 209. John Listil, Prior of Dudley, seems to have succeeded Brekenok as vicar-general. See Warrants under the Signet, file 1387—a licence to Listil to hold the office.
2. *Cal. Patent Rolls*, II, 358.
3. Early Chancery Proceedings, bundle 47, no. 58.
4. Selwood addresses Wenlock's widow as "Dame Alys Fray," but in her will, which is

faith that was in me towards you in such things as were betwixt my Lord
Wenlock, your husband, and me, I recommend me unto you. Madam, where
I was well-willed in late days to have do such things as should have pleased
you and, as I deemed that time, not hurt me, howbeit if I had so do I had
undo myself, as ye know right well, Madam, I am informed that ye propose
to trouble me in the law. If ye so do, I may say that I was simply occupied to
show you such love and favour in opening to you such counsel as was betwixt
my lord your husband and me, the which I did, as I take God to record, for
very true love that I have to you for the good lord's sake, my Lord Wenlock, on
whose soul God have mercy. Madam, if ye will trouble with me, I promitt you I
shall open such things that shall turn you to as much trouble as I shall have by
you, I doubt me thereof right naught. And I trust to God the best man of law in
England will be on my side and right stiff against you. Madam, in such doing
is none avail, ne to you ne to me. Wherefore, if it please you to be in peace, I
will thank you thereof. If ye will needs go to plea, I trust to God. Answer you.
Madam, the Blessed Trinity have you ever in His keeping. Amen. Amen.[1]

---

1. *Ancient Correspondence*, Vol. XLIV, no. 65.
   dated 11 June 1478 (*Testamenta Vetusta*, I, 347) she calls herself "Dame Annes Say" and
   directs that a priest shall sing for the souls of "my Lord Wenlock, Sir John Fray, and
   Sir John Say, my husbands." Her list of her husbands is not chronologically correct,
   however, as Fray, who was Chief Baron of the Exchequer and died the year Edward
   IV ascended the throne, was her first consort, Wenlock her second, and Say her third.
   See the articles on Fray in Foss, *Judges of Eng.*, and on Say in *Dict. Nat. Biog.*

2

THE MERCHANT KING AND SOME OF HIS
FELLOW MERCHANTS

The customs records would probably show, if they were more complete, that Edward IV was engaged in the exportation of wool, and perhaps of other English products as well, from the very beginning of his reign. Even as they are, they prove that at least by the spring of 1463 he was a full-fledged wool merchant. Two galleys leaving London for Italy on 20 May of that year were loaded almost exclusively with wool belonging to the king which had been shipped for him by three factors or attorneys, Henry de Monte, "merchant of Liguria," James de Sanderico, "merchant," and John Godfrey, "alien." The first of these galleys, of which one Francesco Bambow was "patron," carried 22 sacks and 13 cloves[1] of wool for Hugh Wyche, the London alderman who was made a Knight of the Bath at the time of Elizabeth Woodville's coronation, but otherwise the entire cargo belonged to Edward—9½ sacks of wool which had been shipped by Henry de Monte, 84 sacks and 2 cloves which had been shipped by James de Sanderico, and 119 sacks and 15 cloves which had been shipped by John Godfrey; while in the second galley, which was probably a much smaller vessel and of which Marco Dalege, or de Loge, was patron, there were 24½ sacks and 10 cloves of wool which Godfrey had shipped for the king. A ship called the *Christopher* of Flushing, departing from London four days after these two galleys, also carried 14½ sacks and 8 cloves of wool which was Edward's property and which likewise had been shipped by Godfrey. But in this last instance the king's wool was to be transferred at Sandwich to a galley of which one Thomasyn was master and which probably joined the galleys of

---

1. A clove was seven or eight pounds, and there were fifty-two cloves in a sack. Martin, *The record interpreter: a collection of abbreviations, Latin words and names used in English historical manuscripts and records*, 1892.

Bambow and Dalege before the voyage through the Straits of Marrok began. In fact, there must have been a considerable amount of unloading and reloading before the fleet of galleys was ready to start for Italy; for when, four days later still, on 28 May, the *James* of London cleared for Calais, she carried another small consignment, 9½ sacks, of the king's wool which Henry de Monte had shipped and which, as it too was destined for Italy, must have been reshipped on arriving at Calais. Perhaps these few sacks came from one of the king's estates in the distant Welsh marches and, having reached London a little late, were sent on to Calais in the hope that they would overtake the galleys there. But the *James* took to Calais other wool belonging to the king besides the 9½ sacks going to Italy. On its deck were also 84 sacks and 2 cloves which Sanderico was shipping for the king "versus partes exteras" and 158½ sacks and 7 cloves which Godfrey was shipping for him to the same vague destination. Indeed, the *James* carried a very large cargo, as, in addition to the king's shipments, she had on board nearly 170,000 pells and over 300 sacks of wool which belonged to the merchants of the staple, to say nothing of 748 dressed hides belonging to the Earl of Kent and 22 sacks and 13 cloves of wool belonging to Hugh Wyche.[1]

In the summer of 1464 Edward's factors were again busy. Francesco Bambow and Marco Dalege, after a safe voyage to Italy, had returned to England, and when their galleys sailed from London again on 20 April 1464, Bambow's carried four shipments of wool made by the king's factors—9½ sacks shipped by Henry de Monte, 84 sacks and 2 cloves shipped by Sanderico, 97½ sacks and 6 cloves shipped by Sanderico, Godfrey, and another alien, called Barnard, and 21 sacks and 9 cloves shipped by Godfrey alone; while Dalege's galley carried 24½ sacks and 10 cloves of the king's wool shipped by Godfrey. And again, as in the preceding year, there was a small shipment sent separately on the *Christopher* of Flushing to be transferred at Sandwich to Thomasyn's galley, and this time also the amount was 14½ sacks and 8 cloves.[2]

These shipments of wool from London in the years 1463 and 1464 seem to have been entirely for Edward's personal gain, but at the same time other large shipments of wool were going out from more than one English port which, though made in the king's name, were not for his personal profit. For on 1 July 1463, it will be remembered, twenty thousand pounds were assigned to Walter

1. Custom Accounts, London 63/35.
2. Customs Accounts, London 73/36.

Blount, treasurer of Calais, with orders to purchase wool and wool-fells to be shipped to Calais and sold at the king's "aventure" for the purpose of raising the money which was needed to pay what had been due to the soldiers and other creditors of the crown at Calais, Guines, and Hammes at the moment of Edward's accession.[1] Means are lacking to follow all of Blount's shipments, but certain it is that he was shipping wool and woolfells from London and Boston in accordance with these orders in the following year, and in large quantities. When a fleet of seventeen ships left Boston for the staple of Calais on 31 May 1464, fifteen of them carried wool or woolfells or both shipped by Blount for the king, and other ships departing from London on 20 and 26 September and 27 November carried, all told, 290 sacks and 1 clove of wool which was also being sent by Blount to Calais in the king's name.[2]

But it was not on wool and woolfells alone that English exporters were making such big profits in these days that Edward was anxious to obtain a share in them. For some time past, to the distress, as we have seen, of the cloth manufacturing towns in the Duke of Burgundy's domains, England had been turning more and more of her wool into cloth; and by the summer of 1464, if not earlier, Edward had become an exporter of cloth as well as of wool and woolfells.[3] It was on 21 May 1464, that Edward sent to the chancellor of England the already quoted letter in which he enclosed "the copy of a patent unto us sent by the lords and other of our council from our city of London for shipping of eight thousand woollen cloths, grained and not grained, thought necessary and expedient to be done for chevisance of good towards our great charges borne and to be borne at this time."[4] Two days later Sanderico was commissioned to take charge of the shipment of the eight thousand cloths, and the customs accounts show that three thousand of them, that is to say, 2,997 undyed cloths[5] worth £6,561 13s 4d, two half-dyed cloths worth £16, and one cloth of the precious scarlet worth £12, were shipped by Sanderico from Southampton in

---

1. Warrants for Issues, 3 Edw. IV, 1 July. See above, Vol. I, p. 298.
2. Customs Accounts, Boston 10/5, and London 73/37.
3. Edward seems to have taken an interest in improving or increasing the varieties of cloth made in his kingdom. In the last year of his reign he granted a licence to two merchants, apparently Italians naturalized in England, to bring to England some twenty masters "to make and dye cloths of another fashion to those now made in the realm, so that the king's subjects may be able to learn the art." *Cal. Patent Rolls*, III, 343.
4. Warrants under the Signet, file 1377. See above, Vol. I, p. 331.
5. *Panni sine grano*.

five Italian galleys on 11 June and 20 July.[1] The remaining five thousand cloths probably followed soon after, though the gaps in the customs records make it impossible to discover when they left England or from what port.

Sanderico's services to the king did not terminate with the shipment of these eight thousand cloths. On 28 March 1465, Edward sent another message to the chancellor of England stating that he contemplated shipping eighty sacks of wool and four hundred undyed cloths "to divers foreign parts" and directing that letters patent should be issued to Sanderico authorizing him to make the shipments in one or more carracks or galleys or other vessels.[2] Consequently a galley which left Sandwich on 31 May 1465, carried a small shipment of wool made by Sanderico as the king's attorney, and another which sailed on 19 June was loaded with one hundred and thirty cloths shipped by Sanderico "by virtue of the king's writ"; while in three other galleys which left during the two following days there were smaller shipments by Sanderico, in one case six cloths, in another eighty-four, and in the third ninety-seven.[3] But again it is impossible to trace all Sanderico's shipments, although he probably completed them within a very short time, as on 3 July Edward directed that he should be given a new commission, this time to ship fifteen hundred sacks of wool and seven thousand woollen cloths through the Straits of Marrok.[4]

Sanderico, although he was evidently a much trusted servant, was by no means the only factor the king employed at this period. On 26 April 1465, Edward chose two other men, Luca de Pausano and Francesco de Lawrens, or Lawtans, to export two hundred sacks of wool to Italy for him, and all this wool, and apparently even a little more, was shipped by them from Sandwich in the following month.[5] Moreover, in two of the galleys which left Sandwich in June with shipments of cloth made by Sanderico there were nearly three hundred cloths shipped by John Forster "by virtue of the king's writ." Two other galleys which left the same port on 26 and 29 June also carried shipments of cloth by Forster, and at the same time one John

---

1. French Roll 4 Edw. IV, 23 May; Customs Accounts, Southampton 142/2 and 142/3. Cf. Receipt Roll, Easter 4 Edw. IV, no. 885. The customs and subsidies on these three thousand cloths amounted to £747 5s 2d.
2. Writs of Privy Seal, file 802, no. 1625.
3. Customs Accounts, Sandwich, 128/8.
4. Writs of Privy Seal, file 804, no. 1717.
5. *Ibid.*, file 803, no. 1660; Customs Accounts, Sandwich, *ut sup.*

Defford, or Desford, was shipping pells—"shorlings and morlings" and lamb skins—from Sandwich for Edward.[1]

Regarding Edward's commercial ventures during 1466 and 1467 little can be found out, as the customs records for those years are exceedingly scanty. But the king undoubtedly continued to dabble more or less extensively in trade, and before the end of 1466 still another Italian was engaged as his factor. On 30 November of that year Edward commissioned Alan de Monteferrato, merchant, to ship for him through the Straits of Marrok six thousand sacks of wool, twenty thousand woollen cloths, grained or not grained, ten thousand blocks of tin, and ten thousand barrels of vessels of pewter or tin;[2] and by February 1467, if not earlier, Alan had begun to make these shipments. The entire cargo of the *Barbara* of Skedam (Schiedam), leaving Boston on 18 February 1467, consisted of one hundred and nineteen undyed cloths worth £238 which Alan de Monteferrato was shipping for the king, while of two other ships setting sail on the same day, the *Clement* of Harflet (Harfleur?) carried as its only cargo eighty-nine pieces of tin worth £222 10s and eight undyed cloths worth £16, and the *Mary* of Boston three barrels containing three thousand pounds of pewter vessels worth £44, all of which were being shipped by Alan for the king.[3]

Even less information about Edward's commercial activities can be picked up during the years 1468 and 1469. All that can be stated with certainty is that in the galley of Marco Giustiniani, which sailed from London for the Straits of Marrok on 28 August 1468, there were 180 sacks and one clove of wool belonging to the king—or perhaps more correctly to his mother, as the shipment was made by Peter de Furno, who is described as the attorney of Cecily, Duchess of York[4]—and that in another galley which left Sandwich on 20 August 1469, when Edward was Warwick's prisoner, there were 521 sacks and one clove of what is called the king's wool but which again may have belonged to his mother, as it was shipped by Marco de Pesaro, Stephen Contarini, and another Italian, all of whom, like Peter de Furno, are described as attorneys of the Duchess of York.[5] There can be no

---

1. Customs Accounts, Sandwich, *ut sup.*
2. Writs of Privy Seal, file 810, no. 2023.
3. Customs Accounts, Boston 10/7.
4. Customs Accounts, Divers Ports 162/1—an injured document which seems to belong to the customs accounts of London.
5. Customs Accounts, Sandwich 128/10.

doubt, however, that up to the moment that Warwick chased him from his kingdom Edward continued to be a very busy merchant; and by the summer of 1470 he had found another factor in one Alan Mounton, an alien and apparently, like Sanderico and Alan de Monteferrato, an Italian.[1] Mounton, indeed, seems to have played a much more important part than that of an ordinary factor to the king, as he had a number of other factors under him, men who are spoken of as "factors and attorneys of Alan Mounton, factor of the lord king"; and perhaps he might appropriately be called the king's business manager.

Certainly the king had need of a business manager by this time, for he was now engaged in the importing as well as in the exporting business. A carrack of which one Jerome Saluagus was master brought to Sandwich on 12 June 1470, not only treacle, "spendable paper," oil, etc., for Gerard Caniziani and 831 bales of woad for Lord Mountjoy, but 390 bales of woad and 27 butts of sweet wine which had been shipped by John de Nigro,[2] factor of Alan Mounton, factor of the king, and 613 more bales of woad, 32 barrels of alum, 7 bales of wax, 23 bales of "paper scribable," 14 sets of "harness complete," some white wine, wormseed, and other articles which had been shipped by Thomas de Pounte, another factor of Alan Mounton, factor of the king. And when this carrack left port again on 10 August, it carried, in addition to 27 undyed cloths which belonged to two private merchants and were to be unloaded in Portugal or Castile "and nowhere else," 16¾ sacks of wool which had been shipped by Louis Penyll, factor and attorney of Alan Mounton, factor of the king, and were evidently going to Calais, and 1,884 undyed cloths which had been shipped by John de Faune, alien, still another factor of Alan Mounton, factor of the king.[3]

In all probability the carrack of Jerome Saluagus was only one of many which brought to or took from the port of Sandwich cargoes in which the king of England had a personal interest. Nor was it only at Sandwich that Alan Mounton and his factors were busy on the king's behalf. Such customs accounts of the port of London as have escaped destruction go to show that

---

1. No doubt Alan Mounton is identical with Alan Mounttane, alien merchant, mentioned in *Cal. Patent Rolls*, II, 244.
2. John Antonio de Nigro is mentioned in *Cal. Patent Rolls*, III, 198, 216, as the owner of a carrack of Genoa called the *Santa Maria de Gracia*.
3. Customs Accounts, Sandwich 128/12.

Mounton was transacting far more business for the king at that port than at Sandwich. In February 1470, no less than twenty-five ships entering or leaving the port of London contained goods owned by the king and shipped by Alan Mounton's factors—factors who bore such surnames as Pouns, Dues, Russeley, Van Lyr, Van Wale, Claysson, Jacobesson, and Johnson. And very motley were the cargoes of these ships. For example, one of them brought for the king, among other articles, figs, raisins, oil, sugar, oranges, and a popinjay! Another carried alum and rice, another copper, lead, salt fish, and wainscots, and still others hops, madder, hats, cards, baskets, wire, pins, packthread, fans, soap, brushes, and that highly useful invention, spectacles. Also, in each of three ships leaving London on 15 February there were a hundred and twenty quarters of grain which had been shipped by Mounton himself for the king and which were probably going to help feed the people of Bruges and other towns in the Netherlands through whose marts the king's heterogeneous importations, products partly of the Netherlands and partly of more distant countries, had passed.[1]

Edward's flight from England interrupted his commercial enterprises only for the moment. As soon as he recovered his throne, Alan Mounton and Alan de Monteferrato began again to make shipments for him. The customs accounts of the ports of Exeter and Dartmouth show that in the *Bark* of Guernsey which sailed from one of those ports on 16 September 1471, Alan de Monteferrato shipped for the king thirty pieces of "Denysshe" (Devonshire?) tin called blocks and ten blocks of Cornish tin, the value of the whole amounting to £45.[2] And from other customs records we learn that a few weeks later, on 30 October, one Joos Swarfeld, a citizen of Veere[3] who was acting as a factor of Alan de Monteferrato, factor of the king, shipped twenty-four pieces of tin worth £60 from London, and that a little later still, on 10 December, one Hervi Bovyan, alien, factor of Alan de Monteferrato, factor of the king, sailed away with sixteen pieces of lead which were worth £20 and which Edward was probably sending, like the tin Swarfeld took in charge, to the land which had so recently given him an asylum. Also, on 12 March 1472, the ship of one Danyelt Symondson departed from London

---

1. Customs Accounts, London 73/33.
2. Customs Accounts, Exeter and Dartmouth 41/4.
3. See Customs Accounts, Divers Ports 194/20.

with fourteen pieces of lead shipped by John Bedyan, alien, factor of Alan de Monteferrato, factor of the king, and the galley of Jerome Morasyn (Gieronimo Morosini) carried away on 20 April eighty undyed cloths shipped by John de Pounte, factor of Alan Mounton, factor of the king.[1]

It would seem from this list of shipments that, while Alan Mounton probably continued to have charge of the king's exportations of cloth and perhaps some other things, Edward was now exporting much tin and lead, and that in this field Alan de Monteferrato, instead of Alan Mounton, had become his business manager. This conclusion is upheld by the customs records of two other ports, Plymouth and Fowey; for they reveal that eight ships leaving those ports between Michaelmas, 1472, and Michaelmas, 1473, carried shipments of tin and lead made by several different factors of Alan de Monteferrato for the king. But the cloth and wool Alan Mounton handled for the king were doubtless far more valuable than the tin and lead Alan de Monteferrato shipped for him; for the tin Monteferrato sent out from Plymouth and Fowey within the year just mentioned was reckoned as worth, all told, only £96, and the lead £30. That is to say, Monteferrato shipped only forty-eight blocks of tin worth £2 the block and six fothers of lead worth £5 the fother.[2]

That Edward continued to the end of his reign to export quantities of cloth and wool and woolfells, as well as tin and lead, there is every reason to believe, as the Croyland chronicler lays much stress on the importance and large returns of the king's ventures in trade in his later years. But as far as the scanty records are concerned, they tell us nothing more about what the king exported or imported during the second half of his reign, except that a carrack sailing from Southampton on 30 April 1473, carried 114½ sacks and 13 cloves of wool which belonged either to Edward or to his mother, whose attorney, Peter de Casasse, made the shipment, and that in another boat which seems to have left London on 22 September 1481, a factor of the king named Marcellus Mawrys shipped lambskins to the value of £14 10s.[3]

Edward may have owned some trading ships of his own, but it is not an

1. *Ibid.*, 194/19. Gieronimo Morosini was captain of the Flanders galleys in 1475. *Cal. Venetian Papers*, I, cxxxiii.
2. Customs Accounts, Plymouth and Fowey 114/4. A fother of lead was 1950 or 2000 lbs. Martin, *Record Interpreter*.
3. Customs Accounts, Southampton 142/8, Divers Ports 194/25.

easy matter to distinguish between those of "the king's ships" which may have been his private property and those which were undoubtedly crown property, forming a part of the small royal navy that was enlarged whenever need arose by the requisitioning of merchant ships from their owners. The great *Grace Dieu*, which Edward seems to have granted to Warwick (in the same way Henry VI had previously granted it to the Duke of Exeter) when the earl undertook to keep the sea, but which came back into his hands after Warwick's death, was unquestionably crown property.[1] And three other ships that belonged to Edward in the first year of his reign, the *Margaret* of Orwell, which is described as "a great ship," the *Margaret* of Ipswich, and a barge called the *Nicholas de Marche*, were probably purchased especially for the purpose of strengthening the navy, as they served in the fleet the king sent to Wales in the autumn of 1461.[2] Two galleys under construction at London in the summer of 1462 by workmen brought from Sandwich were evidently also ships of war and destined to serve in the fleet with which the Earl of Kent made his descent on the coast of Brittany in September of that year; and the *Carvel* of Leybourne, which the Earl of Worcester bought in the summer of 1463 by the king's order for the sum of £133 6s 8d, was "for the keeping of the sea."[3] It was with a view to the needs of the navy again that Avery Cornburgh, also in the summer of 1463, was "entreated" by the king to pay out of his own money "for the buying of five parts of a ship called *John Evangelist* of Dartmouth, 100 marks, for the victualling, tackling, and manning of the same, £40, for the buying of a carvel of Saltcombe, £80, for the setting forth of the same, 40 marks, for the victualling and manning of our carvel being at

---

1. *Cal. Patent Rolls*, I, 99, II, 495, III, 211, 240. It is quite possible, of course, that there was more than one *Grace Dieu*. In April 1473, Edward ordered the payment of £52 8s 2d to Mark Symondson of Camfere (Veere) for masts, pitch, tar, wainscot, etc., bought by him "for the making of our ship called the *Gracedieu*." Warrants for Issues, 13 Edw. IV, 27 April. But "making," as used here, probably means repairing. It has been suggested by Dr Gairdner (*Paston Letters*, I, 109) that the name *Grace Dieu* may have become traditional, as it was used also in Tudor times, "when, with the king's own Christian name prefixed, it was always given to the largest of the fleet." At one time the purser of the *Grace Dieu* was allowed a month for its "keeping." Tellers' account, Exchequer T. R., Council and Privy Seal, file 92, m. 24.
2. Warrants for Issues, I Edw. IV, 20 July, 20 Oct; Issue Roll, Mich. 1 Edw. IV, 20 Oct., 7 Nov.; *Cal. Patent Rolls*, I, 229, II, 87. Perhaps the "Kyngesbarge" which served in the Earl of Kent's fleet in 1462 (Issue Roll, Easter 2 Edw. IV, 18 June) was the *Nicholas de Marche*.
3. Warrants for Issues, 3 Edw. IV, 24 July.

Fowey, 26 marks, for the victualling, anchors, cables, stays, and shrouds and other apparelments of the same ships and carvels, £60."[1]

Throughout his reign Edward found occasion to buy ships. In the summer of 1467 he paid Nicholas Faunt of Canterbury, who four years later allied himself with the Bastard of Fauconberg and lost his head in consequence, the sum of £170 for a ship;[2] and about three years after his return from Burgundy he seems to have bought the *Antony*, the ship of Veere which had brought him home and which, like the *Margaret* of Orwell, is spoken of as "a great ship of the king's."[3] For what purpose Faunt's ship was purchased there is nothing to show, but the *Antony*, unless the king owned two ships of that name, saw service sometimes as a man of war and sometimes as a trading vessel. For Edward issued letters of protection for his ship the *Antony* on 16 July 1478, and we find her sailing from London on the following 26 August for the Mediterranean with a cargo of wool which, though the king probably had an interest in it, was shipped, according to the record, by William Heryot, a London alderman, and his factors.[4] On the other hand, we find a ship called the *Antony* in the fleet sent against Scotland in 1481. Again, the two ships which were sent to assist in wresting St Michael's Mount from the Earl of Oxford in the winter of 1473–1474, the *Garce*

---

1. *Ibid.*, 5 July. The *John de Evangelist* is also mentioned as one of the king's ships in Tellers' Roll, Easter 5 Edw. IV.
2. Issue Roll, Mich. 7 Edw. IV, 31 Oct.
3. As the *Antony* of which Mark Symondson was master was requisitioned in June 1472, to assist in keeping the sea (Tellers' Roll, Mich. 12 Edw. IV), it would seem that she did not belong to the king at that time. Yet an entry in *Cal. Patent Rolls*, II, 266, might be taken to mean that she was owned by the king as early as July 1471, if not at the time she brought him home from Burgundy. And an entry in a Tellers' account of 1478 (Exchequer T. R., Council and Privy Seal, file 91, in. 86) mentioning a payment to Thomas Rogers, "patron of the king's ship called the *Antony*," for gunpowder which had been delivered to the Earl of Worcester when the earl was treasurer of England would force the conclusion that Edward owned some ship of the name of *Antony* even before his flight, were it not so likely that the recording clerk slipped into an anachronism in implying that Rogers was patron of the *Antony* at the time the gunpowder was delivered. On the other hand, it is certain that Edward owned an *Antony* by 8 November 1474, and also that he bought the *Antony* of Veere sooner or later. See *Cal. Patent Rolls*, II, 471, and Exchequer T. R., Council and Privy Seal, file 92, m. 15—the record of a payment of 100 marks to Mark Symondson "late master and owner of the *Antony*, late of Camfere, in full payment of 80 li. to him due for his part of the same ship by the king's Highness of him bought."
4. French Roll 18 Edw. IV, m. 6; Customs Accounts, London 73/40; *Cal. Patent Rolls*, III, 240; *Household Books of Duke of Norfolk*, 9-10.

and the *Carican*, are also described as the king's ships;[1] and the *Carican* seems to have been sent abroad on one occasion to bring home a cargo of wine for the king, while at another time she was engaged in conducting the wool fleet from London to Calais.[2] Another of the king's ships, the *Falcon*, the ship which carried the Duchess Margaret to and fro when she visited England in 1480, also conducted the wool fleet from Boston and London to Calais on one occasion; on another she conducted "the king's wools" from Southampton to Calais, and several times she seems to have been sent to Bordeaux, probably to get wine for the king.[3] The *Burnet*, still another ship which Edward owned in the latter part of his reign and which was probably only a small trading vessel, as she does not seem to have been used at any time as a ship of war, carried a cargo of wheat, rye, and beans to Spain in the spring of 1478.[4]

It was also in the spring of 1478 that Edward bought a ship from John Alos of Spain for £100;[5] and very likely *la Spaynard* which served in the fleet sent against Scotland three years later was this self-same ship. At any rate, four other ships acquired by the king in 1481, the *Mary Howard*, which he secured from Lord Howard for £333 6s 8d, the *Holy Ghost* of Portugal, which he purchased from two Genoese merchants for £600, the *Marie* of Bilbao, for which he paid £300, and the *Trinity* of Eu, which cost him £100, were all bought especially for the fleet about to be sent to Scotland. And perhaps the *Mary Asshe*, the *Clement*, and the *Michael de la Toure*, which also served in that fleet and are likewise spoken of as the king's ships, were purchased at the same time.[6] Even the *Mary de la Toure*, which came into

---

1. Tellers' Roll, Mich. 13 Edw. IV. Richard III ordered the payment of £7 "for old arrearages" to William Parker, "late master under God of our ship called the *Portingale* and now master under God of our ship called the *Caragon*." Warrants for Issues, 1 Richard III, 21 Dec. Parker had been master of another of Edward's ships, the *Prynce*. *Cal. Patent Rolls*, III, 308.

2. Tellers' account, Exchequer T. R., Council and Privy Seal, file 91, m. 86; Exchequer Accounts, bundle 55, no. 8.

3. Devon, *Issues of Exchequer*, 500; Tellers' account, Exchequer T. R., Council and Privy Seal, file 92, m. 15, 24, 26; Tellers' account in Warrants for Issues, 20 Edw. IV, 17 July. At one time ten guns with thirty-six chambers were bought and delivered to William Fetherston "for the apparel and defence of the king's ship called the *Fawcon* passing from the port of Sandwich to Bordeaux." Warrants for Issues, 21 Edw. IV, 12 Jan.

4. Signed Bills, file 1514, no. 4976.

5. Issue Roll, Easter, 18 Edw. IV, 22 May.

6. *Cal. Patent Rolls*, III, 240; Accounts, etc. (Exchequer K. R.), bundle 329, no. 2. See also above, Vol. II, p. 303.

the king's possession sometime before the end of November 1481, when her steersman, Robert Michelson, the man who had guided the *Antony* and her royal passenger safely across the sea in 1471, was granted an annuity, may have been bought to assist in the attack on Scotland. And so may the *Prynce*, although of this ship, named evidently in honour of the king's eldest son, we hear nothing until July 1482, when she was under orders to go to sea with an armed force, apparently in company with the *Mary de la Toure*.[1]

Yet, however many ships Edward may have owned as a private individual, and however common a custom it may have been to employ for trading purposes any ship belonging to the crown which was not needed at the moment for purposes of war, the customs accounts supply abundant evidence that it was not English bottoms, as a rule, which carried across the sea the various wares England's merchant king wished to send to foreign markets. Not only did Edward make use of Italian ships when he wanted to send cloth or wool through the Straits of Marrok, but even when he was trading with the nearer ports of the Netherlands, he seems to have employed foreign ships more frequently than English ones—and this in spite of the fact that in one of the first parliaments of his reign it had been enacted that no inhabitant of his kingdom except "merchant strangers" should "freight nor charge within this realm or Wales any ship or other vessel of any alien or stranger with any merchandises to be carried out of this realm or Wales, or to be brought into the same, if he may have sufficient freight in ships or vessels of denizens of this realm."[2]

Why Edward made use of foreign ships instead of ships owned and manned by Englishmen is a question easily answered. It was because English ships were much smaller than their foreign rivals—so much smaller that probably few of them wanted to undertake so long a voyage as the one through the Straits of Marrok.

The need of encouraging his subjects to build more ships and larger ships Edward fully recognized. Just as John Taverner of Kingston-upon-Hull had been rewarded by Henry VI for building that wonderful ship, "as large as a carrack or larger," the *Grace Dieu*, of which we have heard so much, so in 1476 Edward,

1. *Cal. Patent Rolls*, III, 253, 308.
2. *Rolls of Parl.*, V, 504. And it will be remembered that after his treaty with Louis XI in 1475 Edward issued a proclamation warning his subjects that the old requirement that only English owned vessels should be used to bring the wines of southern France to England was still in force.

because he desired to see the shipping of his realm increased, requited one John Seman of London, mercer, who had newly built at his own expense a ship called *le George Cobham*, with a licence to load her on her first voyage from London with woollen cloth and other merchandise for Gascony and Bordeaux and to bring home other merchandise from foreign lands without paying customs or subsidies.[1] Nor does this appear to be the only instance in which Edward bestowed a reward for such a reason. In October 1474, when he was preparing to go to France, the king visited Bristol, and it would seem that, while he was there, he promised a reward to every man in the town who would build a ship; for in the following May he granted certain letters patent to a Bristol merchant named William de la Founde because the merchant had "fully made and apparelled a ship of the portage of 220 tons or under to the intent that the same shall at all times be ready to do us service when we shall command her, upon trust of our promise late made at our said town that if any man within the same would do make a ship of any value, he or they so doing her to be made should have her laden in and out custom free and pass free for the first voyage."[2]

In spite of all encouragement, however, most English ships continued to look very small by comparison with many of the ships from foreign ports which brought goods to England. The *Grace Dieu* was always so much of a wonder ship that to say that a ship was as big as the *Grace Dieu* was equivalent to saying that she was a very big ship indeed.[3] It is true that William Canynges of Bristol possessed a ship, the *Mary and John*, of 900 tons burden; and although we do not hear of his receiving any reward such as was given to Taverner and Seman, he had built this ship, Worcester says, at Bristol, and at a cost of four thousand marks. In fact, Canynges had no less than nine ships which had been built at Bristol. But the others were much smaller than the *Mary and John*. The *Mary Redcliffe*, which was next in size to the *Mary and John*, was only 500 tons burden, the *Mary Canynges* 400 tons, and the *Kateryn* of Boston 220 tons; and from the *Kateryn* they ranged downward in size to the *Galyot* of only 50 tons burden.[4] Moreover, Canynges

---

1. *Cal. Patent Rolls*, II, 594. The *George Cobham*, under the command of Lord Cobham and carrying 160 men, served in the fleet sent against Scotland in 1481. *Household Books of Duke of Norfolk*.
2. Writs of Privy Seal, file 853, no. 4156. Cf. French Roll 21 Edw. IV, m. 8.
3. See *Paston Letters*, IV, 57.
4. Worcester's *Itinerarium*, 99.

did most of his trading with Iceland, and it was probably only because there were few foreign ships which he could hire to make the voyage to that lonesome island that he took the trouble of building ships of his own.

William Canynges was not the only subject of Edward IV who owned a whole fleet of trading vessels. On 30 August 1464, when the prohibition against the importation of Gascon wine had been temporarily suspended, Edward granted the Earl of Warwick a licence for two of his servants

> to go out of this our realm during a year with the *Marie of Clyff*, of the portage of
> 280 tons, the *Marie of Grace* of 240 tons, the *George* of 140 tons, the *Great Marie* of
> 500 tons, the *Giles* of 240 tons, the *Marie Richardson* of 80 tons, the *Trinitie* of 350
> tons, and the *Katerine* of 220 tons, and every of them, of the which our said cousin
> is owner, laden or unladen, with all manner lawful merchandise unto Bordeaux
> and there to unlade the same and recharge the said ships and every of them with
> Gascoigne wine, and with the same to return to what port or place of our said realm
> that them shall list, there to sell and dispose it at their pleasure, freedom, and liberty.[1]

Nor is it likely that this is an exhaustive list of Warwick's ships; for the *Cristofer Warwick*[2] probably belonged to him also, as well as other ships of names now unknown. And yet, though Warwick owned many ships, and though no doubt those ships made many profitable voyages to foreign lands, the existing customs records reveal nothing about the great earl's commercial enterprises. His name occurs only once in the customs records of Edward's reign, and then all that we learn is that on 5 December 1462, a carrack of which Thomas Giustiniani was master brought to Sandwich, among a miscellaneous cargo shipped for the most part by John de Bardi, "two horse harness of boiled leather, one for the king and one for Lord Warwick." We are not even given the pleasure of knowing whether the Kingmaker provided his own body as well as that of his horse with elegant trappings, though the king evidently did, as "one pair bolsters for the king" and "an helmet for the king" also arrived in the carrack.[3]

Another English nobleman who probably owned a goodly number of ships

---

1. Warrants under the Signet, file 1378. Compare this list of Warwick's ships with the ships mentioned in a commission issued by the king on 16 June 1462. *Cal. Patent Rolls*, I, 204. The *Mary Grace* and the *Trinity* are spoken of in the *Paston Letters*, IV, 57, as belonging to Warwick.
2. *Cal. Patent Rolls, ut sup.*
3. Customs Accounts, Sandwich 128/4.t

was Lord Howard, who, as we have heard, sold one ship, the *Mary Howard*, to the king and who, occasionally at least, exported hides and Welsh cloth.[1] And Lord Herbert was the owner of at least one ship, the *Gabriell*, which seems to have ranked with some of the king's ships in size, as she is referred to as "a great ship." But the *Gabriell* came to grief on the coast of Ireland in the equinoctial gales of the spring of 1465, when she was returning from foreign parts with a cargo of wine and other merchandise, and the exasperating right of the crown to all wreckage made it necessary for her unfortunate owner to seek a special grant of the salvage from her.[2] Whether Herbert owned other ships is not known, but if names count for anything, Lord Duras must have owned at least two ships, the *Katerine Duras* and the *Barge Duras*.[3] It was another *Katerine*, however, the *Katerine* of Calais—unless the *Katerine Duras* could boast of two names—which took two loads of white herrings across the sea for Lord Duras in the spring of 1466. And eleven barrels of salt fish, two barrels of white herrings, and four barrels of cod-heads shipped by Duras in the preceding November had made their voyage in the *Christopher* of Sandwich, which may also have belonged to him.[4]

It is evident that King Edward was not the only Englishman of haughty lineage who stooped to turn a penny by trade. And the names of Warwick, Howard, Herbert, and Duras do not exhaust the list of the king's noble fellow merchants. Twelve days after he was proclaimed king, Edward told the chancellor that, in consideration of Lord Fauconberg's "great labour and charges," he had given him permission

> to ship or do ship in our port of London in carracks or galleys to be carried over the mountains by the Straits of Marrok an hundred sacks of wool freely without payment of any customs or subsidies therefor to be paid unto us in any wise.[5]

Nor did these hundred sacks of wool constitute Fauconberg's only venture. Two weeks later the *George* of Sklewse (Sluys), leaving London for Calais, took, as a part of her cargo, 63 sacks and 6 cloves of wool and 545 pells belonging to Fauconberg, and in the galley of Marin Dandolo, which departed from the same port for Venice on the following 27 June, there were 68½ sacks and one

1. *Ibid.*, Divers Ports, 194/17, 194/22.
2. *Cal. Patent Rolls*, I, 427.
3. *Ibid.*, I, 204, 302, 349.
4. Customs Accounts, Divers Ports 194/18.
5. Writs of Privy Seal, file 782, no. 9; French Roll 1 Edw. IV, m. 38.

clove of the same nobleman's wool; and as the usual duties seem to have been paid on these shipments, it would appear that they were not covered by the king's grant.[1] Moreover, on 29 October 1462, by which time he had become Earl of Kent, the king's uncle sent 408 dressed hides from London to "foreign parts," and on the following 28 May 748 more by his factor, John Rede. Several months after Fauconberg's death, in fact, hides which had belonged to him were still being shipped by Rede.[2] And Fauconberg's successor in the earldom of Kent was also an enterprising merchant. In October 1467, Edmund Grey, Earl of Kent, was licensed to ship over the sea 180 oxen yearly for ten years—a grant which sounds generous enough, though it probably amounted to less than a ten years' monopoly of the right to export mares which the king had previously granted to one Andrew Rede of Calais.[3]

Another person who stood very close to Edward's throne at the beginning of his reign and who seems to have tried his hand at commerce now and then was George Neville, Bishop of Exeter and chancellor of England. The bishop engaged a Florentine merchant named Louis Bernardo to act as his factor, and the *Mary* of Lushbourne (Lisbon), which left London soon after Edward's accession, was laden with 200 sacks and 25 cloves of the bishop's wool.[4] But a more extensive trader than George Neville, apparently, was the Earl of Essex. In the fourth year of Edward's reign Essex obtained a licence to export sixteen hundred woollen cloths without paying customs, and in the closing years of his life, when he was treasurer of England, the earl exported large quantities of tin, lead, coal, tanned hides, cloth, and other merchandise from Plymouth and Fowey, Bristol, Exeter, and Dartmouth.[5] Like King Edward himself, Essex was an importer as well as an exporter. In October 1475, a number of factors, some of whom were Englishmen and others Italians, were employed in bringing to England all sorts of useful things for the treasurer of England, as well as for the man who had twice been Speaker of the House of Commons, Sir John Say. As Essex no doubt had a large household to supply with the necessities of life, and as Say too probably lived on a large scale, it is

---

1. Customs. Accounts, London 73/32.
2. *Ibid.*, 73/35, 73/36.
3. French Roll 6 Edw. IV, m. II; Writs of Privy Seal, file 790, no. 813, file 814, no. 2248.
4. Customs Accounts, London 73/32.
5. Dugdale, II, 229, citing French Roll 4 Edw. IV, m. 21; Customs Accounts, Plymouth and Fowey 114/10–114/13, Divers Ports 262/7, Bristol 19/14, Exeter and Dartmouth 41/6.

easy to believe that some of the goods they imported were intended for their own or their families' use. Of a dozen shirts, for example, either gentleman could easily make good use, and some of the furs, buckram, linen cloth, wine, almonds, dates, prunes, white plums, sugar, treacle, rice, paper, and soap which appear among their importations may also have been consumed in their households. But two thousand ostrich feathers, two hundred tennis balls, twelve "harness complete," fifty-two pairs of brigandines, and many other things on which they paid customs they must have been hoping to sell to their fellow countrymen at a handsome profit.[1]

Still other noble names which appear here and there in the customs records of Edward's reign are those of Margaret, Duchess of Burgundy, of whose success in securing trading concessions from her brother we have already heard something, Lord Mountjoy, and Lord Hastings. Hastings was even a merchant of the staple of Calais, and one day in the summer of 1478 he sent out from London as many as 3,400 pells in one ship, 866 in another, and 220 cloves of wool in a third.[2] But among the important merchants of Edward's time there was one man who, although he was not blessed with a title and was not even an Englishman by birth, meant more to the king than all the rest. This was Gerard Caniziani.

Although on only one or two occasions is he directly so called in the English records, Caniziani was the factor and attorney of the "fellowship of the Medici of Florence";[3] and that he came to England before Edward ascended the throne is proved by a petition which was sent to the chancellor of England sometime before September 1464,[4] by Thomas Wenslowe, a

---

1. Customs Accounts, Sandwich 128/15.
2. Customs Accounts, Sandwich 128/10, Divers Ports 194/17, 194/25, London 73/40. Another person who made extensive shipments on the same day on which Hastings shipped his wool and pells was Margaret Croke, who is also described as a merchant of the staple of Calais.
3. From the English records in general one might easily conclude that Caniziani transacted all his business with the king entirely on his own account. But in the petition about to be quoted he calls himself "merchant, citizen, and mercer of London, sometime of the fellowship of the Medicis of Florence and factor and attorney of the same." See also the letters of protection, to be cited later, which were granted during Henry VI's readeption to Caniziani and Lorenzo Bardoce and "all other of the fellowship of Medici."
4. It must antedate September 1464, because it is addressed to the Bishop of Exeter as chancellor.

London draper, who complained that Caniziani had cheated him in a bargain. On 22 June, 37 Henry VI (1459), Wenslowe declared, he sold to Caniziani seventy-two woollen cloths of divers colours, containing 2,273 yards, for 4s 8d the yard, on the understanding that he was to receive in payment, first, two ouches of gold "with a balys[1] and certain diamonds in either of the said ouches infixed," which were reckoned to be worth £100 apiece, second, a bishop's mitre garnished with divers stones, which was also worth £100, third, one hundred rings set with rubies, which altogether represented another £100, and lastly, £130 6s 4d in cash. Unfortunately, however, the sale, which was made through a broker of the name of Jacob Falleron, was "written and made by a bill indented in Lombardy, the which your said suppliant could not read," and afterwards, when it was "transposed in English," the said suppliant discovered that it contained no mention of the value of the said ouches. Of this omission, he asserted, Caniziani took advantage and delivered to him in payment an ouche "of simple value, without any balys therein," whereas Caniziani declared that he did not guarantee the stones to be balyses, that he showed the jewels beforehand to Wenslowe, who agreed to accept them, and that he was bound to deliver the jewels thus shown and no others.[2] How the dispute was settled we do not know, but either Caniziani succeeded in proving himself an honest man or dishonesty was no bar to royal favour, as the factor and attorney of the Medici established close business relations with Henry VI's successor soon after Edward seized the crown.

In the very first months of his reign Edward seems to have turned to the merchants of Venice and Genoa when he wanted money and thought the foreign merchants in London might be willing to help him;[3] but by November 1462, at the latest, he had entered into communication with Caniziani, and in the course of that month he obtained two small loans through him, one of £200, of which £170 was repaid a few days later by assignments, and another of 100 marks, which was repaid in cash in the following January.[4] And once begun, Edward's appeals to Caniziani never ceased and apparently were never made in vain, with the natural result that the relations between the king and the Florentine became exceedingly close and friendly. On 24 April

---

1. A kind of ruby.
2. Early Chancery Proceedings, bundle 29, no. 467.
3. Receipt Rolls, 1 and 2 Edw. IV.
4. Issue Roll, Mich. 2 Edw. IV, no. 827, 16 Nov., 27 Jan.

1464, Edward granted his obliging friend, in return for a loan of 800 marks, the right to ship two hundred sacks of wool from London or Sandwich to the staple of Calais and thence beyond the mountains (in other words to Italy) without paying customs or subsidies.[1] But Caniziani handled other English commodities besides wool, for the same boats which carried some of Edward's own shipments from Southampton shortly after this licence was given to Caniziani contained also some cloth and lead which the Florentine was exporting.[2] At the same time, too, that he was exporting English wool and cloth and lead, Caniziani was importing into England many of the products of his native land, such as olives, prunes, oil, sugar, brimstone, saltpetre, and the rich fabrics so much admired and so much worn by Edward and his wealthy subjects. 21½ virgates of velvet ingrain and 27¾ virgates of crimson velvet imported by Caniziani at Sandwich in December 1464, and three pieces of damask and some cloths of silk of divers colours also belonging to him which reached the same port a few years later,[3] are probably only a few samples of many additions which were made through his instrumentality to the gorgeous wardrobes of Edward and his courtiers.

Even before he made the king of England the loan of 800 marks above referred to, Caniziani was probably a householder in London. Certainly he was a London householder before the end of 1464, as he and John de Bardi were the only Florentines in the city who paid, for the year running from Michaelmas, 1464, to Michaelmas, 1465, the tax of forty shillings levied each year on all foreign merchants who were householders.[4] By this time, too, he was so much in Edward's confidence that in the course of the winter he was employed on a delicate and important mission. This was the period when Edward was fighting the influence of Margaret of Anjou in Scotland, and when Caniziani was probably about to set out for the kingdom of James III on business of his own, he was intrusted with the task of conveying two hundred pounds to the Bishop of St Andrew's "for divers secret matters" and four hundred pounds to the Bishop of Aberdeen. The king also authorized him to spend the additional sum of £71 12s 6d "for certain

---

1. 'Writs of Privy Seal, file 797, no. 1400.
2. Customs Accounts, Southampton 142/2–142/3.
3. *Ibid.*, Sandwich 128/6, 128/10, 128/12.
4. Alien Subsidies, no. 96.

things," which may mean that he was to try to buy up some other Scottish prelate or nobleman.[1]

As time went on, Edward leaned more and more on Caniziani for financial assistance. On 27 October 1466, he secured from him a loan of no less than £5,254 19s 10d,[2] and in the following year we find him acknowledging that the Florentine had "paid and lent for and to us at our special desire and pleasure" £8,468 18s 8d. To cancel this large debt, the king granted letters patent which ceded to Caniziani temporarily the profits arising from one half of all wards, marriages, reliefs, escheats, forfeitures, custodies of heirs during minority, and temporalities of ecclesiastical benefices, and also all customs and subsidies, except those set aside for the staplers of Calais, in all the most important ports of England, with the added privilege of exporting wool, woollen cloths, tin, and lead through the Straits of Marrok free of customs and subsidies. Even the power to nominate the customer or collector in the ports from which he did his shipping was bestowed on the king's creditor.[3] And yet a few months later, apparently because Caniziani found that even after all this his money came back to him too slowly, at his "humble supplication" the king granted him three thousand pounds, in part payment of the £8,468 18s 8d, out of the tenth granted by the clergy of the province of Canterbury.[4]

When Edward was making a hard struggle to provide his sister Margaret with a dowry, Caniziani again proved a useful friend. For with Thomas Portinari, Angelo Tany, and Lorenzo Bardoce, he acted as attorney for the Duke of Burgundy, and consequently through the hands of these four Florentines passed the money which Charles received with his English bride.[5] It is even possible that a part of the dowry money was obtained from Caniziani, as he loaned Edward a thousand pounds in August 1468, and £2,600 9s in

---

1. Treasurer's account, Warrants for Issues, 5 Edw. IV, 1 March. Cf. Tellers' Rolls, Easter and Mich. 5 Edw. IV.
2. Warrants for Issues, 6 Edw. IV, 12 Nov.; Writs of Privy Seal, file 809, no. 1999; French Roll 6 Edw. IV, m. 1; Receipt Roll, Mich. 6 Edw. IV.
3. Warrants for Issues, 7 Edw. IV, 11 Dec.; *Cal. Patent Rolls*, II, ii. Cf. Issue Roll, Mich. 7 Edw. IV, 26 Oct.
4. Warrants for Issues, 8 Edw. IV, 30 Sept. A final payment of £2,625 3s 10d ob. to Caniziani to clear off this debt is entered on Issue Roll, Easter 8 Edw. IV, 21 July.
5. See above, Vol. I, pp. 453-454.

November of the same year; and this may also account for the fact that sixteen hundred pounds' worth of poor Thomas Cook's forfeited possessions were handed over to him.[1] Another loan of £3,225 6s 8d which he made to Edward on 8 January 1469, and still another of £700 which the king got from him and Lorenzo Bardoce sometime before 29 May 1469,[2] may also have been used to meet a delayed payment towards Margaret's dowry. It is interesting to find, too, that at this time Caniziani was probably again doing secret errands for the king, as in the autumn of 1468 he handled the sum of £2,210 9s which was spent for "certain secret matters concerning the defence of the kingdom."[3]

In return for the two loans he had received from him at the beginning of 1469, Edward again licensed Caniziani (and in the case of the loan of £700, Bardoce also) to export wool, woollen cloth, tin, and lead and bring back other merchandise without paying customs or subsidies. But the troubles which broke out in England soon after these grants were made seem to have prevented Caniziani from reaping any benefit from them. The agent of the Medici suffered no violence during the readeption of Henry VI, for on 16 February 1471, Henry, by the advice of the Archbishop of York, the Duke of Clarence, and the Earl of Warwick, took under his protection and safeguard Caniziani, Bardoce, their clerks and servants, "and all other of the fellowship of Medici." But for the payment of Edward's debts Henry did not hold himself responsible, and when Edward was again on the throne, he had to acknowledge his indebtedness to Caniziani anew by sending orders to the Exchequer for the entry in the pell of a *mutuum* of £3,225 7s 8d.[4]

Edward's recovery of the throne must have been a great relief to Caniziani and those whose money had been intrusted to him, and he showed his satisfaction by making another loan to the king two months after the battle of Tewkesbury. Sixty-six hundred pounds was the amount the Florentine advanced to Edward this time, and as usual his reward was a licence to export wool, woollen cloth, tin, and lead and bring back other merchandise without the payment of customs or subsidies.[5] In fact, Caniziani was so

---

1. Receipt Rolls, Easter and Mich. 8 Edw. IV; Issue Roll, Easter 8 Edw. IV, 5 July.
2. *Cal. Patent Rolls*, II, 132, 160.
3. Issue Roll, Mich. 8 Edw. IV, 3 Nov.
4. Writs of Privy Seal, file 780, no. 11096; Warrants for Issues, 11 Edw. IV, 17 August.
5. Warrants for Issues, II Edw. IV, 17 August (another document of the same date as the one just cited); *Cal. Patent Rolls*, II, 273.

pleased with the way affairs were now going in England that he not only continued to find loans for the repatriated king and to give him other assistance, such as redeeming some of the royal jewels from pawn at a cost of more than forty-five hundred pounds,[1] but he decided to take unto himself an English wife and become an English subject. The wife he chose, and whom he married sometime before Easter, 1474, was Dame Elizabeth Stokton,[2] and in acknowledgment of his "laudable and acceptable service" on many occasions, the king sent him a wedding gift of jewels which cost £73 12*d* and about two years later, when his first child was born, a cup of silver gilt for the baptism.[3] Moreover, the letters of denization which were granted to Caniziani and his heirs (probably including James Caniziani, who had joined him in London some time before Michaelmas, 1466,[4] and who may have been the son of an earlier marriage contracted in Florence) on 3 November 1473, were issued to him without fee or fine, although he had to pay 6*s* 8*d* "pro homagio suo ligeo."[5] Straightaway, too, he was given an office. The month after he received his naturalization papers he and William Hatclyf were made joint custodians for seven years of the exchange at Calais, and also of the exchange within England for foreign parts.[6]

Caniziani's change of allegiance got him into some trouble, as it was deeply resented by his former associates of the fellowship of Medici. The new "factor and attorney general" of the fellowship was Christopher Spyng, and Caniziani found occasion, a few months after he became an Englishman, to send a long petition to the chancellor of his newly adopted country setting forth the unjust treatment he had received from Spyng and the fellowship. When a certain carrack of Genoa was in the port of Southampton, Caniziani stated in his petition, and two galleys of Naples were about to come to England from

---

1. Warrants for Issues, 33 Edw. IV, 28 Feb.
2. Warrants under the Signet, file 1392, 24 Dec 1483. Cf. *Cal. Patent Rolls*, II, 466.
3. Tellers' Roll, Mich. 13 Edw. IV, and Tellers' Roll, no. 51A. The cup must have been a handsome one, as it cost £11 16*s*.
4. Alien Subsidies, no. 107. James Caniziani paid the tax of 20*s* demanded from foreign merchants who were not householders.
5. *Cal. Patent Rolls*, II, 401; Receipt Roll, Mich. 14 Edw. IV; Tellers' Roll, Mich. 14 Edw. IV.
6. Fine Roll 13 Edw. IV, m. 2. This was not altogether new work for Caniziani, as early in Edward's reign he had been for a time an *appruator* of the exchange for foreign parts, serving with John de Bardi and other Italians. Exchequer Accounts, Mint, bundle 302, no. 11.

Flanders, a "communication was had" between him and Spyng regarding "divers reckonings and accounts" between him and the fellowship of the Medici, and as he had a licence from the king at that time to ship wool belonging to himself and others by the Straits of Marrok without paying customs or subsidies until the amount of the customs and subsidies thus released to him rose to sixty-six hundred pounds,[1] it was agreed between him and the said Christopher, at the special desire of the latter, that five or six hundred sacks of wool or more should be bought for the fellowship and shipped in the said carrack and galleys. The customs and subsidies due on the wool, according to the agreement, were to be retained in Caniziani's name by force of the king's licence, and the sum of money which the customs and subsidies represented was not to be demanded by him from the fellowship or from Christopher until a full reckoning was made between him and the fellowship, when he was to be credited with the amount. But afterwards, Caniziani complained, Christopher, "because the said Gerard was well acquainted with merchants English and understanding how the purveyance of the said wools might be made," asked him to help him to "purvey and ordain the said wools and be surety with him for such payments thereof as should require," promising faithfully in his own name and that of the fellowship that he would afterwards pay for all the wool and for all the incidental expenses. Trusting in this promise, Caniziani, according to his story, then bought 711 sacks and 20 nails[2] of wool from divers persons for which £6,795 16s 5d was to be paid, partly "in hand," and he also spent £952 for canvas, packing, carrying, and other necessary expenses; yet, when he had done this and when, thanks to him, the wool had been shipped to the use of the fellowship without payment of customs or subsidies, which would have amounted to £1,738 12s 3d, Christopher, after having paid nothing except a part of what had been given in hand for the wool, refused to do more. What was worse, having got possession of the wool, he planned "privily to avoid out of this realm and so to leave the said Gerard to rest only in the charge of the said sums payable for the said wools." So what Caniziani petitioned for was that Spyng should either be required to give surety not to leave the realm until the matter was determined or be committed to ward.[3]

---

1. This evidently refers to the grant made to Caniziani in 1471.
2. A nail of wool was 8 lbs. Halliwell.
3. Early Chancery Proceedings, bundle 50, no. 414.

Caniziani did not make his complaint altogether in vain, but neither did he get all that would have been agreeable to him, as the judgment rendered on 25 February 1475, was that Spyng should pay for the society of the Medici two thousand pounds of what was still due to the English merchants from whom the wool had been bought and that Caniziani should pay the rest.[1] In the meantime, moreover, life had been made so uncomfortable for Caniziani that on 13 January the king was moved to grant him letters of protection for five years, stating that he did so because he understood the Florentine merchants of the society of the Medici were very indignant with Caniziani on account of his services to him, the king, and his marriage solemnized in England and were intending to annoy him without cause.[2]

After he severed his connection with the Medici and his native land, Caniziani was known simply as a citizen and mercer of London, and sooner or later he became a merchant of the staple of Calais.[3] But even under these altered conditions he was still useful to the king. When the French expedition was in preparation, he loaned Edward a thousand marks and received his customary reward, a licence to export wool, woollen cloth, tin, and lead and bring back other merchandise without paying customs or subsidies. And when, in the following year, Edward desired to make a settlement with him, Caniziani, as we have already heard, promised that, upon receiving one thousand pounds in ready money, one thousand pounds in assignments on the last tenth granted by the clergy, and one thousand pounds "in sufficient and ready payment" at Michaelmas, 1476, he would restore to the king all assignments, tallies, and patents which he held.[4] Even this settlement did not terminate Caniziani's services to Edward IV, though it does seem to mark the end of his loans to the king. It was into the hands of Caniziani that one instalment of Margaret of Anjou's ransom was paid by Louis XI in the autumn of 1478; and a few months later he is described as a factor of the king and receives £233 6s 8d at the Exchequer because that amount was due from him to certain persons for wool bought for the king's works.[5] Finally, on 14

---

1. See the endorsement on the above document.
2. *Cal. Patent Rolls*, II, 481.
3. Early Chancery Proceedings, *ut sup.*, and also bundle 59, no. 69; *Cal. Patent Rolls*, II, 547, III, 362.
4. Warrants for Issues, 15 Edw. IV, 22 June, 16 Edw. IV, 30 March; *Cal. Patent Rolls*, II, 547. And see above, Vol. II, p. 215.
5. Rymer, XII, 91; Issue Roll, Mich. 18 Edw. IV, 26 Jan.

July 1480, he and Hatclyf were again made custodians for four years of the exchange at Calais and of the exchange in England for foreign parts.[1]

Caniziani outlived the king who had so much to thank him for. But if he did not enjoy an equal amount of Richard III's favour, at least both he and his wife seem to have met with just dealing from the new king, as not only were they granted a general pardon, probably a merely formal affair, on 21 July 1483, but on the following 24 December Richard notified the chancellor that, as he had that day received from them the sum of five hundred marks in cancellation of a "bill obligatory payable at the feast of St Thomas the Apostle last past," and as the said bill "cannot by us as yet be found," they were to have "letters of acquittance specifying the said sum" under the great seal.[2] Caniziani's earthly pilgrimage was nearly over, however, when this order was sent to the Chancery, and unless the letters of acquittance were drawn up and sent to him very promptly, he never saw them, as he was dead before 19 March 1484.[3]

1. Fine Roll 20 Edw. IV, m. 5.
2. *Cal. Patent Rolls*, III, 362; Warrants under the Signet, file 1392.
3. Close Roll 1 Richard III.

3

EDWARD AS A BUILDER AND AS A PATRON OF LETTERS

The Rows Roll gives Edward IV the credit of being "a great builder," and although the description is one which the compiler of the roll is inclined to apply rather freely, in Edward's case at least it seems to be fully deserved. For disturbed as was the condition of England for some years after he took possession of the throne, and greatly as he needed all the money he could scrape together for much more essential purposes, Edward began almost immediately after his accession to indulge his taste for building, and this he continued to do until the end of his life. In the improvement and beautification of Westminster Palace he seems to have taken a special interest. He had been king little more than a year when he wrote to the treasurer and chamberlains of the Exchequer that "for as much as our new work within our privy palace of Westminster late by us is begun," two hundred pounds were to be delivered at once to Thomas Stratton, clerk of the works, "to the intent to be employed upon our said new work."[1] And when his reign was drawing to a close, not only was Simon Dowsynge, gardener, paid 53s 4d for laying out a new garden within Westminster Palace "to the king's great pleasure"—and also, apparently, to the pleasure of the Duke of Gloucester, as Dowsynge was afterwards appointed by Richard III to be keeper of the king's garden in the Tower—but orders were given for the repair of "certain ruinous houses" within the palace, for "the making of a great chamber unto our dearest wife the queen in her lodging, and for a privy kitchen of new to be made within the said palace."[2]

Edward did not by any means confine his building activities to his Westminster home. In 1463 he spent a hundred and thirty pounds on repairs

1. Warrants for Issues, 2 Edw. IV, 16 April.
2. Tellers' Roll, Mich. 22 Edw. IV; *Cal. Patent Rolls*, III, 384; Warrants for Issues, 22 Edw. IV, 6 Nov.

at Queenborough Castle, Kent, at another time he repaired Nottingham Castle, and the year before his flight to Burgundy it pleased him to restore the Prince's Wardrobe in the Old Jewry, an undertaking which may not have been very serious but which at least necessitated the purchase of many new tiles and the expenditure of ten shillings for "mending of the glass windows in the chapel and the glass windows in the great chamber and in the same chamber by the chapel, and mending of the glass windows in another chamber over the garden." In the year 1480 he was particularly busy. During that year, in addition to what was being done at Westminster Palace, Clitheroe Castle, in Lancashire, was being repaired, very extensive repairs calling for twenty hundred thousand bricks were also going on at Dover Castle, the walls of the city of Carlisle were being restored under the eye of the Duke of Gloucester, a new hall was being built at Eltham, and works of one sort or another were in progress at the Tower and at Greenwich.[1] It was at Edward's instigation, too, Ross says, that the walls of the city of London were rebuilt. Yet, after all this has been told, what was by far the most important of the king's "new works" still remains to be mentioned. For it was the building he did at Windsor Castle that is Edward's chief title to be called "a great builder."

From the foregoing list of his building operations, it would appear that Edward was inclined to spend his money on secular buildings rather than on churches. It is true that he founded a couple of chantries in the church of Allhallows, Barking ("in Our Lady Chapel of Barking Church within our city of London"), in which two priests appointed by him were to sing and pray for the souls of "our noble progenitors," and that he presented to Canterbury Cathedral a stained glass window of which an interesting fragment, representing him and his family, is still to be seen there in the north transept, while Elizabeth Woodville evinced her piety by building the chapel of St Erasmus in the monastery of Westminster.[2] But in general the king seemed

---

1. Issue Roll, Easter 3 Edw. IV, 23 June; Tellers' Rolls, Easter and Mich. 20 Edw. IV; Tellers' accounts in Exchequer T. R., Council and Privy Seal, file 91, m. 86, file 92, m. 15, 24, 26; Exchequer Accounts, Works, bundle 474, no. 2, bundle 496, no. 21; Ross, *Hist. Regum Angliæ*, 211; Stow, 434. It is stated in Lewis's *Topographical Dict.* that Edward repaired the palace at Eltham and enclosed one of the parks, and that he enlarged and beautified the palace at Greenwich. While he was staying at Dover in 1482, he sent to London for some painters, who were probably to put the finishing touches to the new work in Dover Castle. Tellers' Roll, Easter 22 Edw. IV.
2. Warrants for Issues, 4 Edw. IV, 22 April; Issue Roll, Easter 4 Edw. IV, 11 June; *Cal. Patent*

to be content to leave the building and beautifying of the churches of his kingdom to his subjects; and he was justified in doing so, as stonecutters and carpenters were at work in all parts of England at this period constructing and adorning churches at the expense either of the communities which worshipped in them or of pious and wealthy individuals, such as William Canynges, the great merchant to whom the city of Bristol is chiefly indebted for that gem of parish churches, St Mary Redcliffe. Nevertheless, by far the greatest of Edward's achievements as a builder was a church, though it was a church dedicated to an unusual purpose.

It was apparently not until the beginning of the year 1473 that Edward began to lay plans for the rebuilding of the chapel erected by Edward III at Windsor for the use of the knights of the Order of the Garter which he had founded. For it was not until 19 February of that year that Richard Beauchamp, Bishop of Salisbury, within whose diocese Windsor lay, was appointed master and surveyor of the king's new works at Windsor Castle and the chapel of St Mary and St George, with power to take stonecutters, carpenters, and other workmen, as well as stone, timber, tiles, glass, lead, and other necessaries.[1] Once begun, however, the erection of the new buildings, which were to include before all was done not merely the new chapel, but, to the north of it, houses for the dean and canons and, at the west end, other houses for the petty canons grouped on the ground-plan of a fetter-lock, one of the badges of the house of York, was carried on with such eager haste that not even the expedition to France was allowed to interfere with it. On 12 June 1475, five days before the citizens of London were asked for another benevolence for the expenses of that expedition, the Bishop of Salisbury was authorized to tear down certain buildings, walls, and houses adjoining the old chapel to make place for the new one which the king was proposing to erect to the honour of St Mary and St George, and to use the material therefrom for the works in Windsor Castle.[2] And reference has already been made to the fact

---

Rolls, III, 133. It may be added that in 1478 Edward remitted to the prior and convent of Christ Church, Canterbury, £77 14s 5d ob., the amount due to him as their share of one half of a tenth which had been granted to him by the province of Canterbury, that they might use the money towards the repairing of the cathedral. Warrants for Issues, 8 Edw. IV, 3 Nov.

1. *Cal. Patent Rolls*, II, 368.
2. *Ibid.*, II, 535.

that, before he started for France, Edward was careful to point out to the bishop just where in the new chapel he desired his body to lie in case death overtook him during his expedition. More than that, in the will he drew up at Sandwich, on the eve of sailing, the king took pains to insure the completion of the chapel under Beauchamp's supervision by ordering that the issues and profits from lands which had come into his hands through the minority of the heirs of the late Earls of Shrewsbury and Wiltshire and through the attainder of Sir Thomas Tresham should be used for that purpose and that, should these resources fail before the chapel was finished, an equal amount of money should be set aside for the work out of the revenues of the duchy of Lancaster. He also provided for the suitable amount of singing and praying at his tomb by giving directions for the foundation of a chantry of two priests, who were to be chosen preferably from doctors of divinity, "or bachelors of divinity at the least," of the Universities of Oxford and Cambridge and were to be paid a salary of twenty marks a year for their services, and for the appointment of thirteen poor men, who, for a reward of twopence a week, were likewise to put up daily prayers at his tomb.[1] But happily the king lived to return to England, and when, on 8 October, just ten days after his entry into London, he hastened down to Windsor to see what had been accomplished during his absence, he must have been well pleased with what he found, as two days later he rewarded the Bishop of Salisbury for the zeal he had shown on behalf of the Order of the Garter by making him the first chancellor of the Order and by providing that the new office thus created should pass to the succeeding bishops of Salisbury.[2]

As Edward brought back from France so much of Louis XI's money, he was able, after his return, to hurry on the work at Windsor as much as he wished. By March 1478, he had drawn so many stonecutters into his service that the supply was exhausted, and in order to secure workmen to complete the Divinity School at Oxford the chancellor of the university had to appeal to the generosity of the Bishop of Winchester, who was then engaged in building Magdalen College and who had secured a grant of the assistance of some stonecutters from the king.[3] Nor were stonecutters the only craftsmen

---

1. *Excerpta Historica*, 366-379.
2. Privy Seals; *Cal. Patent Rolls*, II, 554.
3. *Epistolæ Academicæ Oxon*, II, 445-447. Cf. Chandler's *Life of Waynflete*, 138-139, 360-362, where this letter is referred, wrongly, it would seem, to March 1475. The

the king had use for at Windsor. There was wood-carving as well as stone-cutting to be done, as the carving of the stalls in the choir of the new chapel had now been contracted for, and bell-hangers also would soon be needed.[1] In the meantime, too, the king had become an ardent collector of holy relics and rich ornaments of all sorts with which he hoped to augment the sanctity as well as the beauty of his chapel. In the year 1478 fifty pounds were spent "for the making the head of an image of Saint George in the king's chapel of Windsor and for gold to perform the same";[2] and more than likely it was for his new chapel that the king purchased, about the same time, from the Duke of Suffolk a very elaborate jewel. This jewel cost the king one hundred and sixty pounds, and it is described as "an image of Our Lady of gold with Our Lord in her arms and the images of Saint John Baptist and Saint Katharine on either side of Our Lady and two other images with seven angels thereto pertaining, the same image of Our Lady sitting upon a cushion of silver and over-gilt in a pavilion of gold garnished with six sapphires, six balyses, twenty-four great pearls upon five cushions of gold, twenty small pearls upon the crown, four little pearls in little diamonds, a ruby and two emeralds, thirteen very little pearls set in other places, and a ruby set in Our Lady's breast, weighing together by the weight of troy 103 ounces." What is of greater interest, the king promised to pay two hundred and ten pounds to Philip Maisertuell, merchant stranger, "for certain books by the said Philip to be provided to the king's use in the parties beyond the sea," and perhaps these books, about which we would fain hear much more, also became a part of the treasures of St George's Chapel.[3] Even the pots and cups which the king purchased from the Bishop of Elne, and which all but got the poor bishop into trouble when he went home to France, may have found their way to the new chapel. Certainly seven copes of white silk damask "embroidered with angels with divers minstrelsies," which the king had ordered by the

---

expenditures on St George's Chapel amounted in 1478 to £1,178 18s 10d ob., in 1479 to £1,307 6s 3d ob., in 1480 to £1,249 18s 5d qa., in 1481 to £1,145 7s 2d. ob., qa., in 1482 to £960 12s 10d ob., in 1483 to £730 9s qa. Exchequer Accounts, Works, bundle 496, nos. 17, 19, 22, 23, 26, 28.

1. Tighe and Davis, *Annals of Windsor*, I, 373.
2. Account of John Fitzherbert and other Tellers, Warrants for Issues, 18 Edw. IV. The chapel's holiest relic was the true head of St George. Ross, *Hist. Regum Angliæ*, 211.
3. Account of Fitzherbert, etc., *ut sup.*

spring of 1479 from a London vestment-maker named William Morton for the sum of two hundred and forty pounds, were destined for the use of the college of St Mary and St George in the castle of Windsor.[1] And in the course of the following year the chapel received from the king many yards of precious stuffs, including "white velvet with black spots," "blue velvet with branches," "black velvet with white spots," "white velvet branched," "white damask with flowers of divers colours," "blue velvet tissue cloth of gold," and "white velvet tissue cloth of gold"—a list which makes the purple velvet also sent by the king sound almost dull and homely.[2]

On 6 December 1479, a charter of incorporation was granted to the dean and canons of "the king's free chapel of St George within his castle of Windsor," to which parliament afterwards gave the form of a statute; and so near completion was the chapel by the following year that lead was cast for the covering of the roof.[3] But though in 1482 one John Squyer of Windsor, carpenter, received twenty pounds towards the making of the chapel roof, apparently only the east end of the building had been roofed over when, in April 1483, King Edward was laid to rest within its gleaming walls.[4]

Among those who attended the king's funeral in St George's Chapel there was at least one man who must have heaved a sigh as his eye wandered along the graceful arches and over the rich carvings in stone and wood. William Waynflete, Bishop of Winchester, though he himself had found joy in the creation of beautiful buildings, was not likely to forget that, for the endowment of Edward IV's exquisite chapel, Henry VI's two noble foundations, Eton College, of which he had been the first provost, and King's College, Cambridge, had been robbed of almost a thousand pounds a year.[5] Yet Waynflete had reason to rejoice, even while he sighed; for there had been a time, now happily past, when it looked as if Eton College would lose much more than a portion of its endowments, as if the college which stood under the walls of Windsor Castle would be wholly absorbed by the chapel rising within the castle gates.

---

1. Compare Issue Roll, Easter 19 Edw. IV, 7 May, with Exchequer T. R., Council and Privy Seal, file 92, m. 13, 23 May 1480.
2. Nicolas, *Wardrobe Accounts of Edw. IV*, 156, 158, 159.
3. *Cal. Patent Rolls*, III, 172; *Rolls of Parl.*, VI, 208-209; Tighe and Davis, I. 373.
4. Tellers' Roll, Easter 22 Edw. IV; Tighe and Davis, I, 397.
5. Stow, 434; Twyne, *Antiquitatis Academiæ Oxonienses Apologia*, 319.

In the early months of 1461, when no one could be sure whether the crown of England was going to stay on the head of Henry of Lancaster or be transferred to that of Edward of York, the hearts of the provost and fellows of Eton College were heavy with dread; and when Edward, flushed with his victory at Mortimer's Cross, entered London on 27 February, among the persons waiting to greet him was a deputation from Eton College, one member of which was probably the provost of the college, William Westbury. Fortunately, however, the young earl saw the wisdom, in the present stage of his fortunes, of winning all the friends he could, and before the sun went down he put his signature to a document in which he announced that he had received "the provost and fellowship of the College of Eton into our defence and safeguard" and forbade anyone desiring to have "our good lordship" to trouble or vex them or their tenants or servants or to rob them of their goods.[1] But though Eton College must have reverberated with songs of thanksgiving when it was thus assured of the protection of the Earl of March, Edward's kindness, unhappily, did not stand the test of time. Even before his coronation the new king demanded that all rents and profits of King's College, Cambridge, should be accounted for at the Exchequer,[2] and as soon as the crown had been placed on his head and Henry VI had taken flight to parts unknown, his heart hardened against Eton College also. Provost Westbury again did his best to ward off the blow he feared, this time by loaning the king four hundred marks and later discreetly transforming the loan into a gift;[3] but the day of disaster was not long postponed. When parliament met in November, all grants which had been made by the Lancastrian kings, including apparently every one of the grants made by Henry VI both to King's College and to Eton College, were declared null and void.[4]

The immediate result of this act of parliament was not quite as disastrous as might be expected, as not only did Westbury succeed in a very short time (on 5 February 1462) in obtaining a general pardon, but something less than three weeks later Edward re-granted to Eton and King's Colleges many of their

1. Maxwell Lyte, *Hist. of Eton College*, 59.
2. *Cal. Patent Rolls*, I, 33.
3. Receipt Roll, Easter 3 Edw. IV, 22 June and 26 Sept.
4. *Rolls of Parl.*, V, 463-464. Compare two grants of the alien priory of Derehurst made by the king on 3 August 1462, and 25 July 1467 (*Cal. Patent Rolls*, I, 196, II, 66), from which it appears that the endowments of Eton College were definitely revoked by the king with the consent of the council in parliament at Westminster in November 1461.

possessions.[1] Yet the worst, as far as Eton College was concerned, was still to come. Edward had evidently intended to let the college live, as otherwise he would have allowed the act of parliament to take full effect; but the dean and chapter of Windsor hungered to devour their neighbour, and in the following year it was discovered that the king was seeking authority from the Pope to destroy Henry VI's foundation altogether by annexing it to St George's Chapel. Receiving a hint from some source of what was going on, Westbury hurried at once to London and there, on 15 July 1463, in the presence of a notary public, drew up a formal protest and, at the same time, an appeal to the Pope for protection. In the meanwhile, however, the king's proctor at Rome, whom the dean and chapter of Windsor were prepared to reward for his assistance, had been representing to Pius II that the college which King Henry had founded at Eton was practically useless, as the buildings were still unfinished; and on 13 November 1463, probably before Westbury's appeal reached him, Pius issued a bull decreeing the abolition of the college and the transference of its members to Windsor.[2] Nevertheless, the college again escaped with its life. Thanks probably to Provost Westbury's firm stand, St George's Chapel, in spite of the "Bull of Union," never absorbed, in full at least, Henry VI's foundation; and though the dean and chapter of Windsor were still covetous and in 1465 actually secured an order from the king for the removal of the jewels, bells, and other furniture of the college to Windsor,[3] it was but a short time before the king began to show signs of a change of heart, if not of shame. In the summer of 1467 Edward made considerable grants to the provost and college out of the alien priories and excused them for all time from the payment of any fine or fee for charters, letters patent, or warrants under any of the royal seals; and when, in the same year, parliament passed an act of resumption, the possessions of the college were specially exempted.[4] Two years later the king even suffered the college to take home some tapestry which had been carried off to St George's Chapel, and, more

---

1. Pardon Roll 1–6 Edw. IV, m. 44; *Cal. Patent Rolls*, I, 73.
2. Maxwell Lyte's story seems to be somewhat confused at this point, for, speaking of Westbury's appeal to the Pope, he writes: "It is worthy of remark that throughout this appeal he (Westbury) utterly ignored the recent Bull of Union." But if the provost's appeal was made on 15 July 1463, the Bull of Union had not yet been issued.
3. Maxwell Lyte, 60–63. See also *Three Fif. Cent. Chron.*, 277.
4. *Cal. Patent Rolls*, II, 47, 48, 62; *Rolls of Parl.*, V, 606.

important still, he wrote to Pope Paul II that he had been misinformed about conditions at the college and asked that the bull for its annexation to St George's Chapel, the bull which his own proctor had procured from Paul's predecessor, might be revoked. In 1470, consequently, Paul authorized the Archbishop of Canterbury to make an investigation and to cancel the bill of Pius II if the facts revealed were found to justify such action. But before Archbishop Bourchier could carry out this commission—though not before Provost Westbury had received the new bull in triumph and ordered two copies of it to be made—Edward was driven from his kingdom.[1]

Fortunately Westbury did nothing to compromise himself in Edward's eyes during the months of Henry VI's readeption, and although he was bold enough to go up to London, on 24 May 1471, to attend Henry's funeral, it would have been hard to find fault with him for that, since Henry had been the founder of the college over which he presided. Nor did Edward take offence. On the contrary, he seemed to regard Eton College with increasing kindliness as time went on. During the summer of 1471 he and Queen Elizabeth visited Eton no less than three times, and the third time they rode over from Windsor Castle they were accompanied by some foreign envoys, probably the ambassadors the Duke of Burgundy had sent to invite his brother-in-law to invade France. Westbury was not one to overlook the golden opportunity these royal visits gave him to ingratiate himself with the king and to obtain some further concessions for his college, and it was no doubt owing to his persuasive pleadings that the king issued an order that the valuables of the college which had been removed to St George's Chapel should be restored, as the tapestry had previously been.[2] The king was even led to show a mild interest in the completion of the church of the college, and on 21 March 1472, he announced that, because of his desire "to see the furtherance of the work begun upon the church of Our Blessed Lady of Eton," he had given permission to the provost and fellows to take as much chalk and flint from "our little park" at Windsor as they required for their building.[3] He also made further grants to the college in that and the two succeeding years, the last

---

1. Maxwell Lyte, 64-65.
2. *Ibid.*, 65-68.
3. Willis and Clark, *Architectural Hist. of the University of Cambridge and of the Colleges of Cambridge and Eton* (Cambridge 1886), I, 408.

grant being a gift of two parts of a wharf, crane, houses, etc., in the parish of St Martin in the Vintry in London, the remaining part of which belonged to Earl Rivers and was probably presented to the college by the earl at the same time, as in consideration of his services in securing for the college a grant of a tenement called "the Crane" in the Vintry, it was agreed that daily prayers should be put up in the college church for Rivers and his family and a yearly obit kept for them.[1] Finally, in August 1476, the Archbishop of Canterbury was induced by the counsel of the college to act upon the commission given to him by Paul II in 1470, and when the long delayed decision was rendered, it was all that could be desired, as the chapter of Windsor was ordered to abstain from molesting Eton College on pain of excommunication.[2]

Westbury died a few months after this victory crowned his devoted services to Eton, but his successor, Henry Bost, must have succeeded in keeping Edward's goodwill, since not only were the provost and scholars of the college pardoned, on 30 July 1478, all debts and accounts due from them to the king, but Edward visited the college once more a few months before his death and, by fresh letters patent, renewed its right to the alien priory of Goldclyff in the marches of Wales.[3] The epitaph on Provost Bost's tomb intimates, too, that through his influence large gifts were made to the college by Elizabeth Woodville, though the story commonly told is that Bost was the confessor of Jane Shore and that it was the king's beautiful and warm-hearted mistress, two portraits of whom are still preserved at Eton, who was the best friend and champion of Eton College at court.[4]

Although Eton College and King's College, Cambridge, so narrowly escaped destruction during Edward's reign, it would be a great injustice to the king to draw from this fact the conclusion that he was hostile, or even indifferent to the welfare of the educational institutions for which England was already renowned. He disliked those two colleges solely because they had been founded by the king he had deposed, and as he ultimately relented towards Eton College, so did he also relent in time towards King's College. For not only did he suffer King's College also to live, but in 1479 he promised it a thousand marks, a gift which seems to have swelled to considerably more

---

1. *Cal. Patent Rolls*, III, 328, 394, 553; Maxwell Lyte, 68-69.
2. Maxwell Lyte, 74.
3. *Cal. Patent Rolls*, III, 121, 334; Maxwell Lyte, 80.
4. Maxwell Lyte, 79-80.

than a thousand pounds before his death. Moreover, as at one time he had condescended to give a little aid towards the completion of the church at Eton, so in 1480 he encouraged the building then going on at King's College by buying wood for the work from the Abbot of Walden and providing for its conveyance to Cambridge. A year or two later he even took dinner at the college and attended services in the chapel.[1] In fact, Edward was a frequent visitor at Cambridge, especially in his early years when he was so often on his way to or from the north, and his interest in this already ancient seat of learning was sufficient to lead him, in 1477, to contribute towards the paving of the streets and places of the university, if not to undertake the whole work at his own expense.[2] Yet perhaps Cambridge has more reason to remember Edward's queen than Edward himself. Margaret of Anjou had passed as the foundress of Queen's College, Cambridge, and at the laying of its cornerstone she had been represented by Sir John Wenlock; but Elizabeth Woodville, even before her coronation, usurped Margaret's place at Queen's, and it was from her, as the "true foundress," that the college received, in 1475, its first statutes.[3]

Edward probably paid many visits to Oxford as well as to Cambridge. He was frequently at Woodstock,[4] and it is not likely that he would fail, whenever he was so near, to ride over to the university which had enjoyed the generous patronage of his father's old chief, Humphrey, Duke of Gloucester, and of which, throughout the first half of his reign, Warwick's brother, George Neville, was chancellor. There came a time later on when George Neville's connection with Oxford might have proved a little unfortunate for the university had Edward been inclined to bear a grudge. But when, on 28 June 1471, the masters wrote to congratulate the king on his victory over his enemies at Barnet and Tewkesbury and to beseech him to continue the favour he had shown to the university in the past, Edward not only magnanimously ignored the fact that the masters had sent a similar letter of congratulation to Henry VI a few months before, but confirmed the privileges of the university and

---

1. Willis and Clark, I, 472-473; *Cal. Patent Rolls*, III, 203. Edward's visit to King's College cannot have taken place, as Willis and Clark say, during Whitsuntide (26 May–2 June) 1481, as he was at Sandwich at that time. He was in Cambridge, however, on 31 May 1482. Privy Seals.
2. *Cal. Patent Rolls*, III, 55.
3. Willis and Clark, I, lxiv; *Cal. Patent Rolls*, I, 495.
4. Privy Seals.

even announced, a little later, his intention to be its special protector.[1] When George Neville's complicity, or supposed complicity, in the Earl of Oxford's attempt to invade England brought about his final disgrace, he was forced to resign the chancellorship of Oxford, and Thomas Chaundler, Warden of New College, who had held the chancellorship in the last years of Henry VI's reign, succeeded to his place. But in 1479 Chaundler resigned, and then the choice of the university fell on one of Elizabeth Woodville's brothers. As the members of the Woodville family, both men and women, were endowed not only with good minds but with literary tastes, the intellectual gifts and attainments of Lionel Woodville, Dean of Exeter, probably fully justified his choice as chancellor of Oxford. And yet, even granting this, there is still only too much reason to fear that his near relationship to the king was regarded as his best qualification for the office. However, if Oxford stooped to court the favour of the king through his wife's family, Edward was far from conceiving any prejudice against the university on that account. When he sent the Abbot of Abingdon to Italy in the spring of 1479, he permitted the university to employ the abbot to obtain from the Pope a confirmation of certain of its privileges. What was a still greater mark of kindness, he consented, at the university's entreaty, to send his nephew, Edward de la Pole, the son of his sister Elizabeth, Duchess of Suffolk, and also Lord Stanley's son, to study at Oxford. Finally, moved apparently by the honour paid to him by the entire university at the time he visited Magdalen College as Waynflete's guest in September 1481, and by what he saw and heard at the disputations and other exercises of the university which he attended on that occasion, he undertook to establish a free lectureship in theology at Oxford. His death probably deprived the university of this gift, but his wish to make it proves that he entertained a more than kindly feeling for Oxford.[2]

From all these facts it is plain that, although he was not a founder of schools and colleges like Henry VI, Edward never lacked a genuine interest in the great universities of his kingdom.[3] If he built no counterpart of King's

---

1. *Epistolæ Academicæ Oxon*, II, 391-396, 400-401; Maxwell Lyte, *Hist. of the University of Oxford*, 328-329; Twyne, *Ant. Acad. Oxon*, 322.
2. *Epistolæ Acad. Oxon*, II, 447-448, 453-457, 461-462, 478-479, 483-484; Twyne, *ut sup.*; Maxwell Lyte, 330-331.
3. In 1465 steps were taken to found a university, with privileges similar to those of Oxford, at Drogheda, in Ireland, but the plan came to nothing and there is no evidence that Edward showed any interest in it.

College, Cambridge, at least he evidently looked on with hearty approval while Waynflete brought into existence the magnificent buildings which still rank among Oxford's chief ornaments. What is more, his proposal to found a free lectureship at Oxford reveals a true desire to further the new intellectual awakening of which some signs were already discernible in the gloom that had so long pervaded both of England's universities. In addition to this, we have the testimony of the Croyland chronicler that Edward took much pleasure in encouraging wise and learned men.

Nothing is easier than to exaggerate the intellectual darkness of England in the latter part of the fifteenth century. The brilliancy of the Tudor period tends to blind the eye to the feebler light of the century which went before, and those who turn the pages of history hastily and carelessly are apt to jump to the conclusion that Englishmen of the period of the so-called Wars of the Roses had neither time nor inclination to think of anything save the killing of their fellow countrymen—unless, it might be, the killing of Frenchmen. Picturing to themselves a kingdom reduced to chaos by years of civil war, such readers take it for granted that for the time being the intellectual life of the land was practically dead; and if they are reminded that Duke Humphrey of Gloucester was a true disciple of the new learning already bearing rich fruit in Italy, they perhaps reply that Duke Humphrey was the exception which proves the rule and call attention to the fact that the duke himself fell a victim to the civil war. Even if they read the Paston Letters and discover that the members of that family were not only able to read and write, but went to college and owned books and treasured them, this discovery makes less of an impression on their minds than do the bitter private war raging around Caister Castle and the many other illustrations of the lawlessness and contentiousness of the time which those letters supply.[1] But happily, though there was great disorder

---

1. No student of the *Paston Letters* can fail to be struck by the ability and intelligence of the women as well as of the men of the Paston family. Little is known about the education of girls at this period, but certainly in some cases daughters were sent to the houses of religion for instruction. Among the Early Chancery Proceedings, bundle 44, no. 227, there is a petition addressed to the Bishop of Bath and Wells, chancellor of England, by the prioress of the house of Our Lady of Cornworthy in Devon for the recovery of £21 13s 4d from the estate of one Lawrence Knighte, gentleman, who had agreed with a former prioress of the convent that she should have his two daughters, Elizabeth, aged seven, and Jahne, aged ten, to "tecche them to scole" and that he would pay 20d a week

at times and laws were broken too frequently and with too much impunity, it is not true that the Wars of the Roses produced general chaos in England. The changes consequent upon the removal of one king and the setting up of another were, in reality, curiously superficial, and in the midst of what looks like appalling political instability the life of the people as a whole, mental as well as physical, flowed on much as in normal times. Naturally that life was more or less disturbed and hampered by the confusion and destruction which civil war inevitably causes, but, in spite of all, it continued in a fairly healthy condition. Otherwise the wonderful achievements of the following century would not have been possible, since not even all the rich intellectual influences which penetrated England from the outside world during Tudor days could have suddenly galvanized utter death into such glorious vitality.

Hence it happens that, while no one would venture to describe the reign of Edward IV as a time of literary productiveness, a second look at the period will disclose that, civil disturbances notwithstanding, some minds were dwelling on other matters than war or even trade and some pens were busy with other things than family letters or state documents. To say nothing of the ecclesiastics who composed sermons and similar religious writings as a part of their professional duty, both Sir John Fortescue and Sir Thomas Lyttleton lived and wrote in Edward's time. Fortescue's writings constitute some of the most valuable contributions ever made to the legal and constitutional history of England, while Lyttleton's treatise on "tenures," compiled for the instruction of his son, was subsequently described by the great Coke as "the most perfect and absolute work that ever was written in any human science." Some chronicles were also being produced, and while they were fewer in number than in the past, and inferior in quality (though William of Worcester had the spirit of a true antiquarian), they are still our chief source of information concerning the events of Edward's reign. And be it remarked, both John Hardyng's chronicle and the English annals of John Capgrave were dedicated to the king.[1] Nor were lighter themes than religion,

---

for their meat and drink. The two girls, the petitioner states, had been in the convent five years or more, and yet not a penny for their costs and charges had the convent received.

1. The description of Scotland with which Hardyng's chronicle closes was written to assist Edward in the invasion of Scotland which the chronicler hoped the king would undertake, and as Hardyng had spent several years in that country, his description was of real value.

law, and history altogether neglected. It is the sad truth that England was graced in Edward's day by no poet even so worthy of the name as the tedious John Lydgate of Henry VI's reign. Hardyng's chronicle, and also George Ripley's "Compound of Alchemy," which, like Hardyng's work, is dedicated to Edward, are poetry only in form; the political poems and songs of the period are poor stuff indeed, and of two self-styled "poet laureates," John Kay has left not a verse behind him, while the only surviving specimen of the work of Petrus Carmelianus of Brescia which belongs to Edward's reign is a Latin poem in couplets dedicated to the Prince of Wales in 1482 and now to be found in Royal MS. 12 A. XXIX. Yet let it not be forgotten that it was in the ninth year of Edward's reign, the year of the first revolt of Warwick and Clarence, that Sir Thomas Malory completed that masterpiece of English prose which has exerted so lasting an influence on the spirit and form of later English literature, poetry as well as prose, Le Morte Arthur.[1]

It is not enough to speak of these few subjects of Edward IV whose writings have earned for them a more or less important place in the history of the literature and thought of their country. There were other men living during Edward's reign who, in a different but equally vital way, were helping not only to preserve the intellectual traditions of the past, but to prepare the soil from which a new and vigorous growth was so soon to spring. These were the men who sought the light Humphrey of Gloucester had discerned from afar and who were more fortunate than the duke because while he, being a scion of the royal house and cursed with the ambitions royal blood commonly implants in human breasts, had to content himself with dreaming of Italy and with sending thither for his books, they were able to journey in person to that land of delight, to search among her bookshops, to hire the services of her scribes and illuminators, and afterwards to carry home with them the treasures they had gathered up.

In days gone by many English students had found their way to the University of Paris and many French students had come to Oxford and Cambridge. But the Hundred Years' War had checked this exchange of students, and although the ten years' truce signed between England and France during Henry VI's readeption contained a provision that Englishmen wishing to study in the universities of France, and Frenchmen

---

1. Warton, Hist. of English Poetry.

wishing to study in the universities of England, should enjoy all the privileges of native students and be admitted to all honours and degrees accorded by the university they chose to attend, that truce never went into effect; and in the treaties afterwards signed by Edward IV and Louis XI no such provision was inserted. It was less of a cross, however, for Englishmen to be cut off from the University of Paris at this period than it would have been at an earlier time, for the reason that the great French university now offered fewer attractions than the universities of Italy, whither the scholars of the East, fleeing before the Turk, had brought their priceless treasures and where the most famous teachers of the day were translating and expounding the Greek and Latin classics. Paris had one advantage over Italy for the English student; it was much nearer home. And because the journey to Italy was long and expensive, the number of English students who went abroad to study was no doubt smaller than it would have been had the portals of the University of Paris stood hospitably open. Yet in spite of expense and other difficulties, an occasional English student or tourist had gone to Italy even in the Middle Ages, and among the men destined to play a more or less prominent part in the events of Edward IV's reign were several scholars or literary dilettanti who had visited Italy and who, after their return home, helped on, directly or indirectly, the progress of humanism in England.

Of a small group of English students who went to Italy in the closing years of Henry VI's reign and returned to add lustre to that of Edward IV, the best known is William Grey, who afterwards became Bishop of Ely and, under that title, is already familiar to the reader of these pages. Grey, who was a kinsman of Lord Grey of Codnor and a man of so much wealth that he was able to live like a prince wherever he went, received his early education at Balliol College, Oxford. But some time before 1449 he went to the continent and, after studying logic, philosophy, and theology for several years at Cologne, proceeded to Italy. There he visited Florence and then studied at the University of Padua, and afterwards at the University of Ferrara under the far-famed professor of Greek and Latin, Guarino of Verona. He also served as Henry VI's proctor at Rome, and when, in 1454, Thomas Bourchier was translated to the see of Canterbury, he was provided by Nicholas V to the bishopric of Ely.[1] As Bishop of Ely, he returned to England, and he was one of the ecclesiastics who, when civil war broke out, forgot all they owed to Henry VI and gave their allegiance to the house of York. Grey was faithful to the Yorkist cause from the day Edward and Warwick entered London in 1460 until his death in 1478, and for a few months, 25 October 1469–10 July 1470, he held the office of treasurer of England. By taste, however, he was always a man of letters rather than a man of affairs. He gladly spent his last years in scholarly retirement and, being a devoted son of Balliol, bestowed on his college not merely money for the building of a library, but some two hundred manuscripts which he had collected during his sojourn on the continent and many of which had been transcribed and illuminated by his orders.[2]

It was not long after Grey returned from Italy that two other graduates of Balliol, John Gunthorp and John Free, or Phreas, went to Ferrara to study under Guarino. These two men set out for Italy together, and Free's expenses, if not Gunthorp's as well, seem to have been paid by the Bishop of Ely. But the interests and destinies of the two friends and fellow-travellers were totally different, although both spent some time at Ferrara and afterwards enjoyed the distinction of being mentioned in Ludovico Carbo's funeral oration on Guarino. Free, though his writings attest his familiarity with the Greek as well as with the Latin language, and though we know that he studied philosophy and civil law, gave his attention mainly to medicine. For a time he taught medicine at Ferrara, Florence, and Padua, and later, about the year 1465, by which time, it is said, he had accumulated a large fortune, he went to Rome, where, like his patron, Grey, he so impressed the Pope by his learning that he was provided to an English bishopric, that of Bath and Wells. He was never installed in his bishopric, however, and never saw England again, as almost immediately after receiving this mark of the papal favour, he died at Rome, by poison, it was suspected, and the bishopric of Bath and Wells passed to Robert Stillington, Edward IV's keeper of the privy seal and afterwards chancellor.[3] Gunthorp, on the other hand, returned to England, probably before Free's death, as he became Elizabeth

---

1. *Cal. Patent Rolls*, 1452-1461, p. 204.

2. Vespasiano da Bisticci, *Vite de Uomini Illustri del Secolo XV*, I, 230-232; Leland, *Commentarii de Scriptoribus Britannicis* (Oxford, 1709), 461-462; Antony Wood, *Hist. and Antiquities of the Colleges and Halls in the University of Oxford* (Oxford, 1786), 89.

3. Leland, *Com. de Script. Brit.*, 466-469, and *Collectanea* (London, 1774), III, 60; Le Neve,

Woodville's chaplain and secretary as soon as she was recognized as queen, and, about July 1465, was sent by Edward on a mission to Spain with Bernard de la Forsse. But though Gunthorp was employed on several embassies by Edward, and though in 1468 he was made king's almoner and in 1472 elected Dean of Wells, an office which he held until his death in 1498, he, like the Bishop of Ely, kept up his interest in letters even in the midst of his official duties. In another way also he resembled William Grey. He too had collected manuscripts during his stay in Italy, and some of his acquisitions he gave to Jesus College, Cambridge, where he is said to have resided at one time, while others, together with some of his own writings, ultimately passed into the possession of the university library at Oxford.[1]

A fourth English student who sat at the feet of Guarino of Verona was Robert Fleming, Dean of Lincoln, the founder of Lincoln College, Oxford. Fleming seems to have gone to Italy soon after he was made Dean of Lincoln in 1451[2] and to have remained there a number of years, during which he studied not only at Ferrara, but at the other Italian universities as well. He lived for some time at Rome, and if he returned to England before 1467, as there is ground for thinking he did, he probably went back to Rome a few years later, since he enjoyed the patronage of Sixtus IV, who became pope in 1471 and to whom he dedicated his poems, and the friendship of Platina, the librarian of the Vatican. However, though Fleming seems to have found Italy a more congenial country to live in than England, he died in his native land, in 1483, and bequeathed the manuscripts he had collected, as well as copies of his own writings, all stamped with his coat of arms, to Lincoln College.[3]

Another rich and famous Englishman who went to Italy as Henry VI's reign was drawing to an end was John Tiptoft, Earl of Worcester, a man whose career as constable and treasurer of England and lieutenant of Ireland necessarily makes him a well-known figure in any account of the reign of Henry's successor. Tiptoft too received his education at Balliol College, and

---

Fasti; *Dict. Nat. Biog.* See also Einstein, *The Italian Renaissance in England* (NY, 1902), 20-23.

1. Leland, 462-463; *Dict. Nat. Biog.*

2. He was probably already in Italy when Henry VI made him his proctor at Rome in March 1455. Rymer, XI, 364.

3. Leland, 460-461; Wood, 247; *Dict. Nat. Biog.*

so early did his ability win recognition that, when he was still a young man in his twenties, he served Henry VI for several years as treasurer of England. But in August 1457, he was appointed, together with Fleming, Dean of Lincoln, who was probably already in Italy, and Sir Philip Wentworth, to go to Rome and offer Henry's obedience to Pope Calixtus III;[1] and it was probably at this time that his journeyings began. Attended by a large suite, he landed in Venice and soon after, though probably not before he had fulfilled his mission to Calixtus, sailed for the Holy Land. His pilgrimage to Jerusalem accomplished, he returned to Venice and thence went to Padua, where he formed a friendship with John Free and where he stayed some time studying Latin and presumably law, since his fellow countrymen afterwards accused him of judging them by the "law of Padua." In the midst of his studies he, like the rest, caught the book-collecting fever, and when his book hunts drew him to Florence, the abode of clever illuminators, he wandered, like any curious tourist, into every nook and corner of the city and one morning, we are told, dropped in to hear the lecture of John Argyropoulos, who was then teaching Greek in Florence.[2] From Florence he proceeded to Rome, not long after the death of Calixtus III, and on 16 May 1459, he and Fleming were directed to offer King Henry's obedience to the new Pope, Pius II.[3] This commission probably furnished the occasion for the famous oration which the earl delivered before the Pope and the Cardinals and which is said to have drawn tears from the eyes of the cultured Pius by its eloquence. But while Worcester was also one of the men who were selected by Henry VI to attend Pius's diet at Mantua in the summer of 1459,[4] he failed, as did most of the other English delegates, to put in an appearance when the diet met at the end of September, and possibly he had left Italy before that time, although it was not until September 1461, that he reached England.[5] There he was welcomed and received into such favour by the new king, Edward of York, that if he

1. *Cal. Patent Rolls*, 1452-1461, p. 362.
2. Vespasiano da Bisticci, I, 322-324; Leland, 475-481.
3. *Cal. Patent Rolls*, 1452-1461, p. 487.
4. Privy Council Proceedings, VI, 302.
5. *Chron. of John Stone*, 84. On 24 April, 1 Edw. IV two hundred ducats were exchanged for Worcester at the king's exchange. Exchequer Accounts, Mint, bundle 302, no. 11. This would lead one to conclude that the earl reached England in the spring of 1461, but John Stone says very distinctly that he came to Canterbury on 1 September "de Terra Sancta et de aliis partibus diuersorum regnorum."

ever felt a craving to resume his travels, he was unable to gratify it.[1] He never went back to Italy, and perhaps this was fortunate for that beautiful land, as so many were the books he had purchased while he was there that Carbo declared in his funeral oration on Guarino that it was as if the earl had robbed the libraries of Italy to adorn those of England. The library of Oxford was one of the storehouses of learning which Worcester's purchases eventually enriched, for he remembered his Alma Mater in his will by bequeathing to her manuscripts believed to be worth as much as five hundred marks.[2]

After the death of Guarino, which occurred in 1460, English students who went to Italy seem to have been attracted to the Universities of Padua and Bologna rather than to that of Ferrara. Thomas Langton for one, the man whom Edward sent on so many embassies to France during the last years of his reign, went to Padua soon after he left Cambridge University in 1464; and another man, whom we have known as treasurer of Chichester Cathedral and ambassador to Italy in 1479, at least made an effort to study at Padua during the time Langton was there. On 5 June 1464, an agreement was signed between John Doget and one James Fynche, a London shearman, according to which Fynche, in return for the sum of £50 20d, was to give Doget two hundred and thirty-two gold ducats of Venice, deliver fifty-two additional ducats for him to Master Thomas Langton, doctor of decrees, at Padua on the first day of August following, provide him with a letter of exchange for the remaining one hundred and eighty ducats, and lastly, convey to Venice for him a certain chest containing divers goods of the value of £12 10d. As it turned out, however, when Doget reached Venice and presented the letter of exchange Fynche had given him, the person to whom the letter was addressed refused to pay him a single ducat, declaring that he did not know Fynche "to be of any credence in that country." Fynche failed, moreover, to deliver either the fifty-two ducats to Master Thomas Langton or the chest to Doget himself, and in consequence of his rascality the unlucky Doget, as he stated in a petition which he sent to the

---

1. In Hist. MSS. Com., *Report 9*, app., 103, mention is made of a letter sent by the Dean and Chapter of Canterbury to Worcester at Padua asking for his aid in securing the papal licence for celebrating the jubilee of the martyrdom and translation of St Thomas, and the editor decides that the letter must belong to 1468–1469, as the jubilee took place in 1470. But Worcester certainly did not go to Italy again after his return to England, and the letter must therefore be of a considerably earlier date than 1468.

2. *Epistolæ Academicæ Oxon*, II, 389-391.

chancellor of England a number of years later, "was not able nor of power to content his creditors of their duties in Padua ne durst abide in Padua there to apply him to study, as he intended for to have done, but departed from thence, his debts at that time being unpaid, his learning and his credence lost in that country, to his damage of forty pounds."[1]

Doget, as the loss of £50 20d and a chest of goods worth £12 10d appears to have bankrupted him, was evidently not a man of wealth who could make purchases of manuscripts on any such scale as William Grey and the Earl of Worcester, or even Gunthorp and Fleming, had made them. Still, he must have managed to pull himself out of his financial difficulties in some way, as he stayed on in Italy until he received the degree of doctor of canon law from the University of Bologna;[2] and it is pretty safe to assume that he carried home to England a manuscript or two of his own copying, if no others. Langton, on the other hand, who, so far as we know, had no need to fly from his creditors, probably found money enough to buy a number of manuscripts; and certainly another Englishman who came to Padua while Langton was there did his share of manuscript purchasing.

It was in the autumn of the same year Doget started for Padua that two monks of Christ Church, Canterbury, William Tilly of Selling, or William Selling, as he is often called, and William Hadley set out for Italy. The two monks had obtained from their prior a three years' leave of absence which was to be devoted to university studies, and after reaching Italy they divided their time between Padua, where Selling formed a friendship with Langton, Rome, and Bologna. Selling took his degree in theology at Bologna on 22 March 1466, and Hadley his at the same place a year later, but luckily the Canterbury monks, like other Englishmen who had gone to Italy to study, were not content to take home with them nothing but degrees. Selling carried back to Canterbury a number of Greek and Latin manuscripts which he had bought in Italy, and after he was elected prior of his monastery, in 1472, he took much pleasure in decorating the monastic library where his books found their home. Better still, he brought back to England a desire to impart

---

1. Early Chancery Proceedings, bundle 59, no. 252. As Doget's petition is addressed to the Bishop of Lincoln, chancellor of England, it must have been sent to the Chancery sometime between 1474 and 1480.
2. Cooper, *Athenæ Cantabrigienses*, I, 5.

to others the learning he had gone so far to seek. During his priorship, he did all he could to encourage and assist the monks in their studies and to improve the monastic school in which he had received the beginnings of his own education; and to him belongs the imperishable honour of having been the first to introduce the teaching of Greek into England and of having given Linacre his first lessons in that language.[1]

It is not likely that the names of William Grey, John Gunthorp, John Free, Robert Fleming, John Tiptoft, Earl of Worcester, Thomas Langton, John Doget, William Selling, and William Hadley exhaust the list of Englishmen who were students in Italy in the days of Edward IV.[2] And there were some Englishmen of culture who visited Italy during Edward's reign without remaining to study at her universities and who yet probably brought home with them something more than mere reports of her learning and her art. For example, in May 1482, Edward wrote a letter to the Duke of Milan on behalf of Sir Robert Chamberlain, a faithful knight who had accompanied him on his flight to Burgundy and afterwards on his expedition to France[3] and who was now contemplating a journey to Italy. Chamberlain evidently had some special mission to fulfil abroad, since it is stated in the safeconduct granted to him on 20 June that he was setting out for foreign parts at the king's command to transact divers business; but to judge from Edward's letter to Gian Galeazzo Visconti, it was no diplomatic errand, but simply a desire to behold the princely palaces and other wonders of Milan, which drew Chamberlain's footsteps to that city.[4]

Chamberlain was a person of much less distinction than another Englishman who had visited Milan a few years before he arrived there and who had also carried a letter of introduction from Edward to the Duke of Milan. Of the Italian journey of Anthony Woodville, Earl Rivers, which seems to have been partly a pilgrimage, partly a sightseeing tour, and partly a

---

1. See the interesting account of Selling in Gasquet, *The Eve of the Reformation*, 24-33, and in *Christ Church Letters* (Camden Society), xxxvii-xlii. Cf. Leland, *Com. de Script. Brit.*, 482-483.

2. Another English prelate who studied at Padua was Peter Courtenay, Dean and afterwards Bishop of Exeter. *Epistolæ Acad. Oxon*, II, 442.

3. *Arrivall of Edw. IV*, 2; *Cal. Patent Rolls*, II, 515. Chamberlain had also been chancellor of Ireland and one of Edward's carvers. See a pardon granted to him in April 1469. Pardon Roll 8-9 Edw. IV, m. 4.

4. French Roll 22 Edw. IV, m. 14; Signed Bills, file 1521, no. 5342; *Cal. Venetian Papers*, I, 145.

diplomatic mission, and of his loss of the jewels and plate he had taken with him, some account has already been given. It was some time after 1 October 1475, that Rivers left England, and he was at home again within a year, as he was present at the re-interment of the Duke of York and the Earl of Rutland at Fotheringhay in July 1476. But concerning what the earl did in Italy, except to fall into the hands of highwaymen, we have no information beyond what is told us by William Caxton in the epilogue of *The Cordyale*, which Rivers translated shortly after his return from Italy and which Caxton printed in 1480. Before that time, Caxton says, the earl had gone on pilgrimage not only to St James in Galicia (Compostella), a pilgrimage which he made in 1473, but to Rome, to several shrines in the kingdom of Naples, to that of St Nicholas at Bari, and to "other divers holy places," and he had obtained from the Pope an indulgence for the chapel of Our Lady of the Pew at Westminster which was equal in virtue to the indulgence of the *Scala Celi* at Rome. Who can doubt, however, that Earl Rivers, though his taste seems to have run to books of piety rather than to the ancient classics, carried home his share of manuscripts from Italy?

By no means few, therefore, were the manuscripts which were arriving in England from Italy during the reign of Edward IV, and without question these additions to her libraries contributed not a little towards England's intellectual rebirth. But while Italy was the special home of classical learning, she enjoyed no monopoly of the production of manuscripts. Both Latin and French manuscripts, very carefully transcribed and very beautifully illuminated, were to be procured in the Netherlands, where the Van Eycks had already painted pictures as lovely as any the world has ever seen; and from the Netherlands came most, if not all, of the manuscripts purchased by another Englishman who was a lover and collector of books, King Edward himself.

When he was still only Earl of March, Edward rejoiced in the possession of at least one manuscript book, a small one of a hundred and thirty folios, written on vellum, with initials in gold, red, and blue, and containing a number of medical treatises as well as a version, though not the usual one, of the *Liber de secretis secretorum Aristotelis*, with glosses derived in part from Roger Bacon's commentary.[1] And while no evidence exists that during the early years of his

---

1. Royal MS. 12 E. XV. That this book belonged to Edward when he was only Earl of March is proved by an inscription on f. 2b.

kinghood, when the disturbed condition of the country kept his mind fixed on martial affairs, Edward interested himself in the acquisition of a library, if we had fuller records of his personal expenditures, we might find that even at that period he sometimes invested a little of his pocket-money in books. Elizabeth Woodville paid ten pounds for a book of some sort not long after she became queen,[1] and it is not unlikely that her young husband occasionally made similar purchases. It seems, however, to have been not until he was an exile in Bruges in 1470-1471 and became acquainted, during his enforced leisure, with the treasures of the library of the Seigneur de la Gruthuyse, whose collection of manuscripts was second in size and value only to the one owned by the Duke of Burgundy,[2] that Edward became fired with a desire to form an extensive collection of books. Even before he set out for England to make the attempt to recover his throne, he may have taken steps to obtain some specimens of the elaborate workmanship of the scribes and illuminators of Bruges. At any rate, after his return home many a beautiful manuscript was written and illuminated by his order at Bruges, whence it travelled to England to form, with others of its kind, the beginnings of a splendid royal library. A score or more of the manuscripts in the Old Royal Collection at the British Museum have the arms of Edward IV and, in some instances, those of one or two of his sons, inserted in their elaborate borders of fruits, flowers, foliage, etc.; and there are a number of other manuscripts in that collection which

---

1. See the Account Book of her Receiver General, Miscellaneous Books, Exchequer T. of R., no. 207. A copy of the Romance of the Saint Graal, in French prose, which is now catalogued as Royal MS. E. III, belonged to Elizabeth Woodville while she was queen, and in her widowhood, if not before, she owned a copy of the *Recueil des Histoires de Troyes* from Caxton's press. Ames, *Typographical Antiquities*, I, 27. There is also in existence a small book which belonged to her daughters Elizabeth and Cecily. It is an account, in French, of "the death and testamentary disposition of Sultan Amarath." Hist. MSS. Com., *Report 6*, app., 353, 357-358.

2. After Gruthuyse's death, his manuscripts passed into the hands of Louis XII of France, and they are now preserved in the Bibliothèque Nationale, where I had the pleasure of consulting one of them, MS. français 88 (formerly Bibl. du Roi 6762), a beautiful copy, written on vellum, of the continuation of Monstrelet's chronicle. But one manuscript which belonged to Gruthuyse at this time, and which contains the works of Christine de Pisan, is now in the Harleian Collection, no. 4431, in the British Museum. It seems to have been given to Gruthuyse by Earl Rivers, who evidently had received it from his mother, Jacquetta of Luxembourg. It is probably the very manuscript from which Rivers made his translation of the Proverbs of Christine de Pisan. Madden, *Archæologia*, XXVI, 271-274.

were probably executed for Edward. One of the most beautiful books Edward ever owned was a part of a Bible Historiale and was the handiwork of Jehan du Ries. It is now known as Royal MS. 15 D.I, and through its four hundred and thirty-nine folios of vellum are scattered eleven beautifully painted full page miniatures and nearly seventy smaller ones. In the table of contents, which fills the first seventeen folios, the title of this sumptuous volume is given thus: "Cy commence la table des chapitres du quart volume de listoire scolastique, contenant le liure de Thobie, les prophecyes de Jheremye et de Ezechiel, les visions et prophecyes Danyel et aultres, listoire Susane, le liure Judich, le liure Hester, les deux liures des Machabees, lhistoire euuangelique et les fait des appostres, lequel liure fut fait a Bruges par le commandement & voulente de treshault, tresexcellent & tresuictorieux prince Edouart le quart de ce nom, roy dangleterre &cet lan de grace milcccclxx." However, the words "treshault, tresexcellent & tresuictorieux prince Edouart le quart de ce nom, roy dangleterre &cet," are written on an erasure, and from this fact it may be concluded that the book was not originally executed for Edward, but for some other customer or for stock, and was not actually bought by the king until 1479, the year in which two other volumes of the same work, Royal MSS. 18 D. IX, X, were transcribed and illuminated for him at Bruges. The year 1479 seems to have been a particularly important one in Edward's career as a book collector, as to that year belongs also the execution of at least three other manuscripts in his library, namely, Royal MS. 17 F. II, containing "La grant hystoire Cesar" and "Le sommaire de tous les empereurs qui regnerent aprez Julle Cesar," and Royal MSS. E. III, IV, containing a French translation of Valerius Maximus.

Of special interest among Edward's other books are two volumes, Royal MSS. 14 E. IV and 15 E. IV, which are copies of portions of the chronicle of Jean de Waurin, so often referred to in the course of this history, and the second of which has among its twenty-eight miniatures one depicting Edward himself wearing the Golden Fleece and seated on a throne, while the author, in the dress of a clerk, kneels before him offering his book.[1] The subjects of the remaining manuscripts in the Royal collection which Edward apparently owned at one time or another are various, though in general they "tend to entertainment and edification rather than to study and the

---

1. An engraving of this miniature may be found in Strutt's *Royal and Ecclesiastical Antiquities of Eng.* (London, 1842), and reproductions of the arms of Edward IV, taken from Royal MSS. 14 E. V and 15 E. IV, in Madden's *Illuminated Ornaments* (London, 1833).

advancement of learning." Yet it is of interest to find among them French translations of Boccaccio's Decameron (19 E. I) and "De casibus illustrium virorum et feminarium (14 E. V) and of St Augustine's "De Civitate Dei" (17 F. III), as well as a copy of Raoul Le Fèvre's "Recueil des Histoires de Troie" (17 E. II), an English version of which was Caxton's first venture in printing in the English language.[1]

La Forteresse de Foy is mentioned among the king's possessions in the wardrobe accounts for the year 1480, and in all likelihood the reference is to the French translation of that allegory now preserved, bound in two volumes, in Royal MSS. 17 F. VI, VII. The same accounts also speak of other books among the royal effects, including a Bible, a Bible Historiale (probably one of the manuscripts already mentioned as purchases of the year 1479), "a book of the Holy Trinity," Froissart's chronicles (perhaps Royal MS. E. I or E. II, the first of which evidently belonged, in the beginning, to the king's close friend, Lord Hastings), copies of Josephus and Titus Livius, and *The Government of Kings and Princes* (probably a French translation of Aegidius Romanus de Regimine Principum).[2] In other accounts allusion is made to certain religious service books, a "Gospeller" and an "Epistoler," belonging to the king.[3] The wardrobe accounts of 1480 tell us, furthermore, that Edward spent a considerable sum of money for the binding of six of his books in velvet and silk, with laces and tassels of silk, gilt nails, and clasps of copper and gilt ornamented with roses and the royal arms. We learn, too, that, although most of the king's beautiful manuscripts are so large that he must have expected to have them read to him rather than to turn the pages for himself as he lounged at his ease, they were so essential to his daily happiness that, when he went to Eltham to rest from affairs of state, some of them, carefully packed in "coffins of fir," were sent down from the Great Wardrobe for his delectation.[4]

There can be little doubt that, in addition to the volumes among the Royal Manuscripts and the other books already referred to, Edward had in his possession copies of Hardyng's Chronicle, the last part of which was

---

1. For fuller information regarding Edward's manuscripts, see Warner and Gilson's *Catalogue of Western Manuscripts in the Old Royal and King's Collections* (1921).
2. Sir John Paston owned a copy of "De Regimine Principum." *Paston Letters*, V, 3.
3. Tellers' Roll, Mich. II Edw. IV; Devon, *Issues of Exchequer*, 498.
4. Nicolas, *Wardrobe Accounts of Edw. IV*, 117, 125-126, 152, 237-238.

addressed to him, of Capgrave's Chronicle, which was also dedicated to him, and of that work of an unknown author, revised by William of Worcester, *The Boke of Noblesse*,[1] which was "compiled to the most high and mighty prince King Edward the Fourth for the advancing and preferring the common public of the royaumes of England and of France," and which urged him to renew the wars of conquest in France. Last but not least, Edward's library contained, there is reason to believe, at least one printed book, the *History of Godfrey of Boulogne*.[2]

On just what day William Caxton came back to England from Bruges bringing with him a new fount of type which he and his partner, Colard Mansion, had recently tested in printing *Les Quatre Derrenieres Choses*, has never been determined. He certainly came before November 1477, since on the 18th of that month he printed *The Dictes and Sayings of the Philosophers* at his press at Westminster. On the other hand, it would appear that he was not yet in England on 2 December 1476, as on that day letters of protection of one year's duration were issued to "William Caxton, late of London, mercer, otherwise called William Carston of London, merchant," who was serving the king in the retinue of Lord Hastings, lieutenant of Calais, for the safe custody, victualling, and defence of the town and marches of Calais.[3] At whatever moment, however, between 2 December 1476, and 18 November 1477, Caxton terminated his more than thirty years' sojourn abroad and returned to his native land, he was not a stranger to the English king, as Edward had previously intrusted him with diplomatic business on more than one occasion. More than likely he had even met the king personally during the winter of 1470-1471. For although he had given up the governorship of the English merchants in the Netherlands before Edward's flight to Flanders, he had done so to enter the service of the Duchess Margaret of Burgundy, who may have employed him in the first place to manage her extensive commercial ventures, but who soon became interested in his literary labours, urged him to finish the translation of *Le Recueil des Histoires de Troyes* which he had begun at Bruges in March 1469, and was rewarded by having the completed work presented to her two years later. The Duchess Margaret's

---

1. Published, with an introduction by J. G. Nichols, by the Roxburghe Club, 1860.
2. Blades, *Caxton* (condensed edit.), 253.
3. French Roll 16 Edw. IV, m. 8.

relations with the merchant-author, therefore, if not any personal interest of his own, had probably brought Edward into contact at Bruges with the man who was destined shortly to contribute to his reign an event which later generations may feel inclined to regard as its chief title to remembrance.

Although it is so likely that Edward met Caxton during his brief exile, this does not mean that the king saw anything of the new art of printing while he was in Flanders, as it was not until several years after his return to England that Caxton set up a press at Bruges. But reports of the new invention and of the experiments being made with it at Bruges must have reached England long before Caxton determined to re-cross the sea, and when the printer arrived in London with his type, he quickly found plenty of patrons, including the king himself.

Probably at the suggestion of Margaret of Burgundy, Caxton had already dedicated one product of his press, *The Game and Playe of the Chesse*, to the duchess's favourite brother, the Duke of Clarence. But if he looked forward, when planning to return to England, to help and encouragement from Clarence, it was a hope foredoomed to disappointment, as the duke got into fresh disgrace about the time of Caxton's arrival and was executed a few months later. Through this chance it fell to Earl Rivers to give the printer the initial aid he had probably expected to receive from Clarence, and not only did *The Dictes and Sayings of the Philosophers*, a translation made by Rivers from a copy of *Les dits moraux des philosophes* which Louis de Bretaylle had given him during his pilgrimage to Compostella, issue from Caxton's Westminster press in November 1477, but in the spring of 1479 it was followed by *The Cordyale*, a second translation from the earl's pen.

Another of Caxton's early patrons was John Russell, Bishop of Rochester, whose acquaintance he had probably made during the bishop's several diplomatic journeys to Burgundy and whose Latin oration, delivered when Charles the Bold was invested with the Order of the Garter at Ghent on 4 February 1470, he printed soon after he reached England, if not before he left Bruges. Still another noble friend was William Fitz-Alan, Earl of Arundel, to whom he presented his most extensive work, *The Golden Legend*, with a grateful acknowledgment of financial help received. Yet it was not alone from men of noble lineage or from great ecclesiastics that Caxton received patronage. It was "at the request, desire, cost, and dispense of the honourable and worshipful man, Hugh Bryce, alderman and citizen of London," who was desirous of making a present to Lord Hastings, lord chamberlain and lieutenant of Calais, that Caxton translated *The Mirrour of the Worlde*. And probably Bryce's acquaintance with Caxton also dated back to the printer's Bruges days, as Bryce had represented the king of England at the monetary conference held at Bruges in 1469 and had been in the Netherlands again in 1473 to treat with the Duke of Burgundy and the Hansards.

As for King Edward's friendly interest in Caxton and his new enterprise, that seems to have commenced as soon as the Westminster press was installed, although the attempt of Louis XI to show that the Duchess Margaret was mixed up in Clarence's treasonable activities might easily have led the king to look askance at one who had been for a number of years in Margaret's service and had dedicated one of his books to Clarence. In what was probably the very first product of his Westminster press, *A Boke of the Hoole Lyf of Jason*, Caxton was able to state that it was "under the shadow" of the king's noble protection that he had "enterprised to accomplish this said little book." And while he did not venture to present his book to the king, "for as much as I doubt not his good grace hath it in French, which he understandeth," he did presume, by the king's permission and with the encouragement of "our most redoubted liege lady, most excellent princess, the queen," to present it to "our to-coming sovereign lord," the Prince of Wales, "to the intent he may begin to learn read English, not for any beauty or good inditing of our English tongue that is therein, but for the novelty of the histories." We also find Edward giving orders in the summer of 1479 for the payment of twenty pounds to Caxton as a reward for some service rendered;[1] and two years later not only was the printer able to say again in his prologue to *The Mirrour of the Worlde* that he had undertaken the translation under the shadow of the king's protection, but he dedicated *The Boke of Tulle of Olde Age* to the king, beseeching him "to receive the said book of me, William Caxton, his most humble subject and little servant." In his *Godefroy of Boloyne, or the last Siege and Conqueste of Jherusalem*, Caxton even took the liberty of exhorting Edward, after he had declared that he knew "no Christian king better proved in arms and for whom God hath showed more grace," to "address, stir, or command some noble captain of his subjects" to drive the Turks out of Jerusalem.

---

1. Devon, *Issues of Exchequer*, 499.

Caxton did not long enjoy the honour of being the only printer in England. Soon after he began his work at Westminster, a press was established at Oxford, and a little later books were being printed at St Albans as well. By 1480 he had a still nearer neighbour, as in that year John Lettou, who soon found a partner in William de Machlinia, began, under the patronage of a wealthy draper named William Wilcock, to print books in the city of London. But of these rival presses, that of St Albans expired in a few years, and the printed books produced both at St Albans and at Oxford were for the most part of a scholastic character and in the Latin tongue, while Lettou and Machlinia turned their attention especially to law books.[1] To Caxton, therefore, belongs the credit not only of being the first man to set up a press in England, but of having recognized, earlier than most of his contemporaries, the beauty and dignity of the English language and having chosen to employ both his press and his pen almost exclusively in the production of English books.

It would be too much to claim for King Edward that he appreciated the full significance of the new invention which Caxton had introduced into England. Although when death summoned the king to a better world, four presses were slowly and laboriously turning out books within the confines of his kingdom, there is no reason to believe that he foresaw how soon such exquisite volumes as were being written and illuminated for him at Bruges in his last days would cease to be produced because the less costly, though less beautiful, productions of the printing press better met the needs of a world in which a new life, more hurried as well as more diversified than the old, was beginning to stir. Yet it will ever be to the honour and glory of Edward IV that William Caxton found in him one of his earliest and most faithful patrons.

---

1. *Cambridge Hist. of Eng. Lit.*, II, 361-362.

APPENDICES

APPENDIX I

Bibliothèque Nationale, MS. français 6970, f. 361.
Lettre de W. Hasting à Mr. de Lannoy.

Tres honoré seigneur, apres toute due et cordiale recommandation avec tres affectueux et especial desir d'estre souvent acertené de vostre bonne et honorable prosperité et santé. Je vous mercie aussi cordalement que ie puis de vos lettres par le porteur de cettes a moy delivrées par lesquelles il semble que diverses lettres que vous ay envoiées ne vous ont pas eté delivrées, dont suis tres deplaisant, et que semblablement m'avez rescript plusieurs lettres et des nouvelles par icelles que la pluspart ne sont venues a ma connoissance par defaut de passaige vous signifiant que les Ambassadeurs de mon souverain Seigneur sont apressés a estre de brief a la convention appointée a St Omer, ou ils eussent piecha esté n'eust esté la grande entreprise des anchiens ennemis de mond. souverain seigneur, ceux d'Ecosse, confederés avec ses grands traitres et rebelles, Henry, soy apelant Roy, et Marguerite, sa femme, faite sur son Chastel de Norham par le Roy d'Ecosse avec tout le pouvoir de sa terre garny de la grosse ordonnance d'icelle assiege royalement et environne et au default de . . . Chevalerie, assistée par la Reyne d'Ecosse et lad. Marguerite, cuidanté que la crainte et peur de leur grande severité eussent peu vaincre le noble Royaume d'Angleterre, dont un Chevalier, le noble et vaillant S^{r.}, M^{r.} le Comte de Warvich, sujet de mon souverain Seigneur, avec les marchiers seulement du pays d'Ecosse ont remué led. siege, Led. Roy d'Ecosse avec son pouvoir fuyant de peur de sa venue et lad. Marguerite sans surgier outre la mer avec son Capitaine, Sr. Piers de Brezé, et n'en poy effrayé Mond. souverain seigneur cependant estant en ses desports et esbatemens en la chasse sans aucun doubte ou effraiment de sa très honorable personne ne d'aucuns de ses suiets ença lesd. marches et lad. contree n'a pas seulement recouy led. chastel poyenavant rescous d'un autre siege par mon tres honoré frere, le Sire de Montagu, tres honorablement mais aussi mis a fuite led. Roy d'Ecosse et tout sond. pouvoir a leur grand honte et villenie et deshonneur et poursui en Ecosse ars degasté et détruit du meilleur de son pays depouillé et abbatu plusieurs forteresses, tué beaucoup d'Ecossois et recouvers et pris prisonniers en grand nombre et fait la plus grande journee sur eux que ne fut oye estre faite de plusieurs ans passés ainsi que je ne me doute point qu'ils ne s'en repentent, et jusqu'au jour du Jugement s'en repentiront; la faveur et assistance qu'ils ont donné aud. Hery et Marguerite et combien que leurd. repentance n'est ignorée toute parfaite, j'espere que de brief elle prendra tel effect et conclusion que sera a memorance a la perpetuelle desolation et misere de la nation des Ecossois a la grace de Dieu. A Fodringhen le 7 aoust 1463. Vostre W. Hasting.

APPENDIX II

Bibliothèque Nationale, MS. français 6978, ff 69-72.

Instruction a Sire Guillaume Cousinot Cheualier de ce qu'il aura a dire de par le Roy au Roy et Reine de Secille et a ceux depardela.

Premierement, faites la presentation de ses lettres et les salutations et reuerences accoutumées dira aud. Roy de Secille que le Roy tres cordiallement le mercie du bon et grand vouloir qu'il a montré toûjours auoir au bien du Roy et de ses affaires. Ensemble des bons termes qu'il a tenus a la Reine a l'autrefois qu'elle alla pardela, et pareillement a ce fois icy. Et aussy a monseigneur le prince, dont il se repute bien fort tenu a luy, et luy prie qu'il luy plaise continuer de bien en mieux, et auoir toûjours le Roy, la Reine, le prince et tous leurs affaires pour especialement recommandez, et en ce soy montrer bon, vray et naturel pere comme le Roy en a en luy sa parfaite confiance.

Dira au surplus et recitera aud. Roy de Secille de la personne du Roy et des places depardeça. Ensemble de toutes les nouuelles du Royaume, ainsy que led. Sire Guillaume Cousinot le sçait et connoist par experience.

Remontrera aussy comme chacun jour le Roy est pressé par ses sujets de se mettre sus, lesquels de toutes parts ont enuoyé et enuoyent chacun jour deuers luy pour cette cause. Et si le Roy auoit aucun peu d'aide de gens, d'argent et d'artillerie it ne faut point faire de doute qu'en brief temps it recourrast tout son Royaume, car toute la faueur du Royaume est pour le Roy, et au contraire ils héént maintenant Edouard et ses adherants si mortellement que c'est estrange chose d'en ouyr parler de tous costez.

Pour laquelle cause led. Sire Guillaume Cousinot dira au Roy de Secille que le Roy luy prie et requiert taut affectueusement qu'il luy est possible qu'il luy plaise auoir regard en ces choses, et tant enuers tres haut et puissant prince le Cousin germain de France du Roy comme de la part d'iceluy Roy de

Secille trouuer maniere que le Roy puisse avoir aucune ayde de gens, d'argent et d'artillerie, ainsy comme la necessité en est et que le cas le requiert.

Item, et en laquelle chose faisant en ensuiura deux biens, l'un que par ce moyen il recouuera son Royaume d'Angleterre, l'autre que l'on obuiera a l'entreprise du Comte de la Marche et de ses adherans, qui ont entrepris de mettre le siege en l'esté prochain deuant les places que le Roy tient par deça, lesquelles led. Edouard a intention de conquerir, si aucun secours ne vient par deça du costé dedela.

Item, et au Regard des particulieres Requestes que l'on aura a faire au Roy de Secille, semble que l'on luy doit requerir aucune somme d'argent, aucune quantité d'artillerie, et certain nombre de crannequiniers[1] et de couleuuriniers, le tout selon l'auis et discretion de la Reine, si elle est és marches ou le Roy de Secille sera.

Item, parlera led. Sire Guillaume aud. Roy de Secille du fait des treues qu'on dit de present estre en France, le tout aussy selon l'auis de la Reine, et en toutes choses se gouuernera deuers led. le Roy et Reine de Secille et ceux qui seront par dela ainsy que la Reine aduisera et ordonnera.

Item, et au Regard de la creance touchant la Reine de Secille et des autres depar dela, elle cherra en regratiation[2] et remerciemens des bons termes du temps passé et en recommandations, prieres et requestes pour le temps a venir, et aussy és nouuelles et és dispositions des matieres depardeça ainsy que par la Reine sera aduisé estre mieux a faire. Fait a Banbourg le 22ᵉ Jour de feurier, ainsy sign Henry.

Instruction a Sire Guillaume Cousinot cheualier de ce qu'il aura a dire de par le Roy a monseigneur le Duc de Bretagne.

Premierement, apres la presentation des lettres et les salutations accoutumées remerciera de par le Roy mond. Seigneur de Bretagne du grand et bon recueil qu'il fist a la Reyne quand elle descendit en Bretagne, des dons, aussy curialitez[3] et plaisirs, que semblablement il fist adoncques a lad. dame et a ses gens et seruiteurs, et pareillement du bon vouloir en quoy il a toûjours depuis continué enuers le Roy et ses affaires et des mises et depenses que a cette cause it en a faites, dont le Roy se tient tres fort tenu a

---

1. Cranequinier, "soldat armé du cranequin, arbalétrier à pied et à cheval." Godefroy, *Dict. de l'ancienne langue française.*
2. Regraciation, "remerciement, action de grace." Godefroy.
3. Curialité, "courtoisie, civilité." Godefroy.

luy, et a bien volonté, s'il plaise a Dieu qu'il pust recouurer son Royaume, de le reconnoistre tellement enuers mond. Seigneur de Bretagne et d'auoir ses affaires a toûjours si especiallement recommandées que led. monseigneur de Bretagne aura cause de s'en louer.

Declarera en apres led. Sire Guillaume Cousinot aud. monseigneur de Bretagne l'estat et disposition du Roy et des marches depardeça, pareillement aussy de tout le Royaume taut du costé de soubt contrée que de Galles et d'ailleurs tout ainsy qu'il le voit et connoist par experience.

Item, Remontrera a mond. Seigneur de Bretagne comme si le Roy estoit aucunement ayde de gens et d'argent par le costé de pardeça ou de Galles il ne seroit venir si petit d'aide en quoy it eust apparence qu'incontinent tout le pays ne se leuast pour le Roy, car tous les jours il a nouuelles de toutes les parties du Royaume que s'il se veut mettre sus tout le Royaume se leuera avec luy, et ne reste que d'auoir vn peu d'aide de gens et d'argent, dont ne luy est possible finer[1] pardeça, et sans cela ne se peut aucunement ayder ne mettre sus. Et outre plus chacun jour demeure en danger de sa personne, ainsy que clairement on peut voir et connoistre, dont tons princes, en especial ses parens et amis, doiuent auoir pitié et compassion.

Item, et apres ces Remonstrances dira a mond. Seigneur de Bretagne que le Roy luy prie très affectueusement qu'il luy plaise auoir pitié de son cas et se montrer enuers luy son bon parent et amy, et luy aider et secourir en sa necessité, ainsy comme en luy parfaitement it se confie.

Item, et a venir au particulier de l'aide et secours pratiquera s'il luy est possible qu'en toute diligence on enuoye pardeça aucune quantité de vitailles, comme froment, malth, vin, sel, et aucun peu de fer, poudre et artillerie.

Item, et que le plustost apres que faire se pourra on pust auoir aucun bon nombre de gens d'armes payez pour demy an, et aucune somme d'argent, et que lesd. gens de guerre, s'il est possible, vensissent icy, ou sinon qu'ils menassent monseigneur de Pennebroug en Galles et se joignissent auec ceux qui sont par dela, par moyen desquelles choses au plaisir de Dieu tout le pays se leueroit, et pourroient faire au Roy tel seruice que peut estre la recouurance du Royaume s'en ensuiuroit.

Item, Et pour auoir seurete de la recompense des mises et depenses que a cette cause conuiendroit faire, les Commissaires sur ce ordonnez depar

---

1. i.e., trouver, se procurer. Godefroy.

le Roy besongneront en ces matieres avec led. Monseigneur de Bretagne et ses commis par telle façon que par raison il en deura estre content. Et tout ce qu'ils feront et appointeront auec mondit Seigneur de Bretagne ou de ses gens touchant lesd. matieres le Roy le aura agreable et promet de l'entretenir, ratifier et confirmer.

Item, fera et dira led. Sire Guillaume Cousinot au surplus tout ce qu'il verra bon estre et pouuoir servir au bien des matieres dessusd. Fait a Banbourg le 22ᵉ Jour de feurier, ainsy sign Henry.

APPENDIX III

Bibliothèque Nationale, MS. français 6971, f. 388.

Tres haut et puissant et très excellent prince, je me recommande tres humblement a vostre bonne grace et vous plaise scauoir que j'ay receu par Jehan de tairemonde dit Lebegue, vostre secretaire, vos gracieuses Lettres que de vostre grace vous a pleu moy escripre ensemble vostre saufconduit pour moy et autres officiers et seruiteurs de Monseigneur le Comte de Warwich, mon maistre, dont je vous remercie tres humblement et aussi de ce qu'il vous a pleu me faire si grant honneur en faueur et Contemplation de mond. Seigneur mon maistre, Comme j'ay tres bien aperceu tant par vosd. lettres gracieuses que par relacion de vostred. secretaire, pour lesquelles causes je suis grandement tenu et obligié de vous faire service a mon petit pouuoir que de tres bon cœur feray en ce qui me sera possible. Et ne doute point que a l'aide de Dieu Monseigneur mon maistre vous remercie des choses dessusdites et qui vous a pleu adresser vos lettres que j'ay receue par vostred. Secretaire que je luy enuoyeray en toute diligence par ung de ses officiers et seruiteurs nommé en vostred. saufconduit et l'aduertiray de tout ce que m'avez escript. Et suy seur que mondit Seigneur en sera tres joyeux et par especial de la venue de Monsieur de Lannoy. Et quant au dernier message qui me fut donné en vostre nom par M^r. de la Varde[1] de aduertir le Roy, Monseig^r. le Chancellier et mond. Seigneur, le messaige est retourné et m'a rapporté Response de mond. Seig^r. de Warwich taut par escript que par credence, comme par vostre bon plaisir pourrez veoir par la Coppie de sesd. lettres et par article de sa dite credence que vous enuoye enclos cy dedans. Et ne fust la venue de vostred. secretaire je eusse enuoyé vn propre message par deuers vostre hautesse vous porter lesd. Coppies et Credences, Et aussi des nouvelles d'Angleterre qui sont contenues esdits articles.

Tres hault, tres puissant et tres excellent prince, je prie a Dieu qui vous doint tres bonne vie et longue. Escript de ma main au Chastel de Guisnes le xixe jour de feurier 1463. Vostre tres humble seruiteur Richard, Lieutenant de Guysnes.

---

1. The Seigneur de la Barde?

APPENDIX IV

Bibliothèque Nationale, MS. français 6971, f. 394.

Monseigneur, je me recommande a vous humblement. Se je vous escripuoye a quelle peine j'ay passé la mer la Chose seroit trop longue. Toutesfois grace a nostre Seigneur ie suis a the soir arrivé en Ceste ville de Riseste et demain, au plaisir de Dieu, je seré a Dartefort et le lendemain a Londres, ou le Roy d'Angleterre est. Je doy demain trouver, Comme on m'a dit, audit Dartefort gens de par le Roy D'angleterre pour moy Recevoir et doyvent venir audevant de moy pour moy Recevoir pres de Londres Monseig^r le Comte de — —[1] et Mr de Warwich et autres en grand nombre. Suivant je vous ay Rescript de Calais il y a eu grant murmure du siege que le Roy y vouloit mettre, et a Cette cause je n'ay pas esté si bien Receu comme j'ay accoustumé Jusques cy mais en ceste ville j'ay trouvé mieulx et espere aceque ung des serviteurs de Monsr de Warwich m'a dit a ce soir que du Roy D'angleterre et des Seigneurs ie seray tres bien venu et desirent fort parler a moy. Monseigneur, je ne Rescript Riens a Monseig^r Le Duc pour ce que ie ne scay chose que a Rescripre face et a Dieu, etc. Escript a Rocestre le xix. de mars. Vostre tres humble et tres obeissant subiet et serviteur, Le Besgue.

---

1. *sic.*

APPENDIX V

Bibliothèque Nationale, MS. français 6970, ff. 185-187.

C'est le raport et la creance de Messire Guillaume de Menypeny. Premierement dit que l'Evesque de Glasco et les autres Ambassadeurs d'Ecosse qui sont venus d'Angleterre ont raporté que les Anglois entre autre chose leur ont dit que le Duc de Bretagne avoit envoyé son Ambaxade par devers eux et requieroit qu'ils luy voulsissent aider de six mille Archiers en cas que le Roy luy feroit guerre et aussi offroit le Due de Bretagne au Roy Edouard que quant it voudroit venir en France et y amener armée il luy donneroit passaige et entrée par toutes ses terres et pays pour ce faire.

Dit qu'il a eu plusieurs altercations entre les gens dud. Roy Edouard et lesd. Ambassadeurs de Bretagne sur les offres et aussi sur les demandes que chacun faisoit l'un a l'autre et a la parfin les Anglois ont accordée aud. Duc de Bretagne trois mille archers pour venir a son aide dont led. Sieur de Montaigu devoit avoir la charge de mille archers, le S.ʳ d'escales d'autre mille, et James de douglas des autres mille.

Dit que le S.ʳ de Montaigu a refusé la charge qu'on luy vouloit sur ce bailler pour ce que le Comte de Warwick, son frere, ne veut pas qu'il se desempare pour aller hors du Royaume d'Angleterre s'il ne voit les choses.

*   *   *   *   *   *   *

Dit que led. Evesque de Glasco a raporté au Roy et au Conseil d'Ecosse que les Anglois qui furent a Hesdin luy ont dit que le Roy leur dist aud. lieu de Hesdin qu'il ne luy chaloit de ceux d'Ecosse, Et mesque [*mesme que*] le Roy et le Roy Edouard fussent bien d'accord ensemble se le Roy d'Ecosse ne vouloit faire hommage au Roy d'Angleterre comme il devoit, le Roy aideroit au Roy Edouard a conquerir le Royaume d'Ecosse, dont le Roy d'Ecosse et les Seigneurs du pays et tout le Royaume en ont estés esmeus contre le Roy que merveilles. A quoy led. Menypeny a respondu au mieux que faire s'est peu pour adoucir les matieres.

Dit outre que le Conseil d'Ecosse pour ces Causes estoit demouré d'accord avec ceux d'Angleterre que ce le Comte de Warwick passoit pardeça pour assembler avec le Roy, le Roy d'Ecosse envoieroit un Ecossois avec luy bien entendu qui feindroit estre Anglois pour raporter au Roy et au Conseil d'Ecosse toutes les choses que le Roy se diroit aux Anglois touchant le Roy et le Royaume d'Ecosse.

Dit que les Anglois d'un costé offrent grand Mariage au Roy d'Ecosse, d'autre part Monsr de Charolois eut paroles aud. Roy d'Ecosse du mariage de luy et de sa fille et luy.

*   *   *   *   *   *

Dit que l'Evesque de Galoy doibt venir par deça pour requerir au Roy qu'il delivre au Roy d'Ecosse la Comté de Xaintonge ainsi qu' autrefois fut requis au Roy son pere, sur quoy le Roy pourra avoir bon avis a luy faire réponse ainsi que fit le Roy son pere.

Dit qu'il luy semble que le Roy doibt envoyer par dela aucune Ambassade de gens aimes et congnus aud. pays avec son plaisir sur les choses dessusd. et espere qu'en bonne conduite tout se portera bien.

Dit qu'il est necessaire que le Roy escripve hastivement a l'Evesque de St Andrée touchant la venue de Menipeny par deça et qu'on luy donne esperance qu'il aura brief des nouvelles du Roy par maniere qu'il sera Content.

APPENDIX VI

Warrants for the Great Seal, Signed Bills, file 1498, no. 4199.

Memorandum quod vij. die Julii Anno regni Regis Edwardi quarti post conquestum septimo ista billa liberata fuit Domino cancellario Anglie apud Westmonasterium exequenda.

R. E.[1]

Rex Omnibus etc. Sciatis quod cum quedam realis et perpetua pax amicicia alligancia et confederacio inter nos atque illustrissimum et excellentissimum principem Carissimum Consanguineum nostrum Henricum Regem Castelle et Legionis etc. atque nominibus nostris per venerabiles patres Willelmum Eliensem Episcopum Consanguineum nostrum et Alfonsum Ciuitatensem Episcopum Commissarios procuratores et nuncios nostros sufficientem in ea parte hincinde potestatem habentes iam pridem inita facta concordata et conclusa existat prout in literis dictorum venerabilium patrum Episcoporum ipsorum Sigillis et manualibus signis consignatis plenius continetur Nos ex certis causis et consideracionibus Vobis omnibus et singulis intimamus notificamus et declaramus per presentes quod neque fuit neque est aut erit intencionis nostre nos heredes aut successores nostros prefatum Carissimum Consanguineum nostrum Henricum Regem heredes aut Successores suos quoscunque ex Domina Constancia filia celebris memorie Domini Petri quondam Regis Castelle et Legionis per Katerinam filiam bone memorie Domini Johannis dudum ducis Lancastrie et dicte Constancie uxoris sue legitime descendentes seu eorum aliquem circa ius titulum possessionem aut statum suum in Regnis Castelle et Legionis aliisque terris et dominiis suis quouismodo molestare inquietare aut perturbare. Que omnia et singula fideliter tenere et obseruare pro nobis heredibus et Successoribus nostris bona fide et in verbo Regio promittimus. In cuius rei testimonium etc.

---

1. Sign-manual.

APPENDIX VII

Warrants for the Great Seal, Writs of Privy Seal, file 815, no. 2281.

Memorandum quod xiij. die Nouembris anno subscripto istud breve liberatum fuit domino Cancellario Anglie apud Westmonasterium exequendum.

Edwardus Dei gracia Rex Anglie et Francie et Dominus Hibernie Reuerendo in Christo patri Roberto Bathoniensi et Wellensi Episcopo Cancellario nostro salutem. Vobis mandamus quod literas nostras patentes sub magno sigillo nostro in forma sequente fieri faciatis. Rex omnibus et singulis ad quos nostre presentes litere peruenerint salutem. Notum facimus quod nos precibus et instancia Illustrissimi Principis carissimi Consanguinei nostri Karon Ducis Burgundie, Brabancie, Lemburgi et Luxemburgi, Comitis Flandrie, etc., et ob singularem affecionem quam erga eum gerimus, sibi Concessimus atque concensimus, concedimus et consentimus presencium per tenorem quod de cetero mercatores ceterique subditi dictorum Ducatus, Comitatus et aliorum locorum et patriarum diccioni sue subjectarum possint conducere, vendere et distribuere in Regno nostro Anglie ac Dominio Wallia omnia et omnimoda bona, res mercandisas et mercimonia, ante Vicesimum nouum Diem aprilis anno Regni nostri tercio licita et non prohibita. Statutis et prohibicionibus in parliamento nostro apud Westmonasterium predicto vicesimo nono Die aprilis tento in contrarium factis non obstantibus quibuscumque. In quorum testimonium atque fidem presentes literas magni sigilli nostri appensione fecimus communiri. Teste etc. Datum sub priuato nostro sigillo apud Chelchichith xj^{mo} Die Nouembris Anno Regni nostri Septimo.

NANBY.

APPENDIX VIII

Warrants for the Great Seal, Signed Bills, file 1507, no. 4649.

Memorandum quod xxix. die Julii anno regni regis Edwardi quarti post conquestum quartodecimo ista billa liberata fuit Domino Cancellario Anglie apud Westmonasterium exequenda.

R. E.[1]

Rex vniuersis presentes literas inspecturis salutem. Cum de quadam pecuniarum summa propter nupcias carissime Sororis nostre Domine Margarete Ducisse Burgundie, Brabancie, etc. Illustrissimo Principi fratri nostro dilectissimo Carolo Duci Burgundie etc. ipsius nostre sororis marito donata restat dumtaxat in presenciarum summa octoginta et quinque millium Coronarum quinquaginta grossis monete Flandrie pro qualibet Corona computatis eidem fratri nostro non soluta et debita pro cuius quidem summe propter nupcias vt premittitur Donate solucione ipsi fratri nostro sumus obligati Terminique solucionis ejusdem realiter antehac sunt effluxi prout in quibusdam literis superinde inter nos et eundem fratrem nostrum confectis plenius continetur. Notum facimus quod terminis solucionum dictarum octoginta et quinque millium Coronarum sic vt predicitur restancium et debitarum de assensu atque voluntate ipsius fratris nostri ad dies et annos infrascriptos prorogatis, Nos absque innouacione prioris obligacionis seu prerudicio dictarum literarum nostrarum preterquam ad terminos solucionum dictarum pecuniarum sic ex consensu ipsius fratris nostri vt prefertur innouatos et prorogatos promittimus et obligamus nos per presentes quod dictam summam octoginta et quinque minium Coronarum vt prefertur debitarum soluemus aut solui faciemus modis et

---

1. Sign-manual.

terminis subsequentibus, Videlicet soluemus eidem fratri nostro quinque millia Coronarum predictarum in festo Annunciacionis Dominice quod erit in Anno Domini Millesimo quadringentesimo septuagesimo quinto et alia quinque millia Coronarum in festo Sancti Michaelis de Mense Septembris proximo extunc sequenti et sic de Anno in Annum ad dicta festa singula quinque millia Coronarum donec et quousque prefata summa octoginta et quinque millium Coronarum taliter restans vt prefertur eidem fratri nostro Duci fuerit plenarie persoluta. In cuius etc.

APPENDIX IX

Close Roll 15 Edward IV, m. 16 dorso.

Edward par la grace de Dieu Roy de France et Dangleterre et seingneur
Dirlande a tous ceulx qui ces presentes lettres verront salut. Sauoir faisons
que pour acquiter lobligacion en quoy estoit tenu enuers nous treshault
et puissant prince et nostre treschier et treshonnour cousin Roy Loys de
France en la somme de vint mil escuz dor par ses lettres patentes signees de
sa main nostredit cousin nous a fait paier et deliurer en la ville de Londres
ainsi que promis lauoit ladite somme de vint mil escuz dor par les mains de
Noel le barge, tresorier dez guerres de nostredit cousin. Et dicelle somme
nous tenons pour bien contens et paiez et en quictons nostredit cousin et
sondit tresorier dez guerres de la meisme somme de vint mil escuz. Et parce
moien auons faict casser ladite obligacion et icelle Rendue audit tresorier dez
guerres comme quicte. En testmoing de ce nous auons signe ces presentes de
nostre main et fait seeller de nostre graund seel le xxij^{me} iour de Octobre lan
mil CCCC soixant et quinze.

APPENDIX X

Warrants for the Great Seal, Signed Bills, file 1511, no. 4816.

Memorandum quod terciodecimo die Nouembris Anno regni Regis Edwardi quarti post conquestum xv ista billa liberata fuit Domino Cancellario Anglie apud Westmonasterium exequenda.

R. E.[1]

Edwardus etc. Omnibus etc. salutem. Cum inter nos et serenissimum Principem Lodowicum Consanguineum nostrum Francie conuentum et concordatum sit de modis et formis quibus Domina Margareta filia Regis Sicilie sub potestate et custodia nostra detenta in manus et potestatem dicti Consanguinei nostri vna cum transporto donacione et cessione iuris quod ad nos tam in persona dicte Domine Margarete detinenda quam in hijs que racione persone aut detencionis ipsius ad nos pertinent, pertinuerunt aut pertinere poterunt tradi et deliberari deberet, Nos cupientes pro nostra parte ea que nobis incumbunt vigore concordie predicte efficaciter perimplere, Notum facimus omnibus presentibus et futuris nos transportasse, donasse, cessisse, remisisse et relaxasse pro nobis heredibus et successoribus nostris dicto serenissimo principi Lodowico consanguineo nostro francie omne ius quod habemus, habuimus aut habere quoquo pacto possemus in persona dicte Domine Margarete filie Regis Sicilie seu ad ipsius personam detinendam omneque ius quod nobis competit seu competere poterit in futuro tam ratione persone dicte Domine Margarete quam in quibuscumque alijs rebus que nobis possunt aut poterunt pertinere occasione dicte Domine Margarete aut ratione captiuitatis seu detencionis eiusdem vt prefertur, Promittentes bona fide et in verbo Regio quod si quisquam pretenderit aut pretendere

---

1. Sign-manual.

velit ius aliquod in hijs que ad dictam Dominam Margaretam pertinere videbuntur aut dicto Consanguineo nostro obicem ponere quo minus hijs nostris transporto donatione, cessione, remissione et relaxacione libere vti valeat, Nos pretendenti seu pretendentibus obicem ponenti aut ponentibus huiusmodi nullum auxilium, opem seu assistenciam impendemus neque feremus nec partem aut intelligenciam quamcumque cum eo aut eisdem aduersus prefatum Consanguineum nostrum habebimus seu tenebimus in hac parte. Ita tamen quod idem Consanguineus noster nichil eorum que ad dictam Dominam Margaretam ratione matrimonii seu domicilii contracti per eandem infra regnum nostrum Anglie premissorum occasione seu vigore petat aut vendicet petere aut vendicare valeat quoquo modo. In cuius etc.

APPENDIX XI

Bibliothèque Nationale, MS. français 10,187, ff. 123-124.

Instruction de Maistre Olivier le Roux, Seigneur de Beauvoir, conseiller et maistre des comptes du Roy notre seigneur de ce que le Roy luy a charge dire a tres hault et tres puissant prince le Roy dangleterre son frere et cousin.

Premierement, apres la presentation des lettres du Roy et Recommandations accoustumees dira aud. Sieur Roy dangleterre que le Sieur Roy a sceu par ses derniers ambaxadeurs du bon estat et prosperite de sa personne, dont il a esté et est tres joyeulx et comme de la sienne propre.

Aussi le Roy a sceu par sesd. ambaxadeurs la bonne Reception quil leur a faicte, et les grans et honnorables termes quil leur a tenus et fait tenir en besoignant es matieres pour lesquelles il les avoit envoyez devers luy, dont le Roy le Remercye de tous bon cœur.

Pareillement dira audit Sieur Roy dangleterre comme le Roy a sceu, tant par sesd. ambaxadeurs que par nortroy,[1] son Roy darmes, les points et articles qui Restoient a conclure des choses qui avoyent et ont este pourparlees, et que pour y faire fin avoit este faite ouverture de prendre jour Auquel led. seigneur Roy dangleterre et le Roy envoyeroient aucuns personnages ayans povoir dy prendre conclusion.

Item, dira que le Roy sceit et congnoist veritablement quil na point de si bon amy en tout ce qui le touche que led. seigneur Roy dangleterre, parquoy il ne veult point que les choses soient concluses hors de sa presence, Et pour faire lad. conclusion fera partir ses gens et ambaxadeurs devers la fin de ce moys pour aller devers luy avec povoir tout ample et autant que sil y estoit en personne, Et des ce que ses derniers ambaxadeurs allerent devers led. seigneur Roy dangleterre Ils eussent porte povoir tout ample se neust este

---

1. Norroy.

que lon advertissoit le Roy de tous coustez que par le moyen de madame de bourgogne et de monseigneur le chambellan lappoinctement estoit fait de tout couste, et veu que le Roy y alloit a la bonne foy, Il eust en honte destre refuse.

Item, se plaindra de la part du Roy en bonne facon et dira que nonobstant que ceste querelle icy soit du Royaume et que ce soit confiscation escheue ou royaume, comme plusieurs confiscations qui sont escheuttes aud. seigneur Roy dangleterre en son Royaume, Et que par les amitiez et intelligences dentre le Roy et led. seigneur Roy dangleterre lun desd. deux Roys ne puisse recueillir, soustenir, aider, supporter ou favoriser les subjectz rebelles et desobeissans a lautre, et que feu le duc Charles Ait toute sa vie este rebelle et desobeissant subject du Roy et du Royaume, usurpant ses drois souverains, sans jamais avoir voulu faire les hommages et Redevances des terres quil tenoit de la couronne, Et depuis sa mort ma damoiselle de bourgogne a continue en semblable Rebellion et desobeissance, et par ce ayent chacun deulx confisque tout ce quilz tiennent du Royaume, touteffois il a semble que au commancement il vouloit soustenir monseigneur de clerence a avoir en mariage ma damoiselle de bourgogne qui eust este plus en son prejudice et sil eust bien oy les langaiges qui sen disoient pardeca communement, et ce que ma dame de bourgogne en disoit secretement a ceulx du pais en qui elle se fyoit, mesmement a de bien grans personnages qui ne le celoyent pas au Roy, et des choses quil devoit faire en angleterre sil eust eu les seigneuries depardeca, il eust cogneu clerement que led. mariage eust este plus a son desavantage que a celluy du Roy.

Item, dira que neantmoins toutes ces choses le Roy est delibere de conclurre de sa part les choses qui ont este ouvertes, Et pour ce faire envoyera devers luy ses ambaxadeurs Ainsi que dit est pour le tout conclurre en sa presence.

Item, sentira sil y a point dambaxade du filz de lempereur ne dautre prince ou seigneur dallemaigne ne de ma damoiselle de bourgogne ou du pays de flandres devers led. seigneur Roy dangleterre, et quelz termes lon leur tient, Aussi quelles nouvelles courent pardela, et de tout en advertira le Roy en la plus grande diligence quil pourra.

APPENDIX XII

Bibliothèque Nationale, MS. français 4054, f. 229.

C'est ce que les ambassadeurs d'Angleterre distrent au roy en effect au Plesseys du parc le xxvie jour de decembre l'an mil CCCC lxxvii.

Premierement, comme le Roi avoit envoyé par deux fois Monsieur de Vyenne et autres devers son cousin le Roy d'Angleterre lesquelx a chacune fois luy avoyent parlé de secourir et ayder au Roy contre la fille du feu Duc Charles de Bourgogne et de départir entr'eulx les pays quilz conquesteroyent laquelle division et partage n'a point este encores conclue ne declarée.

Item, au dernier voyage que a faict Monsieur de Vyenne et les autres pardelà le Roy neut renvoyé ledit mondit sieur de Vyenne et ses compagnons et en leur [place] luy a envoyé Monsieur de Aulne lequel a este le mesmement receu par le Roy d'Angleterre et a este receu et introduyt en la conduyte des matieres comme estoit mondit Sr de Vyenne.

Item, et que se le roy d'Angleterre n'a si tost faict response touchant les matieres dessusdites qu'on ne s'en doit point esmerveiller car le roy d'Angleterre ne pourroit faire responce qui ne feust conclue par les sieurs nobles barons et autres de son pays et a este cause a differé jusques il eust communique avec les dessusdits et sceu leur conclusion afin que ce qu'il feroit fut ferme et estable.

Item, que ledit roy d'Angleterre a sur ce parle audits sieurs et autres de son pays qui luy ont fait plusieurs difficultés.

La premiere, de entendre a savoir la justice de la querelle qu'ilz auroyent pour commencer et menner la guerre.

La seconde, remonstroyent les guerres et oppressions que a eu le royaume d'Angleterre par quoy ilz estimoyent difficile de soustenir la despense de la guerre et vouloyent bien entendre la forme comme elle se pourroyt soustenir et conduyre.

La tierce, remonstroyent que les marchands d'Angleterre ont accoustumé de faire la pluspart de la marchandise en pays que tiennent le duc de Autriche et sa femme et mesmement en Flandres laquelle marchandise cesseroit des que la guerre seroit commancée ce qui porteroit bien grand dommage au royaume d'Angleterre.

La quarte, la difficulté qui sera de recouvrer les biens que les marchands d'Angleterre ont esdits pays lesquelx seroient perdus incontinent que la guerre seroit commancée.

La quinte, que encores n'a point este prinse de conclusion sur le partaige et division des choses qui se conquesteroyent.

La sixiesme, disent que combien quil y ait amitié entre le Roy et le Roy d'Angleterre toutesfois ladite amitié n'est seulement que pour leurs vies et que mainctenant s'ilz commancent la guerre peut estre qu'elle durera plus longuement que leurs vies et aynsi demoureroyent en guerre d'une part et d'autre dont pourroit venir de grands dommages au Royaume d'Angleterre.

Finallement, disent que le roy d'Angleterre est conclu d'entretenir et observer au Roy l'amitié et toutes les autres choses quil luy a promys mais luy et ses subgectz font grant difficulté de mectre son Royaume et sesditz subgectz aux perils et aventures de la guerre s'ilz ne voyent et entendent en quelle seurté ilz le feront.

APPENDIX XIII

Vatican Transcripts, portfolio 62.
Archiv. Vatic. Supplicat. 1005, f. 234.

Exponitur S.V. pro parte devotissimi illius et sancte romane ecclesie filii Edwardi anglie regis illustris quod esus piscium gravissime saluti corporis sui adversatur, quodque propterea timet verisimiliter aliquam gravem incurrere infirmitatem. Supplicat igitur S.V. prefatus Edwardus rex qui tunc propter morem et consuetudinem Regum Anglie pro tempore existentem tunc etiam propter eius regiam dignitatem sine magna suorum nobilium et procerum comitiva in mensa cibaria sumere non consuevit, quatinus sibi specialem gratiam facientes ut diebus quadragesimalibus ipse cum otto personis sibi in mensa comitivam vel alias servitium facientes per eum eligendis et duobus medicis ac duobus cocis diebus vero Sabbati et aliis diebus extra quadragesimam ieiunalibus solus de concilio medicorum carnium ovorum et lacticiniorum cibis uti et vesci possit et valeat concedere et indulgere ac cum eo et personis predictis misericorditer dispensare in premissis dignemini gratia speciali. In contrarium facientibus non obstantibus quibuscumque cum clausulis oportunis et necessariis. Concessum ut petitur in presencia Domini nostri pape. Per Salern.

Et cum dispensatione perpetua pro domino Rege et otto personis A duobus medicis ac duobus cocis, ut prefertur. Et pro ipso Domino Rege solo in diebus extra quadragesimam.

Datum Rome apud sanctum petrum Quarto Iduum martii Anno octavo.

BIBLIOGRAPHIES

MANUSCRIPTS

PUBLIC RECORD OFFICE.

CHANCERY RECORDS
  Early Chancery Proceedings.
  Charter Rolls.
  Close Rolls.
  Diplomatic Documents: Domestic and Foreign.
  French Rolls (or Treaty Rolls).
  Fine Rolls.
  Patent Rolls.
  Pardon Rolls (or Patent Rolls Supplementary).
  Inquisitions *post mortem*.
  Inquisitions Miscellaneous.
  Miscellanea.
  Warrants for the Great Seal, Series I.
    Writs of Privy Seal.
    Bills of Privy Seal.
    Warrants under the Signet and other small seals.
    Signed Bills and other direct warrants.
    Warrants of the Council.
    Butler's Warrants.
    Treasurer at War's Warrants.

EXCHEQUER RECORDS.
  Exchequer K.R.
    Alien Subsidies.
    Customs Accounts.
    Nuncii Accounts.
    Household Accounts.
    Miscellanea.
  Exchequer L.T.R.
    Enrolled Accounts, Escheators.
    Enrollments of Wardrobe Accounts.
    Foreign Rolls.

Exchequer T.R.

    Diplomatic Documents.

    Miscellaneous Books.

    Council and Privy Seal.

    Warrants for Issues.

    Issue Rolls.

    Tellers' Rolls.

    Receipt Rolls.

Exchequer Accounts.

    Army, Navy, and Ordnance.

    Butlerage.

    Equitium Regis.

    Foreign Merchants.

    France.

    Jews.

    Mint.

    Miscellaneous.

    Works.

Duchy of Lancaster.

    Entry Books of Decrees and Orders. Vol. I.

Ancient Correspondence.

Vatican Transcripts.

    Portfolio 62.

Record Transcripts.

    (Materials for a new edition of Rymer's Fœdera.)

BRITISH MUSEUM*

Additional MSS, 4613-4615.

    Rymer's Collectanea.

Cotton MSS.

    Julius B VI, f. 94. Letter from Francis II of Brittany.

    Vespasian C XVI, f. 118. Instructions to Alexander Lye.

    Cleopatra F VI, f. 309. Letter under the sign-manual relating to a voluntary subsidy in the province of Canterbury.

Harleian MSS.

48,	f. 78. Account of the re-interment of the Duke of York.
69.	Several documents relating to tournaments.
543,	f. 147b. Letter from the Prince of Wales to the city of London, 1461.
	f. 164. "Articles of ye Erle of Warwike comyng fro Cales before ye

---

* Some minor manuscripts which have been cited are omitted from this list.

fild of Ludlow. Anno 1459."

f. 165. "Articles of the comons of Kent at ye coming of therle of March, Warwike, and Sarum," etc.

f. 171. "Tharticles of the proclamation of the duke of Clarence and erle of Warwike at heyr landinge & cominge out of Fraunce," etc.

f. 171b. "The forme of the savegardes graunted and gyven by the duke of Clarence and earle of Warwike to all saintwaries and other personell people."

Lansdowne MS. 285.

f. 2. "The maner and forme of the kyngis and Quenes Coronacion in Englonde." (Another copy is in Lansdowne MS. 260, f. 60.)

LONDON ARCHIVES, GUILDHALL

Journals, 6-8.
Letter Book L.

BIBLIOTHÈQUE NATIONALE

MSS. français.

88. Continuation of Monstrelet's chronicle.

2902, f. 33. Letter from Lord Hastings to Louis XI. Calais, 27 June.

4054, f. 183. Letter from the Earl of Warwick to Louis XI. 31 July 1465.

f. 194. "La creance des ambassadeurs du Roy Dangleterre ensemble les ouvertures quilz ont faictes."

f. 204. Letter from Edward IV to Louis XI. Canterbury, 17 May (1482).

f. 205. Instructions given by Louis XI to the Archbishop of Vienne, M. de la Rocheguyon, and Olivier le Roux.

ff. 213-227. Minutes of overtures made by the ambassadors of Edward IV.

f. 244. Minutes of instructions given by Louis XI to his ambassadors in England.

6960-6962. l'Abbé Legrand's history of the reign of Louis XI.

6963-6990. l'Abbe Legrand's collections.

10,187. Régistre de Pierre Doriolle.

10,375. Account rendered by Guillaume Restout of payments made to the king of England, Lord Hastings, etc. 1476-1478.

18,427. "Interogatoires faicts à Messire Charles de Martigny, Evesque d'Eaulne, ambassadeur du Roy Louis XI en Angleterre, és mois de juillet, aoust, et septembre, 1480." (Cited as Trial of the Bishop of Elne.)

20,488, f. 22. Outline of a proposed treaty between France and England providing for a marriage for Margaret of York, etc.

20,489,   f. 29. Letter from Bourré to Louis XI announcing the descent

of the English at St Malo. 28 August.

f. 46. Letter regarding the Earl of Warwick and the diet of St Omer.

20,496,   f. 91. Order from Louis XI about the victualling of ships for the Earl of Pembroke. 1 June 1468.

20,855,   f. 63. Letter from Edward IV to Louis XI. Westminster, 24 November,

f. 64. Letter from Margaret of Anjou to the king of France asking credence for Lord Hungerford and Sir Robert Whitingham. Edinburgh, 20 July.

MS. Dupuy, 762.

f. iii.   Letter from Jean Carbonnel to the Duke of Normandy. Mont-Orgueil, 27 April (1466).

f. 113.   Letter from the garrison of Mont-Orgueil to the same. 27 April.

f. 114.   Letter from Jacques de Brezé to Jean Carbonnel. Orleans, 15 April.

Portefeuilles de Fontanieu, 138-139.

ff 58-59.   A report of what was said by some English ambassadors sent to France in February 1477.

PRINTED BOOKS*

Accounts of the Lord High Treasurer of Scotland. Vol. I. Edinburgh, 1877.

Acts of the Parliaments of Scotland. Vol. II.

Annals of the Kingdom of Ireland by the Four Masters. Edited by J. O'Donovan. Dublin, 1848-1851.

Annals of Ireland from the year 1443-1468, translated from the Irish by Dudley Firbisse, or, as he is more usually called, Duald MacFirbis. Edited by J. O'Donovan. Dublin, 1846.

Annals of Ross. Printed in the appendix of *Annals of Ireland* by Friar John Clyn. Dublin, 1849.

Annals of Ulster. Edited by B. MacCarthy. Dublin, 1845.

Anstis, J. *The Register of the Most Noble Order of the Garter.* London, 1724.

Auchinleck Chronicle: a Short Chronicle of the Reign of James the Second, King of Scots. Privately printed, 1819.

Baldwin, J. F. *The King's Council in England during the Middle Ages.* Oxford, 1913.

Basin, Thos. *Histoire des règnes de Charles VII et de Louis XI.* Edited by J. Quicherat. Paris, 1855-1859.

---

* Many books which have been cited only a few times are omitted from this list.

Beaucourt, G. du Fresne de. *Histoire de Charles VII*. Paris, 1881-1891.

Beltz, G. P. *Memorials of the Order of the Garter*. London, 1841.

Blades, W. *The Life and Typography of William Caxton*. London, 1861-1863. Condensed edition of the same. New York, 1882.

Bouchart, Alain. *Les Grandes Croniques de Bretaigne*. Rennes, 1886.

Bricard, G. *Un serviteur et compère de Louis XI, Jean Bourré, Seigneur du Plessis, 1424-1506*. Paris, 1893.

Buchanan, G. *The History of Scotland* translated from the Latin of George Buchanan by James Aikman. Glasgow, 1827.

Calendar of Documents relating to Scotland preserved in Her Majesty's Public Record Office, London. Vol. IV. Edited by Jos. Bain. Edinburgh, 1888.

Calendars of the Patent Rolls.

       Henry VI. Vol. VI. 1452-1461. London, 1910.

       Edward IV. Vol. I. 1461-1467. London, 1897.

       Edward IV. Vol. II. 1467-1477. London, 1900.

       Edward IV. Vol. III. 1476-1485. London, 1901.

Calendar of State Papers and Manuscripts existing in the Archives and Collections of Milan. Vol. I. Edited by A. B. Hinds. London, 1912.

Calendar of State Papers and Manuscripts, relating to English Affairs, existing in the Archives and Collections of Venice and in other Libraries of Northern Italy. Vol. I. Edited by Rawdon Brown. London, 1864.

Calmette, J. *Louis XI, Jean II, et la révolution Catalane*. Toulouse, 1902.

Cely Papers: Selections from the Correspondence and Memoranda of the Cely Family, Merchants of the Staple, 1475-1488. Edited by H. E. Malden. Camden Society, 1900.

Chandler, Rich. *The Life of William Waynflete*. London, 1811.

Chartier, Jean. *Chronique de Charles VII*. Edited by Auguste Vallet de Viriville. Paris, 1858.

Chastellain. *Oeuvres de Georges Chastellain*. Edited by M. le Baron Kervyn de Lettenhove. Brussels, 1863-1865.

Chronicles of London. Edited by C. L. Kingsford. Oxford, 1905.

Chronicle of London. (Edited by E. Tyrell and Sir H. Nicolas.) London, 1827.

Chronicle of the Rebellion in Lincolnshire, 1470. Edited by J. G. Nichols. Camden Society Miscellany, Vol. I. 1847.

Chronicles of the White Rose of York. London, 1845.

Chronique Scandaleuse. Journal de Jean de Roye connu sous le nom de Chronique Scandaleuse, 1460-1483. Edited by Bernard de Mandrot. Paris, 1894-1896.

Collection of all the Wills now known to be extant of the Kings and Queens of England, etc. Society of Antiquaries, London, 1780.

Collection of Ordinances and Regulations for the Government of the Royal Household. London, 1790.

Commynes. *Mémoires de Philippe de Commynes*. Edited by Bernard de Mandrot. Paris, 1901-1903. (Except where otherwise indicated, this edition of Commynes' Mémoires has been used in all citations. For uniformity's sake, the spelling *Commynes* has been used throughout.)

Commynes. *Mémoires de Philippe de Commynes.* Edited by Mlle. Dupont. Paris, 1840-1847.

Commynes. *Mémoires de Philippe de Comines.* Edited by M. l'Abbe Lenglet du Fresnoy. London and Paris, 1747.

Commynes. *Lettres et négociations de Philippe de Commines.* Edited by M. le Baron Kervyn de Lettenhove. Brussels, 1867-1868.

Coventry Leet Book: or Mayor's Register, containing the Records of the City Court Leet or View of Frankpledge. Edited by M. D. Harris. Early Eng. Text Soc., 1907-1913.

Cust, Mrs. Henry. *Gentlemen Errant, being the Journeys and Adventures of Four Noblemen in Europe during the Fifteenth and Sixteenth Centuries.* New York, 1909.

D'Alton, E. A. *History of Ireland from the Earliest Times to the Year 1547.* Vol. I. Dublin, 1903.

Daumet, Georges. *Étude sur l'alliance de la France et de la Castille au XIVe et an XVe siècles.* Paris, 1898.

Davies. R. *English Chronicle. An English Chronicle of the Reigns of Richard II, Henry IV, Henry V, and Henry VI.* Edited by the Rev. J. S. Davies. Camden Society, 1856.

Davies, R. *Extracts from the Municipal Records of the City of York during the Reigns of Edward IV, Edward V, and Richard III.* London, 1843.

Dépêches des ambassadeurs milanais sur les campagnes de Charles-le-Hardi, Duc de Bourgogne, de 1474 a 1477. Edited by M. le Baron Fréd. de Gingins la Sarra. Paris, 1858.

Dépêches des ambassadeurs milanais en France sous Louis XI et François Sforza. Edited by B. de Mandrot. Vols. I-II. Paris, 1916-1919.

Devon, F. *Issues of the Exchequer.* London, 1837.

Drake, F. *Eboracum: or the History and Antiquities of the City of York.* London, 1736.

Du Clercq, J. *Mémoires sur le règne de Philippe le Bon, Duc de Bourgogne.* Edited by M. le Baron de Reiffenberg. Brussels, 1835-1836.

Dugdale, William. *The Baronage of England.* London, 1675-1676.

Dugdale, William. *Monasticon Anglicanum.* London, 1846.

Dupuy, A. *Histoire de la réunion de la Bretagne à la France.* Paris, 1880.

Ellis, Henry. *Original Letters.* Series I-III. London, 1825, 1827, 1846.

Epistolæ Academicæ Oxon. Edited by the Rev. Henry Anstey. Oxford, 1898.

d'Escouchy. *Chronique de Mathieu d'Escouchy.* Edited by G. du Fresne de Beaucourt. Paris, 1863-1864.

Excerpta Historica, or Illustrations of English History. London, 1831.

Exchequer Rolls of Scotland. Vols. VI-IX. Edited by G. Burnett. Edinburgh, 1884-1886.

Fabyan, Robert. *The New Chronicles of England and France.* Edited by Henry Ellis. London, 1811.

Flenley, R. *Six Town Chronicles of England.* Oxford, 1911.

Fortescue, Sir John. *The Governance of England:* otherwise called the Difference between an Absolute and a Limited Monarchy. Edited by C. Plummer. Oxford, 1885.

Fortescue, Sir John. *The Works of Sir John Fortescue, Knight, Chief Justice of England and Lord Chancellor to King Henry the Sixth.* Edited by Lord Clermont. London, 1869.

Gachard, L. P. *Itinéraire de Philippe le Bon*. Collection de Chroniques belges inedites. Voyages des souverains des Pays-Bas. Tome I.

Gairdner, Jas. *History of the Life and Reign of Richard the Third*. Cambridge, 1898.

Gilbert, J. T. *History of the Viceroys of Ireland*. Dublin, 1865.

Gilliodts-van-Severen, L. *Inventaire des archives de la ville de Bruges*. Vols. V-VI. Bruges, 1876.

Gilliodts-van-Severen, L. and Scott, E. *Le Cotton manuscript Galba B. I.* Chroniques belges inedites.

Gobellinus, J. *Pii Secundi Pontificis Max. Commentarii*. Frankfurt, 1614.

Grants of King Edward the Fifth. Edited by J. G. Nichols. Camden Society, 1854.

Green, M. A. E. *Lives of the Princesses of England*. London, 1849-1855.

Gregory's Chronicle. The Historical Collections of a Citizen of London. Edited by Jas. Gairdner. Camden Society, 1876.

Hall, Edward. *Chronicle*. Edited by Henry Ellis. London, 1809.

Halliwell, J. C. *Letters of the Kings of England*. London, 1846.

Hanserecesse von 1431-1476. Edited by Goswin Frhr. von der Ropp. Leipzig, 1888-1892.

Hansisches Urkundenbuch. Vols. VIII-X. Edited by Walther Stein. Leipzig, 1899-1907.

Hardyng, John. *Chronicle*. Edited by Henry Ellis. London, 1812.

Hatcher, H. *Old and New Sarum*. (R. C. Hoare's *History of Modern Wiltshire*.) London, 1843.

Haynin, Jean de. *Les mémoires de Messire Jean, Seigneur de Haynin et de Louvegnies, 1465-1477*. Mons, 1842.

Hearne's Fragment. A Remarkable Fragment of an Old English Chronicle, or History of the Affairs of King Edward the Fourth. (Hearne's edition of Sprott's Chronicle.) Oxford, 1719.

Historiæ Croylandensis Continuatio. (*Rerum Anglicarum Scriptores*, Vol. I.) Oxford, 1684.

Historie of the Arrivall of Edward IV in England and the Finall Recouerye of his Kingdomes from Henry VI. Edited by John Bruce. Camden Society, 1838.

Hist. MSS. Com. *Reports of the Royal Commission on Historical Manuscripts*. London, 1870, etc.

Household Books of John, Duke of Norfolk, and Thomas, Earl of Surrey, 1481-1490. Edited by Payne Collier. Roxburghe Club, 1844.

Hume Brown, P. *History of Scotland*. Cambridge, 1909-1911

Kingsford, C. L. *English Historical Literature in the Fifteenth Century*. Oxford, 1913.

La Marche. *Mémoires d'Olivier de la Marche, maitre d'hôtel et capitaine des gardes de Charles le Téméraire*. Edited by H. Beaune and J. d'Arbaumont. Paris, 1883.

Lecoy de la Marche, A. *Le roi René*. Paris, 1875.

Legeay, U. *Histoire de Louis XI*. Paris, 1874.

Lesley, John. *The History of Scotland from the Death of King James I in the year 1436 to the year 1561*. Bannatyne Club, 1830.

Letters and Papers Illustrative of the Wars of the English in France during the Reign of Henry the Sixth. Edited by the Rev. Jos. Stevenson. Rolls Series. London, 1864.

Letters and Papers Illustrative of the Reigns of Richard III and Henry VII. Edited by Jas. Gairdner. Rolls Series. London, 1861-1863.

Letters of Queen Margaret of Anjou and Bishop Beckington and Others. Edited by Cecil Monro. Camden Society, 1863.

Letters of Royal and Illustrious Ladies of Great Britain. Edited by M. A. E. Wood. London, 1846.

Lettres de Louis XI, roi de France. Edited by jos. Vaesen and others. Paris, 1883-1909.

Lettres de rois, reines, et autres personnages des cours de France et d'Angleterre depuis Louis VII jusqu'à Henri IV, tirées des archives de Londres par Bréquigny et publiées par M. Champollion-Figeac. Vol. II. (Documents inédits pour servir à l'histoire de France.) Paris, 1847.

Literæ Cantuarienses. Edited by J. B. Sheppard. Rolls Series. London, 1889.

Major, John. *A History of Greater Britain, as well England as Scotland.* Translated by A. Constable. Scottish History Society, 1892.

Manners and Household Expenses of England in the Thirteenth and Fifteenth Centuries. Edited by T. H. Turner. Roxburghe Club, 1841.

Marténe, E. and Durand, U. *Veterum Scriptorum et Monumentorum Historicum, Dogmaticorum, Moralium Amplissima Collectio.* Paris, 1724.

Maupoint. *Journal parisien de Jean Maupoint, Prieur de Sainte-Catherine-de-la-Couture, 1437-1469.* Mémoires de la Société de l'Histoire de Paris et de l'Ile-de-France. Vol. IV. 1877.

Maxwell-Lyte, H. C. *History of Eton College.* London, 1889.

Maxwell-Lyte, H. C. *History of the University of Oxford.* London, 1885.

Molinet, Jean. *Chroniques, 1476-1506.* Edited by J. A. Buchon. Paris, 1827-1828.

More, Thomas. *The History of King Richard III.* Edited by J. R. Lumby. Cambridge, 1883.

Morice, Dom Hyacinthe. *Mémoires pour servir de preuves à l'histoire ecclésiastique et civile de Bretagne.* Paris, 1742-1746.

Old Chronicle at the End of Winton. (Pinkerton's *History of Scotland*, Vol. I. London, 1797.)

Oman, C. *The History of England from the Accession of Richard II to the Death of Richard III.* London, 1906.

Oman, C. *Warwick the Kingmaker.* London, 1893.

Ordonnances des rois de France. Edited by M. le Comte de Pastoret. Paris.

Palgrave, Sir Francis. *The Antient Kalendars and Inventories of the Treasury of His Majesty's Exchequer.* Record Commission, 1836.

Paston Letters. Edited by Jas. Gairdner. London, 1904.

Perret, P. M. *Histoire des relations de la France avec Venise du XIIIe siècle a l'avenèment de Charles VIII.* Paris, 1896.

Plancher, Dom. U. *Histoire générale et particulière de Bourgogne.* Dijon, 1739-1781.

Plumpton Correspondence. Edited by T. Stapleton. Camden Society, 1839.

Political Poems and Songs relating to English History. Edited by T. Wright. Rolls Series. London, 1861.

Proceedings and Ordinances of the Privy Council of England. Edited by Sir H. Nicolas. London, 1834-1837.

Raine, Jas. *The Priory of Hexham.* Surtees Society, 1864-1865.

Ramsay, Sir James H. *Lancaster and York.* Oxford, 1892.

Records of the City of Norwich. Edited by the Rev. W. Hudson and J. C. Tingey. Norwich, 1906.

Reiffenberg, M. le Baron de. *Histoire de l'ordre de la Toison d'Or.* Brussels, 1830.

Reilhac. *Jean de Reilhac, secrétaire, maître des comptes, general des finances, et ambassadeur des rois Charles VII, Louis XI, et Charles VIII.* Paris, 1886-1889.

Reports from the Lords' Committees touching the Dignity of a Peer of the Realm. 1829.

Ricart's Kalendar. The Maire of Bristowe is Kalendar, by Robert Ricart, Town Clerk of Bristol 18 Edward IV. Edited by Lucy Toulmin Smith. Camden Society, 1872:

Rolls of Parliament. Rotuli parliamentorum. Vols. V-VI.

Ross, John. *Historia Regum Angliæ.* Edited by Thos. Hearne. Oxford, 1716.

Ross, John. *The Rows Rol.* Edited by W. Courthope. London, 1845.

Rotuli Scotiæ. Vol. II. 1819.

Rozmital. *Des böhmischen Herrn Leo's von Rozmital Ritter-, Hof-, and Pilger Reise durch die Abendlande, 1465-1467.* Stuttgart, 1844.

Rymer, Thos. *Fœdera, Conventiones, Literæ,* etc. Vols. XI-XII. London, 1727.

Samaran, Ch. *La maison d'Armagnac an XVᵉ siècle.* Paris, 1907.

Sandford, P. *Genealogical History of the Kings and Queens of England.* London, 1707.

Sharpe, R. R. *Calendar of Letter-Books preserved among the Archives of the Corporation of the City of London at the Guildhall. Letter-Book L.* London, 1912.

Sharpe, R. R. *London and the Kingdom.* London, 1894-1895.

Statutes of the Realm.

Stein, Henri. *Olivier de la Marche.* Brussels, 1888.

Stone, John. *Chronicle of John Stone, Monk of Christ Church, 1415-1471.* Edited by W. G. Searle. Cambridge Antiquarian Society, 1902.

Stonor Letters and Papers, 1290-1483. Edited by C. L. Kingsford. Camden Society, 1919.

Stow, John. *The Annales or Generall Chronicle of England.* London, 1615.

Stow, John. *A Survey of London.* Edited by C. L. Kingsford. Oxford, 1908.

Stratford, L. *Edward the Fourth.* London, 1910.

Three Fifteenth Century Chronicles. Edited by Jas. Gairdner. Camden Society, 1880.

Van Praet, L. *Recherches sur Louis de Bruges, Seigneur de la Gruthuyse.* Paris, 1831.

Vergil, Polydore. *Historiæ Angliæ Libri XXVII.* Leyden, 1651.

Vespasiano da Bisticci. *Vite di Uomini Illustri del Secolo XV.* Bologna, 1892.

Wake, W. *The State of the Church and Clergy of England in their Councils, Synods, etc.* London, 1703.

Wardrobe Accounts of Edward the Fourth. Edited by Sir H. Nicolas. London, 183o.

Warkworth, John. *A Chronicle of the First Thirteen Years of the Reign of King Edward the Fourth.* Edited by J. O. Halliwell. Camden Society, 1839.

Waurin, Jehan de. *Anchiennes chronicques d'Engleterre.* Edited by Mlle. Dupont. Paris, 1858-1863.

Weinreich, Caspar. *Danziger Chronik. Scriptores Rerum Prussicarum,* Vol. IV. Leipzig, 1870.

Whethamstede. *Registrum Abbatiæ Johannis Whethamstede, Abbatis Monasterii Sancti Albani.* Edited by H. T. Riley. Rolls Series. London, 1872-1873.

Wilkins, David. *Concilia Magnæ Britanniæ et Hiberniæ.* London, 1737.

Witte, A. de. *Conference monetaire internationale tenue à Bruges en 1469*. Brussels, 1893.

Worcester, William of. *Annales Rerum Anglicarum. (Letters and Papers Illustrative of the Wars of the English in France.)*

Worcester, William of. *Itinerarium*. Edited by J. Nasmith. Cambridge, 1778.

INDEX